Authenticity in the Kitchen
Proceedings of the Oxford Symposium on Food and Cookery 2005

Authenticity in the Kitchen

Proceedings of the Oxford Symposium on Food and Cookery 2005

Edited by Richard Hosking

Prospect Books
2006

First published in Great Britain in 2006 by Prospect Books, Allaleigh House, Blackawton, Totnes, Devon, TQ9 7DL.

ISBN 1-903018-47-1

The painting reproduced on the cover is by Frances Jaine.

Design and typesetting in Gill Sans and Adobe Garamond by Tom Jaine.
Printed and bound in Great Britain by The Cromwell Press, Trowbridge.

Contents

5

Preface

'Authenticity' overwhelmed us in 2005. Seventy-five proposals for papers were received, of which 46 were accepted and delivered at the Symposium. All but one, published elsewhere, are to be found here, making an unusually large volume.

The Symposium, organised so capably by Patsy Iddison, Registrar, Phil Iddison, Secretary of the Trustees and Jane Levi, Chairman of the Trustees, got off to a fine start with an opening address on the subject of Authenticity delivered by Colman Andrews, editor-in-chief of *Saveur*. Paul Levy has written a full report of this and the panel discussion that followed, and this can be found on the Symposium website at <www.oxfordsymposium.org.uk>.

Saturday lunch marked a departure from the Symposium custom of having a meal provided by the symposiasts themselves, and a luncheon of 'Authentic English Fare' was served in the Lloyd Common Room of Brookes University. Our hearty thanks go to Anne Petch of Heal Farm for providing delicious pies; to Maggie Beer for sending us her excellent Fruit Paste from Australia; to Patricia Michelson of La Fromagerie, London, for her generous donation of cheeses, and to all those, especially Sri Owen, one of our own Trustees, and Donald Sloan, Head of Brookes University's Department of Hospitality, Leisure and Tourism Management and his staff, who worked extremely hard to make the lunch such a success.

Another departure from the previous year was the Saturday night Symposium Dinner, served in the magnificent Headington Hill Hall, preceded by drinks on the Hall's sweeping lawns. For the aperitifs, Ursula Heinzelmann devised a highly successful tasting of German ciders followed by an interesting and equally success-ful matching of German wines with our meal. Ursula has our deepest gratitude, as do the producers who supplied gave us the ciders and wines, and The Winery who supplied them. The authentic Moroccan dinner in Headington Hill Hall was a very grand affair, cooked by Paul Bloomfield of the Fox Club, London; with menu and recipes from Caroline Conran and Anissa Helou. The huge success of the dinner was not only a great tribute to Paul's organisational and culinary skills and to the team who assisted him, but also to the skill and good taste of Caroline and Anissa; to all of whom we offer our hearty thanks.

Sunday lunch was perhaps the most lavish that has been served at any Symposium. Thanks to the great generosity of Tourism Malaysia we were served an authentic Malaysian wedding banquet. Our thanks go to Mr Libra Lee Haniff and Mr Razip Hasan, Directors of Tourism Malaysia UK, who achieved this extremely generous sponsorship for us; to Chef Mohd Shawal Abdul Jalil whose incredibly skilled and hard working team made it all possible, and to Jill Norman whose brainchild it was.

Jill should also be thanked for working with Wine Australia, and Sri Owen for working with Bisol Desiderio in Italy to supply us with fine wines that we could enjoy whilst basking in the knowledge that in drinking them we were raising funds for the Symposium.

As usual, Alicia Rios and Raymond Sokolov entertained us, this time with a sketch entitled 'In the Bureau of Authentification'. As editor, I feel that 'At the Office of Authentication' would have been a more authentic title, and in an effort to preserve authenticity have done my best to keep the insidious neologism out of the following pages.

Patsy and Philip Iddison's Bring and Buy stall has become a much valued Symposium institution, and we heartily thank them for the funds raised, and their hard work in raising them. Another greatly appreciated Symposium institution is the delicious bread provided by Dan Schickentanz of de Gustibus, whom we also thank very much. The American Friends of the Oxford Symposium have also made a notable contribution to Symposium funds, and this year sold many of our first-ever Symposium Aprons thanks to the hard work of Carolin Young and her mother. Carolin also arranged a fascinating, fund-raising visit to the 15th-century kitchens of Lincoln College.

So many people have worked hard for the success of the Symposium, and we thank them all. Our warmest thanks, however, go to Donald Sloan and all at Brookes University who worked so hard to make Symposium 2005 the undoubted success that it was.

Richard Hosking

Deciphering
La vraye mettode de bien trencher les viandes
(1926)

Julia Abramson

Whenever there are discontinuities in the knowledge that accompanies the movement of commodities, problems involving authenticity and expertise enter the picture.

Arjun Appadurai, *The social life of things* (1986)

[A]t the time of its origin, a medieval picture of the Madonna could not yet be said to be 'authentic.' It became 'authentic' only during the succeeding centuries and perhaps most strikingly so during the last one.

Walter Benjamin, 'The Work of Art in the Age of Mechanical Reproduction' (1936)

A special case of this problem of piracies and spurious imprints is that of the modern photographic or type-facsimile forgery of small books possessing a high commercial value.... The type-facsimile forgeries are mostly of short pieces..., printed (or supposed to have been printed—for it is doubtful if some of these 'forgeries' ever had any originals) for circulation among friends. These trifles should never be purchased without a written guarantee.

'Bibliography and Bibliology', *Encyclopedia Britannica*, 11th ed. (1910)

What slender renown attaches to the name of Charles-Marie-Joseph Baconnière de Salverte (1859–?) owes less to the officer's military career than to his passion for the hunt. The volumes he left behind commemorate his riding to hounds with English and French notables, encapsulate the history of the chase in his own country, and revive a hunting treatise traceable to Greco-Roman antiquity. That two volumes bear imprints from Compiègne,[1] whose château and forest French rulers long favored as a summer residence and hunting grounds, explicitly ties Salverte's avocation to antique aristocratic custom. As Third Republic (1870–1940) France moved through the Machine Age and the Great War, the ancient art of cynegetics, or hunting, connected Salverte to the Bourbon monarchs, the Valois kings, and the long-haired Carolingians.

Salverte's short bibliography contains an anomaly of interest to the gastronomic historian. In 1926, he abandoned his signature topic of hunting, to publish a treatise on carving meat, fowl, fish, and fruit at table. Salverte introduces *La Vraye mettode de bien trencher les viandes tant à l'Italienne qu'à la main et les différentes façons de peler et de seruir touttes sortes de fruits et le moyen den faire diverses figures* as a facsimile of a work that dates to 1647 and that was authored by the Swiss carver Jaque Vonlett. In the 1926 edition, 24 leaves illustrated with engravings are accompanied by sparse, type-set text in French, with a few phrases in Italian. The text transcribes manuscript annotations that give titles to the images or comment on carving procedure and service. Intriguingly, Salverte states that *La Vraye mettode* is also the source for the most famous work on carving of the modern era: the *Traité de la dissection des viandes* in the *Manuel des Amphitryons* (1808) by gastronome *extraordinaire* Alexandre Balthazar Grimod de la Reynière (1758–1837). Printed in a run of 110 copies, the facsimile made the seventeenth-century volume available for the first time to a relatively large group of readers. The edition is cited in essential references for European gastronomic history,[2] and copies can be consulted in research collections across Europe and America.[3] A lone scholar and book collector has taken exception to the edition. In 1949, the Swiss hotelier Harry Schraemli (1904–1995) declared that Salverte's scholarship was faulty.[4] Schraemli's remarks imply the following question: Is *La Vraye mettode* authentic [*vraye*], as its title announces? This article seeks to answer that question.

This analysis of *La Vraye mettode* extends our understanding of the tradition of representation associated with carving, and it sheds light on uses to which that tradition has been put. To place Salverte's volume in context, the first section of the article briefly describes key illustrated works on carving printed on the Continent. The carving treatises have double identities. They are representations whose analysis illuminates the evolution, transmission, and significance of table customs. They are also commodities, in some cases rare objects with a high market value. The second section of the article untangles the bibliography of *La Vraye mettode*. Within this context, the third section examines selected images and passages in the facsimile, with attention to authentication. Authenticity is a vexed notion that incites responses from moral grandstanding to intellectual disdain. Few, however, ignore it in the appreciation of historical artifacts and works of literature and art. Where authenticity is a defining concept, fakes focus attention on the production and location of value in culture. Any study of a work of uncertain status must consider that work's significance to its author as well as the interest for readers of accepting the work at face value, or not. The article's conclusion addresses the issue of motivation in the production and reception of Salverte's book.

Carving is a conundrum. It relies on the primitive violence of the knife, tamed through ritual and masked by technical prowess. In late-medieval France, military origins for carving were inscribed into the words that named its practitioners. From a swordsman defending his liege on the battlefield,[5] the *écuyer* became a domestic servant. During the Renaissance, a courtier must cultivate skill at carving, just as he must know how to dance elegantly and converse wittily.[6] Like his warrior ancestors, the early modern *écuyer-tranchant* [carver] wielded a blade to serve his master, but he did so at table. By the early nineteenth century, the duty of carving devolved onto the master of the house. From artful servant, the carver became a technically proficient host adept at the 'dissection' of the roast. The trajectory of the carver charts the increasingly bourgeois nature of French society and the democratization of manners considered refined.

A handful of works shaped carving treatises printed from the sixteenth century onwards in continental Europe, following the spread of printing itself. The most influential treatises appeared in the Italian states, then were copied and embellished in the German states, in the Netherlands, and in France. The contents reflect participation in a trans-national, aristocratic culture. Vincenzo Cervio's *Il Trinciante* (1581), frequently reprinted, describes service as much as carving. A treatise of the same title by the Bavarian Matthias Giegher (Padua, 1621 and 1639) added images of fowl, meat, fish, and fruit. In Giegher's figures, numbered lines indicate the recommended order and disposition of carving strokes.[7] Giegher's images were copied in some form in nearly every subsequent European illustrated manual concerned with the art of the carver. The visual filiation is clear in German-language works such as Georg Philipp Harsdörfer's *Vollständig vermehrtes Trincir-Buch* (1649) and the surgeon Andreas Klette's *Tafel-Decker und Tranchant* (1657). French-language works whose images resemble Giegher's include Jacques Vontet's *Art de trancher* (*c.* 1650); the blocky, lushly inked prints in the *rarissime De Sectione mensaria* (no date), whose tiny format made it convenient for the traveler;[8] the schematic forms in the carving pages of the *École parfaite des officiers de bouche* (1662); and the highly finished plates in the *Traité de la dissection des viandes* in Grimod's *Manuel*. The first important treatise on carving to be published in France after 1789, the *Traité* linked post-Revolutionary to early modern mores, and, as it happens, assured the continuity of the print tradition. In the *Manuel*, the orientation of the accompanying text shifts from the edification of a lord, to pleasing contemporary taste and modern guests, who might themselves be hosts on another day. Subsequent publications follow the *Manuel's* transformation of carving into a science, susceptible of transmission in a book, and of the carver into a relatively autonomous figure.

Beyond the significance of the *Traité* for carving, it is difficult to overstate the importance for European gastronomic and culinary history of its author. Through his food writing and his gustatory exploits, Grimod linked rich currents of ancien régime aristocratic tradition to Enlightenment innovation, transforming both to the purposes of a modern culture that he helped to shape. The politically charged dinners that he staged prior to the Revolution made him famous both as a trickster and as a gourmand; guests (or victims) and other contemporaries recounted Grimod's prandial high jinks in their letters, journals, and memoirs. His fame persisted so

13

that, states one historian, Grimod was the best-known eater in Napoleon's Empire (1804–15).[9] Anecdotes concerning Grimod were passed on by bibliographers Paul Lacroix (1806–84) and Augustin Thierry (1870–1956), who anthologized farces and *attrapes, curiosités* and mystifications. Today, Grimod is remembered as the author of best-selling gastronomic publications. His *Almanach des gourmands* (1803–12) contains the first modern narrative food guides published in the west. His second great gastronomic work is the *Manuel*. A semi-serious reference work for the modern host, the *Manuel* gives menus arranged by season and number of guests, and tips on etiquette, along with the carving treatise. The *Almanach* and *Manuel* reflect on an eclectic mix of topics connected to the table and draw on a broad range of works to renovate old custom for the 'new' post-Revolutionary France.[10] In Grimod's table talk, quotidian objects and gestures connected with eating telescope to reveal important political and social dimensions.[11] Generations of food writers have paid homage to Grimod, through imitation, quotation, plagiarism, myth-making, even the appropriation of his name. His volumes were plentiful at the time of publication. Today, original editions are hard to come by. Their rarity contributes to a prestige so great that it reliably rubs off, as we shall see, on nearly any work with which the author's name may be associated.

The preface to the *Manuel* adduces a mysterious source text for the *Traité*, and in a manner sure to provoke the curious. The *Traité*, writes Grimod, owes its existence to 'un manuscrit trouvé dans un couvent de Bernardins flamands [qui] nous [en] a donné l'idée.'[12] The statement points to the existence of a document that served perhaps as the principal reference for Grimod's discussion of carving. That he consulted such a manuscript is likely. He came of a wealthy family of tax administrators who were patrons of the arts and letters, knowledgeable about cultural matters, and renowned gourmands, and Grimod described himself as one of the *gens de lettres*. It is reasonable to suppose that he saw a manuscript, whether of French or other provenance, and no matter how rare, and that may have passed through the hands of Flemish monks. But the imprecise description leaves the reader in the dark. What document exactly did Grimod consult?

Nearly a century after Grimod's death, Salverte introduced *La Vraye mettode* as follows:

> Au cours de la préface de son manuel des Amphitrions publié en 1808, Grimaud de la Reynière fait une allusion vague... à un manuscrit trouvé dans un couvent de Bernardins Flamands, qui lui aurait donné l'idée de son traité sur la «dissection des Viandes». Il est probable que le voilà.
>
> ... Les planches gravées doivent bien se rapporter à un livre gastronomique imprimé mais actuellement inconnu. Elles sont certainement du seizième siècle, antérieures à l'écriture du manuscrit, et ne correspondent à aucun des ouvrages français ou Italiens de cette époque sur ce sujet (cf. Scappi,

Lancilotti, etc., soit les divers auteurs mentionnés par Brunet, table nos. 10 982 et suivants).
  (Document unique et précieux.) [Appartenait à la Bibliothèque du baron Pichon]. G. Vicaire, *Bibliographie gastronomique*, page 870.

According to Salverte, his volume presents a facsimile of the source for the engravings in Grimod's *Traité*. The references explain the claim and authenticate the original. The gastronomic and culinary collection of the Baron Jérôme Pichon (1812–96), cited for provenance, had few equals through the early twentieth century. More than one hundred years on, Georges Vicaire (1853–1921), author of the *Bibliographie gastronomique* (1890), editorial collaborator with Pichon, and cataloguer of Pichon's library, remains an indispensable reference for any study of gastronomy and cuisine in western Europe. A comparison confirms the claim for similarity between the images in Grimod's treatise and those in Salverte's edition. 'Le Coq d'Inde' in *La Vraye mettode* resembles 'Le Grand Coq d'Inde' in Grimod's *Manuel* [Figures 1 and 2]. 'Pour présenter le cochon [...]' in the facsimile looks like 'Le Cochon de lait' from 1808.[13] The claim that Salverte reproduces the ur-text for Grimod's *Traité* is exciting. Based on the resemblance among these and other figures, it is also reasonable. Why, then, did Schraemli cast doubt on Salverte's edition? Why did he further state, with unaccustomed perplexity, that bibliographical mystery surrounds the illustrated manuals attributed since the nineteenth century to a carver named Jacques Vontet?[14]

15

Schraemli's history of carving in *Von Lucullus zu Escoffier* (1949; 1971) develops from manuscript and print treatises written by the carvers themselves. To this end Schraemli adduces the Swiss Jacques Vontet. Following Vontet's indications, Schraemli writes that the seventeenth-century carver traveled to major cultural centers of central Europe, teaching his 'noble art.' For convenience, Vontet had engravings made that showed 'all kinds of fowl, game, and fruit.' Schraemli reasoned that Vontet distributed pamphlets with the engravings and otherwise blank pages to his students. The students could take notes on the leaves and consult the illustrations during carving lessons.[15] Schraemli's insight into the format of Vontet's work is now its standard description. Beyond this illumination, Schraemli describes problems associated with the engravings. Two of these problems bear on Salverte's *Vraye mettode*.

First, Schraemli notes that different, hand-annotated copies of similar sets of engravings bear different signatures. He concludes that the engravings should be attributed to Vontet, whom he assumes to be their original author.[16] Subsequent scholarship has concurred that a single set of plates was used for later printings. The paper in one booklet containing Vontet's engravings but bearing the signature Pierre Petit has since been 'scientifically' dated to the mid-eighteenth century.[17] Having intuited Vontet's authorship of the engravings, Schraemli follows out the implications for Grimod's *Manuel*. Based presumably on resemblances between the plates in the *Traité* and Vontet's engravings, Schraemli decides that Grimod consulted one 'notebook' or another of Vontet's. He does not, or cannot, specify exactly which *Diktatheft* that was. To test Schraemli's conclusion, one may compare the images in the *Traité* to the documents containing Vontet's engravings. For example, in the *Methode de Trancher les Alouëttes, Becquefis et Ortolans, avec toutes Sortes d'autres petits Oyseaux* (no date) held in the Cabinet des Estampes in the Bibliothèque nationale de France-Richelieu, unsigned manuscript commentary appears to post-date Vontet, but the engravings are his. Referring to this document for comparison, one sees that Grimod's images have counterparts in Vontet's engravings [Figures 2 and 3]. Working with the artist and engraver Jean-François Tourcaty,[18] Grimod caused some alterations to be effected to the images he included in his *Traité*. Clearly, however, their immediate source is a printing of Vontet's engravings.

A rarely cited volume dating to 1966 confirms Schraemli's theory that Grimod knew Vontet's engravings. The sale catalogue for the library of the book dealer and antiquarian Michel de Bry[19] describes a document entitled *L'art de trancher la viande, & toutes sortes de fruits, nouvellement à la françoise*, by Pierre Petit, *écuyer tranchant*, that contains 35 plates showing a coat of arms and carving diagrams as well as 15 drawings in pen. The catalogue also reproduces the frontispiece from this copy of Vontet's engravings annotated by Petit. The engraving shows two hands with fingers curled to grasp fork and knife, positioned to carve a small barded game bird. Sleeves ending in ruffled cuffs clothe the wrists of the carver. An elaborately carved fruit occupies the upper left corner of the frame. The image corresponds to the frontispiece in the *Methode de Trancher les Alouëttes*. The document has a distinguished provenance. According to the Vente de Bry catalogue, it bears 'l'ex-libris de l'illustre gastronome Grimod de la Reynière' and that of Curnonsky[20] [Maurice Edmond Sailland, 1872–1956], the prolific gastronomic writer and journalist. If the description is accurate, then Grimod owned a copy of Vontet's engravings that were embellished with Petit's manuscript commentary.[21] Logically, it is to this document that Grimod referred when he evoked the 'found manuscript' that inspired his *Traité*.

The second problem for Schraemli directly concerns the facsimile of 1926. Salverte, observes Schraemli, has made errors in his introduction. To begin, he has written 'Vonlett' for Vontet.[22] Schraemli ascribes the mistake to 'superficial study,'[23] presumably of the original, and certainly of Vicaire, who lists Vontet.[24] Moreover, continues Schraemli, Salverte described his original as a 'Document unique et précieux.'[25] Rare the document may be, but it is not the sole exemplar.[26] Schraemli concludes by stating that he cannot get to the bottom of this case.[27] What appears to have remained unclear was the relationship of Salverte's edition to the document it reproduces. By 1952, this problem, too, was put to rest. The catalogue of Schraemli's own book collection evokes a 'bad facsimile edition' dating to 1926 of Vontet's *Art de trancher*.[28] Salverte and Vonlett are not mentioned. However, the date can only refer to *La Vraye mettode*. Salverte published a bad reproduction of a set of Vontet's engravings; the case is closed. Yet for lack of explanation, this conclusion leaves open

Figure 1 (right). 'Le Coq d'Inde.' In Jaque Vonlett, La Vraye mettode de bien trencher les viandes, *editor Charles de Salverte (Dijon: Éditions du Raisin, 1926), 16. Photo: Bibliothèque nationale, Paris.*

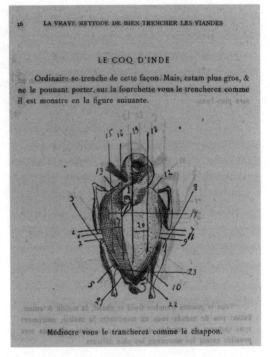

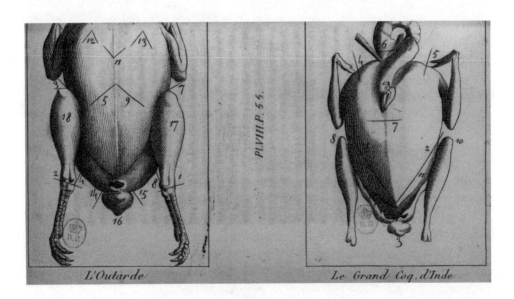

Figure 2. 'Le Grand Coq d'Inde.' Plate VIII in the Traité de la dissection des viandes *in* Grimod de la Reynière, Manuel des Amphitryons *(Paris: Capelle et Renand, 1808), 55. Photo: Bibliothèque nationale, Paris.*

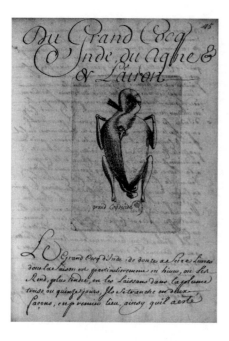

Figure 3. 'Grand Cocq d'Inde.' In [Jacques Vontet], La Methode de Trancher les Alouëttes, Becquefis & Ortolans, avec toutes Sortes d'autres petits Oyseaux (no date), 45. Photo: Bibliothèque nationale, Paris.

18

Figure 4. 'Liur chier de cheuze.' In Jaque Vonlett, La Vraye mettode de bien trencher les viandes, editor Charles de Salverte (Dijon: Éditions du Raisin, 1926), 26. Photo: Bibliothèque nationale, Paris.

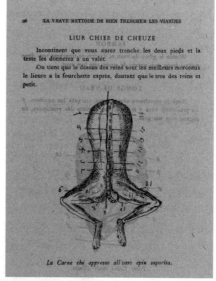

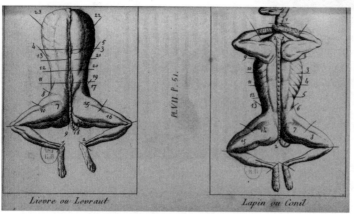

Figure 5. 'Lievre ou Levraut.' Plate VII in the Traité de la dissection des viandes in Grimod de la Reynière, Manuel des Amphitryons (1808), 51. Photo: Bibliothèque nationale, Paris.

a number of questions. What makes the facsimile 'bad'? Why would Salverte produce a bad facsimile of a 'unique and precious' original? To answer these questions, a closer look at *La Vraye mettode* is in order.

Salverte's edition is printed on elegant papers, but the images in it are of a different, lesser quality than those in the documents associated with Vontet and in Grimod's *Traité*. The engravings in the *Methode de Trancher les Alouëttes*, for example, are drawn in sharp, clean lines. Points, hatching and cross-hatching that figure volume and shadow are composed of fine, distinct strokes. The images are heterogeneous in style, in at least four distinctive groups. The pen drawings of game birds are sketches completed with little detail. The engravings showing whole fowl ready for carving on a plate are larger, stylized, and rigorously finished. The engravings of fish resemble illustrations from natural histories. The trout and pike, complete with fins, scales, and glassy eyes, have just been snatched from the water and are not prepared for carving, much less eating. The illustrations for fruit carvings, some geometrical, are hardly naturalistic. Rather, they suggest ingenious mechanical devices and three-dimensional puzzles. Despite the diversity of styles, the illustrations share visual clarity and the logical presentation of the steps the carver must follow.

Relative to Vontet's engravings, Salverte's images lose precision, introduce illogical detail, and present a relatively uniform appearance. To be sure, their subject, form, and orientation mirror engravings attributed to Vontet and reproduced in the *Traité*. But a comparison of, for example, Vontet's 'Le grand cocq d'Inde' to 'Le coq d'Inde' in Salverte shows that the latter marks a decline in quality [Figures 1 and 3]. In Vontet, the neck and head of the bird rest in the depression at the curved top of the breast and next to the wishbone. Through clumsy shading, Salverte's bird has acquired a bristly outgrowth on either side of its face, like dense whiskers. Lines drawn on the pendant shape formed by the neck fuse it into a toru – it will be impossible to unfurl this neck or move it aside. The presumably cooked bird has acquired a lively, open eye. The recommended sequence of carving strokes is 'médiocre,' to say the least. Numerous lateral cuts at the breast will be difficult to execute before the wings and thighs are removed. Salverte certainly offers a bad copy of engravings authored by Vontet. By contrast, unlike Salverte's 'Coq d'Inde,' Grimod's 'Grand Coq d'Inde' matches Vontet's for refinement of execution and for logic [Figure 2].

Beyond the errors Schraemli lists in Salverte's introduction, one may note further inconsistencies. Grimod, writes Salverte, does not discuss the carving of fruit, illustrated in his own edition. Therefore, concludes Salverte, another manuscript 'of the same type' exists. The inference is perplexing. There is no reason why Grimod should have reproduced all the plates in a document from which he drew inspiration. On the contrary, his earlier theatre and food reviews and his literary digest *L'Alambic littéraire* (1803) show him to be adept at picking out salient details. Assuming that he had seen plates illustrating fruit carving, it is logical that Grimod should have rejected such images for his own publication. His treatise – 'qui seul eût exigé un gros volume,

19

[et qui] est sans doute loin d'être complet'[29] – speaks to the practical, modern host. Where comfort trumps ostentation, elaborate fruit carvings are superfluous. These observations may not be sufficient to call into question the identity of Salverte's text. They do lend weight to Schraemli's observation that Salverte's editorial work was sloppy. Additional errors strengthen this impression. Salverte's suggestion that 'another' manuscript may have served as Grimod's model contradicts his claim that the 1926 edition reproduces the document of reference. Finally, Salverte misspells Grimod's well-known and often-printed name (as Grimaud) in the introduction.

Still other elements indicate in what ways exactly *La Vraye mettode* is a 'bad' edition. Throughout, spelling is inconsistent. The French is at times ungrammatical. Sentences are incomplete. Phrases in French and Italian are interspersed. To be sure, the sketchy quality of the text and its small quantity are explained by the fact that it transcribes notes on carving, not a completely worked up treatise. Similarly, the bilingual aspect of the text results, as Salverte states in the introduction, from a transcription of two hands. Yet other elements defy explanation. Salverte writes that his original bears 'no relation' to the texts listed by the bibliographer Jacques-Charles Brunet (cited above). But Brunet's list includes Giegher, a late edition of the *Ecole parfaite* (1708), and Grimod's *Manuel*.[30] In other words, Brunet offers not only an informative bibliography for the general topic of carving, but also one that specifically illuminates the text and images in Salverte's edition. Compare the *École parfaite* to Salverte on carving turkey:

Le Coq d'Inde se tranche en deux façons; sçavoir, ou sur la fourchette, en l'air, ou dans le plat, comme il est aisé de voir en la Figure suivante... . (*École parfaite* [1682], 38)

Le Coq d'Inde, comme il a esté dit au precedent article, se peut trancher en l'air sur la fourchette: toutefois s'il est grand, vous le trancherez dans le plat, cette sorte de dissection estant en ce cas, ce me semble, plus belle & plus commode ... . (*École parfaite* [1682], 40)

Comme j'ai di cy devant & se trenche sur la fourchette en lair, mais estant grand, vous le trencherez dans le plast, & en sera plus beau. (Salverte [1926], 15)

Ordinaire se trenche de cette façon. Mais, estam plus gros, & ne le pouuant porter sur la fourchette vous le trencherez comme il est monstre en la figure suiuante. (Salverte [1926], 16)

Perplexing in Salverte's edition are phrases that do not belong to the primary or secondary languages of the text (French and Italian), such as the heading 'Liur chier de cheuze' [Figure 4]. Corresponding headings for similar images in other carving treatises are far from exotic: Lapin, conil, lapereau, lièvre [Figure 5]. The strange heading may result from a faulty transcription. But if the original manuscript were difficult to decipher as well as 'unique et précieux,' why did not the editor graphically reproduce it along with the images, for a truly complete, and completely accurate, facsimile?

Salverte's edition does not appear exactly to correspond to any document described in the gastronomic histories, bibliographies, sale books, and exposition catalogues. That is, the original upon which Salverte based his copy appears to be missing or unavailable. This state of affairs does not preclude the existence of such an original. Cagle attests two copies of Vontet's engravings which he does not describe but which he understood, at the time of his writing, to be in the possession of the Parisian book dealer Pierre Berès. The original for Salverte's edition may no longer exist, or it may be held in a private collection. It is also possible that no specific original for Salverte's edition ever existed. Instead, the 1926 publication may reproduce elements from one or more sets of engravings by Vontet, and from Giegher and Grimod. *La Vraye mettode* is a 'bad' edition in the sense that its reproductions of visual material are mediocre in quality. To all appearances, La Vraye mettode reproduces images compiled from multiple sources, including works which post-date its alleged original, and produces text that is fabricated, rather than transcribed.

Charles de Salverte's hunting treatises – slim volumes similar in dimension to *La Vraye mettode* – may shed light on his sole gastronomic publication. These works derive significance from personal as well as cultural references. Like the volume on carving, those on hunting multiply names of authors and editors on their covers and title pages. *La Vraye mettode* doubles Salverte's name and also, literally, his signature with that of Vonlett and Vonlettz. Similarly, the hunting treatises carry the pseudonym Thya or Tya Hillaud along with Salverte's name and signature[31] or cite authors whose texts are given in translation or a modern re-edition. Salverte wrote his works on the hunt for a group of intimates who shared his avocation. Like *La Vraye mettode*, the books were printed in small runs, some of numbered copies.[32] One volume lists the names of 44 French and English subscribers who were Salverte's hunting companions as well as his readers.[33] Another includes a phototyped painting of a hunting scene showing figures on horseback at the chase. A schematic table keyed with numbers identifies the figures as Salverte and his companions.[34] This knowledgeable audience would have enjoyed seeing themselves mentioned or pictured in an attractive book on a topic of common, passionate interest.

Salverte's familiarity with the English hunt and English-language hunting terms, and his cosmopolitan peers, point to the intended readership for *La Vraye mettode* as to their milieu. Apparently conversant in English, Salverte could not have failed to be aware of the vibrant community of Anglophone expatriates in France during the 1920s. The creative endeavors of this generation endure as monuments in literature, music, and art. For these individuals, the daily experience of French culture, not

21

least its culinary and gastronomical aspects, fed souls as well as stomachs. Samuel Chamberlain (1895–1975) and Narcissa G. Chamberlain are not the most famous of the Americans to have lived in France between the world wars. Yet they may have been among the most diverse in their creative response. Chamberlain's columns for the new magazine *Gourmet* on food culture in France; his gastronomical memoir *Clémentine in the Kitchen* (1943); his sketches and photos; and Narcissa G. Chamberlain's watercolors and cookbooks, figure the lived experience of France in several dimensions. Chamberlain described learning both lithography and etching in Paris during the early 1920s, in order to print a lavish edition of his own illustrations on luxurious old papers reclaimed from account books and other sources.[35] The Chamberlains were avid book collectors as well as exceedingly well-informed gastronomes. Narcissa G. Chamberlain wrote about her husband that '[h]e never lost an opportunity to explore old bookshops, pick up an eighteenth-century volume on gastronomy or examples of beautiful typography or book design.'[36] With its soft, thick, leaves; its esoteric yet practical gastronomic subject; its 'historical' images of seventeenth-century engravings; and its clever introduction rife with allusion, Salverte's *Vraye mettode* would have been most interesting to cultural initiates such as the Chamberlains. This is born out by the copy of *La Vraye mettode* in the Schlesinger Library, a gift in the name of Narcissa G. Chamberlain. What exactly early readers of *La Vraye mettode* such as the Chamberlains made of the book must probably remain a matter for speculation. It is worth noting that a French study recently cited Salverte's edition as a historical source.[37] In an acceleration of the trend that Chamberlain, among others, helped to shape, the broad topic of food today enjoys ascendancy in commercial, governmental, artistic, and scholarly spheres in Europe and America. In France, both long-standing tradition and self-conscious promotion of the *patrimoine* or cultural heritage increase interest in matters gastronomic and culinary. Food practices and food history are rallying points for Gallic particularity. Taken at face value, *La Vraye mettode* usefully completes a coherent tale affirming the autonomy of the gastronomic in the context of a history that is peculiarly French.

22

In compiling his great gastronomical bibliography, Vicaire benefited from access to the library of the Baron Pichon as well as from the collaboration of his patron. Hardly limited to the gastronomical, Pichon's library notably contained multiple volumes by François Rabelais. One can only imagine discussions that may have taken place between Pichon and Vicaire, of Gargantuan feasts and of the 'library in the Abbaye de Saint-Victor,' which housed only extravagantly humorous, fantastical titles. In the age of the development of bibliographical 'science,' these convivial discussions doubtless included other bibliographers, librarians, and chroniclers of mystifications.[38] This group would surely have been moved to raise a glass to Charles de Salverte's rough bibliographical finesse. Grimod de la Reynière harmonized gastronomy, literary endeavour, and mystification in the course of his career. This triple conjointure also characterizes *La Vraye mettode de bien trencher les viandes*.[39]

Bibliography

Abramson, Julia. 'Du théâtre anatomique à la guillotine: Les enjeux de la découpe dans le *Manuel des Amphitryons* (1808) de Grimod de la Reynière.' (24 ms. pp., under review)

——. 'Grimod's Debt to Mercier and the Emergence of Gastronomic Writing Reconsidered.' EMF: *Studies in Early Modern France* 7 (2001): 141–62.

——. *Learning from Lying: Paradoxes of the Literary Mystification.* Newark, DE: University of Delaware Press, 2005 (forthcoming).

——. 'Legitimacy and Nationalism in the *Almanach des gourmands* (1803–12).' *Journal for Early Modern Cultural Studies* 3.2 (Fall/Winter 2003): 101–35.

Ader, Étienne. *Bibliothèque d'un humaniste* (Vente Michel de Bry). Paris: Georges Blaizot, and Paris: Lucien Scheler, 1966.

Appadurai, Arjun, editor. *The social life of things.* Cambridge, UK: Cambridge University Press, 1988.

Armaillé, Marquis d'. *Chasse à Courre du Chevreuil.* Charles de Salverte [Tya Hillaud], editor. Pau: E. Marrimpouey, 1920.

Benjamin, Walter. *Illuminations* (*Illuminationen.* Frankfurt am Main: Suhrkamp, 1955). Editor Hannah Arendt. Translator Harry Zohn. New York: Schocken, 1969.

Benstock, Shari. *Women of the Left Bank.* Austin: University of Texas Press, 1986.

Berès, Pierre. *Nourritures.* Catalogue 82. Paris: Pierre Berès, 1991.

Bitting, Katherine Golden. *Gastronomic Bibliography.* San Francisco, CA: 1939. Reprinted Ann Arbor, Michigan: Gryphon Books, 1971.

Brunet, Jacques-Charles. *Manuel du libraire et de l'amateur des livres.* 5th edition. 6 vols. and Supplément, 2 vols. Paris: Firmin Didot Frères, 1860–5.

Cagle, William R. *A Matter of Taste.* New York: Garland Publishing, 1990. Reprinted New Castle, DE: Oak Knoll Press, 1999.

Catalogo del fondo italiano e latino delle opere di gastronomia, secoli XIV–XIX. 3 volumes. Sorengo, Switzerland: Fondation Bibliothèque Internationale de la Gastronomie (B.IN.G.), 1994.

Catalogue des ventes des livres de M le Baron de Pichon. Paris: L. Potier, 1869; Paris: Librairie Techener, 1897; and Paris: Librairie Techener, H. Leclerc, and P. Cornau, 1898.

Cervio, Vincenzo. *Il Trinciante, Ampliato et a perfezione ridotto dal Cavalier Reale Fusoritto da Nardi.* Venice: 1581.

Chamberlain, Samuel [Phineas Beck]. *Clémentine in the Kitchen* (1943). New York: Modern Library, 2001.

Duby, Georges. *The Chivalrous Society* (1977). Translator Cynthia Postan. Berkeley, CA: University of California Press, 1980.

Eco, Umberto. *I limiti dell'interpretazione.* Milan: Bompiani, 1990.

L'École parfaite des officiers de bouche, contenant Le Vray Maître d'Hôtel, Le Grand Ecuyer-Tranchant, Le Sommelier Royal, Le Confiturier Royal, Le Cuisinier Royal, Et le Pâtissier Royal (Paris: 1662). 4th edition. Paris: Jean Ribou, 1682.

Elias, Norbert. *The History of Manners. The Civilizing Process* (1939), vol. 1. Translator Edmund Jephcott. New York: Pantheon, 1978.

Faccioli, Emilio, editor. *Arte della cucina, libri de ricette, testi sopra lo scalco, il trinciante e i vini dal XIV al XIX secolo.* 2 vols. Milan: Edizioni il Polifilo, 1966.

Fitch, Noel Riley. *Sylvia Beach and the Lost Generation.* New York: Norton, 1983.

Food and Drink Though the Ages. London: Maggs Bros. Ltd., 1937.

Giegher, Mattias. *Il Trinciante* (1621). In *Li Tre Trattati.* Padua: Paolo Frambotto, 1639. Bibliothèque nationale de France-Tolbiac, Résac. V–11149.

Grimod de la Reynière, Alexandre Balthazar Laurent. *L'Alambic littéraire.* 2 volumes. Paris: Maradan, 1803–An XI.

——. *Almanach des Gourmands.* 8 vols. Paris: Maradan, 1803–8 and Paris: Joseph Chaumerot, 1810 and 1812.

23

——. *Manuel des Amphitryons*. Paris: Capelle et Renand, 1808.

Howth, Earl of. *Leicestershire in France or the Field at Pau*. Translator Charles de Salverte [Thya Hillaud]. Paris: A. Nourry and Librairie Cynégétique, 1907.

Jenzer, E. *Schloss Jegenstorf 1952: Bibliophile Köstlichkeiten der Gastronomie*. Sammlung Harry Schraemli, Zurich. Bern: Berner Handpresse, 1952.

Lacroix, Paul [Bibliophile Jacob]. *Catalogue de la Bibliothèque de l'abbaye de Saint-Victor [...] suivi d'un Essai sur les bibliothèques imaginaires par Gustave Brunet*. Paris: J. Techener, 1862.

——. *Histoire des mystificateurs et des mystifiés*. 3 vols. Brussels and Leipzig: A. Schnée, 1856–8.

——. *Mystificateurs et mystifiés*. Paris: E. Dentu, 1875.

Lancelotti, Vittorio. *Lo Scalco pratico*. Rome: Francesco Corbelletti, 1627.

Livres en bouche. Paris: Hermann and Bibliothèque nationale de France, 2001.

Methler, Eckehard and Walter Methler. *Von Henriette Davidis bis Erna Horn*. Volmarstein-Oberwengern: Evangelische Kirchengemeinde, 2001.

Oberlé, Gérard. *Les Fastes de Bacchus et de Comus*. Paris: Belfond, 1989.

Oettinger, Edouard-Marie. *Un Agathopède de l'Empire*. Brussels and Leipzig: Kiessling, Schnée et Cie., 1854.

Pisanelli, Baldassare. *Trattato della natura de cibi et del bere*. 1583, 1587.

Salverte, Charles de [Thya Hillaud]. *Essai sur la Chasse du Daim*. Ill. Luce Bazire. Compiègne: Decelle, 1906.

Salverte, Charles de. *Notes brèves sur la Chasse du Cerf d'escape à Pau*. Paris: Pairault & Cie., 1907.

Salverte, Charles de [Tya Hillaud], translator and editor. *La Cynégétique d'Arrien, dit Xénophon le jeune*. Compiègne: Decelle, 1909.

Scappi, Bartolomeo. *Opera, divisa in sei libri*. Venice: Michele Tramezzino, 1570.

Schraemli, Harry. *Von Lucullus zu Escoffier* (Zurich: Interverlag, 1949). Bielefeld: Ceres-Verlag, 1971.

——. *De Sectione mensaria*. Paris?: N.d. Bibliothèque nationale de France-Arsenal 80–S 9826.

Simon, André L. *Bibliotheca Gastronomica*. London: The Food and Wine Society, 1953.

Spang, Rebecca. *The Invention of the Restaurant*. Cambridge, Massachusetts: Harvard University Press, 2000.

Thierry, Augustin. *Les grandes mystifications littéraires*. Paris: Librairie Plon, 1911.

——. *Les grandes mystifications littéraires*. Deuxième série. Paris: Librairie Plon, 1913.

Vicaire, Georges. *Bibliographie gastronomique*. Paris: P. Rouquette et fils, 1890. Reprinted London: Holland Press, 1978.

Visser, Margaret. *The Rituals of Dinner*. New York: Penguin, 1991.

Vonlett(z), Jaque. *La Vraye mettode de bien trencher les viandes tant à l'Italienne qu'à la main et les différentes façons de peler et de seruir toutes sortes de fruits et le moyen den faire diverses figures* (Lyon: 1647). Preface author and editor Charles de Salverte. Dijon: Aux Éditions du Raisin, 1926.

[Vontet, Jacques]. *La Méthode de Trancher les Alouëttes, Becquefis & Ortolans, avec toutes Sortes d'autres petits Oyseaux*. N.d. Cabinet des Estampes, Bibliothèque nationale de France-Richelieu, Rés. Lc 16a in-4.

Witteveen, Joop and Bart Cuperus. *Bibliotheca gastronomica*. 2 vols. Amsterdam: Linnaeus Press, 1998.

Notes

1. *Essai sur la Chasse du Daim* (Compiègne, 1906) and a French version of Arrian's *Cynegeticus* (Compiègne, 1909).
2. Bitting (1939; 1971), 480; item 441 in Cagle (1990; 1999), 305; and *Livres en bouche* (2001), 164.
3. Such as the Bibliothèque nationale de France-Tolbiac, the Wellcome Institute for the History of Medicine, the Lilly Library of Indiana University, the New York Public Library, and the Schlesinger Library of the Radcliffe Institute of Harvard University.
4. Schraemli (1949; 1971), 166.
5. 'Écuyer,' *Encyclopédie, ou Dictionnaire raisonné des sciences, des arts et des métiers, par une société de gens de lettres*, editors Denis Diderot and Jean Le Rond d'Alembert, vol. 5 'Do-Esy,' (Paris: Briasson, 1755), 385–9.
6. Elias (1939), 216–7 and 271. On the domestication of the knightly class, see Duby (1977), 187.
7. Images in Giacomo Procacchi's *Trincier- oder Vorleg-Buch* (Leipzig: 1621) similarly show the carver's tools and diagram carving procedure.
8. '[C]ét abregé, fait au profit du Voyageur [...]'. *De Sectione mensaria* (no date), 1.
9. Spang (2000), 152.
10. For Grimod's sources, see Abramson (2001).
11. See Abramson (2003).
12. Grimod, *Manuel* (1808), preface.
13. Salverte (1926), 29 and plate VI in Grimod, *Manuel* (1808), 45.
14. 'Meister Vontet hat mir schon manch Kopfzerbrechen verursacht, denn über seinem „Bilderbuch" schwebt irgendein Geheimnis, das ich gerne lüften möchte'. Schraemli (1949; 1971), 165.
15. Schraemli (1949; 1971), 165.
16. Schraemli (1949; 1971), 166.
17. See Item 265 in Cagle (1990; 1999), 265, who credits Pierre Berès for dating the volume, and Items 146 and 147 in *Livres en bouche* (2001), 164–5.
18. The frontispiece in Grimod's *Manuel* is signed Tourcaty. Pierre Berès writes that '[l]'illustration [est] dessinée et gravée par Jean-François Tourcaty, élève, comme David, du peintre d'histoire Jean Bardin.' Item 59 in *Nourritures* (1991).
19. A passing reference to 'la vente De Bry' appears in Oberlé (1989), 307.
20. Item 158 in Ader (1966), 77.
21. See also Item 147 in *Livres en bouche* (2001), 165.
22. Further: 'Jacque Vonlettz' appears on the last page of Salverte's volume, with no editorial explanation of the discrepancy.
23. '[O]berflächliches Studium.' In Schraemli (1949; 1971), 166.
24. Vicaire (1890), 870. And see Item 577, the listing for Vontet from the collection of Baron Pichon in the sale catalogue to which Vicaire wrote the introduction: *Catalogue de la Bibliothèque de Feu M. le Baron Jérôme Pichon, 1ère partie, livres rares et précieux* (Paris: Librairie Techener, 1897), 167 bound in the *Catalogue des ventes des livres de M. le Baron de Pichon*.
25. Salverte (1926), cited in Schraemli (1949; 1971), 166.
26. Schraemli (1949; 1971), 166 and 168.
27. 'Leider lernt man trotz allem Forschen hier nie aus.' Schraemli (1949; 1971), 168.
28. '[E]ine schlechte Faksimileausgabe aus dem Jahre 1926.' Item 79 in Jenzer (1952), 25.
29. Grimod, *Manuel* (1808), preface.
30. Brunet, *Manuel du libraire*, vol. 6, Table méthodique (1865), 624.
31. Salverte writes: '(1) Thya hillaud est un vieux mot français, dont on a fait Tayaut et Tally ho. Il se crie avec force, pour appeler les chiens à la voie, lorsque l'on en revoit par corps de l'animal de meute.' *Essai sur la Chasse du Daim* (1906), title page.
32. *La Chasse du daim* (250 copies); *La Chasse du Cerf* (150 copies); *La Chasse à courre du Chevreuil* (175 copies).

33. See the 'Noms des Souscripteurs' in Salverte, *Leicestershire in France* (1907) and which includes Salverte.

34. The 'phototype' in Salverte's *Chasse du Cerf* (1907) shows the 44 individuals including 'Ch. de Salverte' (number 34) listed in the 'Noms des personnages du tableau'.

35. Chamberlain, (1968), 46 and see also 5, 23–4, 26–8.

36. In Chamberlain and Kingsland (1984), 15.

37. Item 145 in *Livres en bouche* (2001), 164. By contrast, Cagle (1990; 1999) accords *La Vraye mettode* a full bibliographic description, but offers no further discussion, while the related works on carving receive detailed entries that make connections among them quite clear. His silence is suggestive of caution.

38. Such as Thierry, whom Vicaire acknowledges in the *Bibliographie gastronomique*. On mystification and bibliographers, see Abramson (2005), 20–21.

39. I am most grateful to Barbara Ketcham Wheaton and Keith Arbour, who discussed ideas in this article with me at a very early stage, and to the staff of the Schlesinger Library for research support. For help with bibliographical sleuthing I am indebted to the staff of the rare books room (Sally Y) at the Bibliothèque nationale de France-Tolbiac. A faculty enrichment grant from the College of Arts and Sciences of the University of Oklahoma funded the illustrations.

Authentic Dutch Food and 19th-century Amsterdam Restaurants

Hilary Akers

Dam Square, the heart of the city of Amsterdam, was a good place to start for anyone looking for entertainment in the last quarter of the 19th century. Amsterdam had suffered greatly from a long term economic depression but finally the city was expanding, a new central station was being erected, grand hotels, department stores, concert halls and museums were being built. The city bustled and within five minutes from Dam Square there were streets full of hotels, theatres, places to dance, places to sing, coffee-houses, beer-houses, wine bars, fish and oyster houses, restaurants and night restaurants. This had always been Amsterdam's entertainment centre, but it was now developing rapidly.

Nowadays eating out is a perfectly normal kind of entertainment but it wasn't always like that. In the Netherlands this idea caught on towards the end of the 19th century. So far research on eating out and the development of the restaurant has been published for cities like Paris, London and Brussels.[1] It is commonly accepted that restaurants first appeared in Paris around 1800, followed by other cities later on in the 19th century. Up to now, no research on the development of public eating places in Amsterdam has been published. 19th-century Amsterdam saw an increase in the number of public places where one could eat and I'm researching into why this was and what eating out meant for people in those days.

Because so little has been recorded about this subject my research is progressing at a snail's pace. I started by looking into what kind of places there were and where they were, using mainly travel guides published between 1829 and 1905, newspapers, memoirs and books on Amsterdam written by contemporaries. What was confusing were the titles given to the various eating establishments. Going through many old travel guides I thought that at some point I would be able to see when the first restaurants appeared in Amsterdam and I expected to be able to make clear categories for the various eating places. But it wasn't like that. Let me clarify this with an example.

A famous place in those days was *Die Port van Cleve* (The fortified city of Kleve) just behind the palace on Dam Square, usually referred to as The Poort. The Poort was mentioned in all but one of the guides I consulted published after 1876. The first one referred to it as coffee-house, the second called it a beer-house, in the third we're back to coffee-house again. In number four it appears in the restaurant category. Number five, six and seven use roughly the same description: restaurant and bar or coffee-house, plus The Poort's newly built wine bar. The 1905 guide simply refers to The Poort as a restaurant.[2]

One would expect to find that the changing names meant that The Poort had altered considerably during those years, but in reality it hadn't. It was actually one large room where one could eat and drink, slightly enlarged in the 1870s, just like the kitchens. And in the mid-eighties a wine bar was opened in an adjoining building. The Poort was not the only public eating and drinking place to appear under all these different qualifications in travel guides. It was actually quite common. This made me wonder if a change in name – like from coffee-house to restaurant – was actually due to fashion and not very meaningful in itself. If so, in order to discover what eating establishments that appeared later on in the 19th century were like, whether they were different from earlier eating places, from each other, whether they could be called restaurants and who went there – I had to view them in a different way.[3]

One approach was to look at the kind of food they served. Maybe these new places served a new kind of food, possibly even highly fashionable French food. On the other hand, they might have served the same traditional, authentic Dutch food as eating establishments earlier in the century. A well known Amsterdammer, Justus van Maurik, described in his memoirs how seasonal workers would pass through Amsterdam in summer. They would find themselves a cheap place to sleep and a cheap meal somewhere else, usually along one of the narrow side streets in the oldest part of town. These places, called *schaftkelders*, literally translated eating-cellars, were also frequented by people from Amsterdam without the means to cook at home. The food was simple and plain and hadn't changed for hundreds of years, except of course for the addition of the potato, but that was prepared in exactly the same way as all the other food: as a one-pot meal over an open fire. Everything was either boiled or stewed, e.g. potatoes mixed with another vegetable, often cabbage; brown beans with vinegar and molasses; rice with molasses; mashed carrots and onions. The food never included meat, but the portions were large and cheap.[4]

The same kind of food was served at *gaarkeukens* (a sort of soup-kitchen, but their food wasn't limited to soup). A journalist visited one of the *gaarkeukens* at the end of the 19th century and in the local Amsterdam newspaper he worked for he described the place: rows of wooden benches and long wooden tables with cruets of oil, vinegar, salt and mustard on them. On the wall a blackboard announced the day's dishes in various languages. Our journalist described what his neighbours were eating: *capucijners*, a very popular Dutch kind of dried pea, buttermilk porridge, apple sauce – which can be very thick in Holland – and pea soup. What he said about the customers was most interesting: although these places were meant to properly feed the poor, he noticed students and teachers and people from all social classes. He ends by calling the *gaarkeuken* a cheap *restauratie*, which was the Dutch word for a restaurant well into the 20th century. This man, Jantje van Leyden, was Holland's first culinary journalist and he called an extremely simple place serving traditional food a restaurant. I concluded from these examples that calling a place to eat a restaurant was a matter of fashion and did not necessarily refer to a particular kind of food. The food wasn't new, but this kind of place probably was. So far I haven't found mention of earlier eating places frequented by people who didn't have much money to spend.[5]

Traditional food was also served at places that were mentioned in travel guides. The Portuguese journalist Ramalho Ortigão visited Amsterdam in 1883 and had dinner at a renowned place called The Karseboom (The Cherry Tree). He was told that if he wanted to try classic Dutch food such as *hutspot* – stodgy mashed vegetables, porridge, cream tart and soft cream cheese with cinnamon, sugar and grated rusk, this was the place to go. The journalist was so horrified by the behaviour of the other guests and their lack of interest for the food that he forgot to comment on it. According to him, people barely spoke, glanced at the menu and ordered their food. They tied their napkins around their necks and went through their business papers while waiting for dinner. Most of them had meat and vegetables which they cut into small pieces and smothered in gravy. 'Then', according to Ramalho Ortigão, 'they devoured all of it in one go… which demonstrated a great appetite and a tremendous lack of gastronomical sensitivity.' Having finished they quickly paid and left.[6]

This place was definitely for the well-to-do, and it was popular but not fashionable. The 'eating-basements', the 'soup-kitchens' and restaurants like the Cherry Tree served traditional food for people who ate only because they were hungry. The Poort, discussed earlier, was a fashionable place, but still not a place for gastronomes. A mere fifteen minutes between ordering and leaving the premises with a full stomach was quite common. The Poort was famous for its fried steaks. People would arrive and find themselves a chair, often at a table that already seated people who were total strangers to the newcomer. That was common practice. A waiter would arrive, take the order and shout from wherever he was in the room to the man at the buffet called the 'echo', who would turn round and yell the order to the kitchen. Within minutes the food would arrive, usually the popular steak with fried potatoes or The Poort's other famous dish, a thick Dutch pea soup with rye bread.[7]

The Poort was run by two energetic brothers who were the first to introduce electric lighting at a restaurant. Newspapers also wrote about their other novelty: The Poort's large, airy room with lots of windows. It was immensely popular and people from all over the country paid it a visit.[8] Hotel Krasnapolsky (named after the owner), along a street on the other side of Dam Square was just as popular, particularly because of its Winter Garden. This was a very high construction made of iron and glass full of palm trees and endless rows of tables and chairs. But what was the food this fancy place was famous for? Traditional Dutch pancakes! It attracted Amsterdammers, crowds of people from the provinces and foreigners alike.[9]

So far all my examples have been of eating places serving truly traditional Dutch food, either one-pot meals or pancakes, or one step up: a meal with meat as its main ingredient. Those who could afford it would have meat. As in these places the meat

29

wasn't added to the pot but fried separately it was both a financial and a culinary step up. This kind of cooking required more complex techniques and skilled cooks. But there were people who wanted an evening out enjoying delicacies, either because they were gastronomes or because they wanted to show how affluent they were, or both. For these people a steak or a pancake wouldn't do, and neither would The Poort's wooden floor strewn with sand. For a long time I thought it must have been the new grand hotels who met with these needs. These hotels were especially designed for a new group of travellers: the rich tourist travelling *en famille* wanting the same kind of luxury as at home. These were modern places, so I expected them to have modern restaurants with exquisite food open to the public. But that wasn't so. Amsterdammers did go there to eat, but only if they were invited to a private party.

The grand hotels, built from the late 1860s onwards, served food to residential guests at *tables d'hôte*, not in a restaurant open to the general public. Travel guides always mentioned the grand hotels but only as hotels, never as restaurants. There were two exceptions: the last grand hotel to open, in 1896, had a restaurant as we know it right from the start and it was recommended as outstanding.[10] The other exception was Hotel Krasnapolsky. This never had a *table d'hôte*, and besides its Winter Garden it had a luxury restaurant called The White Room (De Witte Zaal) where people spoke softly and the furniture and decorations were luxurious. The restaurant served French food.[11] The Poort went down the same road and also opened a French restaurant on the first floor, but about thirty years after Krasnapolsky, in 1910.[12]

Other places saw a similar development but changed their whole enterprise into a modern French restaurant. Between 1830 and 1889 Amsterdam's most famous oyster restaurant Van Laar (named after the owner) just off Dam Square, changed from a very basic oyster and fish shop with a simply furnished room where one could eat on the spot, to a richly decorated restaurant with marble, mahogany and gilded iron. The first Van Laar served oysters and toast. According to a French journalist the luxurious Van Laar from 1889 was for the elegant section of the city's inhabitants. To attract these people Van Laar changed from Dutch to French even in its advertisements. One could still order oysters but the restaurant now had a French kitchen and the waiters spoke Dutch and French.[13]

An example of an establishment that was a chic restaurant from the day it opened its doors in 1883 was Restaurant Riche on the main canal leading from Dam Square into the city. Our culinary journalist Van Leyden raves about the interior, especially about the *cabinets-particuliers*, decorated with silk and mirrors, where people could eat in private. There were also various large dining rooms which were decorated in their own particular style. For example Moorish, renaissance or Louis XVI.[14] Van Leyden didn't comment on the food, but luckily I found a menu for a private party in the city archive from 1887. The nine course menu is typically French and also written in French. It featured expensive ingredients such as turbot, langouste, quail and duck.[15] I would call this a typical modern French restaurant. One could only go there if one had plenty of money and time to spend. The interior and the food were luxurious and aesthetically pleasing. It was a fine place to be seen and it was the right kind of place to take one's wife.

There were always places to eat in Amsterdam, both for the rich and for the poor. For respectable, well-to-do men at the beginning of the 19th century there was the possibility to join a *table d'hôte* at a high class inn.[16] We have seen that at The Karseboom in the 1880s well-to-do men would eat simple, traditional Dutch food. But serving the French food that formerly had been served at private dinner parties of affluent families at a restaurant was a development that didn't start until the second half of the 19th century. The earliest reference I have found so far was in a diary describing an Amsterdam family having a French dinner in 1867 at a restaurant just off Dam Square.[17]

It is clear that people who went to these restaurants with a French kitchen had a choice. Poor people ate traditional food at traditional restaurants, rich people could go to both. But apart from the large enterprises that had both a traditional Dutch and a modern French restaurant in the same building, there are no signs of restaurants integrating traditional and imported French food. For that we had to wait until the late 1980s, when high-class restaurants in Amsterdam started serving luxurious ingredients together with typical poor people's food like *hutspot* – the stodgy dish we saw earlier. I think that probably is because there are actually people now who never eat that kind of food anymore, and authentic Dutch food has become popular. Culinary journalists worry about traditional dishes disappearing, but that's also new: Jantje van Leyden, our 19th-century journalist, wasn't in the least concerned about that.

31

Material from archives

City Archive (Gemeentearchief Amsterdam): Menu from Restaurant Riche D.00.184
Universiteitsbibliotheek Amsterdam: Archive Verbeek – Van der Sande: Dl 1–21 Diary of their private life from September 10th 1864 to October 10th 1871 (Not complete).

Bibliography

A guide through Amsterdam: offered to the members of the Holland Society of New-York on the occasion of their visit to this city August 1888 (Amsterdam, 1888).

Amsterdam. Gids met platen (Amsterdam: Van Holkema 1883, reprint Bussum: Unieboek, 1971).

Amsterdam. Gids voor bezoekers der hoofdstad, met 55 gravures. Stadsgezichten en typen van vroeger en later tijd (Alkmaar: P. Kluitman, 1890).

Amsterdam in stukken en brokken (Amsterdam: Uitgave van de vereniging vrienden van het Amsterdamboek 1969. Original edition 1891).

Baedeker, K., *Belgium and Holland. Handbook for travellers* (fifth edition; Leipzig and London: Karl Baedeker, 1878).

Baedeker, K., *Belgique et Hollande. Manuel du voyageur* (twelfth edition; Leipzig: Karl Baedeker, 1885).

Baedeker, K., *Belgique et Hollande y compris Le Luxembourg. Manuel du voyageur* (sixteenth edition; Leipzig: Karl Baedeker, 1897); (eighteenth edition; Leipzig: Karl Baedeker, 1905).

Balbian Verster, J. F. L. de, 'Hotels en restaurants, part 2: "Die Port van Cleve te Amsterdam", *Neerlands Welvaart* 68–69 (1920) 21–38.

Burema, L., *De voeding in Nederland van de middeleeuwen tot de twintigste eeuw* (Assen: Van Gorcum. N. V., 1953).

Collection Thieme à un sou. *Guide populaire pour Amsterdam. Promenade travers la ville et dans les environs. Avec énumeration des principales curiosités* (Nijmegen, 1885).

Ehrman, Edwina, Hazel Forsyth, Lucy Peltz and Cathy Ross, *London eats out. 500 years of capital dining* (London: Philip Wilson Publishers, 1999).

Emeis, M. G., 'Oestersalons: weekdieren voor een zondagsmaal'(in four parts) in: *Ons Amsterdam* 31 (1979) 238–244, 274–278, 302–307, 336–341.

Erens, Frans, *Vervlogen jaren* (Den Haag: Thijmfonds, 1938).

Jobse-van Putten, Jozien, *Eenvoudig maar voedzaam. Cultuurgeschiedenis van de dagelijkse maaltijd in Nederland* (Nijmegen: SUN, 1995).

Leyden, Jantje van, *Eten en drinken in Amsterdam* (Amsterdam: Schalekamp, Van de Grampel en Bakker, 1898).

Maaskamp, E., *A new guide through Amsterdam* (Amsterdam 1829).

Maurik, Justus van, *Toen ik nog jong was* (Amsterdam: Van Holkema en Warendorf, 1918).

Ortigão, Ramalho, *Holland 1883* (Amsterdam: Jacob van Campen 1948. Originally published in Portugese in 1885).

Plantenga, P. B., *Nederland. Handboek voor reizigers. Met reiskaart, plattegronden enz..* (fourth edition; Zutphen: P. Plantenga 1876).

Rössingh, J. H., 'Hôtel en restaurant Krasnapolsky', *Neerlands Welvaart* 31–32 (1920) 1–20.

Scholliers, Peter, 'Brusselse restaurants in de negentiende en twintigste eeuw. Over koks, eters, schrijvers en luxe: Franse dominantie en Belgische respons' in: Marc Jacobs & Peter Scholliers eds., *Buitenshuis eten in de Lage Landen sinds 1800* (Brussels: VUBPRESS, 2002) 57–84.

Spang, Rebecca L., *The invention of the restaurant, Paris and modern gastronomic culture* (Cambridge, Massachusetts, and London: Harvard University Press, 2000).

Vreeken, Bert, and Ester Wouthuysen, *De grand hotels van Amsterdam. Opkomst en bloei sinds 1860* ('s-Gravenhage: Sdu uitgeverij, 1987).

Notes

1. e.g. Spang, Scholliers, Ehrman
2. Plantenga p. 15. Baedeker 1878 p. 233. Gids met platen p. 19. Baedeker 1885 p. 286. Thieme 1885, A guide through Amsterdam 1888, Amsterdam. Gids voor bezoekers der hoofdstad p. 2, Baedeker 1905 p. 379.
3. De Balbian-Verster p. 23,27.
4. Van Maurik p. 26, Jobse 245–247.
5. Van Leyden p. 61–62. His observations were confirmed by Burema, p. 262.
6. Orgigao p. 51, my translation.
7. Amsterdam in stukken en brokken p. 174–175; Erens p. 191.
8. De Balbian-Verster p. 24.
9. Rössing p.8. Vreeken p. 106.
10. Baedeker 1897 p. 315.
11. Rössingh p. 11.
12. De Balbian-Verster p. 27.
13. Emeis, pp. 305, 337–338.
14. Van Leyden p. 198.
15. City Archive D.00.184
16. Maaskamp pp. 276, 278.
17. Archive Verbeek – Van der Sande, September 10th 1867.

The Ambiguity of Authenticity

Joan P. Alcock

Appearance oft deceives.
(Italian proverb, attributed to Torriano, 1666.)

To be authentic is to be genuine or real, but it also means to be original and this may not necessarily be genuine. Authentic ingredients have been used in dishes to entertain and often deceive. There is therefore ambiguity and this is illustrated in culinary history. Roman cooks often made one dish appear to be another to please patrons and create novelty. During the medieval period cooks disguised food in elaborate displays using ingredients as entertainment and to excite the palate. For some Victorians food was an opportunity to provide elaborate displays, for others it was a chance to adulterate foodstuffs with the intention of increasing profit at the expense of the genuine product. Wartime food in the twentieth century had loftier motives. People had to be persuaded to eat what was available. Culinary propaganda ensured authentic ingredients provided nutrition in calculated deception. Over two thousand years the message is often the same: 'appearance oft deceives'.

Surprise dishes

'If it is true that of meats those that are not meats and of fish those that are not fish have the most flavours, let us leave the expounding of this matter to those whom Cato said that their palates are more sensitive than their mouths.' The Roman writer Plutarch (Plutarch, *Moralia. How a Young Man should study Poetry*, 14e) was instructing a young man in writing poetry when he wrote these words but guests would have immediately understood their meaning at a Roman dinner, where they were faced with an ambiguous dish. The hosts vied with others to surprise their guests and so cooks were urged to provide dishes utilising authentic ingredients, often of the more humble kind, which would elicit cries of amazement when the dish was presented.

Trimalchio's cook was a past-master at this. Encolpius, the hero, or anti-hero, of Petronius' *Satyricon*, notes that a wooden hen was brought to the feast, sitting on peahen's eggs placed in straw in a basket. The eggs were distributed to the guests. He hammered at the pastry shell on his eggs with a spoon, 'weighing at least half a pound each', and almost gave up. But his more experienced neighbour commented 'there's something good here' and cracking the eggs Encolpius found figpeckers rolled up in spiced yoke of egg, seasoned with pepper (Petronius, *Satyricon* 33). This dish was akin to the Greek *thrymmatis*, a cake or pastry which when broken open revealed a figpecker or another small bird. Later in the feast as the whole dining room shook and the coffered ceiling began rumbling (thus creating the perfect atmosphere for a surprise), a harp was lowered from the ceiling hung with golden crowns and alabaster jars of perfume. A tray of cakes had in the centre a Priapus made of pastry, holding in his lap apples and grapes. As the guests stretched out their hands to take a cake, a single touch resulted in a spurt of saffron and an irritating vapour reaching them. The bewildered guests thought that this provided such an odour of sanctity that they regarded it as an authentic request and, having raised themselves to a sitting position, loyally cried, 'The Gods save Augustus, the Father of his People' (Petronius, *Satyricon* 60).

Apicius, in his cookery book, also provides recipes of *patinas* (pâtés) where authentic ingredients are used to create something completely different. There are three recipes headed 'Salt fish without fish' (Apicius 13 1–3), which use hare, kid, lamb or chicken liver, moulded into a fish-like shape, sprinkled with oil and mixed with herbs, liquamen and even ground walnuts in order to produce an intriguing dish. One recipe is even noted as being 'excellent for a sick stomach and facilitating digestion'. Another, 'a *patina* of anchovy without anchovies' utilises the authentic ingredients of boiled fish mixed with pepper, rue, liquamen and eggs, together with jellyfish, 'taking care by cooking in steam that these do not mix with the eggs'. This recipe confidently states, 'at table no one will know what he is eating' (Apicius 14 2 12).

The surprise might take the guests even more aback. A nursery rhyme, once well known to British school children, about five and twenty blackbirds baked in a pie, illustrates this.

When the pie was opened, the birds began to sing,
Wasn't that a dainty dish to set before a king?

Trimalchio had produced this effect centuries earlier. A great dish was brought in on which was a wild boar. A huge, bearded fellow, presumably the cook, advanced with a knife and when the boar was cut open out flew a flock of thrushes. Fowlers with nets caught them so that the birds were either to be used again for this trick or were prepared for table (Petronius, *Satyricon*, 40). To carry the joke further, Trimalchio asked the guests to look at the delicious acorns on which the boar had been fed. The guests recoiled when these 'acorns' were handed out but they turned out to be two kinds of juicy dates. A similar trick was played later in the feast when the boar, seemingly cooked, was carried in again. Trimalchio 'looked closer and closer' at it and then complaining that it not been gutted, ordered the cook to be whipped. The cook pleaded for mercy and was ordered to gut the pig in front of the guests. As soon as he did this, out poured sausages and blood puddings (Petronius, *Satyricon* 49).

A surprise could be at the expense of the lower classes. Juvenal (*Satires* 5 80–86) says 'look at the lobster which is brought to the master. It is carried on a dish walled with asparagus as high as a tall attendant'. Guests waited in anticipation for this treat, 'but you are served with a crayfish, hemmed in by an egg cut in half; a funeral supper upon on a tiny plate'.

More elaborate surprise items in the medieval period, which had the intention to entertain and excite, came in the form of subleties or sotelties. These were elaborate confectioneries made of sugar or 'marchpane' (marzipan) which decorated the tables of royalty and the nobility. These 'art works for sugar bakers' may have originated from those made for the eleventh-century Caliph Al-Zahir who preferred his in the form of a mosque (Mintz 1985). Though made of traditional and authentic ingredients, their shape resembled nothing like a traditional cake. Usually produced at the end of each course (Pullar 1977, 92–93) their aim was two-fold: to show off the ingenuity of the cook or pastry chef, which reflected on the skill of the host, and to make a political statement, as did that produced at the coronation banquet of Henry VI in 1429. Henry had succeeded his father Henry V in 1421 as King of England and France, when he was only nine months old. This claim could not physically be substantiated, but the political claim was made clear in the three subtleties. The first displayed Henry between the English saints Edward the Confessor and the French St Louis. The second depicted Henry sitting between Henry V and the Emperor Sigismund, who had supported Henry V in his wars against France. In the third, Henry is shown being presented to the Virgin, sitting with the Christ child on her lap, by the English St George and the French St Denis (Hammond 1995, 142–143).

The English subleties could not compare with the elaborate confectionery decorations which graced the wedding festivities of the Grand Ducal courts of Italy from the fifteenth to the seventeenth centuries, many of which were decorated with what were described as authentic copies of bronze statues by Giambologna (Watson 1978). Guests marvelled at the likeness. These were planned 'to delight the eye' rather than be eaten. Even more extravagant and powerful was the symbolism of a banquet provided at Lille in 1454 by Philip the Good of Burgundy, which was intended to surpass a series of banquets provided by the nobility. So great was the spectacle that crowds jostled to view the tables loaded with the showpieces all made of authentic ingredients but transmogrified into fantastic creations. These included 'a rigged and ornamental carrack, a meadow surrounded by trees with a fountain, rocks and a statue of Saint Andrew, the castle of Lusignan with the fairy Melusine, a bird-shooting scene near a windmill, a wood in which wild beasts walked about, and lastly a church with an organ and singers, whose songs alternated with the music of the orchestra of twenty-eight persons who were placed in a pie' (Huizinga, 1955, 254). Spectators marvelled at the authenticity of the culinary representations.

By the seventeenth century such showpieces had been consigned to history in England, which provided more humble fare. Yet there were elaborate dishes. A surprise item could be a Yorkshire Christmas pie. This consisted of a poussin, placed within a pigeon, placed within a partridge, placed within a goose, placed within a turkey. This very solid 'bird' would be put into a large dish surrounded by jointed pieces of hare and wild fowl, covered with a pastry top and basted well. The deceit of the authentic ingredients was total. A less lavish dish has been revived for modern tastes. This is a five-bird roast; a pigeon, inside a pheasant, placed within a chicken, set within a small turkey all wrapped round by a goose. In the centre was spiced pork stuffing. The cost of this at Christmas 2004 was about £100, but if that was thought to be too costly a smaller version could be provided: a duck wrapped round a chicken enclosing a pigeon with the spaces filled with sage and apple stuffing. These birds were boned for easy carving and the authentic colours and tastes were revealed in the layered slices.

Modern surprises lie in names, which have become authentic because of popular use but are ambiguous in their descriptions. The English popular dishes Toad in the Hole and Spotted Dick have caused many a raised eyebrow; so have Angels on Horseback and their companions Devils on Horseback. Eve's Pudding, Rock Cakes, Singing Hinny and Sally Lunns are only a few of the many names that hide culinary delights made from humble authentic ingredients. Aunt's Pudding, a steamed mixture of suet, flour, breadcrumbs and dried fruit is found under a variety of names. In some editions of Mrs Beeton there is a recipe for a pudding called Aunt Nelly (Beeton 1861, 1224). The pudding is also found under the names of Aunt Martha, Aunt Polly, Kate, Mary Ann and My Cousin (Norwak 1981, 132). Ambiguity of authenticity may also lie in ingredients. The controversy between Spotted Dick and Spotted Dog is a case in point. Spotted Dog, according to some recipes, is a long suet pudding with currents in it, taking its name from the likeness to a Dalmatian dog. Spotted Dick, on the other hand, a term first used by Alexis Soyer in 1849, is said to be a suet pudding rolled round a filling of raisins and sugar. The term 'dick' is said to be a Huddersfield name merely referring to 'pudding'. (Norwak 1981, 128; Ayto 1994, 331). This pudding is also known as Plum Bolster because of its resemblance to a long pillow or bolster. In many parts of England, however, the term Spotted Dick is a more authentic use than Spotted Dog. It might be suggested that what people think is authentic becomes authentic to a locality. On a less culinary correct scale, the tendency in northern chip shops to provide deep-fried, battered Mars Bars may be regarded as surprise items from authentic ingredients. Indeed, some chip shops boast that they can batter and deep-fry any food if the customer brings it to the shop. Thus authentic foods become the latest surprise gimmick.

There is ambiguity in what has become a food made from a surprising ingredient. Quorn is the trade name for a substance called mycoprotein. This has been described as a 'protein-rich cellular mass' derived from the fungus *Fusarium venenatum*, hence myco (fungal) protein. It is described as being found in 1967 in soil at Marlow in England. Fermenting the fungus in vats produces mycoprotein, which is then mixed with a binder and flavouring to form an authentic meat-like texture that can be used in imitation products, especially beef and chicken. As such it is an extremely useful food for vegetarians. British consumers have accepted this produce since 1995 but its

36

production in the United States from 2002 has caused tremendous controversy. The United States Center for Science in the Public Interest (CSPI) is concerned both for the safety and labelling of the product, one description even going so far as to label it a fungus akin to mildew (Miller and Dwyer, 2001; Wilson 2001). This debate raises the question as to whether a manufactured food can in time become an authentic one. Britain has certainly accepted this.

An even more surprising addition in an attempt to become an authentic food is arum. This is made from pea protein and gluten by the British firm Lucas Ingredients. A note posted on Wired News website reported that to obtain the appropriate 'mouth feel' and flexibility, the substance was tested by the volunteers having electrodes attached to their cheeks to record muscle activity. The mastication test states that a piece of arum required 6.1 seconds and ten chews to eat, while a piece of chicken took just over 5.4 seconds and nine chews to swallow. It was not certain if the extra seconds and chews for arum prolonged an interesting food experience.

Imitation

Imitation of objects in cookery can be authentic but also attempt to deceive. Cakes studded with slivers of almonds to look like hedgehogs come into this category; the Romans had already devised quinces stuck with thorns to resemble sea urchins. The English gingerbread man has a long history but it has been brought up to date in 2004 by 'dressing' him in a sugar-icing football kit in the English colours for the World Cup. Trimalchio provides his guest with piglets made of cake surrounding the wild boar; these were gifts to take home.

Such cakes were purely for entertainment, but there were some cakes that had a serious religious purpose. Elephos in Athenaeus' *Deipnosophistae*, (646e) mentions a cake, made from spelt dough, honey and sesame, moulded in the shape of deer and eaten at the festival of the Elaphebolia. These authentic ingredients and the cake had a serious purpose for they were used to commemorate a desperate event. The Phoenicians during a war with the Thessalians piled all their property in a huge pyre and told the few men left in charge of the citadel that if they were defeated, they were to kill the women and children, put the bodies on the pyre and burn everything together. This gave rise to a Greek phrase, 'Phocian desperation'. The Phocians, however, were victorious and the Elaphebolia was celebrated yearly at Hyampolis with a huge bonfire in which baked animals and human figure were burned on the pyre (Nilsson, 1925, 63).

Spelt flour was presumably chosen because it was rarely used in Greece although it was popular in northern Europe. Honey was revered for its healing properties and sesame was a popular ingredient in cakes. In Syracuse on the Day of Consecration of the Thesmophoria cakes of sesame and honey moulded in the shape of the female pudenda were carried in procession and eaten in honour of the goddess, Demeter, and her daughter Persephone. The festival was in autumn to ensure their fertilizing power enabling the autumn crops to grow (Brumfield 1981, 70–103).

Imitation is a problem when it comes to creating meals of past ages. Often the archive evidence provides details of food at meals and feasts but the present-day historian has no means of deducing the quantities of the ingredients, how dishes were made and how exactly this food could taste. There have been several attempts to solve this problem. John Edwards (Edwards, 1984) produced his version of Apicius' cookery book and was closely followed by Ilaria Gozzini Giacosa two years later (Giacosa, 1986). Edwards attempted a total translation of the recipes whereas Giacosa was more selective. Their respective aims were to recreate the taste of ancient Rome. The problem of recreating certain authentic ingredients in Roman cooking, however, seems to have defeated both of these authors.

To produce completely authentic *liquamen, murum* and *allec* (the residue of liquamen) for example, would entail an enormous effort. Some English translators of Apicius recommend the substitution of Thai *nam-pla*, although this tastes more of salt than fish, or even of Lea and Perrins Worcestershire Sauce, presumably on the basis that this contains anchovies. But the production of authentic *liquamen* or *garum* was a skilled operation. Tunny, sprats, anchovies, even sea urchins and oysters were placed with brine in troughs by the sea shore and left to ferment for anything up to three months. Martial (*Epigrams* 13 103) indicates that mackerel produced the best *liquamen. Liquamen* could be made in any quantities providing that the precise ratio of salt to fish (anything between 1:1 and 1:5) was observed and that the produce was allowed to mature for the required time. There could be no one constantly reproduced taste. Each production area in Spain, North Africa, Italy and Gaul, even Britain, had its own distinct taste which might be due to the addition of herbs, wine and spices, the length of preparation time, the quantity of salt and the temperature (Poinsich and Tarradell 1965; Curtis 1991).

Mark Grant (1999, 26–28) has pointed out the difficulty of recreating authentic Roman tastes. The Roman world relied on charcoal for cooking. Pots and pans were placed on tripods and gridirons, which rested on flat raised surfaces, these being the Roman stoves, over which charcoal was spread. The resulting fumes almost certainly flavoured the food. Grant also comments on the difficulty of creating an authentic Roman cheese. As there was no refrigeration, Roman cheeses were steeped in brine or vinegar or smoked to preserve them. Modern smoked cheese may be akin to Roman ones but the Romans used apple and other woods to give a distinctive taste, which was easily discernable to the consumer, as Martial indicates (*Epigrams* 13 32–33). Grant (1999, 34) suggests that the constant testing of Roman recipes does make a claim for authenticity and cookery writers recreating medieval and later recipes have make the same claim. Grant argues that 'where a gap still remains, medieval and modern recipes can be of assistance if they possess an historical affinity with the ancient recipe'. But this affinity may be slight. Ancient wine was carried in amphora impregnated with pitch. It was often flavoured with herbs. At a 'Roman Bash' event in 2005 at the British Museum, visitors were invited to try 'authentic' Roman wine flavoured with pitch, herbs and garlic. The result was undrinkable. Yet, one wondered, was this akin to the ordinary Roman wine of the fourth pressing?

In another context one can speculate about the 'authentic' medieval banquets laid on for unsuspecting tourists in London and other cities. The food produced at these dinners seems to be based on spit-roasted chicken and a few vegetables, and the guests are invited to throw their chicken bones on the floor 'as was the medieval custom'. Much more appropriate are the attempts to provide authentic food at historic properties such as Hampton Court and those owned or administered by the National Trust or English Heritage. These do try to provide authentic food appropriate to the historic setting of the house. The ironic thing is that the general public, eager to taste this food, is often not allowed to do so because of the Health and Safety regulations. Thus attempted authentic food of one era is deemed possible to give food poisoning to people in the twenty-first century.

There was one area where imitation of authentic ingredients could have lethal consequences. This was in the adulteration of food and drink, which was so common in Britain by the nineteenth century that consumers had to ignore the practice or starve. Adulteration could take several forms. Watering down milk, adding thickening agents, such as brains to cream, and bulk substances such as ground-up bones, gypsum, peas and beans to bread might be acceptable. The addition of substances to boost taste such as vitriol and salt to beer, white arsenic and sulphuric acid to gin, and copper sulphate to pickles was far more serious. The investigations of Fredrick Accum (Accum, 1820) in a *Treatise on Adulterations of Food and Culinary Poisons*, with its sub-title *There is Death in the Pot* alerted public consciousness to this scandal. The first Adulteration of Foods Act passed in 1860, feeble though its recommendations were, began the process of making sure that ingredients included in food were authentic. The 1872 Adulteration of Food, Drink and Drugs Act had more effect but the establishment of adequate legal machinery finally began with the Sale of Food and Drugs Act in 1875 and the statutory standards laid down for spirits, milk, butter and other products from 1879 onwards (Burnett, 1966, 205–208).

Substitution of ingredients.

Surprise dishes merge into imitation dishes, which become ambiguous when authentic ingredients are used to create a familiar food. Nicomedes of Bithynia travelling through his dominions in the late fourth century suddenly wanted to eat anchovies. He was far from the coast so his cook created 'anchovies' out of slices of turnip sprinkled with salt and poppy seeds (Athenaeus *Deipnosophistae* 7 d–f). The King's reaction is not recorded. Turnips were useful for Roman cooks because they were a white vegetable. Pliny says that it could be stained in six colours, the most popular being purple (Pliny, *Natural History* 18 129). Martial (*Epigrams* 11 31) says that Caecilius 'mangles' gourds. He can use them in every course making dishes from them. He uses them in desserts to make insipid cakes and sweets of all shapes. He even imitates 'mushrooms, black puddings and tunny tail'.

Apicius (2 28) has a recipe for rissoles with a thick sauce in which *defrutum* of quinces is further reduced to the consistency of honey by exposure to a hot sun. 'If you do not have this, use *defrutum* of dried figs which the Romans call "colouring".' Trimalchio boasted that his cook could produce a fish out of a pig's belly, a pigeon out of lard, a turtledove out of ham and a fowl out of a knuckle. The guests had already had a taste of this for they had eaten of a dish formed like a goose and surrounded with fish, all made from pork. Encolpius remarks that he is surprised that they were not made from wax for he had seen 'that sort of imitation food produced at the Saturnalia in Rome'. Trimalchio's cook was called Daedalus, probably quite deliberately for in mythology Daedalus was revered for being a great inventor (Petronius, *Satyricon* 69–70).

Cheesecakes have had substitute ingredients. In the medieval period the filling consisted of cheese pounded with egg yolks, spices and sugar. Later milk was added to the filling and curds replaced cheese so that the term curd cakes could be used. In the seventeenth century some cheesecakes did not contain cheese but were merely a custard mixture. At the present time, according to the regulations prescribed for ingredients, anything labelled cheesecake must contain some cheese or curd cheese.

But this emphasis on names does not apply to substitution in some foods authenticated by tradition. The history of the medieval mince pie and the plum pudding reveal the extent of substitution (Alcock 1992–1993, 2–4). The modern mince pie, so beloved in England, is derived from shred pie, so called because of the inclusion of shredded fat, which provided nourishment in cold winters. A medieval mince pie contained minced pork, eggs, fat and spices. Beef, mutton or poultry could be substituted, packed into a pastry case, and then baked. Fruit soaked in brandy, and acting both as a sweetener and a preservative, allowed the pies to be baked well in advance of the Christmas season. A deception came in the shape of the pies for they were of an oval shape, originally called 'coffyns'. Christian tradition, however, soon associated their shape with that of the manger and a moulded pastry figure representing the figure of Jesus was put on the top of the pastry lid or was slipped inside. This allowed the Puritan governance of England in the 1650s to forbid the making of mince pies as being idolatrous. At the Restoration in 1660 the making of mince pies resumed but they were made in a round shape, and gradually the meat content was reduced. The first meatless mince pies appeared in early eighteenth-century cookery books, such as that of Elizabeth Raper (Grant, 1984). Elizabeth Raffald (1782) and Hannah Glasse (1796) give recipes for mince pies with and without the meat, but both Eliza Acton (1845) and Isabella Beeton (1861) eschew the meat.

A similar history relates to the Christmas pudding, which began as one of the earliest foods devised. This was pottage, a thick soup of pulses and/or grains simmered slowly in a cauldron with the addition of scraps of meat or fish and flavoured with

40

herbs. Numerous ingredients could be added. Bread provided an additional thickener; egg yolks were a binding agent and fruits and spices would give variety. Pottage was a filling dish to be eaten before a meat course so that the more expensive meat could be proportionally reduced. For the lower classes it might be their only meal. By the sixteenth century in England plums and dried prunes were being added so that the mixture became plum pottage. Oats were gradually replaced by bread and the meat content was reduced. This dish was not linked exclusively to Christmas. It was especially appreciated at Harvest Homes, the feast when the harvest was finally gathered in. By the eighteenth century the meat content had entirely disappeared leaving only the suet to represent the once authentic meat content of pottage.

With both mince pies and plum puddings new varieties have been produced. In Britain during the Second World War shredded carrots and apples were added to provide a sweetener, because dried fruit was scarce. Gravy browning gave a dash of colour and milk took the place of spirits. A very strange pudding was served during the war at St Bartholomew's Hospital when the recipe included three bottles of lemon Kia-ora and three bottles of orange Kia-ora. Those present say that the pudding was consumed with relish. Belief in the traditional taste of Christmas pudding was suspended in the interests of patriotism.

There were other substitutions in Britain because of the policy of rationing and the shortage of ingredients. When dried egg was substituted for fresh eggs, the dried amount had to be carefully measured with one level tablespoonful of dried egg powder to two tablespoons of water (Patten 1985, 9). People always seemed to believe that more should be allocated than the stated amount but increasing the amount of the dried egg did not produce the authentic quantity. The wartime Ministry of Food tried hard to provide a varied diet but the monotony of the food provided was always a problem. Recipes of oatmeal sausages, mock duck, which had a basis of sausage meat, and mock cream made either from margarine, sugar and dried milk or cornflour, milk, margarine and sugar did not help. These were not the authentic tastes, which had been experienced before the war, and the majority of the population were not deceived. Once rationing was over in 1954, gradually the authentic ingredients returned and the mock recipes were consigned to the pages of history.

At the present time several products are provided for people with vegetarian tastes. Vegetarian sausages and vegetarian lasagne products are sold omitting the meat, mince pies and plum puddings omit suet and butter or may include a quantity of crushed macaroons to enhance the mixture. Puff pastry may surround a mince pie and a meringue topping may replace the pastry lid. Are food products such as these to be considered authentic sausages and traditional mince pies or are people deceiving themselves because of their beliefs? An affirmative answer suggests that authenticity must relate to a person's convictions rather than to an authentic recipe. Perhaps recipes change with circumstances so that continuance of tradition outweighs any alteration of a recipe. There may, therefore, be no such thing as authentic recipes.

41

Recipes change with each generation and consumers can conscientiously and with conviction deceive themselves that they are eating the genuine food product. This may apply to names of products but it cannot apply to individual ingredients. EU regulations make it abundantly clear that what is contained in a product must be stated on any label down to the last condiment. Some exceptions may be made such as in the case of Worcestershire Sauce. Otherwise these products may deceive by their ambiguity but be authentic in law.

Bibliography

Accum, F., *A treatise on the adulteration of food and culinary poisons: exhibiting the fraudulent sophistications* (Philadelphia: A. Small, 1820).

Acton, Eliza, *Modern cookery for private families* (1845) (London: Longmans Green, facsimile edition: Reader and Dyer, 1995).

Alcock, J. P., 'The rare mince pie', *Home Economics and Technology*, December 1992–January 1993, 2–4.

Apicius, *The Roman cookery book. A critical translation of the Art of Cookery by Apicius...* by Barbara Flower and Elisabeth Rosenbaum (London: Harrap, 1958).

Athenaeus, *Deipnosophistae*. Translated and edited by Charles Barton Gulick, 7 vols (London: Loeb Classical Library, 1927–1941).

Ayto, J., *A gourmet's guide. Food and drink from A to Z* (Oxford: Oxford University Press, 1994).

Beeton, Isabella, *Mrs Beeton's book of household management: a specially enlarged first edition facsimile* (1861) (London: Chancellor Press, 1982).

Brumfield, A., *The Attic festivals of Demeter and their relation to the agricultural year* (New York: Arno Press, 1981).

Burnett, J., *Plenty and want. A social history of diet in England from 1815 to the present day* (London: Nelson, 1966).

Curtis, R. I., *Garum and salsamenta: production and commerce in materia medica* (Leiden: Brill, 1991).

Giacosa, I. G., *A taste of ancient Rome*. Translated by Herklotz, A. (Chicago: University of Chicago Press, 1992).

Glasse, Hannah, *The art of cookery made plain and easy* (1796) (Facsimile edition, Wakefield: S. R. Publishers, 1971).

Grant, B. (ed.), *The receipt book of Elizabeth Raper* (London: Nonesuch Press, 1924).

Grant, M., *Roman cookery. Ancient recipes for modern kitchens* (London: Serif, 1999).

Hammond, P. W., *Food and feast in medieval England* (Stroud: Alan Sutton Publishing, 1995).

Huizinga, J., *The waning of the middle ages* (Harmondsworth: Penguin Books, 1955).

Juvenal, *The sixteen satires*, Translated by Peter Green (Penguin Classics. Harmondsworth: Penguin Books, 1967).

Martial, *Epigrams*, 2 vols. Translated and edited by Walter C. A. Ker. Revised edition (London: Loeb Classical Library, 1978).

Miller, S. A. and Dwyer, J. T., 'Evaluating the safety and nutritional value of mycoprotein', *Food Technology*, 55 (7), 2001, 42–47.

Mintz, S., *Sweetness and power. The place of sugar in modern history* (New York: Viking Press, 1985).

Nilsson, M., *Greek popular religion* (Oxford: Clarendon Press, 1925).

Norwak, M., *English puddings: sweet and savoury* (London: Batsford, 1981).

Patten, M., *We'll eat again. A collection of recipes from the war years* (London: Hamlyn, 1985).

Petronius, *The Satyricon and the fragments*, Translated by J. P. Sullivan (Penguin Classics. Harmondsworth: Penguin Books, 1965).

Pliny the Elder, *Natural history*, 10 vols. Translated and edited by H. Rackham, W. H. S. Jones and D. E. Eichholz (London: Loeb Classical Library, 1938–1963).

Ponsich, M. and Tarradell, M., *Garum et industries antiques de salaison dans la Méditerranée occidentale*, Université de Bordeaux et Casa Velásquez. Bibliothèque de l'école des Hautes Etudes Hispaniques Fasc. 36 (Paris: Presses Universitaires de France, 1965).

Pullar, P., *Consuming passions. A history of English food and appetite* (London: Book Club Associates, 1977).

Raffald, Elizabeth, *The experienced English housekeeper* (1782) (Facsimile edition, Trowbridge: Redwood Press, 1970).

Watson, K. J., 'Sugar sculpture for Grand Ducal weddings from the Giambologna workshop', *Connoisseur*, 199. 79. 1978, 20–26.

Wilson, J., 'Making mycoprotein: the Quorn foods story', *Food Technology*, 55 (7), 2001, 48–50.

43

The Rise of Molecular Gastronomy and Its Problematic Use of Science as an Authenticating Authority

Rachel A. Ankeny

Does the menu in front of you describe a dish that blends caviar and white chocolate, or offer smoked bacon-and-egg ice cream served with French toast/tomato jam? Is the main cooking device in the restaurant's kitchen a blowtorch? If so, you likely have entered the realm of a growing number of chefs using the principles of molecular gastronomy to concoct unusual dishes or perfect classic ones. Molecular gastronomy has been defined as a field that 'attempts to link chemistry to culinary science, to explain transformations that occur during cooking, and to improve culinary methods through a better understanding of the underlying chemical composition of food'.[1] The term was coined in the late 1980s by the British physicist Nicholas Kurti and the French food scientist and former journalist Hervé This, who felt that 'empirical knowledge and tradition were as important in cooking as rational understanding'.[2] However as critics of more narrow approaches to molecular gastronomy note, some authors seem to consider taste, appearance, texture, or other qualities of food simply as the necessary end result of exploiting the chemical properties of particular food-stuffs, with little attention to non-scientific or more subjective aspects of the tasting and eating experience.

This paper explores one highly influential and popular work in this genre, Harold McGee's *On food and cooking: the science and lore of the kitchen* (abbreviated henceforth as *OFC*), originally published in 1984 and significantly revised for its 2004 reissue, as a lens for examining trends in molecular gastronomy. McGee's new introduction stresses the idea that although the relationship between science and cooking might have seemed strained and distant when his first edition appeared, it is notable that 'in 2004 food lovers can find the science of cooking just about everywhere'.[3]

This book may well be the 'bible' of molecular gastronomy for professional chefs, who also typically cite the work of Kurti and This, co-founders in 1990 of the International Molecular and Physical Gastronomy workshop now held annually in Erice, Sicily, as well as the experimental cooking of chefs such as Heston Blumenthal of England and Pierre Gagnaire of France.[4] McGee's research has had a much wider impact than most food science research, which until recently was primarily academic, and is more accessible than that of most of his molecular gastronomist counterparts, perhaps since he publishes in English through a mainstream press. As Blumenthal claims: 'Harold McGee's [original] book was the single biggest catalyst of the path I'm following now'.[5] Perhaps more importantly, *OFC* self-consciously uses scientific research to explain – or debunk – traditional culinary techniques, and explicitly defends this approach, as will be discussed below. In addition, frequent publications in technical and popular scientific journals have helped to position McGee's work within a broader context of scientific credibility, although he himself has limited formal scientific training.

As will be illustrated, the scientific language and imagery used in this book are reminiscent of a scientific vision that links power and control to understanding.[6] Experimental techniques are prioritized over observation or experiential data-gathering as the best means for developing a true, 'scientific' understanding, thus implicitly communicating to the reader that there is one best way to cook. It also utilizes myth-making devices to position itself as providing definitive and timeless answers about the fundamental mechanisms of the natural world, about what is real and hence what is authentically scientific.

Thus, as will be shown, this book aims to shape our conceptions of what the qualities of a 'good' cook are, shifting them away from the production of good food by empirical, trial and error methods, to understanding why cooking techniques work in the way they do and how to harness chemical principles to produce the desired effects. Its primary target audience therefore is serious cooks or professional chefs, particularly as more popularized and less encyclopaedic food science texts are now available for mass consumption or bedtime reading.[7] Furthermore, as preparation methods, cooking techniques, and gourmet food have become more accessible, the principles of molecular gastronomy are contributing to a new form of 'cultural capital'. The questions that remain, once 'scientific' data are available about how make a truly fluffy soufflé or why a saddle of lamb is best cooked at a very low temperature, are why we cooked these dishes in other ways previously, and perhaps even why we might prefer the taste of things that are prepared in a manner different from that which has been 'scientifically accredited' by these new experts of the kitchen.

Alain-Claude Roudot argues that the history of food science can be traced back to the mid-1700s, when a significant portion of the inhabitants of Western Europe began to be interested in food as something more than merely a material for sustenance. The type of food science that developed was not focused primarily on food safety – although the field shifted markedly in the 1800–1900s toward these concerns – but instead on sensory perceptions and particularly the study of taste. One of the earliest proponents of using scientific methods to analyse food was Jean Anthelme Brillat-Savarin, who stated in an infamous retort to his cook:

> You are somewhat opinionated, and I have had a little trouble in making you understand that the phenomena which occur in your laboratory are nothing more than the execution of the eternal laws of nature, and that certain things which you do inattentively, and only because you have seen others do them, are nonetheless based on the highest and most abstruse scientific principles.[8]

His principles may have been well-founded if not a bit premature, not in the least part because the chemical theories and techniques necessary to substantiate many of his oftentimes outlandish claims – for example, the concept of an 'osmazome' as a fundamental component of meat – were not available during his time. McGee himself traces his intellectual lineage to Brillat-Savarin, and notes that the Platonic dialogue *Gorgias* along with Samuel Johnson suggested that 'cooking deserves detailed and serious study'.[9]

The original edition of *OFC* was nearly seven hundred pages in length, and took McGee five years to research and write. As McGee states, 'As a cook I wanted to believe that chefs were right, that their experience of doing these things over and over must prove something…but as a scientist I could see that the evidence didn't hold up'.[10] The history of the book's unexpected success permits a glimpse into the process of constructing an audience through the making – and subsequent unmaking – of a myth. Originally intended as a reference book, McGee's editors planned an extremely small print run of 2,500 copies. Just before the book was to be published, McGee undertook one new experiment to test the culinary dogma that egg whites beat up stiffest in a copper bowl: 'the copper bowl claim struck me as unlikely from the start…I figured it was either an old wives' tale or a promotional ploy by the copper industry'.[11] Spurred on by historical evidence of the use of copper bowls, for instance in Diderot and d'Alembert's *Encyclopédie* of 1771, McGee purchased a copper bowl and did what was to become his crucial experiment: 'I would have cried 'Eureka!' if I hadn't been so invested in the idea that it was all a hoax…compared with whites beaten in a glass bowl, the foam took almost twice as long to form. But it developed a lovely golden hue, became stiffer and moister, and stayed that way much longer'.[12]

This conclusion, however, did nothing more than reinforce what chefs had known for at least two hundred years, and so McGee, together with biologists Sharon Long (also his wife) and Winslow Briggs, engaged in spectral analysis to determine why copper bowls caused this effect and to develop a theory of the mechanisms at work in the process. They found that an egg-white protein called conalbumin (ovatransferrin) had taken up copper from the bowl, and as the protein's three-dimensional molecules unfolded during the beating process, the copper ions added strength to the protein's original delicate structure. As protein bonds reinforced by metal are more stable, they are 'more forgiving of a cook's inattention'.[13] Hence it is much more difficult to over-beat egg whites to the point of irreversible collapse if a copper bowl is used.

The publication of this study as a letter in the British scientific journal *Nature* is noteworthy for several reasons. First, its use of technical, scientific language – such as 'chicken albumen foams' and 'copper reaction vessels' – and traditional scientific methodology of hypothesis testing set it apart from typical 'cooking' literature. It established the tone for a new genre of food research that aimed to investigate culinary practice in philosophical and scientific terms. Its hybridisation of source materials ranging from the gastronomic progenitors cited above to Julia Child, along with research articles from the mainstream *Biochemistry* to the less accessible *Poultry Science*, emphasized not only the scientific credibility of the research and the team performing it, but their intellectual authority as a new generation of self-defined 'gastronomists'. Perhaps most notably, McGee had begun to fashion himself as the heir to Brillat-Savarin, explicitly providing modern-day instructions so that the 'inattentive' cook – notice the parallel wording! – could avoid that fallen soufflé or non-fluffy meringue. Whereas Brillat-Savarin could only hint at the eternal laws of nature or scientific principles underlying cooking methods, McGee was beginning to explore them and to substantiate long-held intuitions about the right way to cook.

The letter to *Nature* might have remained buried in the back pages of the journal, but instead was rapidly picked up by the wire services and reported in newspapers from Boston to Bangkok, causing McGee's editors to triple the first print order and market *OFC* as trade rather than reference.[14] The book became extremely popular and allowed McGee to fashion himself as a guru of esoteric questions not only about why cooking methods work as they do, but various issues in nutrition, food chemistry, and food science in general.[15] One of his specialities is myth-busting, or attempting to show through experimental testing that cooking traditions – or less generously, old wives' tales – are not well-founded.[16]

In the period between the publication of the first edition of *OFC* and its reissue, the study of the 'everyday' has been claimed to have gained in respectability within science, for instance through the award of the 1991 Nobel Prize in physics to Pierre-Gilles de Gennes, also an attendee at the Erice workshops, for work on flow of large molecules relating to what happens when you stir a drink or move food around in your mouth.[17] Various notable chefs adopted techniques from what became an increasing number of molecular gastronomists, often inviting them to be consultants in their kitchens. The desire for control had begun within the mass production food industry, which had already embraced food chemistry and science in order to achieve replicability, usually at lower cost, in place of more empirical, 'look and cook' approaches.[18] Although gourmet chefs were less concerned about cost, molecular gastronomy did permit better control over food production, allowing more precision – for instance, using a blow torch to put final browning touches on meat rather than rather inexact oven baking – as well as quicker preparation, shorter completion times, and the unusual concoctions such as those described at the start of this paper.

By the 2004 publication of the revised edition of his book, McGee had a captive audience of converted gastronomists eager to learn the scientific principles that would distinguish their cooking from that of 'non-scientific' cooks. Using classic recipes – which he somewhat derogatorily terms 'time-tested and thought-less' – may allow us to avoid guesswork or having to experiment as we prepare a meal. But using thought and analysis 'free[s] us from the necessity of following recipes, and help[s] us deal with the unexpected, including the inspiration to try something new'.[19] Hence the cook who merely wants to recreate the usual can stick with traditional recipes, for which she likely will not understand the underlying principles that make them work. But the truly cutting-edge chef who wishes to be responsive to problems as they arise and to create innovative dishes needs to absorb the principles of molecular gastronomy, to become familiar with the molecular world and the actions and reactions within it:

> Thoughtful cooking means paying attention to what our senses tell us as we prepare it, connecting that information with past experience and with an understanding of what's happening to the food's inner substance, and adjusting the preparation accordingly.[20]

The reader of *OFC* thus is convinced that only 'thoughtful cooking', by which is meant cooking that relies on scientific principles and particularly those of molecular gastronomy, is creative and worthwhile.

The rise of molecular gastronomy can be partially explained through Pierre Bourdieu's idea of cultural capital, the means by which distinctions between social and other classes can be expressed and reinforced.[21] During the twentieth century, knowledge about food and preparation skills have altered but oftentimes served as forms of cultural capital. So, for instance, once time pressures became more significant, fewer people regularly prepared home-cooked meals; thus having leisure time to cook more elaborate meals became a positive indicator of social and economic status. As Pauline Adema argues, 'the constant variable throughout this transformation is that a wider knowledge of foods, an appreciation for foods that are "acquired tastes," and familiarity with advanced preparation techniques remain cultural capital'.[22] This last point is particularly applicable to molecular gastronomy: gourmet techniques and food itself have become more accessible through a variety of popular media, notably the proliferation of television cooking shows, so that anyone can watch and absorb how to prepare various dishes, though perhaps they cannot access all of the ingredients due to cost or availability, and may never actually cook any of the dishes.[23] But molecular gastronomy requires another level of engagement, a willingness to understand what is going on within the food in order better to control its production. Hence McGee's book reinforces a form of cultural capital that allows elite chefs and gourmands to distinguish themselves from the masses that can watch the Food Network but at best merely ape the motions of celebrity chefs.

Many kitchen traditions are unsubstantiated, and a trained molecular gastronomist can recognise this. Why do we add salt to the water when cooking green vegetables? This question was posed by British chef Heston Blumenthal to Peter Barham, a molecular gastronomist at Bristol University and author of a popular book on kitchen science. The usual responses in classic cookbooks are that salt maintains or enhances colour, or even that it lowers the boiling point of water and thus speeds up the cooking process. The latter rationale is clearly absurd, but its frequent inclusion in classic cookbooks helps to underscore the open niche or downright vacuum of scientific knowledge about cooking in which molecular gastronomy has positioned itself. In short, there is 'no good reason' for adding salt, and 'the practice has continued by tradition rather than as a result of any rigorous testing'.[24] But in a recent interview, McGee notes that 'for the record, as every cook knows, green beans cooked in salted water definitely have more flavour...somehow the salt must inhibit the osmosis of chlorophyll into the cooking water...someday I'll figure out exactly how'.[25]

Exchanges such as these between the proponents of molecular gastronomy reinforce its power as a promissory note, even in the current absence of explicit explanations or valid scientific theories. What is to count as a 'reason' for cooking something in a particular manner is a description of a chemical interaction that accords with our sensory experiences associated with foods produced using this method, and the ultimate goal is to find the answer. As This explains the principles of molecular gastronomy: 'success is guaranteed because the recipe has been tested – scientifically'.[26] Meanwhile, McGee puzzles over bread: 'Something I think that is still mysterious is gluten...there's a new theory about what's going on in gluten; how those protein molecules combine with each other and combine into this amazing, almost living superstructure. But the jury is still out on how it all really works'.[27] But there will be an answer and a scientific one at that, if only enough clever experiments are performed.

However, what this approach appears to rule out is that there might be a multiplicity of answers about why we do what we do in the kitchen, and what we should do, particularly as there is no unanimity with regard to what tastes good or how we want our food prepared, though there may be some common positive or negative human reactions to particular foods. Consider the fact that as long ago as 1930, a study showed that meat cooked at a constant temperature loses less moisture than meat given an initial searing to 'seal in the juices'. As McGee explains, searing actually creates extra flavour through the browning of surface chemicals, but its effect on the juices is to pull them out, hence making the meat drier.[28] John Lanchester puts it more bluntly: 'Seared steak is less juicy, not more. Anyone who tells you different – a trusted cookbook, a beloved grandmother – is wrong'.[29] Or at least according to the principles of molecular gastronomy.

But 'wrong' in what sense? Lanchester warns of a dangerous trend in food literature, riding on the coattails of molecular gastronomy but also in some senses recent encyclopaedic compilations such as *The Cambridge World History of Food*. He notes a downbeat, pessimistic attitude about food, one that stresses the threats of biotechnology and bioengineered foods:

> My principal beef with this is not the over-all moral of the work but its remorselessly exclusive insistence on the scientific...as we stand on the brink of a revolution in food technology, we need to be reminded that food is not primarily a form of medicine; that the story of mankind and food can be reduced to science, but it is not primarily about science; that man's relationship with

49

food is, and always has been, a terrible and passionate drama.[30]

Although McGee and other molecular gastronomists make the future seem very exciting, especially if we can control our food production through better chemistry, the 'meaning' of food seems now to have been reduced to its constituent molecules, without adequate attention to the possible emergent properties that might be produced. Contrast these views on molecular gastronomy with the approaches of the chef Ferran Adrià of Spain, and his cooking as 'deconstruction': food historian Fabio Parasecoli describes Adrià's approach in Wittgensteinian terms, as similar to a game into which we must enter, 'one in which the rules are not fixed beforehand, but created while playing'.[31] The rules of molecular gastronomy are in fact the rules of molecular biology and chemistry, fixed and unchanging, and hence it is questionable whether there is a 'game' to be played. Certainly the rules of the language game that we use to describe cooking are quite fixed, if we adhere to the mandates of molecular gastronomy. But as Lanchester aptly summarizes it:

> We can't talk seriously about food without talking about what we think we are doing, as well as what it looks like we are doing. Food is never without meaning. Searing a steak to 'seal in the juices' may not do anything to seal in the juices, but the truth is, searing makes meat taste juicier. When it comes to food, science can be wrong, even when it's right.

And sometimes the science is wrong. Ironically, that copper bowl theory that propelled McGee to fame was disproved by him by simple trial and error, as he admits in the new version of his book. One day, he tried a silver-plated bowl, and whipped up a perfect light and glossy egg foam.[32] If you want the chemical details, read the book. Otherwise, enjoy the process of making a light meringue in blissful ignorance.

Bibliography

Adema, Pauline, 'Vicarious consumption: food, television and the ambiguity of modernity', in *Journal of American and Comparative Cultures*, vol. 23 (2000), pp. 113–24.

Afiya, Amanda, 'The appliance of science', *Caterer and Hotelkeeper*, (8 July 2004a), p. 26.

——, 'Molecular gastronomy: the early years', *Caterer and Hotelkeeper*, (8 July 2004b), p. 26.

Anonymous, 'To information-hungry author Harold McGee, food is something to pinch, poke and probe', *People Weekly*, (25 February 1985), pp. 78–81.

Bacon, Francis, *The new organon and related writings*, ed. F. H. Anderson (Indianapolis: Bobbs-Merrill, 1620 [1960]).

Barham, Peter, *The science of cooking* (Berlin: Springer-Verlag, 2000).

Bourdieu, Pierre, *Distinction: a social critique of the judgement of taste* (Cambridge: Harvard University Press, 1984).

Brillat-Savarin, Jean Anthelme, *The physiology of taste: or, meditations on transcendental gastronomy*, trans. M. F. K. Fisher (Washington, DC: Counterpoint, 1825 [1949]).

Davis, Mandy, 'Poetry and science in the kitchen (PW talks with Harold McGee)', *Publishers Weekly* vol. 251 (2004), p. 54.

Ennen, Steve, 'Taking flavor to the molecule: Europe's top chef uses science to build creativity', *Food Processing*, (February 2002), pp. 30–4.

——, 'Fighting palate fatigue', *Food Processing*, (April 2003), p. 10.

Ferran, Adrià, *Los secretos de El Bulli* (Barcelona: Altaya, 1997).

Fisher, Lan, 'Bon appetit', *New Scientist*, vol. 171 (28 July 2001), p. 58.

Jouan, Anne, 'La science est anarchiste (entretien Hervé This)', *Le Figaro étudiant*, (14 October 2004). http://www.figaroetudiant.com/formation_dossiers/20041014. FIG0567.html, last accessed 15 July 2005.

Keller, Evelyn Fox, 'Baconian science: the arts of mastery and obedience', in *Reflections on gender and science* (New Haven: Yale University Press), pp. 33–42.

King, Émilie Boyer, 'Food: his passion, his science (Hervé This, a French researcher, helps chefs around the world really sizzle)', *The Christian Science Monitor*, (18 February 2004). http://www.csmonitor. com/2004/ 0218/p11s02-lifo.html, last accessed 15 July 2005.

Kurti, Nicholas, *But the crackling is superb* (Bristol: Institute of Physics Publishing, 1997).

Kummer, Corby, 'An end to al dente: lightly cooked can be exactly the wrong way to taste vegetables', *The Atlantic*, vol. 266 (September 1990), pp. 110–3.

Lanchester, John, 'Edible complex', *The New Yorker*, (27 November 2000), p. 170.

Marks, Paul, 'Molecular gastronomy', *New Scientist*, vol. 176 (23 November 2002), p. 49.

McGee, Harold, 'Recipe for safer sauces', *Nature*, vol. 347 (1990), p. 717.

——, 'Why the rubber chicken leg can bounce across the road', *The New York Times*, (29 April 1998), p. F10.

——, 'In victu veritas (role of spices in reducing food-borne disease)', *Nature*, vol. 392 (1998), pp. 659–60.

——, 'Taking stock of new flavours', *Nature*, vol. 400 (1999), pp. 17–8.

——, *On food and cooking: the science and lore of the kitchen* (New York: Scribner, 2004, revised and updated edition). (Also published simultaneously as *McGee on Food and Cooking: An Encyclopedia of Kitchen Science, History and Culture*, London: Hodder & Stoughton Ltd.).

McGee, Harold R., Sharon R. Long, and Winslow R. Briggs, 'Why whip egg whites in copper bowls?', *Nature*, vol. 308 (1984), pp. 667–8.

McGee, Harold, Jack McInerney, and Alain Harrus, 'The virtual cook: modeling heat transfer in the kitchen', *Physics Today*, vol. 52 (November 1999), pp. 30–7.

Moskin, Julia, 'Isaac Newton in the kitchen', *The New York Times*, (24 November 2004).

O'Driscoll, Cath, 'Good chemists make great chefs', *Chemistry and Industry*, (3 May 2004), pp. 12–3.

O'Neill, Molly, 'Better cooking through chemistry: that's the wisdom of Harold McGee, master of the bunsen burner', *The New York Times Magazine*, (17 August 1997), p. 55.

Parasecoli, Fabio, 'Deconstructing soup: Ferran Adrià's culinary challenges', *Gastronomica*, vol. 1 (2001), pp. 60–73.

Perlik, Allison, 'The kitchen scientist continues to experiment and learn', *Restaurants and Institutions*, (15 October 2004), p. 28.

Raffael, Michael, 'Science serves the chef', *Caterer and Hotelkeeper*, (8 July 2004), p. 26.

Roudot, Alain-Claude, 'Food science and consumer taste', *Gastronomica*, vol. 4 (2004), pp. 41–6.

Schwartz, David M., 'Serving up science for everyday cooks and gourmets alike', *Smithsonian*, vol. 23 (December 1992), pp. 110–8.

Slavkin, Harold C., 'Toward 'molecular gastronomy,' or what's in a taste?', *Journal of the American Dental Association*, vol. 130 (1999), pp. 1497–1500.

Smillie, Dirk, 'Torte reform', *Forbes*, vol. 171 (6 January 2003), pp. 162–3.

Smith, Cynthia Duquette, 'Discipline – it's a 'good thing': rhetorical constitution and Martha Stewart Living Omnimedia', *Women's Studies in Communication*, vol. 23 (2000), pp. 337–67.

Steingarten, Jeffrey, 'Better cooking through chemistry (French gourmet Hervé This)', *Vogue*, vol. 186 (March 1996), pp. 312–5.

Telfer, Elizabeth, *Food for thought: philosophy and food* (London: Routledge, 1996).

This, Hervé, *Une théorie du gout* (Paris: Pour la science, 1999).

——, *Casseroles et éprouvettes* (Paris: Pour la science, 2002).

Weiss, Giselle, 'Why is a soggy potato chip unappetizing?', *Science*, vol. 293 (2001), pp. 1753–4.

Wilson, Bee, 'Wrong ingredients (on Delia Smith)', *New Statesman*, (31 January 2000), pp. 51–2.

Wolke, Robert L., *What Einstein told his cook: kitchen science explained* (New York: W. W. Norton & Company, 2002).

Notes

1. Roudot p. 45.
2. Marks; King.
3. McGee (2004) p. 2.
4. Afiya (2004b); King.
5. Afiya (2004a) p. 26.
6. Many credit this to Bacon; for a critique, see Keller.
7. For example, Wolke.
8. Brillat Savarin p. 128.
9. McGee (2004) p. 2.
10. Moskin.
11. Schwartz.
12. Schwartz.
13. McGee, Long, and Briggs p. 668.
14. Schwartz.
15. See for instance McGee's frequent contributions to *The New York Times* as well as *Nature* in the 1990s, a sample of which are included in the bibliography.
16. See for example information on the nutritional value of fertilised versus unfertilised eggs in Anonymous 1985.
17. Weiss (1985).
18. Weiss (2001).
19. McGee (2004) p. 4.
20. McGee (2004) p. 4.
21. Bourdieu.
22. Adema.
23. See for instance Smith; Wilson.
24. O'Driscoll p. 12.
25. Moskin.
26. King.
27. Davis.
28. Moskin.
29. Lanchester p. 170.
30. Lanchester p. 170.
31. Parasecoli p. 63.
32. McGee (2004) pp. 100-6.

Food as Art and the Quest for Authenticity

Albert Arouh

Introduction

The post-modern predicament has invested (one might say, infested) the quest for authenticity with elusiveness. According to the standard post-modern view, authenticity is an illusion, a slippery concept, a futile quest, and thus there is nothing that can be said about it. Everything is interpretation, text and context, and appeals to ultimate authenticity smack of suspect rhetoric.

Gastronomy, where issues of authenticity are usually discussed in terms of genuine ingredients and their provenance, pure culinary identities and natural tastes, has not been able to avoid the post-modern predicament. For example, in the case of Jonathan Nossiter's film *Mondovino*, 'authentic terroir wine' is posited against 'inauthentic big business wine', yet it was shown that the conflict between 'authentic vs inauthentic wine' is no more than a conflict between economic interests masquerading as the 'good', French producer Guibert, and the 'evil', American businessman Mondavi.[1] The debate between 'ethnic authentic food' versus ' inauthentic fusion', is no more than the loss of national identity in the face of globalization.[2] Finally, the appeal for 'natural, 'fresh' or 'authentic' food is nothing else but (as Daniel Harris calls it), the marketing 'rhetoric with which advertisers make love to our taste buds...'.[3]

Despite this post-modern attack on authenticity, however, there is still, I believe, room for discussion, if we see food as art. If food is seen as art, then ideas, concepts and categories about authenticity in art, which have been thoroughly discussed in aesthetics,[4] may be fruitfully employed in order to examine certain issues of authenticity in gastronomy.

Since I will be discussing food as art throughout this paper, and I will be comparing it to music or painting, in order to pre-empt any possible protestations against such blasphemy, I will first deal with this issue. In the first part, I will try to show that there is nothing in the nature of food that inhibits it from being art, even though, at the moment, the consensus thinks that it is not. Then I will turn to a discussion of what kind of art food might be and finally examine two cases of authenticity. Firstly, the case of the 'missing chef', that is, whether the physical presence of the chef in the kitchen is necessary in order to say that one had an authentic experience. Secondly, the case of the artistic integrity of the chef and the relationship between being authentic to one's own aesthetic principles and transcending those of the ruling culinary canon.

The aesthetics of food
The missing 'artworld' of food:

There seems to be a deeply entrenched belief, almost a prejudice, that food is not art, in the sense we mean art when we refer to music or painting. Allen Weiss believes that 'cuisine is still the victim of lowly and deplorable prejudices. Its most noble geniuses still have not conquered the right to be placed between Raphael and Beethoven...'.[5] People readily accept a can of soup by Andy Warhol as art rather than contemplate the possibility of giving the status of art to the soup that was in the can, let alone to a soup made by Pierre Gagnaire. They acknowledge a urinal by Marcel Duchamp (signifying among other things the bodily) as revolutionary art, while at the same time reject food of being art because, as Carolyn Korsmeyer says, 'eating, drinking and tasting...signify the bodily...'.[6] They are willing to discuss modern, abstract, trash, op, pop and all sorts of other activities as art but not the creations of Ferran Adrià, Joël Robuchon, Marc Veyrat or Heston Blumenthal. It seems that, while the commonplace has been transfigured into art, food, and even more so, aesthete haute cuisine, has not.

In general, when reference is made to food as art, it means either 'craft' or at best 'minor art'.[7] Korsmeyer, for example, claims that 'certainly food does not qualify as a fine art; it does not have the right history... Culinary art can still be considered a minor or a decorative art, or perhaps a functional or applied art...'.[8] Paradoxically, the world of food also believes that food is not art. For instance, Ferran Adrià, the chef artist par excellence, says: 'food is not art because it is ephemeral and a deep biological need, it is not like painting or film'.[9] Nico Ladenis (a great culinary aesthete) unequivocally declares his 'deep conviction that cooking is a science and presentation is an art'.[10] The well-known food critic, Luca Vercelloni, says: 'Cooking...is very different from art...Recipes are not masterpieces to be exhibited in galleries...Chefs must be above all skillful executors, rather than inspired creators'.[11] In a study conducted of the way cooks talk about what they do, it was found that 'the large majority of cooks do not conceive of themselves as involved in artistic production per se [though] they are concerned with occupational aesthetics'.[12]

The consensus believes that there is something in the nature of food and the 'logic' of gustatory taste that prevents food from being art; that, as Korsmeyer again says, 'it differs from the logic of genuine aesthetic judgments'.[13] Philosophers object to food being art by pointing to, among other things, its lack of complexity,[14] its sensuality[15] and its transient nature.[16] Some also claim that food cannot be art because gustatory taste does not represent anything except itself, i.e. it does not have 'content',[17] or 'cognitive' value.[18]

I will very briefly try to respond to these objections. I will also disagree with Korsmeyer when she maintains that good food is based on 'sensory pleasure...and... refined discrimination', which however 'are meager grounds on which to establish aesthetic features of tasting and eating'.[19] There is, I hope, more to food than sensual pleasure and refined discrimination.

The fact that food has no artworld, i.e. a consensus that believes that food is art, is a contingent matter, not a law of nature. Given the appropriate circumstances, food may eventually be recognized as art. It happened to other art kinds, such as novels, cinema and photography, which have in time been admitted to the artistic fold, while gardening, which, though it was accepted as art in the past, is now relegated to the status of 'decorative art'.[20] There is, I believe, nothing inherent in the constitution of food that prevents it from being acknowledged as art.

To begin with, one cannot claim that food is not high art, since this requires, first, a definition of art, i.e. a set of necessary and sufficient conditions for something to be called art, and second, a clear evaluative criterion that demarcates high from low art. Philosophers of art however are still debating the issue of what art is, each one offering different definitions and criteria.[21] It seems from the discussion in aesthetics that art eludes definition, or more precisely, there are as many contending definitions as there are debates. One cannot know for sure what art is and therefore one cannot know what art is not. In the context of what Weiss calls 'new aesthetics', boundaries and borderlines between art and craft, or distinctions between art and non-art, have disappeared.[22] Therefore, one cannot say that food is not art, or that it is a minor art, since we cannot know what art is, let alone major art.

As to the nature of food, which prevents it from being art, the arguments are not very convincing. For example, the bodily dimension of food, and its connection to sensuality, is neither the prerogative only of food nor its only dimension. Music is perceived bodily, as sound waves enter our ears, while there are sensual pleasures in music akin to those associated with food. A good melody titillates the senses as much as a good flavour does.[23] Moreover, such sensual pleasures can be disconnected from the aesthetic pleasures afforded by especially, but not only, haute cuisine. One can enjoy the formal qualities of food and contemplate its aesthetic design, a pleasure that is closer to the mind than to the body, even though such formal qualities are perceived as being in the body.

As to the complexity and expressive potential of food, one has to taste the food created by chefs such as Ferran Adrià, Charlie Trotter or Marco Pierre-White to attest to such qualities. A menu created by Pierre Gagnaire, for example, the so-called cerebral chef, is full of spiritual and sublime, even poetic, values,[24] which take such type of food beyond the bodily and the mere sensual. Gagnaire's set menus, for instance, involve an array of courses each one of which is composed of different dishes simultaneously served that constitute aesthetic variations on a theme (his famous lobster, for example, *en trois services*), each dish relating or contrasting with the other, in terms of tastes, aromas and textures, creating an aesthetic experience that involves a complex, varied and unified formal structure.[25] The aesthetic qualities of a menu by Alain Senderens at the 'Lucas Carton' restaurant, match the aesthetic qualities of any other art form: its carefully arranged harmonies and contrasts within each plate but also the

55

aesthetic synergies that exist between plates, like a symphony or a sonata, where the different movements have autonomous aesthetic characteristics but also they relate musically or thematically to each other, from the amuse-bouches to the après-desserts, to the wines that have been selected by the chef for each course, or the other aesthetic considerations that have been taken into account, from presentation, to atmosphere to the art de la table, appealing to all senses and offering an aesthetic complexity far beyond that of simple, bodily, pleasure. As to the transient nature of food, an argument made especially by Elisabeth Telfer,[26] the simple response is that many art forms are transient in nature, for example ballet and theater. Performance art forms are transient in nature, a characteristic that has not prevented them from enjoying the status of art. As to the argument that food has no content, indeed, in its most artistic manifestation, i.e. in haute cuisine, food represents nothing, it refers to no other meaning or symbolism, religious, ethnic or otherwise, except its appreciation. In fact, its meaning is its aesthetic appreciation. Haute cuisine is non-representational.[27] The same can be said about non-programmatic music, which refers to nothing else except its aesthetic appreciation. If we insisted that art necessarily be about something, then this would lead to the disqualification of Beethoven's last quartets from being art.[28]

Finally, Korsmeyer claims that food has limited aesthetic qualities. She maintains that food relates only to 'relishing fine distinctions', it does not have the 'deepened understanding that [is] expected with encounters with important aesthetic objects'.[29] However, if 'deepened understanding' is seen as a necessary and sufficient condition for something to be art, and which food is lacking, then this would leave out of the classification, along with food, a lot of 'important aesthetic objects', especially of the modern kind. It strains one's imagination to see what the deeper meaning there is of Lichtenstein's cartoons or Warhol's Brillo Box. Perhaps one does not deepen one's understanding with a meal at The Fat Duck, in the sense that one does so with a novel by Kafka, but this condition does not define all art. The point is that food has been more and more 'aesthetized'[30] in the sense of being increasingly vested with a host of aesthetic qualities that go beyond the typical idea that one has of gastronomy, i.e. what goes with what, or what Korsmeyer calls 'fine distinctions'. From Taillevant to Carême and from Escoffier to Ferran Adrià, gastronomic sensibilities and aesthetic qualities have evolved in similar ways, as in other art forms.[31] Judgments of taste, critiques of form, aesthetic questions of balance, elegance, simplicity, beauty, shock or humor, creativity, originality and other aesthetic qualities, have been applied to food as in the recognized arts.[32] Even though philosophers and the world of food object to food being art, the increasing 'aesthetization' especially of haute cuisine shows that food bears a close family resemblance to other art kinds.[33]

What is missing in the case of food, in order to be accepted as art, is not a particular characteristic that relates to its nature. What we could say about food is not that it is (or it is not) art, as this is not easily definable, but that, given its 'aesthetization, it bears a family resemblance to the aesthetic experiences of art forms (such as music).

What is missing in the case of food is an 'artworld', i.e., a critical and professional opinion, which would 'ratify' such family resemblance. But this is a contingent matter, depending on factors that transcend the nature of food as art. Food may not be seen as art yet, but there is nothing inherent to it which prevents it from been seen as art.

The ontology and the music of food

If food could be seen as art, what kind would it be? What sort of artistic entity would it be? 'A physical thing... mental...neither?...a concrete particular bound to a single place and time, or is it a universal or type, existing in an abstract manner?'.[34] What is the ontological status of food, especially as compared to other art forms such as music or painting? If we can stipulate the nature of food as an 'artistic entity', we can shed light on issues of authenticity in food, for differences in ontology imply differences in authenticity.

Broadly speaking, art forms can be classified into two categories: those that are characterized by multiplicity and those that are characterized by uniqueness.[35] Music and drama for example are multiple art forms in the sense that performances of them can be repeated in time and space; they are events. Painting, sculpture and architecture, on the other hand, are singular, non-performance art forms in the sense that there is an enduring physical object, e.g. a painting, that is unique and independent of time and space. Thus a composition by Mozart can be performed many times and in different places by different people, whereas a painting by Vermeer is unique and unrepeatable.[36]

57

In unique art forms, questions of authenticity arise in relation to the true physical original, and in multiple art forms, in relation to the manifest intentions of the artist as interpreted by the performance of his/her work. Food is like music; it needs a performance to be realized.[37] As in music, so in food, there is a creator (composer) of a recipe (score), there is the chef who executes (performs) the recipe, there is a place i.e. the restaurant (the concert hall) where it is served, and there are the diners (audience) who taste the food (listen to the music). Food however has a dual ontology. It manifests itself as physical entity and as abstract performance. In paintings, there is a physical entity on the canvas that is unique and original. In food, there is a physical entity on the plate that is also unique and original.

Unlike paintings, however food is transient. The painting on the canvas does not need to be consumed in order to be appreciated. By contrast, the food on the plate needs to be actually consumed in order to be appreciated. Its appreciation implies its disappearance. The aesthetic qualities of the food on the plate are consumed along with the physical entity.

What characterizes food therefore is its dual ontology. Since the physical food on the plate is consumed, it needs to be reproduced. The chef who reproduces the recipe, the ingredients and the implements used, the context in which it is reproduced, are all unrepeatable and therefore every time a dish is cooked, it is an 'original', even though it is the physical token of the same, abstract recipe-type. What applies to issues of authenticity in painting, where the original endures, does not apply to the food on the plate, where the original is transient. Though the food on the plate is physical and unique, its consumption necessitates its reproduction. In this sense, it is a performance, an event that varies in time and place. It is like the performance of a musical score. Issues of authenticity do not arise in respect to the physical original, since this has disappeared, but in respect to the performance: must the performer also be the creator so that the recipe is executed authentically? This is one case of authenticity. The other case is that of artistic authenticity, i.e. the case of pursuing one's own aesthetic principles.

The next section deals with these two cases of authenticity.

Authenticity served on a plate

The case of the missing chef:
When Roland Barthes proclaimed the 'death of the Author', he could not have foreseen that in the case of cooking, the 'death of the chef' has taken on a more literal meaning. And by this I do not mean the untimely death of Bernard Loiseau or the tragic one of François Vatel, but the disappearance of the chef from the kitchen. From Ramsey and Nobu to Robuchon and of course Ducasse, more and more chefs have gone 'missing', opening one restaurant after another, while consulting many more around the world, rarely being present in the restaurant, let alone in the kitchen. So, the question of authenticity in cooking arises not only from the fact that the diners always 'eat' into the food aesthetic experiences that the chef has never intended,[38] a predicament shared with other art forms, but also arises from the literal absence of the chef. The chef is absent figuratively and literally. Does this mean that, unless the chef is present in the kitchen, actually cooking behind the stoves, the food served is inauthentic?

As we have seen, cooking, like music, is a performance art, an event that takes place in time and space. In music there is the composer who creates the music and the conductor who performs it. If the composer is also the conductor, this still is a performance, i.e. an interpretation, of the work. They can however be a different person without any necessary loss of authenticity. That is, every time the work is performed, either by the composer or by someone else, it is a rendition of the composition, one that necessarily involves interpretation. Every performance is different from another, even if performed by the composer. It is like a poet reading his/her poetry in different times and places, each time affected by the moment and by the mood. This is what makes performance a work of art separate from composition,[39] much like directing a play is a different art work from writing the play.

Similarly, Ducasse is the creator of a recipe, which as a work of art is independent of time and place; it is a type the token of which is performed at a particular time and place, either by him or by someone else who executes it. It can be performed in Plaza Athénée in Paris or Le Louis XV in Monaco or the Essex House in New York at the same time by different chefs/conductors, or in the same restaurant in different times also by different chefs/conductors. This means that the experience of Ducasse's *volaille sauce albuféra* as performed by Christophe Moret at the Plaza Athénée is a Ducasse experience in the same sense that the experience of the *Magic Flute* performed by Karl Böhm at Glyndebourne is a Mozart experience, even though the composer was not present at the time of the performance. Though it is an interpretation of the work, it is nevertheless, to one degree or another, an authentic Mozart experience as rendered by Karl Böhm. The performance may be better or worse but the food could still be a Ducasse authentic experience independently of who actually was the performer or whether Ducasse was present or not. It would of course be a Ducasse experience as performed by Moret. The question of authenticity would arise here in relation to the interpretation of the menu, whether the rendition was faithful to the instructions or allowances and adjustments were made according to the sensibilities and aesthetic predilections of the chef/performer. This again does not make the rendition inauthentic in the same way that a liberal interpretation of *Romeo and Juliet* by Baz Luhrmann does not make the Shakespeare experience less authentic. In fact, a liberal rendition of a Ducasse recipe by another chef who has, in his/her view, captured the 'essence' of Ducasse, might present an authentic Ducasse experience, perhaps even more authentically than Ducasse himself would have cooked his recipe.

59

Even when a chef of another restaurant copies Ducasse's style, there is still no issue of being inauthentic, as Ducasse's style is a type of which a Ducasse-like recipe is a token. Maybe the chef of another restaurant cannot exactly copy a Ducasse recipe but he/she can copy Ducasse's style and still be authentic. But in what sense s/he is authentic will be the subject matter of the next section.

The transcendental chef:
There is another sense of authenticity that relates to being true to one's self, and in the case of art, true to one's aesthetic vision.[40] This type of authenticity, I will call artistic. A chef has artistic authenticity if s/he cooks in a style that follows his/her personal aesthetics in which s/he believes and onto which s/he holds against all odds. By contrast, a chef is artistically inauthentic if s/he uncritically copies other styles, thus sacrificing his/her personal aesthetics for the sake of commercial or other gain.

One of the clearest examples of artistic authenticity is Nico Ladenis and his struggle in the '70s and '80s to impose his aesthetics on restaurant food in Britain. His attitude, which made him notorious, was uncompromising in relation to his aesthetic principles; in fact, his intransigent and tenacious allegiance to his personal aesthetics in cooking had brought Ladenis almost to financial ruin. Nevertheless, he held on to his beliefs and by virtue of his persistence to impose his personal aesthetics of food onto an 'audience' that obviously did not agree with them, finally paid off, as the 'audience' learned to accept Ladenis's aesthetic principles in food. Thus he contributed in a large measure to the gastronomic revolution in Britain. In time, chefs followed Ladenis's aesthetics, as they proved popular; restaurants in Britain tried to cash in on the fashion of elegant haute cuisine, which Ladenis tried to impose. These chefs were artistically inauthentic in the sense of uncritcally imitating Ladenis's style.

Ladenis's case is one of being true to one's own aesthetic vision, i.e. of being artistically authentic. This vision, however, was an ingenious exemplification of the aesthetic canon of French cuisine, a colony, or even a jewel in the crown, of the gastronomic imperium of France. It was the authentic token of an aesthetic type, which is the French canon. He neither transcended the canon nor intended to do so. Ladenis would have been artistically inauthentic if he had believed in a set of aesthetic principles in cooking that diverged from the ones imposed by the French canon and yet continued to serve French haute cuisine. This clearly is not the case, as is evident from his food or from his memoirs.[41] Ladenis is completely faithful to the haute gastronomie of France and at the same time true to his own personal aesthetics. He is authentic in relation to his intentions. Ladenis is like Mozart, who composed in the style and tradition of the music of the 18th century, no doubt ingeniously. Ladenis however is not, nor intends to be, like Schoenberg, who radically broke from the aesthetics that had been followed by western classical music up to then.[42] Schoenberg was a true revolutionary when, against all odds (total incomprehension and scepticism on the part of the audiences then), he pursued his dissonant, avant-garde music and broke from the canon that had dominated music until the beginning of the 20th century. This, according to Adorno, is to be contrasted with Stravinsky, who though he believed in modern music, nevertheless tried to make his music more palatable for the audiences then.[43] This means that Stravinsky stayed within the prevailing canon of music, while Schoenberg transcended it. Which brings me to Ferran Adrià.

Adrià is the best candidate for being a transcendental chef and the one most likely to break from the French canon and create a revolution in food of the same caliber as the one created by Carême in the 19th century.[44] Adrià, however, is not exactly like Schoenberg, he is more like Stravinsky. Adrià does not produce quite as 'dissonant' or 'non-melodious' food, at least not yet. He has not abandoned the goal of producing exquisite flavours, which as he says, at the end, after the elaborate 'show' has ended, aim to please, to make his clients happy. Unlike Schoenberg, but like Stravinsky, Adrià still wants to produce palatable food.

Of course, there are many more aesthetic qualities in Adrià's food than just palatable food. The dishes that he serves, such as provocative Kellogs paella, trompe de bouche olive oil spirals, shocking duck tongues kebab, funny cigars of peanut brittle filled with guacamole, playful popcorn clouds and lollipop sticks of artichokes, surprising caramel served in a spoon filled with quail's eggs, even 'terrible' foie gras 'soil' (powders and grains made from foie gras); his famous foams and froths, balloons filled with scented air and his deconstructed tapas, all serve to indulge in a jeu d'esprit, what Adrià calls the 'sixth sense',[45] i.e. the intellect, when experiencing food. As Thomas Mathews reports, 'many of his dishes are more provocative than delicious...a meal [at El Bulli] is an exercise in breaking down barriers, of confronting fears and insecurities...'.[46] Or as Giles Coren confesses: 'Ferran Adrià did not feed us. He deflowered us. He took our innocence, and left us elated, confused and melancholy'.[47]

All these dishes created by Adrià generate aesthetic dimensions that begin to diverge, slowly but steadily, from the French canon of elegance, harmony, subtlety, luxury, finesse, balance etc, but not entirely. Some of his dishes may not be delicious in the straightforward sense.[48] But he has not yet produced food that would disturb the palate, as dissonant music would disturb the ear; food that would be inedible in the same sense that music could be inaudible; palatable food that would be replaced by artistic food, which would aim to achieve other aesthetic experiences than just gastronomic pleasure, however distasteful these experiences would be. Many say that food should not take this direction.[49] The aim of food is to entertain and please, not to create suspicious and horrible tasting experiences. The same was said of modern music, of course, when it was first performed, or when John Cage 'performed' his '4' 33''', the so-called Silent Concert, i.e. a few moments of silence – like serving an empty plate of food.[50]

But music, unlike food, has progressed to other levels of aesthetic experience. Though Adrià, as well as Blumenthal, Berasategui, Arzak, and many others, have taken food to another, far more interesting level of experience than just refined food in elegant surroundings, still they are bound by the 'pleasure principle'. They still want at the end to produce palatable food in the context of a liberal interpretation of the French canon. Thus all of these chefs have Michelin stars. They are no doubt artistically authentic, since they are true to their own aesthetic principles. They are not however artistic revolutionaries, in the sense that Schoenberg was revolutionary for music, since they still create their food in the context of the French canon. Indeed they have extended the borderlines, and on the whole have operated on the margins of the canon, but they have not transcended it.

Perhaps that is why food is not considered art yet, either by philosophers of art or by chefs themselves. Though Adrià comes very close to being the transcendental chef of our age, the world of food,[51] for better or for worse, has not had its Schoenberg yet. His cuisine, despite enriching food with unprecedented and radically novel aesthetic qualities, has not ignited a gastronomic Big Bang that would derail planet food from its trajectory around Michelin stars and that would perhaps elevate it to a higher artistic plane. Though Adrià is as artistically authentic as one can be, he is not the transcendental chef that would make the world stop seeing food as pure pleasure and start seeing food as pure art. This, as I said, for better or for worse, has not happened, at least, not yet![52]

Notes

1. Olivier Torrès, *La Guerre des Vins: l'affaire Mondavi: Mondialisation et terroirs* (Paris: Dunod, 2005).
2. 'This anxiety over the potential loss of a mythic China is the subtextual tale told by repeated claims of authenticity [in Chinese food]', Malinda Lo, 'Authentic Chinese Food: Chinese American Cookbooks and the Regulation of Ethnic Identity', Presented at the Association for Asian American Studies, March 2001. For a critique of authenticity in relation to national cuisine, see John Matchuk, 'Experimenting with Fusion', *Culinary Connection*, April 1999. According to Alain Weiss, in the postmodern context 'new dishes exist as multiregional and polycultural hybrids, where culinary authenticity has become a function of an ever mobile and dissatisfied nostalgia', *Feast and Folly: Cuisine, Intoxication and the Poetics of the Sublime* (Albany: SUNY Press, 2002), p. 57.
3. Daniel Harris, *Cute, Quaint, Hungry and Romantic: The Aesthetics of Consumerism* (New York: Basic Books, 2000), p. 154.
4. See Oswald Hanfling, *Philosophical Aesthetics: An Introduction* (Oxford: Blackwell, 1992, 1997) and for one of the best presentations of the issue of authenticity in music but also in art in general, see Peter Kivy, *Authenticities: Philosophical Reflections on Musical Performance* (Ithaca: Cornell University Press, 1995).
5. Weiss, *Feast and Folly*, p. 1.
6. Carolyn Korsmeyer, *Making Sense of Taste: Food and Philosophy* (New York: Cornell University Press, 1999), pp. 144–5.
7. Korsmeyer, pp. 103–115. See also Elizabeth Telfer, *Food for Thought: Philosophy and Food* (London: Routledge, 1996), pp. 58–60.
8. Korsmeyer, p. 144. With tongue in cheek, Peter Kivy, says: 'The other day I heard a chef called an artist but was not by any means convinced that the dish he was preparing was a work of art', in *Authenticities*, p. 123. In another context, he also says that 'We are not dealing here with ice cream cones but with a level and complexity of satisfaction that cannot be cashed out in the coin of direct titillation of the senses simpliciter', ibid., p. 181.
9. Interview given to Dimitris Antonopoulos, published in the magazine '*EU*', January 2004, p. 102, in Greek.
10. Nico Ladenis, *My Gastronomy* (London: Macmillan, 1987, 1989), p. 42.
11. Luca Vercelloni, 'Searching for Lost Tastes', *Slow, The International Herald of Taste*, issue no 31 July 2002.
12. Gary Allen Fine, 'Wittgenstein's Kitchen: Sharing Meaning in Restaurant Work', *Theory and Society*, Vol. 24, No. 2 1995, p. 262. There are of course exceptions to this rule, most of which interestingly enough come from France, where cooking has, as expected, gradually ascended to the loftier levels of 'high art'. It is indicative of the high esteem that the French have of food that the art journal *Beaux Arts* now accepts articles on cuisine as art, see Weiss, *Feast and Folly*, pp. 8–9. Although some Anglo-Saxon philosophers have equated food with art, they nevertheless believe, to one degree or the other, that taste and smell present limited artistic possibilities. See Korsmeyer, *Making Sense of Taste*, pp. 104–5.
13. Korsmeyer, *Making Sense of Taste*, p. 104.
14. David Cooper has argued that food lacks formal complexity and aesthetic structure, in his *A Companion to Aesthetics* (Oxford: Blackwell, 1992/99), pp. 251–2.
15. Aquinas of course claimed that taste and smell lack cognitive complexity and are irrelevant to aesthetic appreciation (see, Neil Cambell, 'Aquinas' reasons for the aesthetic irrelevance of tastes and smells', *The British Journal of Aesthetics*, 33:1993), while Santayana maintained that bodily pleasures are distinct from aesthetic pleasures and cannot thus be identified with beauty (see Korsmeyer, *Making Sense of Taste*, p. 104).
16. Korsmeyer, *Making Sense of Taste*, pp. 106–109.
17. Food, especially in religion, has symbolic content, but this is not what matters for food to be accepted as art, since it is the secular, non-symbolic, abstract haute cuisine that claims artistic status. Korsmeyer misses this point when she talks about the cognitive function of symbolic food, pp. 137–140.

18. Ibid., p. 110.
19. Ibid., p. 7. For further discussion see Albert Arouh, 'Is Taste Tasteful' (in Greek), *Cogito*, Nefeli, 1 July 2004.
20. Hanfling, *Philosophical Aesthetics*, p. 7.
21. For an introduction to the debate see Hanfling, *Philosophical Aesthetics,* especially the first essay. Also for a critique of the distinction between high and low art see Pierre Bourdieu, *Distinction: A social critique of the judgment of taste* (Cambridge, Mass: Harvard University Press), 1984. For a discussion of the various definitions of art and their dependence on context and history see Cynthia Freeland, *But is it Art?* (Oxford: OUP, 2001), especially pp. 43–4 as well as Noël Carroll, *Philosophy of Art* (London: Routledge, 1999), especially the last chapter.
22. Weiss, *Feast and Folly*, p. 10.
23. Telfer makes a similar point in her *Food for Thought*, pp. 30–31.
24. For the spiritual dimension of food see Leon R. Kass, *The Hungry Soul, Eating and the Perfecting of Nature* (Chicago: University of Chicago Press, 1994, 1999), pp. 183–194. For the sublime in food as an art form see Allen Weiss, *Feast and Folly*, especially the Preface.
25. Noël Carroll identifies as aesthetic properties 'unity, diversity and intensity' and says that attending to these properties amounts to an aesthetic experience. 'That is, a work has the capacity to afford aesthetic experience...in as much as the work has features of this sort. An artwork is something intended to present features like these for the audience to apprehend.' Noël Carroll, *Philosophy of Art*, p. 170.
26. Telfer has made a spirited defense of food as art involving formal organization, but she concludes, for various reasons, amongst which the most important is the transience of food, that 'food can be the basis of a simple but minor art form', *Food for Thought*, p. 3.
27. In addition to being non-representational, in the sense of having formal aesthetic qualities without content, some commentators have attributed meaning and content to food. About the semantics and meaning of food and its significance as text, see especially Alain Weiss' essay on 'The Epic of the Cephalopod', in his *Feast and Folly*, where he says that 'A dish is a symbol; inspiration comes from aromas, tastes techniques; but meaning derives from elsewhere, from a place most often unnamable and unattainable...The hint of the abyss that spices up the squid's welcoming void is a subtle manifestation of the sublime in cuisine...that establishes the metaphysical piquancy of gastronomy...[which] is, quite exceptionally, related to death itself', pp. 80–82.
28. Telfer, *Food for Thought*, p. 59. For a discussion of a representational theory of art, see Carroll, *Philosophy of Art*, pp. 19–56.
29. Korsmeyer, *Making Sense of Taste*, p. 114.
30. Post-modernism rears its relativist head even here: 'the transformation of food into art...provides a subtle way of flattering the consumer...aesthetophage...who dines on paintings and sculptures, sending masterpieces on an inglorious journey down his alimentary canal...', Harris, *The Aesthetics of Consumerism*, p. 177.
31. It must be noted however, that the development of cuisine as an aesthetic object has taken place in the context of the French culinary canon. The canon itself changed, with its aesthetics giving emphasis either to baroque complexity or natural simplicity to tradition or to modernity, but it stays within the context of French cultural sensibilities that have to do with, for example, bourgeois pretensions of fine dining, elegance, finesse, lightness and subtlety, in the context of luxurious surroundings. These aesthetic qualities may have marked modern haute cuisine everywhere in the world, but this does not mean that the history of the aesthetics of food has reached its end. Already, a different aesthetic model of food is emerging, especially from Spain, modernizing cooking in the same way that Spain modernized painting in the previous century. (For the development of the aesthetics of French cuisine, see Weiss, *Feast and Folly*, pp. 90–91 and Jean François Revel, *Culture and Cuisine, A Journey through the History of Food* (New York: Da Capo, 1984), especially chapter 6.)
32. See also W.B. Fritter, 'Is Wine an Art Object', *Journal of Aesthetics and Art Criticism*, 30:1, 1971. Also for the 'aesthetization' of food see Weiss, *Feast and Folly*, pp. 5–8, P. Clark, 'Thoughts for Food:

63

French Cuisine and French Culture', *The French Review*, 49:1, 1975, p. 35 and Luca Vercelloni, 'A Branch of Fashion', *Slow*, no 22, 2001.

33. The idea of 'family resemblances' of course implies an open definition of art, inspired by Wittgenstein's aesthetics, according to which food could easily be counted as one of the arts. For a discussion of this as well as criticism, see Carroll, *Philosophy of Art*, pp. 207–224.

34. J. Levinson, *The Pleasures of Aesthetics: Philosophical Essays* (Ithaca: Cornell Univ. Press, 1999), p. 129.

35. Hanfling, *Philosophical Aesthetics*, pp. 94–96.

36. Things of course are more complicated but such a classification will suffice for the purposes at hand. See Noël Caroll, 'The Ontology of Mass Art', *The Journal of Aesthetics and Art Criticism*, 55:2, 1997. p. 192; see also Gregory Currie's *An Ontology of Art* (Basingstoke: Macmillan, 1989), in which he shows that all art is multiple, even painting!

37. Interestingly enough, the great chef Jacques Maximin, the originator of nouvelle cuisine, having restored an old theater in Nice, went on to place the diners where the audience used to sit and his brigade of cooks on the stage from where they performed their art. Curtains closed and opened with the beginning and the end of each dinner.

38. Hanfling, *Philosophical Aesthetics*, pp. x–xi and Weiss, where he discusses a menu composed by Mallarmé, that 'it would be difficult to discern something 'mallarméian' about this menu...Except for the mousseline, attempts to relate this meal to his poetry are seemingly futile. Perhaps this may serve as a lesson that the intentional fallacy operates in gastronomic as well as in literary analysis', *Feast and Folly*, p. 111.

39. Kivy, *Authenticities*, pp. 155–161.

40. For the many meanings of authenticity, see Kivy, *Authenticities*, p. 3.

41. Ladenis, *My Gastronomy*.

42. Theodor Adorno, *Philosophy of Modern Music* (London: Sheed and Ward, 1948, 1973).

43. Ibid. pp. 212–217, p. xiii.

44. Revel, *Culture and Cuisine*, p. 214.

45. *Wine Spectator*, 15 December 2004, p. 49.

46. Ibid.

47. *Times*, January 11, 2003.

48. Grant Achatz, chef of the avant-garde restaurant Alinea in Chicago is reported as saying that 'food should be not only delicious but also exciting and theatrical and intriguing', *New York Times*, reprinted in Kathimerini, 20 May 2005, p. 8.

49. See for example Vercelloni, *Searching for Lost tastes*.

50. Revel writes about how people in the 18th century resisted the emergence of modern haute cuisine. Voltaire is quoted as saying 'I confess that my stomach cannot get used to the new cuisine', *Culture and Cuisine*, p. 173.

51. Tracy MacLeod of the *Independent* says of the El Bulli experience: 'With no menus to anchor us, and no idea of what was coming next, we trustingly opened our beaks like baby birds and gave in to pleasure...It was great, great fun – and the tastes were out of this world.' *The Independent Magazine*, 4 June 2005, pp. 23–4. One would like to think that 'out of this world' is meant literally, i.e. food that is beyond the constraints of good (gustatory) taste, food that would take cooking into more complex and perhaps bad tasting experiences. But of course, it is meant figuratively. As Giles Coren concludes: 'I have no idea whether a chef can change the world, as some European food writers believe he will. But then Adrià is not really a chef. Like Mozart wasn't really a musician and Picasso wasn't really a painter.'

52. It is interesting to note that Alain Weiss claims that not only food is art but 'Culinary taste would transform aesthetics by redefining the role of art within the human sensorium, transforming the aestheticisation of the senses and eliminating the previously held limits between the arts. The gastronomic must no longer serve as mere metaphor for the arts, but should take its place with the muses', in his essay 'Tractatus-Logicus-Gastronomicus' in *Feast and Folly*, p. 91.

Tafelspitz, More than a Recipe: a Tribute to the Late Chef Louis Szathmáry

Fritz Blank

Chef Louis Szathmáry (1919–1996) once said to me and later wrote: 'The kitchens of every nation have one dish which is not a dish, not even a meal, but rather exists as "an event".'

These culinary events are usually named with one word, and that word elicits a catholic understanding within a culture of the fullest meaning of the term. Thus it is that Boulibase, Pepperpot and Gumbo, Bar-BQ, Pot Au Feu, Cassoulet, and Brunswick Stew, are examples of what helps define 'authenticity'. Furthermore, such gastronomic events evoke memories which are the essence of 'authenticity,' which is probably best described as 'a state of mind.'

Studies continue to demonstrate that the complexity of flavors – which depend upon all five senses – produce the most vivid memories in our mind's eye. And so it is that 'authentic' chicken soup is that which each of us remembers in our minds eye and recalls the flavors and circumstances surrounding the chicken soup which our mother, or cook prepared. Indeed, the variations of chicken soup are global and uncounted. The question is not which is authentic, but rather which rendition is best remembered.

And so it is with the Austrian culinary event called *Tafelspitz*, which Joseph Wechsberg all but beatified when he wrote the delightfully profound essay 'Tafelspitz für den Hofrat.' What then is *Tafelspitz*? *Tafelspitz* is a very special cut of beef carefully dissected from the top hind quarter of a steer; it is considered by many to be the best piece of beef from which to prepare 'boiled beef'. The word *Tafelspitz* might also imply simply 'to dine from or at the top'. Probably no other written account personifies the reverence *Tafelspitz* holds than an essay written by the late, great journalist, Joseph Wechsberg, which describes the dedication and ritual associated with the traditions of the famous boiled-beef houses of nineteenth-century Vienna, in particular the restaurant named Meissl & Schadn.

As an introduction and in order for *Tafelspitz* to be properly understood and appreciated one must first be aware of how Austrians – especially the Viennese – eat. The fact is they love not only to eat, but to eat well. Furthermore, they take the time and make the effort to do so, and the average Austrian may have and enjoy five meals a day.

Breakfast is usually sometime between 7.30 and 8.00 a.m. and consists of a roll (*Semmelbrötchen*) with butter, coffee, perhaps some jam and maybe a slice of cold *wurst* and/or cheese. Hard-cooked eggs may also be offered. Albeit that a wide assortment of breads and soft pretzels are appropriate and often available for breakfast, *Brödchen* is required fare. This is also the only meal for which butter is offered, which usually always shocks neophytes from America.

At 10.00 a.m. school children often have a small meal for which small sandwiches, hard-cooked eggs, sausages and fruit are served. Workmen usually take a mid-morning half-hour to visit a beer house for a small plate of *guylás* or *beuschel* and a glass of beer. At noon a proper albeit small lunch is enjoyed – usually at home rather than in a restaurant. Two in the afternoon demands a coffee break and maybe a pretzel. At four or 4.30 in the afternoon a meal called *Jausse* is most often enjoyed by ladies of all ages. *Jausse* loosely translates as 'Gossip' – *Kaffeeklatsch* being the German equivalent. Large cups of coffee topped with *Schlag* (whipped cream), assorted Viennese pastries and idle talk reign supreme.

The evening meal is for family members and on occasion invited guests. The table is set and everyone gathers to enjoy conversation and a meal of soup, salad, meat, potatoes, noodles or dumplings, vegetables, and dessert. Sundays are reserved for a special meal, which more often than not means *Tafelspitz*, a very popular, if not universal favorite.

Side dishes associated with *Tafelspitz*: in the same manner of seasonal and holiday feast-celebrations such as Clambakes, Picnics, Crabfeasts, Christmas, Thanksgiving, New Year's Breakfasts, and *Reveillon du Nouveau An*, certain side dishes are considered *de rigueur*, but often depend upon the culture and ethnographic backgrounds and family traditions of the celebrants. So it is that *Tafelspitz* is akin to such culinary tradition, except that *Tafelspitz* is not associated with any one holiday, or even a particular season or time of the year. *Taffelspitz* stands alone as an 'everyday dish' with a tradition and a reverence solely dedicated to aristology.

Accordingly, in addition to particular favorite cuts of beef, certain side dishes are usually requisite for devotees of this most revered meal. Some of the most popular of these are: a horseradish sauce such as *Apfelkren* or a variety thereof; a pot of excellent quality commercial mustard; potatoes of some sort – pan roasted, creamed, mashed, or a family favorite; some sort of creamed vegetable; and a sweet-and-sour vegetable salad such as beets, green beans, or cucumbers.

66

The recipes

Viennese style 'boiled beef' – *Gekochtes Rindfleisch/Tafelspitz*
Gekochtes literally translated means 'boiled'; however, the most knowledgeable and reverent chefs never 'boil' their beef but rather poach or simmer it with great care. One of the best ways to achieve this is in a roasting pan which is placed into an oven at 300°F. Carefully following the directions below will produce a perfect rendition of 'boiled beef' that will delight the most discriminating *Tafelspitz* aficionado.

Various cuts of beef can be used to make this dish but in Austria, most aficionados agree that the portion of beef known as *Tafelspitz* produces the best results. This is difficult if not impossible to find in American butchers, but a sirloin tip or a well marbled 'fresh' (meaning not corned or pickled) brisket will be quite suitable.

1 or more tablespoons of shortening (veal kidney fat, clarified butter, corn, peanut, safflower, or 'Canola' oil)

1 meaty beef shank, cross cut into one-inch thick slices so that the light, creamy-pink marrow is visible.

(Optional additions: some boneless beef shank meat and/or a piece of veal or beef tongue, and/or oxtail cut into 1-inch pieces to be added later in the cooking process as a final embellishment)

1 sirloin tip of beef or a fresh beef brisket

1 yellow fist-sized Spanish onion, peeled (leaving the dry papery brown skin on)

1 large firm leek, trimmed

3 or 4 white golf-ball sized 'boiling' onions

1 small tight head of white cabbage cut into 4 or six wedges

1 green jalapeño *pepper*

1 small head of garlic

4 shallots – unpeeled

1 kohlrabi* peeled and cut into 2-inch cubes

2 large thick carrots (sometimes called 'horse carrots') peeled and roll-cut into 2-inch pieces

3 parsnips* peeled and cut into 1-inch x 1-inch rounds

4 parsley roots* peeled and cut into 1-inch lengths

1 celery root* peeled and cut into 2 x 3-inch rectangular pieces

1 bouquet garni: 2 bay leaves – fresh if available – 6 white and 6 black whole peppercorns, and 3 whole cloves tied together with a bunch of fresh flat-leaf parsley

67

[* These vegetables may be difficult to find in a corner 'convenience' supermarket. Try locating them in a market that is located in, or caters to a German or Polish or Eastern European neighborhood or a rural farm community. In addition, many US cities and towns now have farmers' markets and food speciality stores where these items may be found, or ordered ahead. While you are shopping look for a fresh horseradish root to use for making a traditional sauce served with Boiled Beef – see separate recipe.]

1. Pre-heat oven to 300°F. Next, place 1 or 2 tablespoons of shortening into a large heavy (cast-iron preferred) skillet, and place over medium-high heat. Carefully add the shank bones, sprinkled with a little salt and brown them, turning then and adjusting the heat as necessary, until they are well browned but not burnt or blackened. Deglaze with a small amount of water and transfer bones and liquid to a roasting pan.

A Guide to Austrian Cuts of Beef

68

2. Cut one of the yellow onions in half and add it, skin and all, to the pan, also include one or two cloves of garlic, plus all of the vegetable trimmings and peelings. Add about 4 to 6 cups of water – enough just to barely cover – and bring to a boil on top of the stove. Transfer to a 300°F oven, and cook for about 30 minutes turning the bones occasionally. Increase the heat to 450°F for another 10 minutes. Carefully strain and transfer the liquid and any recoverable bone marrow fat, discarding the spent bones, trimmings and peelings.

3. Return the strained broth to the roasting pan.

4. Sprinkle and rub the brisket or sirloin tip with seasoned salt (1 part paprika, 1 part ground white pepper, 1 part salt) and place it back into the roasting pan along with the strained broth, along with the prepared vegetables. Add the *bouquet garni* and enough water just to cover.

5. Cover the roasting pan with a lid and return to the oven adjusting the temperature back between 300° or 325°F. Add the optional boneless shank meat, tongue and/or the pieces of oxtail after 1½ hours and continue to cook in the oven for a total of 2½ to 3 hours.

In the meanwhile, prepare the side dishes and garnishes. Have some excellent crusty fresh bread and butter ready to serve, as well as an appropriate wine or beer of your choice. Serve the piping hot broth as a separate first course or along with the sliced boiled beef along with offerings of the boiled vegetables and side dishes and accoutrements. Dessert, if any, should be light, perhaps a small offering of *Kaiserschmarrn* or *Palatschinken mit Marillensösse* or *Zwetschken Geröstige* and *Kaffee mit Schlag*.

Top of the stove pan-roasted potatoes – *Kümmelerdäpfel*

The cooking methods used for this potato dish are essential in order to achieve the 'authentic' flavor preferred by the Viennese. Especially important is the par-cooking technique applied to the potato cubes before roasting them. Chef Louis Szathmáry was committed to the use of recipes… but, only as a guide, and that attention to cooking methods and directions were as – if not more – important than the measurement of ingredients. Also he subscribed to the view that good cooks – especially chefs – must adhere to the habit of constantly tasting and smelling things – beginning with raw, and proceeding in intervals during the entire cooking process. This careful monitoring allows for correction and adjustments so that the endpoint will be as perfect as perfect can be. We must use all six of our senses (smell, taste, sight, sound, feel, as well as common sense) to achieve the best possible culinary results.

one heavy skillet (well seasoned cast-iron preferred)
2 lbs all-purpose common local potatoes
±3 tablespoons lard
1 tablespoon sweet paprika
8 freshly crushed black peppercorns
3 tablespoons butter
±1 teaspoon salt (times two)
±2 tablespoons of chopped or chiffonnaded fresh flat-leaf parsley.
±1 tablespoon bruised caraway seeds

69

1. Wash and peel the potatoes, then wash them again. Carefully cut them into cubes measuring ±⅔ of an inch each.

2. Place them in a large accommodating pot with enough cold water to cover the potato pieces plus one inch. Add the bruised caraway seeds and ±1 teaspoon of salt.

3a. Bring to a full boil over medium heat, but as soon it boils, remove the pot from the fire and allow it to stand for 5 full minutes.

3b. Carefully pour off the water using a lid or strainer and place the drained potatoes into a large bowl and allow to stand at room temperature until cooled.

4. In a small bowl, or on a piece of paper, or whatever is handy, combine the remaining one teaspoon of salt, the cracked black peppercorns, and the sweet paprika.

5. Place the butter and lard into the skillet than add the cold potato cubes and sprinkle the salt mixture evenly over the top. Place the cold frying-pan containing

the seasoned cold potatoes onto a stove over medium heat. Turn the potatoes slowly, gently and carefully with a spatula once in a while. Continue until the potatoes heat through and become a light golden brown.

6. Sprinkle with the parsley; taste and adjust seasoning if necessary. Serve hot ! [*Methodology Notes*: Precooking the potatoes slowly as prescribed above will produce cubes which are just barely cooked but without raw centers.

The pre-cooked potatoes must be allowed to cook before frying them! If they are fried while still warm they will break and fall apart, becoming shapeless and mushy.

This method of 'pan-roasting' will not be greasy or starchy and will have a deep, genuine potato flavor.]

Creamed spinach, Viennese style – *Spinat Wiener Art*
The use of milk-infused crustless bread to thicken creamed spinach negates the harsh flavor of oxalic acid which so often is associated with spinach, thus resulting in a smoother, mild yet heightened spinach flavor.

2 or 3 slices of white bread, crusts removed
1 cup of milk or half-and-half
1 whole egg
2 or 3 lb of freshly washed and de-stemmed spinach
water and salt q.s., for quick-cooking the spinach
1 small to medium peeled clove of fresh garlic
½(±) teaspoon salt
2 tablespoons flour
1 cup or slightly more of rich chicken or turkey stock
salt, freshly ground pepper and freshly grated nutmeg q.s., tasting by titration [To season food by titration: to adjust and produce a desired flavor endpoint by the incremental addition of seasonings to a product (from the French word titrer: *'to add the minimum needed to achieve a particular result').]*

1. Soak the crustless bread in the milk.
2. Mash the garlic and salt together into a paste and set aside.
3. Bring a large amount of lightly salted water to a full boil. Add the spinach leaves, and cook for 5 minutes. Drain in a large colander and cool by rinsing with cold water. Allow to drain well then chop finely by hand on a cutting board using a large knife. Do not use a food processor or meat grinder.
4. Stir the milk-infused bread into a pulp then incorporate the egg, and set aside.
5. Mix together the flour along with the garlic/salt paste into the cold chicken stock.
6. In a large wet saucepan, or skillet place the blanched spinach and heat for a few minutes until it starts to bubble and steam. Add the salt and garlic seasoned chicken

stock, and bring to a boil while stirring vigorously with cook's spoon. Adjust heat to low and cover and cook for ±10 minutes while stirring occasionally.

7. Just before serving, stir in the bread and milk pulp. Taste carefully and adjust seasonings as necessary.

Bean salad – *Bohnensalat*

'String beans' – whether they be ordinary garden-variety green beans, Italian broad beans, tiny thin French haricots verts, yellow wax beans, or Chinese yard-long beans, – they all are candidates to be made into delicious salads. Seasoned and tossed with any one of a number of 'dressings' and served cold or at room temperature, bean salads are catholic candidates as a side dish for almost any repast.

1 lb fresh green beans, ends trimmed, and usually cut into 1-inch pieces
2-3 tablespoons red wine, white wine, cider, or herbed vinegar
¼ cup olive oil
2 garlic cloves, peeled and mashed with 1 teaspoon Kosher salt
salt and freshly cracked (or ground) black peppercorns
sugar
½ cup chiffonnaded flat-leaf parsley, coarsely chopped

1. Place the prepared beans in enough water to cover and cook for about 10–12 minutes, until the beans are tender but *al dente*.
2. Remove and place in a serving bowl.
3. Whisk together olive oil, vinegar, salt and pepper. Toss the beans with the parsleyed vinaigrette. Serve warm or at room temperature.

NB: parsley is the traditional herb most favored in Austria, but fresh dill weed, tarragon, and even coriander can provide a flavor shift for a change. Likewise, sour cream or yogurt can also be added to change the character

71

Apple-horseradish – *Apfelkren*

4 medium-sized fresh crisp apples (Fuji, Gala, or Yellow Delicious are good candidates)
2 tablespoons butter
6 tablespoons sugar (to be divided and used as 4 plus 2)
salt q.s.
a two-inch piece of lemon rind
water, as needed
1 cup losley packed freshly grated horseradish
the juice from ½ a lemon (discard the seeds)

1. Peel and core the apples and place the peelings and trimmings into a small pot

with 4 tablespoons sugar. Add enough water just to cover. Simmer over medium heat.

2. Cut each apple into small uneven pieces and place into a small heavy pan with 2 tablespoons of butter, 2 or 3 tablespoons of water and the remaining 2 tablespoons sugar. Cover and cook over medium heat stirring every 2 or 3 minutes.

3. Strain the liquid (now a syrup) from the simmering apple peelings and trimmings. Add this syrup to the simmering apples pieces. Taste and add more sugar as your personal taste dictates.

4. Remove the pan from the heat and add the freshly grated horseradish, the lemon juice and season by titration with a pinch or two of salt.

Beet salad

This salad, a global favorite of beet lovers is a most appropriate accompaniment for *Tafelspitz*. It can be and often is made using commercially canned sliced beets. Better results will be apparent if recently boiled and peeled fresh beets are used. However, to achieve the sweetest and most intensely flavored beet salad, the best cooks take the time to oven-roast the beets.

6 fresh, tangerine-sized beets with 1-inch of the stem attached
2 shallots or a small onion peeled and roughly chopped
2 sprigs of fresh rosemary
1 tablespoon of good quality olive oil
1 large red Spanish or sweet Vidalia-type onion halved and sliced thinly
1 bouquet garni (fresh tarragon, fresh bay leaves, a clove or two, a short cinnamon stick, black pepper, etc.)
1 cup red-wine vinegar
1 cup water
½ cup sugar
optional fresh herbs and spices (and/or sour cream) by personal preference
salt q.s. by titration

1. Preheat oven to 400°F

2. Wash and dry the beets and place them in a bowl along with the the olive oil, shallots and rosemary. Toss well.

3. Place the beets onto a large piece of heavy-duty aluminum foil and loosely form an open topped bundle. (Do not seal tightly.) Place onto a baking sheet and into the oven for about 45 minutes. If the beets become slightly charred, that's just fine.)

4. Using your hands (plastic gloves recommended), peel the beets, and cut into ¼ to ⅓ inch slices.

5. Bring vinegar, water, sugar and salt to a boil and allow and pour over the slices beets.

6. Add optional herbs and spices and toss gently. Chill and serve.

72

Bibliography

Beer, Gretel, *Classic Austrian Cooking* (London: André Deutsch, 1993).

Digby, Joan & John, *Food for Thought* (New York: Morrow, 1987).

Lang, George – Personal Communication.

Prato, Katharina, pseud. Katharina Edle von Scheiger, *Die Süddeutsche Küche* (Gratz: 1858).

Szathmáry, Louis – Unpublished documents.

Szathmáry, Louis – Personal Communication.

Szathmáry, Louis, *The Bakery restaurant cookbook* (Boston: CBI, c. 1981).

Wagner, Christoph, *Österreich für Feinschmecker: das kulinarische Jahrbuch* (Wien: Deuticke,1995).

Wechsberg, Joseph, '*Tafelspitz* for the Hofrat' in *Blue Trout and Black Truffles* (New York: Knopf, 1953).

Wechsberg, Joseph and the editors of Time-Life Books, *The Cooking of Vienna's Empire* (New York: Time-Life Books,1968).

Authenticity and Gastronomic Films – A Sybaritic Study

François Brocard

> Gastronomy is the art of using food to create happiness.
>
> Theodore Zeldin[1]
>
> Cooking is much more than recipes.
>
> Alain Chapel

Authenticity : two approaches

Authenticity is the quality of being authentic. It stresses fidelity to fact. The concept of authenticity can be used in two modes :

1. Analysis of the present by reference to the past: 'factual authenticity'. The concept is used in art, history, and similar fields involving artefacts from the past. Authenticity is the truthfulness to origins and not a reproduction or forgery.
2. Analysis of the present for itself: 'existential authenticity'. The concept has been developed by existentialist philosophers. There is a distinction between mental and physical realities and therefore between self and non-self or world. Authenticity concerns a person's relationship with the world. The impetus to action must arise from the person and not be imposed. Authenticity is the negative space outside imposed inauthenticity.

A. Factual authenticity

1. Quantitative observations on food and dishes shown in films

The sample consists of 140 films available in Europe as DVDs or videos. The universe is that of 'art films'[2] and excludes documentaries.

1.1 Quality index of films with a gastronomic content (Graph I)

Films are rated between 0 and 20 for gastronomic and cinematographic quality. An annual index equal to the sum of the grades of all the films is computed reflecting the quality and quantity of films produced in a given year. The ranking is personal but, as the author of the preface to François Marin's cookbook wrote in 1742: 'Cooking is a free art whose only rule is good taste, which everyone can be a judge of according to one's ideas'.[3] What is true for cooking must be true for food films.

The 69-year time series shows three periods:

Phase I (1935–39): quality production of a few films;

Phase II (1940–1955): lack of production during WW II and the reconstruction period;

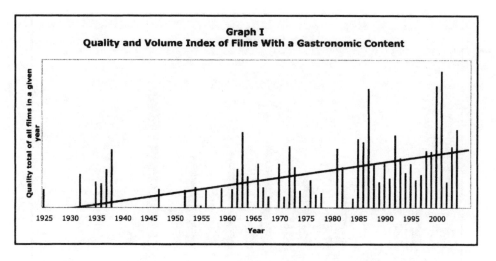

Graph I
Quality and Volume Index of Films With a Gastronomic Content

Phase III (1956–2004): steady increase of the number and quality of food films. The index shows substantial volatility from year to year as a result of the weight given to high-quality films.

There is a definite increase in the annual index with time. Should it continue during the present decade, the index would be around 35 in 2010. Should the volatility stay high, there could be intermediary peaks as high as 100 corresponding to five films of the maximum quality in an exceptional year.

1.2 Time series of all dishes

300 dishes are mentioned in the sample: meat, fruits and vegetables, fish, sweets, eggs and pasta, and cheese (Graph II).

Meat is the most dominant dish. Meat is always cooked. There is no steak tartare. Meat's pole position probably reflects its psychological status as the main dish to be shared, i.e. the archetypal convivial dish in the mind of film directors and spectators.

Fish strongly increased in the '90s. Following the nouvelle cuisine advocacy for simpler cooking, sea species are mostly present including cod, haddock, red snapper and sole as well as salmon (a sea-farmed anadromous fish). One has to go back to 1963 to find a pike dish[4] and 1956 to find an eel dish[5] (a lake or river catadromous fish). Fish is often cooked. Although sashimi is eaten in *Gohatto* (1999),[6] no sushi or sashimi is seen being prepared.

If we categorize meat into birds, quadrupeds and offal (Graph III),[7] the pre-war and immediate post-war decades show the pre-eminent share of birds. Since 2000, there is a 50:40:10 ratio between birds, quadrupeds, and offal.

The percentage of offal as the main ingredient in dishes in films has varied around 15 per cent and has presently decreased to 10 per cent. However if one looks at the number of dishes where offal is present and not just the main ingredient – e.g. liver in

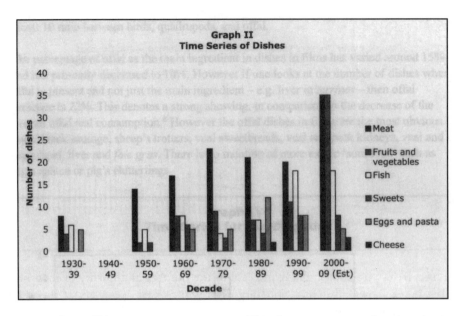

terrines – then offal presence is 22 per cent. This denotes a strong showing, in comparison to the decrease of the overall offal real consumption.[8] However the offal dishes in films are the most obvious ones: black sausage, sheep's trotters, veal sweetbreads, veal and pork kidneys, veal and pig's head, liver and foie gras. There is no mention of more exotic 'soul food' such as pig's spleen or pig's chitterlings.

Among quadrupeds, lamb has been gaining at the expense of beef in the last four years (Graph IV). The leg of lamb is becoming the typical convivial dish at the

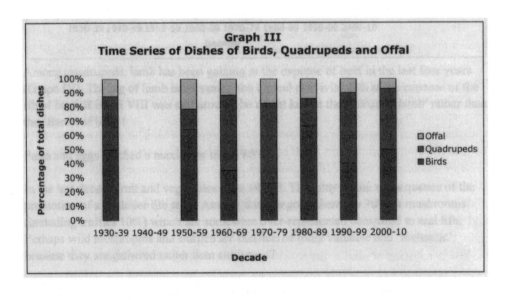

76

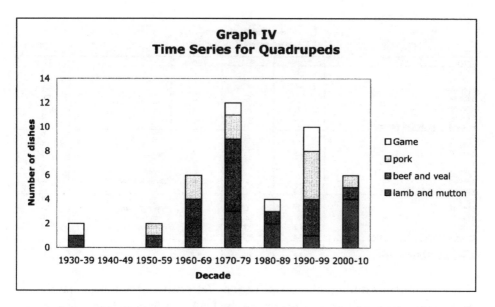

Graph IV
Time Series for Quadrupeds

Number of dishes

Game
pork
beef and veal
lamb and mutton

1930-39 1940-49 1950-59 1960-69 1970-79 1980-89 1990-99 2000-10

Decade

expense of the rib of beef. If Henry VIII was still around, he might knight the 'Baron of lamb' rather than the 'Baron of beef'!

Pasta and eggs reached a maximum in the '80s.

In the last decade fruit and vegetables have tripled. This may be the consequence of the promotion of a healthier life style. Among this category, there are 30 per cent of mushrooms (including truffles, 10 per cent) which are somewhat over-represented compared to real life. Perhaps wild mushrooms and truffles are considered more valuable and 'authentic' because they are gathered rather than cultivated?

The gathering of food is shown in only one film.[9] Markets are not often described.[10] This lack of interest could be linked to the idea of consumers not wanting to link what they are eating to live animals.

The recent deconstruction of meals with various snacks taken in between meals or instead of meals is not really illustrated in these foodie movies.

2. Films and nationality, cultural zone and style of cooking

Determining the main nationality of a film has been done for the 32 best films (rating of 13/20 or above) (Table I).

Conclusions:

Phase A (1935–64, 30 years): France is the only source, with four major films.

Phase B (1965–1989, 25 years): 10 major films produced worldwide: France: 4.5, USA: 1, and others: 4.5. Time of the nouvelle vague.

Phase C (1990–2004, 15 years): 18 major films. The USA takes the lead: 8.5, followed by France: 4.5 and others: 5.

Table I
Films and Nationality
(32 films with a grade of 13/20 or above)

Years		France	USA	Others		Total
1935-39		3				3
1940-44						0
1945-49						0
1950-54						0
1955-59		1				1
1960-64						0
Phase A 1935-64 (30 years)		4				4
						0
1965-69		1				1
1970-74		2.5		0.5	Italy	3
1975-79		1				1
1980-84				1	Sweden	1
1985-89			1	3	Denmark, Japan, UK	4
Phase B 1965-89 (25 years)		4.5	1	4.5		10
						0
1990-94		1	1	2	Mexico, Taiwan	4
1995-99		2	3	1	Denmark	6
2000-04		1.5	4.5	2	Germany, UK	8
Phase C 1990-2004 (15 years)		4.5	8.5	5		18
Total 1935-2004 (70 years)		13	9.5	9.5		32

Is this authentic during this 70-year period? Yes when one considers that the two main cultural zones of film production are the USA and France. France lost its pole position when the USA started to wake up on the gastronomic front. In other terms, Hollywood film production power could only be harnessed to produce food films after the cultural model had evolved domestically with the advent of a food, wine and restaurant culture in the '90s.

I looked at cultural zone and cooking style with only the top eight films since 1960 (Table II).

The cooking styles are diverse across the globe. We observe the emergence of a multicultural gastronomic world in films which seems consistent with real life restaurants. In the metropolises like London and New York, there is a good balance between classic, comfort, nouvelle cuisine and soul.

3. Historical films and factual authenticity
Historical films have staged the historical reconstruction of a single significant meal or of a series of significant meals.

3.1 Single significant meal
(i) Middle Ages: *The Devil's Envoys* (1942)[11] from Marcel Carné. This is a Middle Ages fiction which includes a spectacular medieval banquet in May 1485.

(ii) Early XVII century: *Carnival in Flanders* (1935)[12] from Jacques Feyder. In 1616, troops from Spain, Piedmont and Friburg invade Boom, a city in Flanders. The wife of the burgomaster decides to hold two banquets with lobsters and pâtés whilst the men hide in fear.

(iii) Late XVII century: *Vatel* (2000) of Roland Joffé is the story of a steward of the Chantilly castle. Vatel is reputed to have invented Crème Chantilly. He commit-

Table II
The Eight Best Films since 1960

Rank	Quality	Country	Film	Year	Cultural Zone/Cooking Style
1	20	Denmark	Babette's Feast	1987	French/Classic
2	19	Taiwan	Eat Drink Man Woman	1994	Chinese/Classic
2	19	Germany	Mostly Martha	2001	French/*Nouvelle Cuisine*
4	18	Japan	Tampopo	1985	Japan/Comfort
4	18	USA	Tortilla Soup	2001	Mexican/Comfort
4	17	French	American Cuisine	1998	French/Classic
6	17	USA	Dinner Rush	2000	Italian/*Nouvelle Cuisine*
6	17	USA	Soul Food	1997	American/Soul

ted suicide on Friday 24 April 1671 when he thought that fish would not arrive in time for a lunch hosted for King Louis XIV. The table setting is true to history and was used later for preparing an ambigu table at a learned cookery books exhibition.[13] Since almost nothing is known of Vatel, authenticity concerns table dressing and table manners. Without the beautiful Uma Thurman – of *Kill Bill* fame – the movie would have been a little dull, even if authentic.

(iv) XVIII century: *Tom Jones* (1963) of Tony Richardson adapted from Henry Fielding's 1749 novel. The food orgy scene between Tom Jones and Mrs. Walters contributed to the success of the film.

(v) Early XIX century: *The Supper* (1992) of Edouard Molinaro. After Napoleon was defeated at Waterloo (18 June 1815), Talleyrand (Foreign Affairs Minister) hosted an imaginary private dinner for Fouché (Minister of Police) in his hôtel, Place de la Concorde. Carême, the great chef, was in the kitchen. The dinner was served to perfection and dishes represent an interesting selection:

79

Asparagus in the shape of small peas, a recipe which is in Carême;[14]
Salmon à la Royale;
Breasts of partridge à la financière.

There is a lack of authenticity in a bottle of Champagne. Its shape and label look like that of Dom Pérignon, a bottle shape which was designed a century later by the glass designer Emile Gallé.[15]

The scene was filmed in the Hôtel Sagon, the Paris residence of the Polish Ambassador, in exchange for redoing the kitchens. In compensation for this small inauthenticity, maybe the actors have had the benefit of eating real food from the modernised kitchen!

(vi) Japan, late XIX century: *Gohatto* (1999) of Nagisa Oshima takes place in a samurai school and includes a 22 December 1865 banquet. Each participant uses two to three individual *o-zen* tables.[16] *O-zen* tables were used less after the introduction of collective tables, although the tradition persists for wedding banquets in the Kanazawa vicinity.

3.2 Series of significant meals.
Historical films can also use a sequence of significant meals to structure the story:
(i) *Fanny and Alexander* (1982) from Ingmar Bergman. Meals structure the history

of the Ekdahl family as seen by two children starting with a Christmas dinner in 1907. Colours are used to define the meals : (a) colour (red and green) for luxury, family warmth and sexual freedom, (b) black and white for a wake dinner, (c) sombre colours for frugality, austerity, guilt, punishment and power relationships and (d) pastel for a baptism dinner of the re-founded family unity where men are weak and women become emancipated by becoming artists or independent.

(ii) *The Age of Innocence* (1993) of Martin Scorcese. Seven meals illustrate and structure the behaviour of New York high society in the Gilded Age of the 1870–80s. The most sumptuous meal is the third one when Countess Olenska is hosted by the van der Luydens. The setting is perfect. Cooks are French and servants English. Art historian David MacFadden, also a silverware and Venetian glass specialist, advised table decoration. Chef Rick Ellis was consulted for the menus. The authenticity of the dining rooms and table manners is achieved and used to record social behaviour where words and attitude can kill as well as guns in other Scorcese films (*Goodfellas*, 1990).

B. Existential authenticity

1.   Prevailing existential inauthenticity

Four main categories of movies with 'existential inauthentic gastronomy':

1.1 Psychological movies often consider the table as an extension of the bed or of the analyst's sofa.

They are often quite entertaining but bear no relation to gastronomy. The worst offender is Woody Allen with the lobsters of *Annie Hall* (1977) and the three Thanksgiving dinners of *Hannah and Her Sisters* (1986). *American Pie* (1999) and *Diner* (1982) err by using 'food objects' – a pie and a popcorn box – as sexual objects.

1.2 Science-fiction films choose pills over real food.

In *The Matrix* (1999), Neo chooses the red pill over the blue pill and has to feed himself with bland mash while the traitor Cypher is lunching on a steak cooked rare. Cypher says that he prefers a life of illusions which will bring him immediate satisfactions to a life of lucidity without sensations. Neo chooses an existence where senses play no role and relations to other human beings are purely intellectual. In year 10 191, the spice is also red in *Dune* (1984).

1.3 Films taking place in the kitchen or the dining place without any gastronomy.

In *My Dinner with André* (1981) of Louis Malle, quails are prepared with grapes but the spectators are the pigeons of 110 minutes of table monologues without gastronomy. *Picnic on the Grass* (1959)[17] of Jean Renoir represents the antithesis of the eponymous Manet painting. Only boiled cabbage with very few calories is served. In *The Dinner Game* (1998)[18] of Francis Veber, dining is only a pretext to a cruel game. In *Festen* (1998) of Thomas Vinterberg, the secrets of a Danish family are more important than the venison leg with a bilberry sauce. In *Frankie and Johnny* (1991) of Garry Marshall, Al Pacino and Michelle Pfeiffer do not enhance the food of the small New York Greek restaurant where they work. In *Death in Brunswick* (1991) of John Ruane, 'Cookie', a down-on-his-luck chef, prepares a pizza with cockroaches for his boss. A special mention is deserved for *Fisher King* (1991) of Terry Gilliam when Robin Williams and Amanda Plummer wrestle with their elusive dim sum.

1.4 Films of anthropophagy.

In *Do You Like Women?* (1964),[19] writer Roman Polanski has the charming actress Sophie Daumier as a possible meal. In *Fried Green Tomatoes at the Whistle Stop Cafe* (1991), the bad guy ends up in the barbecue sauce. *Delicatessen* (1991), *Soylent Green* (1973), *The Silence of the Lambs* (1991) and *Hannibal* (2001) are all cannibalistic. Anthropophagy is becoming more acceptable in all types of movies with tribal homophagy in the jungle often replaced by individual cannibalism in urban centres.[20] The only redeeming film is the pleasing Brazilian film *How Tasty Was My Little Frenchman* (1971)[21] of Nelson Pereira dos Santos. In 1594, the girl from the Tupinambas tribe chooses the neck, the best part from her French lover and prisoner she has fattened for the ultimate sacrifice. This is less bitter than the most delicate morsel of her roasted lover chosen by Georgina for her husband in *The Cook the Thief His Wife & Her Lover* (1989) of Peter Greenaway : 'Try the cock, Albert, it's a delicacy and you know where it has been.'

81

I.   Authentic gastronomic films

Three main themes:

1. Factual authenticity and multitude of existential messages

Babette's Feast (1987) is the supreme example.[22]

Theme : An exiled catholic French cook (Stéphane Audran) transforms the celebration of the 100th anniversary of the birth of a pastor of an isolated Lutheran community in Jutland (Denmark) – on 15 December 1885 – into the feast of a lifetime. As Theodore Zeldin put it: 'An open mind about food, and about the taste of foreigners, inevitably modifies one's attitude to one's neighbours'.[23] This is the story of such a transformation and the use of a religious context to carry other messages.

Multivalence : the film can be seen from many angles, hence its wide appeal:

Conviviality: Dining brings people together even when they try to resist.

Néophilia: immediate accessibility of new and strange foods.[24]

Equality: Chef and host operate on an equal footing, and the diner's savoir manger both corresponds and responds to the chef's savoir faire.[25]

Fusion of opposites: reconciling the ascetic with the aesthetic, the spiritual with the carnal through a Dionysian banquet.

Mourning and rebirth: overcoming of an inability to mourn.[26] The dinner is a wake or mourning dinner where Babette commemorates her husband and son killed in the repression of the Paris Commune under the orders of the very same General Galliffet who was appreciating her artistic talents at the Café Anglais. She 'entombs' the past and is reborn in Denmark.

Promotion of 'conspicuous consumption' and 'ceremonial differentiation of the dietary'.[27] When the film opened in New York in March 1988, the restaurant Petrossian offered the menu from the film.[28]

Strong cooking authenticity with a few caveats. The ingredients of the dishes – all shipped from France – are quite recognisable:

Turtle soup with veal quenelles. The soup is served with Amontillado. Before they became a protected species, turtles were said to be best in winter and the soup was considered one of the Seven Wonders of the Culinary Art.[29]

Blinis Demidoff with Beluga caviar. Served with Veuve Clicquot 1860. Not a recognised year unlike 1861 which would have kept all its finesse and vinosity in December 1885 if kept in proper conditions.

Entombed quails – *cailles en sarcophage* – stuffed with foie gras and truffles, 'entombed' in puff pastry and served with a demi-glace sauce. Quails and other small birds such as thrush (*grives*), bunting (*ortolans*) and larks (*alouettes, mauviettes*) have been prepared in pies since the Middle Ages[30] and were a favourite of the late XIXth century and the early XXth century. Quails are at their best in autumn when they have gorged themselves on grapes. Eating them on 15 December might be a little late but not that late, given the time to ship them alive in a cage from France to Jutland. The quail's song has three sharp notes which give rise to the imitative name of wet-my-lip,[31] a very good description of this excellent dish! The quails are put uncooked in puff pastry and they would have been severely undercooked. The recipe of the Danish chef provided for the boned quails to be browned in a skillet over medium high heat and pre cooked for ten minutes in a 375°F/190°C oven. He is reputed to have prepared quails more than twelve times for the dinner to serve twelve.

Chef Edouard Nignon[32] who worked at the Café Anglais during the same period recalls that thrushes cooked in parchment – *mauviettes en caisse au gratin* – were famous. He also proposes The Triumphant Dress of Lucullus – 'La Robe triomphale de Lucullus – a pie of six quails in puff pastry similar to the *Babette's Feast* preparation.[33]

The appellation is unusual but similar funeral appellations can be found in Ali Bab:[34] *ortolans en sarcophage* – 'bunting en sarcophage' – stuffed with foie gras and entombed inside large truffles, and *alouettes en linceul* – 'larks in shroud' – entombed in potatoes.

The quails are served with Clos Vougeot 1845. 148 quails were prepared for the filming and Miss Audran insisted on drinking real wine saying she was not a good enough actress to pretend with apple juice. Authenticity in acting as well as in filming!

Endive salad, indeed a winter vegetable
Cheeses : Tome and Roquefort. Tome is good throughout the year and Roquefort is good in winter
Baba au rhum with candied angelica and cherries
Fruits: mangoes, dates, figs, prunes and pineapples.
Water in small glasses and wine in large glasses – excellent!

2. *The nouvelle cuisine*
a) *Mostly Martha* (2001) of Sandra Nettlebeck (Germany) is excellent.
Nouvelle cuisine theme. The film is the epitome of *nouvelle cuisine* which was built around ten commandments centred around the value of truth, lightness, simplicity and imagination of an autonomous chef with short menus requiring fresh ingredients and low inventories.

Nouvelle cuisine arose in the late '60s after new logics were established by the anti-schools of the *nouveau roman* and the *nouvelle vague* initiated in the '50s and early '60s. 'Just as the French revolution was the master movement that sounded the death knell of the ancien régime cuisine and the construction of classical cuisine by Carême and other gastronomic writers, the events of May 1968 triggered the decline of classical cuisine and the growth of the *nouvelle cuisine* movement.'[35]

La nouvelle vague sought to replace the primacy of the script writer with the director and to emphasise natural light, realism and improvisation. *Nouvelle cuisine* sought to replace the primacy of the Carême and Escoffier traditions with the inventiveness of the cook and to emphasise undisguised product quality, cooking 'just in time' with no advance preparation and serving on a plate or à la cloche without interference by the waiters.

The time lag between *nouvelle vague* and *nouvelle cuisine* is attributed by Rao to the professionalization of French gastronomy. There were no professional requirements to write a novel, stage a play or make a low-budget movie. By contrast, it took a long time for a chef to acquire professional accreditation and recruits had to progress through the various phases. Therefore change had to be promoted by activists at the centre of the system who had technical credibility and wanted to become creators and own their restaurants. All those chefs were MOF (*Meilleur Ouvrier de France*).

Factual cooking authenticity: The kitchen work is very well described as Martha prepares dishes inspired by her training at Père Bise at Talloires near Annecy (This implies some feminism since out of four French women chefs to have won three Michelin stars, two were Marguerite and Charlyne Bise.)[36] Under the coaching of the Chef from the Four Seasons in Hamburg, she prepares:

    Salmon with a basil sauce;
    Foie gras (140°C oven, water at 80°C, 25 minutes);
    Pigeon cooked in a pork bladder with black truffles.

b) *Dinner Rush* (2000) by Bob Giraldi (USA).

A film about revenge – 'a dish best served cold' – in a New York trattoria but also a fine example of nouvelle or perhaps fusion cuisine. The food critic orders 'Shellfish, no butter but pasta'. The Chef creates the following dishes:

Montauk caviar and rock shrimp with a Champagne-shallot sauce with vanilla beans. Garnished with salmon eggs, a 'tobiko' caviar[37] with a wasabi flavour, some chives and fried pasta;

Tagliolini with white truffles.

There are few other recipes but all the action is in the kitchen and the dining room. Very funny and a good story of stress in the kitchen, even more so during an electricity breakdown. Among the good taglines: Chef to an apprentice: 'There are only three proper responses when I say something to you: "Yes Chef", "No Chef" and "I don't know, Chef"!'

3. Universality of gastronomy: the global kitchen

Two excellent films – *Eat Drink Man Woman* (1994)[38] of Ang Lee and *Tortilla Soup* (2001) of María Ripoll – have identical scenarios with strong existential authenticity. The former relates the story of a senior Taipei chef with his three unmarried grown daughters (a chemistry professor, an airline executive and a student working in a fast-food diner). The latter tells the story of a Mexican-American chef living in Los Angeles who also has three very different daughters (a chemistry professor, a career woman and a student). Although the film directors are different, both Ang Lee and Hui-Ling Wang contributed to both scenarios. This is proof that a good story can be adapted to different cultures.

Theme: Life revolves around the ritual of an elaborate dinner every Sunday and the love lives of all the family members. The story is the emancipation of the daughters and the father announcing their decisions during the dominical meal: 'I have an announcement …'.

Factual cooking authenticity:
Eat Drink Man Woman:
Very good description of the preparation, cooking and elaborate presentation of a Chinese meal including:

Dim sum
Crab raviolis
Peking duck (showing the traditional method of pumping air through the neck to separate the meat from the skin)
Smoked ham soup
Tofu with chicken and ham
Pea sprouts sautéed in duck fat
Carp with garlic sauce
Winter melon soup

Beggar's chicken cooked in a lotus leaf and enclosed in clay. The clay is broken with a hammer at the table.

Tortilla Soup
The recipes are very good. I have personally tried a few of them, including the tortilla soup[39] and they are good, authentic Mexican recipes. They can be found in three cookbooks written by Sue Milliken and Susan Feniger who are the food and menu designers and co-chefs and owners of Border Grill in Santa Monica and Los Angeles and Ciudad in downtown L.A.[40] This is the only food art film where all the recipes have the backing of cookbooks. Certainly a good way to achieve culinary authenticity!

> Nopales : grilled cactus salad
> Marrow flower soup (courgettes) with or without seeds
> South-American lamb with cabbage and a mandarin sauce
> Meat en papillotte
> Grilled red snappers Tipin-Chik, a traditional Yucatan dish
> Small octopus à la Veracruz
> Tomatoes stuffed with guacamole
> Tamales of green corn (maize) with cream
> Tortilla soup
> Salad with cucumber and bread
> Enchiladas
> Grilled corn on the cob cob

Again a very good scenario joined with culinary accuracy produces overall authenticity.

4. The politics of gastronomy
Gastronomy has been used for political and economic purposes throughout history, mostly with ceremonial banquets. The nouvelle cuisine also has a political and economic agenda with the chefs taking control and ownership of restaurants. Gastronomic clubs have also been used for political or economic purposes and there is an interesting example in *Twelve Hours to Live* (1956),[41] a *film noir* from Julien Duvivier (France) where Jean Gabin is the chef-owner of a restaurant located in the Halles market in Paris.

Towards the end of the film, the chef indicates that he has to leave early and go back to his kitchen because the 'Club of the Hundred' – the *Club des Cent* (founded in 1912 and lunching weekly) – is coming for dinner the following day. We are shown the speech made by its chairman to comment upon the dinner and congratulate the chef. He praises 'the prodigious movements of the new culinary symphony which they have witnessed…a true [meaning authentic?] French cuisine, a cuisine from our land, a tricolour cuisine, Gentlemen, *Vive la France!*[42] The speech is apocryphal, but it illustrates the utilisation of French cuisine to defend political objectives and identity.[43]

85

Conclusions

1. Food film production and quality on the rise. Possibility of a vintage year with five excellent films before 2010?

2. Factual authenticity. Statistical analysis shows that films tend to follow changing food consumption patterns:

Importance of meat; shift from beef to lamb; but over-representation of offal in films;

there is an increased presence of sea fish;

fruit and vegetable consumption has tripled, but over-representation of mushrooms and truffles;

pasta peaked in the 80s;

but lack of coverage of meal deconstruction, gathering of food and markets.

3. Origin of the good movies. For 'good' food movies, the USA is in the pole position since 1990 with France second. For 'best' movies, production is spread internationally. Emergence of a multicultural gastronomic world. The global kitchen.

Good food movies tend to occur only where the domestic cultural model is supportive of gastronomic culture.

4. The very best movies having factual and existential authenticity:

factual authenticity and multitude of existential messages: *Babette's Feast* (1987);

Nouvelle cuisine: *Mostly Martha* (2001) and *Dinner Rush* (2000);

The global village: *Eat Drink Man Woman* (1994) and *Tortilla Soup* (2001), a good story can be adapted to different cultures;

The politics of gastronomy: *Twelve hours to live* (1956).

I hope that I have whetted the appetite and stimulated the imagination. As Jean-François Revel wrote, 'Like sex, food cannot be dissociated from imagination.'[44]

Bibliography – Film

Berry, Jo and Angie Errigo, '*Movies for the munchies*', *Chick Flicks* (London: Orion 2004) pp. 329–32.

Bolter, Trudy and others, *Les Cinéastes et la table* (Paris: CinémAction, Corlet-Télérama, N°108, 3rd trimester 2003).

Chenille, Vincent (1), 'Homophagie au cinéma', Communication in French at the seminar 'De Honestia Voluptate' (Paris, June 2004).

Chenille, Vincent (2), *Le plaisir gastronomique au cinéma* (Paris: Jean-Paul Rocher, 2004).

Fabricant, Florence, in '*Babette*, A Great Feast For the Palate and the Eye', 2 March 1988, article in *The New York Times*, p. C1, 2.

IMDb, The Internet Movie Database, www.imdb.com.

Lee, Ang, '*Eat Drink Man Woman, the Wedding Banquet*', *Two Films by Ang Lee* (Woodstock, New York: The Overlook Press, 1994).

McKee, Robert, *Story. Substance, structure, style, and the principle of screenwritings* (London: Methuen, 1999).

Oshima, Nagisa, 'Tabou, scénario bilingue' ('Petite bibliothèque des Cahiers du cinéma', no.45, 2000).

Rashkin, Esther, *A recipe for mourning: Isak Dinesen's 'Babette's Feast*' (www.karenblixen.com).

Rogov, Daniel (1), *Food as Filmic Metaphor* (www.stratsplace.com.rogov/food_as_film.html).

Rogov, Daniel (2), *Food from Three Films* (www.stratsplace.com.rogov/food_three_films.html).

Rough Guide, 'Food and tasty morsels' in *Cult Movies* (London: Rough Guides, 2004). p.174–75.

Time Out, 'Food', and 'Cooks, kitchens, restaurants' in *Film Guide*, (London: Time Out Guides, 13th ed. 2005), pp. 1658, 1650–51.

Bibliography – Gastronomy

Ali Bab, *Gastronomie pratique* (Paris: Flammarion, 1907 and 1928).

Carême & Plumerey, *L'art de la cuisine française au XIXème siècle* (Paris: 5 vols., 1843–44).

Chapel, Alain, *La cuisine, c'est beaucoup plus que des recettes* (Paris: Robert Laffont, 1980). English: *Cuisine of the Imagination* (Seven Ho., 1987).

Chelminski, Rudolph, *The Perfectionist, Life and Death in Haute Cuisine* (London: Michael Joseph, Penguin Books, 2005).

Csergo, Julia, «Du discours gastronomique comme 'propagande nationale', Club des Cent, 1912–1930» (17–19 March 2005 Colloque «Gastronomie et identité culturelle», Université de St Quentin, Publication aux Presses du CNRS)

Davidson, Alan, *The Oxford Companion to Food* (Oxford: Oxford University Press, 1999).

Edwards, Michael, *The Champagne Companion* (London: The Apple Press, 1994).

Ferguson, Priscilla Parkhurst, *Accounting for Taste. The Triumph of French Cuisine* (Chicago & London: The University of Chicago Press, 2004).

Fischler, Claude, *L'Homnivore* (Paris: Odile Jacob, 2001).

Hosking, Richard, *A Dictionary of Japanese Food, Ingredients & Culture* (Boston: Tuttle Publishing 1996).

Hosking, Richard, *At the Japanese Table* (Hong Kong: Oxford University Press, 2000).

Kagawa, Dr. Aya, *Japanese Cookbook* (Tokyo: Japan Travel Bureau, 1949).

Laurioux, Bruno, *Une histoire culinaire du Moyen Age* (Paris: Honoré Champion, 2005).

Marin, François, *Suite des dons de Comus* (Pau: 'Collection Livres de bouche', Manucius, 2000), reprint from the 1742 edition, preface from Silvano Serventi, 3 vol.

Milliken, Mary Sue & Susan Feniger with Helene Siegel, *Mesa Mexicano, Bold Flavors from the Border, Coastal Mexico, and Beyond* (New York: William Morrow, 1994).

Nignon, Edouard, *Eloges de la cuisine française* (Paris: H. Piazza, 1933).

Poulain, Jean-Pierre, *Sociologies de l'alimentation* (Paris: Presses Universitaires de France, 2002).

Rao, Hayagreeva, 'Institutional Change in Toque Ville: Nouvelle Cuisine as an Identity Movement in French Gastronomy', in *American Journal of Sociology* (AJS v108 n4), 2003.

Revel, Jean-François, *Un festin en paroles. Histoire de la sensibilité gastronomique de l'Antiquité à nos jours* (Paris: Plon, 1978 and 1995). English: *Culture and Cuisine* (London: Doubleday, 1982).

Rouff, Marcel, *La vie et la passion de Dodin-Bouffant, gourmet* (Paris: Delamain, Boutelleau, 1924 & Stock,1970). English: *The Passionate Epicure* (New York: Modern Library, 2002).

Zeldin, Theodore, *An Intimate History of Humanity* (London: Vintage, 1998).

87

Notes

1. Zeldin, Chapter 6: 'Why there has been more progress in cooking than in sex', p. 92.
2. McKee, p. 59.
3. Marin. Vol. I, Préface, p. 53 'La cuisine est un art fort libre, & qui n'a proprement d'autres règles que le bon goût, dont chacun se doit faire une idée à sa mode.'.
4. *My Wife's Husband* (*La cuisine au beurre*), Gilles Grangier, 1963..
5. *Twelve Hours to Live* (UK) or *Deadlier Than the Male* (US) (*Voici venir le temps des assassins*), 1956..
6. Oshima scene 74, p. 46.
7. 'Organ' or 'variety meat' in the USA.
8. Fischler, p. 131.

9. *The Gleaners and I*, 2000.
10. Les Halles (Paris): *Twelve Hours to Live* (Julien Duvivier, 1966) ; Delft (1665): *Girl with a Pearl Earing* (Peter Webber, 2003) ; New York: *Simply Irresistible* (Mark Tarlov, 1999).
11. *Les visiteurs du soir*.
12. *La kermesse héroïque*.
13. 'Livres en bouche', November 2001–February 2002, Library of l'Arsenal, Paris.
14. Carême, Vol. V, p. 413, Asperges vertes en petits pois.
15. Edwards, pp. 149–50.
16. Hosking (1996), plate 7 and p. 47, (2000), p. 177. Kagawa, p. 31. Oshima, scene 74, p. 46.
17. *Déjeuner sur l'herbe* aka *Lunch on the Grass*.
18. *Dîner de cons*.
19. *Aimez-vous les femmes?* aka *A Taste for Women* (USA).
20. Chenille (1).
21. *Como Era Gostoso o Meu Francês*.
22. *Babettes gæstebud*, by Gabriel Axel (Denmark) based on a 1952 novel by Isak Dinesen aka Karen Blixen (Denmark 1885–1962) taking place in Norway.
23. Zeldin, p. 94.
24. Ferguson, p. 193.
25. Ferguson, p. 179. Comments Rouff's novel.
26. Rashkin, p. 15.
27. Veblen, Thorstein, *The Theory of the Leisure Class* (London: Allen & Unwin, 1925), p. 70.
28. Fabricant.
29. Nignon, p. 129.
30. Laurioux, p. 256.
31. Davidson, p. 643.
32. Nignon, pp. 48 and 184.
33. Nignon, p. 184.
34. Ali Bab (1928), pp. 711 and 713.
35. Rao, p. 9.
36. Chelminski, p. 195.
37. Flying fish roe with a wasabi flavour.
38. *Yin shi nan nu*.
39. Milliken & Feniger, p. 98.
40 The food for the film was prepared by Chef Monique King of Border Grill.
41. *Voici le temps des assassins* aka *Deadlier Than the Male* (USA).
42 'les prestigieux mouvements de cette symphonie culinaire dont nous venons d'avoir la primeur' … une cuisine bien française, une cuisine bien de chez nous, une cuisine tricolore. Messieurs, Vive la France!'
43. Csergo.
44. Revel (1978), p. 15: 'Autant que la sexualité, la nourriture est inséparable de l'imagination.'

Aged, but not Old: Local Identities, Market Forces, and the Invention of 'Traditional' European Cheeses

Bronwen E. Bromberger

In *The Physiology of Taste*, written in 1825, Brillat-Savarin counsels his readers, 'Tell me what you eat, and I will tell you what you are.' Indeed, food production and consumption are highly specific, socially conditioned practices that express the common tastes, meanings, and values of those who share them. As the production of food has become increasingly industrialized and consumption patterns more de-localized, a consumer movement has arisen that stresses what Angela Treagear calls 'typical local foods.' These 'authentic' foodstuffs are valued for (and priced according to) their expression of regional identity and their time-honored methods of production.

Specialty food producers have sought protection from infringement on their 'brand name' products since well before the 19th century, and government programs to establish 'registered designations of origin' have been in place in France and Italy since the mid-1950s. In 1992, the European Economic Community (EEC) instituted Law 2081/92, which expanded the domain for registration and legal copyright protection of local foodstuffs to a much wider area. The European Union legislation cites several objectives: protecting local heritage and identity, safeguarding producers' market interests, providing consumers with guarantees about the origins of local products, and bolstering rural economic development. To be eligible for PDO (Protected Designation of Origin) status, a product must possess 'characteristics...exclusively due to...inherent natural and human factors' and 'have a proven, traditional character and an exceptional reputation and renown.'[1]

Authenticity is a powerful but problematic claim in a competitive marketplace. By defining and imposing the use of 'authentic' methods, government-sponsored registration programs participate in what Eric Hobsbawm calls 'the invention of tradition,' codifying practices to serve economic ends and masking the evolution of products as they change to meet consumer demands. This paper will show that the specifications for the production of certain registered cheeses sold on the basis of their 'authenticity' and 'traditional' production techniques are inconsistent with documented historical practice and argue that truly 'authentic' methods were both heterogeneous and dynamic. Certified 'traditional' cheeses are now as much a reflection of market demands and modern collective representations of health and sanitation as they are of the 'traditional methods' and locality that they purport to embody. The case of European cheeses presents an intriguing example of how static constructions of history and tradition obscure the evolving nature of local symbols.

Setting the table

Food, identity, and locality

Anthropologists have long recognized food as a symbol of culture and society. Eating is far more than picking up a convenient edible object and swallowing it. Every society makes its own choices about which foods to embrace and 'grammaticize' into a coherent system that differentiates between 'nature' and 'culture,' 'inedible' and 'edible,' and 'them' and 'us.' The preparation of typical local dishes from raw ingredients is a perfect example of the transformation of 'nature' into an identifiable regional and ethnic 'culture.'

Food is also a symbol of place. During the 19th century, as advances in transportation allowed local products like farmhouse cheeses to be sold far from their places of origin, each cheese became associated with the name of the town or region in which it was made.[2] This practice continues today for many 'traditional' European cheeses, and the idea that both human culture and *terroir* (soil, climate, and geographical factors) contribute to the attributes of typical food products has proven central to efforts to protect them.[3]

Globalization and McDonaldization

The advent of industrial food production has undermined many of the native ties between locality, 'culture,' and patterns of consumption in Western societies. Rather than being producers of 'cultured' dishes from raw materials, modern Western eaters are consumers who have lost the necessary skills – or do not have the time – for the job and delegate it to others. Fast food and industrial, packaged convenience food is 'stripped of its sensory characters, reduced to appearances and signs,'[4] a recent invention without identifiable origin or history.

Coupled with the public's fear of so-called 'McDonaldization' and the desocialization of eating are concerns about the safety of industrial foods, distrust of large-scale farming practices such as the use of hormones, and outcries over BSE, *Salmonella*, and the recent Sudan-1 adulterant scandal.

Fischler's corollary to Brillat-Savarin's aphorism encapsulates the bind of modern consumers faced with industrial, mass-produced, and de-territorialized products: 'If one does not know what one is eating, one is liable to lose the awareness...of what one is oneself.'[5]

The re-valorization of local foods

Faced with this dilemma, some consumers have reacted by reasserting their interest in 'traditional' foods, attempting to 'reintroduce a normative logic into everyday eating, a coherent system...in short, an order.'[6] One example of such a countertendency is the Slow Food Movement, founded in Italy in 1986, 'whose aim is to protect the pleasures of the table from the homogenization of modern fast food and life'[7] and which now boasts more than 80,000 members in 100 countries. Another well-known example is the anti-globalization movement led by French Roquefort producer José Bové and the French Farmers Confederation, which gained international publicity for subverting the construction of a McDonald's restaurant in southern France in 1999. Evidence of this interest at the individual level can be seen in the resurgence of local farmers' markets and the growing popularity of Community-Supported Agriculture programs.

For these social movements and those who join them, food symbolizes not only shared identity through common consumption; it also symbolizes the past. A strong sense of nostalgia is wrapped up in the conception of these typical foods as symbols of a way of life that no longer exists, a topic dealt with at length by David Sutton in *The Remembrance of Repasts*, a study of food and social memory.

'Re-valorization' refers to the re-ascription of status that has taken place for many of the artisanal products popular today. What were once cheap subsistence foods have been reclassified as rare luxury items and command prices to match. In *Distinction*, Bourdieu argues that 'taste' is a product of social conditioning rather than individual judgment and that individuals' consumption patterns serve as a form of boundary maintenance between classes. As items that were once considered exclusive (for example, white bread or French cuisine) have become available to members of lower economic brackets, the upper classes have looked for new ways to demonstrate their economic and cultural capital. By choosing to consume once-plebeian foods like Staffordshire Oatcakes[8] and Caerphilly cheese, elite classes maintain their difference from their less-privileged counterparts through periods of change.

Few consumers of re-valorized foods would embrace Bourdieu's thesis, as it suggests a one-sided motivation – elitism – for their food choices. Consumers themselves report 'quality' as the primary factor that determines what typical foods they buy.[9] People who buy farmhouse cheeses are also in search of novelty: the ability to have a 'cross-cultural' experience at the dining room table.

Finally, I would suggest that farmhouse products, particularly cheeses, present consumers with a chance to escape from their bland, sterile consumption patterns and court dietary taboos. With mundane, predictable industrial foods on one hand and rare, irregular ones on the other, customers have a choice between a set of binary oppositions:

Clean – Unclean (rindless : moldy)
Safe – Dangerous (pasteurized : raw milk)
Modern – Traditional (industrial : artisanal)
Mild – Strong (bland : flavorful)
Standard – Variable (predictable : changeable)
Mundane – Exotic (supermarket : specialty market)
Fake – Authentic ('new' techniques : 'old' methods)
Cheap – Expensive (up to 1:5 ratio of cost)

Governmental regulation and specification programs mediate between the two sides of this set of binary oppositions, allowing people to have an 'authentic' experience within well-defined, 'safe' parameters.

Governmental registration programs

Not such a new idea

The idea of protecting typical local products is not a new one. Roquefort is the world's most famous blue cheese and one of the cheeses with the longest documented history. Made from sheep's milk in the region of Rouergue in southern France, all Roquefort cheese must be aged in a massive system of limestone caves under the town of Roquefort. By the 15th century the cheese was already widely renowned, and in 1407 Charles VI recognized and protected the sole right of the Roquefort producers to use the limestone caves. Over successive centuries, more protections were added that strengthened the *commune* of Roquefort producers. In 1666 the high court at Toulouse imposed penalties for the sale of imitation cheeses that attempted to pass themselves off as the genuine article. By the 19th century, Roquefort production was a huge enterprise.[10] The producers created the official *Société des Caves et des Producteurs Réunis de Roquefort* in 1842, which coordinated and submitted the various 'legal judgments that defined the characteristics of Roquefort' from that point onward, until they were gathered together into the first complete *Appellation d'Origine Contrôlée* (AOC) cheese specification in 1925.[11]

European national registration programs

The French government was the first to develop a comprehensive scheme to regulate the use of regional names for food products. When the Roquefort name was legally coupled with a territory of origin and complete specifications for production in 1925, it marked the first application of the concept to a cheese. Since then, more than thirty French cheeses have been awarded AOC status, and the process of registering AOC cheeses in France continues up to the present.[12]

The governmental agency responsible for the AOC program in France is the *Institut National des Appellations d'Origine* (INAO). According to the INAO website, the AOC 'Identifies a…processed agricultural product which draws its authenticity and typicity from its geographical origin…[It] guarantees a link between the product and the terroir…as well as particular disciplines self-imposed by the people in order to get the best out of the land.' The purpose of the specifications is 'to protect a duly established reputation…the result of a culture and a history: they include local, loyal and consistent customs and are included in the decree.'[13] Cheeses that are produced according to the specifications may bear a label that signifies their registered status.

While the AOC program purports to define and protect 'traditional' practice, the specifications themselves are by no means static. Many of them have been amended multiple times since their inception, changing the borders of the approved territories of origin for particular cheeses as well as the techniques approved for their manufacture. The Roquefort specification has been amended five times since 1925, most recently in May of 2005.

France was not the only nation to develop a system of registration for its typical products. Italy's *Denominazione di Origine Controllata* was started in 1954; Spain,

Portugal, Austria, and Germany also have similar programs, all modeled on the AOC system. Britain, notable historically for undervaluing its endemic food culture, lacked a program to register its typical foods until very recently.[14]

European Union legislation: the 'Protected Designation of Origin'

In 1992 the EEC (now the EU) passed Council Regulation 2081/92, which introduced the 'Protected Designation of Origin' (PDO), more or less analogous to the national registration marks, but equally applicable throughout the European Union.[15]

The legislation's objectives are similar to the national registration schemes': to 'benefit the rural economy,' provide consumers with 'clear and succinct information regarding the origin of products,' and 'protect agricultural products or foodstuffs… which have a proven, traditional character and an exceptional reputation.'[16] The PDO certification process is administered at the national level by the Member States' existing registration programs. Where none previously existed, as in Britain, the legislation mandated their creation.[17]

This paper is about the way in which the registration schemes promote an unrealistic construction of 'tradition.' The EU and national programs are basically identical; the only difference is in their scope. All products certified by the national registration schemes were automatically granted the double-protection of the PDO in 1992, and the national programs continue to thrive alongside the PDO legislation, which depends on them to screen its new candidates. In this paper I will use the term PDO when talking about the certification programs in general and in the present and the names of the national certification schemes (e.g. AOC) when referring to specific pieces of legislation that were passed before 1992.

93

Deconstructing 'tradition'

Governmental registration programs obscure the fact that cheeses and their production methods are changing – and have always changed – to meet consumer and market demands. The PDO specifications are written in a way that reflects these market imperatives, while appearing to enshrine the 'traditional' practices they specify.

Static specifications are incompatible with the nature of farmstead cheesemaking

Cheesemaking is a highly-sensitive, multi-variable process that lies 'halfway between art and science.'[18] Milk from grass-fed animals changes seasonally and even daily, as do natural bacterial starters and ageing-room conditions. Experienced cheesemakers adjust their methods to balance these changes over time, but farmhouse cheese is nevertheless a dynamic product and every batch is unique.

Legal specifications promote a monolithic concept of cheese, not only from day to day, but within a particular region. Before the advent of the railways, most fresh cheeses were consumed in the same area where they were made, but beginning in the mid-19th century, cheeses shipped to metropolitan areas were sold as, for example, 'cheese from Camembert.' There was a great deal of variation between the products of different makers, and those family names, not the regions, were effectively the brand names of the cheeses. By connecting particular localities to specific profiles, the PDO specifications imply that there is only one 'authentic' form of each cheese.

Specifications reflect legal imperatives and modern sanitation norms

Many so-called 'traditional' practices conflict with modern conceptions of sanitation. Pasteurization, now considered standard (and obligatory for fresh cheeses sold in the United States[19]), was unheard of in any context before 1862, and the utensils used to make cheese were often made of porous materials like wood, which absorb bacterial cultures.[20] Other recorded methods might put a contemporary consumer off cheese for ever: when 19th-century Dales cheesemakers ran out of rennet, they put black snails in the milk to start its coagulation,[21] and conventional wisdom held that 'one could not have a good cheese unless a bit of manure or cow dung had fallen into the milk.'[22]

Faced with the imperative to meet health codes and make cheeses that people will buy, the PDO specifications crystallize 'tradition' in a form that is compatible with modern health codes and conceptions of sanitation. The most obvious case is that of pasteurization, designed to eliminate potentially dangerous microorganisms in raw milk. Farmhouse cheese was never originally pasteurized, and pasteurization destroys the aromatic compounds and enzymes that contribute to the complex flavor and aroma of raw-milk cheeses. Farmhouse cheese experts reiterate that farmstead cheeses 'should not need to have recourse to pasteurization...such a need would indicate extremely careless methods of production for which there is no excuse.'[23,24]

Pasteurization does become necessary under industrial conditions, when milk from multiple sources is transported to a central location and mixed in a bulk tank. As of 1988, 15 of the 27 French AOC specifications 'condoned pasteurization or thermisation [heat treatment], obviously as a sop to industrial cheesemakers.'[25] Likewise, there is intense pressure from some producers' groups for all members to pasteurize their milk, for fear that an outbreak of illness from one company's cheese would hurt the sales of all.[26]

Pasteurization is not the only concession that has been made to modern conceptions of sanitation. The Camembert producers of Normandy, writing their PDO specification in 1983, insisted on the use of raw milk, but mandated the inoculation of the cheeses with the snow-white mold *Penicillium candidum*. In the days before commercial mold spores were available, all cheeses were allowed to pick up a combination of different strains of mold in the ripening room. Rather than just the 'virginal white' seen today, cheese from Camembert once came in a wide variety of colors, as betrayed by the name of the grayish-green mold *Penicillium camemberti*.[27]

Specifications are written to comply with modern consumer and retailer demands

Producers of PDO cheeses are aware that contemporary consumers are looking for a variety of attributes (beyond assurance of sanitation) that are not consistent with historical practice. The most striking of these is the demand for vegetarian cheese.

94

Many consumers of organic, artisanal products are also vegetarians. However, the rennet used for cheesemaking is not a vegetarian product: it is an enzyme extracted from the stomach of a suckling calf, lamb, or kid. As a result of demand from vegetarians, most industrial cheeses today are made using vegetarian substitutes, either from a plant source (which tends to impart a bitter flavor to aged cheeses), or more commonly from a synthesized enzyme made using recombinant DNA technology.

Boisard suggests that cheeses have also become milder in flavor to reflect consumer demand. But Randolph Hodgson, Chairman of the British Specialist Cheesemakers' Association and owner of Neal's Yard Dairy in London, maintains that the decreasing amount of flavor in cheese is instead related to the supermarket sales model, in which cheeses are sold prepackaged and the primary factor involved in customers' choice is price rather than taste. Under these conditions, cheeses evolve to become cheaper, more easily packaged and transportable, more shelf-stable, and less variable, but not more flavorful.[28]

Specifications are malleable to meet large-scale demand

PDO specifications tend to place as much – or more – emphasis on locality than they do on method. The advantage of this flexibility is that it permits different makers the leeway to use their own recipes (within specified limits). At the same time, flexible specifications have also been distorted to allow large-scale industrial production under the guise of 'traditional' methods.

A good example of this is the PDO for Camembert de Normandie, which specifies that curd be transferred to the molds using a ladle, hearkening back to the way in which artisanal producers hand-ladled the curds. However, several of the larger dairies that produce PDO Camembert de Normandie have designed a machine that can ladle the curd into the molds much more efficiently, allowing them to increase their volume of production while conforming to the letter of the law.[29]

A similar example is found in the PDO specification for Roquefort. In the past, the blue molds found in the cheese came entirely from the limestone caves in which they were aged, a process that took at least three months. The current PDO regulations endorse the addition of commercial strains of *Penicillium* to the cheeses, which allows them to be cycled quickly through the caves in rotations of two weeks. This provision allows a six-fold increase in the volume of Roquefort that can be produced: nearly six million cheeses were made in 1985 alone.[30]

PDOs benefit only the largest producers

The PDO legislation specifically cites the objective of 'improving the incomes of farmers and retaining the rural population'[31] in areas dominated by subsistence agriculture, but since its implementation it has become clear that its major beneficiaries are not the farmhouse cheesemakers it was meant to help. Instead, the largest producers of PDO cheeses are the ones who benefit the most from the brand recognition and quality assurance associated with the PDO certification.

As a Somerset-based maker of farmhouse Cheddar cheese, James Montgomery

95

joined the syndicate of cheesemakers who applied for the 'West Country Farmhouse Cheddar Cheese' PDO in 1996. He quickly realized, however, that the PDO only benefited the largest producers in the group, who profited from their cheeses' association with the smaller, more traditional producers protected under the same legislation. For Montgomery, PDO status did nothing more than imply that his handmade, bandage-wrapped Cheddar was made in the same way as the industrial block Cheddars made by the largest Somerset members of the PDO group. None of Montgomery's Cheddar cheeses was ever sold with a PDO label, and he is candid about the fact that he quickly 'got bored with having to spend money and time for someone to come round and tell me I was making traditional cheese' and left the consortium. Fortunately for Montgomery, the fact that the name 'Cheddar' is public property means that he can still produce 'Cheddar' cheese, though he is now legally prohibited from labeling his cheese 'West Country Farmhouse Cheddar' – not that he ever did.[32]

The fact that a group of producers who hold a PDO can prevent others from selling their products under the protected name is a concern for many farmhouse cheesemakers, who worry about the ramifications if certain producers decide to band together and apply for PDO certification that affects their ability to make cheese the way they currently do, or worse, excludes them altogether. Far from empowering subsistence farmers to support themselves, many of the PDO certifications are simply tools used by industrial producers to access the specialty cheese market.

Specifications represent revived and invented 'traditions'

One of the most troubling aspects of the PDO legislation is its tendency to enshrine reconstituted 'tradition' as genuine and 'authentic.'

Many makers of recreated cheeses have no experience with the original product. During the 1990s the Catalan cheese advocate Enric Canut set about to help a small group of cheesemakers recreate Garrotxa, a semi-hard goat's milk cheese whose production was banned during the oppressive regime of Francisco Franco. 'The first time the cheeses developed a blue fungus on the outside, and we washed it off,' he recalled. 'And then it grew back, and we washed it off again. And then finally [a] grandmother said: "Well, of course in this climate it always develops that mold."'[33] Given the many variables inherent in farmhouse cheesemaking, it seems valid to wonder to what extent these recreated products resemble the originals, especially when there are no grandmothers around to consult.

Although the PDO legislation requires that registered products possess 'a proven, traditional character and an exceptional reputation and renown,'[34] Angela Tregear points out that 'claims regarding the territorial distinctiveness...or the traditional nature of production practices are not subject to any serious scrutiny.'[35] Buxton Blue is a variation of Stilton that was developed by the large industrial corporation Dairy Crest. The cheese had never been heard of when Patrick Rance wrote his comprehensive *Great British Cheese Book* in 1982, yet in 1996, Dairy Crest was awarded a

PDO certification for Buxton Blue. The PDO application is extremely vague and unclear, and states 'The cheese originates in this area due to Hartington [creamery]'s reputation in the production of blue cheese and its use of authentic unvarying local methods which utilize Hartington's traditional blue cheese skills.'[36] It does nothing to establish a long-standing historical precedent for Buxton Blue cheese; nevertheless it was approved and the cheese was awarded PDO status.

There is inherent tension between the objectives of the PDO legislation

In her paper 'What is a Typical Local Food?' Angela Tregear notes that there are 'fundamental tensions' between the EU legislation's objectives of protecting cultural heritage, promoting sustainable development, and increasing the market value of typical products by providing a seal of authenticity.[37]

As shown by the evidence above, the protection of so-called 'cultural heritage' is seldom compatible with marketing strategy. Commodities must change to meet consumer demand if they are to survive, and the static construction of 'tradition' suggested by the concept of the PDO certification is by definition resistant to change.

Likewise, the EU legislation was geared towards empowering marginalized farmers and revitalizing subsistence agriculture, but many PDOs are held not by cooperatives of small farmers but by large corporations such as Dairy Crest and industrial-scale producers of popular cheeses like Roquefort, West Country Farmhouse Cheddar and Camembert de Normandie. Whether small farmhouse producers benefit (or suffer) from the legislation is debatable, as shown by the case of Cheddar maker James Montgomery.

97

The 'invention of tradition'

The PDO as 'invented tradition'

In 1983's *The Invention of Tradition*, Hobsbawm and Ranger argue that 'tradition' is a symbolic construction that imposes practices consistent with the values of contemporary society. They also point out the 'long-term inadaptability of pre-industrial ways to a society revolutionized beyond a certain point,'[38] a perfect encapsulation of the contradiction within the PDO legislation. The apparent 'maintenance of tradition' represented by the PDO certification masks the fact that the products continue to adapt to meet the demands of the market. The idea that farmhouse cheeses are relics of the past that need to be protected in their 'genuine' form is reflective of modern Western values and our relationship with 'tradition.' As Appadurai points out, 'authenticity' is a modern invention.

The very presence of a PDO seal suggests that a product has already changed in response to market influence. PDO certification has more to do with creating exchangeable commodities than 'publicly funded museum pieces.'[39] By developing name brands for products in a marketplace that demands consistency and volume, the PDO exerts pressure to standardize and industrialize production methods. The local products with the highest degree of 'typicity' are the ones that resist commercialization beyond a local area and therefore have no reason to apply for a PDO.

Twenty-first century artisans

Small-scale farmhouse cheesemaking is a viable business today because of the revalorization of typical local foods, exemplified by the fact that people are willing to pay up to five times the price for artisanal cheeses as for their industrial counterparts. Contemporary producers are faced with the formidable challenge of balancing inefficient methods of artisanal production with keeping their businesses afloat in a fiercely competitive market.

Under circumstances where producers' and consumers' knowledge differ and products are produced and consumed in different venues, questions of authenticity are bound to arise. The PDO is a visible way to deal with that, a seal of authenticity that signifies that consumers are 'purchas[ing] high quality products with guarantees as to the method of production and origin.'[40] However, it should be clear by now that the PDO legislation serves the market – and often industrial-scale companies – above history.

Finally, it should be noted that the adoption of non-traditional models does not necessarily mean the death of 'traditional' forms. Anthropologist Susan Rogers' 1991 ethnography of a French shepherding village shows that the growth of demand of milk for industrial Roquefort cheese production[41] has recently led to the extinction of local cheesemaking and a focus on the production and sale of liquid milk instead. The superficial transformation of the village (economic growth, modern infrastructure, and the discontinuation of 'traditional' cheesemaking) suggests a complete break with the past and with 'tradition.' However, Rogers found that the new economic model promoted the maintenance of the original sheep farms, which continue to be owned and run by individual families. Within these farms, very 'traditional' household structure and gender roles, dating from long before the new emphasis on the sale of liquid milk, have been unconsciously maintained. Rogers concludes that industrialization has transformed France, but that culture is resilient, and that rather than a destructive force, 'change often preserves and reproduces sociocultural specificities.'[42]

Evolution versus enshrinement

It is tempting to offer a scathing indictment of the PDO legislation as an example of what sociologist Ulf Hannerz calls the 'postmodern world,' with 'little coherent sense of history' and a past that exists only to be 'raided for commoditizable nostalgias'.[43] Indeed, the EU legislation appears to be anathema to 'genuine tradition,' as it promotes the shrewd Disneyfication of local products by industrial interests to serve purely economic ends. In fact, its problem lies in its adherence to a modern, static conception of 'tradition.' Commodities have always evolved to reflect market demands. The problem with the EU legislation is not that it bastardizes tradition, but that, by purporting to protect 'tradition,' it suggests that such a thing actually exists.

Symbolic systems such as those that define 'tradition' and 'modernity' are products of the current state of the world, even as they appear to represent essential, unchanging truths. Conventional ideas about 'native' phenomena are often misguided. Spaghetti Bolognese is often held up as the quintessential Italian dish, despite the fact that its two main ingredients – noodles and tomatoes – were imported from China and the New World in the 15th century. And recent cookbooks, espousing the health benefits of Provençal cuisine, seem to have overlooked the fact that before the 19th century, the Provençal diet had more to do with pork fat and cabbage than fresh herbs and olive oil.[44] Practices evolve with time, and the concept of 'tradition' has more to do with the meaning of the past to those who live today than with the past itself.

Contemporary capitalism has been honed to a fine art, which provides consumers who have sufficient financial resources with the ability to sate their every hunger. The revalorization and canonization of farmhouse cheeses is an example of this economic model taken to its logical end point. It has created products that play to consumers' needs and desires, not only for sustenance, but also for novelty, escapism, social distinction, and quality assurance, allowing them a safe space in which to court dietary taboo and connect with an idealized 'other' and past way of life. The cheeses may be constructions cooked up to feed a voracious market, but that does not change the fact that they are eagerly swallowed as the genuine embodiment of 'traditional culture' in an increasingly hybrid world and integrated international marketplace.

References

Appadurai, A. (1986), *The social life of things: Commodities in cultural perspective* (Cambridge: Cambridge University Press).

—— (1995), 'The production of locality.' In *Counterworks: Managing the Diversity of Knowledge*, R. Fardon (Ed.) (London: Routledge), pp, 204–225.

Bessière, J. (1998), 'Local Development and Heritage: Traditional Food and Cuisine as Tourist Attractions in Rural Areas', *Sociologia Ruralis* 38(1), pp 21–33.

Bodnár, J. (2003), 'Roquefort vs. Big Mac: Globalization and its Others', *European Journal of Sociology* 44(1), pp. 133–44.

Boisard, P. (2004), *Camembert: a national myth* (Berkeley: University of California Press)

Bourdieu, P. (1979), *Distinction: a social critique of the judgment of taste* (London: Routledge).

Brillat-Savarin, J. (1925[1825]), *The Physiology of Taste* (London: Peter Davies).

Commission of the European Communities (1992), Council Regulation (EEC) No. 2081/92 of July 14.

De Roest, K. and Menghi, A. (2000), 'Reconsidering 'Traditional' Foods: The Case of Parmigiano Reggiano Cheese', *Sociologia Ruralis* 40(4), pp. 439–51.

DEFRA Web site. www.defra.gov. Accessed 10 May 2005.

Buxton Blue Specification: www.defra.gov.uk/foodrin/foodname/Ukingdom/buxblue.htm.

Producers' Letter: www.defra.gov.uk/foodrin/foodname/reglocal/pdoproducer.htm.

DiMonaco, M. et al. (2005), 'Valorization of Traditional Foods: The case of Provelone del Monaco cheese', *British Food Journal* 107(2), pp. 98–110.

Douglas, M. (1966), *Purity and Danger* (London: Routledge).

Fischler, C. (1988), 'Food, self and identity', *Social Science Information* 27(2), pp. 275–92.

Goody, J. (1982), *Cooking, cuisine and class* (Cambridge: Cambridge University Press).

Hannerz, U. (1992), *Cultural Complexity: Studies in the Social Organization of Meaning* (New York: Columbia University Press).

Held, D. et al. (1999), *Global Transformations* (Cambridge: Polity Press).

Hobsbawm, E. and Ranger, T. (1983), *The Invention of Tradition* (Cambridge: Cambridge University Press).

Ilbery, B. and Kneafsey, M. (2000), 'Registering regional specialty food and drink products in the United Kingdom: the case of PDOs and PGIs', *Area* 32(3), pp. 317–325.

INAO Web site. www.inao.gouv.fr. Accessed 30 June 2005.

Jenkins, N. (2005), Cheese Guru. *Food and Wine* 28(2), pp. 112–114.

Kopytoff, I., 'The cultural biography of things: commoditization as process', in Appadurai (Ed.), *The social life of things: commodities in cultural perspective* (ibid), pp. 64–91.

Kupiec, B. (1998), 'Specialty and artisanal cheeses today: product and customer', *British Food Journal* 100(5), pp. 236–43.

Leach, E. (1970), *Levi-Strauss* (London: William Collins).

Leitch, A. (2000), 'The social life of lardo: slow food in fast times, *The Asia Pacific journal of anthropology* 1(1), pp. 103–118.

PDO Fast Track Application for Buxton Blue Cheese. Copy provided by Anthony Davis at the British Department for Environment, Food and Rural Affairs (DEFRA).

Rance, P. (1982), *The Great British Cheese Book* (London: Macmillan).

—— (1989), *The French Cheese Book* (London: Macmillan).

Rogers, S. (1991), *Shaping Modern Times in Rural France: The transformation and reproduction of an Aveyronnais community* (Princeton: Princeton University Press).

Slow Food Web site. www.slowfood.com. Accessed 11 July 2005.

Sutton, D. (2001), *The Remembrance of Repasts* (Oxford: Berg).

Tregear, A. (2001), 'What is a 'typical local food'?', Working Paper No. 58 (Centre for Rural Economy, University of Newcastle, Newcastle upon Tyne, UK)

Tregear, A. (2003), 'From Stilton to Vimto: Using Food History to Re-think Typical Products in Rural Development', *Sociologia Ruralis* 43 (2), pp. 91–107.

Watson, J. (2004), 'Don't cut the cheese', *The National Interest* 75, pp. 123–8.

Notes

1. Council Regulation 2081/92 of 14 July 1992.
2. Previously, they were simply described; for example, Valençay, a pyramidal fresh goats' cheese, was known as *chèvre pyramide*; log-shaped Sainte-Maure as *le fromage long*. (Rance (1989), p. 68.)
3. It should not be surprising that cheese, with its links to history, 'culture,' and place, should prove ripe for association with nationalist movements. Camembert, once a regional product of Normandy, is a universal symbol of French identity, and Caerphilly cheese has been imbued with an essentialized 'Welsh' identity that is closely aligned with the other symbols of the Welsh nationalist movement. Several Caerphilly producers insist on writing the name of the cheese in Welsh ('Caerffili'), stressing linguistic separatism from the rest of the U.K., and cheeses are available dipped in wax in the colors of the Welsh flag and shaped like rugby balls (a not-so-subtle reference to the Welsh team's prominence in the sport). Nationalist connotations were never attributed to either Camembert or Caerphilly by their original producers, but these examples show how 'traditional' cheeses are perfect candidates to become powerful symbols of social groups.
4. Fischler, p. 289.
5. Fischler, p. 290.
6. Fischler, p. 291.
7. Slow Foods website.
8. Leitch, p. 104.
9. Ilbery, p. 318.
10. In 1890, the net sale of Roquefort was more than 8 million francs, Rance (1989), p. 180.
11. Rance (1989), p. 180.
12. Obviously, producers of regional products have a vested interest in ensuring that they retain the

monopoly on their own typical products. However, not everyone accomplished this as successfully as the Roquefort producers. Camembert, a much younger cheese whose origins date to the French Revolution, was relatively unknown outside of Normandy until the 1850s, when railway transportation allowed the fresh, soft cheeses to be sold in Paris. By the 1880s, imitation Camembert was produced all over France, and by the time a Norman Camembert-makers syndicate was set up in 1909, it was too late to regain control over the name. Only in 1983 was an AOC certification finally awarded to Camembert de Normandie, a cheese with strict specifications as to its method of production and region of origin. Even so, most consumers do not differentiate between Camembert and Camembert de Normandie; the exclusive right to use Camembert *tout simple* – which is of substantial value – was lost by the Norman producers.

13. INAO website.

14. While the Camembert producers of Normandy were busy fighting for their regional rights during the early 20th century, many British cheesemakers made no effort to protect their products whatsoever. Cheddar is a perfect example. When large numbers of British immigrants left Somerset for the United States and Canada during the 19th century, they took their cheesemaking skills with them, and soon 'Cheddar' cheese was produced all over the world. With an unprotected name and a process that lent itself to industrial production, Cheddar quickly became synonymous with bland industrial block cheese. Faced with this situation (and finding it hard to differentiate their products from the many other Cheddar cheeses on the market), in the late 1990s Cheddar makers from Somerset applied for legal protection for their 'authentic' Cheddar, which they called 'West Country Farmhouse Cheddar Cheese'.

15. The legislation also introduced the 'Protected Geographical Indication' (PGI), a sort of second-tier PDO appropriate for products for which only one stage in production is linked to a specific locality, but which still have regional characteristics deserving of recognition.

16. Council Regulation 2081/92 of 14 July 1992.

17. In Britain, this authority was given to the Regional and Local Foods Branch of the Government's Department for Environment, Food and Rural Affairs (DEFRA).

18. Interview with Randolph Hodgson, 30 April 2005.

19. Watson, p. 124.

20. This phenomenon was very important to early farmhouse cheesemakers, many of whom did not use added starters; the residual bacterial culture started the fermentation by itself.

21. Rance (1982), p. 75.

22. Boisard, p. 218.

23. Dr. J.G. Davis, quoted in Rance (1982), p. 109.

24. The British Ministry of Food did not see it that way, and regarded all unpasteurized soft cheeses as a public health threat. The production of many of these cheeses was effectively outlawed by the government under the aegis of 'Utility standards' during the Second World War, which mandated the sale of small farmers' liquid milk and the factory production of hard, 'safe' cheeses. When the Utility standards were discontinued in 1954, an attempt was made to revive farmhouse cheesemaking under stricter regulations, but many of the local skills had already been lost (Rance (1982), p. 77).

25. Rance (1989), p. xxv.

26. The Stilton Cheesemakers' Association is one example. While pasteurization is not apparently written into the Stilton PDO specification, producers who belong to the syndicate that holds the PDO are required by its internal rules to pasteurize. Recently a new farmhouse producer who wished to make a raw-milk Stilton was denied the right to join the Stilton Cheesemakers' Association and call his cheese 'Stilton.' He plans to continue development of the cheese, which may end up being sold by the name 'Notlits,' a pointed reference to the deceptive nature of the legal statutes (interview with Randolph Hodgson, 30 April 2005).

27. Boisard, p. 73.

28. Interview with Randolph Hodgson, 30 April 2005.

101

29. Boisard, p. 186.
30. Rance (1989), p. 196.
31. Council Regulation 2081/92 of 14 July 1992.
32. Interview with James Montgomery, 9 June 2005.
33. Jenkins, p. 114.
34. Regulation 2081/92 of 14 July 1992.
35. Tregear (2001), p. 22.
36. PDO Fast Track Application for Buxton Blue Cheese.
37. Tregear (2001), p. 24.
38. Hobsbawm and Ranger, p. 8.
39. Tregear (2001), p. 21.
40. Regulation 2081/92 of 14 July 1992.
41. The village she studied, Ste Foy, lies within the territory permitted for the production of milk by the PDO specifications.
42. Rogers, p. 36.
43. Hannerz, p. 35.
44. Goody, p. 36.

The Real Thing? Understanding the Archive at Fairfax House, York

Peter Brown

When Father Hugh Aveling was researching for his book *Catholic Recusancy in Yorkshire*[1] he noted a bundle of over 1000 documents in the Newburgh MSS which referred, not as expected, to the Fauconburg family of that estate, but to the Fairfax family from Gilling Castle, a country seat five miles across the valley.[2] These papers are an eclectic mix of invoices and records covering the period 1735–72 and included a number which detailed the day-to-day living of the Fairfax family. They were not of any particular interest to the priest, and consequently remained uncatalogued until recent times.

When researchers began looking at these in some detail, we discovered a number which covered the building of Fairfax House in York during the period 1759–62, also a large portion recording the purchase of silver, glass, porcelain and other domestic utensils, but the majority were for the daily provisions of the Fairfax household.[3] Not all the bills were continuous, and there were some curious gaps; the housekeeper's records, for example, are limited to the years 1769–72, and whilst the general supplies of wine are well documented, the butler's cellar book, which showed the amounts consumed on a daily basis, only covers a four-year period. Other runs of invoices were more complete, the butcher's supplies of beef, mutton and calf's heads are detailed on a weekly basis and the supply of confections is also well documented.

Less exotic, but just as interesting, are a number of invoices from the York plantsman, John Telford, for the period 1759–60, which itemise a comprehensive range of root and salad vegetables purchased by the head gardener, Ralph Craggs.[4] Over 50 varieties of vegetable were being supplied and these included 8 varieties of cabbage (savoy, white savoy, sugarloaf, ball, red, early Dutch, best, and winter cabbage), 6 different types of lettuce (winter, imperial, capucheen, coss, mix'd and cabbage lettuce), 5 types of bean (Spanish, speckled kidney, bottonia kidney, haricot and early beans), 3 varieties of cucumber (early, long and prickly), some short hotspur and early Charlton pease, curl'd and Italian brocoli, white and red beet, border and ground spinage, Spanish and Welsh onion, white and green endive, together with garlick, shallots, carrots, parsnips, leeks, collyflower (sic), early turnip, white mustard, radish, cur'ld parsley, and purslan. Potatoes and artichokes were seemingly not cultivated in the kitchen garden, but bought in from local markets at York.

Other supplies from Telford included a range of umbelliferous plants, herbs and flowers intended for cooking, including nasturtium, thyme, hyssop, sweet marjoram, double marigold, angelica, caraway and white Dutch clover. From a mid-eighteenth century context, this is a surprisingly sophisticated medley of root and salad growing and suggests that both Telford and Lord Fairfax's gardener, Ralph Craggs, had acquired considerable horticultural knowledge.[5] Also the generally held view is that the products of the kitchen garden were intended mostly for consumption by the servants, but with such a huge range and variety under cultivation in the kitchen gardens at Gilling and Fairfax House, this hypothesis needs to be rethought. The popular recipe books of the period, by the likes of Hannah Glasse (1747), Eliza Smith (1758) and Elizabeth Raffald (1771), have little regard for vegetables, unless they are being boiled to a pulp or used to flavour the sauces.[6] We have tended to assume that because they get little coverage in these texts, they were not part of the rich man's diet, but this may not be the case.

The British medical profession in the first half of the eighteenth century, was also working from a very different theory of diet and health than we understand today,[7] and the doctors were on the whole, rather suspicious of vegetables.[8] They acknowledged, however, that some roots and salads were easier for Europeans to digest than others. The general rule of thumb was: the sooner to maturity (i.e. asparagus and some of the salads), the easier to digest. Those which took longer to ripen (i.e. those taking in more of the solar rays!) were much harder to absorb into the system. Also the smaller the vegetable the better; large onions or apples and pears, for example, were considered difficult for the European stomach. Similarly, the lighter colours were also easier to digest (i.e. turnips, parsnips, potatoes, etc.), whereas carrots, skirrets and beet gave us problems.[9] For some medical conditions, however, certain vegetables were actually recommended; those suffering from stones, for example, needed a 'smooth and diluting regime … Artichoke or Asparagus dressed with Butter or milk, Beets fried, Pease-soup, Turnip-soup, etc.' Also anyone with a 'diuretick' condition must avoid the 'flatulent roots …Pease, Parsnips, Turnips, Carrots, Salads of Nasturtiums, Horseradish, Mint Bawn (sic)', and other 'warming' things. Cucumber, however, was never one of the acceptable vegetables and damned by association with the lower classes. Not only was it considered a poor-man's diet, it was plentiful and cheap during the months of August and September at a time when cholera was most prevalent. Eating too many cucumbers, if you had cholera or a similar intestinal infection, would induce a vomit and this was the last thing the patient needs at this time, and could result in death. The medics also felt that melons and summer fruits are to be avoided if you had cholera, as were swine's flesh, fish, honey and all things sweet.[10] (It is interesting to note that the simplest and most effective treatment for cholera today is to give the patient sugar and water!)

There was also a great distrust of fish and sea-animals amongst the medical fraternity. 'Those who live much on fish are infected with scurvy, or cutaneous eruptions and other deseases of a foul blood', said Dr. Cheyne in his tome, *An Essay of Health and Longlife*.[11] 'Fish was not fit for the Studious and Tender' he said, but acknowledged in a rather lukewarm manner that some fresh-water fish like trout and perch were easier to digest than say carp, tench, salmon, eel and turbot. Also salt-water fish such as whiting, flounder and soal (sic) were considered lighter on the stomach than salmon, sturgeon, herring and mackerel.[12] His final piece of advice on the matter was damning, 'Everybody finds himself more thirsty and heavy after a full meal of Fish, and is generally forced to recourse to Spirits and distilled liquors to carry them off.... and besides, after a full meal of fish, even at Noon, one never sleeps so sound the ensuing Night; as is certain from constant observation.'[13] It is little wonder that most of Britain at this time were not great fish lovers, but Lord Fairfax and his daughter Anne, do seem to be exceptions. The housekeeping records show a regular supply of produce from sea and river, which included: codd (sic), haddock, ells (sic), salmon, lobster, turbot, smelts, whitings, oyster, cockls (sic), anchovies, ling, soles and butt, all being bought in from the local market. Also twice a month the estate labourer, Mathew Robinson, came to York 'with the basket' and this probably included some of the carp cultivated in the fishponds at Gilling Castle.[14] This branch of the Fairfax family were still proclaiming their Roman Catholic faith at this time and the house-keeper's record shows they practised the ritual of eating fish on Fridays. This gesture of penance, however, would not account for such an abundance of fish and sea-animals amongst the weekly provisions.

Also each week a curious reference to a 'wisker', costing either 1s. or 6d. This was a relatively small amount compared to the housekeeper's payment of 2s. 10d. for cod, or even 1s. 3d. for the supply of potatoes – a mystery provision, as yet unidentified, but perhaps no more complicated than the cost of employing a strong arm from the streets to help the cook 'wisk' up her mixtures!

Many of the other purchases are predictable but some are worthy of comment. 'French roles and Bricks' for example were popular in the Fairfax household, as was cheese, but only two varieties ever listed, Cheshire cheese and Double Gloucester.

Also at Christmas time the city chef, William Baker, was paid £1. 16s. 0d. 'to a Pye'. This was a huge amount and comparable to a half-year's wage for the under-cook, Rachel Clement. It was probably one of those complex Yorkshire pies, described as a 'thick crust pie able to travel' in Hannah Glasse's *Art of Cookery*.[15]

Perhaps the most interesting provision, and also supplied around the time of the winter solstice, was 'Brawn', a substance which usually weighed around 16 lb., and cost a staggering 19s. (the butcher charged about the same for a weekly provision of 91 lb. 'Of Beef, Mutton and Calfs feet'). This was obviously something more special than the so-called 'head cheese', the boiled meat and brains of a pig or calf's head moulded into a loaf. Most probably a dish of mediaeval origin, comprising a fully grown domestic boar which has been filleted, cut into joints and tightly wrapped in linen cloths. The meat was then boiled until super-tender (the test was to use a piece of straw as the skewer!) When cooked, the meat is chilled in cold water to set the jelly and the pieces pickled in barrels until needed. To present the dish at the table,

105

the meat is cut into strips (leached) and laid in a shield-like design on a large charger, then decorated in the centre with either a branch of candied rosemary or yew, dusted with 'flower'. Around this are coloured jellies and candied oranges, which complete the display. Ivan Day has argued that this dish was the precursor of the decorated Christmas tree as we know it today, and as such, predates by many centuries, the German tradition adopted by Britain in the mid-nineteenth century.[16]

The most expensive provisions were, as we would expect, those items intended for the dessert. All the usual suspects appear in the invoices: provisions needed for the preparation of wet and dry sweetmeats, the single, double and treble refined loaf sugar, also individual supplies like morrels, trouffles (sic), macaroons, prunelloes, candied oranges, orange chips, small comfits, white candy, cherries, clear cakes, apricot tart and French plumbs, all supplied by Seth Agar from his shop in Stonegate, York.

Three invoices also survive from a French confectioner, a Monsieur Seguin, who had a successful practice in York during the second half of the eighteenth century.[17] Amongst his supplies at Christmas-time, (and written in a naïve French hand) were: 'crystallised fruit, meringlle (sic), candied lemon, coloured sweets, waffles, a bottle of orange flower water, shortbread biscuits for the parterre, sugar figures of sorts' and a payment 'for an effigy'.[18] With Ivan Day's help we were able to recreate a similar sort of display, based on designs which appear in Menon's *La Science du Maître d'Hôtel Cuisinier*.[19]

Knowing the food and drink coming into the house during the occupancy of the Fairfax family was a vital first step in understanding dining practices at this elite level, but exactly how it was prepared and presented at the table was answered partly by reference to a facsimile reproduction of a family recipe book, *Arcana Fairfaxiana*.[20] The original manuscript contains mostly medical potions, written in several hands, but it also includes favourite recipes, tried and tested through generations, for the like of boiling and presenting carp and 'To bake venison in a good crust'. Also the books by Eliza Smith (1758) and Hannah Glasse (1747) were probably included in Lord Fairfax's Library.[21] Other useful clues on how to present the table were provided by invoices for silver from the great rococo silversmith Charles Frederick Kandler.[22] Anne Baker's supplies for blue & white porcelain for the dessert, and references to 'flowered waterglasses' and other glasses needed for the consumption of jellies, wine, old hock, Beer and cider were also helpful.[23] What is missing from the bundle of papers, however, are references to the supply of damask napery for the table. Earlier Gilling Castle inventories, show an impressive selection of damask tablecloths and napkins woven with emblematic patterns of roses, marigolds and eagles,[24] and it seems certain Lord Fairfax would have continued this tradition, perhaps ordering from the developing linen industry in Ireland.[25] We tend to underestimate the European obsession with 'whiteness' during the seventeenth and eighteenth centuries. Apart from the obvious associations with purity and hygiene, the reflective properties of a properly laundered white damask tablecloth, together with a full display of silver and in the presence of candlelight, combine to create a magical atmosphere in which to dine. There is little evidence to support the commonly held belief that the British usually preferred to dine off the bare mahogany table.

At Fairfax House we like think that our set-piece displays are indeed 'authentic' and that the archive is a useful reference point from which to start.

Notes and References

1. Aveling, Hugh, *Catholic Recusancy in York 1558–1791* (Catholic Record Society, 1970).
2. Webb, Gerry, *Fairfax of York* (York, 2001).
3. North Yorkshire County Records Office (NYCRO), ZDV. F: MIC 1128/3462.
4. NYCRO, ZDV, (F) F.G. (bills 52 & 52A).
5. Quest-Ritson, Charles, *The English Garden* (London, 2001), pp. 102–09.
6. Glasse, Hannah, *The Art of Cookery* (London, 6th edn., 1758); Smith, Eliza, *The Complete Housewife* (London, 16th edn., 1758); Raffald, Elizabeth, *The Experienced English housewife* (London, 2nd edn., 1771).
7. For an explanation of the humoral theory of medicine, see Brown, Peter, *Come Drink the Bowl Dry* (York, 1996), pp. 41–44.
8. Quincy, John, transl. *The Aphorisms of Sanctorius* (London, 1712), pp. 124–160.
9. Cheyne, George, *An Essay of Health and Longlife* (London, 1725), pp. 22–23.
10. Strother, Edward, *An Essay on Sickness and Health* (London, 1725), pp. 81–84.
11. Cheyne, op. cit., p. 41.
12. Ibid., pp. 24–25.
13. Ibid., p. 41.
14. NYCRO, ZDV (F) F.G. (bills 103 &109).
15. Glasse, op. cit., pp. 139–140.
16. For an image of a dish of Brawn, visit Ivan Day's website <www.historicfood.com>.
17. Brown, Peter, *Pyramids of Pleasure* (York, 1990), pp. 23–26.
18. NYCRO, ZDV (F) F.G. (bills 122 & 144).
19. Brown, Peter, and Day, Ivan, *Pleasures of the Table* (York, 1997), pp. 27–29.
20. *Arcana Fairfaxiana*, facsimile reproduction, Newcastle, 1894.
21. *York Courant*, 15 May 1793. contains a notice of the sale of Viscount Fairfax's library from Gilling Castle, over 3 days.
22. NYCRO, ZDV, (F), MIC 1132/8663.
23. NYCRO, ZDV, (F), MIC 1129/0628.
24. Peacock, Edward, ed., 'Inventories made for Sir William and Sir Thomas Fairfax of Walton and of Gilling Castle, Yorkshire', in *Archaeologia*, 1881, pp. 123–156.
25. Mackey, Brian, 'Centres of Drawloom Damask Linenweaving in Ireland in the 18th and 19th centuries', in *Leinendamaste* (Riggesberg, 1999), pp. 99–111.

107

Medieval Anglo-Jewry and their Food, 1066–1290

Reva Berman Brown and Sean McCartney

Jews lived in England from 1066 to 1290, when they were expelled by Edward I. The Jewish community lived among their gentile neighbours, both accepted and rejected by them. While the Jews tended to be indistinguishable from Christians, particularly in terms of their clothing, their food remained a point of difference, and sometimes of friction. It was their food that provided a strong foundation upon which they were enabled to maintain the authenticity of their Jewish identity during their period of residence in England. The paper provides a short overview of the medieval Anglo-Jewish community, and then reviews what they ate, when and why, and how these actions contributed to the authenticity of their lives in England.

General overview of the period

Jews, mainly from Rouen and elsewhere in Normandy, were invited to immigrate after the Norman Conquest in 1066 as part of a policy of stimulating commercial development. They were expelled from England by Edward I in 1290. Throughout their period of residence, their presence was both tolerated and also resisted to the point of violence.

During the two centuries that they lived and worked in England, the Jews' status was unique in that they were excluded from the political and social system, but were protected by, and 'belonged to', the Crown. They were literally the King's Jews, and to an extent, were in the same category as treasure trove, a perquisite of the Crown. The Statute of Jewry of Henry III (1253) makes this explicit: 'All Jews, wheresoever they may be in the realm, are of right under the tutelage and protection of the King; nor is it lawful for any of them to subject himself to any wealthy person without the King's licence. Jews and all their effects are the King's property, and if any one with-hold their money from them, let the king recover it as his own.' What is significant about the proclamation is the overt financial claim: it is 'their money' which is at the root of things.

The Jews were outside the hierarchy in which land was given in return for military service, yet constituted a distinct community, owing allegiance directly to the Crown, but largely self-governing, with their own culture, laws, and customs, which both exacerbated and eased their state of internal exile. These rights were proclaimed in the *Statutum de Judeismo* (Jewish Charter), first issued by Henry I, the text of the original of which is no longer extant. It guaranteed liberty of movement throughout the country, relief from ordinary tolls, protection from misusage, free recourse to royal justice and responsibility to no other, permission to retain land taken in pledge as security, and special provision to ensure fair trial. It confirmed the community in a position of privilege as a separate entity, existing for the king's advantage, protected by him in all legitimate transactions and answerable to him alone. This charter was confirmed by succeeding rulers after their accession.

Our information about the lives and activities of medieval Jewry derives from the survival of governmental records such as the Close Rolls (*Rotuli Litterarum Clausarum*), Patent Rolls (*Rotuli Litterarum Patentium*), and the records of the Exchequer of the Jews (*Scaccarium Judeorum*) – what would today be considered as a Department of Jewish Affairs. References to Jewish affairs can be found on many local records such as manorial court rolls and cartularies (monastery records). These records provide evidence of what the Jewish community did or how it was treated, not of how the government of the day directly ran Jewish affairs.

We know nothing about the majority of the Jews, who, for whatever reason, never appear in the records. The records concern the exceptions – the very wealthy, the astute financiers, the victims or perpetrators of crimes, those who paid the taxes imposed by the King, or who come to notice because they could not pay, the converts to Christianity, those attacked or killed in pogroms and riots. The lives lived quietly and unrecorded can be acknowledged, but not explored.

There has been much debate about the question of numbers. Assessment rests on educated guesswork. While the geography of settlement shows a steady expansion through the 1100s to a population of around 4,000 to 5,000 in 1200, it would seem that numbers fell during the 1200s so that there were about 2,500 to 3,000 expelled in 1290. Compared with the total population of England, it is likely that only 0.25 per cent were Jews, though of the urban population, Jews may have composed 1.25 per cent. Whatever the precise figure, it is clear that the Jewish population in England was very small, much smaller than that of contemporary France from which it came.

The Jews were scattered throughout the country, most thickly in the eastern and south-eastern counties. The average community is unlikely to have comprised more than 50 to 100 people, living close together in the same part of town in order to maintain their sense of community and to achieve some sense of protection from the hostility of the Christian majority. Such areas were universally known as the Jewry (from the Norman-French *juierie*), a term which continues to the present time as a street-name in several of the older English cities, though this was not a ghetto. The Jews were not confined to it by law, Christians lived in the same streets and both communities passed freely about their daily business. Nevertheless, the urban Jewish community was close-knit. Everybody knew everybody else, isolated as the Jews were from their Christian neighbours (despite living among them) by their own religious and community traditions. Moreover, the typical family unit was small.

The London community was in existence in 1128; Norwich by 1135; Oxford by 1141, and Cambridge by 1156. The English Jewry was thus made up of a series of urban communities tightly interlocked by their faith, business interests and marriage alliances, and to all intents and purposes exiled from mainstream life. All Jews, whether permanently resident in the town or not, were attached to one of the recognised communities for tax purposes. By the 13th century, they were required to obtain a licence to live in towns which did not have a chirograph-chest (where the documents concerning financial transactions were kept).

From the records, one can gather that there were occasions for friendship between Jew and Christian, although these received clerical disapproval. The fact that the 1215 Lateran Council called for the wearing of the Jewish Badge indicates that, without such identification, Jews could not be readily distinguished from their non-Jewish neighbours. If casual everyday contacts were not normal, there would have been no necessity for moralists of both religions to speak and write against them, nor for there to be mandates forbidding behaviour such as that which decreed that 'no Christian nurse in future suckle or nourish the male child of any Jew, nor any Christian man or woman serve any Jew or Jewess, or eat with them or tarry in their houses'.

Nevertheless, while it can be said that every Jew knew some Christians (even if only on business terms), the vast majority of Christians might never have met a Jew, let alone have developed some kind of acquaintanceship or friendship with him or her. Of course, they 'knew' what Jews were like from the Bible, and from their depiction in miracle stories, mystery plays and the stories of the lives of saints. While, in the main, individuals met Jews when they needed to borrow money or pawn an item – or when they participated in an anti-Jewish riot or pogrom – they consulted Jews for their supposed magical expertise, and, despite the laws forbidding this, were employed by Jews as nurses for their children or as domestic servants.

Life in the Jewish communities centred around the synagogues; these were mostly small establishments, often maintained by wealthy magnates in their own houses. To avoid inflaming public opinion, synagogues were normally constructed out of sight to the rear of the patron's house. (In this respect, the medieval synagogue was similar to the Nonconformist meeting house of the later 17th century.) Here, communal meetings would be held, announcements made and excommunication pronounced. The synagogue formed the channel of communication with the civil authorities, necessary proclamations being made in it, both in Latin and Hebrew on two or three Sabbaths in succession.

Although, as a rule, the Jews were unable to write in Latin characters, whether French or Latin were in question, they understood and could communicate in those languages. All legal documents between themselves were drawn up in Hebrew and according to Rabbinic formulae. Their wills, made in accordance with the Talmudic prescriptions, were recognised as valid by the royal courts. Their own set of the Exchequer rolls recording their transactions were drawn up in Hebrew, in which language they endorsed Latin deeds when necessary.

The main occupation of the Jews – the reason for the toleration which they enjoyed and the sole official raison d'être of their existence in England – was the profession of moneylending, forbidden by canon law, yet indispensable in daily life. It should not be inferred that the church's ban on usury meant that Jews had a monopoly of lending: Christian financiers were not unknown. The prominent role of Jewish financiers cannot simply be explained by the church's prohibition of usury, though that no doubt played a role.

It is out of the question that the entirety of English Jewry can have been engaged in the predominant occupation of money lending. The official records at our disposal relate almost exclusively to the financiers, but a minority of the Jews was engaged in other professions. The records give the names of at least eighteen physicians. An occasional Jewish goldsmith is encountered, including one in the service of King John. At Norwich, there was Diaia le Scalarius (the ladder-maker) and at Gloucester, Abraham le Skirmiseur (fencing-master). In Bristol, a family went by the name of Furmager, and they may have been the accredited cheese-makers to the Jewish community, who would not eat cheese made by Christians without supervision. An alternative explanation of this name, however, is that they were involved in the royal tax collection system (the farm). Hebrew sources indicate that the Jews in England were engaged to some extent in peddling, particularly of cloth, and they certainly imported wine on a large scale, and not only for their own use.

There were special laws governing the Jews. For instance, on death, a Jew's property all reverted to the King, whose property the Jews were. The King was the Jews' universal legatee. Normally, the King did not exercise this prerogative too strictly, as this was would threaten future revenues. In the 13th century, the King contented himself with a third of the estate on average, although in periods of financial stringency, it could be more – for example, in the case of Aaron of Lincoln, where Henry II's dire financial position caused him to take the whole estate.

With the existence of non-Jewish banking facilities provided by the Cahorsins in the 13th century, there was no compunction on Edward I's part, having bled 'his' Jews dry, to expel them from England in 1290.

111

Dietary laws

The extent to which medieval Anglo-Jewry was able to practice and maintain their religious activities is uncertain. For instance, if a community could not muster the necessary quorum (*minyan*) of ten adult males, it was impossible to hold religious services in the synagogue. Additionally, it is also uncertain as to how far it would be possible to follow the prohibitions and regulations concerning food preparation and consumption. Where communities were small, it would be difficult to maintain a dedicated butcher (*shochet*), though it is possible that a community member would have a number of other ways of earning a living, while acting as the *shochet* when necessary.

For the believing Jew, the dietary laws were divinely ordained, and intended to test piety and love for God. It may be, however, that the laws concerning acceptable and forbidden foods and their preparation, and rules, like the washing of hands before eating, may have contributed to the health of the medieval Jews, when compared with their Christian neighbours.

Clean and unclean

The first mention of the distinction between clean and unclean animals appears in Genesis (vii. 2-3, 8). The clean animals were:

1. All quadrupeds that chew the cud and also have divided hoofs. This group includes cattle, sheep, goats, and among the deer, the hart, gazelle, roebuck, antelope and chamois (unclean quadrupeds include the camel, the rock-badger, the hare, and pigs).

2. Fish that have fins and scales.

3. All birds, other than all birds of prey and most waterfowl. A distinguishing feature of clean birds is that they catch food thrown into the air, but will lay it upon the ground and tear it with their bills before eating it.

4. Those winged creeping things that go upon all four legs, of which four kinds of locust are named. (All other creeping things are repeatedly forbidden, including the weasel, mouse, four kinds of lizard and the chameleon.)

It was forbidden to eat an animal, originally clean, which had been torn in the field by a carnivorous best, or had died a natural death.

Many reasons have been provided for these prohibitions, both allegorical and rational. For instance, an allegorical reason for permitting the eating of clean animals is that their split hoofs signify that all actions should be taken with consideration of the right and wrong. Rational reasons include the fact that some of the forbidden animals were worshipped as divine by surrounding tribes, and calling them unclean was both a protest against that worship and also a way of preventing the Jews from participating in the rituals of those tribes. Maimonides considered these ordinances to be mainly sanitary.

112

Blood

The food eaten, or not eaten, by medieval Jews was governed by two basic issues – whether the food was clean or unclean, and the issue of blood. Blood, held to contain the vital element of life, is repeatedly prohibited in the Bible. It was forbidden to Jews at any time or place. The prohibition applied not only to blood itself, but also to the flesh of mammals or birds containing blood; it did not, however, apply to fish. With meat, it is blood in the veins and arteries, or congealed on the surface of the meat, or which has begun to flow from it, that is forbidden. Blood which is a part of the meat may be eaten.

Bread

Bread was the principal food in biblical times, supplemented by meat, vegetables and fruit. The bread was unleavened, and was retained for the Passover ritual as the 'bread of affliction'. Ordinary bread consisted of dough mixed with fermented dough, which raised the mass in a soured bread. The loaf was round. Bread was baked in the form of round loaves by women and could be taken as food: indeed it was enjoined that bread was an essential at every meal. In medieval times, the housewife tended to bake bread for the week on Fridays. A special benediction was instituted for bread – 'Blessed be He who bringeth forth food out of the earth' (Psalm civ.15).

Wine

In Biblical times, wine consecrated to use in idolatrous worship was absolutely forbidden to a Jew, and regarded as defiling, rendering persons and vessels unclean. Consequently wine could not be purchased from a non-Jew, a prohibition that did not apply to other liquors. (Cider and a liqueur made from berries and cherries were not regarded as wine, and could therefore be purchased from a non-Jew.) Anglo-Jewry had originally come from northern France and there the staple beverage was wine, which was regarded not as a luxury but as a necessity, and the grace after meals was recited over wine.

There were different kinds of wine (*yayin* was the generic term): *mazug* was wine diluted with water, *tirosh* was new wine, and *shekar* was an old, powerful wine drunk undiluted (strong drink).

The quality of a wine was known by its colour and by the locality from which it came, red wine being better than white wine. Taken in moderation, wine was considered a healthful stimulant, possessing many curative elements. The Rabbis ordered ten cups of wine to be served with the 'meal of consolation' at the mourner's house – three cups before the meal, three cups between courses, to help digestion, and four cups after the grace.

Vegetable food

There are no restrictions placed on vegetable food in the Bible or in rabbinical literature. There were some laws concerning vegetables and trees, however. Starting as Biblical ordinances, these were extended into medieval times. For instance, the fruit of a tree was forbidden during the first three years after it was planted. The eating of new wheat was forbidden until the second day of Passover.

Milk

Although regarded as a pleasant beverage, milk was probably used more by the poorer classes of the community than by the rich. It was especially used as food for infants. A mixture of milk and honey was regarded as a delicious drink. (Palestine is praised in the Bible as a 'land flowing with milk and honey', milk representing the common necessities of life, and honey referring to the luxuries.) The milk from an unclean animal is forbidden in accordance with the general rule that that which comes from the unclean is unclean. Milk bought from a non-Jew is forbidden, the idea being that the non-Jew, in his carelessness, or from a desire to improve it, may have mixed some forbidden ingredient with the milk. If, however, a Jew has been present at the milking, the milk may be used.

Maimonides suggests that boiling meat in milk was probably prohibited because it was somehow connected with idolatry, forming perhaps part of the services at a heathen festival. A pot in which meat had been cooked should not be used for cooking milk and vice versa. Food prepared with milk and food in which meat is an ingredient should not be eaten at the same meal. The general custom was to wait six hours between a meal at which meat has been eaten and one at which food prepared with milk is to be eaten, although custom varies in this particular, with some people waiting only one hour. There is no need to wait at all after eating food prepared with milk. It is necessary only to see that there is none of the food left on the hands and also to wash the mouth before partaking of meat. It is forbidden to place meat upon the table at the same time as food prepared with milk, in case they are eaten together by mistake.

Cheese

There appears to have been three types of cheese eaten – milk passed through a cloth, and the curd, after being salted, moulded into disks about the size of the hand and dried in the sun. From such cheese, a cool, acid drink is made by stirring it in water. Another cheese appears to have been made of sweet milk and to have been something like cottage cheese.

Eggs

Eggs of unclean birds or of birds suffering from a visible sickness, are forbidden. The Rabbis provided signs by which the eggs of clean birds could be distinguished from those of unclean. If both ends of the egg are sharp or round, or if the yolk is outside and the white inside, it is of an unclean bird. But, according to Maimonides, who provided the laws of terefah, as most eggs sold were those of chickens, ducks or geese, there would be no problem. If there was a drop of blood found on the yolk of an egg, this was considered an indication that the process of hatching had already begun, the egg was forbidden. The roe of unclean fish was forbidden.

Fitness in rabbinical law

There was rigid scrutiny by means of which the fitness or unfitness of a person or object was ascertained according to rabbinical law. The term used is *bediqah*, and applies in the main to four areas.

(a) Condition of the knife (*bediqat ha-sakkin*)

The rabbis interpreted the Biblical injunctions as requiring that animals should be slaughtered according to the method required by tradition, and known as *shehitah*. The throat of the animal must be cut with a perfectly keen and smooth knife, which must be of a prescribed size, and must be drawn to and fro across the throat with a swift and uninterrupted motion, and in such a manner as to sever at least the larger portion of both the oesophagus and the trachea. (In the case of fowls, only one of these tubes needs to be cut.)

The act of *shehitah* can be performed by any person, but a professional slaughterer (*shochet*), who was required to be a well-informed and religious man, was preferred. The slaughterer was required to examine the knife before the slaughtering, to be assured that it was perfectly sharp and smooth, with no dent or roughness, and to repeat the inspection after slaughtering. If a dent or imperfection was then discovered, the animal was declared unfit for food.

(b) Inspection of parts (*bediqat ha-simanim*)

After the animal had been slaughtered, the *shochet* was required to inspect the oesophagus and trachea to see whether they were properly severed. If this were not the case, then the animal was unfit for food.

(c) Examination of the lungs (*bediqat ha-reah*)

The lungs of the animal were examined after slaughter to see whether it was in a sound condition or whether the animal displayed any of the blemishes specified by the rabbinical law which would make the flesh prohibited for use as food. This examination was the most important to be carried out during the process of slaughtering, and required great conscientiousness. The *shochet* looked for a puncture in the lung, the absence of any part of it, a softening, a drying of the tissue, the presence of hard spots, or the hardening of the entire tissue, blister, tubercles, and filaments filled with pus, an unnatural or unwholesome colour. The inspection was carried out by inserting the hand into the body before the lung is removed and feeling it, by putting the lung into lukewarm water, through which hard spots may become soft, and by inflating the lung, which will reveal the presence of puncture. A successful inspection would allow the animal to be considered kosher – fit for food.

(d) Search for leaven (*bediqat hamez*)

This is a ritual carried out on the evening of the 13th of Nisan, when the husband examines, with the aid of a candle, all the corners of the house to discover and remove any stray morsels of leavened matter. The object of this search is to be sure that the house is entirely free from leaven during the Passover festival. Any leavened matter found is to be burned around 10 o'clock the following morning.

Cookery

All Jewish food and its cooking is based on biblical prescription, plus commentary in the Talmud, with further directions and decisions provided by a series of rabbis over the centuries.

It is therefore not surprising that medieval Jewish cookery possessed characteristics of its own that differentiated it from the cooking of the Christian neighbours. The

115

dietary and ceremonial laws to which the Jews conformed had evolved into a particular kind of culinary art. The Sabbath meal, the Passover lamb, the distinction between permitted and forbidden foods, the regulations as to butter and meat, the custom of abstaining from meat at certain seasons, the special foods for the religious festivals all contributed to make Jewish cooking distinctive.

The preparation of food is a matter that is influenced by local conditions, and the Jews of medieval England carried with them the styles of cookery prevailing in the countries from which they had migrated. The kitchen was seen as the chief province of the Jewish housewife, and the influence of the dietary laws and ceremonial customs on Jewish cookery can be traced in the details of the kitchen.

(a) The preparation of fish

The liking of the Jews for fish is mentioned in the Bible (Num. xi. 5). One of the reasons for this is that the need to abstain from meat which has not been killed according to Jewish law puts an emphasis on the eating of fish instead. As fish is not 'meat', it can be prepared and eaten with butter. The eating of fish has been associated with the celebration of the Sabbath; in inland areas, freshwater fish were used. Salmon and herring, being common fish were often used, and it continues to be used, in the smoked form for salmon, and pickled for herring.

(b) The preparation of meat

Not only does meat have to be killed in accordance with rabbinical law, by a qualified slaughterer (*shochet*), it subsequently has to be drained of blood. Before being cooked, meat needs to be sprinkled with salt, to extract the blood more freely, then the meat is soaked in water for 30 minutes, then it is further covered with salt for about an hour, and afterwards washed three times.

The term kosher means 'fit' or 'proper'. Its opposite, for forbidden foods, is terefah. It is not only meat that has to be kosher. Vessels for food and implements used in cooking had also to be ritually fit. At Passover, the entire house had to be cleaned so that any trace of leaven was removed. New metal vessels bought from a non-Jew were immersed in a ritual bath.

Utensils used for preparing and cooking meat could not be used for dairy products. This required two sets of equipment, so that food using butter and milk never came into contact with meat.

(c) Sabbath and festival food and cookery

The Sabbath required special preparations. The Jews were not permitted to cook on the Sabbath, and this led to the development a number of ways to accommodate the prohibition. Many Sabbath meals were based on fish dishes, served cold. In the summer, cold meats were acceptable, but in the winter, a hot dish was prepared by placing a stew of meat, dried peas and beans in the communal oven before the Sabbath. Once the fire is made up and the oven closed, the dish can be left and will cook and retain its heat until it is wanted for the Sabbath midday meal. The hallah, or Sabbath bread, was covered with seeds to represent manna, which the Bible states fell in a double portion on the sixth day.

The institution of the festival of Passover, commemorating the escape of the Hebrews from captivity in Egypt, necessitated the development of special kinds and methods of cooking. The main prohibition against the eating of leavened bread has required adjustment of normal dishes. Where flour or breadcrumbs would be added to thicken a sauce, for instance, during Passover the thickener could only be ground matzo meal.

Some Rabbis were concerned about whether Jews could purchase food from non-Jews, because of their ignorance of the importance of the dietary laws. These Rabbis therefore prohibited the purchase of meat, milk and cheese from Non-Jews, assuming that, by some carelessness or ignorance, the food may have been mixed with some forbidden ingredient. If a Jew was present at the milking and the preparation of the cheese, it could be eaten.

Because of the fear of intermarriage, the Rabbis prohibited the eating of the bread of a non-Jew, or a dish cooked by a non-Jew. But it was permitted to buy bread from a non-Jewish baker. Non-Jewish servants could cook for the families which employed them. Because they were in the house of a Jew, it was assumed that one of the household would give occasional assistance, and if part of the cooking was done by a Jew, the dish could be eaten. (Christians did work for Jews, despite church edicts forbidding this.)

117

Authenticity

Throughout the period of their residence in England, the Jews maintained a strong sense of identification, which enabled their survival despite repeated persecution. Among the factors that were important to their self-definition and their maintenance of authenticity were the strong sense of community responsibility, and the unification of their communities according to the Talmudic precepts, including the dietary laws.

With medieval Jewry, it was not only matter of 'you are what you eat' but also 'you are how you eat'. The dietary laws provided permitted and forbidden foods, as well as particular processes for their preparation. The laws, when observed, had a twofold effect that maintained the authenticity of medieval Jewish life – they marked out the boundaries between the Jew and the non-Jew, and made it difficult to ignore the differences between them, not only in matters of food, but in other aspects of life, from religious belief and practice to work occupations.

Within the boundaries of the dietary laws, medieval Jews could live secure in the knowledge of who they were, creating an authentic and rich Jewish life alongside the majority population whose food was in no way connected as securely to personal and community identity.

Notes

The facts mentioned in the paper have been checked by consulting two sources:

1. Maimonides (Moses ben Maimon/Musa ibn Maimun) was born in Cordova, Spain in 1135, and died in Cairo, Egypt in 1204. Besides his philosophical, astronomical and medical writings, he wrote on religious issues. His aim was to bring system and order into the tremendous mass of traditional law, and to promote knowledge of this by presenting it in a clear and brief form. In his *Mishneh Torah*, he provides the first complete codification of the Mosaic and rabbinical laws, divided into 14 coherent groups. The 3rd book, Times (*Zemanim*), discusses those laws which are limited to certain times, such as the Sabbath and the festivals. The 5th book, Holiness (*Kedushah*), contains laws concerning forbidden sexual relations and forbidden foods. The 7th book, Seeds (*Zera'im*), deals with the laws connected with agriculture and the 10th book, Offerings (*Tohorah*), discusses the rules of cleanness and uncleanness. It is these that have been consulted when writing the paper. Maimonides produced the *Mishneh Torah* around 1170 to 1180, about the mid-point of the history of medieval Anglo-Jewry, and it became an authoritative codification of Jewish Law from that time. Unfortunately, we have been unable to uncover evidence as to whether or not Anglo-Jewry had access to copies of the *Mishneh Torah* in the last hundred years of their residence in England.

2. *The Jewish Encyclopaedia*, conceived, created and funded by The Kopelman Foundation, and which can be downloaded from the Internet at www.jewishencyclopedia.com.

'Real Eating': A Medieval Spanish Jewish View of Gastronomic Authenticity

Jonathan Brumberg-Kraus

In medieval Jewish sources on gastronomy, the authenticity of what or how one eats and drinks is treated primarily as a philosophical and theological issue rather than an aesthetic one. And yet, my consideration of one important term for authentic eating in these sources, *akhilah vada'it*, 'real eating,' raises many of the same sorts of questions about the nature of authenticity that other papers in this year's symposium do, even those concerned primarily with modern and post-modern gastronomy – though it may answer them quite differently.

So what makes eating 'authentic'? If we turn to the rabbinic commentaries on the Torah, the *midrashim* which refer to *akhilah vada'it*, or to the discussions of it in medieval Jewish mystical texts like the Zohar and Rabbenu Bahya ben Asher ben Hlava's *Shulhan Shel Arba'*, the particular text upon which I will focus, these are the questions they pose.[1] Is authentic, that is 'real eating,' a physiological or intellectual experience, or some sort of fusion of both? Is it primarily a matter of a specific selection of foods and drink? Or is a sense of authenticity achieved by performing meals according to certain prescribed ritual words and actions? Is eating authentic because it is rooted in the past, e.g., a re-enactment of Biblical precedents – ancient meals recounted in Jewish mythic history? Or is it authentic because it is both an anticipation and means to a future end, 'salvation' at the eschatological banquet – a 'foretaste of the world to come'? Is the experience of authentic eating only a future hope or something that can actually be realized in the present? Is the experience limited to only certain groups, i.e., an ethnic group like the Jews, or a moral or intellectual elite – the 'righteous' or the *maskilim* (those 'in the know,' that is, who know the mystical secrets of kabbalah).[2] Is a meal authentic because it is connected to a deeper 'reality:' to divine beings, God, the supernatural?[3] Or when it is an ecstatic experience? The medieval Jewish mystics say that 'real eating' is a form of prophecy.[4]

What distinguishes the emphases and answers to these questions from contemporary discussions of authenticity is the teleological moral framework in which they are posed. In other words, medieval Jewish discussions of authentic eating presuppose a theistic world view in which human beings were created for a certain purpose, and 'the good life' is the means by which we realize what we are in potential and perfect ourselves to conform to the end for which we were created. Eating has a moral value, and is good or bad, authentic or inauthentic only to the extent that it contributes to the perfection of our character and purpose as human beings. Medieval Jewish philosophical and mystical thought would define this purpose as knowing and serving God. This is to be opposed to a philosophical perspective which Alasdair MacIntyre calls 'emotivism',

> the doctrine that all evaluative judgments and more specifically all moral judgments are *nothing but* expression of personal preference, expressions of attitude or feeling, insofar as they are moral and evaluative in character.[5]

This perspective characterizes most modern and post-modern thinking, including much of the present discussion of authenticity in food and cookery. In this view, there are no real objective criteria for judging whether a dish or cuisine is 'authentic' or not; it is ultimately an individual's subjective matter of taste. In contrast, the teleological perspective of medieval philosophy and theology informs its consideration of gastronomy, so that authentic, 'real eating,' is an evaluation based on 'objective' external criteria. So for our Jewish medieval sources on gastronomy, MacIntyre's paraphrase of the famous saying is literally true and particularly apt: 'de gustibus est disputandum.'[6] That is, *akhilah vada'it*, 'real eating,' more closely approximates the purpose for which human beings were created – as revealed in Scripture and Aristotelian philosophy – than less authentic, less 'real' forms of eating.

In this paper I will focus on one particular medieval Jewish source which develops the idea of *akhilah vada'it*, and integrates it into a full-blown program of Jewish meal ethics, namely, the short treatise *Shulhan Shel Arba'* ('Table of Four') by Rabbenu Bahya ben Asher ben Hlava, the Spanish kabbalist and Biblical commentator. In this thirteenth-century work on eating, Rabbenu Bahya develops the rabbinic idea that the revelation of the Torah on Sinai was '*akhilah vada'it*' –'real eating'– following a creative interpretation of the verse describing the Israelite elders' experience of divine revelation: 'They envisioned God and they ate and drank' (Ex.24:11). R. Bahya seems to consider the Israelites' past eating of manna in the wilderness and the future promised messianic banquet on the flesh of Leviathan analogous, and consequently more 'real' ('authentic') than eating beef, fowl, or bread ordinarily set before one at the dinner table in the present. But 'authentic eating' for R. Bahya is not a purely spiritual experience. Rather, physical eating combined with mindful talk about it so heightens the experience that one 'sees God.'[7] Saying the right words of Torah about the table while one is dining at the table with other scholars learned in Torah and kabbalah effects an experience of 'real eating,' that is, a prophetic vision of God, analogous to the experience of the past revelation to the Israelites at Mt. Sinai and the future enjoyment of the light of the Divine Presence at the eschatological banquet for the righteous in the world to come.

The crux of R. Bahya's theory of eating is that the soul's intellectual process of conception is somehow analogous to the body's physical process of digestion. Both the soul and the body 'eat' and are nourished by the spiritual or physical 'food' appropriate to their respective natures. Cognition, that is, knowing something by means of one's act of thought, *is itself a kind of eating* – 'real eating'. R. Bahya's distinctive interpretation however is that while one can distinguish conceptually between nourishment of the body and nourishment of the soul, the way it actually occurs is a *fusion* of the soul's 'eating' by means of thought, and the body's physical eating. As R. Bahya himself puts it,

> the limbs of the body which are the vessel of the soul receive power and strength from the meal, and the soul is stimulated in its powers themselves and strengthens them from this thought, and possibly even the holy spirit descends upon [the eater] at the very moment of eating when this thought arises, and his body is clothed in the thought of his soul – *and the two of them together are as good as one* and fit for the Shekhinah to dwell amidst them.[8]

For R. Bahya, fusion, albeit metaphysical, makes the experience of eating more rather than less authentic.

R. Bahya ben Asher's theory of authentic 'real eating,' *akhilah vada'it* appears in *Shulhan Shel Arba'*, a book he intended his late thirteenth century Spanish Jewish audience to read at meals while they were actually eating at the dinner table, in order to dignify the meal with conversations suffused with 'precious sayings,' that is, pertinent references to Scripture and rabbinic and kabbalistic interpretations of them. As R. Bahya says in his preface,

> My heart lifted me…to write about this in brief in a book, and to include in it 'precious sayings,' so that it be in the hand of any person on his table, that he should set it down by his right hand, and that it should be with him, and that he read in it all that is required at his meal. And if at the time one is eating, he merits the drawing of his inclination to what is in this book of mine, and according to its words, he is sure to be at the level of the pious ones who are perfect in their qualities, who wage the war of HaShem, and oppose all their desires.[9]

No doubt R. Bahya had in mind the famous rabbinic saying from the Mishnah Avot 3:3 (compiled in the third century CE):

> If three have eaten at one table and have spoken over it words of the Torah, it is as if they had eaten from the table of God, for it is written (Ezekiel 41.22) 'He said to me, "This is the table which is before the LORD".'[10]

R. Bahya's transformation of a descriptive statement in the rabbinic tradition ('if three have eaten at one table and have spoken over it words of the Torah, it is as if…') to a prescription that one *ought to* recite words of Torah about the table over the table, is typical of the Jewish genre of *hanhagot* literature, manuals of practice, which originated in medieval Spain and Provence, and to which *Shulhan Shel Arba'* belongs.[11]

I do not wish to say too much here about the historical context in which R. Bahya wrote *Shulhan Shel Arba'* since that would exceed the scope of this paper. Suffice it to say what I have said in more detail elsewhere, that *Shulhan Shel Arba'*, and indeed R. Bahya's particular discussion of *akhilah vada'it* in it, reflects many of the important cultural trends of 13th- and 14th-century Spanish Jewish life: adaptation of Muslim literary forms and philosophical ideas, the emergence of Kabbalah as a distinctive stream of Jewish mysticism – for example, the composition and dissemination of the *Zohar*, the anti-Maimonidean controversy, class tensions between Jewish elites and the Jewish masses, strategies of Jewish acculturation to the surrounding Christian society of northern Spain during the period of the Reconquista, and an increasingly aggressive effort on the part of the Church to proselytize the Jews of Spain that culminated in the disputations of Barcelona and Tortosa, and finally the expulsion in 1492.[12] We can also infer that medieval culinary culture in general, and that among the Jews in northern Spain in particular, was part of R. Bahya's cultural assumptions, though he is characteristically vague when referring to the dishes served at the table.[13] R. Bahya's language stressing the inseparability and fusion of body and soul is probably a response especially to a development in thirteenth-century Christian theology and practice emphasizing the incarnation of Christ, the movement which Caroline Walker Bynum masterfully charts in *Holy Feast, Holy Fast*, though she draws few of her examples from Spain.[14] The eating rituals R. Bahya prescribes are an expression of what Ivan Marcus calls

'inward acculturation,' that is, a strategic response to Christian society in which Jews both maintained an unequivocal Jewish identity [and] sometimes expressed elements of their Jewish religious cultural identity by internalizing and transforming various genres, motifs, terms, institutions, or rituals of the majority culture in a polemical, parodic, or neutralized manner.[15]

Bynum's remarks on medieval Christian cultural assumptions about food are particularly suggestive in this light:

Medieval cookbooks make it clear that visual effects were more important to a medieval diner than taste…Given such assumptions about and expectations of food, it is small wonder that medieval mystics considered sounds and sights as crucial to the eucharistic banquet as eating, or that sometimes they felt they 'ate' or 'received' with their eyes or in their minds and hearts.[16]

Such attitudes, which emphasized the visual over the taste experience, not only affected

Christian Eucharistic practice, theologies of transubstantiation, and ecstatic visionary experiences of Christ in the Eucharist, especially among women mystics,[17] but also probably influenced R. Bahya's theory of 'real eating.' But instead of the Eucharistic rituals in which Christian women saw and thus 'tasted' *Christ* – the central symbol of Christian culture, R. Bahya proposes an alternative, almost parodic system of eating rituals in which learned Jewish males through 'real eating' could embody 'the Word' of their Torah and thus 'envision God and eat and drink' (Ex 24:11).[18]

Moreover, though R. Bahya adopted the term *akhilah vada'it* from earlier rabbinic sources, his particular treatment of it in *Shulhan Shel Arba'* singles it out as the most important interpretation of the Scriptural verse Ex 24:11: 'They envisioned God and they ate and drank.' In its original contexts in Midrash Rabbah, the tradition attributed to Rabbi Yohanan which refers to *akhilah vada'i* or *akhilah vada'it* is one positive response to the negative presumption that there was something wrong with the Israelite leaders eating and drinking after seeing God. Ex 24:11 itself suggests this when it says, 'Yet He did not raise His hand against the leaders of the Israelites; they envisioned God and they ate and drank.'[19] The midrashic interpretation of Ex 24:11 in Leviticus Rabbah 20:10 states:

> 'Against the leaders of the Israelites' – Said Rabbi Pinchas, From here it suggests they ought to have had His hand raised against them, because as Rabbi Yehoshua said, Were cakes taken up with them on Mt. Sinai, when it says 'they beheld God'? On the contrary, it teaches that they feasted their eyes on the Shekhinah. 'They beheld God' like a person staring at his friend in the midst of eating and drinking. But Rabbi Yohanan said it was real eating [*akhilah vada'i*], as it is said, 'In the light of the King's face there is life' (Pr 16:15). But Rabbi Tanhuma said, it teaches that it was with an abandonment of their minds and a coarseness of their hearts that they feasted their eyes on the Shekhinah.

123

R. Yohanan insists that what happened was real eating because they *really were* fed by light coming off the face of God, and that it was a good thing to feast on the splendor of the Shekhinah. But Rabbi Tanhuma counters that it was an act of vulgarity and disrespect to have 'glutted' their eyes on the Divine Presence, as one modern interpreter translates the Hebrew word *zanu* in this expression.[20] R. Yohanan's saying about *akhilah vada'i* may be an expression of a mystical tradition which employed eating and food metaphors for visionary experiences that was already current in the rabbinic era.[21] But R. Bahya's positive interpretation of *akhilah vada'it* as a mystical way of seeing God is probably much more dependent on the ideas about 'physical nourishment through mystical experience' developed in the *Zohar*, the central mystical text which emerged from the circle of kabbalists in northern Spain of which R. Bahya was a member, and among the first writers to quote it, in his commentary on the Torah.[22] According to the *Zohar*, Ex 24:11 is intended to praise the leaders of the Israelites:

Rabbi Yosi said this is a way of praising them, as it is written, 'they ate and drank', that is, their eyes were nourished by His light. Rabbi Judah said it was real eating [*akhilah vada'it*], they ate and were nourished from it, that is, they were joined to the upper [heavenly light].[23]

R. Bahya follows the *Zohar* in understanding *akhilah vada'it* as a kind of revelation of God, occurring during a meal, which effects a certain conception of God in the participants that raises their status to that of the angels in heaven. It should be clear at this point that R. Bahya's criteria for authenticity are quite literary, based on Scriptural precedents like the 'meal' described in Ex 24:11, and have very little to do with the actual sensory experience of the flavors of specific foods.

That being said, R. Bahya does want his readers to think about *akhilah vada'it* and focus on the specific literary metaphors and Scriptural verses which evoke it during the performance of quite specific meal rituals, so that his idea of real eating is not wholly devoid of sensory experience. Perhaps it is just that R. Bahya privileges the senses of hearing and sight over taste in the meals he deems most authentic. He divides his eating manual into four 'Gates,' whence the title *Shulhan Shel Arba'* ('Table of Four').[24] Two are devoted to the specific actions to be performed at the table, and two to the specific topics to be discussed there. This suggests that R. Bahya wants there to be an even balance between the things done ('*dromena*') and things said ('*legomena*') at the table, to adopt the language of Jane Harrison's theory of ritual.[25] The First and Third Gates prescribe specific meal behaviors. The First Gate is concerned with the blessings and hand-washing rituals rabbinic tradition requires for meals. The Third Gate is concerned with '*Derekh Eretz*,' that is, rabbinic meal etiquette, and is essentially a brief anthology of the traditions about host/guest relations from the minor Talmudic tractates like *Derekh Eretz Zuta* and *Derekh Eretz Rabba*.[26] Interwoven between these two is the Second Gate, devoted to a discussion ostensibly about the 'physiology of eating' but really the exposition of a mystical kabbalistic theory of eating, and the Fourth Gate, devoted to discussions of the eschatological banquets reserved for the righteous in the messianic era and in the world to come. All the specific references to the term *akhilah vada'it* appear in the Second Gate in the discussion of the 'mystical secrets' of the nature of eating. However, in this discussion, *akhilah vada'it* is associated with certain metaphors or images from Biblical and rabbinic literature which recur throughout all of the chapters of the book, like the meal of the Israelite leaders at Mt Sinai in the verse Ex 24;11, the manna in the wilderness, the meals of the heavenly angelic beings, and the eschatological banquets. Moreover, the preface of *Shulhan Shel Arba'* sets up all these examples of real eating in the context of a story of the Fall. There is a hierarchy of beings who are distinguished from one another by their diet:

heavenly beings who dine without any effort on the splendor of the Shekhinah in heaven, and we earthly creatures who have to work hard and sweat for our food. 'The lowest realm is the one limited by physical dimensions. Our food is not like their food. Their food is by conception, by seeing the face of their Maker. Our food is the bread of sorrow and the water of tears, by hard work and effort, for so the King established it for our first father because of his sin.[27]

We lower beings are under a decree of judgment sort of like Christian original sin, because of Adam and Eve's sin of eating the forbidden fruit. Our difference from the heavenly beings is a consequence of this sin. This sin not only reduced the physical stature of all humankind, but consequently limited our capacity to eat the diet reserved for those higher beings who have no physical dimensions or measurements, and therefore an infinite capacity to take in the nourishment of the glow of the Shekhinah. However, God in His mercy gave a remedy for this condition, the Torah, at least to a select few, the Jews. In R. Bahya's words,

All of us human beings are stained by sin and our souls are sick In this our nation is just the same as the rest of the nations; we and they alike are under the decree of Eve. However, we are distinguished by our regimen of the pleasures [dat sha'ashu'im] from the nations who err, rebel and sin.[28]

In other words, the story of the Fall provides the teleological moral framework for evaluating authentic, 'real eating.' We human beings are not presently what we are supposed to be, but we will be when our food is like their food, that is, the food of the heavenly beings. And God has provided at least some of us with a means to that end, the Torah, a 'regimen of pleasures' that will refine and purify us so that we can realize the purpose for which we were indeed created – to attend and serve God constantly. However this suggests that the Torah-prescribed diet that distinguishes Jews socially from non-Jews is analogous to the diet which distinguishes the upper from lower beings. It is not 'authentic' just because it is the eating typical and peculiar to a particular ethnic group, the Jews. R. Bahya has in a sense generalized his distinctive Jewish ethnic foodways as the 'real eating' for human beings as such.

Akhilah vada'it in Shulhan Shel Arba'

For R. Bahya four types of meals and the Scriptural and rabbinic traditions about them are the most important examples of 'real eating:'
1. The meal at Mt. Sinai when the nobility of Israel 'envisioned God and ate and drank.'[29]
2. The miraculous meals of the Manna in the Wilderness.[30]
3. The Messianic Banquet at the end of time.[31]
4. Rabbinic meals conducted using Shulhan Shel Arba'.

All of these meals stress what Hecker calls the 'psychosomatic unity' of the meal experiences,[32] though apparently there is some confusion about whether R. Bahya imagines a wholly disembodied, metaphorical banquet at the end of time, or one at which one really eats physically.[33] But to focus on R. Bahya's ambivalence about the resurrection probably misses his point. I think he says there are both, the messianic banquet which involves physical eating (albeit of highly refined and pure foods), and a 'meal' in 'the world of souls' after that which is purely intellectual. But he also insists that there is no way even the wisest among us can conceive of it except by analogy to the physical delight we take in eating or walking in a garden:

> However in principle we know by inference through our intellect and through the Torah 'which makes wise the foolish', that just as the body enjoys and takes delight (*mitaden*) in a pleasant and fragrant meal, in its measure of bodily delight, so the soul will enjoy and take delight in this upper world, however, its way of taking delight there is not measured like bodily things which have measures and dimensions…. Come and see how the way of the Holy One Blessed be He is not the way of flesh and blood. For flesh and blood, an empty vessel can contain something, a full one cannot. But it is not so for the Holy One Blessed be He. The full vessel can contain, the empty one cannot … insofar as bodily things have measure and dimension, when they are empty they can filled, but when one fills them, they cannot contain any more since they are already filled to their capacity, and nothing with a capacity can contain something more than its capacity. But among the upper things, the full can contain, since it has no measured capacity. And the world of souls is called 'Garden of Eden' (*gan aden*) among the sages, and they called it this by way of an allegory, using the example of how the body takes delight (*mitaden*) in a garden, and so it is written about the Garden of Eden in the land, 'He set him in the Garden of Eden to work it and keep it,' (Gen 2:5) – this heavenly Garden of Eden is the world of souls comparable but in contrast to [the earthly one], and it too is called 'Garden of Eden', and it is the reward for doing the *mitzvot* in which the soul takes delight, using the image of the body taking delight in a garden.[34]

Since R. Bahya addresses an audience that is not yet disembodied nor eating at the end of time, we can infer that he believes that discussion of Jewish traditions of eschatological banquets, whether there is physical 'eating and drinking' at them or not, at the dinner table with his book at one's side, is indeed an embodied, physical, psychosomatic experience of eating and drinking which can potentially turn into 'real eating.'

R. Bahya explicitly associates present rabbinic meals conducted according to his instructions with the term *akhilah vadai'it* in the final paragraph of the Second Gate of *Shulhan Shel Arba'*:

So you find yourself learning that *when a person stands over his table and eats with this thought in mind*, see! this eating is indeed a physical matter and natural activity, but see! it also returns to a higher, intellectual form of worship…And this is the point of *having the right intention at a meal at the table* – that the body be nourished by it and take its bodily portion from the bodily eating, and the soul by this act of thought is filled, fed, and satisfied as if from the choicest parts of **real eating** of the ways of Ha-Shem and His pleasantness, and regarding this it is said, 'Your table is laid out with rich food.' (Job 36:16)[35]

By having diners say Scriptural passages that convey these metaphors *at the table*, R. Bahya encourages what I have called elsewhere a sort of 'directed free association.'

To summarize, the main components of R. Bahya's definition of 'real eating' are as follows. 'Real eating' is some kind of visionary, prophetic experience.[36] R. Bahya gives numerous examples and references to this dimension of real eating, especially those connected to the verse that he practically turned into a slogan, 'They envisioned God and they ate and drank' (Ex 24:11). But what also seems clear is that real eating is not only cognitive, or just a gastronomic *metaphor* for a visual conception. It is inseparable from the physical experience of eating, a quality of 'psychosomatic unity.'[37] Or as R. Bahya puts it,

> the powers of the soul are not visible and are actualized only through the body. If so, the body is a great necessity for the public revelation of the high degree of the soul and its perfection.[38]

127

This psychosomatic unity is then described in images drawn from the burnt offering sacrifices as analogies to normal human digestion.[39] That being said, the physical component of 'real eating' consists of a relatively ascetic diet.[40] It is kosher, with particular emphasis on not eating meat with blood in it, that is, its soul, and as a way of socially differentiating Jews from non-Jews by maintaining a higher, that is more discriminating diet.[41] What R. Bahya and his kabbalistic contemporaries call 'fine' and 'pure' foods are preferable, because they believed them to be better at purifying and refining both the mind and body.[42] Hecker aptly calls these 'brain foods.'[43] It is not clear what actual specific dishes R. Bahya has in mind, besides recommending small poultry over red meat, since he is pretty vague about this, though it seems he understands 'fine' versus 'coarse' foods as contrast between city and country foods.[44] Also a vegetarian diet appears to be closer to 'real eating' than meat-eating, though Torah sages learned in both the rules of kashrut and the mystical secrets of reincarnation involved in meat-eating need not avoid meat.[45] Presumably R. Bahya does not recommend total abstinence from wine in the 'real eating' that may occur when following his eating manual, since *Shulhan Shel Arbaʿ* is full of specific instructions about the etiquette of drinking wine and saying blessings for over wine at the table, though it is clear that it would be wrong to get too intoxicated.[46] The bottom line is that eating or drinking which tends to reinforce rather than diminish one's intellectual capacity is closer to 'real eating. Real eating is purposeful eating. If there is a form of 'real eating' at the end of time which is disembodied and purely intellectual,[47] it can only be inferred and spoken about allegorically from our experiences of physical eating and drinking in the here and now. [48] Moreover, R. Bahya's 'real eating' is possible in the here and now if one arranges their table talk and conduct properly according his eating manual *Shulhan Shel Arba'*. Doing so makes 'real eating' a form of worship and service of God, the purpose for which God created all His creatures.[49]

This teleological framework obviously supplies the external 'objective' criteria for determining whether eating is 'real', that is authentic. However, I also think R. Bahya's insistence on the psychosomatic unity of 'real eating', the rich imaginative way he has described it, and provided in *Shulhan Shel Arba'* a script for its performance suggests that real eating also has an important social, experiential dimension. Eating and talking about eating with one's companions the way he suggests cultivates an experience of the unification of opposites, knowing the one in the many. There is no delight in the soul apart from the vessel of the body, of bodies living in community. It is this same sense of bringing together of all things that General Loewenhielm evokes with his Biblical image from the Book of Psalms in the speech he makes at the banquet in *Babette's Feast*: 'Mercy and Truth have met together. Righteousness and bliss shall kiss one another.'[50]

128

We have all been told that grace is to be found in the universe. But in our human foolishness and short-sightedness we imagine divine grace to be finite…But the moment comes when our eyes are opened, and we see and realize that grace is infinite…See! that which we have chosen is given us, and that which we have refused is, also and at the same time, granted us. Ay, that which we have rejected is poured upon us abundantly. For mercy and truth have met together, and righteousness and bliss have kissed one another!'[51]

Bibliography

Assis, Yom T., *The Golden Age of Aragonese Jewry: Community and Society in the Crown of Aragon, 1213–1327*, Littman Library of Jewish Civilization (London: Portland, Or: Vallentine Mitchell, 1997).

Bahya ben Asher ben Hlava, *Pirke Avot*, in *Kitve Rabenu Bahya*, ed. Charles Ber Chavel (Yerushalayim: Mosad ha-Rav Kuk, 1969).

——, *Shulhan Shel Arba'*, in *Kitve Rabenu Bahya*, ed. Charles Ber Chavel (Yerushalayim: Mosad ha-Rav Kuk, 1969).

——, *Be'ur 'al Ha-Torah*, ed. Charles Ber Chavel (Yerushalayim: Mosad ha-Rav Kuk, 1966–1968).

Brumberg-Kraus, Jonathan, 'The Ritualization of Scripture in Rabbenu Bahya's *Shulhan Shel Arba'*', *World Congress of Jewish Studies*, 13 (2001), 1–17, in LEKKET [accessed July 7, 2005].

——, 'Meat-Eating and Jewish Identity; Ritualization of the Priestly Torah of Beast and Fowl (Lev 11:46) in Rabbinic Judaism and Medieval Kabbalah', *AJS Review*, 24 (1999), 227–262.

Bynum, Caroline W., *Fragmentation and Redemption: Essays on Gender and the Human Body in Medieval Religion* (New York; Cambridge, Mass: Zone Books; Distributed by the MIT Press, 1991).

——, *Holy Feast and Holy Fast: The Religious Significance of Food to Medieval Women* (Berkeley, Calif.: University of California Press, 1987).

Chernus, Ira, '"Nourished by the Splendor of the Shekhinah": A Mystical Motif in Rabbinic Midrash', in *Mysticism in Rabbinic Judaism: Studies in the History of Midrash*; Bd. 11. (Berlin ; New York: W. de Gruyter, 1982).

Cooper, John, *Eat and be Satisfied: A Social History of Jewish Food* (New Jersey: Jason Aronson Inc., 1993).

Dinesen, Isak, 'Babette's Feast' in *Anecdotes of Destiny; and, Ehrengard* (New York: Vintage Books, 1993), 21–59.

Flandrin, Jean L., Massimo Montanari and Albert Sonnenfeld, eds., *Food : A Culinary History from Antiquity to the Present, European Perspectives* (New York: Columbia University Press, 1999).

Al-Ghazali, Abu Hamid Muhammad ibn Muhammad, *Al-Ghazali on the Manners Relating to Eating : Kitab Adab Al-Akl, Book XI of the Revival of the Religious Sciences, Ihya' `ulum Al-Din*, trans. and ed. Denys Johnson-Davies (Cambridge: Islamic Texts Society, 2000).

Gitlitz, David M. and Linda Kay Davidson, *A Drizzle of Honey: The Lives and Recipes of Spain's Secret Jews*, 1st ed. (New York: St. Martin's Press, 1999).

Goody, Jack, *Cooking, Cuisine, and Class : A Study in Comparative Sociology*, Themes in the Social Sciences (Cambridge: Cambridge University Press, 1982).

Gries, Ze'ev, *Sifrut Ha-Hanhagot : Toldoteha u-Mekomah be-Haye Haside R. Yisrael Ba'al Shem-Tov* (Yerushalayim: Mosad Byalik, 1989).

Hecker, Joel, *Mystical Bodies, Mystical Meals : Eating and Embodiment in Medieval Kabbalah*, Raphael Patai Series in Jewish Folklore and Anthropology (Detroit: Wayne State University Press, 2005).

MacIntyre, Alasdair C., *After Virtue : A Study in Moral Theory* (Notre Dame, Ind.: University of Notre Dame Press, 1981).

Marcus, Ivan G., *Rituals of Childhood: Jewish Acculturation in Medieval Europe* (New Haven, Conn.: Yale University Press, 1996).

Montanari, Massimo, *The Culture of Food, The Making of Europe* (Oxford, UK ; Cambridge, Mass., USA: Blackwell, 1994).

Roden, Claudia, *A Book of Middle Eastern Food* (New York: Vintage Books, 1974).

Rodinson, Maxime and A. J. Arberry, *Medieval Arab Cookery* (Devon, England: Prospect Books, 2001).

Sperber, Daniel, *A Commentary on Derech Erez Zuta. [2], Chapters Five to Eight* (Ramat-Gan, Israel: Bar-Ilan University Press, 1990).

——, *Masekhet Derekh Erets Zuta u-Ferek Ha-Shalom*, Mahad. 3., *murhevet u-metukenet be-tosefet be'ur murhav, mevo'ot ve-nispahim edn* (Yerushalayim: Tsur-ot, 1994).

Talmage, Frank E., *Apples of Gold; the Inner Meaning of Sacred Texts in Medieval Judaism* in *Jewish Spirituality* [Vol. I]: 'From the Bible to the Middle Ages', ed. Arthur Green (New York: Crossroad, 1986), 315–355.

van Gelder, G. J. H., *God's Banquet : Food in Classical Arabic Literature* (New York: Columbia University Press, 2000).

129

Notes

1. Leviticus Rabbah 20:10; Numbers Rabbah 2:25; *Zohar* 1:104a, 2:126a; Bahya ben Asher, *Shulhan Shel Arba'*.
2. Brumberg-Kraus (1999), p. 237.
3. Bahya ben Asher, *Shulhan Shel Arba'*, p. 483.
4. Bahya ben Asher, *Shulhan Shel Arba'*, p. 482. Brumberg-Kraus (2001), p. 7.

5. MacIntyre, p. 11.

6. MacIntyre, p. 177.

7. Brumberg-Kraus, (2001), p. 5.

8. Bahya ben Asher, *Shulhan Shel Arba'*, p. 495, my emphasis.

9. Bahya ben Asher, *Shulhan Shel Arba'*, p. 460.

10. Bahya ben Asher, *Shulhan Shel Arba'*, p. 474 (a reference to m. Avot 3:3); p. 457 (the first words of the book quoting Ez.41:22); p. 513 (a paraphrase of Ez. 41:22 in the book's last paragraph): And now this book is finished, based on precious sayings…by which we have raised the 'table which' will be called 'before the Lord.'

11. Ze'ev Gries (1989), p. 18–22; Brumberg-Kraus, (2001), p. 1. See Jack Goody, pp. 143–5, for a sociological interpretation of the emergence of manuals of etiquette in the medieval period.

12. Brumberg-Kraus (1999), p. 227, 257–62.

13. Particularly relevant for understanding R. Bahya's medieval Spanish Jewish food culture are Gitlitz and Davidson; Assis, pp. 224–8, 282–3; Cooper; van Gelder; Rodinson and Arberry; *Al-Ghazali on the Manners Relating to Eating*; Roden; Montanari (1994); the relevant essays in Flandrin, Montanari and Sonnenfeld; and Goody (1982), pp. 127–133.

14. Bynum (1987,1991); Brumberg-Kraus (1999), p. 262.

15. Marcus, pp. 11–12, though referring to Jews in medieval northern Europe, not Spain.

16. Bynum (1987), pp. 60–1.

17. Bynum, (1987), pp. 51, 60, 230.

18. This is my conclusion, Brumberg-Kraus (1999), p. 262, but here applied to R. Bahya's interpretation of the term 'real eating' rather than 'the torah of beast and fowl. '

19. *Leviticus Rabbah* 20:10; par. *Numbers Rabbah* 2:25 and see also *Pesikta de-Rav Kahana* 26.9; *Midrash Tanhuma Aharei* 6; *Midrash Tanhuma (Buber)* 7, and the discussion of these traditions in Hecker, p. 42–46.

20. Hecker, p. 46.

21. Chernus, pp. 74–87.

22. Hecker, pp. 82–3,and see pp. 84–90, esp. p. 88, for a discussion of these ideas, nearly all which are echoed in R. Bahya's discussion of *akhilah vada'it* in the Second Gate of *Shulhan Shel Arba'*, and p.148 for R. Bahya's relationship to the *Zohar*. Hecker, pp. 82–3, quotes and discusses R. Bahya's reference to *akhilah vada'it* in *Shulhan Shel Arba'*, p. 492, to suggest that while R. Bahya and the Zohar share ideas about 'idealized foods' like the manna, the splendor of the Shekhinah, the meals of angels, Bahya's view is much more 'intellectualist, spiritualizing, and ascetic' than the Zohar's and other kabbalists from its circle. However, I am arguing that R. Bahya advocates a fusion of physical and spiritual eating quite close to what Hecker says is the *Zohar*'s view.

23. *Zohar* 2:126a.

24. Bahya ben Asher, *Shulhan Shel Arba'*, p. 461. Actually, this is but one of four explanations R. Bahya gives in his preface for the title of his book.

25. Brumberg-Kraus (2001), p. 3–4.

26. See the Hebrew and English editions of Sperber (1990, 1994).

27. Bahya ben Asher, *Shulhan Shel Arba'*, p. 457.

28. Bahya ben Asher, *Shulhan Shel Arba'*, pp. 458–9.

29. Bahya ben Asher, *Shulhan Shel Arba'*, pp. 492–3.

30. Bahya ben Asher, *Shulhan Shel Arba'*, p. 493.

31. Bahya ben Asher, *Shulhan Shel Arba'*, pp. 495–6, 501.

32. Hecker, p. 92.

33. Hecker, p. 108.

34. Bahya ben Asher, *Shulhan Shel Arba'*, pp. 508–9. The Hebrew *gan aden* (Garden of Eden) and *mitaden* (take delight) are connected by means of a pun.

35. Bahya ben Asher, *Shulhan Shel Arba'*, p. 497.

36. Bahya ben Asher, *Shulhan Shel Arba'*, p. 492–3.
37. Hecker, p. 92.
38. Bahya ben Asher, *Shulhan Shel Arba'*, p. 492.
39. Bahya ben Asher, *Shulhan Shel Arba'*, pp. 491–2. Hecker, p. 94.says, '[R. Bahya's contemporary] Moses De Leon's model of spiritual digestion follows directly from his understanding of the physiology of digestion.'
40. Hecker, p. 83.
41. Bahya ben Asher, *Shulhan Shel Arba'*, p. 459, 460, 506.
42. Bahya ben Asher, *Shulhan Shel Arba'*, pp. 496, 501 and *Pirke Avot*, p. 588.
43. Hecker, p. 108: 'brain foods rather than culinary delights.'
44. Bahya ben Asher, *Pirke Avot*, p. 588.
45. Bahya ben Asher, *Shulhan Shel Arba'*, p. 496; Brumberg-Kraus (1999), p. 227.
46. Bahya ben Asher, *Shulhan Shel Arba'*, pp. 493, 492.
47. Bahya ben Asher, *Shulhan Shel Arba'*, p. 506.
48. Bahya ben Asher, *Shulhan Shel Arba'*, pp. 504, 508.
49. Bahya ben Asher, *Shulhan Shel Arba'*, p. 497.
50. Ps 85:10. Cf. Bahya ben Asher, *Shulhan Shel Arba'*, pp. 508–9.
51. Dinesen, 'Babette's Feast, ' p. 52.

Western Mediterranean Vegetable Stews and the Integration of Culinary Exotica

Anthony F. Buccini

Introduction[1]

In her book on Mediterranean food, Elizabeth David says of *ratatouille* that it has 'the authentic aromatic flavour of Provençal food' (1965: 131). That this dish is indeed an authentically Provençal dish, few would dispute; one might say that *ratatouille* is even the quintessential representative of Provence's cuisine. Yet, to anyone familiar with the regional cuisines of the western Mediterranean, it is striking that almost all feature a similar vegetable stew, one that has as its base onions cooked in olive oil and includes peppers, tomatoes, often also eggplant and/or zucchini and in several cases potatoes and green beans as well; common but not universal regional additions to these dishes are garlic, chillies and herbs. And just as *ratatouille* is regarded as an authentic, emblematic dish for Provence, so too *xamfaina* for Catalonia, the various *pistos* for Castile, and *cianfotta* or *ciambotta* for southern Italy.

It is perhaps ironic that these emblematic vegetable stews are composed principally of ingredients originally from elsewhere: eggplant from Persia; from the New World tomatoes, zucchini, peppers, potatoes and green beans. The stews in question are thus in the first instance remarkable examples of how exotica may be thoroughly integrated into an established cuisine. Furthermore, since these exotic vegetables were introduced to the western Mediterranean in the course of the latter Middle Ages in the case of the eggplant and during the early modern period in the case of the American items, there is a good chance that all these regional stews that feature the same exotic vegetables did not evolve independently but rather are reflections of an original dish from one region which subsequently was spread from region to region.

Though many have noted the similarity and possible relatedness of some of these western Mediterranean vegetable stews, the relationships between the regional variants and possible paths of spread have not been investigated. In this paper, we examine the linguistic evidence of the names of these dishes together with evidence for the socio-historical settings in which the culinary and linguistic transfers occurred and offer a comprehensive picture of the developments. The linguistic evidence indicates in some cases diffusion from a primary point of innovation in southern Spain but also shows an intimate connexion between the *Països Catalans* and Campania, a connexion which allows no simple assignment of priority to either. The evidence points, moreover, to the first widespread consumption of the American exotica and thus too the development of the stews having occurred among the poorer strata of society, who rapidly integrated the new foods into their diets. Indeed, the culinary and linguistic evidence related to these vegetable stews, when taken all together, reflects to a remarkable degree the political and socio-economic history of the western Mediterranean basin in the early modern period.

Variations on a theme

From the various western Mediterranean vegetable stews one can abstract a core, basic version: a base of onions fried in olive oil, to which are added the originally exotic vegetables, including the *de rigueur* tomatoes, then the very common peppers, eggplants and zucchini, and finally the more regionally restricted potatoes and green beans.[2] In virtually all the particular regional dishes, however, there is some variation with regard to the major ingredients used and sometimes variation with regard to aspects of the cooking process. With these qualifications in mind, we can give a brief survey of notable regional versions of the western Mediterranean vegetable stew.

Països Catalans (the Catalan-speaking lands): *xamfaina*, also *samfaina* with further minor dialect variants.

Known throughout the Catalan-language area is a dish conforming completely to our abstract basic version: a base of onions cooked in olive oil, usually also with garlic, to which are added peppers, eggplant, zucchini and tomatoes.[3] Catalan *xamfaina* is a dish unto itself but it is also cooked down until the vegetables lose their independent character completely; in this state *xamfaina* is used as a sauce and it is considered one of the fundamental sauces of Catalan cuisine.[4]

Castile, neighbouring Castilian-speaking regions (e.g. Extremadura): *pisto*.

In Spain, *pisto manchego*, from La Mancha, is the best known version of the western Mediterranean vegetable stew from the Castilian language area. Recipes for *pisto manchego* resemble closely those for *xamfaina* and *ratatouille* but without eggplant – olive oil, onions, sometimes garlic, with tomatoes, peppers and zucchini – though there are versions which add eggplant to the mix, as well as versions which forego the zucchini and include instead ham. While the Catalans and Provençal also consume their stews on occasion alongside eggs, the addition of eggs and/or sliced ham is a popular way of finishing a dish of *pisto* in central and southern Spain.

Andalucía: *alboronía* (also *boronía*, *moronía*).

In Andalucía the local vegetable stew, *alboronía*, fits well into the family of dishes discussed here; it begins with the base of onions, often peppers as well, fried in olive oil, to which are then added tomatoes. The subsequent necessary additions are eggplant and squash; in this latter case, many recipes call for *calabaza amarilla* ('yellow squash'), clearly the traditional choice, though some recipes sporting the name *alboronía* call for *calabacín* ('zucchini').

North Africa (Tunisia, Algeria, also Morocco?): *shakshouka* (French spelling: *chakchouka*, also *chouchouka*).

Shakshouka typically includes both onion and garlic and normally contains only

133

tomatoes and peppers, though versions which add zucchini or eggplant exist. The dish is, however, commonly finished with the addition of eggs to the top of the vegetables, which are cooked until they set.

Southern Italy: *cianfotta* (Campania), *ciambotta* (Campania and elsewhere), *ciambrotta* (Calabria and elsewhere), *ciammotta* (Calabria), *ciabotta* (the Abruzzi).

The southern Italian stews show a fair amount of variation with regard both to the name and the ingredients. In general, garlic is often absent from the base and the added vegetables most often are – beyond tomatoes – peppers, eggplants and potatoes. Other common ingredients are zucchini, green beans, and chiles. Occasionally other vegetables are present, such as celery or carrot, as well as olives and capers.

North-western Italy (Liguria, Piemonte, Lombardia): *ratatuia*.

North-west Italian *ratatuia* varies between versions rather close to the Provençal counterpart and others differing significantly. First, the base is often not simply onion (and garlic) fried in oil but sometimes a full *battuto* with celery and carrot as well. In some recipes, celery and carrot are added later, in large pieces, as major ingredients. Tomatoes, eggplant, peppers and zucchini are typically present but green beans and, especially in Piemonte, potatoes are also commonly included; thus these north-western Italian versions bear a noteworthy resemblance to their southern counterparts.

South-eastern France: *boumiano* (Camargue, Rhône Valley, generally western Provence?) and *ratatouia* (standard French *ratatouille*; Côte d'Azur, Nice, generally eastern Provence?).

Most recipes for these dishes conform to the base version described above, though occasionally omissions of an ingredient or additions (potatoes, green beans) are found.[5]

The angels' kitchen

That the vegetable stews under discussion all include as primary ingredients two or more food products introduced to Europe from the Americas and that this introduction occurred in the context of Spanish colonialism is good reason to look to Spain as the place where these stews first developed. That the other exotic ingredient, the eggplant, had been especially popular among the Moors in Al Andalus further strengthens the connexion. This evidence finds graphic support in the painting of 1646 by Bartolomé Esteban Murillo known as 'The Angels' Kitchen', as noted by Grewe (1988: 110). This work depicts a group of angels preparing food, including eggplant, squash and tomatoes, three of the four essential ingredients of our vegetable stews and more specifically, the most prominent ingredients of the Andalucian *alboronía*. Murillo's painting was executed for a Franciscan convent in his hometown of Seville, then the largest city of the Spanish empire and the central point for the regulation of trade with the New World (Elliott 1963, 2002: 182–3). Clearly to Murillo these vegetables were sufficiently delicious to be fit for Heaven, implying that by the mid 17th century, either singly or together as Seville's *alboronía*, these were well-known foods.

The arrival in southern Spain of each of the American foodstuffs of interest here surely belongs to roughly the first half of the 16th century. It is, however, generally assumed that, while peppers and the New World squashes and beans were quickly and widely accepted as comestibles, the tomato was generally regarded with suspicion and only gradually accepted in Spain and Italy as a foodstuff. This point is important here, since the tomato is a constant in all the related western Mediterranean vegetable stews, alongside the base of onions fried in olive oil. Grewe (1988), in his brief article on the tomato, concludes from references in the contemporary literature that through the 16th century, even in southern Spain, there was only limited cultivation of the tomato; Davidson, following Grewe, adds that from this initial century after the introduction of the fruit to Europe, 'there is little evidence to suggest that people had begun cooking or eating tomatoes except rarely and by way of experiment' (2002: 962).

For 17th-century Spain, there is no extant cookbook indicating how tomatoes and other American exotica were incorporated in the diets of Spaniards but there is evidence which indicates that use of the tomato had progressed well beyond the purely experimental stage. Murillo's depiction of tomatoes in the angelic kitchen shows clearly that by mid-century the tomato, certainly in Seville but surely more broadly in Spain as well, was an appreciated foodstuff. And if we consider further the two recipes with tomatoes in Antonio Latini's *Lo scalco alla moderna* which appeared in Naples in the 1690s, recipes both characterised as '*alla Spagnola*', that is, 'Spanish style', it seems the strong suggestion of Murillo's depiction is confirmed (Grewe 1988: 109, cf. Davidson 2002: 962). But while most food historians have insisted on the very gradual and late acceptance and popularisation of the tomato, there are indications that it was already consumed in the 16th century, including the remark by Pietro Mattioli who, in a work that appeared in Venice in 1568, states that tomatoes were eaten in the same manner as eggplants.[6] Another Italian, Costanzo Felici, in a manuscript from *ca.* 1570, also refers to the consumption of tomatoes, though he dismisses them as something desired by 'gluttons and those eager for new things' ('*ghiotti et avidi de cose nove*') and as a food that looks better than it tastes. Also dismissive, though on different grounds, is Castor Durante, who in a publication from Rome in 1585 observes that tomatoes are eaten in the same manner as eggplants 'but give little and bad nourishment' ('*danno poco e cattivo nutrimento*'). To whatever degree Felici and Durante thought ill of tomatoes themselves or of those who enjoyed them, already in the third quarter of the 16th century we find three Italians, all apparently writing outside the parts of Italy that during this period belonged to the Spanish empire, who were quite aware not only that tomatoes were eaten ('*si mangiano, mangiansi*') but also how they were prepared.

An instructive parallel can be drawn to another American import, namely, peppers. Textual evidence for consumption of peppers, at least in Italy, is also quite sparse – according to Milioni (1992: 93), they are barely mentioned in Italian sources from the 16th to 18th century and are not even listed in the dictionary of the Accademia della Crusca – but virtually all food writers agree that peppers were diffused through Europe, including Italy, soon after their importation from America and that from early on different varieties of pepper were developed and consumed. But when the silence on peppers in Italy is broken, Corrado, in the 1781 edition of *Il cuoco galante* says the following:[7]

> [A]lthough peppers are a rustic food of the masses, there are many who like them... they are eaten when they are green, being fried and sprinkled with salt or cooked over the coals and flavored with salt and oil.

The implication here is that, despite peppers being a popular food among the lower classes, some members of the higher classes also enjoy them and that Corrado's readers should look past the stigma attached to this common food.

The claim here is not that tomatoes were consumed very widely in the 16th century but rather that they were eaten already within decades of their arrival in Europe but then primarily by the poor. Note too that indications for similarly early acceptance of the potato exist.[8] The lack of textual evidence indicating any appreciable consumption of the imported vegetables must therefore be relativised. On the one hand, the habits of the poor, illiterate masses were largely ignored by the privileged and literate until fairly recent times and at best only incidental and indirect mention of the spread of the new foods among the lower classes could be expected. On the other hand, quasi-learnèd and cultural prejudices against these foods, which clearly operated to varying degrees among the upper classes, were surely of little consequence to people living regularly under the threat of starvation. All the exotic vegetables common to these Mediterranean stews, including perhaps the potato, insofar as they grew well under local conditions, were surely adopted by the peasantry throughout the region well before they were embraced by the literate classes.

Returning to the vegetable stews, we find indirect historical support for the assertion that the new ingredients were used to create the stews by the poor, well before any particular note of the developments made its way onto paper.

First, there are good reasons to conjecture that Gypsies played a part in the introduction of a version of the vegetable stew to western Provence, where the dish is known as *boumiano*, that is, 'Bohemian', Provençal for 'Gypsy'. Starting in the 15th century, many Gypsies settled in Andalucía and especially in the area around Seville. These Spanish Gypsies also established communities throughout the Catalan-speaking lands and in the Camargue region of Provence; all these Spanish Gypsy communities have maintained close contacts and form a natural social bridge between Seville, where the exotica were first introduced, and the Camargue, where we later find *boumiano*. Given the social standing and economic condition of the Gypsies over the centuries, it seems certain that a dish associated with them was a dish of the poor, whoever may have first invented it.[9]

Second, support for a relatively early acceptance and agricultural exploitation of some of the exotica from the Americas, if not actually for an early development of a version of the vegetable stew, can perhaps be seen in relation to the history of the 'Moriscos,' the Muslims who remained in Spain after the fall of Grenada in 1492 and were forced to convert to Christianity. After roughly a century of uncomfortable coexistence, the Moriscos were expelled from Spain, with some 300,000 emigrating from 1609 to 1614.[10] Of these, many thousands relocated to the coasts of Morocco, Algeria and Tunisia, with especially large numbers settling around Tunis and on the Cape Bon peninsula.[11] Among the contributions these refugees made to Tunisia was the introduction of New World foodstuffs, including corn, tomatoes, green beans and peppers (Latham 1986: V.56). This further supports the notion that these items, including tomatoes, were already well accepted as foodstuffs in Spain before the end of the 16th century. In addition, one notes the strong similarity between north Africa's *shakshouka* and the *pistos* of Castilian Spain: they both often are a minimalist – perhaps especially old – version of our western Mediterranean vegetable stew with only onions, tomatoes and peppers, a dish commonly fortified with eggs in both central Spain and along the north African coast.

Mixed, trampled, crushed?

The evidence discussed above suggests that the exotic ingredients and perhaps the stews themselves were first consumed by the late 16th or early 17th century by the peoples inhabiting southern Spain, namely the Castilian-speakers of Andalucía and immediately neighbouring areas, the Gypsies, the Arabic-speaking Moriscos, including many in Valencia, and surely also the Catalan-speaking Valencians. For further clues concerning the development of the vegetable stews, we now examine the linguistic evidence of their names.

Setting aside for now Catalan, it is striking that the names for the stews linked more or less directly with southern Spain show no overlap. Castilian *pisto* is transparently derived from a verb *pistar(e)* meaning 'to pound' and is a direct cognate of the name of Genoa's famous pounded sauce, *pesto*.[12] There is clearly no direct relationship between *pisto* and Arabic *shakshouka*, which appears to be derived from a mimetic verb, presumably referring to the sound of the dish cooking.[13] Of a name of any vegetable stew in the Gypsies' Caló language I have found no evidence but around Seville and more broadly in Andalucía one encounters in Spanish the aforementioned *alboronía*. This name is obviously Arabic in origin and related in no way to *pisto*. The development of both the dish and the name in the Arabic-speaking world is described by Perry (2001) but for current purposes it suffices to say that in late medieval Arabic recipes, including some from Moorish Spain, the dish is not a vegetable stew but rather a combination of fried eggplant (or squash) and meat. Whether the Moors also had a vegetarian version of *bûrâniyya* from which the stew including American vegetables directly grew is possible, as Perry (p. 247) suggests, but it is also possible

137

that the name came simply to be strongly linked to fried eggplant in areas where there was a large Arabic-speaking presence and when the vegetarian stew was developed, the name was applied to it, a misapplication but one to which no Arabic speakers were present to object after 1614.

Perhaps the most interesting and complex matter in the development of these vegetable stews is the relationship between dishes and names within the Romance languages beyond southern Spain. There are five Romance names for the stews and of these, we can set aside the term *boumiano*, which is of historical interest, as discussed above, but sheds no light on the development of the other names; we can also set aside the already discussed term *pisto*. Remaining then are the Catalan *xamfaina* or *samfaina*, the eastern Provençal and north-west Italian *ratatouia* or *ratatuia*, and finally the group of closely related forms in southern Italian dialects, namely, *cianfotta*, *ciambotta* etc.

Provençal *ratatouia* has as its French cognate *ratatouille* and it is this latter form that is first attested in 1778 in the sense of '*ragoût*'; it is subsequently attested more generally in that sense or pejoratively to denote a coarse or bad stew.[14] In specific application to the famous vegetable stew, the first attestation dates only from 1930 (Davidson 2002: 784), which has led some to believe that the vegetable dish itself is a relatively recent creation. *Ratatouille* is also attested in the sense of a 'volley of blows' and this meaning in turn points to the family of verbs to which the noun is related. The base form for the verbs is *touiller*, attested since Old French times, meaning 'to stir, agitate, mix' and this verb has by-forms with intensifying and affective prefixes, including *ratouiller*, *tatouiller* etc., with a range of meanings from 'to stir (intensely)' to 'to wallow, soak' and especially 'to soil'. The further etymology of the base verb is, however, well worth noting: it is the reflex of Lat. *tudiculare* 'to grind, crush' and this in turn is derived from the noun *tudicula* 'mechanism for crushing olives'. Semantically, *ratatouille* has developed along two lines, one denoting the act (e.g. 'volley of blows'), the other the result ('ragoût, bad food, mess') of intensified forms of a verb originally meaning 'to pound' or 'to crush', associated with the crushing of olives.

The standard etymology of Catalan *xamfaina* (<x> pronounced as English <sh>) or *samfaina* is that of Corominas (1954: vol. II, p. 16–7). According to him, the Catalan form is a 'semi-learnèd word' derived from Lat. *symphonia* 'concert'. In support he offers a number of music-related words from Catalan and other Romance varieties (e.g. 'bagpipe') which can be derived from *symphonia* but which also show irregular, presumably mimetic or phonæsthetic (and thus not according with general sound laws of the dialects in question) alterations; e.g. Cat. *sanfoina*, Occitan *sanfónia*, Cast. *zampoña*. The key to making such an etymology convincing lies in the semantic link and Corominas' suggestion that the stew could have been metaphorically likened to a harmonising of voices in concert is conceivable but seems rather more learnèd and poetic than one might expect.

For the southern Italian dialect names for the vegetable stew, the few, unconvincing etymologies proposed assume the word was originally borrowed.[15] We suggest, however, that they represent a genuinely native southern Italian formation. To begin, we recognise that a word initial sequence of *cia-* (pronounced like Eng. <cha->) is in general not a normal, '*lautgesetzlich*' outcome of an inherited sound sequence in the dialects in question; thus, if not borrowed, then the initial sequence must be attributed to mimesis or a phonæsthetic process. And indeed, not only in southern Italian but also in other Italian dialects and the standard language, there are many words with this ('non-*lautgesetzlich*') initial sequence *cia-* or *cio-*, words with mimetic and/or affective force and semantically associated with speaking (excessively or badly), eating, shoes or feet (and related sounds) and persons or things that are bad or useless.[16]

Particularly interesting here are the terms for feet and shoes and their close association with things and persons that are useless, bad or slovenly. In standard Italian and most dialects, there occurs a word *zampa* meaning 'paw, animal's foot' and, presumably on phonæsthetic grounds (directly connected to the semantic values), this form *zampa* and its derivatives occur with specialised or affective meanings in the standard but especially widely in the dialects (n.16). Throughout the southern Italian dialects, sets of forms exist both with *za-* and *cia-*, as in Camp./Np., Cal. *zampa/ciampa* 'paw, big foot', *zampare/ciampare* 'to stamp, crush (e.g. grapes)', *zampata/ciampata* 'slap, stamping'. In turn, these words sometimes have derivative forms indicating a bad person or thing, as in Cal. *zampitta* 'sandal, peasant's shoe' and *zampattu* 'coarse peasant', and *zamparu* 'rogue, boor', or Np. *zampitto* 'peasant's shoe; rogue, boor', *zampruosco* 'rogue, boor' but also *ciampruosco* 'shoe; rogue, boor' (Salzano 1986). Finally, and of paramount importance here, the Neapolitan and Campanian dialects – but for the most part not the other southern Italian dialects – have a further and common variant of the *zampa/ciampa* word, namely *cianfa*, and its derivative *cianfata*. In light of this, we posit that at some point, a derivative of this form was created, *cianfotta*, presumably with a pejorative sense. The question is, how can we link *cianfotta* to food and the vegetable stew in particular?

Clues to a possible connexion can be found in dialects neighbouring Campania, specifically, those of Lazio and Calabria. In Lazio we find as the reflex of Latin *sampsa* (standard Italian *sansa*) the form *ciancia* (e.g. Chiappini 1945: 88), meaning 'olive pomace', the mushy residue left from crushing olives in the process of making oil, which is then variously used, including as animal feed.[17] This form in turn calls to mind apparent relict forms in the dialects of Calabria, *cianciana*, *ciancianu*, which refer to stews made from sheep's or goat's pluck or the pluck itself (Rohlfs 1977). The evidence of these relict forms, on the periphery of Campania, suggests that forms similar to *cianciana* meaning 'offal stew' may once have existed more widely, including in Naples and elsewhere in southern and central Italy. The major steps in the linguistic development posited here are:

139

1) Lat. *sampsa* > It. *sansa* 'olive pomace'.

This development involves straightforward sound changes.

2) It. *sansa* –> Central, southern It. dialects *ciancia*.

There are two related developments: a) a mimetic change of consonants; b) a semantic development by which *ciancia*, through the use of olive pomace as animal feed, takes on a secondary meaning of 'messy food', 'food noisily eaten', 'slop' or 'mush'. At this stage, *ciancia* comes in various dialects to be associated increasingly with humble stews made with poor ingredients and in particular with offal stews.

3) Dialectal It. *ciancia* 'offal stew' is reformed further for mimetic/affective reasons, yielding such forms as:

– Tuscan *cioncia*, known today as a stew of calf's snout, cheek, ears, lips.

– Calabrian *cianciana*, *ciancianu*, *ciacialiddra* (diminutive), (a stew made with) sheep's or goat's pluck (heart, lungs, spleen, trachea).

4) In Campania, there is a crossing of the jocular/pejorative form for the offal stew, *ciancia*, with an affective derivative of *cianfa*, i.e. *cianfotta*, perhaps originally bearing the meaning of 'something of little value, something boorish'. The semantically crossed form envisioned here, *cianfotta* meaning 'offal stew', would have brought together several complementary phonæsthetic associations and ultimately, except in peripheral areas, have fully supplanted the older forms of the *ciancia*, *cianciana* variety.

5) The name *cianfotta* as 'offal stew', perhaps also with a more general sense of 'coarse peasant stew, slop' was expansive within continental southern Italy but as it spread beyond its area of origin, where the base form *cianfa* was native, it was adapted in form to the local cognates of the *ciampa/ciamba* variety, giving rise to *ciambotta* and further minor variants.[18]

6) The final step in the development to the attested modern situation is the transfer of the name *cianfotta* and the majority of its variants across southern Italy from a meaning of 'offal stew' or a more general meaning of 'messy, peasant food' to indicating the vegetable stew with tomatoes, eggplant, peppers, potatoes and zucchini. While such a transfer may at first seem unlikely, one should note that there is a general resemblance between the southern Italian pluck stews and *cianfotta*: starting with the fact that they both begin with a *soffritto* of onion, both (ultimately) include tomato and feature several further ingredients of differing textures cut up in roughly similarly sized pieces. If our arguments in the third section above are true about the status of the exotic vegetables following their introduction to Europe, then both stews were quintessentially humble dishes of the poor. They both seem even to have necessarily included one bitter ingredient, spleen in the case of the pluck stew and eggplant in the case of the vegetable stew. From this perspective, the two can be seen as variants of one another, with the vegetable stew, which in Italy is traditionally strictly vegetarian, being the dish appropriate for the many fast days which Catholics observe.[19]

Given that Corominas' etymology for *xamfaina* is semantically unpersuasive, we suggest the Catalan name is linked to *cianfotta*. From a linguistic standpoint, there is no problem: the initial *cia-* (Eng. <ch->) in Italian, not present in that position in Catalan, would naturally be adapted to native phonology as *x-* (Eng. <sh->), and with regard to substitution of the suffix, *-aina*, a specifically north-east Iberian feature which itself has a strongly affective semantic value, it is not surprising that adaptation and integration would involve a change of this sort.[20] But if Catalan *xamfaina* is an adapted borrowing from Campanian *cianfotta*, the borrowing must have taken place at a time before *cianfotta* had switched in its reference from an offal stew or more generally a messy, peasant stew to specifically a vegetable stew. The basis of this assertion is that there exists throughout the Castilian-speaking world the term *chanfaina* which a) consistently is used in Castilian to refer to a stew of offal and b) for linguistic reasons is almost without doubt a borrowing from Catalan into Castilian. Assuming this path of expansion of *cianfotta* to Catalonia and thence, after adaptation, subsequent borrowing into Spanish is correct, the attestation of Spanish *chanfaina* in the first decade of the 17th century in secondary, non-culinary meanings ('mixture, criminal world') apparently affirms our contention that the expansion of *cianfotta* to Iberia occurred early enough to pre-date or coincide with the period when the vegetable stews first developed.[21] Thus, we might surmise that the American vegetables and possibly the stews themselves were first consumed in Spain, but evidence of the spread of the name of a humble dish from Campania to Spain calls attention to the two-way nature of cultural and culinary exchange between these two parts of the Spanish empire.

141

One last point concerning the spread of the term *cianfotta* brings north-western Italy and its versions of *ratatuia* back into the discussion. I know of no early attestations of *ratatuia* in Liguria, Piemonte or Lombardia and given the name perhaps the dish is – as natives of those regions think – an import from neighbouring France. Two interesting facts, however, prompt us to question that view. First, note that in Liguria and especially in Piemonte and Lombardia, there is a tendency to include several vegetables in the stew not typically added in nearby Provence and Nice, including potatoes and green beans and notably carrots and celery; these additions are all found in some versions of the stews consumed in southern Italy, implying some connection – if only of shared aesthetics – between the two parts of the country. Second, in the dialects of at least two of these three north-western regions, there exists a term *cifute*, *cifotu*, *cifutti* in Ligurian, meaning 'awkward, boorish, or worthless person; scoundrel' and in Piemontese *cifota* meaning 'bad wine'.[22] The standing etymology for these words, offered by Meyer-Lübke and repeated elsewhere, links them via Arabic to a word meaning 'Jew' in Turkish. Whatever merit this proposal has, we might well wonder – given the previous discussion – whether Campanian *cianfotta* also reached Genoa and Liguria and spread to Lombardia, both integrally tied to the Spanish empire during the 16–17th centuries, and thence on to Piemonte. Perhaps then the word *ratatuia* is a late arrival in north-western Italy, but one which entered the region as a more respectable moniker for a vegetable stew of southern Italian origin. In any event, one is struck by the coincidence of the presence of both vegetable stews and traces of the *cianfotta/ciambotta* family of names in those regions of continental Italy that were linked to the Spanish empire during the early modern period and their general absence in those regions, such as Tuscany and Lazio, that were not.

Fritta è buona persino una scarpa'

While the etymology for *cianfotta/xamfaina* proposed here includes some steps not directly attested, support for each of the steps can be adduced, and while this derivation of such a humble and jocular term as *cianfotta* may seem unduly baroque, the fact is that the hitherto proposed etymologies both for the Italian and the Catalan names for the vegetable stews simply do not address the material broadly or convincingly. On the other hand, our proposed solution to the problem brings together two previously poorly explained names and additionally offers a view of the semantic developments in the southern Italian dialects which is remarkably parallel to what we know of the more transparent history of the name *ratatouille*.

This last point calls to mind a general observation regarding the development of the entire family of western Mediterranean vegetable stews, namely, that the family falls into two closely related but distinct branches. On the one hand, in the west and south, we have an area including the Castilian *pisto*, Andalucian *alboronía* and north African *shakshouka*, all dishes which typically either include more limited sets of exotic ingredients or else emphasise one above the others, and which bear names that are strikingly unrelated to one another. To the east and north, from Catalonia to France, north-western Italy and on to southern Italy, we have, however, dishes which all typically include at least three, if not more, of the exotic ingredients and do not feature one above the others; in addition, in this second area, as discussed above, there is noteworthy unity in the names, with a direct connexion between Catalonia and southern Italy and a remarkably parallel semantic development lying behind *cianfotta/xamfaina* on the one hand and *ratatouia* on the other. The overall picture is then of a probable zone of original innovation embracing several ethnic and linguistic groups in the southern half of Spain, but then also a second area of innovation, spanning from Catalonia to Campania but with no obvious priority being reasonably assigned to the one or the other.

The claim that this family of stews necessarily derives directly from Moorish cuisine in Al Andalus, as often asserted by Andalucians and writers who approach the topic from an Arab perspective, is not supported by the facts in any meaningful way and the denial of the complex origins of this family of dishes would be, in light of the evidence presented here, no less misguided than would be any attempt to deny the strong possibility of direct participation in the development by the Moriscos and the certainty of a significant historical, background rôle of Moorish culinary traditions in southern Spain. In the end, the origins of *cianfotta*, *xamfaina*, and *ratatouia* are no less a jumble and ultimate harmonisation of the culinary efforts of humble people of several distinct ethnic backgrounds than these stews are themselves a jumble and ultimate harmonisation of inexpensive ingredients from far-flung places. In a very real way, this family of western Mediterranean stews reflects through its diversity and unity a particularly important period for the region as a whole, when Spain, as centre of a great empire, served as both actor and audience on a world stage.

References

Andrews, Colman, *Catalan Cuisine* (New York: Atheneum, 1988).

Aprosio, Sergio, *Vocabolario ligure storico-bibliografico sec. X-XX* (Savona: Marco Sabatelli Editore, 2003).

Bloch, Oscar, & Walther von Warburg, *Dictionnaire étymologique de la langue française* (Paris: Presses Universitaire de France, 2002 [1932]).

Boris, Gilbert, *Lexique du parler arabe des Marazig* (Paris: Klincksieck, 1958).

Chantot-Bullier, C., *Vieilles recettes de cuisine provençale/vieii receto de cousino prouvençalo* (Marseille: P. Tacussel, 1988).

Chiappini, Filippo, *Vocabolario romanesco* (Roma: Casa Editrice 'Leonardo Da Vinci', 1945).

Corominas, Joan, *Diccionario crítico etimológico de la lengua castellana* (Berna: Editorial Francke, 1954).

——, *Breve diccionario etimológico de la lengua castellana* (Madrid: Editorial Gredos, 1961).

Cortelazzo, Manlio, & Carla Marcato, *Dizionario etimologico dei dialetti italiani* (Milano: Garzanti, 2000).

David, Elizabeth, *A Book of Mediterranean Food* (Harmondsworth: Penguin, 1965).

Davidson, Alan, *The Penguin Companion to Food* (London: Penguin, 2002).

De Sales Mayo, F., *Los Gitanos, su historia, sus costumbres, su dialecto* (Madrid, 1869).

De Vaux de Foletier, François, *Mille ans d'histoire des Tsiganes* (Librairie Fayard, 1970).

Diccionari Català-Valencià-Balear (Palma de Mallorca, 1959).

Elliott, J. H., *Imperial Spain 1469–1716* (London: Penguin, 1963, 2002).

Frisoni, Gaetano, *Dizionario moderno Genovese-Italiano e Italiano-Genovese* (Bologna: Forni Editore, 1910).

Grewe, Rudolf, 'The Arrival of the Tomato in Spain and Italy: Early Recipes', *Proceedings of the First International Food Congress in Turkey* (1988), pp. 106–113.

Harvey, L. P., *Muslims in Spain, 1500 to 1614* (Chicago: University of Chicago Press, 2005).

Lapesa, Rafael, '«Chanzón», «chanzoneta», «chancha», «chanza», «chanzaina», «chanfaina» y sus derivados', *Homenaje a Félix Monge* (Gredos, 1995), pp. 233–47.

Latham, J. D., 'Contribution à l'étude des immigrations andalouses et leur place dans l'histoire de la Tunisie' (1973); in J. D. Latham, *From Muslim Spain to Barbary* (London: Variorum Reprints, 1986), pp. 21–63.

Meyer-Lübke, W., *Romanisches etymologisches Wörterbuch* (Heidelberg: Carl Winter, 1935).

Migliorini, Bruno, *Vocabolario della lingua italiana* (Torino: Paravia, 1965)

Milioni, Stefano, *Columbus Menu: Italian Cuisine after the First Voyage of Christopher Columbus* (New York: Istituto Italiano per il Commercio Estero, 1992).

Perry, Charles, 'Bûrân: Eleven Hundred Years in the History of a Dish', *Medieval Arab Cookery:* essays and translations by Maxime Rodinson, A. J. Arberry & Charles Perry (Totnes: Prospect Books, 2001) pp. 239–50.

Pharies, David A., 'The Ibero-romance Suffix -aina', *Romance Philology*, 43 (1990), 367–99.

143

Rey, Alain, Marianne Tomi, Tristan Hordé, & Chantal Tanet, *Dictionnaire historique de la langue française* (Paris: Dictionnaires Le Robert, 1998).

Rohlfs, Gerhard, *Nuovo dizionario dialettale della Calabria* (Ravenna: Longo Editore, 1977).

Salzano, Antonio, *Vocabolario Napoletano-Italiano Italiano-Napoletano* (Napoli: Edizione del Giglio, 1986).

Notes

1. In researching and writing this paper, I benefited greatly from the aid and input of Amy Dahlstrom, to whom I extend my gratitude. I should also like to thank Ernest Buccini Jr. and Joseph Grano for their input in discussions on certain aspects of this project.

2. The slow-fried base of onions in olive oil, optionally with further ingredients, is a fundamental element in Castilian (*sofrito*), Catalan (*sofregit*) and Italian (*soffritto*) cooking.

3. Surely the dish is also well known on the Balearic Islands but then perhaps as part of the Catalan national cuisine, for there occurs there also a different local version, tumbet, which includes potatoes and is baked. The term (and dish) *xamfaina* is also known in the Catalan-speaking enclave of Alguer (Alghero) in Sardinia. For details of the dialect distribution of phonetic variants of the name, see the entry for *samfaina* in the *Diccionari Català-Valencià-Balear*.

4. For detailed recipes and further discussion, see Andrews 1988, esp. p. 42 ff.

5. See, for example, Chanot-Bullier's 1988 bilingual (French-Provençal) cookbook, with *ratatouia/ratatouille* in the section of recipes from Nice (p. 212–3) and *boumiano/bohémienne* in the section of recipes from the Camargue, Arles and the Comtat-Venaissin. The recipe for *ratatouia* omits tomato but I believe this omission to be an editorial mistake rather than a genuinely tomato-less recipe.

   Apparently around Nîmes, this style of vegetable stew is known as *bourbouillade* (Davidson 2002: 784), though that name (Occitan *borbolhada*) is known to this writer primarily as a dish composed of wild greens from Languedoc. Further investigation is required.

6. I have not yet had the chance to consult this work directly; Mattioli's comments are widely referred to in the literature but an actual citation of the original Italian of the 1568 text I have only found on the internet, at the following Italian site:

   <http://www.racine.ra.it/russi/webscuola/alimamer/pomodoro.htm> [accessed 13 July 2005]

   These passages have been copied over and translated at the following English-language site:

   <http://home.comcast.net/~iasmin/mkcc/MKCCfiles/16thCITomatoReferences.html> [accessed 13 July 2005]

   Also quoted in these same web-pages are the passages by Felici and Durante referred to directly below.

7. The translated passage from Corrado is from Milioni 1992: 93.

8. The potato, like the tomato, is generally thought to have been only very slowly accepted in Europe but Milioni (1992: 34) cites two rather early indications of the potato's acceptance and exploitation as food of the poor in Spain. According to Milioni, potatoes were 'listed in 1573 among the provisions of the Sangre Hospital in Seville' where they were 'used to supplement the diets of the ailing poor.' Milioni also calls attention to another of the works of Seville's Murillo, who in a painting of Saint James dating to 1645 'shows the saint distributing potatoes to the famished.'

9. For general discussions of the history of the Gypsies in Spain, see De Sales Mayo 1869 and De Vaux de Foletier 1970. The questions of what rôle the Gypsies may have played in bringing the new foods or the stew to Provence and when they may have done so need to be investigated further.

10. For a recent and detailed account of the Muslims in Spain from 1500 to the mass expulsions, see Harvey 2005.

11. A detailed discussion of the settlement of Muslim emigrants from Spain in Tunisia is Latham 1973 [reprint 1986].

12. There are reasons to believe that the specific form *pisto* is not a '*lautgesetzlich*' development of Castilian and thus that the form must have been borrowed from some other Romance dialect; see,

for example, Corominas 1961: 450. Unfortunately, due to time and space restrictions, I cannot address this problem here.

13. For the Arabic of the Marazig in Tunisia, for example, Boris (1958: 317) gives the verb in question as follows (phonetic spelling here adapted): '*shakshak*, inacc. *ishakshek* «produire du bruit; bouillonner» (boisson versée); «gargouiller, chanter» (liquide sur le feu)...'

14. This discussion draws especially from the entries for *ratatouille* and *touiller* in vol. III of Rey et al. 1998, as well as from those in Bloch & Wartburg 2002.

15. Of more recent suggestions, there is that of Rohlfs (1977: 170), who suggests that one of the Calabrian variants, *ciambrotta*, which he defines as a 'liquid or brothy mixture of things', is to be derived from *ciambra*, meaning 'a kind of shelter from the sun' and ultimately from the French *chambre*. The semantic basis of this etymology is, at best, opaque. As an alternative, Cortelazzo & Marcato (2000: 140) have suggested instead that the same Calabrian form be derived from the French dialect term *chabrot*, which they define as a 'mixture of wine and broth'. While this originally western Occitan word seems to fit *ciambrotta* as defined by Rohlfs tolerably well, the link to the broader family of vegetable stew names is tenuous at best and the historical path for the transfer from western Languedoc to southern Italy clearly needs elaboration. Given the more proximate relationship of *ciambrotta* to Neapolitan *cianfotta* and thence to Catalan *xamfaina*, this etymology seems not especially compelling.

16. Some examples of such forms from standard Italian, Genoese and Roman: 1) speaking, e.g. It. *ciarlare* 'to chatter'; 2) speaking nonsense or stuttering, Gen. *ciambrottâ* 'to babble', Rom. *ciancicagnocchi* 'stutterer'; 3) lying, It. *cianciare* 'to lie, chatter, gossip'; 4) eating, Rom. *ciancico* 'eating'; 5) shoes or feet and the sounds made by them, It. *ciabattare* 'to shuffle along', *ciampicare* 'to stumble along', Rom. *cianfarone* 'large, badly made shoe', Rom. *ciocia* 'poor peasant's shoe'; 6) persons or things that are bad or useless, It. *ciarpame* 'rubbish', *cianciafruscola* 'bagatelle', It. *cialtrone* 'scoundrel, rogue, slob'.

17. Migliorini (1965: 1243): '*Sansa* s.f. Quel che resta delle olive spremuto l'olio, e che, sottoposto a nuova macinazione e sprematura, fornisce l'olio d'infima qualità e lascia un ulteriore residuo che serve all' alimentazione dei bovini...'

18. Note that the existence of Pugliese *ciambotto*, *ciambotta* in the sense of a sauce for pasta made with a soffritto, tomatoes and mixed small fish provides evidence for the word having been expansive with a general meaning, allowing for such relatively local and exceptional re-lexicalisation.

19. Cf. Perry's (1988: 246–7) comments in connexion with the rise of a meatless version of *alboronía* in Spain.

20. On the history, distribution and value of *–aina*, see Pharies 1990.

21. On the earlier attestations of *chanfaina* in Castilian, see Corominas 1954: 16–7 and Lapesa 1995: 242–4.

22. For the Ligurian forms, see Aprosio (2003: Part II, vol. 1, p. 307) and Frisoni (1910: 79); the Piemontese form is cited in Meyer-Lübke (1935: 309).

Communicating Authenticity

John F. Carafoli

How do we market and communicate the authenticity of food to the consumer through its visual presentation?

In an era of food conglomerates, round-the-clock marketing, over-hyped restaurants and advances in modern technology, what constitutes culinary authenticity? With so many players in the food presentation chain, from suppliers of the raw ingredients to those who style, photograph, represent and sell the finished products, each player brings to the table a different idea of what authenticity means.

This paper addresses the 'visual authenticity' of food, meaning its origins, how it is processed and prepared, and the link between what the eye sees and what the mind concludes about its taste. It is discussed from the perspective of a food stylist who authored the first and only book on food styling, and who acts as middleman in the food supply chain. It is the food stylist's job to understand the multiple realities that define the authenticity of food and the ways that authenticity can be communicated visually.

Why is visual authenticity important? Because we as visual communicators are responsible for creating 'appetite appeal,' for seducing the public into buying a product or trying a recipe by means of tempting photos. We are charged with creating visual fantasies around a particular food or product by invoking the senses. And in order to do this effectively and well, we need to understand not only the characteristics of the food or product we're presenting, but also the perceptions and expectations of the consumer to whom it's being targeted, and what is authentic to them. Authenticity, after all, is all in the eye of the beholder.

Creating 'visual authenticity' is truly a team effort. Consider the variety of players involved in understanding the consumer's perspective and then interpreting it to create an enticing visual. For any given assignment, there typically is the food editor, the corporate styling manager (if a large corporation is involved,) the marketing and advertising departments and the ad agency, as well as the food stylist and food photographer. Each brings a different viewpoint of what constitutes visual authenticity and how best to create the right mood, attitude and setting to appeal to a food's or product's target consumer.

Advertisers typically take more of a 'hard sell' approach than magazine editorials do. In both cases, however, the goals are the same – to sell a product. Let's look first at how advertising approaches 'visual authenticity,' and then contrast it with the editorial approach taken by magazines.

Authenticity and advertising

A striking case of achieving 'visual authenticity' at all costs is illustrated by the efforts involved in a Special Advertising Section appearing recently in *Bon Appetit* which featured a well-known pasta and pasta sauce. While the public may perceive little 'real authenticity' in a pasta sauce from a jar, the client's objective was to convey a sense of a traditional, homemade Italian product. 'It was our job to create this illusion of authenticity,' St. John Frizell, promotion copy director of *Bon Appetit*, told me. In order to do so, the team knew that ' the setting for the food is very important. We wanted to make it look like it was being served in someone's home.'

Maryellen Mooney, creative marketing director of *Bon Appetit*, says, 'What we had to do to create what appears to be very simple food shots was painstaking. It was a step by step process, like putting another piece of asparagus here, putting a second string of pasta on the fork, moving a fleck of sauce from that piece of pasta, moving the tip of the asparagus over and putting a bit of sauce on it, then putting it behind the spaghetti. It was a mosaic puzzle for us.' In addition to striving for an appetizing, authentically Italian look, the editors also were mindful of truth in representation. 'We had to be sure you could see in the greatest detail what would tempt the consumer without being unrealistic about the serving portion the consumer would get in that jar.'

After a long and painstaking photography session, the editing was arduous as well. 'We spent five weeks on re-touching and moving things around digitally,' Mooney adds, 'all the while continuing to support the client's idea visually, constantly trying to reinforce their concept of authenticity.'

There are many devices used to promote a product as authentic. As food stylists, we often put products in environments with flavor cues to support what the client is trying to portray as authentic. An example was a recent advertising photo shoot in which two identical cups of iced coffee were placed side by side to be photographed. In order to 'cue' the fact that one was blueberry and the other coconut-flavored (flavorings did not change the color of the drinks), a few blueberries and chunks of coconut were placed next to each cup to differentiate and emphasize the individual flavors.

'The relationship between the setting and the environment is very important in creating an authentic look to our product,' says Neil Martin, art director and designer for Hill Holiday, the ad agency for Dunkin Donuts. 'Photography also plays a huge part in enhancing products, particularly through special lighting techniques.'

The issue of food stylists using artificial food or ingredients in their work has been a big controversy over the years. The trend today is to use only genuine ingredients. Martin discusses this issue. 'Using real and natural ingredients always helps to make the product look more authentic. This is important because today's consumer is sophisticated. People know when something is fake. Trying to trick them is the quickest way to destroy a sense of authenticity.'

147

Ethical and legal issues

In the business of advertising and food packaging, it is critical for manufacturers to remain within legal and ethical bounds with respect to representing portion size, quality, and overall attributes of a product. How does a large corporation maximize the sense of authenticity and culinary appeal of its product, while at the same time maintaining truth in advertising?

I posed this question to Cindy Lund, food styling manager for General Mills and Betty Crocker. 'From our viewpoint we feel it is our ultimate responsibility to truthfully represent our products,' Cindy stressed. 'For example, we are legally and ethically obligated to depict the actual color, the true consistency, and the accurate ratio of particles to broth in our soups.

'I have been with General Mills for 20 years and we have established guidelines. Everyone knows what they are and relies on us to interpret them and make sure we all follow them.

'Therein lies the challenge to us as food stylists. We must respect and reflect our clients' ethical and legal responsibilities, calling upon our artistry and innovativeness to accentuate the appeal of products while in no way misrepresenting the product by changing its color, adding fresh ingredients that aren't actually part of the product, or altering any critical aspect of it.

'On occasion, based on marketing research findings, we make recommendations... to add an herb or something to give [the product] a little bit of interesting color. In particular I am thinking about a microwave product that may not brown, so you have to look at other ways to create a certain appetite appeal, and the sauce and herbs might create a little more visual interest. Sometimes recipe developers do go back and revise the produce or reformulate it to add a little bit more appetite appeal to it.

'In our area of food styling, we veterans know the industry better than a lot of the new young marketers. We have the experience, we know what our competitors are doing, and we have a passion about food and what represents appetite appeal. We look at our products and know what the consumer is going to see. It is all a matter of best judgment.

'The marketing department relies on our expertise. They might not always like what we have to say, but they do tend to listen to us.'

Authenticity in magazines

Magazines also have products to sell – the magazine itself, as well as its recipes. While an editor may use more of a 'soft sell' approach than advertising does, nonetheless editorial features also employ various devices to promote a product's authenticity. These frequently are evident in the photos that are added to enhance a story.

John Willoughby, executive editor of *Gourmet Magazine*, thinks there are two schools of thought with respect to food photography in magazines.

'The question is, Do you want to show them what it really looks like, or do you what to show them the best possible way it can look? Which one is more authentic depends on your point of view.' He points out that magazines take different approaches depending on whom they're appealing to.

'If you take something and cook it and just put it on a plate without much styling and propping, it will probably look more like it will when someone cooks it at home, so that is an authentic version of what it will look like.' Having said that, he adds that he doesn't think that that is what people want. 'They want it to look the best it can possibly look, with the right plate, the right lighting and props and all the things that go into styling and photography. And people do respond better to that. People aren't fooled – they don't think it's actually going to look like that when they make it, but this is the best and ideal way this dish can look. This is an ideal version of this recipe. It gives them something to aspire to.'

Romulo Yanes, staff photographer at *Gourmet*, shared Willoughby's views about editorial and visual authenticity. Yanes uses certain techniques he feels are important for creating an authentic look when photographing food. Like Martin, who shoots for advertising, Yanes thinks lighting is an extremely important part of this process, particularly the use of strobe versus natural light to enhance food.

He finds an increasing number of photographers are using daylight because they feel it is closer to what we see, hence more authentic. But he adds that sometimes shooting in daylight does not bring out the best in certain foods and products. Under certain circumstances strobe lights elicit a better effect and result. He considers the strobe a legitimate tool, and feels that just because daylight is 'the real thing,' it doesn't necessarily translate into making food appear more authentic. He told me, 'The idea of shooting in daylight is very romantic and very wonderful, but you have to give the subject whichever treatment brings out the qualities you want to get across in that particular plate of food and recipe. Sometimes it is not always a great picture, but one that will sell that recipe by making the person looking at it want to make that recipe.'

149

Yanes continues, 'Communicating visual authenticity is sometimes a little bit of trickery. If you want to bring an authentic look to a photograph, one of the ways I have always used has been letting a crumb fall on the plate or shooting that smudge on the spoon. It gives a feeling that someone has been here. It brings a human, relaxed element into the photo without showing a hand or a real person. It is a little bit of a tease, but it conveys something is happening beyond a dish being placed in front of the camera.'

A very different point of view was put forth by Chris Kimbell, founder and editor of *Cooks Illustrated*. Chris doesn't think anybody in the food world is trying to create authenticity. 'I think it's just the opposite. Nobody is trying to sell you on authenticity. They are trying to sell you on a lifestyle, and are trying to create a fantasy. Authenticity has nothing to do with ninety-eight percent of what is going on in the editorial world. They are selling you a concept. This culture does not appreciate or honor authenticity in almost any sense, especially as it relates to food.'

He continues, 'We at *Cooks Illustrated* don't take advertising so we can be honest about what works. We create recipes that people can rely on. Our whole gig is saying that most food really sucks, so let's start with bad food. We made these six brownie recipes and they are all bad. Now let's figure out why they are bad and how to make a pretty good one. We are not going to lie about what it takes or how long it takes – we'll be pretty straightforward about it.'

Darra Goldstein, editor, *Gastromonica: The Journal of Food and Culture* takes a more skeptical approach to visual authenticity. She is not convinced that we can claim anything to be truly authentic at heart, but feels rather that authenticity comes from what the food preparer puts into it. 'For example, take an old family recipe that was made a certain way in the 19th century. If someone is making it now in the 21st century it still can be an authentic recipe even if the polenta is not ground by hand and even if the ingredients are not put together and cooked in exactly the same way as they were when using 19th-century technology. So I have some trouble with the idea that for something to be authentic, it has to be done exactly the same way as it has been done in the past. Authenticity is an idea that can incorporate new methods or modern ingredients as long as the impetus behind it is genuine.'

She adds that immigrants underscore this point. 'There has been so much movement around the world that while immigrants are adapting to the newer ingredients that they find in the place they come to, their preparation is just as authentic – they are doing it the way they know best.'

At times Goldstein has used very graphic images to create controversial visual authenticity in her magazine. I refer to one in particular, a cover called The Tomato Eater, which is very tight shot of a man with a mustache and dirt under his nails. The shot is so close that at first glance the viewer is not quite sure what he or she is looking at. Goldstein observes, 'Now, this to me is as authentic as you can get. I mean, here is a guy in the fields with dirty hands, and so if you are confronted with something that is this real it makes some people uncomfortable.'

Conclusion

Anne Mendelsohn, culinary historian and author of the book *Stand Facing the Stove*, puts it well when she says, 'Visual presentation can lie as much as it can tell the truth. When you talk about authenticity you are implicitly allowing that there is inauthenticity. What is authentic? The camera does not tell the truth on its own – it is how it is used.'

So what can we conclude? Some would contend that visual authenticity is an illusion created by people in the business of selling something, achieved by manipulating light, perspective, and photographic technique. But there's also the illusion that the viewer or consumer himself imposes – the belief that a doughnut, some pasta sauce straight from the jar, or a can of soup on the grocer's shelf can be just as authentic and credible as a family recipe created from scratch in one's own home. It does seem, in the end, that visual authenticity truly is in the eye of the beholder.

I would like to acknowledge my gratitude to a true friend, April Eberhardt for her time, effort and support in writing this paper.

151

The Authenticity of Wild Boar in England

Caroline Conran

If you would like to be liked by my sweetheart, then know, friend,
      what troubles her heart:
The boars, they come at night from the grove
And break into her cabbage garden
And tread and wallow in the field
The boars – shoot them you hunter hero.

Wilhelm Müller

Recently wild boar, *Sus scrofa*, once a popular game animal, but extinct in Britain for hundreds of years, has again become a favourite meat in this country, and there are now many wild boar farms. It appears disguised as ropes of sausages in butchers' windows, on restaurant menus, and at last year's Symposium a wild boar from a farm near Oxford was roasted on a spit, carved up and enjoyed by about 140 people.

I first saw wild boar in Tuscany, a splendid sow and her procession of furry piglets, striped with a soft brown and gold camouflage, trotting across the road close to the famous Vipore restaurant near Lucca, where, of course, they served pappardelle with wild boar (*cinghale*) sauce. The boars looked and acted like nervous wild animals, and were, to me as an uninformed observer, considerably less threatening than the legendary animals that were mythologised by the Greeks and others in the past.

In fact this is a serious question; are they still the same animals that were, together with stags, bears and wolves, known in France as *les noirs*, regarded as both heroic archetypes and formidable warriors, boars being the most dangerous adversary in any hunt, liable to rip open the stomachs of dogs, horses and men with their much-feared tusks?

It has been estimated that there are hundreds of thousands of wild boar in the wild in France, while in Germany up to 200,000 are shot every year. In addition there are farms, all over Europe, where they are reared, for meat, in strongly fenced pens, often covering large areas of maquis and woodland.

These wild boar have often, over hundreds and perhaps thousands of years, interbred with their relatives, domestic pigs; with whom they will readily mate. Wild boar have also been cross-bred deliberately in order to improve the quality or quantity of their meat, or to enable them to be fattened faster or produce more piglets than is natural to the wild boar.

But all species have evolved over the centuries and standards change. In an advanced scientific age, can authenticity be proved scientifically, or can it still be ascertained by looking at traits, and in the case of the wild boar by looking at and tasting the meat?

I shall start by looking briefly at the wild boar's history and the history of man's relationship with it in order to define the authentic, magnificent wild beast of legend and history. It would be sad if man's interference has turned it into a different, perhaps less courageous, semi-domesticated, hybrid animal.

The wild boar in history
In the past, the wild boar has always represented something noble, even spiritually superior to other animals; in ancient Greece hunting and killing a boar was a rite of passage. Usually undertaken on foot with dogs, it was an initiation for young boys to hoplite (foot-soldier) status, and 'one could not recline at dinner until one had speared a boar without a hunting net'.[1]

Boar hunting was, by definition, a masculine activity and considered, together with athletics, to be a suitable training for warfare. Plato himself applauded the chase on horseback or on foot with dogs, and disapproved of nets, snares, night trapping and poaching. Odysseus was gored in the leg by a 'mighty boar which sallied out from his lair' and 'gave him a long flesh-wound with a cross lunge of his tusk'.[2]

Odysseus and his companions hunted with a pack of hounds and a long spear; clubs, tridents, swords, special serrated spears and bows and arrows were also used. The Spartans hunted it with hands and teeth.

153

Homer frequently used the wild boar as a metaphor for heroism – for example Idomeneus, in the *Iliad*, waits to confront Aeneas 'with the self-reliance of a mountain boar when he is caught by a crowd of huntsmen in some lonely spot and faces the hue and cry with bristling back and eyes aflame, whetting his tusks in his eagerness to take on all comers, hound or man'.[3]

The boar was also invested with magical or god-like qualities. Ancient man experienced a feeling described by André Bonnard as 'Otherness'. For them 'The divine may exist everywhere, in a stone, in water, in a tree or an animal'.[4] To the ancients hunting the wild boar was a symbolic quest.

In myth, the boar, depicted on pottery as large, with stiff bristly crest, huge shoulders and curved tusks like the crescent moon, symbolized the agent of the wrath of deities in many parts of the world. The boar in the Adonis legend is an aspect of the deity himself and Adonis was killed by a boar.

In Celtic mythology, on the top of Mount Ben Bulben in County Sligo, a magical wild boar attacked Diarmaid the young lover of Grainne, Finn McCool's wife. Finn, the giant, arrived to see them both expire after the boar, the agent of Finn's wrath, had ripped the young man open.

In the myth of Tristan and Isolde, Tristan, like Odysseus, bore a scar on his thigh from a boar's tusk, and his shield was inlaid with the image of a boar as sable-black as coal.

In all the myths, the authentic boar is described as huge and black, and he represents something heroic, powerful or, as in the Buddha myth, transforming. We can see what he looked like in the past, as there are many images of hunting.

Some of the most vivid are on Greek vases, mainly made between 60–425 BC, which demonstrate the importance of boar-hunting. In these the boar has a fine upstanding mane and gigantic tusks. One red-figured cup in the British Museum shows Theseus and the huge Krommyonian sow, another shows Herakles chasing the bad-tempered Erymanthian boar. A superb vase in the Louvre dated 450 BC depicts the dangerous hunt of the boar, fought down in the dirt, emphasising the heroic nature of a hunt in which men could demonstrate their courage. Facing a wild boar entailed facing extraordinary danger; at that time he was considered to be more dangerous than any other prey, including the lion, and with the possible exception of the rhinoceros.

The wild animals that inspired such myths and descriptions certainly sound awesome, but when it comes to the wild boar of Italy, France and England up to the Middle Ages and later, things become less clear. Clearly the feeling of 'Otherness' of earlier civilisations had been invested in many things, now it had moved from human gods to an invisible God, and beasts were not revered in the same way.

However the courage of the boar lived on in myths and heraldry, and amongst the landed lords and seigneurs, hunting still kept its importance as a noble sport, while in Germany boar hunting was the dominant form of the chase. Certain animals were considered noble game, including the wild boar, red deer, the hare, the wolf and the bear; these five were also referred to as venery, everything else was categorised as a beast of the chase, folly, vermin or rascal.

Any feast worthy of a great nobleman had to have a boar's head as a centrepiece, and wild boar was considered 'strong meat', even though it is more easily digested than pork, provided that the testicles and guts have been removed immediately, as the meat, due to the thick fur which keeps the carcase warm over a long period, will taint very quickly. Often wild boar was preserved like beef in the winter – that is, salted for 8–10 days, then smoked in the chimney for the rest of the winter. Alternatively, in the summer, it could be put in brine in a vat, then hung to dry in the open air.

Although the live animal was considered noble and spiritually superior to other animals, the fresh meat itself had to be purged with something acid – wine vinegar, white wine in a marinade or in cooking, or a sauce such as *agrodolce* with oranges or lemon and sugar. Treated differently, it offered different flavours from ordinary meat.

In medieval times, 'They believed that they could assimilate strength and noble virtue by eating noble game. Mysterious and dangerous, nevertheless the strength [was] the life-force... the hunter gives the hunted animal the status of fellow-hero, noble to noble, hero to hero.'[5]

It is interesting to note how this philosophy was parodied in Italy, in cruel games reminiscent of the Roman emperors and their gladiatorial combats with wild beasts, when the animal became both object of and metaphor for the savagery that man still carries within.

When Sir Richard Colt Hoare went after wild boar with the King of Naples in 1786, he was appalled to discover that the boar, so far from being wild, came when whistled for, and that the hunters stuck it with spears when it was held fast by dogs. He is quoted as saying, 'I was…thoroughly disgusted with this scene of slaughter and butchery…yet the King and his court seem[ed] to receive great pleasure from the acts of cruelty and to vie with each other in the expertness of doing them.'[6]

In England hunting was the sport of kings, and game was reserved for the nobles – William the Conqueror introduced strict anti-poaching laws in the 11th century, a man could have his eyes put out for poaching deer.

Even so, wild boar were both detested and sought after by the rural populace, since a herd of boar out foraging can do a huge amount of waste and destruction in a single night, by trampling and rooting up a vital crop. Hunt historian Richard Almond tells us that the medieval writer Gaston Fébus is one of the few authors to include common hunting methods such as how to trap a wild boar. He tells how a wild boar raided a farmer's orchard and was trapped in a pit, the entrance to which was concealed with brushwood. 'When one thinks that many a peasant spent much of the year fattening a domestic pig in preparation for the winter, an autumn windfall such as this in one's orchard was probably as welcome as the apples themselves.'[7]

So they were hunted down, and from perhaps as early as the 13th century, were only found in royal forests and private hunting parks. These forests, however, having been established in the Middle Ages to provide 'a favourable environment for beasts of the chase,'[8] covered up to a quarter of England in the 13th century.

In the sixteenth and seventeenth centuries, 'many of these reserves were disparked or given over to cattle, as an expanding market provided incentives for a more profitable use of the land'.[9] In addition, commoners encroached on the land with their herds of pigs, giving ample opportunity for encounters between domestic pigs and wild boar.

There were rules for smallholders about feeding domestic pigs in the forests, an activity called pannage. Swine and cattle were not allowed in during the close season (termed 'the fence month') which was May – when red deer were giving birth to their fawns. This, significantly, shows that they were allowed in for the rest of the year. Interbreeding inevitably took place frequently, since wild boar come into season during the autumn.

But as hunting with guns became common, and close seasons, imposed to conserve various game creatures such as otters, fallow deer, and hares, did not (and still do not) apply to wild boar, by the first half of the 17th century after much indiscriminate hunting, and loss of their habitat through felling of forests and draining of marshes, English wild boar were extinct in the wild, and park-bred animals were used

155

for hunting. In the 18th century General Howe tried to breed wild boar in Wolmer Forest, but 'the enraged inhabitants rose and destroyed them', presumably because they preferred not to have their crops dug up and their hunting dogs gored.[10]

The wild boar in England today

Although they became extinct in the wild in the 17th century, in this country, today, thanks to the reintroduction of farmed wild boar and their subsequent escapes, there are currently several colonies of wild boar at large in England. They have become particularly common in the Forest of Dean and there are several breeding groups in south-east England. Sussex, in particular, is providing an ideal breeding ground with its large and frequent areas of chestnut and oak wood.

These colonies started when several wild boar, *Sus scrofa*, native to France but, as we have seen, not seen in the wild in Britain for at least 200 years, escaped from their pens in a now-defunct licensed East Sussex boar farm, in October 1987, during and after the great storm, when falling trees had damaged the electric fence. Others escaped from the same farm in January 1989, when the electric fence was damaged by a poacher driving through it in his 4 x 4 vehicle, during a chase. Others have got away from the abattoirs at Aldington and Port Lymne.

They seem to be very intelligent and great survivors, adaptable, resourceful and clever. The heavily wooded area near Romney marshes is favourable to them, firstly because of large tracts of Forestry Commission woodland, and secondly because of a large protected area, adjacent to the Forestry Commission land, owned by Paul McCartney, which provides them with a sanctuary.

About 8 years ago Lisa Reeve, who works with her husband on the family sheep farm near Rye, had a Forestry Commission inspector, Martin Goulding, to stay at her bed-and-breakfast. His brief was to do a survey of escaped wild boar and to look into the possibility of eliminating them completely, as potential carriers of disease. In outbreaks of foot-and-mouth, TB and swine-fever, farm animals can be either culled or inoculated, but nobody can inoculate these animals or restrict their movement from farm to farm.

But the wild boar cull did not get under way, and although questions were repeatedly asked in the House of Commons in 1997 and 1999, both Baroness Hayman and Angela Eagle insisted that what were called 'sporadic' sightings 'had not been substantiated and there was no confirmed evidence of established breeding populations in the wild'.[11] The subject was dropped, in spite of the fact that DEFRA acknowledges 'wild boar may have an impact on many areas, particularly agriculture, animal health, conservation and public safety'.[12]

Meanwhile the area they now occupy is estimated to be between 65 to 125 square kilometres, depending on whom you are talking to.

Lisa Reeve and her husband Franco, increasingly fascinated by the animals, started to track and photograph the local boar, and to learn as much about them as they could.

156

Franco has been given permission to shoot some of the male wild boar – in fact they are not classified as 'game' in this country and are, therefore, what is called 'fair game' – they don't, for example, have a closed season during breeding and it is not an offence to kill a wild boar humanely with a licensed firearm.

Franco guts the boars as soon as they are shot, to prevent taint, hanging them up by their back legs and cutting their throats to bleed them, which takes no more than 10 minutes.

They are then skinned, cut up and the meat roasted or slow-cooked in daubes; they think it is excellent. They are fierce protagonists of the wild boar's continued return to the wild.

Over the last several years Lisa has spent hours up trees watching their activities and has become an expert. She believes (and hopes) that it is unlikely that they can be eliminated now; they are too widely spread and too clever at hiding. She reckons there are several hundred in the area.

She has studied the family groups and regards these boars as totally authentic on the grounds that they have all the traits of the original wild boar, and no domestic pig traits. Other escaped colonies, such as those around Aldington and Ashford, are descended from animals that have been cross-bred with domestic breeds, particularly pot-bellied Vietnamese pigs, to improve their growth rate and meat. Others elsewhere have been crossed with Tamworths to obtain the so-called 'Iron-age pig'. But the East Sussex wild boar have all the traits of genuine, authentic wild boar.

157

Authentic traits

They live in family groups.

They have straight noses and straight tails, which they hold aloft when they run. (Crossbreeds have dished noses and tend to have curly tails.)

They have upright, furry ears and black snouts.

They have long, fairly thin legs. (Cross breeds have shorter, thicker legs.)

Their eye sight is poor but the sense of smell is more acute than that of a dog.

They are lean with about ½ to 1 cm of body fat. (Cross breeds have thicker fat.)

When mature, the males have long lower tusks, which lengthen and curve backwards as they get older.

They have thick fur, particularly on the cape, which lies over the shoulder blades and along the neck.

Their fur is long in winter, with a woolly undercoat, and is greyish brown, darkening with age. They moult in spring and have light summer coats.

They live in matriarchal groups or sounders.

These consist of females and immature males.

The sows often come in season in October or November, the eldest sow in the group comes in season first. Then her sisters and daughters follow.

The mature boars are loners but they turn up to be part of the family in the mating season. They see the younger boars off.

Once mating has taken place, gestation lasts 3 months, 3 weeks and 3 days.

The sow makes a nest where she lies up for about 48 hours to farrow. She gives birth to four to six cream and brown striped, furry, young. After 4–6 days she brings them out into the forest and all the females in the group may suckle each others' young.

Piglets stay with the sow and her group until the following autumn, when the young males, called tegs, are turned away, and form little bands.

The females stay with the mother and eventually have their own families. If groups grow large and the foraging is poor, they move on to new areas.

They are good, strong swimmers and love wet wallows in the mud, which they use to get rid of bugs and mites. The mud also acts as a sun screen, and gives a 'tribal', recognisable smell.

They have scratching trees, which are always pine-trees – the resin helps to act as an insecticide.

They are omnivores, eating acorns and beech mast, mice, lizards, beetles, tubers, roots, bulbs, funghi, insects, young birds, pheasants' eggs and so forth. Susan Adams has seen one of her sows catch and eat a crow, and they will hunt down and eat a wounded or sickly rabbit, pheasant or lamb. They sometimes catch and eat fish.

They love rootling, and will dig up whole areas of pasture or orchard when foraging; they also dig up crops, being particularly fond of apples, maize and potatoes. Travelling in groups of up to 20, they can rapidly cause a lot of damage.

Typical weights of males are 66–68 lbs at 9–10 months, and 135 lbs at 20 months. They may live for up to 35 years and can get very large.

The fur can be brown or dark greyish-brown when young, darkening towards black in an older male. A mature animal will have an outer winter coat about 7–10 cms long, and an inner fluffy layer of insulation; they moult when the weather gets warm, in spring. There are also lighter sports, with pale cream-coloured fur. This could be taken to show hybridisation with domestic or feral pigs (feral pigs are domestic pigs that have escaped to the wild), although Lisa Reeve says it is a naturally occurring sport for wild boars.

But establishing authenticity is never that simple; Martin Goulding, conservation biologist and mammalian ecologist, who has worked solely on free-living wild boar over the last six years, and has recently completed a D.Phil. in wild boar ecology, says that feral pigs – the descendants of escaped domestic pigs – and wild boar in the same area will readily hybridize. So distinguishing hybridized animals from pure bred becomes virtually impossible.

Farmed wild boar, too, can have all the traits of free-living wild boar. They are fascinating to watch, as unlike domestic pigs, they never stay still. The distinct family groups of sows wander about, having spats with the others and with the piglets, who run and jump all over the place like sand-crabs, continuously starting mock fights.

Susan and Neil Adams breed what they consider to be a pure strain of wild boar from Eastern Europe at Brampton Wild Boar, near Beccles in Suffolk. When I went to visit, I could finally see why the wild boar was considered a noble beast and worthy adversary. I found their chief boar, in his winter coat, very impressive; Mordred, son of Arthur, is gigantic, with the curving tusks, thick long coat and bristling mane of legend. He is jet black, has twelve sows and is the father of huge numbers of offspring. His grandfather was DNA-tested by the then Ministry of Agriculture some six years ago, to ensure that he was pure wild boar, and he passed the test, although Martin Goulding casts doubt on this procedure as 'there are no definitive samples of pure-bred wild boar against which unknown samples can be compared.'[13]

The younger animals, although somewhat heavier, resemble the wild boar filmed in the wild in East Sussex, but this mature boar is a different-looking animal altogether. This is partly because of his age, his enormous size and the fact that he has his thick, bristly, black winter coat.

His offspring will be slaughtered at one year old, as they take twice as long to reach a mature size as domestic pigs. Their meat is deep red, and resembles venison or beef. The fat is 1–1½ cms thick and the crackling very thin.

As the animals age, they lay down more layers of fat, like rings in a tree. The outer layer becomes very dense and tough – hard to penetrate with sword or dagger, a thrown spear would simply bounce off – a good reason for his reputation as a fierce adversary. Mordred's owner tells me that when cornered they will attack; one of her sows has the evil eye, and she would bite your throat out if you fell over between her and her food. Mordred himself, although a gigantic animal, is completely tame; he lies down to have his stomach scratched by his owner, and looks totally relaxed in human company.

The Sussex wild boar, on the other hand, avoids human company, but will attack if cornered, while sows with young are extremely protective. But there have been no reports of any attacks. In general they are shy, wary animals and it is hard to see them amongst the dappled shade, so effective is their camouflage in soft brown and grey colours. These are lighter specimens than the farm-fed specimens at the Blue Tile Farm. According to historian Denison Bingham Hull, 'the boar hunted by the Greeks was bigger and more dangerous than those at large today.'[14]

However he adds that they have kept their destructive traits – 'Those confined to zoos have been known to destroy macadam paving in only a few days.'[15]

There is one major difference between the wild East Sussex colonies and the farmed boar – they belong to different sub-species. There are 12 sub-species of the wild boar of Eurasia, *Sus scrofa*. The different regions of Eurasia have different types; *Sus scrofa scrofa* is found in France and as far east as the Carpathians, and a mature male will rarely exceed 120–150 kg, while *Sus scrofa ussuricus*, found in Siberia, Scandinavia

159

and parts of Eastern Europe, can reach up to 300 kg in Russia and 250 kg in Poland. Perhaps the enormous wild boar of ancient Greece were similar to this type.

The diploid chromosome number in the wild boar ranges from 36–38. The French type have 36 chromosomes, while the Eastern European type, have 38 chromosomes; the domestic pig also has 38.[16] They can interbreed, when they will have 36, 37 or 38 chromosomes. Therefore the study of chromosomes has not proved very helpful in differentiating the types.

However we can establish that the Sussex boar, with 36 chromosomes, is definitely the French type *Sus scrofa scrofa*, and the Blue Tile boars are of the Eastern European strain.

In *Sus scrofa scrofa* whether from France or from Sussex, in spite of the fact that they live in the wild, the meat is not very dark and not what you could call 'strong meat', although, when old, it can certainly be tough, with fat that no table knife could possibly penetrate. In contrast, the meat of the farmed Eastern European strain is dark, like venison, and tastes similar to beef, goose or venison, in spite of the fact that, although they are free-range, the farmed boar are enclosed in pens of less than one hectare and fed substantially on pig-nuts. These animals are slaughtered at one year and are very tender.

Martin Goulding, author of *Wild Boar in Britain* told me on the telephone, 'There is no evidence that the Sussex groups are not pure wild boar, but wild boar and domestic pigs have been interbreeding for hundreds if not thousands of years, and some ancestral outbreeding is likely. However if the meat is dark, like venison, it would be indicative that it is authentic, a hybrid meat would be slightly paler and domesticated pig meat is white.'

As to whether they are as fierce as the boars of legend, is also hard to answer, but according to all sources, a fully grown boar or a sow will attack, if cornered, if its food is threatened or if piglets are involved. It is definitely not advisable to let one see you standing alone and unprotected on the ground.

But since the advent of guns, it has become less dangerous to hunt wild boar, as it is no longer necessary to close up on them in the same way. To be alone up a mountain, wielding a hand weapon to protect yourself, is very different to pointing a gun from a distance.

Conclusion

I end up with a paradox: one group of wild boar, members of one of the new breeding colonies now established in the wild in the U.K., are self-reliant, live entirely in the wild, avoid humans, breed randomly and have all the traits of wild boar, but are smaller, occasionally have pale fur and have somewhat paler meat; the other group are larger, blacker and have dark meat and are supposed to be DNA-tested to prove they are a pure strain of wild boar, but are reliant on humans, are fed a partly artificial diet and bred selectively. But Martin Gould maintains that these are no purer than the

160

French type. Which, then, are the authentic wild boar?

Unless there was much exaggeration, the boars of legend were large, fierce and very frightening animals, outdone, as a dangerous adversary, only by the rhinoceros.

The Eastern European boars appear to be more akin to this stereotype and look a little more frightening than the French and what we may call the 'English reintroduction' types. These last may have developed differently over the centuries, according to the conditions they have lived under, such as poor, dry countryside and hotter conditions; a look at a Mediterranean sheep compared with a Northern one will give some idea of what 'environmental plasticity', as it is called, can do.

I want to give Martin Goulding the last word, since he is able to say with some certainty that the original East European type of wild boar, such as the ancestors of those at the Blue Tile Boar Farm, were a heavier sub-species originating in Siberia, *Sus scrofa ussuricus*, differing considerably from the lighter-bodied, but equally authentic, French type, *Sus scrofa scrofa* to which he believes the original British type also belonged, since we once shared the same landmass as France. In this case, he concludes, 'Britain has a melting pot of wild boar of unknown purity and consisting of an unknown number of sub-species.... However, no free-living wild boar in Britain has been reported with any characteristics that could be associated with hybrids.... If you are for their reintroduction, purity is not such an important issue, since they look and behave like wild boar.'[17]

161

Bibliography

Almond, Richard, *Medieval Hunting* (Gloucester, England: Sutton Publishing, 2003).

Berland, Hélène-Marie, Barthelemy, G., Darre, R., *Symposium International Sure le Sanglier, Study on Chromosomes* (Toulouse France, Toulouse University: 1984)..

Berringer, Judith M, *The Hunt in Ancient Greece* (Baltimore and London, John Hopkins University Press, 2001).

Bingham Hull, Denison, *Hounds and Hunting in Ancient Greece* (Chicago: University of Chicago Press, 1964).

Bonnard, André, *Greek Civilisation* , trans A. Lytton Sells (London: George Allen & Unwin, 1958).

Campbell, Joseph, *The Mythic Image* (New Jersey, U.S.A: Princeton University Press, 1974).

Cummins, John, *The Hound and the Hawk, The Art of Medieval Hunting* (London 1988).

Goulding, Martin, *Wild Boar in Britain* (Stowmarket, Suffolk: Whittet Books 2003).

Homer, *The Iliad*, Book xiii, trans E.V. Rieu (Harmondsworth: Penguin Books, 1950).

Homer, *The Odyssey*, Book xix, trans E.V. Rieu (Harmondsworth: Penguin Books, 1950).

House of Commons Questions, June 1997 (www.britishwildboar.org.uk/housecom.htm).

Macdonald, David, ed. *The New Encyclopaedia of Mammals* (Oxford: Oxford University Press, 2001).

Norwak, Ronald M., Paradiso, John L., *Walker's Mammals of the World*, Vol 11 (London: John Hopkins University Press, 1983).

Salvadori, Philippe, *La Chasse Sous l'Ancien Régime* (France: Fayard, 1996).

Thomas, Keith, *Man and the Natural World* (London: Allen Lane,1983).

Notes

1. Berringer, p. 14.
2. Homer, *Odyssey*, p. 306.
3. Homer, *Iliad*, p. 246.
4. Bonnard, p. 133.
5. Salvadori, p. 131.
6. Thomas, p. 143.
7. Cummins, p. 21.
8. Thomas, pp. 200–201.
9. Thomas, p. 202.
10. Thomas, p. 276.
11. House of Commons Questions 3, 17, 23 June 1997.
12. ibid.
13. ibid, p. 96.
14. Bingham Hull, p. 103.
15. Bingham Hull, p. 103.
16. Berland, Barthelemy, & Darre.
17. Goulding, pp. 100–102.

162

The Quest for Reality

Daphne Derven and Christian Banfield

What do a London chef/ex-architect and a Rhode Island Red chicken living in New York have in common? A passion for authenticity in how they live. Both Fergus Henderson and the Rhode Island Red have spent time at Stone Barns as part of their separate quests for authenticity, quality and the real thing. Fergus, a chef, author and thinker, embodies authenticity to us. The chickens in the field are living as real chickens in contrast to most chickens that spend their lives toiling in factories far from sky, worms and grass. At the Symposium we visually explored these on-going and intertwined quests for authenticity.

Most would agree that authenticity, reality and genuineness are synonymous qualities. Many would also agree that these characteristics seem to be harder and harder to find due to the increasing global homogeneity of our plates. For some of us, the search for memorable meals, food grown by someone we know and the chef who celebrates ingredients is a consuming passion. The very elusiveness of authenticity seems to run contrary to the ubiquity of food, and for most the source of food is a mystery. In today's world, animals and vegetables are frequently available only as unrecognizable objects in packages, products of production farming which is basically a factory system focused on efficiency. It is no surprise that most of this food lacks flavor and character, just as fast food has its efficiencies in speed, not in flavor. In this presentation, we combined our narrative with original film and photography, utilizing two iconic figures to explore and celebrate this quest for authenticity.

Our first iconic figure is Fergus Henderson, chef/owner of St John's Restaurant, and St. John's Bread and Wine in London. Fergus is an architect who has become famous for his unwavering commitment to seasonal ingredients, purity of style and quality. His restaurant looks at food in a holistic manner, beginning with the entire animal and proceeding to the plate. His book, *The Whole Beast: Nose to Tail Eating* codified it. Fergus is very particular about his chickens in St. John, and all the food that is served there. His vision has helped create a new awareness among chefs and the public that 'Nose to Tail Eating' is a viable, sustainable way to eat.

Chickens represent our other icon. Stone Barns Center in New York raises Rhode Island Red/White Rock cross laying hens that thrive in six flocks of 100–150 on a daily rotation of pasture. Their eggs have egg flavor, bright orange yolks and a firm white. Chicken that actually tastes like chicken. Chuck Klosterman says: 'I honestly believe that people of my generation despise authenticity, mostly because they're all so envious of it.'[1]

We believe this quest for authenticity; the current human condition and the contrasts between both sides of the Atlantic provide much food for thought.

Bibliography
Henderson, Fergus, *The Whole Beast: Nose to Tail Eating* (New York: Harper Collins, 2004).
Klosterman, Chuck, *Killing Yourself to Live: 85% of a True Story* (New York: Scribner, 2005).

Note
1. Klosterman, p. 103.

164

The Strange Tale of General Tso's Chicken

Fuchsia Dunlop

When, in 2003, I decided to go to Hunan Province in southern China to research the local cuisine, I was unable to do more than the most rudimentary preparation. The only exclusively Hunanese cookery book I could find in English was *Henry Chung's Hunan Style Chinese* Cookbook, written in the 1970s by a Hunanese restaurateur in San Francisco. Even in my own extensive library of Chinese-language books on food and cookery, I could find little information about Hunanese cuisine. But the name of one dish did come up again and again in internet searches and in American Chinese cookery books: General Tso's chicken (*zuo zong tang ji*, 左宗棠鸡). In the eastern United States, this dish seemed to have become virtually synonymous with Hunanese cuisine.

General Tso's chicken is a wok-cooked dish, in which large slices of chicken (usually the dark meat) are battered, deep-fried and then tossed in a sour-sweet sauce laced with dried chillies. The precise constituents of the sauce vary: some recipes include hoisin sauce, some tomato paste. The dish is so popular that it appears not only on the menus of supposedly Hunanese restaurants, but also of more mainstream Chinese establishments.

165

The dish is named after General Zuo Zongtang (alternatively transliterated as Tso Tsung-t'ang), a formidable nineteenth-century general who is said to have enjoyed eating it. Zuo was born in 1812 in Xiangyin County, Hunan Province, and died in 1885 after a glittering career in the Qing Dynasty civil and military administration. He led successful military campaigns against the Taiping rebels, a quasi-Christian sect whose revolt tore China apart in the mid-nineteenth century. He crushed another peasant revolt by the Nian Army, as well as an uprising by Hui Muslims in Northwest China, and is widely famed for recapturing the great western desert region of Xinjiang from rebellious Uyghur Muslims.[1] The Hunanese have a strong military tradition,[2] and General Zuo is one of their best-known historical figures, alongside Zeng Guofan (曾国藩), the founder of the Hunan Army (湘军), and the communist leader Mao Zedong.

A number of Chinese dishes are named in honour of the famous personages who are said to have enjoyed eating them. The Sichuanese dish Gong Bao (or Kung Pao) chicken, for example, is named after Ding Baozhen, a nineteenth-century governor-general of Sichuan who was known as 'Gong Bao'. The Hunanese banquet dish Zu'an shark's fin takes its appellation from the assumed name of the early twentieth-century Nationalist premier and legendary gourmet, Tan Yankai, who developed the recipe with his private chef, Cao Jingchen. More recently, restaurants all over Hunan, and their offshoots in Beijing, Shanghai and other cities, have taking to serving 'The Mao family's red-braised pork' (毛家红烧肉), a favourite of Mao Zedong's. All these dishes appear in regional cookery books and on regional restaurant menus, and their associations with the celebrities are widely known.

Although General Tso's chicken conforms perfectly with this tradition, it is generally accepted to be an American-Chinese invention. Precise accounts of its origins, however, vary widely. In a *Washington Post* article entitled 'Who was General Tso and why are we eating his chicken?', Michael Browning wonders, somewhat fancifully, if Chinese immigrants in the United States gave the chopped chicken dish its name 'from the sliced and diced victims of Tso's grim reprisals' against the rebel armies. He also cites author Eileen Yin-Fei Lo in her book *Chinese Kitchen* as saying that the dish is a Hunan classic called *chung ton gai*, or 'ancestor meeting place chicken'.[3] Eric A. Hochman, in his 'definitive General Tso's chicken page' on the internet, argues that the dish was invented by 'Chef Peng' in his restaurant on East 44th Street, New York, in the 1970s, when Hunanese and Sichuanese food were first introduced to the city.[4] At the end of his article, Browning quotes another Manhattan restaurateur, Michael Tong, who claims that his former partner, 'a gifted Chinese immigrant chef named T.T. Wang', devised the recipe for 'General Tso's chicken, sometimes called General Tsung's chicken or General Tsao's chicken'.[5]

What is clear is that the dish is all but unknown in Hunan itself. When I went to Hunan for the first time in 2003, mention of it drew blank looks from everyone I met. None of the major local cookery books make any reference to it, including, for example, the *Hunan recipe book* edited by the state-owned Hunan Non-Staple Food Company and the Changsha Food and Beverage Company,[6] a recent, authoritative series of Hunan cookbooks published by the Hunan Science and Technology Publishing House, and the complete works of Shi Yinxiang, the leading chef of the older generation.[7] All these cookery books include recipes for a whole canon of classic Hunanese dishes, including Zu'an shark's fin (组庵鱼翅), Dongan Chicken (东安仔鸡) and steamed smoked meats (腊味合蒸), but they make no mention of General Tso's chicken or any dish closely resembling it.

Over the last two years, during which I've spent extended periods in Hunan, I have never seen the dish listed on a restaurant menu, and the only people I've met who have heard of it have been members of a small and interconnected circle of chefs in the provincial capital, Changsha. One of them, the 'celebrity chef' Xu Juyun (许菊云), includes the recipe on a VCD in which he demonstrates nineteen classic Hunanese dishes. Another, the founder of the Hunan branch of the state-run culinary association (*peng ren xie hui* 烹饪协会), Yang Zhangyou (杨张猷), devotes a page to it in *Hunan Cuisine*, one of a series of cookery books on China's 'eight great regional cuisines'. In a postscript to the recipe, he writes 'Legend has it that the famous Qing Dynasty General Zuo Zongtang liked eating chicken cooked in this way... The dish has become enormously popular and widely known, and is still a hallmark dish for many restaurants at home and abroad'.[8] Another leading figure in Changsha food circles, the head of the state-run Changsha Food and Beverage Company and private restaurateur Liu Guochu, says in a book published in 2005: 'Zuo Zongtang's Chicken has been handed down on the fame of his name... Zuo Zongtang loved eating this dish, and it has achieved considerable fame, spread widely, and succeeded in becoming a well-known traditional Hunanese dish.'[9]

These assertions that General Tso's chicken is a traditional Hunanese dish and one that the general himself liked eating do not stand up to any scrutiny. Firstly, if there was any shred of evidence connecting the real Zuo Zongtang with the dish that bears his name, it seems unlikely that this would have disappeared from public awareness. In China, there is an almost cultish interest in connections between famous people and food. Long-established restaurants display calligraphic quotations from political and military celebrities, past and present, who have praised their cooking, and photographs of famous visitors. One Changsha restaurant, Huogongdian, publishes a commemorative album that includes images of fifteen famous figures who have sampled its snacks and dumplings, including Zeng Guofan and Mao Zedong.[10] It would be strikingly out of cultural character for the general Hunanese public to 'forget' a tradition linking the legendary General Zuo with a particular dish. (Contrast the Sichuanese dish Gong Bao chicken, whose name is on the lips of every Chengdu taxi driver.)

Is it possible that General Tso's chicken was simply expunged from the historical record during the political upheavals of the Maoist era? Again, it seems unlikely. It's true that some dishes with imperial or feudal connotations were renamed at the height of the Cultural Revolution. Gong bao chicken, for example, was changed to 'scorched chilli chicken cubes' (糊辣鸡丁), a name that still lingers in an official cookery book published in 1988.[11] An official Hunanese cookery book published in 1976, at the end of the Cultural Revolution, includes what is clearly a recipe for Tan Yankai's 'Zu'an shark's fin', but obscures its connection with a Nationalist official by naming it simply 'shark's fin in clear soup' (清汤鱼翅).[12] However, given that General Zuo was a patriotic military hero of the Qing Dynasty rather than an official on the losing side of the Chinese civil war, it seems improbable that his favourite dishes would have been given the same treatment. In addition, Gong Bao chicken and Zu'an shark's fin have been swiftly rehabilitated since the end of the Cultural Revolution: their political stigmatization was just a passing phase.

If General Tso's chicken was based on some long-lost Hunanese recipe that had recently been rediscovered, it is highly improbable that the influential chefs and food-writers mentioned above would not have reintroduced it to the Hunanese public, given hot competition in the restaurant industry, public interest in dishes with a 'celebrity' connection, and constant demand for new menus and innovative cooking.

The strongest evidence that General Tso's chicken is not traditional lies in the nature of the dish itself. It includes some elements of traditional Hunanese cooking,

167

especially in the combination of hot and sour tastes (in this case given by dried chillies and vinegar). Most recipes for General Tso's chicken, however, include generous amounts of sugar. In particular, the famous Hunanese chef Xu Juyun can be seen adding two heaped spoonfuls of white sugar to the sauce as he demonstrates the dish on his VCD, so the final dish would have a marked sweet-and-sour flavour alongside the spicy taste of the seared chillies. In Sichuanese cookery, this would be unremarkable, as the Sichuanese are known for their complex combinations of flavours, and a tendency to mix sweet, sour and spicy tastes in a single dish.

In Hunanese cookery, however, sugar is generally absent from the mise-en-place of seasonings in restaurants, and rarely added to savoury dishes. The dominant flavours of Hunan are salty, hot and sour; sweetness is very much a supplementary taste, found in a few sweet soups, dumplings, and other sweetmeats that are not eaten at mealtimes. Although some cookbooks include recipes for sweet-and-sour pork, various dishes with sweetened tomato sauces, and tonic soups flavoured with crystal sugar, these dishes are very untypical of what is actually served in local restaurants and homes.

I was led to the real origins of General Tso's chicken during a visit to the Peng Yuan Hunanese restaurant in Taipei, in the autumn of 2004. As I scoured the menu before an interview with the manager, my eye was caught by a dish called, in Chinese, Zuo Zongtang's farmyard chicken (*zuo zong tang tu ji*)[13], and translated as 'Chicken a la Viceroy'. During our interview, the manager of the restaurant, Peng T'ieh-cheng (彭铁诚), told me that his father, Peng Chang-kuei (彭长贵), had created the dish. According to Peng T'ieh-cheng, his father first cooked General Tso's chicken when he was in charge of catering at Taiwanese government functions in the early 1950s. The dish appeared on the menus of national banquets (国宴), including those provided during a visit by the US Admiral Arthur Radford, who went to Taipei on a secret mission in 1955.[14]

Peng Chang-kuei himself, a tall, dignified man now in his eighties, can no longer remember exactly when he first cooked the dish, although he says it was sometime early in the 1950s. 'Zuo Zongtang's chicken did not pre-exist in Hunanese cuisine,' he says, 'deep-frying is not a traditional cooking method, and I used much larger chicken pieces than was normal. Originally the flavour of the dish was typically Hunanese – heavy (*zhong* 重), sour (*suan* 酸), hot (*la* 辣) and salty (*xian* 咸).'[15]

Peng Chang-kuei has one of the finest professional pedigrees of all Hunanese chefs. He was born in 1919 into a poverty-stricken household in the Hunanese capital, Changsha. As a teenager, he argued bitterly with his father and ran away from home. Then, with the help of relatives, he was taken on as an apprentice by Cao Jingshen (曹敬臣), the former private chef of the Nationalist official Tan Yankai, who had opened his own restaurant in Changsha, the Jianleyuan. Peng Chang-kuei was smart and diligent, and soon won the approval of his Master (师傅), who came to treat him like a son.[16]

Tan Yankai (1879-1930) was a highly-educated scholar-official who began his political career in the dying days of the Qing Dynasty, rose through the ranks of the revolutionary Nationalist Party (Kuomintang), and in 1928 became president of the Executive Yuan, a position equivalent to that of premier. He came from a Hunanese family and served several times as governor of Hunan.[17] Although the history books remember him mainly for his political and military activities, in culinary circles he is regarded as the father of modern Hunanese haute cuisine.

Tan Yankai's kitchen was by all accounts a hothouse of culinary innovation. Although Chef Cao was in charge of the practical work in the kitchen, Tan took an active role, issuing precise instructions on how each dish should be cooked, and offering detailed criticisms of the end results.[18] The dishes they created were based on Hunanese tastes, but incorporated influences from eastern Huaiyang cuisine (Cao had previously served in the household of an official from Jiangsu Province), southern Cantonese cuisine (Tan's father had served as a provincial governor in the south), and other places where Tan Yankai had served in office, including Zhejiang, Qingdao, Tianjin and Shanghai. Some famous Hunan banquet dishes are still named after him, including Zu'an shark's fin and Zu'an beancurd.[19]

The late Qing and Republican periods are generally remembered as the heyday of Hunanese cuisine. High officials, like Tan Yankai, hired top chefs to serve in their official residences, and they were imitated by powerful businessmen and merchants. Chefs who had served in the homes of fine-living mandarins opened public restaurants, and ten grand restaurants in Changsha became known as the 'ten pillars'. By the 1930s, the capital Changsha had four celebrity chefs and a number of famous dishes, and there were even said to be four mini-schools of Hunanese cookery, one of them, Zu'an Cuisine (*zu an cai*) derived from the style of cooking developed in the household of Tan Yankai.[20]

After the Japanese invasion of China in the 1930s, Peng Chang-kuei moved to the temporary Nationalist capital in Chongqing, where he won acclaim as a chef in his own right. By the end of the Second World War he was serving as head chef at Nationalist government banquets, and in 1949, after the victory of Mao Zedong's communists in the Chinese civil war, he was part of the great Nationalist flight to Taiwan.[21] At that time, one-and-a-half to two million Chinese people left the Mainland,[22] including the remnants of the Nationalists and their entourages, and others who were rich enough to emigrate. Among them were large numbers of Hunanese who, with their strong military tradition, had had a disproportionate influence on the army, and a number of important chefs from all over China.[23]

The Communist takeover was to have a devastating effect on fine dining on the Chinese Mainland. The 1950s saw political campaigns against private businesses, and then the state takeover of the private sector (including restaurants).[24] By all accounts, this removed incentives for chefs and other staff, and led to a fall in the quality of restaurant cooking. The Great Leap Forward of 1958 was followed by a famine that cost some thirty million lives.[25] In the 1960s and 1970s, the 'Cultural Revolution' provoked an all-out assault on bourgeois culture which further damaged the restaurant industry.[26]

The near-collapse of sophisticated culinary culture tends to be glossed over in Mainland Chinese publications. For example, Liu Guochu's account of the history of Hunanese food has nothing at all to say about the years between the pre-war Republican period and the 1990s (when, he says, Hunan cuisine had 'another great turn for the better'[27]). One unpublished government document on the restaurant industry that was given to me by a local official is more revealing: it mentions that in 1958 (the year of the Great Leap Forward) 'the supply of natural resources was tight and the quality of products declined'. According to the same document, during the Cultural Revolution (1966–1976), 'management [in the restaurant industry] was disturbed, manufacture was simplified, some famous restaurants had their names changed and customers had to serve themselves'; furthermore, the whole sector 'was disrupted, and some of its traditional skills and specialities were attacked'.[28] Aside from hints like these, there are great lacunae in published accounts of food and restaurant culture, often accounting for about half a century between the 1930s and the 1980s.

Oral accounts by chefs and elderly people support the suggestion that the communist period was a disaster for Chinese cookery. Even as late as the mid-1990s, when many larger restaurants remained state-owned, the standards of cooking, decor and hygiene were poor, and many chefs complained of the lack of incentives for workers.[29] It was only after the economic reforms of the 1990s took effect that Mainland food culture embarked on a rapid recovery.

As China was turned upside down by the crazy economic policies of Mao Zedong, and the violent political movements he unleashed, Taiwan experienced an economic boom. Restaurants run by chefs from different regions catered for the homesick Mainland elite, many of whom never accepted that they had left China for good. Different regional cuisines were represented in microcosm on Taiwan, and were inevitably influenced by their neighbours. Junior chefs moved around between different regional restaurants, and there was a constant cross-fertilisation of ideas and techniques. And as the Mainland closed in on itself, the people of Taiwan travelled abroad, and their island republic engaged with the world.[30] It was in this context that Peng Chang-kuei invented General Tso's chicken.

The route to America is very straightforward. In 1973, Peng Chang-kuei went to New York and opened his first restaurant on 44th Street. Despite his great fame in Taiwan, no one in New York had heard of him, and there was little interest in the unfamiliar regional cuisine of Hunan. The restaurant folded, but Peng felt unable to return home and admit his failure. After a period of working for others, he saved enough money to open a small restaurant on 52nd Street that served American-Chinese food, and eventually returned to the original premises on 44th Street, near the United Nations, where he opened Peng's Restaurant (*peng yuan*, 彭园).[31] The place attracted the attention of officials at the UN, and eventually of Henry Kissinger, who was instrumental in promoting Peng Chang-kuei's innovative Hunanese cooking. 'Kissinger visited us every time he was in New York,' says Peng Chang-kuei, 'and we became old friends. It was he who brought Hunanese food to public notice.'[32] In his office in the Peng Yuan restaurant in Taipei, Peng still displays a large, framed black-and-white photograph of Kissinger and himself raising wineglasses on their first meeting.

Peng Chang-kuei, having been taught to cook by one of the most creative and influential Chinese chefs of the twentieth century, was no hidebound traditionalist. Faced with new circumstances and new customers, he worked creatively, inventing new dishes and adapting old ones. 'The original General Tso's chicken was Hunanese in taste, and made without sugar,'[33] he says, 'but when I began cooking for non-Hunanese people in the United States, I altered the recipe. Of course I still love the old flavours, the hot and sour and salty tastes, but people these days don't like them, so I've always had to change and improve my cooking methods.'[34]

In the late 1980s, having made his fortune and earned enough 'face' to go home, Peng sold up and returned to Taipei, where he opened several branches of the Peng Yuan. His New York venture had had an enormous impact. In 1979, an article in the dining out section of the *New York Times* mentioned that Hunanese food had 'won many American devotees' in recent years, and that 'one of the most respected of the Hunanese chefs in New York has been Peng Chang-kwei, owner of Peng's restaurant in Manhattan since 1976'. The reviewer, M.H. Reed, noted that 'some of the most zestful dishes are inventions of Mr Peng, clever interpretations of the Hunanese style', and included General Tso's chicken in a list of recommended dishes.[35]

The fact that General Tso's chicken was not a traditional Hunan dish is further illustrated by the confusion with which another Hunanese restaurateur, Henry W.S. Chung, describes it in his Hunanese cookery book, written just a few years after Peng's restaurant opened in New York. Chung's recipe appears to be a combination of Sichuanese Gong Bao (Kung Pao) chicken and General Tso's chicken. It is entitled 'Kung Pao Diced Chicken', and its introduction claims the dish 'was created during the latter part of the Chin [Qing] Dynasty by the chef of a scholarly Hunanese general, Tso Tsung-tang [Zuo Zongtang].' The introduction also includes an almost certainly spurious anecdote that muddles Zuo Zongtang with the Sichuanese governor-general Ding Baozhen.[36]

Peng Chang-kuei's cooking has been hugely influential in the Chinese diaspora. After the success of Peng's in New York, as one Mainland source rather charmingly puts it, Hunanese restaurants 'sprouted up like spring bamboo shoots after rain'.[37] Not only General Tso's chicken, but also other dishes that he invented, have been widely imitated. In Hong Kong, the popular Superstar restaurant chain offers 'Peng's homestyle beancurd' (彭家豆腐), a dish that appears to be a direct imitation of one

171

on the menu of the Taipei Peng Yuan.[38] Even in London, the Hunan restaurant in Pimlico, until recently the only supposedly Hunan restaurant in the city, has a repertoire that is clearly derived in many respects directly from the Peng Yuan restaurant in Taipei.[39] 'My father has taught generations of Hunan chefs, who have in turn taught their own apprentices,' says Peng T'ieh-cheng.[40]

But if this is a dish created in Taiwan after the end of the civil war, when the doors slammed shut between the island and the Mainland, what is it doing on an otherwise authoritative VCD of traditional Hunan dishes made in Changsha, and why do some leading food-writers there describe it as a traditional Hunanese dish?

After China began to open up to the outside world after the end of the Cultural Revolution, it became possible for Taiwanese exiles to return to their hometowns for the first time in more than thirty years. Peng Chang-kuei returned to Changsha in the spring of 1980, and was reunited with the wife and two children he had left behind at the chaotic end of the civil war. The communist authorities in Changsha lavished him with hospitality during his two-month visit, hoping he would return to live on the Mainland: 'But I was unwilling. Life there was unbelievably bitter and I couldn't get used to it,' he says.[41]

When conditions on the Mainland did improve in the wake of the economic reforms, Peng Chang-kuei returned once more to Changsha, where, in 1990, he opened an upmarket restaurant in the Great Wall Hotel (*chang cheng fan dian*), again called the Peng Yuan. During his sojourn in Changsha, Peng was feted by local chefs and officials, and was also reunited with his old childhood friend, the famous Changsha chef Shi Yinxiang. Yang Zhangyou, the witty and vivacious founder of the Hunan Culinary Association, now in his seventies, remembers all the details. 'I went to the opening of the Peng Yuan with Shi Yinxiang, and Peng Chang-kuei sat with us and all the top chefs. Peng's son from his earlier marriage to a Mainland woman was in charge of running the restaurant. Peng brought over two chefs from Taiwan, and Tso's chicken was one of the dishes on the menu.' Despite its grand beginning, Peng Chang-kuei's Changsha restaurant was not a success, and closed after about two years. 'All the dishes were a bit sweet,' says Yang Zhangyou.

Yang freely admits that General Tso's chicken was invented by Peng Chang-kuei and has no connection with General Zuo Zongtang. 'It was invented *years* after he died,' he told me, 'and although the *legend* is that General Zuo liked chicken cooked in this way, the fact is that we just don't know.'[42]

Although it seems clear that General Tso's chicken was only known in Hunan itself from the early 1990s, some locals still insist that it is a traditional dish. The famous chef Xu Juyun, who knows Peng Chang-kuei, Shi Yinxiang and Yang Zhangyou personally, acknowledges that Peng popularised the dish in the United States, and that the name 'General Tso's chicken' may be a recent invention, but avers that Zuo Zongtang did like chicken flavoured in this way.[43] Xu Juyun's own star apprentice, Wu Tao (吴涛), says she has 'heard of' Peng Chang-kuei, and that Tso's chicken was not invented by him but is a traditional local dish. 'We used to serve it in our restaurant [the famous Youloudong] in the 1990s, but it's no longer on the menu because it's not popular. Hunanese people don't like sweet dishes.'[44] Liu Guochu also maintains that it is a traditional dish, dating back to the late Qing.[45]

The fact that these key figures in the food scene of Hunan have incorporated Tso's chicken into their narrative of local culinary tradition makes it likely that the legend will stick. After all, the Hunanese cookery book edited by Yang Zhangyou and Lin Shide bears the stamp of authority of the Culinary Association of China, Liu Guochu's book is the most detailed, well-written and authoritative account of Hunanese culinary history and culture in print, and Xu Juyun is one of the best-known and most accomplished Hunanese chefs of his generation.

The question that remains is *why* a dish that has been proven unpopular with the Hunanese public and has little affinity with local tastes is now in the process of being reclaimed as part of the local culinary culture. I would suggest that there are a number of possible explanations.

One is related to the opening up of China to the outside world in the last two decades, and the growing international contacts of Hunanese chefs and restaurateurs. The chefs and food-writers mentioned in this article have all travelled abroad. Xu Juyun has visited the United States and been to Taiwan several times;[46] Liu Guochu has also travelled abroad. In 1998, Yang Zhangyou led a Hunanese culinary delegation that included Shi Yinxiang and Xu Juyun to Hong Kong, where they spent 21 days demonstrating Hunanese cookery and networking with Hong Kong chefs. The trip took place amid a blaze of publicity, and among the dishes they demonstrated was General Tso's chicken.[47]

173

The importance of Peng Chang-kuei and the chefs he taught in making Hunanese cuisine known abroad has been outlined above. While China was consumed with its own internal struggles, Taiwan was the source of what in Hong Kong and the United States became known as Hunanese cuisine. And as Yang Zhangyou told me, Tso's chicken appeared in Hong Kong before it was known in Hunan.[48] So when the Changsha culinary delegation went on their promotional trip, it seems likely that the Hong Kong chefs they met would have expected them to be able to cook that famous 'Hunanese' dish, General Tso's chicken. Perhaps it would have seemed senseless to refuse to acknowledge a dish upon which the international reputation of Hunanese cuisine was largely based – especially when very little if anything else was known about Hunanese cuisine. It might also have made the Hunanese delegation appear ignorant in the eyes of their Hong Kong audiences – something that Mainlanders, sensitive at that time to the relative 'backwardness' of their economy, would have been keen to avoid.[49] Xu Juyun's VCD, on which General Tso's chicken appears, is also clearly aimed at a wide audience of Chinese speakers, and Liu Guochu's 2005 book was written mainly for the Taiwan market.[50]

It may be that a kind of cultural embarrassment is another factor in the silent incorporation of General Tso's chicken into the public narrative of Hunanese culinary history. China's 'decade of chaos' in the Cultural Revolution, and the wasted opportunities for economic (not to mention culinary) development are a source of pain and embarrassment for many in China. Perhaps it is simply too hard to acknowledge that the most famous 'Hunanese' dish in the world is the product of the exiled Nationalist society of Taiwan and not of Hunan itself, with all the implications of the relative success of Taiwan's development over the course of the twentieth century. The deliberate adoption of the dish serves to paper over the cracks in China's recent past and helps to create the sense of a continuous history. General Tso's chicken is, perhaps, the tartan of Hunan: historically spurious, but invaluable in the recreation of a Hunanese culinary identity.[51] And perhaps it will eventually lead outsiders into an appreciation of *Hunanese* Hunanese cookery.

Perhaps, too, there's a sense in which Tso's chicken really does belong in the narrative of Hunanese culinary history. After all, Peng Chang-kuei is a Hunanese chef par excellence, not only Hunanese himself but 'descended', according to the old apprentice system, from Cao Jingshen. An 'Album of influential Hunanese figures', published in Beijing in 1993, included mention of only two Hunanese exiles in Taiwan, one of them Peng Chang-kuei – a measure of the great esteem in which he is held in Mainland China.[52] It should also be pointed out that Taiwan is generally regarded on the Mainland as being part of China, so there may not be any great contradiction for food-writers such as Liu Guochu and Yang Zhangyou in including a Taiwan-Hunanese recipe in the repertoire of classic Hunanese dishes. Given the popular view of Taiwan, Peng Chang-kuei's impeccable culinary lineage, and his own strong personal ties with Changsha, why not view General Tso's chicken as a member of the family of Hunanese cuisine?

It's also worth noting that the Chinese economic boom has led to a promiscuous mixing among different culinary regions. People are travelling more, and many regional restaurants are opening branches in other parts of China. At a recent meal in Sichuan, for example, I tasted Sichuanese, Cantonese and Hunanese dishes at the same dinner table; and a recent dinner I attended at a famous old restaurant in Changsha included dishes from Zhejiang Province. This recalls the cross-fertilisation found in Taiwan after 1949, when chefs from different regions suddenly found themselves working in close proximity. As Hunanese cuisine becomes more cosmopolitan and the boundaries blur between it and other regional cuisines, it's not hard to envisage a day when Tso's chicken no longer stands out as incongruous.

Which brings us to the final question: is General Tso's chicken an 'authentic' Hunanese dish? And, from a personal point of view, should I include it in the 'authentic' Hunanese cookery book that I am currently writing? Certainly, attempts by chefs in Hunan to pass it off as a dish of long-standing tradition may seem fraudulent (though in themselves they offer fascinating insights into recent Chinese history), and the connection with Zuo Zongtang is clearly invented.

But, in the end, General Tso's chicken has to be seen as part of the story of Hunanese cuisine. It doesn't tell the same story as the dishes eaten in remote Hunanese villages, where some cooking methods haven't changed for millennia, or as those cooked up in the capital Changsha, which is finding its gastronomic feet again after half a century of confusion, but it seems to me that it is nonetheless equally valid, and a key part of recent culinary history. After all, General Tso's chicken embodies a narrative of the old Chinese apprentice system and the Golden Age of Hunanese cookery; the tragedy of civil war, exile and homesickness; the struggle of the Chinese diaspora to adapt to American society; and in the end the opening up of China and the re-establishment of links between Taiwan and the Mainland.

Besides, any attempt to seek a kind of pure, essentialist Hunanese cookery is stymied by the unavoidable fact that *the* key symbol of the local cuisine is the chilli, a fairly recent Mexican import.[53] If even supposedly 'authentic' Hunanese cookery as practised in households across Hunan is contaminated by Mexican influences, where do we draw the line?

Bibliography

English-language sources

Accinelli, Robert (1996) *Crisis and Commitment*, University of North Carolina Press, Chapel Hill and London.

Becker, Jasper (1996) *Hungry Ghosts*, John Murray, London.

Boorman, Howard L. (ed.) (1970) *Biographical Dictionary of Republican China*, Columbia University Press, New York and London.

Browning, Michael (17 April 2002) 'Who was General Tso and why are we eating his chicken?', *Washington Post*, p. F01.

Chung, Henry W.S. (1978) *Henry Chung's Hunan Style Chinese Cookbook*, Harmony Books, New York.

Gray, Jack (1990) *Rebellions and revolutions*, Oxford University Press, Oxford.

Hobsbawn, Eric and Ranger, Terence (eds.) (1983) *The invention of tradition*, Cambridge University Press, Cambridge, 1983.

Hochman, Eric A., 'The definitive General Tso's chicken page', http://www.echonyc.com/

Hummel, Arthur W. (ed.) (1944) *Eminent Chinese of the Ch'ing period*, United States Government Printing Office, Washington.

Lu Wenfu, *The Gourmet* (美食家), published in English in *Chinese Literature*, Winter 1985.

Reed, M.H. (14 October 1979) 'Keeping the Hunan fires burning', *New York Times*.

Roy, Denny (2003) *Taiwan: a political history*, Cornell University Press, Ithaca and London.

Spence, Jonathan (1990) *In search of modern China*, W.W. Norton, New York.

Yen, Stanley (29 September 2004) 'Taiwan's Global Cuisine', *Sinorama magazine*, Taipei.

Chinese-language sources

成都市饮食公司川菜技术培训研究中心 (1988) 四川菜谱.

火官殿 promotional brochure and matchbox cover album, 2003.

湖南省副食品公司, 长沙市饮食公司(编) (1976) 湖南菜谱, 湖南人民出版社, 长沙.

湖南省副食品公司, 长沙市饮食公司(编) (2002) 湖南菜谱, 湖南科学技术出版社, 长沙.

江玉祥 (2001) '川味杂考', in 川菜文化研究, 四川大学出版社, 成都.

林世德, 杨张猷 (编者) (1997) 湘菜, 华夏出版社, 北京.

刘国初 (编者) (2005) 湘菜盛宴, 岳麓书社, 长沙.

石荫祥 (2001) 湘菜集锦, 湖南科学技术出版社, 长沙.

王兴国, 聂荣华 (编者) (1996) 湖湘文化纵横谈, 湖南大学出版社, 长沙.

潇湘风云人物墨迹画册, 北京燕山出版社, 北京, 1993.

VCD: 许菊云, 许菊云先生湘菜教学专.

Notes

1. See Hummel (1944) p. 762.
2. According to a local saying, an army without Hunanese troops doesn't even count as an army – *wu xiang bu cheng jun* 无湘不成军.
3. Browning, Michael (2002).
4. Hochman, Eric.
5. Browning, op.cit.
6. 湖南省副食品公司, 长沙市饮食公司(编) (2002).
7. 荫祥(2001). Shi Yinxiang was born in Changsha in 1917, and served as head chef at the Hunan provincial guest house, a role in which he supervised the catering for Chairman Mao on his occasional return visits to Hunan, his home province.
8. 林世德, 杨张猷 (编者) (1997) p. 104.
9. 刘国初(编者) p. 102.
10. 'Huo gong dian' promotional brochure and matchbox cover album, 2003. The same restaurant has on museum-like display a fairly ordinary armchair, simply because Chairman Mao sat in it when he dined there in 1958.
11. 成都市饮食公司川菜技术培训研究中心 (1988).
12. 湖南菜谱 (1976) p. 315.
13. 左宗棠土鸡.
14. Interview with Peng T'ieh-cheng, 11 October 2004. While I was in Taipei, I tried to pinpoint the exact date on which General Tso's chicken was first served at national banquets, but although staff at the Grand Hotel in Taipei (which manages such official functions) confirmed that Peng Chang-kuei had worked with them in the 1950s, and showed me a few state banquet menus from the archives, we were not able to find Tso's chicken on any of them, and they said they had no record of whether, or when, the dish was served.
15. Interview with Peng Chang-kuei, 14 October 2004.
16. Interviews with Peng T'ieh-cheng, 11 October 2004, and Peng Chang-kuei, 14 October 2004. See also biographical entry on Peng Chang-kuei in 潇湘风云人物墨迹画册 (p. 347)
17. Boorman (1970) pp. 220-223.
18. Interviews with Peng T'ieh-cheng, 11 October 2004, and Peng Chang-kuei, 14 October 2004. See also 刘国初 (2005) pp. 26-7.
19. Zu'an was Tan Yankai's zi 字, an assumed name taken in early adulthood.
20. 王兴国, 聂荣华 (编者) (1996) , pp. 308-9; 刘国初 (2005) . p5-6.
21. 潇湘风云人物墨迹画册, p.347
22. Roy (2003) p. 76.
23. Interview with Peng T'ieh-cheng, 11 October 2004; see also Yen (2004).
24. Gray (1990), Spence (1990).
25. Generally-agreed estimate, see Becker (1996).
26. For a fictionalised account of the effects of China's political upheavals on the culture of food and dining out, see Lu Wenfu, *The Gourmet*.
27. 刘国初 (2005) p. 6
28. The same document mentions that a famous noodle restaurant which was founded in 1883, the *gan chang shun* 甘长顺 was renamed 'The East Noodle Restaurant' at the start of the Cultural Revolution; and that the signboard of another restaurant, the *he ji fen guan* 和记粉馆, was 'smashed'

during the same period, after which it was renamed 'The present is superior to the past' (*jin sheng xi* 今胜昔).

29. Personal observations in the Sichuanese capital, Chengdu.

30. See Yen (2004). Yen says the flight of the Nationalists to Taiwan 'brought about an important revolution in Chinese food. As a result of this huge migration, independent chefs from all the different provinces were now gathered in Taiwan, and they left the households of the wealthy and came out into the marketplace… Taiwan cuisine went through a period of study, when it was absorbing the advantages of various Chinese regional cuisines.. This represents an even bigger revolution than the one that occurred after the southward migration during the Song Dynasty [1127–1279], when the wealthy all moved to Hangzhou and developed 'northern cooking with southern ingredients'.'

31. Interview with Peng T'ieh-cheng, 11 October 2004.

32. Interview with Peng Chang-kuei, 14 October 2004.

33. The dish, as it is still served in the Taipei Peng Yuan, is not sweetened with sugar. It has a deep, salty, sour, garlicky taste, with a gentle kick of scorched chilli. The glossy sauce clings deliciously to the large, crisp slices of chicken.

34. Interview with Peng Chang-kuei, 14 October 2004.

35. Reed (1979).

36. Chung (1978) p. 66.

37. 潇湘风云人物墨迹画册, p. 347

38. Superstar menu, seen in Hong Kong in October 2004.

39. It is the only place in London, to my knowledge, to serve a version of Peng Chang-kuei's minced chicken, pork and game soup served in a bamboo tube, and it also offers minced chicken in lettuce leaf cups (a variation of a prawn recipe Mr Peng invented in New York). The manager of Hunan, another Mr Peng, says he learnt to cook from 'a Hunanese master chef in Taiwan'.

40. Interview with Peng T'ieh-cheng, 11 October 2004

41. Interview with Peng Chang-kuei, 14 October 2004.

42. Interviews with Yang Zhangyou in Changsha, 12 and 16 April 2005.

43. Interview with Xu Juyun in Changsha, 12 April 2005.

44. Interview with Wu Tao in Changsha, 12 April 2005. I ate General Zuo's chicken in Hunan Province for the first time in April 2005, as part of a dinner at Yuloudong with Yang Zhangyou. It was not on the menu, but Mr Yang discovered that one young chef knew the recipe – he had learnt it, he said, from Xu Juyun. The dish he made was delicious, but, in its sweetness, very un-Hunanese. 'This tastes just the way it did in Peng Chang-kuei's restaurant,' said Yang Zhangyou.

45. Interview in Changsha 16 April 2005.

46. Interview with Xu Juyun in Changsha, 12 April 2005.

47. Interview with Yang Zhangyou in Changsha 12 April 2005.

48. Interview in Changsha 16 April 2005.

49. Presumably this is also what induced Henry Chung (1978) to include allusions to General Tso's chicken in his Hunanese cookery book, even though he was clearly unfamiliar with the Peng Chang-kuei recipe.

50. Personal communication from Liu Guochu. Taiwanese readers would, of course, very likely have encountered the dish through the fame of Peng Chang-kuei and his restaurants.

51. See chapter by Hugh Trevor-Roper in Hobsbawn and Ranger (eds.) (1983).

52. 潇湘风云人物墨迹画册 p. 347. Peng T'iehcheng pointed out that only two Taiwanese exiles were included in the book.

53. I haven't seen any research that precisely identifies when the chilli came into widespread use in Hunan, but Professor Jiang Yuxiang of Sichuan University suggests that it was first popular in the lower Yangtze region in the mid-eighteenth century, and commonly cultivated in Sichuan in the early nineteenth century. It is tempting to suppose that the chilli entered Hunanese cookery sometime between these dates. See 江玉祥 (2001).

Is it the Real Thing™?
Lidwina of Schiedam, Chocolate Eclairs, and GM Cornbread

James G. Ferguson, Jr.

As teacher of the honors seminar in Food and Culture (aka Eats 101) at The University of North Carolina at Chapel Hill, I admonish my students at the outset that, among other things, this highly idiosyncratic and gruelling course is preoccupied with 'how we know what we know'. Satisfactorily meeting this challenge demands satisfying the rule of Occam's Razor and thus illumines the path we are following this year at the Oxford Symposium. Few topics are more vexing and intriguing for one professionally preoccupied with studying judgment than 'authenticity'. Once past the etymological trace in the Merriam-Webster 11th Collegiate Dictionary to Middle English autentik, the interpretive ground is littered with terms variously implicating 'falseness', 'imitation', and 'actuality'. Nowhere, however, is there mention of how such attributes are determined or defined. Rather, they are, *ipso facto*, simply assumed to be. Hence the problem for judgment – what is an 'authentic' croissant, for example, against which others can be judged? Is there an undiscovered template from Plato's bakery?

Among other requirements in our seminar are responses to the readings assigned for the week. I think the excerpt by Michael Jerch from this spring's program at the University of Burgundy in Dijon helps to illuminate the problem before us.

A friend recently told me an anecdote about a time when after purchasing a baguette at the nearby Epicerie de Gaulois she was accosted by an older man who chastised her for buying bread made in a machine. It wasn't a flute from an enormous department store or even one from a local miniature grocery shop. It was a piece of French bread purchased from a Frenchman, with French money, at a French establishment. Apparently, however, those conditions were not enough to ensure French authenticity. The man could not have possibly been old enough to have been around at the time when bread in this style was made by hand from local ingredients, but he maintains that connection as sternly as if he were.

As I sat contemplating 'authenticity' over a 'double expresso' [sic] at Café de Flore on Boulevard St. Germain some months ago, a serendipitous event played directly into my hands as the pastry case was being charged with onctueux temptations for the luncheon faithful. Any pâtissier/ière worth his/her Beurre de Normandie knows that an éclair's glaçage holds the key to the flavor of the crème waiting within. But what's this… someone had ordered chocolat et sacré bleu, the crème patissière within, while no doubt delicious, was… vanille. In this instance, at least, the 'outward and visible sign' proved untrustworthy. In Clyde Coombs's psychophysical terms, the 'mapping rule' by which one moves to and from the observed to the hypothesized had been violated. 'So what', one might mutter, 'it's simply an éclair. It was probably a tourist who wouldn't know the difference'. But what if the difference mattered? What if, for example, it were a matter of life or death?

My students get more than a passing fair exposure to medieval studies, both to ground them in the antecedents to some contemporary food practices and to furnish a potential hermeneutic path to unpacking anorexia and bulimia. Caroline Walker Bynum's *Holy Feast and Holy Fast* remains a comprehensive landmark source in the field in part due to the thoughtful and careful way in which she deals with what we would call disordered eating behavior. Nested in this topic, moreover, is a concern of literally life and death – which is perhaps closer to us than its date might imply. Bynum gives considerable attention to Lidwina of Schiedam (1380–1433) for a rather extraordinary array of pietistic behaviors, among which was her relationship to the eucharist. As Bynum notes,

> The eucharist was at the core of her devotion… Her biographers emphasize that during this period [her final years], only the holy food kept her alive.

For our purposes a particular episode underscores the epistemological quandary which in my view, noted above, frames this year's conference, how do we know what we know?

Again, Bynum:

> For much of her life she was embroiled in conflict with the local clergy over her eucharistic visions and hunger. One incident in particular… the way in which a woman's craving for the host, although it kept her under the control of the clergy, could seem to that same clergy a threat – both because it criticized their behavior and because if thwarted, it could bypass their power. Once an angel came to Lidwina and warned her that the next day the priest would bring her an unconsecrated host to test her. Then the priest came and pretended to adore the host, but Lidwina, when she received it, vomited it out, declaring that she could easily tell the Lord's body from unconsecrated bread. The priest swore that the host was consecrated, however, and returned angrily to the church.

Farfetched dusty medieval history? Fast-forward to 28 May 2005 and the hamlet of Uxeau in *la Bourgogne profonde*. Our class was on a field trip to archaeologist colleague and longtime Eats 101 contributor Carole Crumley's research site to visit one of her excavations, hear of her current work in the impact of climate change on agriculture (including some vivid images from the summer of 2003), and to tour two artisanal farms, one devoted to raising goats (for cheese making) and the other iconic Charolais cattle – the *usines de viande* upon which much of the regional economy rests. As our genial farmer/hostess led us around the barns and pastures under a perfect *agence de voyages* blue sky, two of my students, Mary Archer and Brian Sykora (whose research papers respectively concerned Mad Cow Disease (BSE) and the EU and agricultural policy), and I drew closer while she explained the quotidian rhythms of the sturdy white animals which dotted the landscape.

Gesturing expansively toward the pastures, she pointed out that 'most' of the cattle's feed came from grazing, but that nearer to the time they are taken to the market, she said 'we add this to their diet to improve the flavor and texture of the meat.' As she talked, she ran her fingers through a handful of a pelletized mixture which, she explained, was made of three or four grains, of which soy was an important constituent. She added that the supplement came from the United States and had been completely approved by the French government for such use. Brian turned aside to me and said *sotto voce*, 'Jim, you know that must contain GM grain – it's almost impossible to avoid it in the States.' Mary added a similar comment, musing about what else the feed might contain with a possible link to BSE.

As I thought of the *affiches* all around the wonderful *boucheries* at Dijon's *les halles* proclaiming 'pure' Charolais beef, I also thought of Barber's point in *Jihad vs. McWorld* that control of rhetoric in a globalizing world is more important than the control of a concrete resource because rhetoric is a resource. What would Lidwina have done? (The second confirmed case of BSE in the United States has just been acknowledged by the FDA. The revision was due to a delay by the FDA as well as reanalysis of the data by a British laboratory equipped with more sophisticated methodology.)

Suddenly our enquiry becomes more nuanced. Is it 'authentic' beef? Of course. Is it Charolais beef? *'Mais oui, monsieur'.* Is it 'authentic' Charolais beef? *'Ça dépend'.* In fact, Charolais cattle were raised on the second farm we visited. These animals were fed entirely on grass and hay cultivated *in situ*, and it would have been interesting to have posed the question to our two farmers as to which one was raising the more 'authentic' Charolais and to note the criteria they might have invoked. Now, however, our concern has become more complex than Lidwina's and that of the Café de Flore éclair eater. No longer solely a semiotic issue based on observing the mapping rule between a signifier and an internal or 'real' state, the thicket of complications athwart our path is composed of at least three hypothetically separable but nonetheless interrelated strands of the authenticity tangle. First, there is the matter of 'naturally' fed beef versus beef fed with supplements. Second, how does the highly probable presence of genetically modified soy products (and the spectre of potential BSE carrying material, depending on the supplier) affect the designation of something as 'safe' for human consumption by virtue of its 'authentic' status according to accepted Charolais criteria? Finally, for the diner, whether at Troisgros for the Château Fleuri or la Maison de quelque chose for a *steak frites*, do the taste and texture differ, holding other things constant as best as one can? Does it taste like the 'real thing'?

180

Now we confront the thorniest question of all – what is the 'real thing'? In the case of Coca-Cola™, this is more a creature of Madison Avenue advertising than it is some rigorous replication of Dr. Pemberton's original formula in an Atlanta pharmacy. Indeed, cognoscenti know that the key ingredient whose name 'Coke' still bears was eliminated decades ago. Historians among us are concerned with locating the first recorded instance of a thing or a technique, for which we are increasingly indebted to our archaeological colleagues. Thus, the appearance of complex cooking utensils, techniques, and ingredients has been recently pushed back to 3200 BCE. in the Middle Babylonian Kingdom. However, one must pose the question as to whether the earliest appearance or recording of something constitutes sufficient evidence for authenticity, i.e., is the first thing the real thing or simply the first thing? I argue it is the latter, that we must look elsewhere for evidence of authenticity. Further down in the Merriam-Webster authenticity entry is this – 'it can also stress painstaking or faithful imitation of an original'. At this point, two divergent paths appear, one leading toward discovering the 'original', the second to defining and locating a 'faithful imitation'. Indeed each intersects and redirects the other. For example, those of us interested in the Cistercian monastic 'order's' role as a medieval template for agribusiness had our apple carts overturned recently by Constance Berman's *Cistercian Evolution* in which she notes, after reciting the conventional wisdom about the 'apostolic gestation' of nearly 2,700 monasteries and convents,

> This is not how the Cistercian Order began. Early twelfth-century Cistercians were at first simply the monks of a single house called Cîteaux. Later they became a small congregation in Burgundy. Later traditions would date an enormous expansion of the Order to the 1130s and 1140s, but many of the houses counted for those decades were still pre-Cistercian or proto-Cistercian after mid-century... We have no evidence of a Cistercian Order as an administrative institution that attempted to enforce specific practices on member abbeys until after the death of Bernard of Clairvaux in 1153. Indeed, only gradually in the 1150s and 1160s were the first steps taken to create such an institution after pre-Cistercian reform communities began to adopt the Cistercian *ordo* as a way of life.

Why does it matter? Listen to the redoubtable Hugh Johnson:

> By the death (and canonization) of St. Bernard in 1153, he and his colleagues had founded some 400 abbeys, and filled his own abbey of Clairvaux with 700 monks. A century later, there were almost 2,000 Cistercian monasteries and 1,400 nunneries across the length and breadth of Europe.

Alas, Michael Novak runs equally amok:

The Cistercians, who eschewed the aristocratic and sedentary ways of the Benedictines and consequently broke farther away from feudalism, became famous as entrepreneurs.... Their monasteries 'were the most economically effective units that had ever existed in Europe, and perhaps in the world, before that time,' Mr. Gimpel writes.

How do we know what we know? Go to the Dijon archives and research original documents in Latin as Berman did. Although judgment contours both the 'original' and 'faithful imitation' trajectories, I think the latter most widely engages the attention of food and culture studies.

Be it about philosophy, eating disorders, connoisseurship and food criticism, or research methodology, Eats 101 students cannot escape immersion in the topic of judgment. Early on in the semester they confront a scrap of writing I did for a class with philosopher/colleague, close friend, and long-time Eats 101 contributor, Ruel Tyson, in which I try to capture some of the pitfalls of the judgment process – determining authenticity is anything but linear. The wide-ranging narrative takes the students many places, among which the Tour d'Argent at which 'our hero' Ruel (nephew of none other than Marvin Shanken, publisher of the *Wine Spectator*) encounters the ravishingly beautiful Alicia Asch, formidable wine connoisseur and employee of the *Wine Spectator*. The Shankens have flown to Paris for two reasons – to give Uncle Marvin a chance to assess Ruel's progress in oenology after six weeks intensive study with Robert Parker and to introduce Alicia and Ruel. Here is a clip as they select three 1985 red Burgundies from Tour d'Argent's nearly bottomless *cave*:

182

The table grew quiet as contemplation of luxuriant possibilities encountered remembrances. Uncle Marvin made his choice in a matter of a minute or two and waited graciously as you and Alicia were in earnest consultation. Then, choices made, he asked that each commit them to paper so there would be no undue influence. Let's listen in...

Uncle Marvin: Starting with the last selection, I have Henri Jayer's Echézeaux. It has just the voluptuous body and strength to pair with the acidity in the final sauce. Lots of leather and tobacco in the bouquet.

Alicia: That's precisely the one we selected. Robert Parker said it was rare among red Burgundies for its explosive richness.

You: This is a good omen. Let me go first on the second one. Alicia and I selected Mme Bize-Leroy's Nuits St. Georges 1er Cru. I remember tasting it in a lab section in Dijon, and it was spectacular. I believe Parker said he was 'blown away' by it.

Uncle Marvin: Perfect choice. Mr. Parker was not the only one to take note of it, the *Wine Spectator* made a very strong buy recommendation. You learned a great deal in Dijon. I'm impressed. I selected a Chambolle-Musigny for the opener. What did you two select?

Alicia: We did, too. Again Mme Leroy. Her reputation is so strong.

You: I voted for Chambolle-Musigny as well, but Ponsot's Les Charmes. Alicia won me over, however. What grower did you select?

Uncle Marvin: Actually, the same one as you did. I remembered that Parker said Mme Leroy's Chambolle-Musigny was 'bland,' which corresponded to my own memories, whereas the Ponsot is stupendous. I think we should get the Ponsot, but remember, the Leroy would not have been bilge. We are dealing with entries at the upper end of the reference scale – the area of 'delicious complications'.

I plead *mea culpa* to stacking the deck in this scenario with many of the preeminent powerful blue meanies which haunt the judgment process. Performance anxiety, impression formation, halo effects, reference scales, and status differentials are among the usual suspects represented, but I want to draw attention to an aspect of connoisseurship whose generality is not implicit in the excerpt – sensitivity to small differences. This ability which undergirds connoisseurship is a sine qua non for determining authenticity. Uncorrelated with the monetary value of the objects or situations being evaluated, connoisseurship is not the exclusive province of those choosing from among 1985 Burgundies at Tour d'Argent – rather it is the domain of the observant and experienced.

If one were to aggregate all the countries visited by this year's Oxford attendees, I suspect few would be left unvisited, and at our conference noshing-intervals we are no doubt regaling each other with tales of discovering the latest gastronomical watering hole. Once back home, however, I imagine there is another type of watering hole that beckons us all—one that keeps some sort of flame of authenticity. It may be as localized as Roast Chicken and Shoestring Fries at Judy Rodgers' Zuni Market Café in San Francisco – hence the 'original' – which poses one sort of task for our authenticity sleuth. Or the watering hole may be one of a vast number of variously affiliated or unaffiliated regional establishments sharing a coherently codified culinary tradition. Complications now abound for the authenticity squad in that its task is informed by the parameters noted by Graham Ward in discussing food and religious ritual:

The Jewish food proscriptions create and patrol ancient Israel's cultural boundaries, they establish and maintain a certain order of creation against its potential contravention.

For an admittedly adopted American southerner it is an easy segue to our regional cuisine as a case for study. Indeed, through enduring and thorough survey work, eminent sociologist and colleague John Shelton Reed maintains 'southernness' is tantamount to 'ethnicity'. There are 'boundaries' to 'patrol' and 'potential contraventions' to worry about, but how are we to study them? How do we represent these practices? In *Philosophical Investigations*, Wittgenstein devotes much of his attention to the 'language games' we play – of which this symposium is an example. Citing the ultimate limitation of language as a comprehensive descriptor, he argues for the need of 'friction… the rough ground [of experience]' to gain genuine understanding. So, do we study American southern cuisine by poring over cookbooks or by engaging the 'rough ground?' How do we best locate and patrol the boundaries? One answer appeared in spring 2004 via an excellent research paper on politics and barbecue by emerging professional journalist and Eats 101 XII student, Debra McCown, who is currently finishing her Study Abroad semester in Mongolia – studying and writing about barbecue. She notes in her introduction:

Barbecue, of course, is different things to different people. Depending on the region, barbecue can be pork, beef, chicken, fish, mutton, or just about any other meat. Sauces vary widely, as do use of smoke, cooking times, and what sort of pit the barbecue is cooked in.

The common thread among all of these barbecue traditions, however, is the traditional method of slow cooking over wood coals. Many barbecue pit masters still take pride in the long, slow method that they believe both produces a superior product and resonates with important cultural values.

Today, many barbecue restaurants use gas or electric cookers, which produce barbecue with all of the characteristics of the traditional method except for the smoky flavor that comes from using wood. Allowing for this to be called 'real' barbecue (though many would dispute such an assertion), barbecue is simply meat that is cooked for a long time at a low temperature. This method of cooking keeps the meat tender and allows for the seasonings to permeate it, giving it a unique flavor. These seasonings exist in several different forms: rubs, which are put onto the meat before it is cooked; basting sauces, which are used while the meat is cooking; sauces used for seasoning the barbecue after it is pulled and/or chopped; and dipping sauces.

Most good barbecue guides divide the South into seven distinct barbecue regions, each with its own ideas about what constitutes barbecue and what food and beverages should be served with it. These differences provide the basis for never-ending arguments about what constitutes 'real' barbecue, but while grilling (which is not the same thing as barbecue) is a phenomenon that spans America, barbecue remains a Southern regional concept.

The paper continues with a detailed summary of regional variations on the barbecue theme—always within the 'boundaries' – and concludes with historical and political scientific perspectives on the traditional relationship between barbecue events and the ballot box. Three points about authenticity from her work inform our concern here at Oxford. Phenomenally, barbecue occasions are a statement in which barbecue as a food becomes a metasymbol for cultural boundaries and thus inclusion or exclusion. Participation and enjoyment are essential to orthodox southern identity. Per Ward,

> [Such] rituals are, then, about the creation and control of experience. They perform a cultural identity and a cultural ideology; they are a means of consolidating a community and articulating its value system.

At a more microscopic level the food consumed comes under scrutiny for compliance with various stated or implied canons about accompaniments, sauces, cooking methods, sliced versus chopped meat, pork versus other meats, provoking lively and typically unresolved debates – excursions into connoisseurship over items typically costing less than $10/€7/£6. Finally, without barbecue, a southern political occasion is not authentic, as European leaders assembled by President Jimmy Carter discovered to their surprise and some even to their delight. Debra notes that politics and barbecue have been intertwined in the United States since the 1600s.

The ancient association between politics and food, however, foreshadows the darker side of our contemporary preoccupation with authenticity. Organized religion has been involved from the beginning – the Levitical dietary codes provide ample and clear opportunities for orthodoxy boundary 'patrol', as does the Quran. Historians Constance Berman and Constance Bouchard have amply documented the intricate interconnection in medieval France between Roman Catholic monasticism, political power, and agriculture. The Carolingian period saw an important politically based change in food access as hunting rights in the forests previously enjoyed by peasants and nobles alike were restricted to nobles, thus limiting (but not eliminating) access to protein sources. Indeed it is only after the Black Death (1348–50) that dietary patterns for peasants begin to seriously deteriorate. Bober notes the considerable influence beginning in the 10th century of the Medical School of Salerno whose dietary regimes influenced courts throughout Europe well into the 15th century, thus in a sense intertwining politics and the study of nutrition. We could devote our entire session to this complex entwinement, but I turn now to what we might call concern for antiseptic, or perhaps even survival, authenticity – the stuff of which Eric Schlosser and Marion Nestle write in *Fast Food Nation* and *Food Politics*, respectively.

Returning to judgment, let us make the operational assumption that we can judge something according to some criteria of authenticity, one of which might be loosely defined as nutritional value or safety for consumption. In addition, let us assume the 'average American consumer,' who probably would give Thomas Jefferson pause.

185

Before we contour the task, let us consider the required assumptions. First, there is an object/experience to be selected for assessment as to authenticity. Also we want to assume some sort of 'rational' choice. Note this is not the dispassionate, perhaps untenable, Cartesian process, but rather a procedure wherein, as noted by neuropsychologist Antonio Damasio, there are 'somatic markers' conditioning the weighing of alternatives. The personal consequences of a choice are anticipated and impact the weighing of other 'objective' attributes associated with that being chosen – the judge is assumed to be capable of projecting some future state which will change as a function of the choice to be made. In addition the choice is assumed to be at once a choice and informed – it is neither simply throwing darts nor is it controlled by some algorithm as 'I always choose chocolate on Mondays.' But how does our judge know what he knows? Who or what 'informs' the choice? 'Aye, there's the rub.' Discussing the sources of information for judgment, Hannah Arendt writes,

> Facts inform opinions, and opinions, inspired by different interests and passions, can differ widely and still be legitimate as long as they respect factual truth. Freedom of opinion is a farce unless factual information is guaranteed and the facts themselves are not in dispute. In other words, factual truth informs political thought just as rational truth informs philosophical speculation.

186

Let us join our consumer/judge in front of the dairy case at the local Whole Foods/Stop & Shop/Carrefour et alia. 'Somewhere' our subject read or heard 'something' about the potential benefits of soy-based 'milk' products. Then there were those television commercials for cow's milk that showed Bill Clinton and Bob Dole urging people to 'Vote: Strengthen America's Backbone' and Larry King saying 'Listen to the King and drink up, America' – just as Alicia urged Ruel to choose the 1985 Ponsot's Les Charmes. How could anyone question such publicity – aren't these 'facts'? After all, milk is the all-American authentic health beverage, i.e. as the Sealtest commercial said, 'You never outgrow your need for milk.' In a thorough research paper for Eats 101 XII, Hilary Lundquist (whose father works for Land O'Lakes) fairly demolished the myth that cow's milk is a majority beverage in the United States and elsewhere, asserting that 'lactose intolerance' is the dominant rather than minority reaction. More to our point, however, is her documentation of milk promoters' covert and powerful ties to Washington.

The main lobbyist groups, the National Milk Producers Federation (NMPF) and the International Dairy Foods Association (IDFA), invest considerable energy and capital so that Capitol Hill policies reflect the interests of American dairy farmers. Interestingly, the dairy lobby's opposition to Richard Nixon's proposed cut in price supports led to its involvement in the Watergate scandal. By laundering funds totaling $2 million to Nixon's re-election campaign, lobbyists successfully maintained price supports. The dairy lobby influenced considerable policy during the Carter administration as well. In fact, the $1.3 million disbursed by the dairy lobby to political candidates in the 1976 election was the second-highest special interest group to the American Medical Association, surpassing the lobbies representing labor, oil, gas, education, maritime unions, and the United Auto Workers. In 1983, Congress responded to declining dairy popularity by enacting the Dairy Production Stabilization Act. This act established a National Dairy Promotion and Research Board with the express purpose of 'dairy product promotion, research, and nutrition education as part of a comprehensive strategy to increase human consumption of milk and dairy products.' A mandatory 15 cents per hundredweight (100 pounds, or 11.63 gallons) of fluid milk produced within the contiguous 48 states and marketed commercially provides funding for ongoing programs in this legislation. The National Dairy Promotion and Research Board (together called simply the Dairy Board) utilizes its substantial budget ($84.7 million in 2001) to boost the public's perception of milk. While all promotions can present a biased and potentially erroneous perspective, the Dairy Board has been very pleased by the broad acceptance of its marketing efforts.

Marion Nestle emphasizes this point by demonstrating that the Dairy Board lobbied successfully to modify significantly the FDA's 2000 food pyramid.

> Bossy and Elsie are not culprits in this scenario as they simply are doing what comes naturally, however not far from their pastures and feed troughs can be found corn – the source of one of the 20th century's most insidious nutrition developments. The all-American sine qua non of July Fourth feasts, grits, cornbread, 'liquid corn', and now ethanol indeed has a chequered past. UNC-Chapel Hill anthropologist Clark Larsen has data from Native American burial mounds of Saint Catherines Island dating back three millennia. Located off the coast of Georgia, these early inhabitants became agriculturists circa A.D. 1150, at which time they began growing corn. Discussing Larsen's work, Susan Allport notes the appearance of 'periostitis, an inflammatory response to a long-term infection that had eventually spread into the bones.' Further, the incidence rose from 'four and one half percent... to fifteen percent... soon after the advent of agriculture.' Most pronounced are the changes in teeth, especially the incidence of cavities. She writes, 'before farming, only about ten percent... had cavities; after farming sixty percent did.'

187

She concludes, quoting Larsen,

> These people [hunter-gatherers] didn't have cavities; they didn't have overbites; they didn't have crooked teeth. We see these things developing because of the change in the diet and the way food was prepared. Corn had to be ground and cooked to be digestible, and soft sweet foods stick to the teeth.

John Groopman, Chair of Environmental Health Sciences at Johns Hopkins School of Public Health and Professor of Oncology at Johns Hopkins School of Medicine, is a guest lecturer in Eats 101. Chief among the horrors he highlights for the class is the alarming obesity trend in the American population. Indeed tables now show data not available at the 2003 Symposium. Is there a single culprit? No, as it is an environmentally and demographically complex causal matrix. Are there some usual food suspects? There are, but chief among them appears to be high fructose corn syrup. Formerly the exclusive stealth weapon of the carbonated beverage industry, it now cuts a wide swath across the culinary landscape, touching such seemingly innocuous items as nonfat frozen yogurt and the flavored syrups (often made in France) at your local espresso bar. Health implications are alarming as consuming this 'sugar substitute' tricks the body into thinking it has received an energy boost, only to trigger a hunger sensation as the sugar is metabolized – even though the body needs no more calories. Because high fructose syrup is more concentrated and tastes sweeter, habitual consumption elevates the threshold at which 'sweetness' cravings are satisfied, thus one consumes more high fructose containing foods, often with high saturated fat and high carbohydrate accompaniments. The movie *Supersize Me* caricatured such behavior *in extremis*, but this from Marion Nestle does not:

188

> Rates of obesity are so high among American children that many exhibit metabolic abnormalities formerly seen only in adults. The high blood sugar due to 'adult onset' (insulin-resistant type 2) diabetes, the high blood cholesterol, and the high blood pressure now observed in younger and younger children constitute a national scandal.

Moreover, recent research by Bray et al and Basciano et al unequivocally implicates high fructose corn syrup in the dramatic rise of both obesity (U.S.) and type 2 diabetes, respectively, since the 1960s.

Julia Child decried the 'fear of food' she saw overtaking the culinary domain as we became obsessed with avoiding anything the 'fat police' deemed the least bit naughty. Instead she exhorted us to revel in the sensual pleasures of preparing and consuming 'real' food. Now a genuine 'fear' stalks the land as the authenticity sleuth must ponder whether the Real Thing™ is even safe. 'All is not as it seems.'

References

Allport, Susan, *The Primal Feast* (New York: Harmony Books, 2000).

Arendt, Hannah, as quoted by Maurizio d'Entrèves in 'Arendt's Theory of Judgment'. In *The Cambridge Companion to Hannah Arendt*, Dana Villa, ed., pp. 245–60 (Cambridge: Cambridge University Press, 2000).

Barber, Benjamin R., *Jihad vs. McWorld* (New York: Random House, 1995).

Basciano, H., Federico, L., and Adeli, Khosrow, 'Fructose, insulin resistance, and metabolic dyslipidemia', *Nutrition and Metabolism*, 2005; 2:5.

Berman, Constance H., *The Cistercian Evolution* (Philadelphia: University of Pennsylvania Press, 2000).

——, *Medieval Agriculture, the Southern-French Countryside, and the Early Cistercians: A Study of Forty-Three Monasteries*. Transactions of the American Philosophical Society 76, 5 (Philadelphia: American Philosophical Society, 1986).

Bober, Phyllis P., 'Late Gothic International Style', in *Art, Culture & Cuisine – Ancient & Medieval Gastronomy* (Chicago: University of Chicago Press, 1999), pp. 219–66.

Bouchard, Constance B., *Holy Entrepreneurs: Cistercians, Knights, and Economic Exchange in Twelfth-Century Burgundy* (Ithaca: Cornell University Press, 1991).

Bray, G.A., Nielsen, S.J., and Popkin, B.M., 'Consumption of high-fructose corn syrup beverages may play a role in the epidemic of obesity', *American Journal of Clinical Nutrition*, 2004; 79: 537.43.

Bynum, Caroline W., *Holy Feast and Holy Fast* (Berkeley: University of California Press, 1987).

Coombs, Clyde H., *A Theory of Data* (New York: John Wiley, 1964).

Damasio, Antonio R., *Descartes's Error* (New York: Avon Books, 1994).

Ferguson, James G., Jr., 'Just For Laughs', unpublished manuscript, UNC-Chapel Hill, 1997.

Jerch, Michael, private communication, Honors 45, Université de Bourgogne, 21 March 2005.

Johnson, Hugh. 'The Cloister and the Press', in *Vintage: The Story of Wine* (New York: Simon and Schuster, 1989), p. 120–37.

Lundquist, Hilary, 'Consume with Caution: The Politics of Milk', Honors 30, UNC-Chapel Hill, spring 2003.

McCown, Debra, 'The Politics of Barbecue', Honors 30, UNC-Chapel Hill, spring 2004.

Montinari, Massimo, 'Peasants, Warriors, Priests', in *Food: A Culinary History*, Jean-Louis Flandrin & Massimo Montanari, eds. (New York: Columbia University Press, 1999), pp. 178–85.

Nestle, Marion, *Food Politics* (Berkeley: University of California Press, 2002).

Novak, Michael, 'How Christianity Created Capitalism', *Wall Street Journal*, 23 December 1999.

Ward, Graham, 'Flesh Sweeter than Honey', in *Consuming Passions*, Sian Griffiths and Jennifer Wallace, eds. (Manchester: Mandolin, 1998), pp. 192–208.

Wittgenstein, Ludwig, *Philosophical Investigations* (Englewood Cliffs: Prentice Hall, 1958).

Food and Modernism

Anna Marie Fisker

A photo —

A kitchen with a fish on the kitchen table.

We look at the kitchen and the eye of the fish.

What has happened here?

And can we form an idea of the historical development and its constituent occurrences, which are actualised in history?

Are we, as Norman Mailer states in regard to the uncanny in cubism, placed in a landscape of the psyche, where past and future live, the entire inner world of night, dreams, memories and primitive premonitions? (Mailer, 1996: 310)

And are we aware that the past and the future are even more closely bound up with each other than the present moment?

I will attempt to uncover the iconography of the motif, which involves its cultural, historical and design-wise importance in the broadest sense. I will attempt to demonstrate coherences, on the one hand of a period in architectural history, and on the other, of the representation of the unprepared meal, and that there is an immediate connection between these two independent phenomena.

Does the photo represent an invitation to give up on the simple and classical point of view, to which we are almost doomed, and freely, at least in our thoughts, move around the object represented as the motif, the fish, a *Merluccius merluccius,* and further around the house in order to meet the historical reality behind this specific house, Villa Stein, designed by Le Corbusier? The simultaneous representation of the object from several angles in the motif is implicated like it is in cubism. At least a virtual mobility from the viewer's part is allowed, and it would be a contradiction to pass on such an invitation – we are invited.

In order to unfold this creation in the material, it is necessary to go back in time and study the movements that reformed the figurative arts from around 1908 and the following years, and which affected Le Corbusier's design of Villa Stein. The rate at which the development and also the resemblance with the results that were attained simultaneously by different artists, who followed different paths like painting, sculpture, architecture and literature, showed that a very vital process was taking place. I am going to explore whether or not this tendency also applied to gastronomy.

Around 1910, the notion that the artist's means of expression had lost its connection to the modern world started to emerge.

Between 1907 and 1908, the first cubistic works by Picasso and Braque were produced, and that was the starting signal of the increasing radical contributions from e.g. Gris, Léger and Delaunay (Benevolo, 1989: 390).

The method that the cubists developed as a means of representing spatial relations led to the design principles of the new conception of space. Both Picasso and Le Corbusier found their inspiration in Paris. Here, I will draw attention to Sigfried Giedion's perception of space-time: 'As a consequence of a new understanding of space Picasso and Braque about 1910 showed the inside and the outside simultaneously. In architecture Le Corbusier in line with the same principle developed the mutual penetration of the interior and exterior space' (Bek et al., 1997: 254).

According to Giedion, the results did not gain sympathy among the general audience. From the Renaissance and up till 1900, the central perspective had been one of the fundamental elements in painting; across all styles. This four-hundred-year-old tradition of perceiving the external world in a Renaissance manner, which means in three dimensions, had taken root deeply in man. It was impossible to imagine other forms of perception. But in the 19th century, the perspective was misused and, says Giedion, this led to its disintegration. His explanation is that the cubists not only attempted to depict an object's external appearance from one point of view. They moved around it, and tried to get a hold of its internal composition. They thus sought to expand the sphere of the emotions (Bek et al., 1997: 263).

191

As such, cubism settles with the perspective of the Renaissance. It perceives the object relatively, hence from several points of view, of which not one single viewpoint dominates. By dissecting the objects in this manner, cubism conceives them from all angles. Therefore, a forth dimension is added to the Renaissance's three; namely time. The poet Guillaume Apollinaire was the first person to recognise and express this change around 1911, and in 1913 his book *Les Peintres cubistes* was published. The same year, the first cubistic exhibition at Salon des Indépendants took place.

The scientific crisis regarding the traditional concept of time and space linked up the history of the conventions of perspective (Benevolo, 1989: 392).

To present an object seen from different perspectives, introduces a principle which is closely connected to the modern life of the past – contemporaneousness. In 1905, Einstein initiated his famous work *Electrodynamik bewegter Körper*, which contains a thorough review of the notion of the contemporary (Bek, et al., 1997: 264).

Einstein's theory of relativity would not only link up time and space, but also gravity, and he thus tried to create some sort of uniformity in his perception of the universe.

In the beginning, it was not *a priori* that the cubistic perception of spatial construction could be utilised in other areas than painting. The symbols of cubism were not rational and could not be used directly in architecture and handicrafts, but they were still ahead of and guidelines for artistic creations. As a follow-up to this, Le Corbusier among others tried to rationalise cubism. Converted to the plane of practical spatiality in architecture, the new mobility presented an opportunity to break with the classical static systems. These are the pure visual progressions that were composed on the conditions for axes and symmetry as a means of reintegrating the sum of the total complex experience of movement in architecture (Leymarie,1968: 41). Le Corbusier called his art purism. It emerged in relation to constructivism in Russia and neo-plasticism in the Netherlands, closest to cubism's own goals and to architecture (Bek et al., 1997: 265).

In 1927, Le Corbusier created Villa Stein de Monzie. The residence, if anything, constituted the central problem in modern architecture, and Le Corbusier expressed his ideas about this in the precept 'une maison – un palais'. At the end of the 1920s, Le Corbusier tried to carry out research on both the new technological cultures and the architectonic systems of the past, simultaneously, in his puristic architecture. He chose living-quarters as a type in the completion and the actualisation of this research. To focus on living-quarters as an object of architectural discourse was, according to Le Corbusier, to bestow dignity on modern life (Gans, 1987: 60). As Le Corbusier in this way intended to monumentalise living-quarters, he was charged with the task of creating a personal and modern equivalent. A weekend house for Gabrielle de Monzie, former wife of the Minister of Housing and Building, Anatole de Monzie, in whom Corbusier found a client with status, culture and wealth, for whom he could construct a house with the grandeur of a palace. The other client in this unusual joint venture was Michael Stein, Gertrude Stein's brother, and his wife Sarah, painter and collector of Matisse (Gans, 1987: 60).

As an answer, Le Corbusier developed a composition which he called 'mask of simplicity', or Dom-Ino, a sheet-column structure.

When Corbusier settled in Paris at the age of 30, he had not paid much attention to cubism. Nevertheless, it was in the spirit of cubism that he chose to take up his own standing in a manifesto entitled 'après le Cubism'. This manifesto was accomplished in co-operation with the painter Amedée Ozenfant (Leymarie, 1968: 35).

In the manifesto, Corbusier accentuated the ethical value of the principles that had been promoted by the initiators of cubism; namely to reduce the form to its geometrical – and thus clear – elements, and to re-evaluate the idea of composition, i.e. the construction. To Le Corbusier, cubism unfolded an uncertainty in the utilisation of constructive principles. Therefore, Le Corbusier concluded that the new age needed precision, or at least a spirit of precision, which cubism until then had proved to be incapable of (Leymarie, 1968: 38).

Purism marketed its aesthetics in the periodical *L'Esprit nouveau*, 1920–1925, and through Le Corbusier, it was introduced to architecture. In 1929, American architectural-theorist Henry-Russell Hitchcock labelled this form of architecture

'International Style'. He pin-pointed that this style emphasised volume and plane above mass, and also that architecture eschews ornament and utilises the machine as an artistic tool (Skude, 1989: 23).

In e.g. Choisy and Viollet-le-Duc's tradition, Le Corbusier searched for his knowledge in the past. Not for the stylistic characteristics, but for principles regarding the organisation of space and the rational structure.

What is so brilliant about Villa Stein is the way in which systems of historical and modern architecture are brought into relation with one another, and whereby they create a number of interpretations and coherences at the same time.

For Le Corbusier, the fundamental answer to modernity was the Dom-Ino framework of reinforced concrete columns and sheets, and the unbroken layers of space that are generated hereby. A system that extricates the walls in Villa Stein – internally as well as externally. Even though the non-load-bearing walls are extricated from the internal demanding structure and do not need to conform to the division of the rooms so they, more abstractly, express the layers of space from back to front. The continued layers of space are consonant with the compositional planes of layers of overlapping planes. As an example, the façades are organised as a series of overlapping planes, some real, others implied. They either yield or arise in relation to the plane of the white walls (Gans, 1987: 62). In the front façade, the windows appear both as background to the white wall and as fillets on a level with the wall. By finishing the corner of the house, the windows suggest a layer of space parallel to the villa. They give weight to the extreme periphery of the façade, but they are separated from it as to the centripetal composition of cubistic paintings. On the back façade, the proportions of the fillets are reversed, but their ambiguity and their ability to raise the surface are the same. Where the spatiality of the house seems to collapse into a tight front façade with a lot of implied planes, the courtyard façade seems to explode into the surface far away from the other. The horizontal mouldings of the stair's landing, the terrace and the roof garden describe a visual progression, which moves up and back in relation to the reference plane of the right wall (Gans, 1987: 61).

193

I will try to exemplify this. The entrepreneurs, especially Michael and Sarah Stein, were famous art-lovers and collectors. Therefore, there were not only great demands regarding the lay-out of the house, but also a demand for a suitable room for the gigantic collection of paintings and sculptures. The house, first and foremost, contains generous corridors and rooms with enormous spatial qualities, created by means of a perfect inflow of light and proportional balance. Villa Stein is regarded one of the most sumptuous of Le Corbusier's villas, in the sense that he has been prodigal of space in order to attain these architectural effects. Here, Le Corbusier completed what he referred to as 'une promenade architecturale', an architectural pleasure-walk (Statens Museum for Kunst, the Danish National Gallery, Catalogue, 1987: 89).

The Palladian design of Villa Foscari was also reflected in the interior. Not intact of course, but transformed in accordance with modern rules. The ground-plan is very harmonious in its implementation, just like the façade. The distinct shapes and slopes that fill the interior, e.g. the S-shaped plan, which is the expression of the great central room that can be seen from the roof, manifests the same sensibility as the well-formed bottles in Corbusier's still lifes. However, they do not represent these objects. On the contrary, they spring from an eclectic repertoire of architectural, machine-age and historical sources deprived of their original ornamental features.

Transparency constitutes yet another level of interpretation in connection with cubism, and I will try to describe how transparency is uncovered in Villa Stein. In this connection, it is interesting to see how Rowe and Slutzky, in their analysis, make use of Gyorgy Kepe's wording from *Language of Vision*: 'When looking on one or more figures overlapping each other and how much both claim their common share, we are facing a contradiction in spatial relations. To solve this contradiction we must assume the presence of a new optical quality. The figures are provided with a transparency, which means that they are capable of penetrating each other mutually without the optical disappearing. Transparency however implies more than an optical characteristic. Transparency involves a comprehensive spatial order. Transparency means simultaneously handling different spatial conditions. The space is not only drawing back but fluctuates in a continuous activity. The positions of the transparent figures have an ambiguous meaning (alt. significance) when we see the single figure sometimes close, sometimes fare away' (Bek et al., 1997: 275).

As such, transparency can be the object's inherent attribute as e.g. the curtain wall of glass in a building, or it can be the inherent quality of the construction. Rowe and Slutzky distinguish between literal transparency and phenomenon-bound transparency. The sense of phenomenon-bound transparency probably originates from the cubistic painting alone.

They refer to Alfred Barr, who states that Apollinaire 'raises the fourth dimension in a metaphorical rather than in a mathematical meaning'. This is essential in Rowe and Slutzky's presentation of considerations regarding architectonic transparency. The painting can merely offer the third dimension, while architecture cannot suppress it. Since architecture in reality is three-dimensional and is not just an imitation of three dimensions, the sense of literal transparency is, thus, a physical fact. For that reason, phenomenon-bound transparency is harder to achieve than literal transparency, and it is so difficult to discuss that there has been a great willingness to solely combine transparency in architecture with the transparency of materials.

Picasso's *L'Arlésienne* from 1911–1912 supplies the visual support to these reflections, because of the great transparency of overlapping surfaces in the painting. Picasso exhibits surfaces that seemingly are made of celluloid, which gives the audience a sensation of looking straight through. Thereby, a material transparency is experienced. In his slant constructed image space however, Picasso offers unlimited access to alternative interpretations through the constellation of larger and smaller shapes (Bek et al., 1997: 282)

Rowe and Slutzky use Villa Stein in their analysis of phenomenon-bound transparency, where they establish that Le Corbusier does not allow for discontinuances in the horizontal movement of glass. Glass is led around the corner with emphasis. In architecture, Le Corbusier is primarily occupied with the surface-wise qualities of glass and not with its translucent attributes (Bek et al., 1997: 282).

In Villa Stein two of modern architecture's ambitions have, thus, succeeded. Not as an unconscious return of the progress coming from the science of engineering, but as an actualisation of an artist's conscious intention. There is a suspended vertical grouping of planes that satisfy our wish for relational rooms, and there is an extensive transparency that allows for the internal as well as the external to be perceived simultaneously. *En face* and *en profile* like in Picasso's *L'Arlésienne* (Bek, et al., 1997: 269).

Transparency however, did not only apply to the painting. The idea of cubism is followed definitively in the voluminous works of Gertrude Stein, which includes novels, short stories, prose poems, plays, operas and lectures. In these works, Stein developed a literary modernism, which differed in all respects from other contemporary authors. Stein had a desire to operate beyond object-based poetry, which derives from a dismissal of femininity and an urge to create a form in its place. This should reveal continuity between the ego and the environment (Nicholls, 1995: 202).

A study of Gertrude Stein's works confirm that even in the early works, Stein's focus is constantly on a retreat from structure and the conventional composition of writing. Language, thus, started to assume a new opacity (Nicholls, 1995: 202). It can be said that Stein invents another version of modernism, by bypassing the image and studying the concise self-sufficiency of language, which some people find decadent. Stein used past times' modern painting, especially Picasso, as the model. The connection between writing and painting is clearly expressed in the following remarks about Cézanne: 'Up to that time composition had consisted of a central idea, to which everything else was an accompaniment and separate but not an end in itself, and Cezanne conceived the idea that in composition one thing was as important as another thing. Each part is as important as the whole' (Nicholls, 1995: 203).

The incentive to the artist's work is mainly the sight and what is seen. What the artist tries to maintain in his work is, therefore, not reality as such. It is rather the visual structure, by virtue of which the environment appears to be ordered visually by the artist and his contemporaries, in order to be grasped within the given frame of understanding (Bek, et al., 1997: 29).

Allow me to exemplify this. While Picasso studied light and time – he tried to integrate the two – Stein also works with the eyes. Hence, Picasso's 'Fruit Bowl' from 1908-1909 have opposing flows of light – one flows from above and one flows from below (Mailer, 1996: 293). An analogue to Stein, who claimed that she sensed language with her eyes. 'It does not make any difference to me what language I hear, I don't hear a language, I hear tones of voice and rhythms, but with my eyes I see words and sentences' (Stendhal, 1995: 73).

Apparently, none of the cubistic thoughts and experimental currents were connected to gastronomy. In fact, it seemed as if the chefs and gastronomes of the past preferred to avoid contact with these activities, and concentrated their energy on the classical meal.

Curnonsky set the fashion during these years. Perhaps the only indication of something new. But not a new dimension, and certainly not something pointing in the direction of possibilities in terms of moving towards the position of avant-garde and creating a connection to cubism.

What did the cubists eat? What about Matisse and Picasso, these two great characters of twentieth century art, two characters that were perceived as opposites and rivals. In Gertrude Stein's book 'Picasso', the following dispute can be found regarding the matter of eating a tomato. Matisse is asked: '…if, when he ate a tomato, he saw it as he painted it'. No, Matisse said, 'When I eat it I see it as everybody sees it'. And, says Stein, this is because painters like Matisse perceive nature in the same way as all other people perceive it. And they express it more or less emotionally, clearly or intensely in order to depict the tomato exactly how the whole world sees it.

But Picasso is not like that. When he eats a tomato, the tomato is, according to Stein: 'not everybody's tomato, not at all', and she continues 'his effort was not to express in his way the things seen as every one sees them, but to express the thing as he was seeing it' (Stein, 1984: 17).

Gastronomy on the other hand broke with the traditional outer boundaries of the meal. The established foundation was used as a basis on which people worked, and it soon came to liberate the artistic culture from the visual rules of the past.

The focal point in this story is Pablo Picasso, for whom the meal was of great importance. Food affected his life and art deeply. He often drew with wine on the paper table-cloths of the cafés, and caught himself and people around him in lifelike portraits.

As an example of the gastronomical limitation of the time, I will refer to a farewell dinner, which preceded Picasso's trip to Spain in the spring of 1905. Picasso had sold several works of art to art dealer Ambroise Vollard and wanted to travel for the money.

Subsequently, Apollinaire wrote to him about their heroic expedition to the train and the farewell dinner: 'Oh Vatel, Oh Carême, Oh Brillat-Savarin, the dinner we have had and the wines, pouring down the guests starched waistcoats' (Herscher, 1996: 75).

It is definitely a dinner that refers to the classical principles and ideals, where neither of the currents that are underway seem to be indicated nor represented. Apollinaire conclusively refers to the most important culinary front figures of the past. To the famous chief caterer Vatel, to Carême, and last but not least, the father of gastronomy, Brillat-Savarin.

The deeper meaning of the cultural process in cubism was not a modification of the content of artistic representation, but a modification of the traditional concept of art as a representative activity.

In 1908, Picasso was in the middle of cubism's locks when he arranged the famous hommage for le Douanier Rousseau in his studio in Bateau Lavoir, where Fernandes' 'ris à la Valencienne', not a newly composed dish, was served (Mailer, 1996: 278).

There are many descriptions of this grand party, which the cubists held. Not everybody agrees on the course of events, except that the gastronomical highlight of the party was the serving of 'ris à la Valencienne'. This dish could very well have been based on the painter Heni de Toulouse-Lautrec's traditional recipe, the same Toulouse-Lautrec, who had a large influence on Picasso's first late impressionistic works (Rodrigues-Hunter, 1994: 29).

The same traditional level existed when Alice B. Toklas prepared a perch for Picasso one of the times he had lunch at Gertude Stein's. She garnished a finely striped perch in a way she thought would amuse Picasso.

The cold steamed perch was covered with a pattern of different garnishes, and Alice B. Toklas proudly served her masterpiece for Picasso. He praised it enthusiastically for its beauty. But, he said, it should probably have been prepared in honour of Matisse rather than me (Toklas, 1981: 32).

Does a parallel exist in another dish, which Toklas created for Picasso? For many years, Picasso was on a strict diet; red meat was forbidden. But a spinach-soufflé, since spinach was recommended strongly by Picasso's doctor? Perhaps it could become a bit more interesting if a sauce was added (Toklas, 1981: 32).

197

But which sauce would Picasso's diet allow him to eat? Like in the film *Babette's Feast*, Toklas decided to give him a whole selection – the B in Alice B. Toklas is for Babette. In equal areas around the soufflé; hollandaise sauce, a cream sauce and a tomato sauce were arranged. 'Scary puzzle', said Picasso, when he was served the soufflé (Toklas, 1981: 33).

The traditional understanding of gastronomy is not sufficient here. As it has been emphasised, gastronomy has to be seen as a much more complete art form, where not only sight and the olfactory sense but all of the senses are represented.

One of the things that separated purism from cubism was the maintenance of the motif's recognisability. Therefore, as mentioned, articles for everyday use were often represented. Simple standardised objects like glasses, plates and bottles are included because they qualify as simple foundations of meditations over the original meaning of the painting – form and space in infinite interaction – of great poetic power (Statens Museum for Kunst, the Danish National Gallery, Catalogue, 1987: 15).

To let them all meet at the transparent meal at the same time in Villa Stein; Picasso, Braque, Le Corbusier, Gertrude Stein and Matisse, confirms the reciprocal penetration of time and space. As a statement that cubism is fascinating because it is uncanny, resonant and full of disturbing awareness that time itself is being budged. Because while we stare at the objects in cubist paintings, call them depths or phenomena or visions of each of the canvas' parts, we step directly out of our sense of the present and into another mysterious time dimension, which is best described as non-present (Mailer, 1996: 310).

New forms of perception and new feelings are thus indicated as formulations of a meal. A meal that has a plurality of reference levels or reference points and at the same time, in short, includes the idea of space-time.

But who prepares the *Merluccius merluccius*? The hake. As has been pointed out, Apollinaire's epoch-making *Les Peintres cubistes* was the first presentation of cubism. An astounding amount of what separates 20th-century poetry from 19th-century poetry is caused by Apollinaire. Not least that nature and technology are placed on an equal footing as artistic objects.

One of the chefs that separate the 21st century from the 20th century in Scandinavia is the very young and competent Nikolai Kirk. There is no doubt that Nikolai Kirk seeks stagnation and movement, growth and dissolution, the sense perceptions of childhood and subversion at the same time. To do everything at the same time in one single dish. I believe that he is as set on capturing the whole as Einstein was in his search of a general theory that would include movement, space, gravity and energy in one single formula. In the preface to his book, *Kirks Fisk*, Nikolai Kirk says that he was born for water, that Aquarius is his sign. That he grew up with water over his head, namely a small fish-tank. He slept side by side with his fish, and they shared his nightmares. He is extremely fascinated by water. Water plays an important role in his life. In almost mythological phrases, he describes the taste of the fish, its smooth surface, its agility and how it almost flies, but without noise and without a tail of smoke. 'It is close to perfection' (Kirk, 2000: 12).

The cubists broke with naturalistic continuity in painting and introduced superimposed or overlaying points of view that referred to different points of view, none of which were used as an absolute reference point (Benevolo, 1989: 393).

They broke down the totality into its basic components: lines, surfaces, colours. That is exactly Kirk's motif in his composition 'Hake baked with smoked peppers served with warm lamb's lettuce (mâche) and macaroni in lemon oil' (Kirk, 2000: 60).[1]

This dish reveals liberating elements of new qualities and new meaning, which have been hidden behind the hake's conventional skin from the beginning. New elements begin to exist between the elements, which are organised according to new rules. Through the smoked pepper that has an almost fluorescent orange transparency, the hake's white and yet transparent flesh is sensed.

Kirk not only tries to depict the smooth external appearance of the fish; he also tries to get a hold of its fine and delicate internal appearance. We are forced to move around the fish through the layers of the smoked pepper, and we can thus establish that Kirk's fascination with the fish expands the sphere of our feelings. In the preparation it is the interplay between nervousness, seriousness and the ability to keep one's head that gives the dish its ambiguous meaning. One looks at the fish almost at close range and almost from a distance. Exactly such a transparency of overlapping sheets exists in the composition – like in Picasso's *L'Arlésienne*. Sheets that seemingly are made of celluloid, we get a sense of looking through the layers in the baked fillet; we not only experience material-transparency but an evident phenomenon-bound transparency.

The dish, thus, contains cubism's precepts or some sort of dichotomy, which does not automatically follow the development that was founded by cubism and its repercussions on architecture. The dish also points to the future.

This leads us back to Villa Stein's kitchen. In an entirely practical and inconceivably simple room cleared of all decorations, where the fish's eye, even in death, is the only seeing or living thing.

Raymond Cogniats described how Picasso and Braque reached a total conceptualisation of the painting, which from now on was an object in itself, independent on the realistic representation of an object. An object, which has its own architecture, its own space and perspective, and which is not a series of planes that are procured through the methods of traditional perspective. An object that makes the work form a homogenous whole and which is closed around itself (Mailer, 1996: 308).

I assert that Nikolai Kirk's dish both thematises cubism's formal problem, the many layers on layers, the internal and external appearances that are shown at the same time and, thus, it passes on some of the universal elements from cubism.

By incorporating the fish on the kitchen table in Villa Stein in his dish, the connection between time and space remains intact. And the meal, thus, represents a definite result, which holds past, present and future at the same time.

199

Bibliography

Bek, Lise og Oxvig, Henrik (1997), *Rumanalyser*, Århus.

Benevolo, Leonardo (1989), *History of modern architecture I & II*, Massachusetts.

Gans, Deborah (1987), *The Le Corbusier Guide*, Princeton.

Herscher, Ermine (1996), *Dining with Picasso*, London.

Kirk Axelsson, Nikolai Ibsen (2000), *Kirk's Fisk*, København.

Lemaire, Gérard-Georges (1998), *Die Künstler Cafes von Paris*, München.

Mailer, Norman (1996), *Picasso. Portræt af den unge Picasso*, København.

Skude, Flemming (1989), *ISMERNE, det 20. århundredes arkitektur*, København.

Nicholls, Peter (1995), *Modernism*, London.

Rodrigues-Hunter, Suzanne (1994), *Genfundne Måltider Fra Den Fortabte Generation, Opskrifter og anek-doter fra 1920'rnes Paris*, London.

Stendhal, Renate (1995), *Gertrude Stein. In words and Pictures*, London.

Statens Museum for Kunst, the Danish National Gallery (1987), *Katalog*, København.

Stein, Gertrude (1984), *Picasso*, New York.

Toklas, Alice B. (1981), *Alice B. Toklas' kogebog*, København.

Note

1. 'Hake baked with smoked peppers, served with warm lamb's lettuce and macaroni in lemon oil'.
    (serves 5)
    500 grams of hake fillet without skin and bones
    5 peppers without skin and seeds
    100 grams of rice
    100 grams of clayed [semi-refined, Demerera] sugar
    100 grams of jasmine tea
    100 grams of pasta dough, thinly rolled out
    ½ decilitre of lemon oil
    ½ kilo lamb's lettuce (mâche)
    20 grams of finely chopped pine nuts
    1 tablespoonful of cherry vinegar
    1 decilitre of light junket
    4 sprigs of dill
    5 grams of granulated sugar
        (Kirk, 2000: 60).

Running a 15th-century Restaurant in the 21st Century

Judy Gerjuoy

Olde Hansa, founded in 1997, is the most popular restaurant in Tallinn, and therefore in Estonia. The 'persona' of the restaurant is that of a mid- to late-15th-century merchant's home. This is carried out with its décor, the way the wait staff is dressed, and most importantly, the food. Unlike the Medieval Times restaurants in the United States, which have little or no concern with authenticity, but rather are putting on a show, the people of Olde Hansa are concerned with authenticity, and spend a great deal of time and money researching and working with medieval scholars on several continents to recreate their chosen time-period more accurately.

They are not content with the status quo, but rather seek to improve what they are doing, and to bring it closer to what would have been done in the 15th century, within the constraints of 21st-century health and safety issues. For instance, in the last two years, they have redone all their bathrooms so they appear at first glance to be a medieval garderobe (bathroom). The flush toilets are built into a wooden throne-like chair, that resembles a medieval privy. The flushing mechanism is a large wooden button in a wooden box, built into the wall, and does not look like a modern handle. Water comes out of a copper pitcher, which is discreetly attached to a pipe, giving the illusion of a pitcher and basin set-up. The doors to the bathrooms are made from hand-hewn planks and use hand-forged hinges.

Obviously this is not 100 per cent authentic, but it looks authentic, and meets 21st-century health codes. As we will see in this article, most of the compromises that Olde Hansa makes come from conformity to 21st-century codes.

One of the advantages that Olde Hansa has is that Tallinn is one of the most intact medieval cities left in Europe, with some of the walls and towers that surrounded medieval Tallinn still extant. This means that there is a medieval atmosphere both in the restaurant and outside of it. The building that Olde Hansa uses for its restaurant is a 15th-century building that has been modernized in some parts, but retains most of the original structure. The major changes include electricity, piped water and sewage, and modernizing the kitchen. The kitchen is a modern kitchen, with gas and electric appliances.

The building has three floors plus a basement. The kitchen is on the second floor and there is dining on all three floors as well as outside in the summer months. The second floor has a musicians' gallery where musicians frequently play medieval songs using replica medieval instruments, and the third floor has a freestanding wood-burning fireplace. The walls are decorated with designs from illuminated manuscripts and tapestries. The tables and chairs were made for Olde Hansa. The tables are medieval trestle tables, or are wooden boards on saw-horses, as was done in the Middle Ages, and the chairs are based on medieval designs. The public part of the restaurant is lit by candles and well-hidden electric lights.

All of the wait staff are dressed as 15th-century servants, including shoes that look medieval. The shoes are not 100 per cent accurate, as they have modern soles instead of medieval soles, so they will last longer and be more comfortable for the staff. The staff is not allowed to have hair that is dyed in non-normal colors, piercings that show except earrings, visible tattoos and other 21st-century items.[1] The wait staff is trained in maintaining the illusion that it is the 15th century by avoiding modern references and making medieval ones.

The place where Olde Hansa is farthest from authentic is in their kitchen and menu, and therefore their food. This is due to several reasons, all of which impact upon their authenticity. Some of these could be changed, while others cannot, at least in any practical way.

The first issue is the cooking equipment. Medieval food was prepared in a number of different ways. First, of course, was cooking in a pot over a fire. Cooking in a pot over a modern gas stove will give you the same results as was done in the Middle Ages, so those dishes don't have a problem in terms of authenticity. Second was cooking in a medieval oven. A medieval oven is not really comparable to a modern oven. In general, when things were cooked in a medieval oven, the oven was filled with wood and heated up. When the oven was hot enough, the coals were removed, the items to be baked were put into it, and the oven was sealed.[2] This resulted in items cooking in an oven which gradually decreased in heat. At Olde Hansa the food is cooked in a modern oven. A modern oven gives you approximately the same temperature the entire time of the cooking cycle, which means the resulting food comes out differently. Third, food in the Middle Ages was cooked on a spit over an open fire.[3] Olde Hansa does nothing comparable to that. And, of course, the food is stored in modern refrigerators and freezers, which are not medieval. However, they serve in many ways as a modern substitute to going to the butcher every day, and have no major effect on the authenticity of the food.

The second issue is the ingredients themselves. Modern species of animals, fruits, vegetables and spices have been bred in ways that make them a lot different from the medieval species in size, taste, color, and texture. For instance, modern cattle are a lot larger than medieval cattle[4] and have a much higher percentage of fat. The medieval carrot was available in many colors, not just orange. In *Le Ménagier de Paris*, written in 1393, translated by Eileen Power, it says in a carrot recipe, 'Carrots be red roots which be sold in handfuls in the market.'[5]

The third issue is the recipes themselves. Some of the dishes at Olde Hansa are done from extant medieval recipes, but some are constructed by the cooks, based on medieval ingredients of the time and medieval cooking techniques.

The fourth issue is the fact that modern people come to the restaurant and want modern food and drink. Olde Hansa offers coffee and tea, neither of which was drunk in 15th-century Europe. They offer tomato juice, which comes from a New-World fruit that was not used in 15th-century Europe. On the other hand, they are moving towards more authenticity in what they offer. When they first opened, they would serve potatoes – again, something not used in 15th-century Europe – because people in Estonia do not feel that a meal is complete unless it contains potatoes. After several years they stopped serving them, deciding that authenticity was more important than how people might feel. This switch to greater authenticity does not seem to have hurt their business.

The fifth issue is that not all medieval ingredients and practices would be considered safe today. For instance, one medieval subtlety (a table decoration served at the end of the course which may or may not be eaten) that was meant to be eaten was serving a peacock in its full plumage. The peacock would be carefully skinned, so all the feathers would be kept whole and attached to the skin. The bird would then be roasted, and then the raw peacock's skin would be carefully put back on the bird, and it would be served to the diners.[6] While it makes a very impressive sight, our modern knowledge of food safety forbids such a practice. Foods were colored with assorted coloring agents, some of which we now know are poisonous, such as elder bark.[7]

The sixth issue is eating utensils. While spoons and knives were used for eating in the 15th century, forks were not commonly used for eating, though large forks were used in kitchens to aid in food preparation and serving. Olde Hansa provides forks for their guests along with the other silverware. They provide them because their customers are, in general, unwilling to eat without them.

Another way that Olde Hansa must deviate from strict authenticity is through observance of modern fire codes. The restaurant has lighted exit signs and disguised, but there if you look for them, sprinklers and smoke detectors.

Olde Hansa serves meals from a menu, plus assorted feasts. The feasts are patterned after medieval feasts. When the guest comes in, the wait staff wash their hands for them, using a bowl and pitcher, and a linen towel for drying, something that was typically done in a medieval feast.[8] For two hours, dish after dish of food is brought out, in messes of 6 to 10 people depending on the dish. This is typical of a medieval banquet where a mess, a group of people, would share dishes of food. These feasts offer foodstuffs that were eaten in the Middle Ages, but are not common today. For instance, the Royal Hunting Feast sells for 710 Estonian Crowns (roughly 47€) and consists of:

Dry game spiced with herbs
French royal poultry liver pâté
Andalusian salmon
Earl's pickled cucumbers Livonian style
London merchant's saffron pickles

Berries of the Highly Blessed Olive Tree
Spice merchant's berry sauce
Herb-bread with nuts
Rye bread with ham
Castle's fresh cheese
Game fillets
Wild Birds favoured by the richest of Venice
Fillet of elk or wild boar, baked and flavored with the most expensive spices in honor of Waldemar II, the King of Denmark
Game fillets of the season
Honorable cook Frederick's game sausages with figs and almonds
Well-cooked spelt with saffron
Baked smoked-sauerkraut
Crusader's lentils sauce
Ginger turnip
Velvet delight of the nobility – Rose pudding savoury
St. John's cake[9]

One of the problems that Olde Hansa has in its quest for authenticity is that you cannot go out and buy much of what they need. They had to have all their furniture built for them, after they researched medieval furniture. They had to research medieval plates, bowls, glasses, silverware, etc., and then have it custom-made. The wait staff's clothes are made for them by local seamstresses, who have studied medieval costume and fashion. Their shoes are made by a local shoemaker, who first had to learn what medieval shoes look like. Putting together the proper setting for Olde Hansa has been a learning experience both for them, and for the craftspeople they employ. For instance, one glassblower made them lovely replica medieval goblets – which broke after going through the dishwasher several times. The first model plates didn't stack very well, which meant that they had to be redesigned in order to save storage space, etc. Because Olde Hansa has to design all of its equipment and have it made, they are constantly researching and refining their equipment, striving to come closer and closer to what would actually have been there.

In conclusion, while there are many ways that Olde Hansa falls short of perfect authenticity, they are making a good attempt to recreate 15th-century life, and are continuing to grow and be more authentic. In a lot of cases their lack of authenticity comes from matters beyond their control, such as availability of items or health and safety issues. In matters that are within their control, they are improving and growing closer to their goal. The truth is that they will never be perfectly authentic; there are too many issues beyond their control. But, they are producing a useful, good tasting, educational and fun product as well as a successful one.

Bibliography

Adamson, Melitta Weiss, *Food in Medieval Times* (Greenwood Press: Westport, Connecticut, 2004).

Anonymous, *Le Ménagier de Paris*, trans by Eileen Power (Harcourt, Brace and Company: New York, 1928).

Dobney, K. M., S. D. Jaques and B. G. Irving, *Of Butchers and Breeds* (Lincoln Archaeological Studies, No. 5).

Harrison, Molly, *The Kitchen in History* (Charles Scribner's Sons: New York, 1972).

Henisch, Bridget Ann, *Fast and Feast: Food in Medieval Society* (Pennsylvania State University Press: 1976).

Olde Hansa Staff Manual, 2002.

Redon, Odile, Francoise Sabban, and Silvano Serventi, *The Medieval Kitchen* trans by Edward Schneider, (The University of Chicago Press: Chicago, 1998).

Renfrow, Cindy and Elise Fleming, *The Colorful Cook*, 1999.

Scully, Terence, *The Art of Cookery in the Middle Ages* (The Boydell Press: Suffolk, 1995).

I would also like to thank the people of Olde Hansa for allowing me to interview them for this paper, and for letting me read their staff handbook. For more information about Olde Hansa go to www.oldehansa.com.

Notes

1. Olde Hansa Staff Manual.
2. Scully, Terence, pp. 93–94.
3. Harrison, Molly, pp. 20–21.
4. Dobney, K.M., et al., p. 33.
5. Anonymous, p. 298.
6. Scully, Terence, p. 106.
7. Renfrow, Cindy and Elise Fleming, p. 21.
8. Scully, Terence, p. 171.
9. Menu taken from the Olde Hansa website at www.oldehansa.com.

Towards an Authentic Roman Sauce

Sally Grainger

There are many problems associated with reconstructing Roman recipes and I spend a good deal of my time wrestling with these problems. Is it possible to be 'authentic' and what is the value of achieving 'authenticity' compared with only being able to get close to the real thing? If the purpose of experiments is just to give a flavour of Roman food to your colleagues or the public, then surely getting close to the real thing would be close enough.

This kind of thinking is the normal justification for using a Thai fish sauce such as *nam bplah* when reconstructing the Roman recipes in *Apicius*. It is close enough and we don't want to have to think about the possibility of using authentic *garum* if that means that we have to eat rotting fish intestines! So it is a convenient and satisfactory compromise and one that I have accepted until now. But is it a safe assumption to make?

With my husband Dr Christopher Grocock I have recently completed a new edition and translation of *Apicius*, and the question of the definition of *liquamen/garum* has taxed me greatly during the process. I felt able to tackle this momentous task because I had developed skills in reconstructing Roman recipes using 'authentic' equipment and techniques. I was able to reconstruct comparable conditions under which cooks worked and it has therefore been possible to create 'authentic' dishes. If I was able to be true to the cooking techniques then compromises such as inadequate substitutes and alternative ingredients were no longer acceptable. And it was from this perspective that I re-considered *liquamen*.

It has generally been accepted that *garum* and *liquamen* were the same thing: a form of fermented fish sauce used in Roman cooking. This much is true, but the wider issue of precisely what *liquamen* is in relation to *garum* has not been considered fully or understood. Diocletian's price edict of AD 301 is written in both Greek and Latin, and the two terms are used to reflect the same item in the list. However I am less willing to trust the civil servants who surely wrote the text of this edict and would seek other evidence before taking this at face value. It is also true that the 10th-century agricultural manual known as the *Geoponica* – part of which is 6th century – also uses the term interchangeably. Basically it says 'you make *garum* this way…*liquamen* is the result'. This ought to be clinching evidence, but if we look elsewhere at other data derived from the manufacture of fish sauce and also from the use of it in the kitchen by the cook and by the gourmet at dinner, then the generality that *garum* and *liquamen* are the same is less clear; in fact we are told quite categorically that they are not the same.

Cooks, in the guise of the Apician recipe text, have always contradicted this generality, though it has seldom been acknowledged. *Garum* appears in references to the early Greek compound sauces such as *oenogarum* while the standard term in the text for fish sauce is *liquamen*. Why don't we find *garum* referred to in these recipes? It has been assumed that the recipe collection was compiled in the late Empire by gourmets from the literary elite who used the term *liquamen* rather than *garum* because it was, at that time, the standard term for the basic kind of fish sauce available. *Garum* is found mentioned in all kinds of late literature, so this cannot explain the omission, but crucially *liquamen* is not found in any early literature. My explanation for this strange omission is that true *garum* is a sauce handled largely by the consumer after the food is served – a table condiment like table soy sauce for instance – and so would feature in culinary literature, while *liquamen* is a sauce used by the cooks in the kitchen and would be little understood and therefore never mentioned in literature. It is clear that the cooks wrote the recipes and the collection was compiled over many centuries. The recipes were written in a particular style of vulgar cooks' Latin that was not discernibly altered or regularised when, on completion, it may have passed into the hands of the literary elite. We ought to be able to trust the cooks to use the terminology accurately, so that when they say *liquamen* they mean a specific fish sauce rather than the general one referred to in the *Geoponica* and Diocletian's price edict.

So we must define *garum* and *liquamen*. *Garum* was originally a Greek term, though we know no more than that it was a smelly fish sauce. It was made, according to Pliny, from a fish of the same name, the size of which will prove to be the crux of the question. He goes on to say that *garum* in his day was made from the waste that would normally be thrown away – the viscera – defined as the blood and entrails of particular fish such as mackerel, and salt and, it appears, only these things. We might imagine the mackerel (once it had been drained) being thrown in too, and this is reflected in the recipe from the *Geoponica* which describes small fish, pieces of fish and fish entrails all going in to make a sauce which is both *garum* and *liquamen*. Martial tells us in his list of Saturnalia presents[1] that *muria* was another form of fish sauce of an inferior quality made from tuna and here we must assume the waste matter – head, skin, entrails, fins etc. Any tuna meat would surely not be used to make fish sauce, but be sold at a premium. The *Geoponica* recipe tells us to leave the mixture for a few months to dissolve, ferment and clear into layers: the fluid at the top is the fine free flowing liquid called *garum/liquamen*. The paste at the bottom called *allec* was also a condiment – a true pickle in appearance and the precursor to anchovy paste no doubt. The *Geoponica* also has a recipe for a Bithynian sauce which is made from small fish alone with salt and a few herbs. Some are said to add extra *allec* to it, no doubt in order to start the dissolving process.

It is clear from the way Thai sauces are made that it is the enzymes in the guts of the fish which cause the product to break down, rather than bacteria – the salt allows for no other scenario. I suspect that the use of fish viscera was only introduced in order to speed up the dissolving process. Any small fish used would dissolve both from the inside out and the outside in. A further consideration is the modern-day practice in Thailand of taking the first fluid from the vessel it is made in, diluting the residue with sea water, and allowing it to separate and clear again. This second batch is then blended with the first in order to produce sufficient quantity of good quality fish sauce to supply the large market for it. A second-grade fish sauce is referred to in Diocletian's price edict, which may indicate such a practice.

It is also necessary to consider the possibility that fish sauce manufacture developed and evolved over the 600 years of production through the Greek and Roman periods. The first product from Greek manufacture might not necessarily be the same or even recognisable a few HUNDRED years later. This can only make my attempts at defining fish sauce all the more difficult.

So we have the possibility, over the whole period, of sauces made from fish entrails alone; from fish that is drained but also thrown in; from pieces of fish, whole fish and blood and entrails from the cut fish, and also from whole small fish such as anchovy, all mixed with salt and/or herbs, and apart from the first, each of these processes would as a matter of course produce a paste at the bottom and a liquor at the top if left for long enough. All would also allow for a second grade sauce if the residue was diluted again. Trying to put a specific name to each of these possibilities seems impossible but it does highlight just how complex the whole issue is and how simplistic it is to assume that *garum* and *liquamen* are the same.

A key piece of evidence that these two sauces were at one stage very different comes from a letter by Ausonius. In *c.* AD 390 Ausonius wrote from Bordeaux to his former pupil Paulinus, thanking him for a gift of *muria*:[2]

208

> Fearing that the oil which you had sent was not pleasing, you repeated your gift and distinguished yourself more fully by adding in addition a *condimentum* of *muria* from Barcelona. But you know that I have neither the custom, nor the ability to say that word *muria*, which is in the use of the common folk, although the most learned of our ancestors and those who shun Greek expressions do not have a Latin expression for the appellation *garum*. But I, by whatever name that liquor of our allies is called, 'will soon fill my *patinas*…'

Ausonius is a gourmet with an obvious interest in the details of these fish sauces. He would wish to have the best products and to understand the complexities of designation and definition. We therefore must have confidence in the information he gives us. *Garum* and *muria* seem to be of a similar nature according to Ausonius and our other sources already mentioned confirm this: fish entrails and waste matter are a primary ingredient and it appears that they may be defined by this addition of blood and viscera. Ausonius states categorically that the Latin language does not have a term for *garum*. *Garum* was a Greek word and also the fashionable Latinised term for this kind of fish sauce, but if you shunned Hellenistic things there was no corresponding word you could use. For Ausonius at least *liquamen* is not *garum* and whatever it may be, it is of no interest to him. He does also suggest I think that the 'I' in the quote is the diner filling his *patinae* with *garum* rather than the cook.

The evidence for manufacture comes from Pompeii of course. It was a Greek colony where the three sauces were made and sold separately: amphora labels describe *gari flos* (flower of *garum*), *liq. flos* (flower of *liquamen*), and *muria flos* (flower of *muria*).[3] Fish sauce manufacturers made all three kinds and took pains to identify and advertise each one separately. Despite the fact that *gari flos*, made from mackerel, was supposed to be the most expensive of the fish sauces, it is the most common label and is often found in relatively modest houses and *popinae*. *Liquamen* and *muria* are also very well represented. Fish sauce amphora finds elsewhere in Italy do not contradict these findings.

The *Astronomica*, a poem by Manilius, provides considerable detail (albeit in poetic form) about fish sauce production that may shed light on the issue. It describes activity on a beach where fish are landed and prepared, described in great detail, and as a consequence is worth citing in full:

> Nor is it enough to have caught them: their bodies struggle against the net and they await fresh battles and are put to the sword (i.e. cut up with a knife): the sea is stained, mixed with their blood. Then again, when the catch lies all along the shore (or perhaps brought ashore whole, with transferred epithet: see the phrases following), a second slaughter is made of the slaughter: they are jointed (lit: cut into their limbs) and from the one body different purposes are allotted: one part is better with its juices drained, another with them kept in. From some a precious fluid flows out, pouring out (lit. vomiting up) the flower of the gore, and mixed with salt, balances taste in the mouth.[4]

209

This is the blood drained to make *garum*: we appear to have confirmation that blood alone was used. The choice of words here suggests that the consumer has some role in making the balance of taste in the mouth happen rather than the cook, especially when contrasted with the 'juice for food' mentioned below. The text continues (vv. 673-5):

> The whole of the remainder – a mass of decaying slaughter (i.e. the drained carcasses) sinks to the bottom and mingles its shapes in a second demise, serving up a common compliment and a juice for food.

Here there seems to be a separation of solid and liquid matter; the solid will clearly become *allec*, the fish paste, and the implication is that it was also a table condiment. The *sucus* (juice) above this paste is another fish sauce: perhaps this is the origin of *muria* or perhaps a form of *liquamen*. However, the issue is complicated by what seems to us to be a description of a different operation which immediately follows upon the last one in the text of Manilius:

> Or, when a cloud of scaly creatures comes to a halt and sticks fast in an unmoving shoal, closely resembling the blue-green sea itself, it is hauled out, besieged all around with a vast net, and fills huge tanks and wine-jars, and it exudes the shared wealth of its fluid over itself, and dissolving from the inside it flows out into liquid gore.[5]

This is a reference to a sauce made from very small uncut fish: small fry or anchovy, with no additional blood. This, it appears, is *liquamen*. We are told as much in a late (though often unreliable) source, Isidore of Seville's *Etymologiae*. Isidore wrote in the 6th century AD about the origin of familiar words, but his reasoning on the derivations and origins of words is doubtful on many occasions, to say the least. We have already heard that he thought Greek *garum* was so-called because it was originally made from a fish called *garon*. He then talks about *liquamen*:

> *Liquamen* is so called because little fish dissolved during salting produce the liquid of that name. Its liquor is called *salsugo* or *muria*. Now strictly speaking, *muria* is the name of water mixed with salt...[6]

210

We have to view this evidence with care, as Isidore is obviously unreliable elsewhere, but when his evidence is added to the description cited above from Manilius, it is clear that small fish such as anchovy were turned into a separate kind of fish sauce, which is of course the same as the kind of fish sauce used in South-East Asian cooking today. Thus we can be reasonably confident that *liquamen* is the same product as Thai fish sauce. So when I use Asian fish sauce to make my Roman food I truly believe I am not using a substitute, not just close enough, but the real thing – the authentic sauce. The 'assumption' appears to be a safe one after all.

[At the symposium I offered a number of sauce tastings to test this theory. Recipes from *Apicius* and also from Martial's satires were made with a good quality Thai sauce as well as the sauce now being manufactured in Sorrento according to an ancient recipe.]

Notes

1. Martial 13.103. *Muria* is also Latin for 'brine', either clean or that generated from the salting of fish.
2. Ausonius, *Ep.* 21, from Prete's Teubner ed. (Leipzig, 1978); no. 19 in R.P.H. Green's *OCT* (Oxford: 1999).
3. See Curtis, *Garum and Salsamenta*, Appendix II, for details of these *tituli picti*.
4. Manilius 5. 664–72.
5. Manilius, 5. 676–81.
6. Isidore of Seville, *Etymologiae* 20.3.20.

Naming Authenticity and Regional Italian Cuisine

Alexandra Grigorieva

– What are you calling a *sfincione?* – this is a *pizza*, that is a *sfincione*.
– Now really, that is a *sformato*, but this definitely is a *sfincione*.

The articles in question were a thick *pizza*-like item liberally smeared with tomato sauce (called *sfincione* by the girl from Palermo and *pizza* by her colleague from Marsala) and a kind of cold green vegetable soufflé (called *sformato* by the girl from Palermo and *sfincione* by her colleague from Marsala). As for me, I (using my mainstream Italian) would have called the former a *pizza* (albeit of the particular Sicilian variety with a thick crust) and the latter a *sformato*. So much for naming authenticity. And we hadn't even started with the recipes yet!

Situations like this are fairly common when you start talking to people in Italy about their cuisine. Instantly friends that have grown up just some miles apart can't see eye-to-eye. They use different names for the same classical regional dishes or the same name for different ones. Some of the names go back to Roman times and even beyond. The dialect word *sfincione*, for example, like its relative *sfincia* (representing savoury and sweet spongy Sicilian pastry respectively[1]) is usually thought to be a development of the initially ancient Greek *spong-* root (meaning 'sponge') perhaps via the Roman culinary vocabulary, where a kind of sweet omelet was called *ova sfongia* ('sponge eggs').[2] Both seem to be linguistically related to the north Italian *spungata/spongata* cakes of Liguria and Emilia-Romagna that date back at least to the Renaissance period and their modern Greek cousin is the savoury *sfungato* omelet of Crete, although the recipes *per se* have nothing in common.

The now ubiquitous *pizza* word is probably an irregular medieval perfect passive participle of Latin verb *pinsere* (to crush, pound)[3] meaning 'flattened (cake)' not unlike its modern local (mostly Tuscan) cousin *schiacciata*[4] formed regularly from Italian verb *schiacciare* with the same meaning. The 'flattened cake' has been obviously popular throughout Italy, and all its archaic regional varieties I've found are sweet, not savoury, contrary to most of the present-day *pizze*. They can vary in form and taste, but they still keep their old 'flattened' name. There is a rather flat *pinsa* from Pordenone[5] traditionally baked for Epiphany with fennel seed, dried figs and even some grated pumpkin mixed into the dough and there is rolled Christmas *pinza* from Bologna[6] with jam, currants and *mostarda*[7] filling. There are also bulky well-raised *pinze* of the Friuli Venezia-Giulia and Veneto region baked for Easter and soft *pinze* made of stale white bread soaked in milk that were once part of poor man's fare in the Trentino Alto-Adige region.[8] The earlier preponderance of sweet *pizze* is also evident in the classic 19th-century Italian cookbook by Pellegrino Artusi[9] first published in 1891 (there have been 111 editions since): his 3 *pizza* recipes are all sweet as are his 3 *stiacciata* recipes.[10] His recipe for *pizza alla napoletana* must seem especially strange to the modern reader who, even if only slightly acquainted with Italian cuisine, would expect tomatoes and mozzarella from such a name – but finds sweetened ricotta[11] and custard instead. In the classic 20th-century Italian cookbook by Ada Boni (first published in 1927) that is even more popular than Artusi's cookbook the *pizza alla napoletana* recipe is already what we expect with both tomatoes and mozzarella present, and the recipes for savoury *pizze* are even more numerous (13, including potato *schiacciatine*) than those for the sweet ones (10, including *stiacciata alla fiorentina*).[12]

The meaning of *sformato*, a newer and more straightforward word than *pizza* or *sfincione* that mostly exists in the language of educated classes but not in the dialects, is reasonably clear: something that was cooked in the mould and then extracted from it – a substantivized perfect passive participle of the verb *sformare*. So far, so good. But if we look at the usage of this word in the two Italian classics, 19th-century Artusi and 20th-century Boni, we'll discover that whereas Artusi has 18 recipes of different *sformati*, Boni has none at all, although in the 20th century *sformati* featured (as they do now) quite prominently on Italian menus. What's the reason for this strange omission? After reading Boni's book more thoroughly we can however observe that there are quite a few (11 to be precise) *sformato*-like recipes present in Boni's book but the name itself is absent and replaced with *timballo* (originally meaning a kind of drum[13]). Now Artusi also has one *timballo* recipe, but the difference between his *timballo* and his *sformati* is well-marked, *timballo* being also a moulded dish but encircled within a characteristic ring of pastry.[14] Boni's *timballi* are mostly without pastry or breading of any kind though several instances of the latter occur. I could hazard a guess that just a few decades after the establishment of the Kingdom of Italy in 1861 Pellegrino Artusi was seemingly all for authentic Italian words to describe the dishes of the new Italy patriotically (*sformato* is really quite tame compared to his calling *béchamel balsamella*), but Ada Boni, who till the end of her life looked like a lady of the Belle Époque,[15] must have favoured European sophistication and so opted for the very international (though primarily French, of course) 19th-century *timbale-timballo* word both for *sformato* and *timballo*-style dishes. In 21st-century Italy *sformato* and *timballo* are definitely two separate culinary entities,[16] the balance as far as I can see being firmly redressed towards *sformato*, that is found twice as frequently on the internet[17] as the slightly old-fashioned *timballo*.

These three examples of *sfincione*, *pizza* and *sformato* give us just a taste of how very complicated and tangled the history of culinary words can be. So where is one to start exploring the naming principles of Italian regional cuisines and their authenticity?

I've decided to begin my preliminary investigation with Ada Boni's posthumous collection of regional Italian recipes.[18] It is not without flaws but as far as I know there are no universally appreciated Italian books on regional cuisine, though there exist many excellent books on regional Italian cuisine seen from outside.[19] Still our quest for authenticity restricted me to using only the sources of Italian origin (at least for that part of research and this paper's purposes). I actually wanted to find out region by region which recipes of Ada Boni's collection were still popular and which were forgotten and also hoped to discover more historical names of the regional dishes that could be traced back to antiquity to enrich my work on the Roman culinary vocabulary. With this project I came as a runner-up for Geoffrey Roberts Award in 2004 and thanks to it was granted a wonderful opportunity of some first-hand field research in Italy. Some fifty-odd towns, five seas, four ferries and one earthquake later I surfaced in Moscow loaded with precious data, primarily seventy-two hours of registered gastronomic small talk with chefs, waiters, hotel-owners, bakers, farmers, wine-makers and simply interested and enthusiastic passers-by (lots of those).

There were also some unwelcome revelations. It has been established that whereas the book's selection of recipes from Lazio, Tuscany and Liguria is entirely trustworthy, the recipes from Valle d'Aosta and Sardinia for example incite the righteous anger/laughter (depending on the temperament) of the 'locals'. One cook from Valle d'Aosta especially resented the presumably traditional eggplant recipe 'melanzane al forno all'uso valdostano'[20] in the chapter on her region, because she remembered the time – just a few decades back – when they only began to appear in the valley and there were lots of people who had never tasted eggplants in their lives. She put her finger right on the problem of non-authentic 'regional' naming – a recipe is named after the unlikely region just because a certain local ingredient (here Fontina cheese) is called for. This is the usual source of recipes masquerading as regional. Although nothing beats Escoffier who once called a salad of rice, carrots and peas with vinaigrette dressing Italian just because its colours were those of the Italian national flag.[21]

213

At the same time many fascinating traces of Roman cultural practices were discovered. My hostess from Calabria assured me that 'only uncultured people eat dormice, although shepherds will do it from time to time'. In central and southern Italy grape must is still boiled down and reduced to a thick syrup *vin cotto*[22] though it hasn't kept its Roman name *defrutum* (once one of the most-used ingredients in Roman cuisine), and in the province of Bari (Apulia) *vin cotto* is made of figs like it was also done in antiquity, etc. etc.[23]

And it is back to antiquity that we can turn in order to look for the continuity and authenticity of onomasiologic patterns in modern Italian regional cuisine. Writing my thesis on Roman culinary vocabulary I divided all the names of Roman dishes present in *Apicius* into three types, each formed after an onomasiologic model and name pattern of its own. Let us see whether they survive in the present times. The first type is when the name of the dish corresponds to the name of the main ingredient(s) used for the dish (incidentally, if I am not mistaken, a naming style currently favoured by the most famous restaurants in the world). It is almost absent in modern cookbooks but we find some examples of it in Boni's regional recipes, for example Calabrian '*zucchine e peperoni*' (courgettes and bell-peppers) or '*agnello, cacio e uova*' (lamb, cheese and eggs) from Molise.[24]

The second much more popular type of pattern is naming the dish after the main ingredient and adding a modifier. The modifier can reflect the method of preparation of the dish, the additional ingredients, the cooking utensil used or even some other specification (but it was comparatively rare in *Apicius*), such as the name of the place where the dish presumably comes from or the name of the person to whom the dish is allegedly dedicated or who is supposed to have created it. Of course some of the recipes' names of the second type include several modifiers. It is quite popular in modern cookbooks and Boni's collection has many instances of it:[25] Ligurian '*funghi alla foglia di vite*' (mushrooms in vine leaves), Tuscany's '*pollo fritto*' (fried chicken) and '*fagioli nel fiasco*' (beans cooked in the bottle), Sicilian '*pomodori ripieni alla siciliana*' (stuffed tomatoes Sicilian style – two modifiers being present), '*cavolo lessato all'aceto*' (cabbage cooked with vinegar – two modifiers) of Friuli-Venezia Giulia etc.

The third type of pattern is the most interesting one, the dish receiving as a name a special culinary term, a proper dish name. However it can also be, and most often is, specified with additional modifier as the second type model. Half of *Apicius*' recipes are named using this type of pattern, and so are half of Boni's regional recipes some twenty centuries later:[26] '*peperonata*' (bell-pepper stew) of Campania, '*fritto di fiori di zucca*' (a fried dish of pumpkin flowers) of Lazio etc.

I have tried really hard but I couldn't find any other naming patterns either in Boni's regional recipes or other Italian cookbooks, so I think that we can safely assume that these are the authentic patterns that worked for Latin and still work for Italian recipes. Another important thing about them is that the second and the third pattern type constantly interact and the modifier of the second substantivized changes into the dish name of the third, i.e. '*pollo fritto*' becomes a '*fritto*' and so on. De-substantivization is also not infrequent. Although pepper sauce was called *piperatum* in *Apicius*[27] and *peperata* in the 15th-century Maestro Martino's cookbook[28] it is back to *salsa peverada* in Boni's Venetian recipe.[29]

Onomasiology is all very fine, but it is even more interesting to find out whether there are any authentic patterns of culinary word-formation that remain from antiquity. One of the best-witnessed and the most productive suffixes in *Apicius* is *-atus* that is present in the above-mentioned *piperatum*.

Now the names of the recipes of all the twenty regions of Italy in Ada Boni's collection contain words with this prolific suffix (that has generally become Italian *-ato*) in one form or other (in many dialects it is pronounced and spelled *-ado*), even beef *roulade rollé* of Molise[30] does it via the French transformation of Latin *-atus* into *é*. Of course partly it's due to the fact that a lot of *-atus* forms come from verbs of the former Latin first conjugation (such as *lessato* – something boiled) but still many more *-ato* words are often substantivized adjectives derived from food-naming nouns (like

214

peperonata from *peperoni* , 'bell-peppers') and mostly they are used by the language to show that such or such ingredient is present in the dish.

Suffix -*ato* is used throughout Italy's regions from the mountains of the north to the islands of the south and nowhere is its prominence as evident as in regional restaurant menus; there one sees names of the dishes that are not in any Italian dictionary but are perfectly understandable because of their inner clarity. This suffix is one of those few diachronic things in Latin-Italian that haven't changed in the slightest and it is still working just the same it did in the time of Caesar and Cicero. Moreover it's a part of greater European culinary heritage, we encounter it in French *jambon persillé* and *mouclade*, Spanish *paella mariscada* and *fabata*, the already mentioned Greek *sfungato* etc. In fact we can trace its presence everywhere the Romans went. And no wonder, it has been leaving its unmistakable imprint on the world culinary vocabulary for more than twenty centuries of authenticity!

Conclusion

The global authenticity of culinary words on -*ato* is proved beyond doubt but how should we deal with single regional recipes, their names and their authenticity? During the Oxford Symposium on Food and Cookery in 2002 Andrew Dalby delivered his 'Fat words butter no parsnips' paper where he talked about the necessity of creating a food word database. I second that – especially as it would be a perfect tool for mapping out the elusive authenticity of regional cuisines. Because frankly there is no such thing as transcendental authenticity of a regional recipe – why must we be forced to choose between the 1st-century version and the 21st-century one, when it was recorded, this and that village, where the dish is cooked? Ideally (I am not speaking of bad cookbooks or bad chefs here) every version is authentic and different. It might be more interesting to consider the life of the traditional recipe as a series of authenticities, the older transforming itself into the newer with each new cookbook and each new person that cooks the dish.

215

The recipes could change name from region to region, or their names might remain the same and the recipes themselves would change – but we could still follow every important metamorphosis if we could make a really good electronic database, both synchronic and diachronic, that will show us what was this recipe when recorded in Rome in the 15th century and how the same/not the same recipe fared in Venice in the 18th. How did the name change? How did the recipe? Did any traveller write about it in his journal and what did he write? Only this tentative mapping out of all the possible two-dimensional recipe 'versions & mentions' mosaic could help us capture, however fleetingly, the Proteus of authenticity.

Notes

1. See http://www.palermoweb.com/panormus/gastronomia/*sfincione*.htm and http://www.palermoweb.com/panormus/gastronomia/lesfince.htm .

2. Apicius, *L'Art Culinaire* (Paris: Les Belles Lettres, 1987), p. 83, the only Roman cookery book extant (with recipes dating as it is currently supposed from 1st till 4th century CE) it is ascribed to the legendary Roman gourmet Apicius. As far as I know that's the only instance of *spong-* derivatives being used in a culinary context in Roman times, if we don't count Martial's epigram (XIII, 47) on the famous Picenum bread variety (*panes Picentini*), where he compares bread imbibing wine to a light sponge swelling with water.

3. Pianigiani, Ottorino, *Vocabolario etimologico della lingua italiana* (Genoa: Polaris, 1993). Other researchers indicate a possibility of Old High German root *bizz-* (meaning 'a bite', 'a piece of food' cf. modern German 'Bissen' and English 'to bite') or at least its influence, see Devoto, Giacomo e Oli, Gian Carlo, *Nuovo vocabolario illustrato della lingua italiana* (Milan: Felice le Monnier e Selezione dal Reader's Digest, 1992). For my part I find the former etymology much more convincing.

4. Also called *stiacciata* in some dialect versions.

5. http://www.ilpasticciereitaliano.it/scheda.asp?IdArticolo=66

6. http://www.fornocalzolari.it/pinza.htm

7. Italian fruit mustard (pieces of various fruit cooked in mustard syrup or mustard-flavoured fruit jam), especially popular in the north of Italy, the region of Lombardy (Cremona, Mantua etc.) is famous for its manufacture.

8. *L'Italia dei dolci* (Bra: Slow Food Editore, 2003), p. 120 and p. 373 respectively.

9. Artusi, Pellegrino, *La Scienza in cucina e l'Arte di mangiar bene* (Florence: Giunti Marzocco, 1991).

10. One of his *pizza* recipes (*pizza a libretti*) contains as an introduction words of a certain lady that had allegedly provided Artusi with this recipe and cautioned him against calling it *stiacciata* ('guai a lei se la chiamerà stiacciata'), because the *pizza* wouldn't come out flat at all, Artusi, p. 186. It is a good indication that by the 19th century the initial meaning of *pizza*, contrary to the same 'flattened' meaning of *stiacciata/schiacciata*, was no longer clear.

11. Bar the absent traditional *grano* (wheat berries) the recipe is not unlike the second version of the famous Naples cake *pastiera napoletana*, see the classic of Naples cuisine – Francesconi, Jeanne Caròla, *La cucina napoletana* (Rome: Newton Compton, 1992), p. 672.

12. Boni, Ada, *Il talismano della felicità* (Rome: Colombo, 1961).

13. Pianigiani, p. 1432.

14. Devoto e Oli's Italian dictionary seconds this in its *sformato* and *timballo* definitions.

15. http://www.pariopportunita.gov.it/I-SERVIZI/PUBBLICAZI/Italiane/pagine_da_26_a_37.pdf

16. Compare recipes for both in *Ricette di Osterie d'Italia, 630 piatti di cucina regionale* (Bra: Slow Food Editore, 2003).

17. *Timballo* gets 27 100 hits on Google, whereas *sformato* – 51 400. Just for the record *pizza* with its worldwide popularity amounts to 16 200 000 Google hits.

18. Boni, Ada, *La cucina regionale italiana* (Rome: Grandi Tascabili Economici Newton, 1995).

19. Chamberlain, Samuel, *Italian Bouquet, an Epicurean Tour of Italy* (New York: Gourmet books, 1968), Roden, Claudia, *The Food of Italy* (London: Vintage, 1999); Sälzer, Sabine und Hess, Reinhardt, *Die echte italienische Küche* (Munich: Gräfe und Unzer, 1990) et al.

20. Boni (1995), p. 360.

21. Escoffier, Auguste, *Ma cuisine* (London: Mandarin 1991) p. 130:

22. In most of the regions *vin cotto* is made from black grape must but in Lazio white grape must is used.

23. *Apicius*, p. 229.

24. Boni (1995) p. 29, p. 210.

25. Boni (1995) p. 147, p. 315, p. 327, p. 299, p. 84.

26. Boni (1995) p. 51, p. 114.

27. *Apicius* p. 16, p. 39 et al.

28. Martino, Maestro da Como, *Libro de arte coquinaria* (Milan: Terziaria, 1990), p. 4, p. 54.

29. Boni (1995) p. 386.

30. Boni (1995) p. 211.

Bede's World – Harvesting Knowledge on an Anglo-Saxon Farm

Christopher Grocock

'Bede's World' is a museum and heritage attraction begun in 1993 and opened to the public in 1996. It made use of a generous source of European funding and the availability of 11 acres of formerly derelict industrial land, formerly a dockyard and oil refinery, which had been 'regenerated' by the Tyne & Wear Development Corporation at no cost to the project itself. Its aims are to celebrate the achievements of the Venerable Bede and to explore the economy and culture of the early Middle Ages. From the outset the 'vision' behind the project was authenticity. This was the project's watchword, and as a concept – especially as it relates to food – it was to be explored in a variety of ways.

First, the landscape was devised to reflect the impact of Anglo-Saxon practice overlaid on a late Roman managed landscape. Every hump and bump had an explanation behind it! Second, within this landscape, appropriate – let us say 'authentic' – genotypes of plants were to be sown, as woodland areas, pasture, and in particular as crops to be cultivated, concentrating on wheat types (einkorn/ emmer/ spelt). Then the small areas of pasture were to be stocked – I want to say 'peopled' – with appropriate/authentic unimproved breeds of cattle, sheep, and other farm animals. Finally, the site was to be a vehicle for experimentation in authentic techniques – building in wood, tilling the ground with ards drawn by oxen, harvesting crops by hand, and processing them in an appropriate way.

From the outset, the 'vision' was clouded by the need to meet modern heritage standards and health and safety requirements. In place of a 'working authentic Anglo-Saxon Farm' came a demonstration area, including a tarmac path for wheelchairs.

Visitors were not the only obstacle to this vision of authenticity; the lack of an adequate trained or experienced labour force (peasants being in short supply these days), lack of funds, and above all a lack of time to develop the necessary skills and put them to good use, constituted another obstacle; most difficult of all was the pollution encountered in the soil, which was dredged from the adjacent River Don and turned out to have unhealthy levels of industrial residue – cadmium, mercury, and lead included.

Nevertheless, the project did produce a vast amount of useful data for museums, and many indicators which I think are of help on a more general level to food historians, especially as far as the vexed question of 'authenticity' is concerned, and these are the main topic of my paper.

First, the project established beyond doubt that what at first appeared to be a simple, almost naïve, socio-economic system was in fact highly complex and inter-connected. This became evident from a consideration of the activity for which Bede is most notable – writing. The inks used in Jarrow's scriptorium required honey, soot, egg white, and (possibly) gall; colours were made from plant extracts and imported materials. The books themselves were written on parchment – both sheepskin and calfskin being used in what appears to be an enormous quantity; they were written with quills. Thus these documents demanded bee-keeping, chickens or geese, cattle or sheep, and geese (again), let alone the probable cultivation of specific herb types. Sheep of course also provided the wool for the monks' habits.

Animals surprised our board of directors – many of them academics supposedly expert in these fields, but who were repeatedly caught out by reality – by their need of a constant human presence if they were penned or kept in fields, requiring additional feed, water, and checking on a regular basis to make sure they were (a) unhurt and (b) still there. The specific animal types we kept were a lesson in themselves. The unimproved breeds of sheep (Manx Loghtan, Hebridean, Shetland) were good wool producers, less effective as producers of milk, and very poor as makers of a meat carcass by modern standards. These breeds did not produce an adult carcass over 10kg kill-out weight. Our flock was small, but one dedicated person could have coped with a larger flock of over 100 head, producing some 100 fleeces and 50 meat carcasses per year – the manpower demands for sheep were in fact slight, apart from milking.

218

Pigs were another matter. Here we made use of a Tamworth x Wild Boar to breed the so-called 'Iron-Age pig'. These proved much better meat producers, reaching a kill-out weight of about 25kg in six months, and moreover took up little space on the site. They were also valuable as waste-disposal units, eating any surplus feed not consumed by the sheep.

Again, it would have been straightforward to multiply our swine without putting a strain on human resources.

Cattle were present on the site for their visual aspect and for the specific purpose of providing traction, both for building and for tillage. With advice from the Centre for Tropical Veterinary Medicine, a training programme lasting 2 hrs per day for 6 days per week over 16 weeks turned two feral steers into tractable animals docile enough to move half-ton timbers and to pull ploughs and ards in short bursts. Ploughing made demands on our human resources – at least 2 for training, 1 carrying on with feeding and watering, and more likely 3 persons required for ploughing. This is significant because multiplying up draught oxen teams would have necessitated an additional human ploughing team in a way that other animal types do not, and make the demands and sophistication of arable farming more obvious when compared to raising stock for wool, milk and meat.

A useful point which arises from all this experience is that all these personnel are mouths to feed, and not just from the aspect of agriculture in which they are involved:

in academic circles there is a marked tendency to split off the different aspects of agricultural activity, whereas in fact they are interdependent; arable farmers wear sheep, and shepherds eat bread!

This brings us to cereals. Cereal cultivation took time to develop because of the poor quality of the soil, to which I have already referred. Crops were at first sown in small patches prepared by hand; attempts at ploughing were thwarted by the appallingly artificial nature of the site, being compacted and having no natural layer of topsoil. What was noticeable however was the ability of primitive types of wheat to prosper in our very poor soils, and in experimentation it became evident that if they were sown thickly enough, the wheat types (particularly emmer and spelt) grew faster than the competing weeds and required no additional attention until harvest – 'wheat and tares together sown'. This diverges from the practice instigated by Peter Reynolds at Butser Ancient Farm, where wheat is sown in rows and then periodically weeded. If the Bede's World results are a reflection of authenticity in this respect then we can visualize that wheat cultivation demands intensive activity at two specific periods – the first, in soil preparation and then sowing once conditions are right; and second, a much more intensive and hectic period at harvest, when all must be safely gathered in ere the winter storms begin… (or the autumn storms, or indeed any kind of storm, or drizzle, etc.) and all available labour was presumably encouraged to participate. The harvest was particularly labour-intensive because of the peculiar nature of our wheat types, which do not grow at an even length – so they have to be plucked by hand, or cut and stacked into stooks and then threshed at a later date.

219

Sadly, in the case of the wheat there seems never to have been enough time to do more than sow demonstration crops at Bede's World, and its heritage side has in this respect overtaken the experimental archaeology side; some small-scale trials with emmer and spelt wheat have been conducted on our allotment since moving to Grayshott with a view to building up a seed-corn stock and carrying out experiments to measure yields on better soil than was available at Jarrow.

Nevertheless, some basic points arise from the 'Bede's World experience' which are foundational, and need to be incorporated in any hypothetical model of an ancient economic system (and which indicate areas of potential research in experimental archaeology):

The volume of harvest must be at least enough to feed a posited population on a regular basis, or else a society ceases to exist through famine;

There is always a 'peak' demand on human resources at the key time of harvest, which must be met from that posited population or else part of the crop will remain un-harvested (this is an obvious point but it seems to be overlooked frequently in hypothetical scenarios of ancient economies);

There is a symbiosis between animal and arable farming, which is the source not only of food products but also of clothing and what might be called non-essential items for survival (inks and other writing materials/gut strings for musical instruments are two examples which spring to mind).

In conclusion, although the project has never attained 'authenticity' in its heritage sense, and the idea of operating a 'working Anglo-Saxon farm' had to be modified considerably, there are aspects of Bede's World in which the aim of authenticity were fully met: the experience of farming using authentic technologies has provided valuable insights into the sequence of activities and human requirements in maintaining a farmed landscape; most important, the raising of authentic animal and arable types has provided a platform for reaching a better understanding of the usage and availability of food products, and the interdependence of animal and arable activity. In respect of food types, authenticity is an achieveable goal.

The Work of Food in the Age of Molecular Gastronomy Authenticity versus Artistry in the Contemporary Food Scene

Naomi Guttman

> Works of art are received and valued on different planes. Two polar types stand out; with one, the accent is on the cult value; with the other, on the exhibition value of the work.
>
> Walter Benjamin, *The Work of Art in the Age of Mechanical Reproduction*

The dangers of an insistence on authenticity are well catalogued by the twentieth century's tragic history of ethnic division and 'cleansing' and are all the more insidious because of the ways in which 'the revolutionary can turn reactionary.'[1] Ultimately, as Regina Bendix suggests, the proper question for study is not whether we can distinguish the authentic from the inauthentic, but rather to inquire how a particular discipline negotiates questions of authenticity.[2] This paper seeks to examine how questions of authenticity have been negotiated between what might appear to be opposing camps in the contemporary debate about food – the Slow Food movement and the movement in haute cuisine toward what has been variously named molecular gastronomy, deconstruction, fusion, or *nueva cocina*. Applying theories developed by Walter Benjamin in his essay, *The Work of Art in the Age of Mechanical Reproduction*, this paper will explore particularly the practices and rhetorical strategies of these two food movements both of which, ironically, owe their development in some way to the rise of globalization and fast food. While Slow Food and molecular gastronomy may seem at the outset to have quite divergent philosophies and ideas as concerns authenticity, a closer study reveals that they share many fundamental beliefs. All the same, in applying Benjamin's theories it is unclear which can lay a stronger claim to authenticity.

Fast food, slow food and molecular gastronomy

Eric Schlosser argues in his book *Fast Food Nation* that fast food is in part the result of the green revolution, giant agribusiness and modern living, including the ubiquity of the automobile and the U.S. highway system. Sociologists have noted that women's increased employment outside the home has also been instrumental in the decline of the family meal and the rise of processed and fast foods. In addition, fast food and junk food production increased dramatically with the technology afforded to produce, preserve and ship food products in mass quantities. The result is that presently most packaged products now contain large quantities of high-fructose corn syrup, salt and artificial flavorings and are aggressively marketed in our media.

As its name suggests, the Slow Food movement came to life in response to the global phenomenon of fast food. First established by the Italian Carlo Petrini in 1986 as a reaction to a McDonald's franchise opening in Rome's Piazza Spagna, Slow Food now claims 80,000 members in 50 countries. According to the Slow Food USA web site, Petrini 'recognized in 1986 that the industrialization of food was standardizing taste and leading to the annihilation of thousands of food varieties and flavors.' The Slow Food remedy is an approach that, among other things, 'seeks a rediscovery of authentic culinary traditions and the conservation of the world's quality food and wine heritage.'[3] Not surprisingly, 'authenticity' is a frequent term in Slow Food literature, and one can find it peppered throughout the web sites and books devoted to explaining and promoting the movement. Corby Kummer's book of essays and recipes, entitled *The Pleasures of Slow Food, Celebrating Authentic Traditions, Flavors and Recipes*, uses the 'A-word' in the title as well as in the text: in a portrait of German sausage-maker Torsten Kramer, Kummer emphasizes Kramer's integrity as an 'ideal Slow Food artisan' who preserves old sausage recipes without using the saltpeter which gives modern sausages their bright color. Kummer writes that Kramer's 'recipes and where he makes them are as authentic as is imaginable.'[4] Authenticity here is obviously associated with honesty and history, other qualities Kummer extols in his portrait. But in using this term, Slow Food can be seen to be betraying in its rhetoric the longing Bendix associates with the modern quest for the authentic, a longing which is reactionary rather than revolutionary.

The Slow Food movement sees itself as authentic because of the value we place on uniqueness. Each micro-climate that produces a particular type of grass will necessarily produce a particular type of cheese, and cheese-producers, even ones who live close to one another, will note how the weather in any given year will also affect the taste of their product. Given how sensitive cheese-making and other small, Slow Food activities are to the particular environment in which their product is grown, can it be that any of their products is not authentic? In other words, where each block of American sliced cheese produced in a Michigan factory will taste more or less exactly the same – this is the goal of standardization after all – each wheel of Vermont Shepherd from Major farm in Putney, Vermont will be slightly different, and this is exactly what the epicure wants.

In contrast to Slow Food, which attempts to recover and preserve old traditions, *nueva cocina* or molecular gastronomy seeks to renovate tradition by emphasizing the new: new flavors, textures and techniques, most of which employ some modern scientific process. Ferran Adrià, whom other chefs have 'the most imaginative cook in all history' and 'stratospheric, a Martian' in the world of haute cuisine, is largely responsible for the direction this movement has taken.[5] Adrià, who began the famous restaurant El Bulli on Spain's Costa Brava over twenty years ago, spends half a year in the restaurant and the other half in his workshop-laboratory in Barcelona. One

222

of Adrià's most significant contributions to contemporary cooking has been 'foam,' which is a sauce aerated 'with a nitrous-oxide siphon ordinarily used to whip cream.'[6] Adrián and Juan Mari Arzak were two of the most flamboyant members of the 2005 Madrid-Fusion gastronomic conference, where they

> showcased exploding desserts and solid soups, smoking cocktails and electric milk. There were lessons in liquid nitrogen technology and calcium chloride applications, and new ways with foams and gelees.[7]

Another, younger chef allied with molecular gastronomy is Homaro Cantu, whose innovations include using computer technology to create facsimiles of food which he serves at his Chicago restaurant, Moto. Using the edible paper bakers use to transmit designs onto birthday cakes, Cantu prints images of sushi 'using organic, food-based inks of his own concoction.' He has used this process to create edible menus that can be crumpled up and sprinkled into soup. Some critics have lauded Mr. Cantu and compared him 'to Salvador Dali and Willy Wonka for his peculiarly playful style of cooking.'[8] Mr. Cantu's ambitions do not stop with his restaurant. In one interview, Mr. Cantu claimed that his experimentation could contribute to space exploration:

> Maybe a mission to Mars, I don't know. Maybe we're going to find a way to grow something in a temperature that liquid nitrogen operates at. Then we could grow food on Pluto. There are possibilities to this that we can't fathom yet. And to not do it is far more consequential than just to say, hey, we're going to stick with our steak and eggs today.[9]

223

Cantu's cuisine stresses invention and technology, going way beyond the limits we usually associate with haute cuisine.

Hand in hand with pushing the envelope as far as technology is concerned, most chefs in this movement are also devoted to a more spectacular presentation style. For many years, nouvelle cuisine has emphasized plating, whetting appetites in part by a meal's visual effects, and certainly spectacular effects are part of any restaurant's repertoire. But the new chefs bring the spectacular, the interactive and the visual to new levels. Chef Grant Achatz claims that his cooking should be delectable but also 'theatrical and intriguing.'[10] Above all, he believes that he 'should take fuller advantage of the senses of touch, sight and smell as well as taste' and that plates can be opportunities for interaction and sculpture.'[11] Juli Soler, manager and co-owner of El Bulli, defends the spectacular emphasis in Adrià's presentation: 'Nous voulions récompenser les clients qui se donnent la peine de venir jusqu'à nous par une sorte d'œuvre de théatre.'[12]

Where Slow Food emphasizes the old, *nueva cocina* is infatuated with science, technology and artifice. What the movement does have in common with Slow Food is its emphasis on taste. Through the Ark of Taste, one of Slow Food's main goals is to conserve traditional tastes and increase their public profile. But *nueva cocina* also sees itself as defending and refining taste. Instead of using traditional thickeners, for example, chef Angel Leon of Casa del Temple in Toledo uses fish eyes to thicken a sauce that goes onto his fish, because using fish products 'brings the dish, and the diner, closer to the sea.'[13] Adrià himself claims that his techniques are developed to provide a more thorough engagement of all the senses, but that he is above all interested in 'the pure taste of things,' and hopes to achieve that purity by separating flavors so that they surprise the diner.[14] As Frank Bruni writes in a composite report on this state of the art cooking, at El Bulli he experienced the best of what the deconstructionists have to offer:

> More often than not, the oddball shapes, textures and temperatures of Mr. Adrià's food represented methods for delivering more consistent or concentrated flavors. He has devised ways to encase purees, oils and other liquids in translucent membranes, which do not compete with the taste of what's inside them but let them explode in a heady rush across a diner's tongue.[15]

While the emphasis on taste and the types of taste promoted are very different in the two movements, we see in each of them an interest in 'authenticity.' Molecular gastronomy's concern with taste is to isolate flavors and to create surprising contrasts, and some of its chefs are not afraid to employ junk food as a means to achieve a new twist on the old. Slow Food sees itself traveling hand in hand with environmental and land preservation movements; it insists on the primacy of taste, but only insofar as these tastes are 'authentic,' by which they mean old and traditional. The premise is reactionary and aim is conservative – a reaction to the onslaught of fast food and industrial food processing with the concomitant goal of conserving varieties of old flavors before they are lost. What separates and what unites Slow Food and molecular gastronomy can be further explored by looking into the relationship between authenticity and aura proposed by Walter Benjamin.

Authenticity and aura

Bendix and Benjamin both see the quest for authenticity as a reaction to the pressures of modernity, including technology and the capacities that technology affords, such as, in Benjamin's terms, 'mechanical reproduction.' Addressing the problem of authenticity and the emergence of European nationhood, Regina Bendix writes:

> The quest for authenticity is a peculiar longing, at once modern and anti-modern. It is oriented toward the recovery of an essence whose loss has been realized only through modernity, and whose recovery is feasible only through methods and sentiments created in modernity.[16]

The reaction to modernity thus sets into motion the anxious quest for the inaccessible 'authentic' which, paradoxically, only emerges once authenticity is threatened. In Benjamin's view, 'artistic production begins with ceremonial objects destined to serve in a cult.' Thus, he argues, 'the unique value of the "authentic" work of art has its basis in ritual, the location of its original use value.' This uniqueness or authenticity diminishes and loses what Benjamin terms its 'aura' when we reproduce artwork by means of mechanical reproduction:

> ...for the first time in world history, mechanical reproduction emancipates the work of art from its parasitical dependence on ritual. To an ever greater degree the work of art reproduced becomes the work of art designed for reproducibility. From a photographic negative, for example, one can make any number of prints; to ask for the 'authentic' print makes no sense.[17]

In Benjamin's paradigm, the authentic work of art is imbued with an 'aura' because it is one of a kind, an original; however, it only attains the aura once it is threatened by technology, such as photography, that enables mass reproduction. As an example, however, Benjamin uses not a work of art, but of nature. For Benjamin, a mountain perceived directly provides us with its 'presence' and has an 'aura'; however, when the actual mountain is replaced with a photograph of the mountain, we can no longer experience this 'aura,' for we are no longer encountering directly the mountain's presence.[18]

225

Note that in the quotation above Benjamin does not hold the 'authentic' cult-laden work of art in higher esteem; but in fact sees mechanical reproduction as a possible salvation from the cult object of art: 'for the first time in world history, mechanical reproduction *emancipates* the work of art from its *parasitical* dependence on ritual' (emphasis added). His essay thus celebrates the potential for democracy and liberation from the 'authentic' and may be seen as a reaction to the Romantic cult of the sublime. In other words, Benjamin sees a possibility for human progress away from religion and toward a more democratic access to the work of art – or propaganda.

What do these ideas imply about the future of food? Fusion chefs emphasize the entertainment value of cooking and the wit and surprise available to the diner if the chef engages our taste and eyes in unfamiliar ways. Arzak says, 'Ferran and I like our food to be fun and entertaining, and science is a big part of that.'[19] However, critics of deconstruction, such as Michael Steinberger, insist that the Emperor has no clothes when it comes to taste. In his lambasting article on the subject titled 'Cooked Senseless,' Steinberger, claims that the purpose of deconstruction is to 'shock' and that his cooking is 'making a joke' of haute cuisine. Steinberger sees 'little sensual gratification' in what Adrià's expensive meals have to offer.[20] Even Frank Bruni, an admirer of Adrià's cooking generally, admits that there is a limit to the purpose of deconstruction for its own sake, and is particularly underwhelmed by Homaro Cantu's desserts, such his 'green curry' ice cream which was, Bruni writes, 'a blast frigid heat without any virtue beyond that oxymoronic effect. This was food as props in a theater of the absurd.'[21]

That said, there is a philosophy among some American chefs that it is their responsibility to reeducate the public palette; this can express itself in Cantu's desire to avoid 'the usual steak and eggs' found in common restaurants and replace them with his printed food.[22] It can also appear in the desire to push the envelope in unexpectedly low-brow directions. Chef Graham Elliot Bowles, at Avenues in Chicago's Peninsula Hotel, seeks to develop his own brand of theatrical cooking by using junk food in his haute cuisine menus. Instead of the traditional dollop of mint jelly, Bowles might serve crushed Altoids with his lamb. He has also been known to serve 'lollipops of foie gras encrusted with Pop Rocks.' As Bruni writes, 'his cooking typifies another facet of this cuisine: the way it recruits junk food into the service of fancier dishes or creates highbrow versions of lowbrow classics.'[23] The ultimate goal for Bowles is to avoid being the kind of chef who would repeat 'that horribly boring quote, "I love to use farm-fresh products and local ingredients and European technique." '[24]

These examples underscore the values each side gives to food and raise particular questions: is food a medium in service of art, or is it a fundamental element of human experience? Is the ultimate goal of a restaurant meal to entertain and delight us in new ways or to participate in and educate us about an identifiable culinary tradition?

226

Food and/as art

One of the questions Benjamin's essay raises when applied to food is whether cookery qualifies as an art form and if so, what is the tension between the authentic and the inauthentic within the boundaries of what we call cookery? While cookery is mostly a domestic pursuit – a chore that until very recently every marriageable woman was expected to know something about – at its most rarified it is considered an art form, divorced somewhat from its quotidian function by virtue of special ingredients, techniques, time and presentation. This is clearly depicted in literature and film: Isak Dinesen's famous short story 'Babette's Feast,' for example, celebrates Babette's artistry which she pursues even as she recognizes that her art depends on the patronage of her political enemies. In Stanley Tucci's film *Big Night*, two Italian brothers attempting to open up an authentic Italian restaurant in New Jersey struggle over the competing values of Primo the chef, who is insulted by the philistinism of his new world clientele and Secundo the manager, who is willing to compromise in order to succeed in America. But even within the realm of good cooking, there is a tension between the craft-like approach of the artisan, and the higher scale, more flamboyant realm of the chef. Thus, when applying Benjamin's thesis to food, we must ask ourselves whether or not simply working from a recipe, a set of instructions for the reproduction of a particular dish, does not automatically rob food of its possible 'aura' in Benjamin's terms. While each chef or cook will necessarily produce a dish that is slightly different, and thus his/her own, the effect of following a recipe can be said to be akin to reproducing a photograph. But in the case of food, unlike the instance of the Mona Lisa, reproduction is assumed, for there is no 'authentic' osso bucco, no single Platonic ideal to which all osso buccos will be compared.

In his essay, Benjamin writes the following:

> [w]orks of art are received and valued on different planes. Two polar types stand out; with one, the accent is on the cult value; with the other, on the exhibition value of the work.[25]

If we replace the phrase 'works of art' with 'food' here, we may see a crystallization of some of the debates taking place between proponents of the new wave of haute cuisine – fusion or deconstruction – and those who promote the Slow Food philosophy of the preservation of tradition and 'authenticity.' The new sentence would read: 'Foods are received and valued on different planes. Two polar types stand out; with one, the accent is on the cult value; with the other, on the exhibition value of the work.'

We may well ask how far this goes: would Benjamin have lauded the liberating and democratizing effects of industrial food practices, for example, or would Agribusiness's and the industrial food giants' capitalist schemes have made him nostalgic for the authenticity of local and 'slow' food? Does Slow Food accent 'cult value' in the terms Benjamin posits? Or does deconstruction's emphasis on ritual paradoxically return it to the realm of the cult? Deconstructionist chefs believe that their work is not simply entertainment for the moment, but critical to the future of haute cuisine. In an interview with Frank Bruni, Anya Von Bremzen claimed that the new techniques of deconstruction have given chefs around the world 'a fresh perspective':

> In 20 years deconstructed food will be passé, but the revolutionary methods they developed will still be here. It's similar to the way the Impressionists completely destroyed figurative painting.'[26]

In this scheme food is simply an artistic medium, much as paint was for the Impressionists; whereas for the artisan food is connected to a sense of place, culture and perhaps even family, the chef is freer to explore the boundaries of the other worldly – as seen in Adrià's use of aerated foams – and perhaps even outer-space – as seen in Cantu's ambitions for growing food on other planets.

One could see that Slow Food's attempts to return to the authentic flavors of the past is somewhat akin to the attempt in art to capture the 'aura.' By returning to original and authentic techniques and flavors Slow Food attempts to bring us into the presence of the aura, while molecular gastronomy hopes to provide us with the experience of the exhibit. Deconstruction has turned the restaurant experience into something increasingly theatrical; does this mean that it is privileging 'high art' over the common or is its form merely a means to compete in a world of entertainment and diversion? Chef Grant Achatz claims that his cooking should be delectable but also 'theatrical and intriguing.'[27] Above all, he believes that he 'should take fuller advantage of the senses of touch, sight and smell as well as taste' and that plates can be opportunities for interaction and sculpture.[28]

This emphasis on sight – one of the cognitive senses Plato privileges over the more bodily senses, taste, touch and smell – causes one to wonder whether nueva cocina's insistence on the artifice is yet another way to remove food from its everyday animal function. Fundamentally, however, both sides claim to be after a certain kind of purity and even authenticity. Adrià's goal is to increase sensuality, particularly through taste, texture and sight as well as originality. Like any great artist, his focus is on originality, 'making it new.' Slow Food, by returning us to a sort of cult of the original, the authentic, of whatever kind of food is being recreated, envisions itself as a guardian of the origins of foods, of regional specialties and thus of culture generally. This could mean that Slow Food's drive is to maintain 'aura,' whereas deconstruction's goal is, in Benjamin's terms, to exploit its 'exhibition value.' However, in that they have created ritualized menus aimed at an elite audience, it could be said that this theatricality returns us to the ritual value of food and that the deconstructionist chef is in fact reintroducing ritual to the restaurant experience.

228

Bibliography

Bendix, Regina, *In Search of Authenticity* (Madison: U. Wisconsin Press, 1997).

Benjamin, Walter, 'The Work of Art in the Age of Mechanical Reproduction', *Illuminations* (New York: Schocken Books) p. 217–51.

Bernstein, David, 'When the Sous-Chef Is an Inkjet', *New York Times*, February 3, 2005. Circuits. G1, Column 2

Bruni, Frank, 'Sci-Fi Cooling Tries Dealing with Reality', *New York Times*, May 11, 2005. Dining In, Dining Out, Style.

Clark, Melissa, 'The Latest from Spain: Way Beyond Foam', *New York Times*, January 26, 2005, F2 column 1.

Korsmeyer, Carolyn, *Making Sense of Taste, Food and Philosophy* (Ithaca: Cornell University Press, 1999).

Kummer, Corby, *The Pleasures of Slow Food: Celebrating Authentic Traditions, Flavors and Recipes* (San Francisco: Chronicle Books), 2002.

Lubow, Arthur, 'A Laboratory of Taste', *New York Times Magazine*, August 10, 2003, Section 6. pp. 38f.

Schlosser, Eric, *Fast Food Nation: The Dark Side of the All-American Meal* (Boston: Houghton Mifflin, 2001).

Slow Food USA Web site: www.slowfoodusa.org

Steinberger, Michael, 'Cooked Senseless', *Financial Times*, London, April 30, 2005, Food & Drink. Online. Lexis Nexis Academic. 23 June 2005.

Style, Sue, 'Chef's Laboratory dishes: Eating Out: Sue Style visits El Bulli', *Financial Times*, Sept. 1, 2001, Saturday, Food and Drink.

Vetil Comellas, Virginie, 'Les bonnes affaires du meilleur cuisinier du monde', *Le Figaro*, Jan. 10, 2005. 'Etranger.' Online. Lexis Nexis Academic. 23 June 2005.

Notes

1. Bendix, p.8.
2. Bendix, p. 23.
3. Slow Food USA website.
4. Kummer, p. 40.
5. Quoted in Lubow.
6. Lubow.
7. Clark.
8. Bernstein.
9. Bernstein.
10. Quoted in Bruni.
11. Bruni.
12. Vetil Comellas, Virginie, 'Les bonnes affaires du meilleur cuisinier du monde', *Le Figaro*, Jan. 10, 2005, 'Etranger,', p. 16. (Trans: 'We want to reward clients who take the trouble to come all the way to our place by creating a type of theater piece.')
13. Ibid.
14. Bruni, p. 1.
15. Ibid.
16. Bendix, p. 8.
17. Benjamin, p. 224.
18. Benjamin, p. 223.
19. Clark.
20. Steinberger.
21. Bruni.
22. Article on Cantu—Ink Jet Sous Chef.
23. Bruni.
24. Bruni.
25. Benjamin, p. 224.
26. Bruni.
27. Quoted in Bruni.
28. Bruni.

History in the Baking:
Taste, Authenticity, and the Legacy of the Scotch Oven

Roger Haden

Writing in 1891, Italian cookery authority Pellegrino Artusi complained:

> If I knew who invented the oven, I'd erect a monument to him at my own
> expense. He certainly deserves it far more than many others who've been hon-
> oured in this monument-crazed century.[1]

From Artusi's culinary perspective, the evolution of the oven was a story of great
cultural significance and overdue for some public recognition by his countrymen.
Moreover, what has remained an unremarked evolution may have proved particularly
poignant for Artusi, as he witnessed first-hand the onrush of change which modernisation brought to cookery, baking, and indeed, to the form of the oven itself during
the last decades of the nineteenth century.[2]

    In this paper I explore the notion that, over time, indeed spanning millennia, an
accumulated gustatory wisdom was embodied in the generic design of the pre-modern oven, which during modern times was quickly and almost entirely outmoded.
Artusi's comment therefore underscores a broader process: how a dominant culture
based on self-interest historically overshadows what could be called authentic human
invention.

    The history of the oven also discloses a history of the sense of taste. This history
has always been fragile, because a physiological mode of knowing the world by understanding specific sensations constitutes a knowledge always susceptible to dominant
institutional forms of knowing, like applied science, for example. The latter can also
influence the degree to which sensory taste is historically devalued. The disciplinary
discourse of the philosophy of science has paid more attention to sight and hearing
as preferred epistemological tools of trade. In contrast, I suggest that the oven is an
authentic gauge of what the sense of taste has contributed to our species' corporeal,
culinary, and cultural experience. This old-world sensory wisdom (*Homo sapiens*
means the 'thinking,' but arguably also, the 'tasting' human) of the premodern era is
embodied in the technology of the domed stone oven.

    Historically, taste invested oven technology with a kind of sapience, not by
conscious act on the part of an inventor, but by a slow accumulation of traditional
knowledge formed by the constant receipt of taste's unique sensory register. Taste is a
living sense negotiating between bodily life and environment. The form of the oven

gives material form to this slow evolution. Siegfried Giedion writes:

> The form of the baking oven has passed down almost unchanged throughout the centuries. Like the axe or the knife, it is the basic tool of the human inventory. The oven developed into an egg-shaped chamber, which is excellently adapted to retaining and distributing heat... the baking oven was an oval chamber encased in a thick, fireproof vault of clay, brick or stone... every detail of this simple device – the vaulting, the inclined hearth, the position of the flue – was the product of unfathomably ancient experience.[3]

The generic form of premodern domed oven was thus not an invention, per se, but emerged as an outcome of an organic evolution, the technical extension of an empirical wisdom. Historian Peter Brears describes a 16th-century English example:

> The oven itself was of the beehive variety, consisting of a large domed masonry structure, entered by way of a small rectangular door. A fire of fast-burning kindling was first lit inside the oven so that its floor, walls and roof were brought up to a high temperature. The fire was then raked out, the bread swiftly inserted, and the oven door sealed in place with mud. After a short while, the oven door was broken open, and the bread, baked by the heat retained by the masonry, was withdrawn and allowed to cool.[4]

231

Many medieval illustrations of ovens feature the domed stone arch of this generic oven style.

Humoralism and the oven: a technology of taste

This type of oven clearly produces different sorts of flavours, but to understand how such a taste-informed technology developed we need to understand the premodern context in which the domed stone oven evolved. It was much more than merely a means of cookery. It was I suggest an organon ('An instrument of thought or knowledge; a means of reasoning, discovery... a system of rules or principles of demonstration or investigation' – *OED*), a unified practical and symbolic source of a tangible, indeed, tastable knowledge. The oven made everyday sense of the cosmos itself. It graphically demonstrated by analogy the humoral concept of correspondence, central to humoralism, which up until the scientific revolution of the seventeenth century had been the dominant system of medical knowledge in Europe for 1500 years.

Both the wheat from which bread was made, and bread itself, were thought to 'ripen,' for example; one by the sun, the other because as the loaves of bread baked in the oven they 'rose' and also took on the golden colour of the sun, and, moreover, resembled the ripened wheat from which the bread was made. The bread was also thought to expand like the fœtus within its mother, and so the oven – already womb-like in form – was a powerful fertility symbol.[5] Italian peasant women were known to ritually dance before the oven while pregnant. The oven demonstrated the validity of knowledge based on correspondence and analogy. And as Piero Camporesi writes:

> in peasant mythology the oven had a magic dimension... [it] was where food passed from the raw to the cooked state... the rising of dough was associated with the rise and 'growth' of the solar orb in the sky.[6]

Similarly, the baked bread itself,

> like a fleshy and tangible sun captured and shaped, fed, gave life, and repro-duced... a process which imitated, reproduced and captured the sun's strength in order to transform it into another small sun, a source of life, bread.[7]

But how did humoralism relate more specifically to taste, cookery, and the oven? One way of looking at this question is to link them both to heat itself, which ovens by their very nature serve to produce. According to the tenets of the humoral system taste, ovens, cookery and heat were all fundamentally connected. When it came to know-ing how to gauge the heat of the oven by outstretching one's arm inside the chamber, cooks might tell the correct 'temperature' in the older sense of that word: by thinking in terms of the four elements of fire, air, earth and water, and of their mixture.

At its heart, humoral lore endorsed an ideal of balance; the harmonious 'tempera-ture' (Gk. *eucrasia*) or mixture of the four elements, and of the respective human corporeal humors. Accordingly, the sanguine, choleric, phlegmatic and melancholic humors suggested individual 'temperaments,' each implying a specific mixture of the four elements within the human body, but also of differing thermal qualities and degrees of wetness and dryness. Temperature was literally a qualitative term describ-ing a state of mixture of fire, earth, air and water, and of heat, cold, wet and dry. It was also the product of a whole constellation of physical forces which could affect the balance and nature of these elements.

Thus, the macrocosmic world of stars and planets, according to laws of 'corre-spondence,' also affected the human body, plants and animals, and substances of all kinds: medicines, foods, and indeed, tastes. Tastes were considered to play an active part in preserving bodily 'balance,' and so a healthy constitution, and were under-stood in their cosmological, earthly, and physiological registers as material forces which could affect the organs of the body. Tastes were also linked to their governing celestial bodies, as historian, T. Sarah Peterson, explains:

> Taste, too, is correlated with the planets. Bad tastes attract Saturn; sweet and mellow ones, Jupiter; the hot, dry and bitter, Mars; sweet and rich, the sun; all good tasting sweet things, Venus; all sour things, Mercury; all insipid things, the moon.[8]

Within the humoral context tastes were also attributed 'thermal' qualities, as is still the case in Indian Ayurvedic and traditional Chinese pharmacy.[9] 'Heating' foods affect the liver, and 'cooling' foods must therefore be included to 'balance' the diet. Spicy tastes, not surprisingly, often indicate heating properties.

Importantly, the humoral system employed a language of analogy which connected cooking, ovens, heat (and cold) directly with human physiology and the macrocosmos; 'cooking' was a term used to describe the body's 'coction' of food, just as the oven figured as a microcosmic replica of a great cosmic 'oven.' Above all other everyday symbols, the baker's oven staged the very kinds of thermal transformation which Nature itself creates. Like Nature, the oven seemed to be a powerful transformer of the four elements.

From a culinary perspective, it was arguably a different kind of heat – 'temperature' – that the old oven reproduced, a heat which had its miraculous effects on the flavour of food. The taste of food cooked in a brick oven has a complexity which 'corresponds' with the complex system of knowledge in which premodern taste was culturally configured. One could say in passing that today taste is far less complex because ours is an age not only of diminishing biodiversity, but more blatantly, in modern times tastes have been simulated, synthesized, and replicated; simplification by approximation, and a form of inauthenticity which certainly betrays a richer past.

The clearest indication of a culinary and gustatory shift between past and present, comes in the late eighteenth century, at which time heat was theorized as a form of 'pure' energy. This history of 'heat,' as it were, is marked by a shift in emphasis from quality to quantity. By 1800, a quantifiable, measurable heat no longer resembled the qualitative 'substance' which thinkers since the time of Aristotle had described with regard to heat.

233

'Temperature,' in the context of cookery, therefore implies taking a holistic view of how heat has material qualities which were historically overlooked in the rush to modernize. Such qualities 'translate' into gustatory effects. Critical of modern rationalism, French philosopher Michel Serres has remarked that 'modern' heat 'has no dimension, it is... statistical... Cartesian, it subsumes disorderly multiplicities.' It is, he continues, 'a concept from the scientific era... [which] covers the mythical concept of chaos.'[10] 'Chaos' in this instance corresponds nicely with the complexity of caramelized flavours which a domed brick oven produces; the layers of 'chaotic' flavour produced by the composite technology of 'temperature.'

The Scotch oven

By the early twentieth century baking had become an industrial process on a massive scale. Drawplate, moving floor, reel, rotary, and finally, conveyor ovens, thoroughly outmoded the old 'manual' variety of 'peel,' or 'Scotch,' oven, the last in the line of generic premodern ovens.[11] The authentic tastes of the past have left a material trace of their history in these ovens, which can still be found in many rural townships all over the Western world. They are now the 'monuments' to a world of taste which over a century ago Artusi knew to be in passing. The long established understanding of temperature as something substantial was still in fact echoed by the last commercial bakers who worked in the heyday of the Scotch oven. They referred to the oven's heat as 'necessarily 'solid,' because the whole structure of the oven was solid and was heated in all its material to a high degree of intensity.'[12]

Typically, in Australia as elsewhere, Scotch ovens were '…solidly built [of] brick… with arched crown[s] nearly 3 feet from the sole, the latter being constructed of large stone slabs or bakery tiles'.[13] Perfected for the commercial baking of bread in the early 1800s (Diderot and D'Alembert's *Encyclopédie* includes an illustration of a similar style of oven, *circa* 1740) Scotch ovens were the commercial bakery's standard for almost a century. Three (and up to seven) thousand loaves could be baked in a Scotch oven over the period of a week.[14]

In 1995, in the Blue Mountains town of Blackheath, west of Sydney, New South Wales, I was privileged to work with Australian restaurateurs, Phillip Searle and Barry Ross, in opening their aptly named restaurant, Vulcan's, which featured an 80-year-old Scotch oven.[15] We experimented at first by roasting various larger items (legs of pork and whole ocean trout) and baked sour-dough bread. The tastes which resulted were complex, satisfying, and exciting. Meats were tender and juicy inside but well caramelised outside, showed little sign of shrinkage, while producing a lot of jus which accumulated inches deep in the roasting pan, but which might be lost to evaporation in a conventional oven. The bread was crusty beyond comparison with normal bread.

It appeared that anything and everything could be cooked – and cooked extremely well. Cakes baked and custards set perfectly in the oven as it cooled. The firebox also proved efficient for speed-roasting, and such favourites as 'fire-box squid' could be cooked in seconds. Whole halved zucchinis, split lengthways and brushed with olive oil could also be blasted with intense heat in this way; in half a minute they emerge, still green, caramelized down the middle, but tender, and quite delicious.

To taste the difference between foods cooked by temperature, rather than by heat, reminds me of a remark of Brillat-Savarin's, that 'the instinct of taste anticipates science.'[16] This sage of gastronomy also mourned the passing of spit-roasting, and thereby the art of roasting itself as something which could not be taught but rather that could only be intuited by a lucky few born with an innate talent. This talent is the instinctual, sensual knowledge which precedes abstraction and codification. Just as temperature historically precedes heat.

The brick oven at Vulcan's is a state-of-the art cooking machine which gives a palpable sense of heat-as-temperature: a qualitative, tangible, humoral substance. The 'climate' inside the oven appears humid, while the bricks seem to provide their own 'earthy' qualities. Fire is literally present, lending a smoky character at times, and air too plays a part, mixing as it does in abundance with the moisture present in the oven's atmosphere. Vulcan's oven had become a graphic teacher of a seemingly lost art of culinary transformation.

Such generically ancient ovens were not designed by some gustatory council who applied their knowledge in pursuit of culinary excellence! Rather, the 'instinct of taste' calls to mind the idea that, historically, the sense of taste acting within established patterns of social activity and oral culture, found expression in the form of the oven. Out of absolute need springs pleasure, as the world's greatest cuisines confirm. A slow evolution, analogous to the concentrating and intensifying complexity of flavour which develops over hours of cooking.

Precisely because this process was not covert, precisely because 'instinct' was at work, meant that the role of sensory taste had some potency for a time in the hierarchy of forces which shaped Western culture. For a time, institutional forms of knowledge let taste take its course. The oven evolved to meet the requirements of taste before the demands of industry and other forms of knowledge shattered the fragile ecology of taste's cultural technology.

Conclusion

It appears that the 'unconscious' historical sensitivity to taste and its fragile cultural technology stood little chance against modernisation. The quantitative priorities of production and of profit would supersede the qualitative virtues of taste as a driver of the food economy. It should be mentioned here that no attempt has been made to romanticise the life of the baker before the age of modern mechanisation and fossil-fuel firing. The working conditions of bakers were generally appalling in the 19th century. The hours were taxing enough on health, but additionally, bakers commonly worked coke or coal-fired ovens in basement bakeries with poor ventilation. In 1848, the average life-expectancy of bakers was lower than in other trades, at 49.[17] The gradual improvement of working conditions as the result in part of technological change was of undoubted benefit. My point, however, is that the passing of an era in oven technology also marked an end to baking skills linked to a deeper vein of empirical knowledge. Handling the peel and understanding heat, but most of all perhaps, the engagement of the senses in the production of a priceless gastronomic product: bread.

235

The premodern oven, still represented by working Scotch ovens today, remains the technological bearer of an authentic history of the senses yet to be thoroughly investigated. The senses are physiological, but they also find expression through technologies like the oven which we make in the image of the world as we find it. Tastes leave no material traces themselves, but the Scotch oven puts us in touch nonetheless with a lost syntax, what Camporesi poetically describes as the 'mute subterranean alphabet of the senses (taste and smell) that lead us into the deep, fragrant soul of things'.[18]

Notes

1. Pellegrino Artusi, *The Art of Eating Well*. Kyle M. Phillips III trans. (New York: Random House, 1996 [1891]) 307.
2. On the paucity of historical studies of the baking industry see, Christian Petersen, *Bread and the British Economy c 1770–1870*. Andrew Jenkins ed. (Aldershot, UK: Scholar Press, 1995).
3. Siegfried Giedion, *Mechanization Takes Command* (New York: Oxford University Press, 1948). 172–173; Cornish 'clome ob'ns,' or clay ovens, are an example of the simplicity, and antiquity, of this generic style of oven. Simple domed structures, sometimes simply 'a hole in the wall of the chimney... there must be hundreds of them walled up in Cornwall, for every house had one' survive as examples of the ancient form of the oven. Often 'oval in shape' they were heated with sticks, 'brimbles,' or furze; the 'favourite fuel' being blackthorn. Cornwall Federation of Women's Institutes, *Cornish Recipes Ancient and Modern*. Seventeenth edition (Truro: A. W. Jordan, November, 1946 [1929]) 72–73.
4. Peter Brears, *Food and Cooking in Sixteenth Century Britain: History and Recipes* (Birmingham: Historic Buildings and Monuments Commission for England, 1985) 13–14.
5. See, H. E. Jacob, *Six Thousand Years of Bread: Its Holy and Unholy History* (New York: The Lyons Press, 1997 [1944]) 77; the Roman goddess of the oven, Fornax, was supposed to dwell in the oven (357). Fornix, Latin for vault, or arch, is the root of the English word, fornicate, indicating a brothel, or arched room.
6. Piero Camporesi, *The Magic Harvest: Food, Folklore and Society*, Joan Krakover Hall, trans. (Cambridge: Polity Press, 1998 [1989]) 4; on the symbolism of bread (and ovens) in medieval Italy, also see, Piero Camporesi, *The Land of Hunger*, Tania Croft-Murray, trans. (Cambridge: Polity Press, 1996 [1985]) 151–154.
7. Piero Camporesi, *The Land of Hunger*, 156.
8. T. Sarah Peterson, *Acquired Taste: the French Origins of Modern Cookery* (Ithaca: Cornell University Press, 1994) 20. Peterson also provides much useful information on the links between Arab and European cookery in the medieval period.
9. Ayurvedic medicine belongs to a long history of Indian dietetics, a therapeutics which still observes humoral lore; on the humoral qualities of foods, see, K. T. Achaya, *Indian Food: A Historical Companion* (Delhi: Oxford University Press, 1998) Chapter 7.
10. Michel Serres, *Genesis*, Genevieve James and James Nielson, trans. (Ann Arbor: University of Michigan Press, 1995 [1982]) 102–103.
11. In the US, 'peel oven' was the term used for what was essentially a 'Scotch' oven (the peel being the long handled device used to move loaves around inside the oven, etc.). *The Baker's Dictionary*, Second edition. Compiled by Albert R. Daniel (Barking: Elsevier, 1971).
12. John Kirkland, *The Modern Baker, Confectioner and Caterer: A Practical and Scientific Work for the Baking and Allied Trades*, vol V, (London: The Gresham Publishing Company, 1908–1909) 272. Heat-related terms were also used by bakers, whose knowledge was not dependent on technical gauges. These included: 'good, sound', 'good', 'sound', 'sharp', 'solid', 'moderate', 'quick', 'ordinary', 'slow', 'very slow', 'slack.' Cited in Robert Wells, *The Pastrycook and Confectioners' Guide*, Second (revised) Edition (London: Crosby Lockwood and Son, 1892).
13. It is worth noting here that the 17th-century French writer Nicolas de Bonnefons' *Les Délices de la Campagne*, emphasizes that the 'bottom' of the oven should be made of 'loamy clay' which is 'much to be preferred before fire stone or brick tile'. See, William Rubel, 'Parisian Bread *circa* 1654,' in *Petit Propos Culinaires* 77 (Dec, 2004): 14.
14. See Wilfred Lovell, *The Craft of Baking: A family tradition of the Lovells since 1877, with family trees* (Daw Park, South Australia: W. Lovell, 1997). 'The largest bakery in the world' at the turn of the twentieth century, situated in Glasgow,... had 130 [Scotch] ovens, 15 hoists, about 140 horses and bakes every week... 450,000 loaves of bread at 2 lbs each', *Glimpses of Co-operative Land: including an account of the largest bakery in the world written for young co-operators* (Glasgow: United Co-opera-

tive Baking Society Ltd, 1899).

15. Vulcan's opened in April, 1996. I had the opportunity to work there during the first month or so of opening, in which time I had first hand experience of using the oven.

16. J-A. Brillat-Savarin, *The Physiology of Taste*, Anne Drayton, trans. (Harmondsworth: Penguin, 1970: 64).

17. Christian Petersen, *Bread and the British Economy c. 1770–1870* (Aldershot: Scolar Press, 1995) 78

18. Piero Camporesi, *The Magic Harvest*, 165.

In the Eye of The Beholder, on the Tongue of The Taster: What Constitutes Culinary Authenticity?

Sharon Hudgins

'Culinary authenticity' is a slippery subject that can be approached from many angles and defined in different ways, from strict constructionist to liberal revisionist. During the past half-century university academics have addressed issues of authenticity in the fields of anthropology, philosophy, art, music, folklore, and literature. Now it appears that my fellow culinarians have caught the bug. From culinary historians to culinary philosophers, from food journalists and cookbook authors to professional chefs and home cooks, conscious or unconscious attitudes toward 'authenticity' underlie many of our actions, discussions, and beliefs about food.

In an essay titled 'A World of Inauthentic Cuisine', historian Rachel Laudan coined the term 'Culinary Luddites' to describe those people who rail against the foods of modern industrial societies and laud those of the past as being 'traditional... true, real and authentic'.[1] Her thesis is that romanticization of, and nostalgia for, an often misunderstood past have created an idea of culinary authenticity that bears lit-

tle relationship to the reality of food production, distribution, and consumption in earlier times. At the 2005 International Association of Culinary Professionals' conference in Dallas, Texas, Laudan was asked about 'the loss of [culinary] authenticity' in many places around the world, as a result of modern food marketing, such as that of American (now global) fast-food companies. After describing how McDonald's adapted its menu to the culinary expectations of its customers in Hawaii (in 1958), she asked the audience, 'Are we *losing* the authentic? I think we're *inventing* the authentic. I don't think it was ever there. I think cuisines *do* change.'[2]

I doubt that any of us would disagree that cuisines do change. And cultural relativists will certainly contend that we are always inventing the authentic. But many people – from romantic nostalgists to cultural relativists and a lot of eaters in between – might question whether the 'authentic' was not 'ever there'. Regardless of your viewpoint – past or present, historically fixed or ever-changing – the 'authentic' does exist, albeit in different forms and different places, in different people's minds.

Perhaps I seem to be stating the obvious. But I think that most people do have their own sense of the 'authentic' in regard to food. Very likely their concept of culinary authenticity is based on their having eaten a particular dish frequently while they were growing up ('Mother [or Grandmother] always made it that way') and/or their having eaten it, at any age, in a place where the dish has become an accepted part of the personal, local, or regional cuisine. Memory and experience thus play a large role in many individuals' concept of culinary authenticity, shaping each person's expectations of how a particular dish should look, feel, smell, and taste.[3]

In addition, a person's own rigidity or flexibility concerning acceptable variations of a particular dish affects his or her notion of authenticity. Today's culinary historians might debate whether it is ever possible to authentically re-create a dish that was made in ancient Greece or Rome, but the contemporary consumer usually has a pretty good idea of what he or she considers 'authentic' about the foods eaten every day. That is one of several reasons why some consumers prefer Wendy's to McDonald's hamburgers, Burger King's to Sonic's french fries, Blue Bell's to Braum's ice cream, Mother's to Aunt Sally's cornbread, their own chocolate cake to mine.

However, I do think it is possible to reach some level of agreement on what constitutes culinary authenticity in regard to certain dishes, not only in a personal sense but also in a broader one. Cultural relativists who deny the possibility of this concept beyond the smallest unit of analysis will always say that any notion of culinary authenticity exists solely on the tongue of the taster and in the eye of the beholder. But if that is true – and if that's all there is – then much of what has been written (and tasted, digested, experienced) about 'traditional', generally agreed-upon dishes has to be taken with a grain of salt. From that point of view, a well-researched book with recipes for Texas-Mexico borderland cooking would be worth no more or no less than a poorly-researched or badly-written book, since all the recipes would be 'authentic' to someone (if only to the author). And serious culinary historians, cookbook authors, food journalists, and recipe researchers would be better off looking for other jobs.

239

Besides, if nothing is 'authentic' or can be 'authentic', then why have two hundred people from all over the world gathered at this symposium to discuss and debate this topic?

I enjoy pondering the philosophical over a glass of wine, but in my own work as a food writer I tend toward the practical. When I became a professional food writer in 1983, I approached my job with one guiding principle (which I naively assumed was the way that all food writers worked): I would write only about foods that I had eaten (preferably many times and in many venues) on their home soil. Without realizing it, I had established my own personal standard for 'authenticity'. And with only a couple of minor exceptions, I've adhered to that principle ever since.[4]

The following essay discusses several aspects of 'culinary authenticity' that I have encountered in my travels, research, and writing, in various places on the globe. But with all of our emphasis on 'authenticity' – and our turning it into a subject for analysis, discussion, and debate – I do hope that writers, readers, cooks, and consumers will not lose sight of what really counts: *eating*.

Dutch treat

The less we know about a culinary practice the easier it is to make assumptions about its authenticity and the more likely those assumptions might be wrong. One of my first encounters with the concept of culinary authenticity was in the early 1970s when my husband and I went on holiday to Amsterdam. We stayed at a small, family-run hotel that had been recommended in a well-known travel guidebook published in the United States. According to the guidebook, the hotel's breakfasts were especially noteworthy. We agreed: Every morning we sat down at a table covered with a white linen cloth and an array of sliced light and dark breads, cinnamon rolls, raisin bread, crisp crackers, a variety of cold meats, three kinds of hard cheeses, fruit jams, savory meat and cheese spreads, honey, and butter – much more than we could possibly eat at one sitting.

Following the suggestion printed in the guidebook, we drank our morning coffee 'the way the Dutch do'. That is, we stirred into our cups of strong, steaming-hot coffee a heaping spoonful of semi-sweet chocolate sprinkles that had been set on the table in a faceted glass bowl. After the chocolate had melted in the coffee, we added sugar and cream.

Every morning for the next five days, we spiked our coffee liberally with chocolate sprinkles – and even showed some other foreigners in the breakfast room how to flavor their coffee 'the way the Dutch do'. On our last day in Amsterdam, as we were checking out of the hotel, the proprietress said, 'May I ask you a question? Why do you always put chocolate into your coffee every morning? Is that a special American way of drinking coffee?' When we replied that we'd been told it was a Dutch custom, she laughed and said she had never seen anyone do that before: The chocolate sprinkles were meant to be strewn over slices of buttered white bread.[5]

This is a good example of being led astray by incorrect information, of making assumptions based on a single, inaccurate source.[6] We had thought we were doing something that was authentically Dutch, tasting coffee the way it was flavored in the Netherlands (an understandable assumption, since the Dutch are such important producers of chocolate).[7] And if the Dutch innkeeper had not inquired about our seemingly strange 'American' way of drinking coffee, we might have continued to think (for who knows how long) that this was an authentic Dutch culinary practice. However, when I told this story to an American culinary historian, he cautioned against drawing the conclusion that no one in the Netherlands spikes their morning coffee with chocolate sprinkles, because maybe that *is* a practice among some people or even just one particular family. His point was that we should distinguish between authenticity in a *particular* sense (i.e., whatever is authentic to the individual) and authenticity in a more *general* sense (i.e., whatever is considered authentic by a number of people, such as an agreed-upon recipe for a certain dish, or a commonly accepted culinary practice).

The case of *Kugelhopf*

The pursuit of culinary authenticity (although I didn't call it that) became a guiding force when I began my career as a food writer in Europe in the 1980s. *Kugelhopf* is a

case in point: When I set out to write an article about Alsatian *Kugelhopf*, I was determined to learn everything I could about this light, delicate, yeast-raised cake made
in that region of France.[8] I was already very familiar with its taste and appearance,
having eaten *Kugelhopfs* in Alsace many times during the previous decade – at elegant
pastry shops in Strasbourg, Colmar, and Obernai; at small country bakeries in villages
from the Vosges to the Rhine; and at local festivals where homemade *Kugelhopfs* were
sold by the women who had baked the cakes themselves.

In addition to researching the history of *Kugelhopfs* in Alsace, I also needed to
develop a recipe for Alsatian *Kugelhopf* (expressed in American measurements, for
my readers), a recipe that was 'my own' but that also produced a cake with the taste,
texture, and appearance of the *Kugelhopfs* I had eaten in Alsace – in other words, an
'authentic' product.

My approach in developing a recipe from other written and/or oral sources is to
collect a number of recipes – usually at least ten, often many more – for the dish I
want to make. The recipes should also be ones for the dish as it was prepared during
the time period I am referencing in my writing (in most cases, a specific time during
my own contemporary era, from the 1950s to the present). Then I make a chart comparing the ingredients and techniques of each recipe to determine which are common
to most or all of the recipes, which are deviations from the norm, and which of those
deviations are within the generally agreed-upon range of variables for that dish.[9]

In the case of *Kugelhopf*, I compared thirty-eight recipes from Alsatian, French
(non-Alsatian), German, Austrian, British, and American cookbooks, with the
majority of the recipes coming from the Alsatian and French cookbooks. I kept the
ingredients and techniques that were used by most of them, weighting those from the
Alsatian and French cookbooks more heavily than those from other sources. When
the techniques differed, I chose the one that seemed most likely to produce the kind
of *Kugelhopf* I was seeking, a cake that would taste like the best I had eaten in Alsace.
Then I baked the dough in a traditional glazed earthenware *Kugelhopf* mold from the
Alsatian pottery village of Soufflenheim.

On my first attempt, that recipe produced a *Kugelhopf* just like those I had eaten in
Alsace.[10] The accuracy of the ingredients, technique, cooking utensil, form, presentation, texture, and taste all contributed to the 'authenticity' of that *Kugelhopf*. I would
stack it up against an Alsatian-made *Kugelhopf* any day.

But wait: Cakes called *Kugelhopf* (or *Gugelhupf*)[11] outside of Alsace – in Germany,
Austria, and even elsewhere in France – are not always made from a yeast-raised
dough studded with raisins and decorated with almonds and confectioners' sugar.
Some recipes for *Kugelhopf* are leavened with ingredients other than yeast, sweetened
with much more sugar, flavored with candied fruits, and sometimes soaked with liquor or covered with a sugar glaze. These dense, rich cakes, with a large heavy crumb
and more assertive flavors, are very different from the light, yeasty, subtle, bread-like
Kugelhopfs of Alsace. The only thing they have in common, besides their name,

is their form: Both kinds of *Kugelhopf* are baked in a round, fluted mold shaped somewhat like a Turk's turban. Many German and Austrian bakers would claim that these dense, rich cakes are authentic *Kugelhopfs* – as indeed they are in those parts of Europe. Authenticity in this case depends on the basic type and regional variations of *Kugelhopf* being considered.

This is where food writers sometimes fall into a trap when writing about an 'authentic dish'. In referring to *Kugelhopf*, or to 'authentic *Kugelhopf*', it is necessary to specify which kind of *Kugelhopf* is meant and what region it comes from. For the sake of accuracy, food writers need to provide both the correct context for this cake as well as the right kind of recipe for it. Some writers make the mistake of mixing up – or not even being aware of – these two very different kinds of *Kugelhopf*, thus adding to the confusion and misinformation about these cakes that have the same name and the same form but very different tastes and textures.[12]

A hill of beans

Authenticity is a concept often applied to various traditional bean dishes around the world, from French *cassoulet*[13] to Spanish *fabada asturiana* to Boston baked beans. In Texas, almost everyone familiar with traditional Texas 'cowboy cooking' can agree on what constitutes authentic 'cowboy beans', 'ranch beans', or 'barbecue beans' (different terms for the same, or very similar, dishes).[14] The basic recipe combines pinto beans[15] with water, salt pork or bacon, onions, salt, and usually black pepper. Many cooks also add fresh garlic, as well as fresh and/or dried chilies (hot peppers) or chili powder.[16] Other variables include the cooking time, as well as the amount of liquid used – both of which contribute to the texture of the dish: a thick mass of soft beans that have been cooked for several hours, or firmer beans cooked for a shorter period of time and usually served with more of their cooking liquid – the 'soup' – surrounding them.[17]

Regardless of these variations, everyone agrees that authentic Texas 'cowboy beans' must be made with pinto beans (although similarly shaped red beans are permitted in a pinch). The same kind of dish made with white beans, black beans, kidney beans, butter beans, or any other kind of beans would not qualify as authentic.

In the case of 'cowboy beans', authenticity is based on a consensus regarding the specific kind of bean that must be used, plus a relatively narrow range of other ingredients that can be included and cooking techniques employed. If these 'rules' are not followed, then the product is more likely to be the kind of so-called 'cowboy beans' (usually bland-tasting, mass-produced commercial concoctions sold in restaurant-size cans) that are served at many restaurants in the United States – beans that do not taste the same as the 'authentic' Texas version of this dish.[18]

In Texas there is less agreement about beans in one of the Great Debates on culinary authenticity, which revolves around what constitutes 'authentic Texas chili', a meat dish halfway between a thick soup and a stew.[19] Purists contend that true Texas chili is made only of finely cubed or coarsely ground beef (or venison) cooked in fat, then slowly simmered in water or meat stock along with fresh and/or dried red chilies, cumin, garlic, Mexican oregano, and salt. The addition of beans would be heretical. But other Texas cooks choose to add onions, tomatoes, and many other ingredients, including beans. Given that different versions of chili made with a wide range of ingredients are eaten across the large land area of Texas, there is no real consensus on the ingredients of an 'authentic' Texas chili. (The rules of various chili cook-offs in Texas do specify which ingredients are allowed and which are not permitted – but these rules, too, vary greatly from place to place and among the different cook-off sponsors and 'sanctioners'.) In this case, the concept of authenticity varies so much that it is difficult to define it in regard to Texas chili – which leads to the conclusion that the controversies over 'true Texas chili' don't amount to a hill of beans.[20]

Whose potato salad is it?

I first encountered 'Russian Salad' in the mid-1960s, in cookbooks published in English by Russian emigrés in the United States and England. But I never tasted this dish until several years later, at a somewhat sinister restaurant in Istanbul (reputedly a meeting place for Cold War spies), which was run by a pair of elderly Russian sisters. From the menu printed in Russian and Turkish I ordered a rather exotic-sounding appetizer called '*Salat Oliv'ie*', which turned out to be the 'Russian Salad' or 'Potato Salad with [Whatever]' published in those Russian emigré cookbooks: a cold salad of cubed potatoes and carrots, green peas, chunks of white-meat chicken, and pickled capers, dressed with a lemony mayonnaise.

243

In Paris a couple of years later, I came across a similar dish – with the addition of chopped onions and hard-cooked eggs – listed as '*salade russe*' (an appetizer) on restaurant menus and also sold as a cold take-out item at some charcuteries. And traveling around Spain in the 1980s, I discovered that a tapa often served in bars was '*ensalada rusa*' (or '*ensaladilla rusa*') – similar to the French version of Russian potato salad but with a Spanish twist: plenty of garlic infusing the mayonnaise, along with canned bonito or tuna added to the mixture. At one bar in Castile the memorable *ensalada rusa* was even bound with traditional alioli, made solely with extra-virgin olive oil, raw garlic, and salt.

Finally, in the early 1990s, I ate Russian potato salad on its home soil. But the desultory versions served in Moscow and St. Petersburg restaurants tasted merely like drab cousins of the more fully flavored French *salade russe* and Spanish *ensalada rusa* that had already won my allegiance in Paris and Madrid.

When my husband Tom and I moved to Vladivostok in the Russian Far East in 1993, we began making Russian potato salad at home. Inspired by ingredients found in the local markets,[21] Tom soon developed his own version that we called 'Vladivostok Potato Salad'. Starting with the basic recipe (which itself permits several variations), he added ingredients that contemporary Russians did not usually include in this dish, but which were available in the Russian Far East: olive oil, lemon juice, fresh garlic, Kamchatka crab meat, and shiny red-orange Pacific salmon roe. Russians who tasted Tom's version of 'their' potato salad were invariably seduced by his take on an old theme. They dropped heavy hints about hoping to eat it again at our dinner parties, and they asked for the recipe to add to their own culinary repertoire. And who knows? Tom's 'Vladivostok Potato Salad' might now be a 'family recipe' among some people in the Russian Far East, already handed down to the next generation – or might even be offered (under another name) on restaurant menus in Vladivostok.

But whose potato salad is it? Culinary historians tell us that this dish, known in Russian as 'salat Oliv'ie', was created by a French chef named Olivier at his fashionable Ermitage restaurant in Moscow during the second half of the 19th century.[22] An aristocratic recipe that included grouse, crayfish, truffles, and olives, this elegant cold potato salad evolved into more proletarian fare in the twentieth century, usually combining potatoes, carrots, and bottled or canned green peas, occasionally perked up with onions and cucumbers (fresh or pickled), all napped with commercial mayonnaise, sour cream, or a blend of the two.[23]

Although the creation of this dish is attributed to that restaurant chef in nineteenth-century Moscow, it is not hard to imagine that Russian home cooks – in large cities and small villages – also combined chopped leftover cooked meats and fresh or cooked vegetables, including the increasingly available and acceptable potatoes, binding them together with soured cream to make a cold salad. My Russian friends and I did this all the time in late 20th-century Siberia. Why should our predecessors not have done likewise, when they had the same ingredients available more than one hundred years ago?[24] Was this recipe really 'invented' in a single famous restaurant – or also in hundreds of home kitchens after potatoes became a common ingredient in the Russian root cellar?

And how did 'Russian potato salad' travel to France to become *salade russe*? How did it end up in Spain as a popular *tapa* that crosses the boundaries of Iberia's many culinary regions? Where does Tom's crab-and-salmon-caviar 'Vladivostok Potato Salad' fit into the 'authentic' cuisine of Russia's Far East? How many different versions of Russian potato salad are made in thousands of kitchens around the world every day?

These are the kinds of questions that send culinary historians off on their quests. And all roads lead back to the question of authenticity. What is 'authentic Russian potato salad'? 'Authentic *salade russe*'? 'Authentic *ensalada rusa*'? 'Authentic Vladivostok Potato Salad' (with its combination of Russian Far Eastern and Spanish-influenced flavorings)? Whose potato salad is it, anyway?

Paula Wolfert addressed a similar issue in an interview with David Leite, posted in 2005 on his website, 'Leite's Culinaria':

David Leite: There's so much controversy surrounding culinary authenticity. At times I've been called on the carpet because a particular dish that has been in my family for generations has been called 'faux food' by someone whose family makes it a different way. And in the Azores [where Leite's family comes from], the same dish can vary from town to town, neighborhood to neighborhood, even family member to family member. To you, what's an authentic dish?

Paula Wolfert: Their way? Your way? What's authentic? Nothing. I veer away when anyone says the word *authentic*, because authentic isn't what I'm interested in. I'm interested in the truth. There's a difference between the two. The integrity of the dish is important, but I'll change the recipe to make it work. Integrity is using the ingredients of an area, it's using what people recognize as what comprises the dish, but there's not just one way to make something. Even Bordelaise sauce has seven different ways to make it.... The recipes in all my books are, for lack of a better word, authentic in that they were taught to me by locals, but there are people down the road where I would be learning a dish who cooked it differently. I just try to make it as good as I can and frame the recipe in a story. It is all authentic.

Leite: Well, the reason why I asked is I took the idea out of your introduction, where you wrote, 'Authenticity is always my guide, but I try not to let it become my straitjacket.'

Wolfert: Oh, okay, that's different – it's a guide. I'm trying to get to the truth of a recipe, to use the right ingredients, the things that people generally agree comprise the dish. But how they make it is personal.

Leite: So it's being selective within an area.

Wolfert: Exactly, and that's why I said it's not a straitjacket, because with a straitjacket, I'd have to go with the first person who said, 'This is the way of doing it.' Well, how would I know if she knows, and does she know which is the right way? Does *anyone* know which is the right way? It's all subjective. Isn't it? [25]

Culinary cloning

Although my own sense of culinary authenticity is tied to time, place, and custom, I also believe that it is possible to recreate authentic versions of traditional dishes such as Alsatian *Kugelhopf* and Texas 'cowboy beans' in almost any part of the world, if – Big If – you follow a classic (i.e., generally agreed-upon) recipe, use the same ingredients and cooking techniques (including the right kind of heat source and cookware), and know what the dish is supposed to look and taste like (because you have eaten it – preferably several times and in several places – on its home soil).[26] But fudge on any of these variables and you are likely to produce only a semblance of the traditional dish, one that would not necessarily be recognized as authentic by an Alsatian or a Texan. (Yet of course your dish would be 'authentic' – in the sense of an authentic variation – from the cultural relativist point of view.)

In support of my contention that it is possible – if not always easy – to accurately reproduce a dish outside its own culinary context, I offer the example of goulash soup (*Gulaschsuppe*/German, *polévka gulásová*/Czech), a popular Hungarian-inspired dish eaten in many parts of Central Europe, including Germany and the Czech Republic. Goulash soup is made at home (from scratch or with commercial dried soup mixes that have been a convenience product available to home cooks for at least two decades), and also in restaurants where this thick, spicy soup is a common item on German Gasthaus and Czech beer-hall menus.

In my quest to develop a recipe for a classic Czech beer-hall version of this dish, I followed my standard procedure. I ate goulash soups in many beer halls in the Bohemian part of Czechoslovakia, compared recipes published in both Czech and German, and devised my own recipe to produce a goulash soup equivalent to the best I had eaten in Bohemia. Then I tested it at home (in Germany), using Hungarian paprika (commonly available to Czech cooks), and included the recipe in an article about Czech foods that I wrote for *Chile Pepper* magazine in 1991.[27]

Another food writer also published my recipe for Czech goulash soup in an American newspaper (with credit to me). Later he received a letter from a reader thanking him for that recipe. She wrote that her father had emigrated to the United States from the Sudetenland of Czechoslovakia shortly after the end of World War II. The food from 'home' that he missed the most was goulash soup – but, no matter how many recipes she tried, none of the goulash soups she cooked for him in America had ever lived up to his memories of the dish he had loved so much in south-western Czechoslovakia. Then she made my Czech beer-hall version. Upon tasting the first spoonful, her elderly father looked at her with tears in his eyes and told her that, after all those years, she had finally succeeded in making a true goulash soup like the one he had always eaten 'at home'.

This story makes two points: First, it is possible to accurately reproduce a dish from one place in another place, if you know what the dish is supposed to look, smell, and taste like; if you use the right ingredients and techniques; and if you do not cut corners on any of these variables. Second – and this is a factor that you cannot control – one of the primary constituents of many people's sense of culinary authenticity is their own personal taste memory, the standard against which many a dish is judged.

Conclusion

Each of us eats food every day (if we are fortunate), yet relatively few people are conscious of the issues of culinary authenticity addressed in this essay and at this symposium. Authenticity exists on the tongue of the taster, in the nose of the inhaler, and in the eyes of the beholder – all of which come together in the mind as a culinary experience, whether it's the comforting cinnamon-sweetness of Grandmother's peach cobbler or the post-modern frisson of Ferran Adrià's sardine foam. As Darra Goldstein pointed out in the Winter 2004 issue of *Gastronomica*:

With careful research in material and written culture, we can sometimes determine the Ur-recipe for a dish, which is definitely of historical interest. But why should we aspire to recreate this original concoction on our modern-day plate? Like beauty, authenticity should reside in the eye (and the tongue, and the nose) of the beholder – in this case, also the eater. If a dish resonates for us, evoking memories of another time or place, if it connects us with something beyond the present moment, then it should be considered authentic enough, even if its ingredients and methods have changed.... Instead of seeking a fictive original, let's admit that innovation can be authentic, too.... A recipe is authentic not only when it has been conveyed unchanged across the ages. Food can take new forms in different times and places yet still remain genuine in spirit. We should continue to pay attention to tradition, to understand what's come before. But to remain vital, recipes, like people, need to change.[28]

I especially like Goldstein's statement about food's taking new forms in different times and places, but still remaining genuine in spirit. That's the whole point: genuine in spirit. At the same time we also have to recognize that no matter how hard we, as serious food writers, strive for accuracy – and for genuineness of spirit – in our own writings and in our efforts to communicate the authenticity of our subjects to our readers, we cannot be held responsible for those readers who misread or misinterpret what we have written (despite what we assume to be the clarity of our own prose), or those who make changes in our recipes and then are disappointed because the resulting dishes do not turn out the way they had expected. Surely every food writer has had this experience sometime in his or her career: the book review where the reviewer completely missed the point of what you wrote, or misquoted you, or quoted a statement of yours out of context;[29] the complaint from a reader who used one of your recipes but made so many changes that the recipe failed, or the dish was edible but bore little resemblance to the 'authentic' one that you presented in your cookbook or culinary article.

Despite our earnest efforts to be accurate – and to approach authenticity – in our food writings, we should always remember that our noblest attempts cannot withstand the blatant blunders of readers like the woman depicted in the comic strip, 'Piranha Club', by B. Grace:

[Setting: *Woman in her kitchen, preparing to bake cookies, with an open cookbook, an electric mixer, and a mixing bowl on the table in front of her.*]
Recipe: 'Beat until soft, 1/3 cup butter...'
Cook: I'm out of butter...I'll use lard.
Recipe: 'Sift two cups all purpose flour...'
Cook (*looking quizzically at an unidentified cardboard container*): No flour...
I'll use cornstarch.

Recipe: 'Resift with 1/4 teaspoon double-acting baking powder...'
Cook (*holding up a jar of something white*): I'll have to use foot powder...
Recipe: 'Blend in two egg yolks...'
Cook (*peering into the refrigerator*): No eggs...Mustard's yellow.
Recipe: 'Add one can flaked coconut...'
Cook (*looking into a kitchen cabinet*): I've got a can of tuna.
Cook's Husband (*to his wife, after taking a bite of these 'cookies' presented to him on a serving platter*): How could they turn out so BAD?!
Cook: Don't ask me...I followed the recipe![30]

Notes

1. Laudan, Rachel. 'A World of Inauthentic Cuisine', <http://food.oregonstate.edu./ref/culture.html> (Corvallis, OR: Oregon State University, January 2000), p. 1.

2. 'A Conversation with Scholar-in-Residence Rachel Laudan,' International Association of Culinary Professionals, Dallas, Texas, April 16, 2005. Lawrence Iliff, in "Mexico's gift to the world" (*Dallas Morning News*, Sunday, March 27, 2005, p. 81) provided a recent example of culinary invention and change in regard to a traditional Mexican product: Evelio Arias, proprietor of Chocolatería Mamá Sarita in Mexico City, offers 80 different varieties of hot chocolate, 'plus those you are free to invent on your own.... Patrons are free to pick their chocolate base (from bitter to sweet), their hot liquid (water, different types of milk and even soy milk) and their sweetener (from cane sugar to diabetic-friendly fructose and maguey honey). Customer recommendations are welcome.... A Colombian customer said hot chocolate in that South American country includes chunks of yellow cheese, and now it's on the menu. A Greek customer suggested hot chocolate with marshmallows, which is not traditional in Mexico, but that's now on the menu, too. "The traditions that die are the ones that are not open to change," says Mr. Arias. "The ones that will survive are the ones that can change without losing their essence".'

3. A personal example: Having eaten a large number of excellent French pastries in France during the 1970s, I was taken aback by the perfectly formed – but nearly tasteless – 'French' pastries sold at French-style pastry shops in Tokyo when I lived in Japan in the latter part of that decade. They looked like French pastries, but most of them had the texture of Styrofoam garnished or filled with something like unflavored Cool Whip. To me, they were certainly not 'authentic' French pastries. But I've always wondered if the Japanese (and any other people) who ate them in Tokyo used those peculiar pastries as their standard for what constitutes 'authentic French pastries' when they encountered those foods elsewhere in the world.

4. To me, this is a fundamental principle: A food writer must go to the country or region whose food he or she plans to write about. This might seem an obvious statement – but I have known food writers in the United States who thought they could write about another country's cuisine(s) without ever traveling there themselves. They claimed they could do all the necessary research in the United States, eat at restaurants featuring that country's cuisine in America, and then write authoritatively about the foods of the foreign country they were assigned to cover, even though they had never been to that country at all. I strongly disagree with that approach. To me, a particular place's cuisine is rooted in its geography, climate, agriculture, animals, cooking methods, religions, and customs. You must go there to experience it on site, so that you will have both a basis and a context for whatever you write about the foods of that place (even if your article is about how that country's cuisine has migrated to, and been interpreted in, your own country).

248

5. Adapted from 'Dutch Treat', letter to the editor of *Gastronomica: The Journal of Food and Culture*, Vol. 5, No. 1, Winter 2005, p. 1. Later I discovered that the Dutch make several kinds of chocolate sprinkles (*chocoladehagel*, also known as *hagelslag*) for strewing over buttered bread – including milk chocolate, dark chocolate, white chocolate, mocca, and caramel-chocolate versions. According to <www.hollandring.com>, the 'Dutch people eat about 14 million kilos of "*hagelslag*" per year on about 850 million slices of bread'.

6. Errors of ignorance like this crop up in published works all the time. One of my favorite examples comes from an English-language newspaper article about Spanish foods, published in the 1980s. The story focused on a well-known restaurant in Spain where the specialty was roasted suckling pig. But throughout the story the writer referred to the restaurant's chef-owner as 'Maestro Asador', as if that were the man's actual name. (Perhaps she had seen displayed on the wall a certificate awarding him that culinary status and mistaken the title for his name.) Such basic lack of accuracy in a food article perpetuates misinformation among less knowledgeable readers, while making more knowledgeable readers doubt the accuracy – and hence the authenticity – of the rest of the information in the story.

7. Regardless of the 'inauthenticity' of our actions and beliefs – at least as they related to Dutch culinary practices – we had stumbled upon a delicious new vice: chocolate sprinkles in our morning coffee!

8. In Alsace there are two basic kinds of *Kugelhopf*: a slightly sweet version containing raisins and sometimes flavored with lemon zest, which is traditionally eaten for Sunday breakfast but can be served at other times, too (including as a dessert, where the slice of cake might be sprinkled with kirsch or another liquor, garnished with whipped cream, or accompanied by a caramel sauce); and *Kugelhopf salé*, a savory version containing chopped smoked ham or bacon (instead of raisins), often served with a glass of chilled Alsatian white wine. Both are baked in a special kind of pan or mold – round, with high sides, a tube in the center, and flutes or ridges along the bottom and sides. Part of the outer surface of the cake is usually decorated with almonds (whole or flaked, blanched or unblanched) inserted into the mold before the dough is added and hence baked onto the cake. After the cake has baked and cooled, it is usually dusted with confectioners' sugar, which looks like a light sprinkling of snow. There is also a rich frozen dessert called *Kugelhopf glacé*, consisting of an outer layer of vanilla ice cream and a filling of egg mousse flavored with raisins and liquor, which derives its name from the shape of the mold in which the mixture is frozen. In this paper, I am referring only to the cakes called *Kugelhopf*.

9. Of course I realize that this 'consensus' approach to recipe development can also perpetuate errors made by one or more recipe writers and copied by others afterward. That is why I try to collect a large number of recipes for a dish when developing my own recipe for it – to compare as many versions as possible and ferret out variations over time. Thus I approach this stage of recipe development as a kind of culinary detective work.

10. Not all of the recipes I have developed using this method have been as successful on the initial test. I remember making seven different batches of German gingerbread before I came close to the taste and texture of a certain kind of commercial *Nürnberg Lebkuchen* that I was trying to replicate in my home kitchen in Munich.

11. Other spellings include *Gougelhof, Kouglof, Guglhupf, Kougelhopf, Kugelhoff, Gougelhopf, Kugelhupf, Gugelhopf, Gougelhop, Kougelhof, Kougloff*, and *Kuglof*.

12. A similar example: 'Barbecue' is a term that must be explicitly defined when referring to this or that 'authentic barbecue'. In some parts of the world, 'barbecuing' is a synonym for 'grilling' (high heat, fast cooking, on an open grill). In other places – such as Texas, the Deep South, and much the American Midwest – 'barbecuing' is a technique of slow-smoking on a closed grill, over relatively low heat for a long period of time. Hence, 'authentic barbecue' in California is very different from 'authentic barbecue' in Texas. After making that basic distinction between two very different cooking techniques described by the same term, it is also necessary to distinguish among various regional variations of slow-smoked barbecue, as well as sub-regional varieties. 'Authenticity' in regard to

249

barbecue is very much a function of place, meat, and technique.

13. For a description of competing kinds of *cassoulets*, see Paula Wolfert, *The Cooking of South-West France* (Garden City, New York: Doubleday & Company, Inc., 1983), pp. 232–40.

14. Admittedly, some people do make a distinction between the 'cowboy beans' eaten on cattle trail drives in the nineteenth century, which were made with fewer ingredients, and 'ranch beans' or 'barbecue beans', which are cooked in a more stationary setting and often include more ingredients than were available to trail cooks. These distinctions are apparent in the rules for contemporary chuck wagon cook-offs that prescribe the ingredients permitted to be used, based on those available to cooks at certain times in the history of the American West. At some of these cook-offs, 'trail wagon' cooks are allowed fewer ingredients than 'ranch wagon' cooks.

15. Speckled brown-and-white beans, also known by several nicknames, such as 'prairie strawberries,' as well as the general Spanish term '*frijoles*' (beans).

16. A dry spice blend of powdered chilies (mild, medium, and/or hot) combined with ground cumin, Mexican oregano, garlic powder, salt, and sometimes other spices. ('Chili powder' is the correct spelling of this term because it refers to the particular dish known as 'chili', of which the spice powder is an important ingredient.)

17. Variations on this dish can also include the use of beer as part of the cooking liquid, as well as chopped tomatoes, bell peppers, and fresh hot peppers (usually *jalapeños* or *serranos*) – either raw or cooked with onions in melted lard or vegetable oil to make a *sofrito* – added toward the end of the cooking period. If diced fried bacon is added, this dish is known along the Texas-Mexico border as '*charro* beans' (Mexican cowboy beans), '*frijoles à la charra*' (beans, horsewoman style or ranchwoman style) or simply '*frijoles rancheros*' (ranch-style beans).

18. On the other hand, it should be noted that some restaurants do serve excellent versions of authentic 'cowboy beans', which are just as good as our usual benchmark: Homemade with a capital 'H' (notwithstanding that even some home cooks can manage to screw up a mess of beans).

19. In 1977 the Texas Legislature declared chili to be 'The Official Texas State Dish' – an indication of the importance of chili in Texans' notions of their state's cuisine, as well as the political effectiveness of the 'chili lobby'.

20. Although Texans don't agree on what constitutes 'true Texas chili', most of them do agree on what is not Texas chili – e.g., regional variations such as Cincinnati chili, Midwestern 'chili macs', and non-spicy California chilis made with black beans, corn, avocados, bean sprouts, black olives, and goat cheese. For more information on chili (the dish) – not chilies (hot peppers) – see my entry on 'Chili' in Smith, Andrew F., ed., *The Oxford Encyclopedia of Food and Drink in America* (Oxford: Oxford University Press, 2004), pp. 230–33.

21. Russians often refer to potatoes as their 'second bread'. But this hardy tuber has not always been so popular or widespread in that country. Most sources say that potatoes were first imported into Russia in the early 1700s, during the time of Peter the Great (1682–1725). Others claim that potatoes did not come to Russia until several decades later, during the reign of Catherine the Great (1762–1796). Despite a government decree in 1797 that potatoes be planted throughout the country, they were not accepted as a food by most of the Russian population until the second half of the 19th century. Potatoes are now one of the staples of Russian cuisine, served in many forms at breakfast, lunch, and dinner – at home, on picnics, in cafeterias, canteens, and restaurants, and at street stalls.

22. None of my Russian friends in Vladivostok and Irkutsk called this dish '*salat Oliv'ie*', however. They all used its other names, '*stolichnyi salat*' ('capital city salad') or '*Moskovskiy salat*' ('Moscow salad'), both terms in reference to its supposed origin in Moscow.

23. 'Russian potato salad' recipes indicate a number of other ingredients that can also be included, such as cooked beef or veal, cooked chicken, smoked or boiled fish, salted herring, marinated mushrooms, capers, white or green cabbage, sauerkraut, French beans, white beans, orange and apple pieces, artichokes, cauliflower, and asparagus tips. When beets are added – and especially when this mélange is tossed with an oil-and-vinegar dressing (instead of dressed with mayonnaise or sour cream) – this

salad is often called '*Vinegret*'. But writers of Russian cookbooks are not always in agreement about the names of these salads. Some call potato-based salads dressed with mayonnaise or sour cream '*Vinegret*', whereas others make the distinction between 'Russian potato salad' (*salat Oliv'ie, stolichnyi salat*, with a mayonnaise or sour cream dressing) and similar mixtures made with beets and a vinegar-and-oil dressing (*Vinegret*). And when you combine beets with potatoes and other ingredients, and mix them with mayonnaise or sour cream, you end up with a creamy-pink-colored salad that has different names in different cookbooks. Admittedly, the nomenclature of Russian potato salads can be somewhat confusing, both in Russian and in English, because the naming of these salads is based on definitions that are highly flexible and not generally agreed upon.

24. On the other hand, this same question occurred to me when I was living in Siberia in the mid-1990s: Just because people in different locations have the same ingredients available to them doesn't mean they will necessarily combine them in the same ways, to produce the same kinds of dishes. For example, to my knowledge southern Siberians have never developed a dish like Andalucian *gazpacho* to eat during the humid heat of the short Siberian summer, even though they have tomatoes, cucumbers, bell peppers, garlic, vegetable oil, vinegar, salt, and white bread available from their *dacha* gardens and local markets.

25. 'La Bouche Speaks: A Passionate and Often Rambling Discourse on the Past 45 Years of Food, by Paula Wolfert, High Priestess of Mediterranean Cooking', interviewed by David Leite, <www.leites-culinaria.com/interviews/wolfert/wolfert01.html>.

26. Yes, I know that white flour is not the same in north-eastern France and the American South, but a good Southern baker can compensate for that and produce a yeast-raised *Kugelhopf* with the correct taste and texture. Similarly, I have made Texas 'cowboy beans' in Germany and Russia, using local and imported ingredients, that tasted the same as the ones I have eaten since childhood in Texas.

27. Hudgins, Sharon, 'The Spicy Foods of Czechoslovakia,' *Chile Pepper*, Volume V, No. 6, November/December 1991, pp. 16–21, 37–8.

28. Goldstein, Darra, 'From the Editor,' *Gastronomica: The Journal of Food and Culture*, Vol. 4, No. 1, Winter 2004, no pagination.

29. This happens in both negative and positive book reviews, which I think is an indication of how the gods of literary justice keep the universe in balance.

30. Grace, B., 'Piranha Club', King Features Syndicate, *Dallas Morning News*, Comics Section, April 9, 2005.

Adulteration as Part of Authenticity

Jan Krag Jacobsen

A typical definition of authenticity may be 'entitled to acceptance or belief because of agreement with known facts or experience'.[1]

The common use of the concept 'authentic food' signifies genuine and unadulterated products unspoiled by a modern combination of industry, ignorance and greed. This interpretation is not in line with the dictionary's claim of agreement with known facts or experience.

Adulteration of valuable foods with less valuable ingredients is an old phenomenon whether it was done because of hunger, greed or a combination of both. Each era and place had and has its specific kinds of and reasons for making foods up.

Adulteration or improvement?

It may indeed be difficult to distinguish between adulteration and improvement. Saffron has been used to simulate eggs in pastry. When hops first were added to beer as a flavour some 600 years ago it was not at first appreciated. But hop resins showed as preservatives to keep the beer well. Upper-class Romans had a preference for bread whitened by alum just as the wealthy Europeans had until the end of the nineteenth century.[2]

Scientific and industrial adulteration

The fraud remained on a rather limited scale as long as the production methods remained unsophisticated and the communities small and transparent. But this changed with the development of modern science, especially chemistry, the industrial revolution and the growing physical and mental distance between the consumer and the producer in Europe in the 18th and 19th centuries. A cornucopia of new and often rather dangerous substances and methods came into use by ignorant and unscrupulous food producers with the purpose of cheating the consumers.

'In London there are two sorts of bakers, the "full priced", who sell bread at its full value, and the "undersellers", who sell it under its value. The latter class comprises more than three-fourths of the total number of bakers.... The undersellers, almost without exception, sell bread adulterated with alum, soap, pearl ashes, chalk, Derbyshire stone-dust, and such like agreeable nourishing and wholesome ingredients.' Sir John Gordon stated before the committee of 1855, that 'in the consequences of these adulterations, the poor man, who lives on two pounds of bread a day, does not now get one fourth part of nourishing matter, let alone the deleterious effect on his health'.[3] It may be added that a great part of the numerous people crammed together in the cities starved and did not have the money to buy expensive bread from the full-priced bakers.

Adulteration and law

Since the quality of food is pivotal in human society, adulteration has long since been of great concern. In 1202 King John of England made one of the first European food laws, 'The Assize of Bread', prohibiting the adulteration of bread with ground beans and peas.[4] In Great Britain in the 18th and 19th centuries the quality of expensive foods like coffee, tea and cocoa became protected by law. Perhaps not so much in the interest of the consumer as to keep up the internal revenues in the trade.[5]

The industrial revolution and the parallel development of modern science paved the way for new sophisticated forms of adulteration as well as dramatically improved methods for revealing it, especially the analytical chemistry.

Frederick Accum

In 1820 the German chemist and apothecary Frederick Accum published his best-seller *A Treatise on Adulterations of Food and Culinary Poisons* in London. On the cover it states 'There is death in the pot' under a skull and cross bones together with a snake writhing around a spider's web, in which a large spider is grabbing a fly.

Frederick Accum named and shamed brewers adulterating beer with water and making it up with green vitriol, alum, salt and *Cocculus indicus*, a poisonous bitter agent used in the tanning industry. He also described adulterations of wine, bread, brandy, cream, lozenges, custard, olive oil, tea, coffee, pepper, cheese and pickles with chemicals like lead, mercury and copper compounds.[6]

253

During the 19th century the emerging national food controlling agencies in Europe and USA undertook the controlling role of the old-time cupbearer and diminished the risk of the public being poisoned. But they still have to be on the alert.

In 1959 many thousand of people in Morocco and neighbouring countries died or became seriously ill from cooking oil adulterated with motor oil containing the neurotoxic orthocresylphosphate. In 1985 several Austrian wines were adulterated with the poisonous antifreeze agent diethylene glycol. In 2004 some Indian chilli products sold in Europe were coloured with the carcinogenic colours Sudan I, II and III. These cases combine classical greed, ignorance and industrial chemistry.

Legal and illegal adulteration

Modern adulteration can be divided into illegal and legal adulteration. The former includes the use of hazardous ingredients and the concealed use of non-hazardous ingredients. Adulteration is widely permitted as long as it is transparent. The legal adulteration is based on the use of governmentally approved adulterants stated on an information label on the product. In Europe these matters are regulated by the EU and the national governments.

In 1914 The Danish Supreme Court decided that only the use of compounds hazardous to health could be forbidden in foods[7] and this still seems to be the practice in the EU and many countries in the case of flavours.

The legal adulterations are typically based on a combination of cheap inferior ingredients, often water and fat, and food additives. This might be a meat sausage containing an inferior meat product and fair amounts of water and fat bound by soy flour or/and various chemical compounds and made up with colours. On the information label the consumer might read several of these numbers E 200, E 210, E 214, E 235, E 249, E 315, E 100, E 120, E 150, E 160, E 162, E 338, E 620, E 626, E 630, E 634, E 420, E 421, E 953, E 965, E 966, E 967, E 959, E 170, E 260, E 261, E 262, E 263, E 270, E 290, E 296, E 300, E 301, E 302, E 304, E 306, E 307, E 308, E 309, E 322, E 325, E 326, E 327, E 330, E 331, E 332, E 333, E 334, E 335, E 336, E 337, E 350, E 351, E 352, E 354, E 380, E 400, E 401, E 402, E 403, E 404, E 406, E 407, E 410, E 412, E 413, E 414, E 415, E 418, E 422, E 440, E 460, E 461, E 463, E 464, E 465, E 466, E 469, E 470a, E 470b, E 471, E 472a, E 472b, E 472c, E 472d, E 472e, E 472f, E 500, E 500, E 501, E 503, E 504, E 507, E 508, E 509, E 511, E 513, E 514, E 515, E 516, E 524, E 525, E 526, E 527, E 528, E 529, E 530, E 570, E 574, E 575, E 576, E 577, E 578, E 640, E 938, E 939, E 941, E 942, E 948, E 949, E 1103, E 1200, E 1404, E 1410, E 1412, E 1413, E 1414, E 1420, E 1422, E 1440, E 1442, E 1450, E 1451. After having consulted his/her library the consumer will perhaps be able to judge the quality of the sausage. No wonder that the state control apparatus is growing.

During the 1970s the principle of having positive lists with approved additives and ingredients gained ground in Europe. Positive listing of aroma compounds was and is still an unsolved problem because of the very large number of possible compounds. Only negative lists of aroma compounds have been made.

In 1973 The Danish Ministry of the Environment made the first draft of a positive list of food additives. This list is very interesting because of the way it was created. The producers were asked which additives and amounts they used and their practice was then by and large codified in the positive list. The list mirrored the actual practice of the food industry until then hidden behind the veil of 'trade secrets'. The consumers might until then have lived in the naïve belief that for instance marmalade was made of fruit, sugar and perhaps a preservative. Now they could se in print that it also might contain considerable amounts of 42 food additives, among them 16 colours of which several had a questionable toxicological record.

Another valuable source of information on the practices of the food industry at the time were the journals of the industry where the food producers and their suppliers of raw materials communicated in a lingo not intended for the eyes and ears of the consumer.

Below is what can be seen and read in typical advertisements in *Food Technology* of 1975:

Texture and binding of water and fat

Bakery goods being transported by a money transport service:

> Today's moneymakers start with Methocel…Methocel cellulose ether products thicken, emulsify, suspend or bind at very low levels…are used by the money-makers. (Dow Chemical USA)

A plate with food and a football:

> Supro 620 is a modified soy isolate containing a minimum of 90% protein on a moisture free basis. It has been especially developed for use in meat products where water and fat binding properties are desired. 620 forms a firm resilient gel when thermally processed. Imparting a meat like bite to emulsified meat products…Supro 50 is a texturizer, shrink controller, extender and improver perfected to simulate natural meat fibers. (Ralston Purina Company)

A shopping cart with 12 small boxes with brownish powders and granulates:

> ADM supplies ingredients rich in protein and with excellent water and fat holding characteristics for canned and frozen foods, processed meat, bakery goods, cereals, candies, food drinks and more. ADM textured protein provides the unique combination of high quality and lowered costs in your food formulations. (Archer Daniels Midland Company)

255

Artificial aromas

Black text on yellow background:

> Maggi flavors hit elusive taste targets. RFB: Faithfully duplicates the hearty taste, and aroma, of oven-roasted beef. RFC: Provides a flavor profile similar to stewed chicken. RFP: Achieves the succulent flavor of roasted pork. Promac 20: Mild roasted meat flavor for application in thermally processed foods. Type 17B: Smooth beefy flavor with a charcoal-broiled character. Type 33C: Adds a juicy chicken flavor to poultry dishes. Type 44: Cheese flavor intensifier and enhancer. Artificial Bacon: A hydrolysate with the flavor of crisp smoky bacon. Artificial Mushroom: Achives a smooth mushroom flavor without mushrooms. Artificial Ham: The country-cooked flavor of smoked ham. Artificial Clam: Brings a smooth clam flavor to chowders and bisques. (Food Ingredients Division, The Nestlé Company, Inc.)

Eve with a red apple:

> So good, it could have fooled Eve…new apple fooler smells like the real thing, tastes like it too! It's a brand new flavor that imparts the aroma and tangy, tasty goodness of ripe apples to all kinds of food products, hot or cold. (Wm. M. Bell Co.)

Six laboratory people in white coats sitting behind music stands with laboratory glassware held like musical instruments:

> And now we would like to do our variations on fruit flavors. It is not so difficult to duplicate perfectly ripe fruit flavours, but often the perfectly ripe flavor of a particular fruit isn't right for your product. Sometimes you need a variation. Like the flavor of a new strawberry – a little crispy, not quite ripe, but definitively strawberry. Or the ripe, mellow banana we all know. And peach, the kind you remember in jams. These variations exist in nature and are duplicated by Norda…Norda takes nature further. (Norda)

Three laboratory people in white coats:

> Looking for new artificial flavors? Talk to one of our great imposters. (Ottens Flavors)

A piggy bank:
'Use Ottens artificial bacon flavor and laugh all the way to the bank'
(Ottens Flavors).
Six wine bottles locked up in a metal chain:
'Ottens locks in wine flavours. 200x stronger than natural'
(Ottens Flavors).

Colours

Nineteen different kinds of foods on a table:

The natural look is in. Since 1957, retail sales of carotenoids have increased ten-fold... And the reasons are simple. When you use Carotenoids, you can duplicate nature's colors. But unlike nature, we can assure your product will be the same color in January as it was in June. (Roche)

Food imitations

A small conical laboratory flask and 4 tomatoes:

How did Griffith get four big tomatoes out of one little flask? After we stretched one the rest was easy!...When added to water and tomato paste or puree, TOMATO STRETCH will extend these products 100%, and still retain the zesty flavor, color, texture and viscosity of the original tomato product. (Griffith Laboratories)

A half ripped picture of tomatoes:

'Now get rid of half of your tomato requirement or all of it…Tomato Extender and Total Tomato replacement. (The Baltimore Spice Company)

258

Two ladles with a red sauce:
One of these delicious tomato sauces costs significantly less than the other. Can you tell which? …-The MATE-O-Mate line is a series of dry granular mixes that hydrate instantly to form rich tomato-like pastes. They contain coloring and flavoring agents that complement the sharp, acidic flavor of tomatoes; and

they offer a proven solution to the problem of rising costs and the unpredictable supply of pastes and powders. (Staley)

Tomatoes, a heap of red powder and a laboratory glass with water:

> Durkee improves on the fickle tomato. Durkee synthesized tomato complement improves your inventory and storage pinch. 20 lbs. of complement plus 80 lbs. of water equals 100 lbs. of tomato paste. So why waste space storing tap water? Now you can quit hassling nature's fickleness-crop failures, labor costs, supply problems, quality fluctuations...just 2 ounces approximates the flavor and aroma of 30 bushels of ripe tomatoes. (Durkee)

A grocer handing a ham and a cheese to two customers:

> They don't know our name. You should. Families taste our full bodied, natural hickory smoke flavor in cheese, meats, cheese spreads, fish, canned beans, sausage, salad dressings, snack items, sauces, specialty foods. But they don't know the name of our natural, hickory smoke flavor...can be employed by direct action, dipping, brushing, spraying, injection blending etc. Liquid smoke – the smokers choice. (TRI-K Industries. Inc)

Cakes and sweets:

259

> puritein combines two key ingredients: protein and profit...Puritein can be used as a partial or total replacement of more expensive non-fat dry mil solids. (Purity Cheese Company)

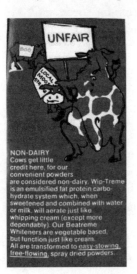

A violet cow with a picket-line poster saying 'unfair':

> NON DAIRY. Cows get little credit here, for our convenient powders are considered non-dairy. Wip-Treme is an emulsified fat protein carbohydrate system which, when combined with water or milk, will aerate just like cream (except more dependable). Our Beatreme Whiteners are vegetable based, but function just like cream. All are transformed to easy stowing, free flowing, spray dried products. (Beatrice Foods Inc.)

A cook presenting a cake with a white topping:

> 'Voila. Dairy fresh cream…unexcelled rich in flavor, and unpredictable in handling characteristics. For centuries, there was no substitute for its functions in fine foods, desserts, and coffee whitening applications. That is until Beatrice did nature one better with powdered whipped toppings and non-dairy creamers. (Beatrice Foods Inc.)

Ghosts emerging from Aladdins lamp:

> Hocus-Pokus-A-New-food-Opus. There's no magic in formulating new foods. Just hard work, and accumulated know-how. But our Create A Food Service can help. Help you use ATLAS surfactants and polyols to modify lipid, carbohydrate, or protein foods. Achieve special effects. Even develop new food forms. (ICI United States Inc.)

The style of today's advertisement

Today's advertisements in *Food Technology* are more subtle and lack the frankness of those of 1975. One example: The company Ottens Flavors, Quakers of origin, have changed the piggy bank to a red strawberry and writes:

> Clarity. It is what separates us from others. With over 100 years of personal attention, innovative ideas and application solutions, Ottens continues to be committed to making every product a success. Ottens combines collaborative R&D with the latest technologies to create the right flavor to meet your every need. Add to that a staff of knowledgeable professionals who know your business inside and out, and you have the perfect recipe for success. We are dedicated to managing our customer's objectives and goals in clear focus. (*Food Technology* 2003)

The meaning is probably the same as in 1975 but the clarity of the 1975 version is missing.

Adulteration of raw materials

This paper has until this point dealt with different kinds of adulteration in the processing of raw materials. But another important kind of adulteration is at work in modern Western society. The raw materials themselves have to a large extent been adulterated. New breeds of animals and plants as well as new production methods of poor gastronomic quality have been developed.

Most of today's chickens offered on the market are very different from their ancestors 100 years ago. They are cheaper and with less taste. One hundred years ago chickens were a luxury food as tasty chickens are today. In a Danish supermarket one can buy 7 tasteless chickens for the price of one chicken of high quality from Bresse or elsewhere.

The old-fashioned species of strawberry were tasty but posed problems to producers and retailers because they were fragile and did not keep well. Today's species keep extremely well and often look more strawberry-like than the old ones and are probably cheaper, but the taste and the sweetness have gone.

The deterioration of the raw materials has been going on for many years. The driving force is primarily a combination of the efforts of the producers and retailers to lower their expenses and gastronomic ignorance and stinginess among the consumers. During this development the consumers have lost gastronomic competence to a degree that has made it difficult for producers of high quality foods to find a foothold on the market. Why should people spend money on expensive high quality foods when the capacity to appreciate them is missing?

The deterioration of the raw materials is not a matter of legislation since health is not directly at risk and nobody is getting cheated economically speaking.

Epilogue

Food is the basis of life and the foundation of every society. Confidence in the consumed food and the people preparing and controlling it is of pivotal importance for societal coherence. For this reason adulteration of food is a very serious matter. Much more serious than many other kinds of adulteration and fraud.

261

The political discussions and decisions in the realm of adulteration are usually about health and sometimes economy. The problem is rather of moral, aesthetic and existential character and can only be solved by a vivid public discussion of gastronomic practices and values hopefully leading to an altered relationship between consumers, producers and retailers.

It is encouraging to witness that this discussion has gained momentum during the last 10 years and is very slowly beginning to influence the market. There are at present many signs of a change. The growing slow food movement and the fact that it is getting easier to get hold of good products are just two of them.

Notes

1. *Webster's Encyclopedic Unabridged Dictionary of the English Language* (New York: Gramercy Books, 1994).
2. Kiple, K. F., Ornelas K. C., *The Cambridge World History of Food* (Cambridge: Cambridge University Press, 2000).
3. Marx, Karl, *Capital*, vol. 1, chapter 6, footnote.
4. FDA backgrounder, <www.cfsan.fda.gov/mileston.htm>.
5. <www.encyclopedia.com/html/f1/foodadul.asp>.
6. Royal Society of Chemistry, <www.rsc.org/images/cw01_accum_tcm18-23432.pdf>.
7. Zinck, O. and Hallas-Møller, T., *E-nummerbogen* (Denmark: Ashehoug,1996).

Feeding Pharaoh: 'Authentic' Ancient Cookery for Schools?

Cathy K. Kaufman

During the past decade, progressive primary and secondary school curricula in America have introduced culinary history as a means of teaching social studies. Students research and prepare foods from ages past to learn about culture, technology, and trade, with the complexity and sophistication of the recreations tied to the grade level. Textbooks describing the daily life of past civilizations and cultures have been popular for some time. Most have covered food from agricultural and nutritional perspectives and give cuisine short shrift, offering only the occasional illustrative recipe, and usually not in a form that can be prepared by students. As a cooking teacher specializing in culinary history, I have directed teachers, students, and parents to more practical sources and cookbooks that will help them stage medieval banquets and Roman bacchanals (yes, the question about the vomitorium inevitably, if sheepishly, arises). These audiences are amazed by the extensive primary and specialized secondary source materials available to help resurrect a taste of the past. Educators believe these exercises spark curiosity and capture pre-teen and adolescent attention spans in ways that dry recitations of kingly successions and trade routes cannot.

As culinary history is a current darling of school systems nationwide, it comes as no surprise that textbook publishers are rushing to fill the void by collecting and contextualizing historical recipes and practical information on foodways. For the past year, I have been writing a cookbook to enrich history and social studies curricula for secondary and middle school students (and their teachers, who may have little cooking expertise). Mine is the earliest volume chronologically in series designed to cover the foodways of Western civilization. It illuminates the culinary habits of Mesopotamia, pharaonic Egypt, Greece, and the Roman Empire through approximately 175 recipes that students can prepare in modern kitchens. The occasional recipe for sow's womb or flamingoes' tongues (using ducks' tongues for those with access to Chinese markets) is included for the sake of representing the range of ancient foods, but most of the recipes are for foods that can be prepared either in school kitchens or at home.

Considerations and biases in cooking ancient cuisines

This paper addresses how I tried to make these recipes as 'authentic' as possible, focusing primarily on creating recipes for pharaonic Egypt, which has no known cookbook tradition. Egypt contrasts sharply against the Greco-Roman world, with its hundreds of ancient recipes and abundance of culinary literature in which to ground modern redactions. And even with this reservoir of historic recipes, it bears stating that most Greco-Roman foods cannot be 'authentically' recreated, at least in a way that is practical for school systems: modern kitchens and 21st-century ingredients can, at best, evoke, but not duplicate, ancient foods. Students will use flours that differ slightly in their fineness, extraction rates, or protein content to make breads that differ from those that Galen wrote about.[1] There are also intractable questions of the comparative purity and freshness of imported spices, the relative sharpness, sweetness, or bitterness of ancient fruits, vegetables, and herbs, and the toughness, tenderness, and butchery of ancient meats.

We can disclose these practical differences to students and minimize grossly anachronistic or inappropriate ingredients, but a fundamental challenge remains in that we are outsiders attempting to create foods of which we have no first-hand experience. Even when ancient recipes exist, most do not specify quantities or proportions of ingredients, leaving both modern interpreters and ancient practitioners considerable latitude in seasoning dishes. Ancient cooks, immersed in their culinary cultures, knew how a dish 'should' taste; modern cooks less so. Although it was tempting to write recipes that simpley said, 'make of dough from flour and water, work in fat, and cook,' my experience as a cooking teacher told me this was not practical. Students and their teachers would have too many questions about recipes, so I deliberately used contemporary recipe-writing conventions and specified quantities to help inexperienced student-cooks. These measured ingredients result in flavors and textures that my 21st-century palate finds in keeping with the piquancy of the few Roman recipes that specify quantities. Whether this has inappropriately skewed the balance of flavors is open to debate, but at least the Greco-Roman redactions are grounded in ancient texts that give some modest reassurance that the ingredient combinations and cooking techniques might approximate the ancient originals.

263

By contrast, writing recipes for the chapters on Mesopotamia and Egypt felt like swinging from trapeze to trapeze without a net. While there were plenty of dry lists of what the Egyptians and Mesopotamians ate, there is little to suggest what these foods were like. Putting aside the fragmentary and enigmatic Yale Babylonian Collection,[2] which offers some tantalizing glimpses into the elite cookery of Babylonia, how was I to create recipes that would be accessible to students, educational, and fairly reflect, as far as practicable, 5,000 year-old food? Moreover, I wanted the recipes to focus on the cuisine of pharaonic Egypt from predynastic times to that point in the Late Period when Egypt fell to the Persian armies of Cyrus the Great, exploring Egyptian food before extensive contacts with Northern Mediterranean foodways. Part of the reasoning was to provide a contrast against the subsequent Greco-Roman chapters. Deliberately excluded as source materials were the writings of Herodotus and other Greek and Roman visitors, both for reasons of cultural bias and reliability for pre-Hellenistic foodways. Although pharaonic Egypt's food had already been influenced by Near Eastern and sub-Saharan African crops, my goal was to present the 'purest' ancient Egyptian cuisine, before the influx of Greco-Roman crops, particularly free-threshing bread wheat, and technologies, particularly the substitution of the rotary for the saddle quern, that would make Egyptian food appear to be merely a variation on Greco-Roman cuisine.

Issues specific to undocumented cuisine

To write 35 recipes illustrating Egyptian foodways from the greatest pharaoh to the humblest slave required answers to the obvious questions of what Egyptians ate and how the foods were prepared. Here the century of research by Egyptologists, archaeologists, botanists, and other scholars quickly provided basic answers, based on artistic renderings in tombs and temples, the translations of bureaucratic records, and evidence from archaeological digs. Some of the archaeological evidence dated back to the early 20th century, where relatively simple chemical analyses of pot residues gave clues as to the presence of foodstuffs – cheese, for example – for which there was scant independent evidence. More useful was work conducted by Delwen Samuel at Amarna and Michael Lehner and Ed Wood at Giza. Their work will be touched on in detail later, but their experiments with bread baking and electron microscopic analysis of various artifacts suggested ways of writing recipes that previous listings of foodstuffs found in burial chambers could not.

264

Armed with a basic knowledge of the what and how of Egyptian foodways, actually writing the recipes raised three much more interesting questions. Firstly, where should the balance be struck on practicality, that is, how far could the search for ancient-style ingredients and cooking methods go and still be a useful student laboratory experience? Second, how complex or simple should the recipes be to neither over- nor underestimate the sophistication of Egyptian cookery? Lastly, how palatable should the food be to 21st-century students?

The single most serious issue involved bread and beer, the staple foods of Egyptians of every social class. I needed to explain these grain-based foods and the ancient preparation techniques, even if they could not be faithfully imitated in modern kitchens. Recipes had to minimize the intrusions of the modern world while remaining practical for experimentation by students in different settings. Few classes below the university level could realistically be set up for students to grind grains on a saddle quern or to have access to a tannur-style oven. Yet some previous forays into ancient cookery, such as those suggested by the Oriental Institute through the University of Chicago, seemed to pull too many punches in the interests of accessibility. The Institute offers on-line lesson plans for teachers in middle schools, including preparing 'ancient-style' breads allegedly from Mesopotamia and Egypt. The recipes specify flour, water, and salt to make a simple bread that is baked in the oven for 30 minutes. Notwithstanding Egypt's reputation as the birthplace of leavened bread, no yeast or leavener is used in the Egyptian recipe. Yet the 'Student Stuff' worksheet breathlessly exclaims, 'for an authentic Mesopotamian experience, eat the bread with a raw onion.'[3] This dumbed down the historical lesson too much. Although a painstaking analysis of the genetic and chemical structure of the wheats widely used by Mesopotamians and Egyptians may be beyond the abilities of ten-year olds, use of whole wheat flour (preferably stone-ground) is not; this simple adjustment in a basic recipe could illustrate some of the differences between the ancient world's quotidian loaf and the modern world's white bread.

Given that high schoolers are the target audience for my volume, I could go beyond the mere substitution of whole wheat for white flour and grapple with the fact that hulled emmer was the predominant wheat of pharaonic Egypt. Free-threshing bread wheat, aptly named by anthropologists for its strong and very elastic gluten that effectively traps carbon dioxide, came into meaningful use only in the Greco-Roman period. Leavened bread made from emmer has been found in many archaeological locations, and modern experiments with emmer conducted by master baker Fred Martin indicate that hulled emmer can be carefully processed to preserve its some-what elastic gluten-forming proteins, although breads made from emmer are never as light as those made from bread wheat.[4] Nowadays emmer is nearly impossible to find commercially,[5] so specifying the historically correct emmer as the grain for bread making would have prevented students from attempting the bread recipes. But using bread wheat would result in bread unlike anything the Egyptians would have enjoyed. A minor conundrum if 'authentic' bread was the goal.

My solution was to specify semolina flour, made from durum wheat, as the practi-cal substitute for emmer. I choose durum even though it is a relatively modern wheat dating only to the classical period, and thus anachronistic for pharaonic Egypt. The reasoning follows: both durum and emmer are tetraploid wheats (meaning they have 4 sets of 7-chromosome groups, for a total of 28 chromosomes) and are the result of matings of a wild wheat with wild goatgrasses; bread wheat is hexaploid (6 sets, 42 chromosomes), and is believed the result of a cross of a tetraploid wheat with a goatgrass. Both emmer and durum are characterized by somewhat inelastic gluten, compared with bread wheat's very elastic gluten.[6] Using standard bread wheat would have misled students about the quality of Egyptian bread. Although durum is an imperfect substitute, it seemed closest to emmer, closer even than the spelt wheat that some authors confuse with emmer.[7] Once the students know how and why they were deviating from ancient foodways, they could evaluate the modern adaptations.

Two other practical issues arose from the lists of foods eaten by Egyptians: what cooking fats should be used and how to compensate for changes in fruits and vegeta-bles over 5,000 years of botanical flux. The biggest problems with cooking fats is that Egyptians seemed to use lots of animal fats, a modern dietary bugaboo, and that the vegetable fats that were used are unusual by modern standards. Also, contemporary audiences might expect, based on current Egyptian cuisine, to douse foods in olive and sesame oils. Contrary to modern practice, these oils were not native in pharaonic Egypt. They were imported through much of Egypt's ancient history and presumably would have been expensive and limited to the elites. Domestic cultivation of these crops came relatively late in Egypt's pharaonic history, so while they would not be completely anachronistic, extensive use of these oils would skew the recipes to elite tables. Linseed oil, ben oil from the moringa tree, and oil pressed from the seeds of radishes and lettuces were much more common in earlier Egyptian times, but harder to find currently. My solution was to point out these facts and suggest a bland seed oil, such as rapeseed (distantly related to radishes) or grapeseed oil, as an all-purpose substitute, or to use safflower oil, which also arrived in New Kingdom times. Students were told that they could choose to substitute olive or sesame oil, but to keep in mind that these imported oils probably elevated the dishes to something found on elite tables rather than in lower echelon worker and peasant households.

Fruit and vegetable choices also required many cautionary notes, especially given the difficulties in interpreting foodstuffs represented in tomb paintings and hiero-glyphics. The cucumber is a prime example. Claimed in many sources to have been part of ancient Egyptian foods based on linguistic and artistic depictions, recent botanical research has cast doubt on whether they had arrived in pharaonic Egypt.[8] The chate melon, however, often eaten like cucumbers, clearly was in predynastic Egypt. It seemed fair to substitute ubiquitous seedy cucumbers (not the seedless, gourmet varieties of modern breeding) for the rare chate, while noting the issue for students.

Finally came the question of adapting cooking equipment and techniques. Whipping up pesto in a food processor is fine for cooking classes teaching time-saving shortcuts to harried future cooks, but most of us probably agree that the 'authentic' learning experience for a history or social studies curriculum requires laborious pounding of herbs, garlic and cheese. Users were urged to make the modest investment in a mortar and pestle. Although the recipes were written for modern stoves and ovens using standard modern equipment, whenever possible, open-air grilling was encouraged, as well as clay pot cookery. Bake stones or griddles stood in for *tannur*-style ovens. Grain mills for grinding whole grains were encouraged, as manual grinding by querns would be unlikely at best and probably would discourage too many schools and students. The purchase of stone-ground grains was recommended as the next best substitute, with industrially milled flours identified as the poorest substitute. The occasional food processor, with heavy heart, found its way into a few recipes to make them more practical, as will be detailed below.

How complex and delicious would 'authentic' cuisine be?

The remaining two questions, how complex should the food be and how should it taste, required the greatest creativity and offered many opportunities to go astray. I was pulled between the Scylla of writing overly simplistic recipes that might underestimate the elegance of ancient Egyptian cuisine and the Charybdis of making food that was too sophisticated, too familiar, too accessible, too much like modern Egyptian cuisine. I wanted neither to glamorize Egyptian food nor to downplay its potential. Previous writers had concluded either that ancient Egyptians never developed elegant cuisine, or that ancient Egyptians 'probably' seasoned foods in ways that would be familiar and appealing to modern palates.[9] I returned to Phyllis Pray Bober's fundamental question,

> [What is] the essential community of expression in any given era between the culinary arts and other arts more regularly termed 'fine'?[10]

On the one hand, the sophistication of Egyptian art and the magnificence of Egyptian furniture and tablewares suggests that some Egyptian cuisine was more than mere sustenance, yet the alabaster chalices, turquoise-tinted glassware, and other drinking and dining accoutrements tell us nothing specific about the foods and beverages these luxurious containers held 3,500 years ago. At best, they hint at a sense of table refinement that may have peaked in the New Kingdom. Egyptians themselves distinguished among different foods, assigning more prestige to some dishes. An etiquette book, probably first written in Old Kingdom times, counsels a social inferior who has been invited to dinner not to be jealous of the superior foods that the host will enjoy:

> If you sit at the table of one who is greater than you, take what he gives you, what is set before you. Do not look [greedily] at what is in front of him, but only at what is in front of you.... Laugh when he laughs.... When a great man hosts, his actions depend on his *ka*, and a great man can be motivated by good *ka* to be more generous.[11]

267

The variety of foodstuffs found in burial chambers also communicated a gourmet's broad palate, yet none of this soft evidence hinted at flavors.

Deciding whether and how to season the foods was educated guesswork. Traces of local herbs, spices, and fruits have been found in beer and bread, as well as in various tomb offerings, although it is unclear whether the dill found in Tutankhamun's tomb was used as an insecticide or as a flavoring. Medical papyri recommended local herbs and spices, as well as exotic imports, in unguents, fumigants, suppositories, and, occasionally, elixirs. These last preparations were added to wines for medicinal purposes. It seemed unnecessarily pessimistic about the quality of Egyptian food to deny the Egyptians local seasonings in their daily fare. Culinary uses of the expensive, exotic imports, even among the elites, is more problematic, as all of the evidence points to the use of such luxuries as cinnamon and pepper for perfumes, medicines, or embalming. Lack of evidence certainly does not prove that elite Egyptians never enjoyed exotically spiced cuisine, but there was no good reason to suspect that Tutankhamun's roast beef was seasoned with pepper or his carob cakes enlivened by a soupçon of cinnamon.

Ultimately this dilemma was resolved with a pedagogical model in mind: Egyptian cookery would rely only on local herbs and spices, notwithstanding access to Eastern spices, to set up the contrast of the more limited trade of Egyptian civilization with the extensive trade and heady spices of Apicius's Rome. I thus omitted eastern spices from even those recipes identified as appropriate to elites. Elite cuisine could easily be distinguished from plebeian by the use of documented Levantine imports, such as olive oil or wine. I judged it better to delay introducing eastern spices until the chapter on Roman cookery, both for the 'authentic' comfort that Apicius's recipes give and the opportunity for teachers to explain the ever-widening role of trade in the Roman Empire, the discovery of the monsoons, and other nifty bits of traditional history.

How complicated could or should the culinary preparations be? The complexity of several of the recipes in the Yale Babylonian Collection proves beyond doubt that second millennium civilizations were capable of intricate, multi-step, *haute* cookery, but did this Mesopotamian complexity find parallels in contemporaneous Egyptian cookery? Although accidents of history and preservation may account for the failure to find any recipes on gastronomic literature among the scads of papyri and bureaucratic records, I inferred that the lack of Egyptian culinary recipes meant that complex cookery either did not exist or, much less likely, complex cookery was not deemed sufficiently important in that record-obsessed civilization to write it down. I concluded that Egyptian cuisine was simpler, less *haute*. Accordingly, the most complex recipes in the Egyptian chapter were technically simpler than the most complex ones created for the Mesopotamian chapter.

268

Reconstructed, invented, and fanciful recipes

Each of the 35 recipes fell into one of three basic categories, 'reconstructed,' 'invented,' or 'fanciful.' Each category has different amounts and quality of evidence to support each redaction.

The 'reconstructed' recipes presumably come closest to 'authentic' Egyptian foods. They have been reverse-engineered from the archaeological analysis of remains, the chemical properties of foods, and sometimes from field experiments written up by scholars such as Samuel or Lehner and Wood. These recipes tended to be for staple foods such as bread and beer, which have understandably been the focus of tremendous amounts of research. In addition to bread and beer, meats grilled simply and dried fish roe seemed reasonable reconstructions from the artistic record.

Some reconstructed recipes were involved to prepare. Samuel's analysis of bread remains under an electron microscope showed that some breads were made from sprouted emmer; some remains also showed breads flavored with dried figs that appeared to have been mashed to a paste. By combining these bits of information, I reconstructed an 'Emmer Bread with Figs' that requires students to sprout whole wheat berries (ideally from farro, which may, depending on the source, be emmer rather than bread wheat),[12] a process that might take three days of careful moistening and partially drying of the grains. Once the grains were sprouted, they are pounded with the dried figs in a mortar and pestle, or failing the strength and perseverance, a food processor, and left to rest before shaping and baking. Practical cooking advice came from the field research of bakers Jeffrey Alford and Naomi Duguid, who have documented in popular form many traditional bread recipes from the Mediterranean, Near East, and Central Asia.[13]

Other reconstructed bread recipes offered an opportunity to mimic ancient techniques by seasoning small, clay flowerpots with lard or other solid fat, heating them in an oven, and placing a leavened wheat dough therein. Baked upright in a conventional oven that was turned off once the dough was inserted, and covered by a preheated clay 'shard' (which could be a saucer), the modern equipment imitated the experiments of Wood and Lehner at Giza. To make the reconstruction complete, an alternative was offered for those who could indulge in the modest cost of ordering the 'Giza' sourdough starter marketed by Wood based on his efforts to capture the ambient wild yeasts surrounding the Great Pyramids.[14]

Brewing Egyptian beer also depended on recent electron microscopy to help tailor the recipe. Conventional wisdom holds that Egyptian beer was made by fermenting lightly baked loaves of bread in water, perhaps with additional grains, yeasts, or dates added. Part of the reasoning has been the proximity of breweries and bakeries in Egyptian estates, the fact that modern bousa is made from such par-baked loaves, as well as the detailed recipes from Mesopotamia ca. 1800 BCE that use under-baked loaves to make beer.[15] The Mesopotamian chapter contains just such a recipe that results in a light, refreshing, and cloudy brew. Recent research by Delwen Samuel, however, has cast doubt on this process, at least for beers brewed during New Kingdom times.[16] Her electron microscopic analysis of beer residues focused on the degree that starch molecules had fused under heat and suggested that two different grain mixtures were used, a cooked grain plus uncooked, malted grain. Thus, the Egyptian beer recipe was reworked from conventional descriptions to become a combination of a cooked barley porridge fermented with raw malted wheat.

269

Invented recipes relied largely on the artistic record or less detailed archaeological evidence. Archaeological evidence always seemed more reliable, even if many details had to be inferred. An otherwise nondescript dish of stewed figs discovered in a Second Dynasty tomb of a wealthy woman became, as a dish for the elite, figs stewed in wine, with a variation of stewing the figs in water or beer for the hoi polloi. Tomb paintings of beef legs being boiled in large cauldrons inspired a braised beef osso buco with garlic and wine vinegar, although placing turned wine into the stew pot as a way of tenderizing and flavoring the meat may say more about my classical French training in the 20th century than anything 'authentic' about ancient Egyptian cookery. Ditto for the 'chate' melon salad, dressed with honey, vinegar, raw onions, and mint.

A useful counterbalance to these recipes was provided by an archaeological find at an early, predynastic burial site. The dry conditions preserved the stomach contents of a suddenly deceased man, offering archaeologists a chance to discover his last supper. The fellow had dined on what was termed a 'soup' of barley and chopped tilapia, complete with bones, fins, and skin. This crude-sounding preparation was written as a crude recipe, with students boiling barley with onions and, towards the end of the cooking, whacking up a gutted fish with a cleaver and cooking the bits of fish—head, bones, fins, and all – in the soup base. I can imagine the squeals of disgust from finicky students, but it is a not-too-subtle reminder of the dangers of over-refining the most ancient cuisines.

Fanciful recipes were the 'invented' recipes writ large, that is, recipes using ingredients confidently placed in ancient Egypt but for which virtually no preparation information has been discovered. The Egyptians force-fed many of their domesticated animals and are believed to have been the first creators of *foie gras*, so opportunity knocked to inject some information on Egyptian animal husbandry. Moreover, what chef could resist the opportunity to write a recipe for *foie gras* and what food scholar could forego commenting on the current state legislative fracas that will soon ban the force-feeding of ducks in California and may well in New York? One would have to be of stronger stuff than I. Yet how to present the dish in any way that might resemble an ancient preparation? Rather than create a recipe that pretended to have roots in Egyptian cookery, I took a contemporary preparation and adjusted the ingredients slightly to use ones appropriate to ancient Egypt. Thus, instead of the ubiquitous sautéed *foie gras* with balsamic reduction, students can prepare *foie gras* with pomegranate molasses and poached figs. The introduction to the recipe confesses that we have no knowledge about how *foie gras* might have been prepared, and that this preparation derives from modern models, but it draws attention to the range and refinement of Egyptian husbandry. The deliberate fattening of animals for the table implies some sophisticated gastronomy.

Tentative conclusions about historical cookery in school systems

Complete authenticity obviously cannot be the standard against which exercises in historical cookery for school systems are judged, particularly those that attempt to plumb prehistoric and unwritten cuisines. Experimental archaeologists and cooks, including the fine efforts by people such as Jacqui Woods,[17] can present wonderful research and can offer small groups the opportunity to use early technologies. These set-ups, however ideal they may be, are of little practical avail to most school systems and students.

The information presented must be tailored to the educational level, but to make the exercise meaningful requires teachers and students to step out of their normal expectations and conveniences about food. Baking white bread from modern bread wheat as an homage to Egyptian foodways seems misleading; the daily fare of the Egyptians was quite different, so puffy soft loaves teach little. For those of us with adventurous palates, ancient foods can often be pleasing, but many will be put off by bony barley and tilapia soup or dry, unleavened flatbreads. Encouraging students to refrain from judging these different foods negatively, especially because they cannot walk in the sandals of a hungry young student living in the Middle Kingdom, may be the most 'authentic' history lesson these foods can teach.

Notes

1. Galen, *On Food and Diet* (Mark Grant, trans.), Routledge (2000), pp. 78–82.
2. See, e.g., Jean Bottéro, *The Oldest Cuisine in the World* (trans. Teresa Fagen), Chicago (2004).
3. <http://oi.uchicago.edu/OI/MUS/ED/TRC>
4. Thomas Braun, 'Barley Cakes and Emmer Bread', in *Food in Antiquity* (John Wilkins, David Harvey, and Mike Dobson, eds.), Exeter (1995).
5. There is disagreement about the availability of emmer wheat; some claim that it is grown commercially only in limited areas in Russia, while others claim it is still raised in France and Italy. Italians confusingly refer to it as farro, a term they often apply to spelt as well. Non-commercial crops of emmer have be found in England and California, but regardless of the existence of these small enclaves, emmer was not going to be practical for school systems.
6. See, Harold McGee, *On Food and Cooking* (rev. ed.), Scribner (2004), pp. 464–8.
7. Many ancient sources conflate emmer with spelt, but this confusion in the ancient record seemed a poor reason to substitute readily available spelt for emmer. First, spelt seems never to have made it to Egypt in any significant amounts, although it was well distributed in the ancient Near East and Europe. Moreover, spelt is hexaploid, like bread wheat, and thus seems structurally further removed from emmer. Finally, the book contained several spelt recipes for other civilizations, so using spelt would have downplayed the uniqueness of Egyptian foodways.
8. Compare, William J. Darby, Paul Ghalioungui, and Louis Grivetti, *Food: The Gift of Osiris*, Academic Press (1977), vol. 2, pp. 694–5, with Daniel Zohary and Maria Hopf, *Domestication of Plants in the Old World* (3rd ed.), Oxford (2000), pp. 194–5.
9. Peter Kaminsky, personal communication; Selima Irkam, 'Food for Eternity: What the Ancient Egyptians Ate and Drank', (in 2 parts), *KMT, a Modern Journal of Ancient Egypt* (5:1, 25–33 Spring 1994) and (5:2, 53–60; 75–6 Summer 1994)
10. Phyllis Pray Bober, *Art, Culture, and Cuisine*, Chicago (1999), p. 3.
11. Adolf Erdman, *The Literature of the Ancient Egyptians*, Methuen & Co. (1927), see, The Instruction of Ptahhotep.
12. Because whole grain durum wheat is not a common market item, I forewent my preferred substitution of semolina for emmer, thinking it was more important for students to have the experience of sprouting wheat berries in this particular reconstruction.
13. Jeffrey Alford and Naomi Duguid, *Flatbreads and Flavors*, Morrow (1995). My recipe borrowed from the 'Hunza Sprouted Wheat Bread' of the Hunzanots of northern Pakistan, who make a flatbread from dried apricots and sprouted wheat; whether there ever was any connection between these breads is beyond my expertise, but I was struck by this unusual use of dried fruits with sprouted grains, similar to that found in New Kingdom sites, in a technologically simple setting.
14. Ed Wood, *World Sourdoughs from Antiquity*, Ten Speed Press (1996).
15. *Hymn to Ninkasi*, translated by Miguel Civil, in Solomon H. Katz and Fritz Maytag, 'Brewing an Ancient Beer', *Archaeology* 44: 4 (1991), pp. 24–33, at p. 29.
16. Delwen Samuel, 'Brewing and Baking', in *Ancient Egyptian Materials and Technology*, Paul T. Nicholson and Ian Shaw, eds., Cambridge University Press (2000), pp. 537–76; see especially discussion at pp. 555–7.
17. Jacqui Woods, *Prehistoric Cooking*, Tempus (2001).

271

Nostalgia and Authenticity in Low-carbohydrate Dieting

Christine Knight

In his chapter on 'Real Food' in his book *Authenticity*, David Boyle suggests that 'there is a growing demand for what is authentic, local and trustworthy'.[1] Amongst his many examples, Boyle discusses Martha Stewart, the anti-GM backlash, raw food restaurants, the Campaign for Real Ale, organic produce, the Slow Food movement and farmers' markets. The global food scene Boyle describes is one with which contemporary food scholars are very familiar, and to which we could add numerous examples of our own from both elite and popular culture. In this paper I want to consider the extent to which the ideology of authenticity – what Boyle calls, in the subtitle to his book, the 'lust for real life' – has permeated an area of Western food culture which has hitherto appeared to be the antithesis of 'real food': namely, dieting. My work focuses on some of the most popular diet books of the last decade, including strict low-carbohydrate regimes such as *Dr. Atkins' New Diet Revolution*, and more recent low-glycemic index bestsellers such as *The South Beach Diet*.[2] What these books share is the idea that health in general, and slenderness in particular, can be achieved through a return to a more natural, traditional and authentic way of eating.

Defining authenticity in food

In everyday usage outside the world of food, *authentic* is generally synonymous with *genuine* or *real*, as opposed to *fake*.[3] An authentic Rolex is the 'genuine article', the 'real thing'. Authentic emotion is true, not pretended; an authentic Leonardo is an original, not a copy or a forgery. The everyday meaning of *authenticity* supports the postmodernist cliché that we live in a world of 'simulacra', given the value placed on the real. In relation to food, however, perhaps the most common use of the word authentic, in both popular and scholarly parlance, refers to so-called ethnic cuisines. Lisa Heldke discusses this concept of 'cross-cultural authenticity' in her recent book *Exotic Appetites*.[4] Heldke suggests that Westerners view ethnic food as authentic if it is prepared in accordance with cultural tradition, 'the way it would be in its culture of origin'.[5] Moreover, a food or preparation technique will only be considered authentic in relation to a particular cuisine if it originated in that particular country or culture – *pad thai* is authentically Thai, for instance, to cite one of Heldke's examples.[6]

Increasingly, alongside notions of cross-cultural authenticity, authenticity has come to refer to certain foods which belong to Western food culture. In this context, authenticity often approaches its ordinary, everyday meaning, referring to foods which are *real* and *genuine*, not processed or artificial. This is the sense in which David Boyle uses the term in his chapter on 'Real Food': authentic food is *natural*, not manufactured, synthetic, or modified.[7] These qualities are most likely to be found in foods and dishes which are traditional – in other words, which originated before the development of advanced food processing techniques. Elspeth Probyn discusses this 'new traditionalism' under the rubric 'sincere food' in her recent book *Carnal Appetites*. 'The new "food sincerity"', Probyn writes, 'dwells on the supposedly simple pleasures of cooking, in an explicit yearning for yesterday'.[8]

I will return in a moment to the culinary 'yearning for yesterday'. To sum up, however, current definitions of authenticity in food and cuisine emphasise two inter-related concerns. Firstly, authentic foods should be real and natural, not synthetic or modified from their original state. Secondly, authentic food-*ways* should follow long-standing cultural traditions. In other words, both foods and cuisines should exist in their original state. Foods and foodways which are newly-invented, hybridised, or which incorporate elements of the new or the Other are not authentic. First and foremost, the authentic is the *not-modified*. What is implicit is that both foods and food cultures exist in some original untainted, uncorrupted state which can, however, be recovered by nostalgic post-industrial Westerners.

In contemporary low-carbohydrate diet discourse, the *not-modified* – in the form of natural, unprocessed foods and traditional, pre-industrial foodways – functions as a nutritional and moral imperative. Crucially, low-carbohydrate logic places responsibility for contemporary health crises (especially obesity and diabetes) on modern changes to traditional foods and foodways, especially the increasing refinement and processing of grain foods. Correspondingly, authenticity in food and diet is presented as the key to health. The point I want to stress is that this logic incorporates a specific temporal dimension. Authenticity in food and diet is located always *prior* to particular events in the history of food production and processing, beginning with the Agricultural Revolution and accelerating after the Industrial Revolution. Because of this, low-carb is an inherently nostalgic nutritional paradigm which looks back to discover the key to health in earlier, 'authentic' diets.

273

Real food and traditional diets in low-carbohydrate discourse

Media representations of the low-carb trend – and even some academic analyses – tend to associate the Atkins diet with fatty processed meats such as bacon and sausage.[9] But despite these grotesque images, low-carbohydrate diet books such as *Dr. Atkins' New Diet Revolution* repeatedly stress that dieters should eat 'real', natural foods, not synthetic or processed products. Atkins urges dieters to 'aim for unprocessed natural foods and select the freshest produce [they] can find'. He even recommends buying organic.[10] In Atkins's terms, authentic food is *pure*: free of synthetic and processed ingredients, including flour, sugar, and trans fats.[11] As these definitions indicate, Atkins constructs real food in opposition to *fake* food. Here, for instance, is how Atkins describes low-fat processed foods, including specific diet foods, but also staples such as white bread:

> This is not real food; it's invented, fake food. It's filled with sugar and highly refined carbohydrates and with chemically altered trans fats ... not to mention plenty of other chemical additives.[12]

Trans fats come in for particular attack, not just for being unhealthy (which few would dispute) but for being 'unnatural': in other words, modified from their original state. Atkins views these 'so-called "foods"', as he describes trans fats, with moral as well as nutritional suspicion. '[H]ydrogenated and partially hydrogenated oils,' he writes, 'contain fats never found in Nature.' The molecular structure of trans fats, he tells us, is 'twisted' and 'unnatural'.[13] The subject matter may be diet, but the terminology is that of sexual perversion.

Like Atkins, *The South Beach Diet* markets itself as a 'real food' regime, in contrast to the synthetic, flavourless horrors of low-fat dieting. In testimonials included in the book, dieters celebrate the fact that they can eat 'real olive oil', 'real dressing', and 'real butter'.[14] Agatston, like Atkins, constructs processed foods as morally questionable – interestingly, not for being unnatural, but for being too easy to digest. In an ethic verging on the Calvinist, *South Beach* continually deplores the ease and convenience of modern Western life. Hard work, temperance, and domesticity are the keys to moral and physical health. Processed grains, argues Agatston, have had the work of digestion done for us, in contrast to 'real, old-fashioned bread', which 'puts your stomach to work'.[15] Uncooked broccoli, he writes, is 'crunchy, hard, cold, and covered with a layer of nutritious fibre ... your stomach has really got to work in order to get at the carbs'.[16] Refined carbohydrates such as white bread and sugar are described in terms reminiscent of drugs, and carrying a similar weight of moral censure:

> Consider that loaf of sliced white bread. First the wheat is stripped of the bran and fibre. Then it's pulverized into the finest white flour. The baking process puffs it up into light, airy slices of bread. No wonder your stomach makes such quick work of it. A slice of white bread hits your bloodstream with the same jolt you'd get by eating a tablespoon of table sugar right from the bowl! Marie Antoinette would have a hard time telling it from cake, and the truth is that there's not much difference.[17]

In this passage, white bread's lack of *physical* substance (it is 'light' and 'airy') translates to a lack of *moral* substance, associated with the notorious frivolity of Marie Antoinette. Worse, the 'jolt' to the bloodstream caused by white bread is the same as that of taking in fine white powder off a spoon! Many low-carbohydrate diet books routinely describe sugary and starchy foods in terms of addiction reminiscent of drugs;

a particular example is Rachael and Richard Heller's *Carbohydrate Addict's Diet*.[18] Yet the Hellers (like Atkins) use this trope to excuse carbohydrate 'addicts' from moral responsibility for binge eating, instead blaming overeating on carbohydrate cravings caused by inappropriate dietary advice.

As well as privileging 'real food' over processed food, low-carbohydrate diets such as Atkins and South Beach privilege 'authentic' traditional food cultures over those of the modern industrial West. In *South Beach*, the foodways constructed as authentic are frequently 'ethnic' cuisines, as in Lisa Heldke's critique of cross-cultural authenticity in *Exotic Appetites*. Agatston advises South Beach dieters to '[g]o to restaurants serving Mediterranean-style food ... I'm thinking of Greek and Middle Eastern food'.[19] However, while Agatston gives Mediterranean and Asian cuisines the nutritional seal of approval, he also laments the 'corruption' of these originally healthy culinary traditions by American restaurants and home cooks. He writes:

> In Italy, you don't sit down in front of a huge dish of pasta with a bottomless bread basket and call it dinner. That's why Italians can eat pasta twice a day and not suffer the obesity rates we see in the United States.[20]

He advises dieters to eat *authentic* ethnic food. 'If you *do* go Italian,' he cautions, 'try to structure the meal the way they do in Italy' – a 'modest serving' of pasta followed by meat or fish and vegetables.[21] Agatston is similarly wary of Asian restaurants in the West, especially the type of rice they use. 'Asians have always used the whole grain,' Agatston claims. 'In this country, and even increasingly in Asian cities, a more processed variety of white rice is used'.[22] In this example, the authentic ethnic is said to be under threat from industrialisation even in its original location in Asia. The effect of this claim is to render authenticity doubly distant from the modern West, in time as well as in space.[23]

Notwithstanding this trope, *South Beach* also harks back to Western culinary traditions which have been destroyed by modern developments in food processing. Agatston writes:

> Once, the carbs we ate were less processed than they are today. More of our bread was baked at home or in local bakeries, not factories, and was made with whole grains, not flour that had been overly processed and stripped of all fibre. Back then, convenience and speedy preparation weren't the highest ideals food aspired to – we were in less of a rush, and home cooking meant starting with raw ingredients. Rice had more of its fibre intact, and had to be cooked slowly. Potatoes weren't sliced and frozen or powdered and bought in a box. Children's after-school snacks weren't limited to what could be microwaved.[24]

In this passage, authenticity is constructed by contrasting an idealised, generalised past against a frenzied, dystopic present.[25] The passage is structured according to a

275

temporal comparison between *once, back then*, and today. *Back then* represents local production, whole foods, and a slower pace of life. *Today*, on the other hand, means industrial production, instant food, and parents who are too busy to cook for their children – if they're home at all. Yet the very structure of the passage, by constructing an opposition between yesterday and today, posits an authentic original prior moment against which subsequent changes can only appear as corruptions.

In her article 'The Other Atkins Revolution: Atkins and the Shifting Culture of Dieting', Amy Bentley identifies a similar nostalgia for traditional Western ways of eating in Atkins. 'Because of the centrality of seemingly unlimited portions of animal flesh', Bentley suggests, 'the cuisine formula of the Atkins diet has a 1950s American gestalt' – meat + two veg, 'but minus the starch'.[26] Bentley concludes:

> the current popularity of Atkins is due in part to its Americanness – built on large chunks of animal flesh, particularly red meat – the same high-status food that has traditionally stood for abundance, wealth, and power.[27]

In Bentley's reading, Atkins, like *South Beach*, draws on a nostalgic ideal of American life popularly centred on the 1950s. Like *South Beach*, Atkins posits an original and authentic Americanness against a vision of a contemporary America which has run monstrously amok. Atkins envisions a post-industrial dystopia lashed by nutritional forces beyond our control. He asks:

> what has caused the *avalanche* of degenerative diseases that now threaten the health of our species? ... About a hundred and ten years ago the lid *blew off* the sugar canister. In the 1890s, the craze for cola beverages *swept* the nation.[28]

In an image straight out of mythology, the initial lifting of the lid has set in motion a chain of disasters, destroying humanity's primordial, sugar-free innocence.

Bentley's analysis at this point in her argument is based primarily on testimony from Atkins dieters and the collection of recipes included in *Dr. Atkins' New Diet Revolution*. In the explanatory chapters of *New Diet Revolution*, however, Atkins idealises a wide variety of traditional food cultures. As in *South Beach*, these authentic cuisines are under threat from Western (and, especially, American) influence. Regarding France, for instance, Atkins writes:

> Only a few decades ago, the Frenchman with his butter-, cheese- and goose-liver-pâté-laden diet had a heart disease rate sixty percent lower than his American peers.... The French also have far lower rates of obesity than Americans do, despite the fact that their diet is higher in fat.... [However,] the French have now discovered fast food. As their diets become closer to American ones, they are losing some of their health advantage.[29]

Chief amongst the authentic foodways touted by Atkins is that of Paleolithic hunter-gatherers. Atkins writes:

> the human body evolved and primitive humans thrived as hunter-gatherers who subsisted primarily on meat, fish, vegetables, fruit, whole grains and seeds and nuts. ... Consequently, your body's capacity to deal with an excess of processed foods is pretty poor, which is why our twenty-first-century way of eating so often gets us into trouble.[30]

The logic of low-carb dieting is that by replicating this hunter-gatherer way of eating, people today can also achieve the supposedly excellent health and physique that Paleolithic people enjoyed.

As these examples from Atkins and *South Beach* show, low-carbohydrate diet rhetoric locates authentic food and foodways in other times and other places. Even authentic ethnic cuisines outside the West are now said to be under threat, so that authenticity (even cross-cultural authenticity) is always *past*, never present. To low-carb authors, the history of agriculture, industrialisation and food processing is one of degradation of an original state of nature. The natural, the original, the authentic is therefore posited always prior to one or more of these historical events and processes. Accordingly, low-carbohydrate texts idealise a multitude of different 'pasts', all of which are envisioned nostalgically rather than accurately. What this suggests is the *self-reflexivity* of low-carb nostalgia. In other words, in privileging tradition, Atkins's and Agatston's primary goal is to critique the state of nutrition and food production in the contemporary West via a constructed opposition with an imagined past.[31] This rhetorical opposition, however, effectively sets up these imagined pasts as originating moments in food culture, against which future modifications may be judged (and found wanting). By virtue of this structuring opposition, nostalgic visions of hunter-gatherer life, of 1950s America, of fatty French feasts all become authentic pasts, static images against which the modern West appears in unflattering silhouette. Once rhetorically fixed in time, these nostalgic images become timeless, accorded the full ideological weight of tradition and authenticity.

Fake food: the Atkins Advantage™

Low-carbohydrate authors like Atkins may extol the benefits of natural food and traditional foodways, but they also simultaneously advocate certain processed diet foods and nutritional supplements. The Atkins brand incorporates a host of processed low-carbohydrate food products, including Atkins Morning Start™ breakfast bars, Atkins Advantage™ nutrition bars, and Atkins Endulge™ candy.[32] While he is careful to avoid mentioning his own brand, Atkins explicitly recommends such products to readers of *New Diet Revolution*:

Today, a person choosing to follow a controlled carbohydrate nutritional approach has almost as many packaged and prepared food options as people who are, unwittingly, following a low-fat diet. Visit your local natural food store, drug store, supermarket or even mass market store and you will see the wide variety of food products available to someone who understands the benefits of controlled carbohydrate nutrition.[33]

Atkins also represents vitamin and mineral supplements as a core component of his diet. Chapter 23 of *Dr. Atkins' New Diet Revolution* is entitled: 'Nutritional supplements: don't even think of getting along without them!'[34] Atkins' list of essential supplements for dieters includes vitamins and minerals such as chromium, pantethine, selenium, vanadium, and biotin. Conveniently, these are all available in the Atkins-brand 'Basic #3 Formula' supplement – although Atkins is careful to acknowledge his financial interest in Atkins Nutritionals.[35]

To a cynic, the real food/fake food contradiction in low-carbohydrate diet discourse simply indicates the extent to which authenticity has become a pre-packaged and well-marketed commodity in contemporary Western culture. In her study of primitivism, Marianna Torgovnick makes this point with regard to cross-cultural authenticity. In Western commodity culture, she points out,

278

> urban and rural, modern and traditional Africa and South America and Asia and the Middle East merge into a common locale called the Third World which exports garments and accessories, music, ideologies, and styles for Western … consumption.[36]

David Boyle makes a similar point in his discussion of 'Fake Real and Virtual Real' in *Authenticity*.[37] Boyle points out that 'many of the big brands are trying to build a hint of authenticity into their products'[38] – McDonald's McCafé and Salads Plus™ being perhaps the ultimate examples. But Boyle's more subtle point is that it is technology – in itself 'inauthentic' – which allows authenticity to be commodified in this way, both in food and other products. Boyle asks, 'how do you deliver authenticity to a mass market?', answering:

> if you're going to reach a mass market, you need that authenticity to be helped along by something which doesn't seem real at all – either the internet, or computer technology, or the mass media.[39]

I would add that it is frequently the technologies of mass *production*, not just mass communication, which enable the commercialisation of authenticity, including authentic food and foodways. In the low-carbohydrate diet movement, advanced food manufacturing technologies have allowed the development of a plethora of low-carbohydrate processed foods, and hence the rise of a commercial low-carbohydrate industry – despite the fact that the nostalgic ideology of low-carb is strongly *anti-*commercial. In an article in the online food industry periodical *Nutraceuticals World*, Julie Hirsch describes the development process for low-carbohydrate products:

> creating low-carbohydrate products requires removing easily digested carbo-hydrates and replacing the macromolecular mass with protein, longer chain less digestible carbohydrates like fibers (including resistant starch and fructo-oligosaccharides like inulin) or water. If some sweetness needs to be added back into products, high intensity sweeteners (like aspartame, sucralose, or acesulfame potassium), or sugar alcohols (such as sorbitol, mannitol, xylitol, isomalt, maltitol, lactitol, erythritol, or polydextrose) are used.[40]

In fact, creating a low-carbohydrate product is as easy as planting a row of lettuces. But the technologies Hirsch describes enabled low-carb manufacturers, in 2003 alone, to 'churn' out 600 new low-carbohydrate processed foods, an industry valued that year at over US$1.4 billion.[41] Arguably, the food industry has 'hijacked' low carb, transforming a 'real food' movement into just another way of making money.

I want to conclude this paper, however, with a somewhat more optimistic reading of the real food/fake food contradiction in low-carb. In chapter 4 of his book *White Identities*, Alastair Bonnett suggests that advanced technology, like the nostalgic turn towards an authentic past, may function as a way to escape the deadening or devitalis-ing influence of modern industrial life.[42] Bonnett explores this idea in relation to the body modification performance artist Stelarc, whose work involves technological and prosthetic modifications to his own body, but in ways which echo 'Modern Primitive' (or 'Neo-Tribal') practices such as body-piercing. Bonnett describes Stelarc's aesthetic as 'techno-primitivist'. In his interpretation,

> Stelarc's self-consciously grotesque attempts to intertwine cable with veins, electricity with blood, are striking precisely because they appear to be provid-ing a techno-primitivist critique on the bland, safe and bloodless nature of modern life. It is a process that seems to offer an escape from the normal, European body into more extreme, more exotic, realms of experience.[43]

In Bonnett's view, the alienated post-industrial Westerner, seeking authentic expe-rience, may well turn towards so-called 'primitive' cultures. A case in point is the archetypal 'food adventurer' whom Lisa Heldke describes, who seeks new and exotic experiences in the authentic cuisines of non-Western ethnic groups. Yet the alienated Westerner may equally, and at the same time, seek authentic experience via high tech-nology. David Boyle describes this phenomenon as *virtual real*. To Boyle, the virtual real 'provide[s] authentic experience by using modern delivery systems that look a little virtual'.[44] He gives the example of IVF, an advanced technology which paradoxically allows women to achieve the ultimate 'natural' experience: having a child.[45]

However, Boyle contrasts *virtual real* with *fake real*: the spurious claims to authenticity by manufacturers of inauthentic or synthetic products, such as 'the pictures of happy chickens gambolling in the countryside on the boxes of eggs from battery farms'.[46] If Atkins Advantage™ bars epitomise fake real (processed foods dressed up in the rhetoric of nature), 'nutraceuticals' and vitamin supplements provide an excellent example of virtual real. Bonnett's notion of techno-primitivism, and Boyle's notion of the virtual real, both seek to explain the myriad ways in which contemporary Westerners seek the natural and the authentic via advanced technological pathways. According to Atkins, the reason we might do this is because advanced industrialisation has corrupted our environment to such an extent that 'nature' must now be sought elsewhere: in a bottle of factory-produced pills. 'With the increasing depletion of nutrients in our soil', Atkins claims, 'there is simply no way we can ensure that we get all [the nutrients] we require from food'.[47] Ultimately, eating real food and emulating authentic foodways is no longer enough. The level of vigour and vitality which Atkins attributes to a natural, unrefined diet can only be achieved – in this denatured world – through the technologies of nutrient supplementation. Paradoxically, in low-carbohydrate logic, the sickness of advanced civilisation is also its own cure.

Notes

1. Boyle, David, *Authenticity: Brands, Fakes, Spin and the Lust for Real Life* (London: HarperCollins, 2003), p. 76.

2. Atkins, Robert C., *Dr. Atkins' New Diet Revolution* (New York: HarperCollins, 2002); Agatston, Arthur, *The South Beach Diet: The Delicious, Doctor-Designed Plan for Fast and Healthy Weight Loss* (London: Headline, 2003).

3. The *OED* lists two current and closely related senses in its definition of authentic. Sense 3 is 'Entitled to acceptance or belief, as being in accordance with fact, or as stating fact; reliable, trustworthy, of established credit.' Sense 6 reads: 'Really proceeding from its reputed source or author; of undisputed origin, genuine.'

4. Heldke, Lisa M., *Exotic Appetites: Ruminations of a Food Adventurer* (New York & London: Routledge, 2003), p. 26.

5. Ibid., p. 29. The quotation is from Steingarten, Jeffrey, *The Man Who Ate Everything* (New York: Random House, 1997), p. 243. See also Abarca, Meredith E., 'Authentic or Not, It's Original', *Food & Foodways*, vol. 12, no. 1 (2004), p. 3.

6. Heldke, pp. 313. Earlier in the same chapter (pp. 279), Heldke points out that much of the time, Westerners designate as authentic foods which are simply new and unfamiliar to us, even if they are not authentic in any other sense.

7. Boyle, pp. 74103.

8. Probyn, Elspeth, *Carnal Appetites: FoodSexIdentities* (London & New York: Routledge, 2000), pp. 245.

9. See, for instance, the sausage-and-egg cover design of the first critical anthology on the Atkins diet: *The Atkins Diet and Philosophy: Chewing the Fat with Kant and Nietzsche*, ed. Lisa Heldke, Kerri

Mommer and Cynthia Pineo (Chicago and La Salle, Illinois: Open Court, 2005).

10. Atkins, p. 130. In fact, the low-carbohydrate paradigm of health and nutrition overlaps considerably with that of the alternative health movement. See for instance, Coward, Rosalind, *The Whole Truth: The Myth of Alternative Health* (London: Faber and Faber, 1989), especially ch. 1 (pp. 1541) 'Nature – Not "Red in Tooth and Claw"', and ch. 5 (pp. 12349) 'The Meanings of Health Foods'. Both Atkins and Mary Dan Eades (co-author of *Protein Power* (New York: Bantam, 1996)) have published books on vitamin supplementation, while Leslie Kenton, author of *The X Factor Diet* (London: Vermilion, 2002), has published numerous books on raw food eating, health foods, and personal and spiritual development.

11. Atkins, p. 123.

12. Ibid., p. 25.

13. Ibid., pp. 3534.

14. Agatston, pp. 3, 14, 5.

15. Ibid., p. 48.

16. Ibid., p. 47.

17. Ibid., p. 48.

18. Heller, Rachael F. and Richard F. Heller, *Carbohydrate Addict's Diet* (New York: New American Library, 1993). Atkins also refers to carbohydrate addiction – see Atkins, pp. 44, 2001.

19. Agatston, p. 79.

20. Ibid., p. 80.

21. Ibid. (Original italics.)

22. Ibid. Although Agatston is writing as an American, when he refers to 'this country' he may well be meaning Britain; this particular passage of the book has been adapted for the UK edition because of Britons' penchant for Indian food. As food scholars will know, Agatston's comment regarding Asians' use of whole-grain rice is inaccurate. As with white and brown bread in the West, white rice in Asia has always been preferred and has therefore functioned as a mark of social status, with brown rice reserved for the lower classes.

23. The other effect of this claim is to imply that ethnic cuisines should be somehow 'preserved' intact for Western exotic tastes; see Torgovnick, Marianna, *Gone Primitive: Savage Intellects, Modern Lives* (Chicago: University of Chicago Press, 1990), p. 187; Knight, Christine, '"The Food Nature Intended You to Eat": Low-Carbohydrate Diets and Primitivist Philosophy', in *The Atkins Diet and Philosophy: Chewing the Fat with Kant and Nietzsche*, ed. Lisa Heldke, Kerri Mommer and Cynthia Pineo (Chicago and La Salle, Illinois: Open Court, 2005), pp. 545.

24. Agatston, p. 73.

25. As I note elsewhere, it is impossible to date Agatston's nostalgic vision with any accuracy. Some aspects of the culture he describes are mid-nineteenth-century, others mid-twentieth-century. See Knight, pp. 489.

26. Bentley, Amy, 'The Other Atkins Revolution: Atkins and the Shifting Culture of Dieting', *Gastronomica*, vol. 4, no. 3 (Summer 2004), p. 40.

27. Ibid., p. 44.

28. Atkins, p. 23. (My italics.)

29. Ibid., p. 25.

30. Ibid., p. 48.

31. See Knight, pp. 469.

32. See the official Atkins diet website at www.atkins.com. Sean Scheiderer points out the contradiction between Atkins's appeals to 'Nature' and the Atkins company's processed low-carb food products in a note to his master's thesis. See Scheiderer, Sean R., 'Mass Consumption: Scientific Fact-(Un)Making in Popular Diet Literature' (unpublished master's thesis, Ohio State University, 2002), n. 31 (unpaginated).

33. Atkins, p. 26.

34. Ibid., p. 301.
35. Ibid., pp. 3025.
36. Torgovnick, p. 27.
37. Boyle, pp. 5673.
38. Ibid., p. 59.
39. Ibid.
40. Hirsch, Julie, 'The Low-Carb Evolution', *Nutraceuticals World* (July/August 2004) <http://www. nutraceuticalsworld.com/JulyAug041.htm> [accessed July 28 2004] (para. 8).
41. Bentley, p. 34; Hirsch (para. 1).
42. Bonnett, Alastair, *White Identities: Historical and International Perspectives* (Harlow, Essex: Prentice Hall, 2000), pp. 878.
43. Ibid., p. 88.
44. Boyle, p. 60.
45. I am grateful to Dr Karen Throsby for initially pointing out the example of IVF. I subsequently read Boyle's book in which he also discusses 'test-tube babies'.
46. Boyle, p. 59.
47. Atkins, p. 135.

Riverworld: the Vanished World of Illinois Riverfolk

Bruce Kraig

Marking the boundaries and draining its central prairies, rivers flow around and through the state of Illinois. In the century before World War II the largest and slowest flowing gave home to groups of people who lived on the rivers, along their banks, and who made their meager livings by harvesting the waters. In those days, the rural societies that bordered the river formed themselves into social hierarchies: farm owners and town folk; tenant, farmers; share croppers; and at the bottom people described in Southern Illinois communities along the Ohio River as 'them river rats.'[1] The same opinion held for the musselers of the Illinois River in the western side of the state. Although mostly of the same American stock as their neighbors, mostly of German, Irish, English, and 'American' (meaning Appalachian) origin, these river people were recognized as distinct not only by their occupations, family ties, and relative lack of cash, but partly by their diets. Except in hard times, they tried not to eat fish but to eat 'normal' meat and potatoes diets. Ecological disaster, population demands, and changes in commerce ended these generations-long traditions, but they are remembered by some as authentic folkways that are now lost. (Note 1)

Chillicothe, Illinois is a modest town of some six thousand people with the now familiar signs of small-town American economic decline. It was once a lively commercial center for railroaders, farmers, businessmen, and especially fishermen who harvested fish and freshwater mussels, usually called 'clams.' Virginia Smith, now in her 80s, worked in her mother's tavern from the 1920s onward: 'it was rough little town back then, thirteen taverns, bootlegging, ladies...not what you see today.'[2]

I was talking with Jay Close, now in his sixties and a life long resident of Chillicothe, Illinois about the history of food in his native town. Once home to a large musseling industry, I asked if he had ever eaten shellfish as a youth. 'No, not until I was an adult,' he replied, 'but once in a while, turtles. Club Lacon [in nearby Lacon, pronounced LAY-con] still serves fried turtle on Friday nights. Especially for the EYE-talians from Toluca, you know, the coal miners there.' He went on, 'There was Mrs. Gurdy's tavern in Rome, IL that served more turtle dinners in 1952 than anyone in the United States. Or so a wire story said. She later worked at the nursing home run by a friend of mine with another great cook, Mrs. Leggio. The manager always said that he had the best restaurant in Illinois. But, when they cooked they had to cut back on heavy spices like oregano, because only the EYE-talians would eat food with it.' Such are the flavors of the Anglo-German Midwest and along the Illinois River.

The setting

The Illinois River is formed by the confluence of the Des Plaines and Kankakee rivers, about 50–80 miles southwest of Chicago, Illinois. It then flows 273 miles to join with the Mississippi River about 31 miles northwest of St. Louis, Missouri. Except in flood conditions, the Illinois is a placid river that flows through a chain of marshes with small lakes scattered up and down its whole length. Early French explorers preferred navigating it to the parallel Mississippi, calling it 'a paradise.' With an enormous wealth of wildlife of all forms and rich soils, paradise was a good description of the Illinois valley. The river bottom was sand and gravel laid down by the last glacial moraine. Older river residents remember when they could see clear through to the river bottom. It was an ideal environment for game fish and mussels, or clams, *was* being the operative word.

The river bottoms give rise to once heavily wooded low bluffs on either side. Beyond them, to the west and southeast, the land levels out into prairie lands. Both river bottoms and bluffs are remarkably fertile, among America's best farmland. Once the prairies were cut (after the invention of a hardened steel plough) they became fabled corn and bean producers. Bluff settlements in the region began in 1820, with settlers from New England and New York, both having their own eating patterns. Chillicothe, right on the riverside, dates to 1834, named for the town in southern Ohio from which the founders hailed. From the start, riverbank settlers built levees, some small, some extensive, against river floods. When these became larger after 1910, especially along the river's southern reaches, they could be planted with small gardens, and folks living in shanty boats did so.

Early settlement patterns remained stable, a world of growing towns providing agricultural products to external markets via flatboats in early years, steamboats later, until the 1870s. Fishing and hunting wild fowl was mainly local, duck and catfish, smallmouth bass, and bluegill eaten fairly regularly. New technology and the press of commerce brought changes in occupations and industry along the river. At the same time, enormous changes in America's foodways were also taking place, changes from local farming and home production to large scale agriculture, food processing, and marketing. Life on the rivers would be transformed.

Fishing

The invention of box cars refrigerated with natural ice made commercial fishing in the Illinois River possible and a new fish species created a new market. German carp were introduced in 1885 because of their use as a food fish by the many new immigrants from Europe to America's cities. By the 1890s, Illinois River fish were being sent up river to Chicago and from there to cities of the east coast. A history of Chillicothe reports that carp and buffalo were harvested for Chicago and eastern markets: 'At these cities they were known as Illinois River Kefelta Fish and were a delicacy to the Jewish and other ethnic populations.'[3] Old World eating patterns and religious practices drove a new industry.

The carp population grew exponentially. In 1894 about 600,000 pounds were caught and processed and by 1908 the catch was 24 million pounds or 64 per cent of the total catch from the Illinois River and its lakes. Live and dressed fish were sent over long distances urban markets.

Commercial fishermen worked seine nets on both the river and lakes to catch carp, catfish, and buffalo. The latter two and game fish such as bass, perch, and bluegill declined in numbers after 1908 for several reasons: competition from the new carp; the increase in water from the Chicago Sanitary and Ship Canal; sewage from that canal, and the leveeing of lands from 1910 onwards to gain and protect arable land against floods.[4]

As a result, fish catches were regulated by state officials beginning in the 1920s. Carp were legal but real money came from game fish that could be sold in Chicago. Jimmy Mattox, a former excursion boats captain (including the *Delta Queen*) and a native Chillicothian says of the fishermen: 'They packed shipping barrels this way: carp 4 inches high, then ice, then game fish like catfish, bullheads, bass, crappies, and others, then carp on top, then another layer of ice again. So inspectors would not get wise. The barrels were sent by Santa Fe Railroad to Chicago, to the Fulton Street fish market.' He went on: 'River people were always getting away with something. They used illegal seine and hoop nets, big seines a city block long across the river with 15 people pulling in. They used seine boats, boats with flat bottoms and shallow drafts. That's a good way to get catfish, they just pulled them in and fish flopped onto boat decks.

'Another way to fish was "hogging". Flatheads are really big catfish that dig themselves into holes in the river backwaters. Fishermen get down into the water and pull them out by hand – 50, 60, 70 lbs or more in size.'[5]

Virginia Smith remembered that fishermen had sheds on the side of the river where they processed the fish-skinning and scaling fast: 'they could do it fast as lightening.' Carp, she says, used to be good to eat when the river was clean. It was filleted and fried in a corn meal batter, seasoned with salt and pepper. Once, every tavern along the river served this delight. Fried carp is still a local specialty in Bath, just south of Chillicothe and anywhere where old German food traditions remain. The fish has to be scored first. That means slicing across a piece of fish every quarter inch to a depth of about two-thirds of the way through. This allows the cooking process to soften the fish's many small bones.[6] Frying makes it perfectly American.

Typically, fishermen rowed for hours in the early morning to reach their nets, traps, or lines, where they would collect their catch and deliver it to the local market. Almost every community along the Illinois River once supported a fish market. Traditionally, small, family-operated markets sold fresh fish to local buyers, but with increased demand from wider markets, the small floating markets became transfer points for shipping fish destined for tables in Boston, New York, and Chicago. Large scale commercial fishing became possible after railroads linked the Midwest with the eastern seaboard. Wives and daughters of the market owners assisted with cleaning and packing (called dressing), although in the larger markets, hired hands performed these chores.[7]

But the river was to decline. One of the 20th century's greatest engineering feats helped destroy river ecology. The Chicago River that runs through the city flowed into Lake Michigan carrying with it all the city wastes. Typhoid fever and dysentery were a constant danger. That and a perceived need to link Chicago with the Mississippi River for barge traffic led to Chicago Sanitary & Ship Canal in 1900 and later the reversal of the Chicago River. Illinois River communities protested that Chicago was sending garbage downstream, but to no avail.[8] Initially the canal raised the water level from the diversion of water from Lake Michigan. A fisherman could pull 80,000 pounds of fish per day. However, this water carried raw sewage from the residents of Chicago and would soon begin harming the fish and their habitat.

Overfishing became a problem as early as 1915 when a fisheries scientist reported that fish had been seined out along the southern end of the river. A 1931 law made the Canal divert less water (this to control floods that raged across the United States), the Illinois became muddier and more shallow, increasing stress on the remaining fish species. Fishermen could still pull thousands of tons of fish from the river in the 1930s, though selling them in a depressed market was another matter. By the end of World War II the fishing industry was but a shadow of its former glory. A few local fisheries remained, such as Roberts in Chillicothe (Virginia Smith's step-father) and were completely gone by 1960.

Other pollutants infected the river. New levees made for new fields and with it much more agricultural chemical runoff. A rubber tire plant at the river bend near Henry spewed black waste straight into the river until the 1970s. And the federal munitions plant upriver in Joliet, producing more than five tons of TNT per day during the war, sent its waste down the river. Jay Close says that he could almost walk on the black crusted waters in the back bays by the 1970s.[9] By the 1960s the river was almost dead and so were former ways of life.

Clams/mussels

'Freshwater mussels are bivalve mollusks (*Phylum Mollusca*, Class *Bivalvia*) distantly related to marine clams, oysters, mussels, and scallops. They have soft inner bodies and hard outer shells consisting of two valves. Historically, North America had the richest fauna of freshwater mussels in the world.'[8]

The rivers within and around Illinois harbor many species of freshwater clams. With extremely hard shells, the mussels spend most of their lives partially or completely buried in the bottom of a body of water. They prefer sandy bottomed rivers and streams with a good current. These animals have experienced dramatic declines in both actual numbers and species due to pollution.

Another human activity is reason for the decline. From about 1890 to 1948 most buttons for clothing in the U.S. came from clams, many from Illinois. 40,000–60,000 tons of shells a year were used to make buttons in various sizes. Waste parts were used in chicken feed and road fill, but rarely for food. In the 1890s pearl buttons as the clothing fastener of choice, created a large market.

Fresh-water mussel shells were a cheaper and higher quality source that salt-water shells and other materials such as wood, glass, metal, and bone. Other events helped to create this industry. In 1890, the McKinley Act prohibited the importation of buttons. This protection continued with the Dingley Act of 1897. The design of shell-cutting machines was improved to work better and faster. The primary use of shells was the manufacture of buttons, although some shell was made into decorative parts for items such as handles of knives, hairbrushes, and cigarette cases. Illinois River button factories mainly cut the unfinished blanks and shipped them overland to be ground and polished into buttons in much larger facilities, such as those in Muscatine, Iowa that opened in 1891 and transformed museling from parties of waders searching shallow waters to fleets of motorized boats plucking huge numbers of mussels from the deepest pools.[10]

287

Museling boats and tools were specialized instruments, the first flat bottomed, the latter varieties of hooks, pikes and nets. Mussels were processed by steaming. A large wooden vessel containing some water was set over a fire and filled with mussels, then covered. After 20 minutes, the dead shellfish were removed with wide pitchforks and allowed to cool. Sorters, mainly women and children, pried open the shells with a knife, scooped the meat from the shells, searched for pearls, threw out the meat, this to be used for pig feed, or fish bait. 'Saw shops' as they were called washed sorted, and categorized the shells by use, color, size, and species. By season's end the shell middens had overwhelmingly sickening odors. That smell stuck with the muselers and set them apart from their neighbors.

The shell collectors manually scooped the shells into tubs that held 100 pounds and loaded them onto trucks that came by weekly: payment was by the ton. Shells were then delivered to factories that made buttons and other decorative items. Soon small plants opened near the mussel beds and a new industry grew.

By 1910 at least 2500 museling boats worked the river bringing higher levels of income to those who clammed and those who worked in the button factories. Many workers were women from poorer farms, but many also were from fishing families. However, like fish, mussels began to decline in numbers from overfishing, pollution and changes in fashion and technology. When Japanese manufacturers introduced celluloid buttons in 1926 with buttons made of celluloid, metal, and ivory nut (the seed of the South American tagua palm *Phytelepas macrocarpa*), American button income declined. Zipper and metal clasps introduced in the 1930s also hurt business. And by 1930, local mussel had been over-harvested, killed by pollution from the Sanitary Canal and silted out by farm runoff. Perhaps worst, the heat produced by the new automatic washers and dryers of the 1940s caused pearl buttons to yellow and exfoliate. So, too, another river industry and way of life was lost (Endnote 2).

Society and foodways

When speaking with the 'old timers' in small towns like Chillicothe, people in their 70s and 80s, about food memories, almost all refer to times of greatest stress, the Great Depression. This is the same period in which John Bennett, Herbert Passin and others studied life along the Ohio River in Southern Illinois (see Endnote 1). There are differences between the Illinois River region and the Ohio, but also some interesting parallels. In Southern Illinois, the researchers defined several ecological zones, each with somewhat different cultural styles, yet each interacting with one another. At the bottom of the Ohio River social heap were people living on the river by fishing, many in 'shanty boats.' Small farmers, squatters, occupied the riverbanks, making their livings by fishing or farm labor. Along the rich Bottoms were tenant farmers and sharecroppers and farm laborers. Several levels of hills stand above them, living on badly eroded lands as sharecroppers, tenant farmers, or land renters. Only people of German extraction, their way of life different from their 'English' neighbors, were more prosperous. The region's town served as a business center with a permanent, non-agricultural population, and income based partly on bootlegging done during Prohibition and not completely dead by 1938–39.

Food was a means of self-identification among the groups. Though most were poor, their staples being potatoes, beans, and pork, there were distinct differences in food prestige. That is, fish was at the bottom of the social scale, scorned as food fit only for the river people, hardly eaten by folks at the 'higher' end of the spectrum. Because of changes in American food production, many of the tenant farmers and sharecroppers ate more store-bought food than raised their own. Corn meal and flour, even canned vegetables and canned milk were usually purchased. Gardens were sparse among these groups, non-existent in shanty boat life. Only to people living on the Bottoms, some of them black, and among the German farmers, were vegetable gardens with subsequent canning important. As Thelma Renshaw from New Athens [AY-thens] near St. Louis, related, during World War II people made money for the first time in many years, and after it could not wait to quit eating homemade bread in favor of good 'store boughten' white bread. Wonder Bread, that is. So much for authentic farm food.[11]

This model has some application to Chillicothe in the first part of the 20th century, beginning as a center for farm products meant to be sent to external markets.

Grain shipping businesses and a bank appeared in its early years, the 1850s, followed by more white-collar businesses. In 1886 the Atchison, Topeka and Santa Fe ran its tracks nearby, thus linking California to Chicago. Before long, Chillicothe became the railroad's headquarters and source of much local income (and also was responsible for a small Mexican community dating to 1906). By time the fishing and musseling industries were in full swing, and the Great Depression (1929/30–1940), Chillicothe's divisions were geographic, social, and economic. On the rivers were the 'river people,' who lived in 'shanty boats' all along the river. Mainly fishermen, they were despised by the others. Railroaders were those employed by the Santa Fe. By no means were these white-collar workers, but ranged from the elite engineers to manual laborers. Many became unionized and thus had an entirely different work-ethic than the river people. They were almost entirely dependent on store-bought food. On the bluffs and interior were farmers. Many were self-sufficient, producing enough grain, legumes, meat and dairy for the market. In the 1880s a large canning company opened in town, buying produce and giving farmers a cash income. Others were less fortunately placed, tenant farmers, though never as poor as the share-croppers of the Ohio River region. Thelma Renshaw describes her father's life as a share-cropper in the 1930s: they got a four room house, $1 a day, and all the skim milk they could drink. Almost everything else they grew or reared themselves. And that was a cut above the commercial catfish fishing he had had to do when they were really down and out. Finally, there were the townspeople, the storekeepers, bankers, and artisans who were once familiar sights in small-town America. Most of these provided cash wages to employees of various kinds, especially those who had graduated from the town's schools. Of these, there was one subset, tavern keepers. All along the river were taverns patronized by fishermen, railroaders, farmers. Some were of more dubious reputation, closer to the river people than to townspeople. Such a place was Marge's.

289

Virginia Smith was born on a farm in nearby Elmwood, Illinois and has lived in Chillicothe all her life, as does her family. Married three times, she says that she 'never married the others, and wouldn't do it again.' Her stepfather was the biggest fisherman between Peoria (10–12 miles south) and Henry (10–12 miles north). His name was 'Kokomo' Roberts, so named because he had been a baseball player who was so good that 'he whipped everyone's butts.' Kokomo was the name of a stellar professional baseball player of the era. Roberts' was one of the few fisheries to survive into the 1960s.

Not just what people eat but how they get it is a social denominator. Virginia's mother owned a tavern called Marge's. During Prohibition (1919–1932) her mother took to bootlegging in order to feed her children. 'There was always someone with 15 cents for whiskey or a dime for beer.' Her mother made home brew, and got the first retail license after Repeal at a cost of $20. Virginia remembers when three officials from Pabst Brewing Co., a large brewery south of town, came in and told her to keep bootlegging because her stuff was so good that they didn't want to spoil it. It could be, she adds, that the brewers knew that Al Capone used to come down to

Chillicothe on his houseboat and stopped in for a quick one at Margie's. 'Wives were always angry with Marge,' Virginia continues, 'because there they would be with 6 or 7 kids at home waiting for husbands who stopped at the "evil" tavern to have a drink or two.'

Virginia's mother came from a farm family, her stepfather was a fisherman, so she knew both societies and Marge's was a place where they met. River people, she declares, were always second-class citizens. They had the lowest paying, dirtiest job, they stank, and they were often dishonest. Railroaders were never dirty and looked down upon the river people. There was always conflict between the river people, the railroaders, and the town people …and sometimes the Mexicans who worked in agriculture and railroads. The river guys got into fights all the time because 'banging heads meant nothing to them.' Fights often broke out this way: when the fishermen were done for the day, they headed to Marge's where they drank whiskey shots with beer chasers. They sat around the pot-bellied stove and were pretty quiet. Then the railroad men came in, would have a few, then they'd comment on how bad the river-men smelled, comments were exchanged, and soon a fight broke out. Virginia says that almost always the railroad men were sorry they ever came in. For instance her uncle George Neal, a real character, was a riverman who was always drinking and fighting. He was short but really powerful from pulling seine nets, and was never beaten in a fight. (Fishermen were usually described orally and in newspaper accounts as thickset and strong.) But he never learned to swim.

290

Jimmy Mattox reinforces the idea of river people's perceived dishonesty. Many of the river people were market hunters, meaning, poachers. One family, the Hamms, were notorious. They would kill ducks, can them with peaches, and sell them in Chicago in the 1930s. (Evidently this was a popular item.) The Hamms killed many thousands. Virginia and others remember that they killed several thousand in one day using shrapnel in their shotguns. It was during migration season, this being the famous Mississippi Flyway. The Hamms often hung out on an island in the river, Grand Island, for their illegal activities, like pirates.

Houseboat, or 'shanty boat' life flourished along the Illinois River from the 1890s to the 1930s. They were literally flat bottoms, low in the water with cabins set on them. The 'house' might have had several rooms with the most basic furnishings, such as a stove, table and chairs and a bed. A federal researcher described one thus:

The exterior of this houseboat is nicely painted. The inside walls are sealed, though unpainted. All the four rooms were furnished like an ordinary cottage: linoleum on the floors, a kitchen range, a polished table, a stand made of walnut, an iron bed covered with an attractive spread, an air-tight heater, a rocking chair, and dining chairs. One window was filled with plants and vines. Dainty drapes were at the one-panel windows. Small framed pictures were on the walls. Everything was neat and very clean.[12]

Most shanty boat dwellers made every effort to eat the same kinds of foods as landed people. Partly because of its low prestige value, few would admit to being serious pis-cophages. Shellfish were especially abhorred. Perhaps because fish were so abundant, or so easily caught, those who lived on them were thought lazy, and thus not part of American social norms. The quote below is telling in this regard. Since most of the shanty boaters worked (hard) for cash they had some disposable income to spend on store foods. By the 1890s and thereafter, commercially produced goods were available everywhere. Nor could cooking facilities on shanty boats have been sophisticated. A stove meant not a bake-oven, but small wood-fired thing used only for stovetop cook-ery: frying and boiling. Nonetheless, Virginia Smith says she and others associated with the river ate lots of fish, the land dwellers only on Friday.

Shanty boat residents varied: some were year-round houseboat residents, others sea-sonal migrants, or seasonal river workers. As one former dweller, Dale Ward, put it:

> Cabin boats, people lived on cabin boats. They thought maybe it was a kind of utopia. This came as near as anything I know of. They had one family or more living on a cabin boat. It might have been a big one, nice with two rooms, you know, that they fixed up. And they fished on the river. They might have stopped and had a garden on the levee. Keep a sow and some little pigs. And they had the fish all the time. They had easy livin'. Maybe had a garden up there. They'd drive a stand pipe for water. And, of course, there was plenty of wood. There was a lot of driftwood on the bays, you know. If the wood got scarce, they moved off.[13]

291

Mobility, and freedom, prized by Ward, was the reason for shanty boat people's lower prestige. Because they weren't part of the networks of land-based church and social organizations, they were outsiders, even though they might have come originally from farms or towns. Besides, as fishermen, they probably 'stank.'

Most shanty boat dwellers owned their boats, but almost never the land on which they moored. Some were squatters, hence all the more scorned. Fishing and musseling were the major activities.

> Shanty boats had the advantage over land-based homes of being tax-free, low-rent, and portable to move to where there was work or harvesting opportuni-ties. This was important for fishermen and musselers, and for many others, especially during the Depression, when the number of people on the river increased after farms began to fail and industrial jobs were lost. Another advan-tage of the houseboat was that one could not get flooded out, with possessions damaged, as many Illinois River inhabitants did in high flood years.[14]

The Great Depression drove people to the shanty boats, in much the same was as on the Ohio River. Virginia Smith knew at least ten families who lived in them. Most of the families who lived in them came from farms, but during the dry years of the Great Depression people were driven off their farms. They fought to keep them, but failed because the drought and dust storms were so great. She can picture even now the large mounds of dry earth piled up against farm fences. (The Dust Bowl, usually thought of as covering the Great Plains of the American west, actually began in the Midwest in 1931.)

Hungry and broke people took to the river boats. Of course, there were people already there, so population swelled. The only food available in the early years of the Depression were fish. People ate fish before, but it was déclassé fare except for on Friday nights for Catholics or festive cookouts. The original shanty boat dwellers far preferred eating what dry-land people ate: pork, beef, potatoes, beans, and sweets. But poverty made fish-eating a necessity. One might think that consuming one's cash crop was not an attractive prospect, but in 1931 many dry-land farmers destroyed crops and farm animals because they could not get anything like a fair market price for them. A major fishery at Meredosia at the same time had to horde its catch in large tanks for the same reason. Virginia Smith well recalls farmers bringing their slaughtered animals in to her mother's tavern to be cooked up for the poor.

'People were lucky to even be eating back then,' Virginia recollects. 'When FDR got in my mother got food from the government for free, 100 lb flour, or cornmeal, and the like, and she cooked it at the tavern for free lunches and dinners, for the poor. Many of the poorest were the river people, so they came to Marge's – where on Saturday nights there was always some conflict.'

Or folks could go to Mrs. Webb's. This estimable lady, who once cooked at Prairie Shores (the automobile club and club for the well-to-do including politicos and Al Capone), owned Webb's Inn which was famous for its fried chicken dinners (chicken not a commodity as it is today, but a Sunday dinner). Fish and pork were cheap and that's what people got. She received free food from the government and cooked for the poor, river dwellers, too: People could just walk in and get a free lunch, especially after 1933.

When people were really hungry Marge's and Mrs. Webb and others resorted to something they would never think of eating: clam (mussel) soups and stews. This was truly food for the poor but Virginia says that the dishes were really good. 'Just throw them in the pot with some carrots or whatever vegetables you have, add some salt and maybe pepper and cook them down.' The original settlers of Chillicothe, from New England, would surely have recognized such dishes.

World War II ended shanty boat life. War industries soaked up all available labor. Money saved during years of rationing went directly into new land housing after the war. With factories such as Caterpillar in nearby Peoria, large breweries and even the world's largest whisky distiller, also in Peoria, the old river life ended. It could hardly have gone on anyway given the imminent death of a once-great river.

292

If there were a natural Riverworld Cuisine, excluding store-bought foods, what would it be? Certainly fish, not carp, but the 'better' sort such as bass and definitely catfish. Turtles were also part of the diet, maybe of higher status than fish because the flesh is considered to be 'meat.' Jimmy Mattox tells how they were captured. Big ones could be found, 'as big as washtubs.' They were caught in traps that look like boxes, just baited with meat. The only good turtles are snappers. Soft-shelled turtles are not. Snapping turtles are still caught and eaten, Jimmy's uncle one such hunter. The way to get them was to stick a pole into soft mud along the banks. When the snapper grabbed on it, it was a simple matter of pulling them out – using iron hooks to grapple them. Mostly hunting was done in the autumn when they settled in to hibernate and before the mud froze. There are said to be seven kinds of meat in a turtle, from its flesh to internal organs. These might be indistinguishable when properly fried up.

Since it was hard to fish in the winter, river folks hunted and trapped. Mink (inedible), raccoons, muskrats, possums and beaver were all on the menu, the latter giving up its tail to the table. The preferred cooking method would be to roll the meat in cornmeal and then fry it, normally in lard.

Waterfowl were always on the menu, though Jay Close relates that he once got a mud hen, that's a coot, and brought it to his mother to cook. She did and it was so foul that he never hunted for duck again.

Pork, beef when possible, potatoes, beans (often), and perhaps some greens would have made up the shanty boat diet, with the exception of beef, similar to that other shanty boat culture across the state on Ohio River.

293

Endnotes

Endnote 1. In the late 1930s a team of anthropologists from the University of Chicago studied the society of a small Illinois town and its region along the Ohio River, actually near Metropolis or Cave-in-Rock (see note 1 below). The ways of life the team described in the Great Depression have long disappeared. In many ways, these studies mirror another riverside region, Chillicothe, located on the broad Illinois River. This paper uses some of the materials and conclusions from the Southern Illinois study.

Endnote 2. Mussel harvesting resumed in the 1960s to provide the shell implant or 'nucleus' for producing cultured pearls grown in Japan. Commercial harvesting continues in the Mississippi River and some of its tributaries, but is currently prohibited in the Illinois River except for one short harvest season. Over seven-million pounds of mussels, valued at over six-million dollars, were harvested in 1990. Jimmy Maddox recalls barges laden with shells worth a million dollars rolling down the river and he knows some current musselers

Notes

1. John W. Bennett, Harvey I. Smith, Herbert Passin, 'Food and Culture in Southern Illinois – A Preliminary Report,' *American Sociological Review*, Vol 7, No 5 (Oct., 1942), 645–660; Herbert Passin, 'Culture Change in Southern Illinois,' *Rural Sociology*, Vol 7, No 3 (Sept., 1942), 303–317.
2. Interview with Virginia Smith, Chillicothe, IL, June, 2005.
3. Jack L. Bradley (ed.), *The History of Chillicothe, Illinois* (Chillicothe, IL: the Chillicothe Historical Society, 1995), 52.
4. Records of fishing and musseling along with some oral histories can be found at the Illinois Museums and Illinois Natural Resources website: www.museum.state.il.us/RiverWeb.
5. Interview with Jimmy Mattox, Chillicothe, IL, June, 2005.
6. <http://www.museum.state.il.us/RiverWeb>
7. *Chillicothe Bulletin*, Friday, April 3, 1893. Put out a call for a meeting to protest Chicago's plan to build a sanitary canal: 'Chicago wants to unload its garbage into the Illinois' thus hurting 'the Valley people.'
8. <www.museum.state.il.us/RiverWeb>.
11. Interview with Jay Close, Chillicothe, IL, July 2005.
10. Ibid.
11. Interview with Thelma Renshaw, New Athens, IL, August, 2002.
12. <http://www.museum.state.il.us/RiverWeb/harvesting/transportation/boats/houseboats.html>
13. Dale Ward, Oral History, 07/17/1981. <http://www.museum.state.il.us/RiverWeb/harvesting/transportation/boats/houseboats.html>
14. Ibid.

294

Traditional Philippine Vinegars and their Role in Shaping the Culinary Culture

Pia Lim-Castillo

Filipinos and vinegar – from a need to an acquired preference

The person who led me to do research on Philippine food and foodways was Doreen Fernandez. She was a friend and mentor who shared her passion for Philippine food, culture and history with me. Her presentations at the Oxford Symposium were always about the Philippines because she wanted to put the Philippines on the culinary world map. Before she passed away, she wanted someone to continue to carry the torch of the Philippines at the symposium so here I am presenting a paper on the topic of authenticity and I've chosen to write about traditional Philippine vinegars.

In the Philippines, vinegar is an important ingredient in cooking. Centuries ago, vinegar was used as a preservative when refrigeration was non-existent. This has formed our taste for sourness that is ingrained in our culinary culture. Vinegars are made from saps of palm trees, sugar-cane, fruits and alcoholic beverages. No Philippine kitchen is complete if there is no vinegar. In rural areas, one will see rows of glazed jars called *tapayan* where vinegar is allowed to ferment. Villagers would come with their empty bottles for a refill of either toddy or vinegar. Nowadays, traditional vinegar making has become a specialty trade and the kind of vinegar made depends on what is locally available. In Northern Luzon and Pangasinan, the typical vinegar is made from sugar-cane, as the land is suitable for growing sugar-cane. In the central plains and in areas near unpolluted rivers, vinegar is made from *nipa* palm sap. *Nipa* palms grow along the banks and help in soil erosion control. From the southern part of Luzon all the way to Mindanao, coconut sap is turned into vinegar. In forested areas where sugar palms grow, these too are tapped for their sap to turn into vinegar. These four are the most common vinegars that one would find in the country: *kaong*, *tuba*, *paombong* and *iloko*. The choice of vinegar to be used for cooking is dependent on what is locally available. One need not go very far to find good natural vinegar.

Traditional vinegar making is a biological process whereby sugars in fruit juices are converted into alcohol. This conversion is facilitated by wild yeasts found in nature. After this conversion takes place, these wines are allowed to sit in open containers which are partially filled to allow the free flow of air and for acetobacters to work on the wine to turn it into vinegar. Acetobacters are aerobic microorganisms (they need oxygen to live) and non-sporiferous (they do not form spores). They reproduce by duplicating themselves (Diggs, p. 73). In unpasteurized vinegars, a mat is commonly found floating on the top of the fermenting vinegar. This is called the mother of vinegar. It is a coin-like gel or cellulose produced by the harmless vinegar bacteria. Vinegar containing the mother is not harmful and may continue to grow in the bottle.

This is how our traditional vinegars are made. What started as a need to preserve our foods eventually became an acquired taste for anything sour whether it be foods cooked in vinegar to sour fruits. It is this simple flavor that we come to miss when we can't have it.

The craft of vinegar-making in the Philippines

The Philippines is blessed with an abundance of different kinds of palm trees that can be tapped for sap, a variety of fruits and even grass (sugar-cane) that can be turned into vinegar. Due to fertile soils and conducive weather, grown trees can be tapped for years to make toddies and vinegar. Vinegar making could have been discovered by mistake by toddy brewers when their alcoholic beverages turned sour as in the case of wine vinegar. Later on, toddy brewers also became vinegar makers when their toddies weren't all sold. Vinegar became a secondary product for toddy brewers. This is the case with coconut, *nipa* and sugar-cane.

Coconut vinegar

The most commonly used vinegar in the Philippines is coconut vinegar. The best coconut vinegar is made from the sap of the coconut inflorescence. Early in the morning, men climb up coconut trees to collect the previous day's sap drippings. These are transferred to bamboo containers which the climber or *mananguete* brings up with him. After transferring the coconut sap (which by that time has started to ferment into alcohol), he cleans the emptied container and slashes the spadix again to allow the sap to flow until the following day. Harvesting is better done in the morning because the sucrose level of the sap is higher as measured on a Brix refractometer. This sap is sweet, clear, and colorless, containing about ten to eighteen per cent sugar. In a few hours, alcoholic fermentation takes place and turns the sap into a toddy (*tuba*). The toddy is a heavy, milk-white opalescent suspension of live yeasts and bacteria with a sweet taste and vigorous effervescence. Toddies are consumed throughout the tropics and contain as much as 83 mg ascorbic acid per liter. During fermentation, beneficial minerals such as thiamine, riboflavin and pyridoxine increase. It also contains considerable amounts of vitamin B-12. Palm toddies play an important role in nutrition among the economically disadvantaged in the tropics. They are the cheapest sources of B vitamins (Steinkrauss, p. 30). Some coconut vinegar makers start by transferring their unsold toddies to vitrified earthen jars, fifty-gallon food-grade plastic drums or stainless steel vats where they are allowed to come into contact with acetobacters in the air and thus turn the toddy into vinegar. This fermentation process lasts anywhere from forty-five to sixty days until such time that the acidity level hits five to six per cent titratable acidity when it is bottled for ageing and sale. Others start straight from the sap.

As the vinegar ages, sediments will appear at the bottom and the color changes from cloudy white to light yellow, to a clear light brown as it further matures. These sediments that form inside the vinegar bottle contain protein, starch, crude fiber and ash. They settle as the vinegar ages and mother of vinegar forms.

Coconut palm vinegar contains nutrients such as potassium (164 mg/100 ml), sodium (16 mg/100 ml), phosphorus (9 mg/100 ml), beta carotene (6 mg/100 ml), magnesium (5 mg/100 ml), calcium (0.6 mg/100 ml) and iron (0.26 mg/100 ml).

The flavor of coconut vinegar varies slightly depending on the location where the coconut trees grow. Like wine and its terroir, trees growing close to the sea will produce saltier vinegars as against coconut trees inland. It is sharp in flavor, mouth-puckering and has the highest titratable acidity of all Philippine vinegars.

Nipa sap vinegar

The next most common vinegar is made from *nipa* sap or *Sukang Paombong*, so called after the flower of the *nipa* palm. *Nipa* grows in muddy soil along rivers and man-groves to keep soil from eroding. It is unusual in having an underground stem which branches to form new above-ground plants. The pinnate leaves of the palm appear to come from a stemless rosette. This places the inflorescence very near the ground where it can easily be tapped for its sap.

The seeds of the *nipa* palm float and germinate in the water, and when deposited on a muddy bank, can establish themselves. The bases of the fronds are characterized by air-filled cavities, which keeps them upright. These fronds have an especially wide usage in weaving household articles and can be used to cook food in.

Twice a day, men kick the fronds to stimulate the sap to flow (*pag-uuntag*). The stalk is slashed to allow the sap to flow to a bottle attached to it. Sap is harvested twice a day and is more prolific during the dry season. The sap contains from fifteen to twenty-two per cent sugar, and wild yeasts immediately start the fermentation process. The sap toddy is fermented for fifteen to thirty days in glazed jars where acetobacters found in the air turn the toddy into vinegar. The vinegar is checked for acidity and when it reaches four per cent, it is bottled for sale.

With an acidity level of four to five per cent, *nipa* vinegar isn't as sharp as coconut vinegar and is slightly salty because these palms grow in brackish water. It is also relatively sweeter than coconut vinegar. *Nipa* sap vinegar has a tendency to darken as it ages, because it contains quite a bit of iron. In fact, old folks claim that if *nipa* vinegar doesn't darken, it isn't pure.

Nutrients that *nipa* sap vinegar contains are iron, potassium, calcium, sodium and magnesium. These are among the few that the vinegar has been tested for.

Sugar palm vinegar

The third kind of palm vinegar in the Philippines is made from the sap of the sugar palm (*Arengga pinnata*). These trees take ten to fifteen years before they can be tapped for their sap which contains ten to twenty-five per cent sugar. These palm trees best thrive on ravines along rivers. The life-cycle of an *Arengga* tree is about fifteen to twenty-two years. Sap is only taken from the male flowering stalk. The natural allies in the propagation of these trees are palm civets. These civets eat and excrete the seeds of the *Arengga pinnata*.

Collecting the sap of the *Arengga pinnata* requires more steps than coconut or *nipa*. A few months before the flowering stalk can be cut to extract sap, the caretaker (*mangangarit*) has to rock the flowering stalk daily until the flowers bloom and attract hundreds of fruit flies. It is only then that the flowering stalk is ready for tapping and collection. This is a necessary step to ensure a good drip from the stalk. The caretaker collects the drippings daily, climbing as high as seven meters, using bamboo poles to collect the sap, and transferring it to bamboo container known locally as *tukil* which he carries on his shoulder.

The sap of the *Arenga pinnata* is transferred to vitrified earthen jars called *tapayans* or *bangas* for acetobacter fermentation. The process takes three to four weeks to complete. It is stored in these glazed jars until the acidity level hits four per cent. In the case of the brand *Arengga Vinegar*, they have opted to standardize their vinegar by transferring collected vinegar from earthen jars to stainless steel tanks where it is pasteurized for thirty minutes and cooled to 60°C. It is aged in airtight food-grade plastic drums (to minimize oxidation) for ageing anywhere from two months to three years before it is bottled. This process, done before bottling, ensures standard acidity and sugar levels favored by restaurateurs. Sugar palm vinegar has a final acidity level of 4.2 to 5.5 per cent.

Nutrients that sugar palm vinegar has been tested for and found to have are benzoic acid in beneficial quantities, potassium, sodium, iron, magnesium and calcium.

Sugar palm vinegar is the least sour of all the palm vinegars and is sweeter. It can be used for salad dressings as well as for cooking.

Sugar cane vinegar

Sugar cane vinegar is different from the first three because it comes from a family of grasses. This is a traditional vinegar made mostly in Northern Luzon where there are many sugar-cane plantations. It is commonly called *Sukang Iloko* and most vinegars sold in the north to the central plains of Luzon are made from sugar-cane.

Of the major crop grasses, cane is remarkable because it is a perennial. Typically, a stem of sugar-cane grows to a height of four or five metres in ten to fourteen months and then produces a flower stalk. Just when a flower stalk forms, the solid stem of this plant is loaded with sucrose, which can be easily removed from the stem by crushing.

Stems are subdivided into four-foot lengths and transported in carts or rail cars to a nearby processing mill. Cane must be processed within two days of harvesting, otherwise fermentation and bacterial growth destroy the crop and the sugar content decreases sharply. Stems are harvested when sucrose content in the stems is fifteen to sixteen per cent. At the sugar mill, the fresh stems are fed into a mechanical crusher. The juice is boiled to remove impurities and cooled down to lukewarm before being transferred to vitrfied jars for fermentation. This will take about a month to turn into vinegar before bottling. Of all the vinegars, this is the cheapest because the yield of harvested raw material is the highest per hectare. A hectare of sugar-cane generates about 50 cubic metres of raw juice which can be turned to wine, sugar and vinegar.

Sometimes, *Sukang Iloko* is also made from sugar-cane wine called *basi*. In *basi* production, a yeast called *bubud* is added to ferment the sugar-cane juice and to give it a bittersweet flavor. Vinegar made from *basi* is done if the wine turns sour. Flavoring agents such as tanbark and leaves are added to impart a different flavor and coloring and is aged in glazed jars to complete the acetous fermentation.

The flavor of this vinegar is sweetish with a reminiscent smell of freshly cut sugar-cane. It is best used as a dipping sauce. When used for cooking, the resulting dish will have a sweetish aftertaste.

A summary of the salient features of each of the above-mentioned vinegars is included as a table in the end of this paper.

Culinary uses of vinegar in the Philippines

From the times of our forebears, vinegar was used in pickling vegetables, seafoods and meats to preserve them. It was also used as a dipping sauce for all kinds of fried, broiled and boiled dishes. Cooking foods in vinegar and salt are ways of preserving foods. Traditional cooking methods using vinegar are *adobo, kinilaw, sangkutsa* and *paksiw*. These were the main cooking methods in the country then and continue to this day especially in the rural areas where foods can be left in its cooking vessel unrefrigerated for days without getting spoiled.

Adobo is the essence of Philippine stews. It was thought to be of Mexican origin because it is similar to the Mexican *adobado* which is meat cooked in wine. However, food historian Raymond Sokolov believes that the name was applied to the native dish, which already existed before Spanish contact, proof being that many *adobos* exist that Spain never knew (Fernandez, p. 34). The stew is usually chicken, pork, seafoods and vegetable that are boiled in vinegar, garlic, cracked peppercorns, soy sauce and bay leaves. In some areas of the Philippines, soy sauce is replaced by salt, turmeric or annatto seeds for color rather than the dark soy sauce. The main flavoring agents are vinegar and garlic.

Kinilaw is a method of preparing the freshest seafoods and was probably developed by sea-faring people (Fernandez, p. 6). Fish or other seafoods are dressed with vinegar and flavored with onions, ginger and chilis. It is a way of eating raw fish and shellfish particularly oysters without subjecting the meat to heat. The meat turns opaque white, giving it a texture of having been cooked. In the Visayas, coconut milk is added at the last minute to lessen the sourness of the *kinilaw*. This dish is similar to the Latin American *ceviche*.

Sangkutsa was traditionally a method of pre-cooking meats in bulk to be used the following day for different dishes. This method was used for chicken, beef and pork which were sliced into big chunks and half fried in plenty of lard and sautéed in a lot of garlic, onions and salt. Vinegar was poured in and allowed to cook uncovered in large enamel wash *basin*s. On the day of the actual use, the cook concocted different recipes from the basic *sinangkutsa* (Fernando p. 28). This method is rarely used today except in the provinces prior to a fiesta, wedding or other large functions.

Paksiw is similar to *kinilaw* except that the dish is subjected to heat. It is a way of cooking fish in a clay pot with vinegar, ginger and chilies until the fish is cooked or until the vinegar has completely evaporated. Sometimes, vegetables like eggplant and bitter gourd are added to complete the meal. In coconut growing areas, fresh coconut cream is added for flavor. This dish can be left in the pot unrefrigerated. eaten at any meal and served hot or cold. In Cebu, it is called *inun-unan*. Cebuanos have this packed in cans and shipped to Mindanao or wherever Cebuanos have migrated. This is another case in which the practical need for preservation brought about a flavor preference that nourishes while speaking of home (Fernandez, p. 10).

In cooking Philippine dishes where vinegar is used such as in *adobo, paksiw, sangkutsa*, from the moment the vinegar is added to the dish, it cannot be stirred until the mixture has boiled for at least 15 minutes otherwise you end up with a raw-tasting sourness and there will be no way to fix it. Interviewing all the native cooks for the reasons behind such a practice is difficult because they cannot explain the raw flavor. The only reason I can think of is that allowing the vinegar to boil releases the esters and gives the dish a less sour finish.

Vegetables and seaweeds are also pickled (*atsara*). Practically any vegetable can be pickled, like mustard greens, bamboo shoots, bitter gourds, green papaya. Pickled seafoods such as sea urchins, clams, oysters, fish and seaweed usually require much more salt to preserve them for a longer period of time.

No Filipino meal is complete without the *sawsawan* or dipping sauces. The purpose of the *sawsawan* is to individualize the food, thus making the diner the final cook, the diner having the right to adjust it to his palate. It is an expression of the communal nature of food (Fernandez, p. 66). Vinegar is blended with garlic and salt for fried spring rolls or grilled seafoods, with onions and soy sauce for pork dishes and with fish sauce for those that like the taste of fermented fish. Bird chilies are added to make it spicy. A sour *sawsawan* is the perfect antidote to greasy and fat laden foods such as pork, a Filipino favorite.

All of the above are dishes that preserve foods with vinegar. The traditional Filipino ingredients that are combined with vinegar are limited to garlic, ginger, onions and bird chilies and the salt may come in the forms of sea salt, fish and soy sauce. In a third-world country such as the Philippines where the majority of the people do not have refrigeration facilities, these ways of cooking extend the shelf life of food with the use of vinegar. Our penchant for sour foods was shaped out of a need to preserve our foods and since then, it has been ingrained in our taste buds.

Health benefits of natural vinegars

As early as 4000 BC, Hippocrates used vinegar to treat his patients, using it as an antibiotic and an antiseptic. He also prescribed honey and vinegar for coughs and other respiratory problems. In traditional Chinese medicine, vinegar is used in the processing of herbal preparations. It is thought to possess yin qualities that arrest bleeding, disperse blood coagulation and counteract toxic effects. The Chinese have used vinegar in the treatment of pneumonia, hepatitis, influenza and catarrh (Diggs p. 215). During the 19th century, vinegar was used as a healing dressing because of its antimicrobial properties. In the 20th century, people drank vinegar cocktails of all kinds (Orey, p. 12).

In the rural areas of the Philippines, vinegar was given to those with pulmonary, arthritic and skin disorders, hypertension, as well as a cure for fever and fatigue. They did not know why it was good, they just felt better after drinking the vinegar. Thanks to research done on vinegars, old folk remedies now make sense.

With the resurgence of eating more natural foods, people are looking back into the goodness of the foods of yesteryear and vinegar is one of them. A lot of research went into finding health benefits in apple cider vinegar and there is conclusive evidence that apple cider vinegar contains many beneficial vitamins, minerals, antioxidants and enzymes such as potassium, calcium, copper, iron, manganese, beta-carotene, amino acids and pectin. Research was also done on wine vinegars where it was found that wine vinegars contained flavonoids, specifically *resveratrol*, which can help prevent high blood pressure and other cardiovascular diseases. It was also found to be rich in antioxidants that help lower cancer risk (Orey, p. 66). Vinegar also plays an important role in human metabolism – the acetic acid in vinegar releases energy from fats and carbohydrates (Diggs, p. 211). Vinegar helps the stomach produce hydrochloric acid which aids digestion. The acetic acid in vinegar is believed to help detoxify the body from foreign substances such as drugs and alcohol. It unites the toxic substances with other molecules to produce a new compound. The combination of sulfanomides with acetate forms a compound that is biologically inactive and more easily excreted.

Other healthy minerals and nutrients found in natural vinegars are:

Potassium – a mineral that counteracts the damaging effects of too much sodium and prevents high blood pressure. It also inhibits fluid retention which is caused by an accumulation of sodium in the body. Potassium also helps energize the body and battles levels of fatigue by ensuring that muscles can contract and relax.

Beta-carotene – a carotenoid and trace element that is a potent antioxidant. It helps neutralize the free radical molecules that cause normal cells to become cancerous.

301

Boron – a mineral essential for good health and strong bones. It plays a major role in utilizing calcium and magnesium, which are necessary for beating bone loss.

Calcium – a mineral necessary for transmitting nerve impulses and regulating muscle contraction.

Enzymes – protein molecules that digest foods.

Fiber – contains pectin and soluble fiber which blocks fat absorption, lowers blood cholesterol and reduces risk of heart disease and high blood pressure.

Iron – a mineral in absorbable form to avoid anaemia.

Carbohydrates – enhances mental performance because the brain requires glucose all the time.

Amino acids – building blocks of all protein molecules essential to brain chemistry and emotion. Vinegar contains trace elements of some of these amino acids (Orey, p. 33–38).

The health benefits of natural vinegars are highest in the unfiltered and unpasteurized ones because they contain a living mixture of good bacteria and enzymes. Organic versions are better because trees are not sprayed with chemical insecticides and pesticides and are free of chemicals, additives such as artificial colorings, dyes and preservatives. The nutrients found in apple cider vinegars are also in palm sap vinegars. Some may contain more of one than others but in general, their health benefits would probably be the same.

302

These are just a few of the health benefits of natural vinegars. In summary, the most important health benefits of natural vinegars are that:
it fights fat and is fat and calorie free;
it enhances the immune system;
it lowers blood pressure;
it lowers the risk of heart disease;
it can prevent cancer;
it can slow down the ageing process (Orey p. 10);
it is sodium chloride free, containing only natural salts beneficial to man, and;
it avoids bacterial contamination of food.

Artisanal versus commercial vinegar

Vinegar is essentially acetic acid, but acetic acid is not vinegar. Acetic acid can be made in a number of different and cheaper ways than traditionally fermented vinegar and there have been and continue to be attempts to pass it off to consumers as vinegar. Science and industry are able to make acetic acid by means other than fermentation. Fermentation is an inconsistent process – almost more of an art than a science – so commercial food processes developed techniques to standardize more consistent yields and to shorten the processing from months/days to hours. There is nothing wrong with commercial or quick vinegars, for they serve a purpose.

Most commercial vinegar in the Philippines starts off from natural ingredients such as sugar-cane, coconut water and pineapple. However, commercial vinegars are now processed using acetators designed to accelerate the traditional fermentation process of vinegar from months to days, even hours. Other ways of producing cheap vinegars is to start with synthetic acetic acid which has a much higher titratable acidity and then mix it with water to bring down the acidity to four per cent. Sometimes, caramel or burnt sugar is added to improve the taste and appearance. These methods bring down the cost of the vinegar and makes it quite cheap.

These kinds of vinegars are inferior in flavor and aroma to vinegars which are solely the product of alcoholic and acetous fermentation of saccharin liquors. In fermented vinegar, we find many chemicals not found in commercial vinegars. In traditional vinegars, the esters are not as strong and pungent and can be drunk without hurting one's throat. One also doesn't get a whiff of anything chemical or synthetic when smelling it. In terms of flavor, traditional vinegars (even if their origins are the same) may vary, as so many factors affect the final product such as the raw material, alcohol concentration, temperature, motility, light, oxygen, storage and ageing.

The survival of traditional vinegars in the Philippines

Traditional vinegar making in the Philippines started as a backyard operation serving the community. It provided a livelihood for people in the rural areas. Anyone living amongst coconut trees, sugar-cane, *nipa*, sugar and other palms made vinegar. The number of traditional vinegar makers has diminished because it is no longer a lucrative venture. The reasons are many. First is the time element. To allow for proper fermentation takes a minimum of 15 days to a few months when no income is generated. Second, the manufacturers of good traditional vinegars are at a disadvantage when they have to compete with cheap commercial vinegars. In a third-world country, price is a very important factor in the choice of ingredients. Third, local vinegar makers lack the marketing knowledge and the funds to compete against commercial vinegar producers who have the budgets for marketing, distribution and advertising. Fourth, even if they know that their products are good, testing their products for their nutritive values so it can be marketed properly is far from affordable. Fifth, those that know how to make vinegars are not able to because the cost of starting up a traditional vinegar business is prohibitive. Sixth, consumers that can afford to buy these traditional vinegars may either have the colonial mentality that imported is better or they are not aware of how good our native products are. Those that have continued to make these vinegars know they cannot rely on the local market but hope to get into the export market of specialty vinegars.

The traditional vinegar industry should be kept alive in the country because it is part of our culinary heritage and it is a food product at par with the best from other nations. Not only is it good in flavor, these vinegars are also excellent sources

303

of vitamins, minerals and enzymes that can improve the nutritional status of the underprivileged at a much cheaper cost than medicines. It also provides livelihoods in the rural areas where it is much needed and the livelihood is environmentally friendly and sustainable.

If these skills and livelihoods are to continue, their survival rests on assistance and incentives from both the public and private sectors. First, the technical knowledge must be disseminated to the areas where vinegar making can be done to provide a livelihood for the people. Start up equipment should also be provided at low cost by the government or non-governmental organizations to get them off the ground. Currently, training programs are being undertaken by the Department of Science and Technology for those interested in setting up small-scale vinegar businesses. Aside from assistance in learning the technology and setting it up, constant checking is necessary to ensure that the end product is done correctly. Producers also need assistance in product packaging, marketing and distribution. Demand must be created both locally and internationally through re-education with the help of mass media. In marketing traditional vinegars locally, a niche must be created with the possibility of selling the vinegars as a beneficial food ingredient since most Philippine recipes use vinegar. For the export market, the possible entry will probably be in the specialty vinegars and health food stores provided that the necessary testings be made affordable to them. All these requirements cost money but the costs must be subsidized in order to provide incentives to current and future producers. In one case, four different vinegar producers have grouped themselves together to assist each other in marketing. An information campaign about the health benefits and how their purchase upgrades the lives of the producers is necessary to make people aware of the benefits of traditionally made vinegars not only to themselves but to others as well. With proper marketing, those that can afford to buy them can make the switch.

These are just some ways that the traditional vinegar industry can be kept alive in the Philippines and with that, a better life for both the producer and consumer and the survival of traditional Filipino cuisine as well. After all, if we are indeed champion lovers of sourness as Doreen says, our source of sourness must also be kept alive.

Table 1: Comparative Analysis of Philippine Vinegars.

	COCONUT SAP	*Nipa*	SUGAR PALM	SUGAR CANE
Sugar level of sap upon harvest	10–18%	15–22%	10–25%	15–16%
Seasonality of raw material	All year round but best from April to November	All year round	October to May	Once a year, mid November to mid April
Alcoholic fermentation time	30 days	2 hours to 5 days	2–5 days	1 week
Acetobacter fermentation time	45–60 days	15–30 days	21–30 days	21 – 30 days
Vitamin and Mineral content	Potassium, Sodium, Phosphorus, Beta-carotene, Magnesium, Calcium and Iron	Iron, potassium, calcium, magnesium and sodium	Benzoic Acid, potassium, sodium, magnesium, calcium and iron	Potassium, iron, calcium and phosphorus
Acidity level before bottling in titratable acidity (TA)	5–6%	4.5–5.5%	3.8–5.5%	4%
Final acidity level	5%	4.5–5.5%	4.2–5.5%	4%
Aging time in vats/drums	45–60 days	N/A	up to 3 years	Up to 1 year
Aging time in bottles	60 days	N/A	N/A	Depends on what is bottled and not sold
Selling price of 750 ml. bottle	75 pesos = £.75	65 pesos = £.65	95 pesos = £.95	55 pesos = £.55
Taste descriptors	Sour–sweet and sharp when young, mellows as it ages	Slightly salty in comparison with others, sharp but mellows as it ages	Mild and sweetish	Distinct aroma of sugar-cane, sweetish
Best use	Cooking, pickling, marinades, dipping sauces and salad dressings	Cooking, marinades and dipping sauces	Salads and dips	Dipping sauce, for cooking
Other biproducts from raw materials	Sugar, sugar syrup, mother of vinegar into pickles, toddy	Syrup and toddy	Syrup and toddy	Different forms of sugar and wine

References

Cordero-Fernando, Gilda, *Philippine Food and Life* (Pasig:Anvil Publishing, 1992).

Diggs, Lawrence J., *Vinegar: The User Friendly Standard Text, Reference and Guide to Appreciating, Making, and Enjoying Vinegar* (New York: Authors Choice Press, 2000).

Fernandez, Doreen G., *Palayok* (Makati: Bookmark, 2000).

Mindell, Earl with Larry M. Johns, *Amazing Apple Cider Vinegar* (Los Angeles: Keats Publishing, 1999).

Moore, Melodie, *Vim and Vinegar* (New York: Harper Collins Publishers, 1997).

Orey, Cal, *The Healing Powers of Vinegar* (New York: Kensington Publishing, 2000).

Quillin, Dr. Patrick, *Honey, Garlic and Vinegar* (Ohio: The Leader Co., 1996).

Scott, Cyril, *Cider Vinegar* (New York: Benedict Lust Publications, 2003).

Steinkraus, K. H., *Fermentations in World Food Processing* (Institute of Food Technologists, Comprehensive Reviews in Food Science and Food Safety, Vol. 1, 2002).

Internet Sources:

McMillen, Bonnnie, Vinegar:An Ancient Medicine and Popular Home Remedy <http://www.pitt.edu/~cjm6/s98vinegar.html>

Player, Cheryl, The Value of Authentic Vinegar <http://www.celtic-seasalt.com/valofautvin.html>

Products of mixed fermentations, <http://www.fao.org/docrep/x0560e/x0560e12.htm>

Regulations Prescribing the Standard of Identity and Quality of Vinegar <http://www.bfad.gov.ph/AO/ao_134_1970.htm>

The Benefits of Cider Vinegar, <http://www.harvestfields.netfirms.com/CookBooks/Vin/05.htm>

<http://www.versatilevinegar.org/>

Eating Postmodernity: Fusion Cuisine and Authenticity

Mark McWilliams

What is 'fusion cooking'? It's brushing skewers of beef tenderloin with a traditional Caribbean jerk barbecue sauce; matching spicy Southwest fried chicken with a sunny ginger apricot sauce; or drizzling watermelon and sweet red onion salad with a raspberry vinaigrette.

The Fusion Food Cookbook celebrates the new American cuisine, in which distinctive seasonings and cooking styles from Asia, Mexico, the American Southwest, New Orleans, the Caribbean, and the Mediterranean are incorporated into familiar home cooking. Highlighting the vivid flavors of these diverse ethnic and regional traditions, authors Hugh Carpenter and Teri Sandison define a major new trend in American cooking, showing us how to mix and match seasonings and cooking techniques and encouraging us to be more creative in our own cooking.

Dust-jacket blurb

Fusion cuisine is postmodern. Its 'vivid colors and cross-cultural style' reflect its fusion of elements from different (and often opposed) traditions. The consciously created results illustrate the dynamic inter-referentiality that characterizes the postmodern in various art forms. While much has been written about the new American cooking, which draws heavily on fusion principles, few have recognized that, as a concrete postmodern practice, fusion cuisine reflects the promises and contradictions of postmodern theory.[1] Such recognition hints at troubling costs not reported on the bill for an evening's gastronomic pleasures at many of America's best restaurants.

While a list of the pioneers of fusion cuisine – including restaurants like Lydia Shore's Biba in Boston and Susan Finiger and Mary Sue Milliken's City Restaurant in Los Angeles – would seem familiar to longtime readers of newspaper food pages and obsessed viewers of the Food Network, a clear definition of the term is more elusive. Claiming that the current use of the term was coined by Norman Van Aiken (of Norman's in Miami), Andrew Dornenburg and Karen Page introduce fusion cuisine vaguely as 'a harmonious combination of foods of various origins' before providing the more precise industry definition that restricts fusion to 'a melding of ingredients and/or techniques of two or more regions' in a single dish. (They use the term 'eclectic' to refer to mixing regional influences across courses or in a menu.)[2] They attribute the force behind the spread of fusion cuisine to shifting demographics; increasingly diverse populations both introduce new traditions and provide an audience for reinterpretations of those traditions.

Pound's famous modernist injunction to 'make it new' can be seen in food culture in two recent, parallel trends: nouvelle cuisine and highly refined ethnic cuisines.[3] The first made classical French cuisine new by reducing the complicated flavors of traditional preparations to seemingly simple, intense essences; the now comic stereotype of the nouvelle cuisine's small portions also reveals its emphasis on few, distinct flavors abstracted from the sheer substance of traditional French cookery. The second can be seen as making other foodways new by applying the ethos of nouvelle cuisine to food traditions outside the dominant sphere of French cookery; the search for the essence of specific foodways led to the rejection of inauthentic methods and ingredients in an attempt to recreate 'pure' cuisines.

If both these trends illustrate the modernist urge to make the familiar new, they also reflect the modernist problem of enacting a separation between art and everyday life. With nouvelle cuisine, the emphasis on flavor over – even to the exclusion of – substance replaced the traditional utilitarianism of food, thus limiting its appeal to a small, highly affluent subculture; with refined ethnic cuisine, the emphasis on authenticity excluded those with untrained (or at least inexperienced) palates, thus limiting its appeal to those, again mostly affluent, with the time and money to cultivate appreciation for 'foreign' tastes.

Fusion cuisine, on the other hand, reflects what John McGowan has characterized as 'the determination of postmodernism's champions to pull arts back into the maelstrom of daily life'.[4] Its diversity of tastes reflects its diversity of influences. As in other postmodern artforms, here fusion dares to combine traditions previously believed relentlessly incompatible.

Wolfgang Puck, whose boyish enthusiasm and ceaseless (self) promotion of the 'new' cooking has made him a celebrity as well as one of the legitimate authorities in the field, is convinced that fusion cuisine is far more than just another food fad. Indeed, he grandly locates fusion cuisine both as the logical culmination of the history of cooking to date and as the very embodiment of the American character:

The past few years will go down in history as the rebirth of American cooking. I speak of neither a fad nor a passing fancy, but rather the result of a culinary evolution. Decades ago, the general population did not think along the same lines as James Beard and other visionaries. The French dominated the restaurant scene, and all else was looked on as second class. But time marches on, and change has brought us back to the food belonging to the land and its unique inhabitants. Past and present join forces as time-tested classics combine with new concepts and techniques. There are still some who laugh at this progressiveness, and they stand clutching their Escoffiers. Maybe they don't change the water in their bathtubs for years at a time either!

That is not to say that a solid understanding of basics has become outmoded. It is a necessary foundation for further creative development, much as it is in painting as in music. But these branches of the arts are also continually moving into new areas. And as Picasso's style became less complicated later in life, so has cuisine in America left behind the showing-off typical of youth, maturing to a greater simplicity. We have the security of knowing that this country's resources are second to none and can stand on their own in preparations that expose the national character, instead of altering it so that you have to guess what you're eating.

> [A] major breakthrough, whose originators were once thought to be crazy, is the mixing of ethnic cuisines. It is not at all uncommon to find raw fish listed next to tortillas on the same menu. Ethnic crossovers also occur when distinct elements meet in a single recipe. This country is, after all, a huge melting pot. Why should its cooking not illustrate the American transformation of diversity into unity?

> … How fortunate we are to be a part of such an adventurous age. No longer fearing to cross borders, the cook goes into unexplored territory without intimidation. You don't need to be a Cordon Bleu graduate to do it. Think of cooking as an outlet for ideas, a release for the artist in you. It took me eight years to break away from the traditions of my European training and feel free to experiment with new ways. But you can start now. Your American heritage is a wonderful one. Let the world know you're proud of it![5]

Though his populist statement blurs the more precise industry distinction between fusion and eclectic cuisine, I quote Puck at such length because he gives us here a kind of Fusion Manifesto, and like most manifestoes it both exposes the exuberant hope and conceals the contradictions and less radical assumptions of its movement.

309

The promises of 'high' fusion expressed here are grand indeed. Cooking in the manner recommended by Puck offers dramatic improvements for both individual and society. Some of the changes promised the individual are familiar; engaging in any new creative act offers the possible 'release of the artist in you', though the untrained home cook has less to gain in escaping the confines of tradition than one trapped by the training of the Cordon Bleu. More interesting are the larger social changes claimed in Puck's manifesto.

Puck echoes Ihab Hassan's seeming endorsement of the frontier narrative of art; the postmodern artist, whether Californian chef or Irish novelist, works on the boundaries, constantly pushing back cultural margins.[6] Unlike the modernist avant-garde seeking to push back boundaries, freewheeling postmodernism is perhaps better understood as working to dissolve those boundaries, as attacking the very notion of boundaries. Here the central promise of fusion cuisine is its democratization of taste. The conglomeration of styles that is fusion cuisine broadens its appeal beyond the traditional audience of 'high' art by incorporating elements of (and occasionally even the ethos of) 'low' art from the ethnic borderlands. In this way, as Puck insists, the traditional French foundation of foodart in Western culture is torn down to make way for a more inclusive and democratic structure.

Here there is at least one success story – and in the ultimate American house-hold. Since its beginnings, the kitchen of the White House was devoted, almost exclusively, to classical French cuisine. While the imported French chefs often had to broaden their repertoire to include the cheeseburgers privately requested by some of the house's occupants, public events from small, intimate gatherings to formal State Dinners revolved around classical French menus.[7] Despite occasional complaints from politicians and food practitioners that the White House should serve and promote American cooking, the White House only recently moved away from these French roots. Dornenburg and Page recount the lobbying effort that followed the Clintons' announcement that they wanted the official residence to be a showcase for American art; many of the leading chefs of the country wrote an open letter to the Clintons urging the adoption of American cuisine in the nation's kitchen. This effort was successful, and Puck would be thrilled at the resulting fusion orientation of the kitchen's New American style.[8]

The change in White House tradition reflects the flip side of the central promise of democratization: fusion cuisine allows traditionally 'low' ethnic traditions increasing access to 'high' cuisine. The chefs who promote fusion explicitly recognize this link. Lydia Shore, whose restaurant Biba helped pioneer fusion, says that other cuisines, especially Asian, 'really opened the doors of my mind, in terms of the way I thought about flavors, textures, and combinations.'[9]

By 'opening the doors of the minds' of many of America's best chefs, ethnic food has dramatically influenced the foodways of the affluent class that patronizes their restaurants. Fusion cuisine effectively becomes, according to many of its proponents, an advertisement for ethnic traditions. As a non-threatening gateway to ethnic cuisines, fusion exposes diners to traditions that they would not otherwise risk – or perhaps even encounter. Fusion thus promotes the exploration of other cultural foodways, which in turn further expands possible combinations for fusion cooks; the spiraling interest is good for business at both ends of the spectrum. And indeed business has exploded. Much of the boom in new restaurants can be linked to the popularity of fusion cuisine – though the bubble economy certainly helped – and the cookbook industry has heartily embraced fusion as well.[10]

Here the promises of fusion cuisine echo the promises of postmodern art in general. For example, Charles Jencks's view of postmodern art defined by double coding is based on his understanding of the way populist architecture references multiple styles to both appeal aesthetically to the untrained visitor and to play with the professional's knowledge. The double coding makes the structures of postmodern architecture accessible to the general public while broadening professional architects' sense of the possible in design.

But I want to return to Wolfgang. Puck combines the enthusiasm of the immigrant with the missionary zeal of the convert, but his journey has left him closer to his roots than he implies. While he claims to have shed the confining ways of his

'European training', make no mistake: the 'basics' which are still required are the basics of classical French cuisine. Puck is careful not to state it – doing so would undermine his claims – but the foundations of fusion cuisine lie in the highly refined methods of traditional French cookery. Puck's celebratory prose reveals this French bias (confirmed by a close reading of his recipes) in its seemingly accidental description of the innovative combinations of fusion:

> experiment[ing] with a variety of foods, using spices from the Far East, chiles from South America, pastas from Italy, sashimi from Japan, and techniques from France.[11]

The ingredients may be lifted out of various ethnic foodways, but the techniques are still French; the hip new cook can toss out the *Escoffier* only after mastering it.

Puck's French emphasis is echoed in statements by other leading proponents of fusion cuisine. Raji Jallepalli, of Memphis's Restaurant Raj, attempts to justify this bias – but effectively only heightens it – when he explains:

> The problem I had with ethnic cooking, as it was, is that it typically doesn't respect the texture of the food. So the food gets overcooked, the presentations are not respected, and the bouquets are overloaded with too many spices and too many herbs and are too strong. By borrowing French technology, I was able to respect the textures and incorporate a lot more items than Indian cuisine typically is known for. But I feel I'm barely scratching the surface.[12]

311

Again, while fusion incorporates new flavors, the techniques – the 'technology' – remain French. More importantly, the standards remain French: 'respect' for texture, presentation, and clear bouquet are hallmarks of classical French cooking. This French bias can also be seen in the choice of foodways fusion chefs most often choose to combine. Lists of fusion restaurants reveal a wide variety of combinations – Japanese/French, Chinese/French, Thai/French, Indian/French – but in almost every case one of the dominant traditions is French.

This French basis is a class bias as well. Fusion cuisine seems open to any number of possible combinations, but this openness is doubly limited, by the classically (that is, it should by now be clear, French) trained chefs who developed fusion on the one hand, and by the taste(s) of the affluent consumers who support such restaurants on the other. In Western culture, where 'fine dining' has for centuries been synonymous with 'French cuisine', this bias has shaped the very language of the food industry (and, to some extent, of the culture at large) to the point where it has become difficult even to discuss food developments without replicating and reinforcing the problem. Consider the language Norman Van Aiken chooses to describe his use of the name of fusion:

> I coined the term fusion cuisine as a response to the melding together of different cultures, although I was not so much initially talking about marrying French and Thai, for example, as I was talking about marrying rustic cuisine, with its boldness and greatness, to classic cuisine, with its intellectuality.[13]

As one of the pioneers of opening fine dining to traditions beyond French (and, to a much lesser extent, Italian), one would expect Van Aiken to be sympathetic to ethnic foodways, yet he too equates 'French' with 'classic' and, much more tellingly, with 'intellectuality', while 'ethnic' still equals 'rustic' and 'bold', exciting perhaps but hardly civilized. In effect, with fusion cuisine, dominant (French) culture merely appropriates other cultures.

Even the blurring of the boundaries between high and low foodways, the heart of much of the promise of fusion cuisine, also signals appropriation. Chris Schlesinger, of the East Coast Grill in Cambridge, Massachusetts, points out that much of what is now called fusion relies on a lack of knowledge of individual ethnic cultures, rather than on an intimate understanding of them. As an example, he notes that a condiment like 'Indian Salsa' – almost a cliché on fusion menus – turns on an ignorance of 'chutney'.[14] Rather than carefully combining traditions through informed synthesis, much fusion cuisine depends on mere ingredient substitution, to the point where Barbara Trapp's differentiation between cooks committed to authenticity and tradition and those interested in creativity (like Wolfgang Puck) begins to make sense.[15]

As fusion appropriates from other traditions rather than building out of them, it also fails as effective advertisement for ethnic cuisines. Fusion's appropriations succeed often by removing much of what could be seen as authentically ethnic from the flavors it steals from various traditions. Gray Kunz, the head chef of New York City's Lespinasse, says,

> A good friend told me, 'What you're doing is taking the rough edge off ethnic cooking.' I knew what he was trying to say. I do see myself as incorporating flavors and fragrances, but in a very subtle way. Doing so successfully has a lot to do with finesse. You want to make sure that the context is still approachable and not go overboard and shock customers.[16]

Indeed.

Kunz's characterization of fusion creativity points to the de-differentiation that several postmodern theorists notice in postmodern art in general. Both Donna Haraway and Jean Baudrillard discuss the ramifications of this homogenization of art. While Haraway sees the potential for revolutionary change in the boundary violation that characterizes postmodern art, Baudrillard views de-differentiation as lowering culture into 'the Hell of the same'.[17] This much more negative interpretation of category breakdown is extended by the metaphors he uses to describe its effects; Baudrillard describes de-differentiation as degradation, as contamination, as virus.[18]

This interpretation seems to gain importance if a culture's cuisine is more than just a set of ingredients. If food helps to define cultural identity, Baudrillard's account of fusion as contamination can perhaps be better understood through Lyotard's notion of incommensurability. While tearing down meta-narratives – the large stories through which a culture explains itself – Lyotard clings for hope to the multiplicity of small narratives. But he insists on irreconcilability across mini-systems. Some sets of discourses, he maintains, simply cannot be brought together without doing extreme violence to one or the other. Here fusion cuisine becomes not only a deterioration of the authenticity of its constituent traditions but even a terrorist attack on the cultural identity behind each of those traditions.

Some of fusion's proponents, of course, argue that it is possible to draw from various traditions without doing violence to them. Joyce Goldstein, of San Francisco's Square One, insists that successful fusion cuisine demands respect for individual ethnic cultures and traditions:

> About 95 per cent of the time, fusion doesn't work. It's only through eating and tasting and travel and understanding where food comes from that you can come to know what flavors work together.[19]

In her cooking, she tries to communicate a respect for the culture and authenticity of the food she's serving. 'That is, unless I'm screwing around,' she notes. 'But then, I'll indicate on the menu that I'm just screwing around'.[20]

Goldstein's comment reserves the possibility of having fun with fusion creativity, but if cuisine and culture are integral this fun comes with high risks.

Fun in fusion cuisine, as in postmodern art in general, turns around parody and pastiche. The very inter-referentiality that forms the basis of what Jencks sees as double-coding is also the basis of self-conscious quotation that characterizes much of postmodern art. While Jencks limits his discussion to the ways double-coding can address multiple audiences, theorists who emphasize the parodic interreferentiality of postmodern art in detail recognize the high stakes for which this style plays. Hutcheon stresses the emphasis on parody because of its potential for political change. She insists that parody is always political in the way it foregrounds the contingency of conventions as constructions, the way it highlights the ceaseless artificiality of tradition(s). Parody marks the

> paradoxical postmodernism of complicity and critique, of reflexivity and historicity, that at once inscribes and subverts the conventions and ideologies of the dominant cultural and social forces of the twentieth-century western world.[21]

313

Hutcheon recognizes the inescapable complicity of parodic critique, if for no other reason than that 'we are all part of the postmodern, whether we like it or not'; given this inescapable complicity, however, she chooses to emphasize the subversive possibilities of parody as the only possible vehicle for political action.[22]

Jameson's view is far grimmer. The possibility for parodic critique is completely undermined in the way

> the prodigious new expansion of multinational capital ends up penetrating and colonizing those very pre-capitalist enclaves ... which offer extraterritorial ... footholds for critical effectivity.[23]

He argues that those who would like to believe in the political role of art cannot help but

> dimly feel that not only punctual and local countercultural forms of cultural resistance and guerrilla warfare but also even overtly political interventions ... are all somehow secretly disarmed and reabsorbed by a system

that is global and inescapable.[24] In Jameson's view, the 'cultural logic' of multinational capitalism has distressingly expanded to the point where it not only assimilates attempts at critique but actually exploits such attempts to expand its socio-cultural hegemony.

This depressing view suits fusion cuisine all too well as a commercially booming phenomenon possible only under multinational capitalism. Fusion cuisine and other postmodern artforms play a central role in maintaining and expanding the socioeconomic system. Jameson argues that

> aesthetic production today has become integrated into commodity production generally: the frantic economic urgency of producing fresh waves of ever more novel-sounding goods ..., at ever greater rates of turnover now assigns an increasingly essential structural function and position to aesthetic innovation and experimentation.[25]

While the best postmodern art is capable of 'restor[ing] proper tension to the notion of difference itself,' all too often recognition of this emphasis dissolves as 'the cultural and the economic ... collapse back into one another'.[26]

Here, finally, seems to be the reality behind the democratizing promise of postmodern art. Claiming to celebrate ethnicity, it instead commodifies it. While some are far more hopeful – Celeste Olalquiaga, for example, believes that by '[a]voiding a rationale for consumption based on functionality ..., postmodernism sponsors consumption as an autonomous practice [that enables] the articulation of novel and contradictory experiences' – others find the hope that consumption can be a liberating act to be limited indeed.[27] John Thompson argues that,

> since no matter how the commodity is revalued, the socio-economic system that delimits the horizons of so many remains in place (not to mention the fact that many people simply cannot afford the acts of creative consumption Olalquiaga valorizes). After carnival, the disenfranchised go back to whatever lives they led before carnival.[28]

By offering an easily palatable form of cultural compensation, fusion cuisine, like other postmodern artforms, risks forestalling radical political change.

It seems too early to say which one of these views is right, but at least one new restaurant may suggest a troubling development. Recently Jean-Georges Vongerichten, the current wonder of the New York food scene, opened a Chinese restaurant named 66. In a town where restaurant openings have become glitzier than Broadway premieres – the *New York Times* article about 66 was titled 'It's Show Time' – Jean-Georges's new venture has raised some culinary eyebrows. Unlike the remarkably inventive French cuisine of his flagship restaurant (where, full disclosure requires me to admit, I had one of the best meals of my life) or the relatively straightforward Thai/French fusion of his Vong, the Chinese food at 66 is, Jean-Georges claims, authentic. Yet with the average food bill expected to run over a hundred dollars per couple, clearly Jean-Georges must do something different to woo diners away from the range of real Chinese cuisine available just blocks away. As the *Times* notes, there's *fleur de sel* next to the chili oil in the kitchen, and 'butter instead of pork fat in the dumplings.'[29] Even so, Jean-Georges insists that '66 will be more authentic' because

> we're using Chinese techniques here even though we're breaking some rules. … Chinese is a great cuisine but they haven't changed some of this stuff in 3,000 years. It's about time.[30]

So 66 offers fusion after all, but here fusion hides behind repeated, if strange, appeals to tradition.

Whether or not such innovations have any effect on our notions of what 'authentic' Chinese means, whether or not 66 takes business away from its more traditional competitors, Jean-Georges's new restaurant does seem to confirm Puck's claim that fusion cuisine is much more than just one of the many food fads that pass through the short-lived restaurants and glossy magazines of a culture hungry for the new thing. Whether Puck's unbounded optimism is similarly justified, however, remains to be seen.

Works Cited

Baudrillard, Jean, *The Transparency of Evil: Essays on Extreme Phenomena*, trans. James Benedict (London: Verso, 1993).

Brenner, Leslie, *American Appetite: The Coming of Age of a Cuisine* (New York: Avon, 1999).

Budra, Paul, 'The Cilantro Cannot Hold: Postmodern Cuisine Beyond the Golden Arches', *Postmodern Times: A Critical Guide to the Contemporary*, ed. Thomas Carmichael and Alison Lee (Dekalb, IL: Northern Illinois UP, 2000), pp. 231–44.

Carpenter, Hugh and Teri Sandison, *Fusion Food Cookbook* (New York: Artisan, 1994).

Dornenburg, Andrew and Karen Page, *Becoming a Chef: Recipes and Reflections from America's Leading Chef* (New York: Van Nostrand Reinhold, 1995).

Dornenburg, Andrew and Karen Page, *Culinary Artistry* (New York: Van Nostrand Reinhold, 1996).

Fabricant, Florence, 'Ladies and Gentlemen, It's Show Time', *New York Times* (22 Jan. 2003, late ed.), pp. F1+.

Haraway, Donna, *Simians, Cyborgs, and Women* (London: Routledge, 1991).

Hassan, Ihab, 'Toward a Concept of Postmodernism', *The Postmodern Turn: Essays in Postmodern Theory and Culture* (Athens, OH: Ohio State UP, 1987), pp. 84–96.

Hutcheon, Linda, *The Politics of Postmodernism* (London: Routledge, 1989).

Jameson, Fredric, *Postmodernism, or The Cultural Logic of Late Capitalism* (Durham, NC: Duke UP, 1991).

Jencks, Charles, *What is Postmodernism?* (London: Academy, 1986).

Lyotard, Jean-François, *The Postmodern Condition: A Report on Knowledge*, trans. Geoff Bennington and Brian Massumi (Minneapolis, MN: U Minnesota P, 1984).

Lukins, Sheila, *All Around the World Cookbook* (New York: Workman, 1994).

Lukins, Sheila and Julee Rosso, *New Basics Cookbook* (New York: Workman, 1989).

Macherey, Pierre, *A Theory of Literary Production*, trans. Geoffery Wall (London: Routledge, 1978).

McGowan, John, 'Postmodernism', *The Johns Hopkins Guide to Literary Theory and Criticism*, ed. Michael Groden and Martin Kreiswirth (Baltimore, MD: Johns Hopkins UP, 1994), pp. 585–7.

Olalquiaga, Celeste, *Megalopolis: Contemporary Cultural Sensibilities* (Minneapolis: U Minnesota P, 1992).

Puck, Wolfgang, *Adventures in the Kitchen* (New York: Random House, 1991).

Puck, Wolfgang, *The Wolfgang Puck Cookbook* (New York: Random House, 1986).

Thompson, John, 'Consuming Megalopolis', *Postmodern Culture* 3.2 (1993).

Notes

1. While fusion cuisine seems to me the primary example of postmodern food, Paul Budra argues that '[t]he image of postmodern plurality in fast food is best found in the mall food court' (p. 241); see his interesting article for a different take on postmodern foodways. For an excellent account of the development of the New American cuisine, see Leslie Brenner's *American Appetite*.

2. Dornenburg and Page (1996), p. 302. Unlike the authors of *Fusion Food Cookbook*, a lavish coffee table book aimed at a popular audience, Dornenburg and Page address food industry practitioners in their volumes.

3. In his work on architecture, Charles Jencks views the emphasis on the new as a misdefinition, even as a fundamental misunderstanding of modernist art which was carried to unfortunate extremes by its practitioners. At best this misunderstanding led to 'such a fetish of discontinuity that now a radical work of quality is likely to have a shock of the old' (p. 43); at worst, Jencks finds this emphasis in modernist art flatly immoral. Here the limitations of Jencks's method become apparent, for by attempting to define postmodernism purely through architecture and only then extending that univocal definition to other artways, Jencks mischaracterizes the history of those other artways in a Bloomian strong misreading which seems nevertheless wrong.

4. McGowan p. 585.

5. Puck (1986), pp. xiii–xv. Note that Puck's populist statement blurs the more precise industry distinction between fusion and eclectic cuisine.
6. See Hassan, pp. 84–96. This notion of the artist pushing back boundaries seems more aligned with the modernist avant-garde than with freewheeling postmodernism, which is perhaps better understood as working to dissolve those boundaries, as attacking the very notion of boundaries. See also Linda Hutcheon's discussion of this view of postmodern art (pp. 18–19).
7. This dominance was complete; even the menus, when provided, were printed in French (without English translations).
8. Dornenburg and Page (1995), pp. 22–5.
9. Qtd. in Dornenburg and Page (1996), p. 68.
10. One of the best examples of this adoption is Sheila Lukins's most recent volume, *All Around the World Cookbook*. Lukins is half of the dynamic duo behind The Silver Palette, the tremendously influential New York restaurant, cookbook, and specialty food products enterprise. The early work of Lukins and her partner, Julee Rosso, reflected a covert adherence to fusion principles (see, for example, their *New Basics Cookbook*), but the introduction to Lukins's work includes an explicit celebration of the potential of fusion cuisine.
11. Puck (1991), p. xvi.
12. Qtd. in Dornenburg and Page (1995), p. 270.
13. Qtd. in Dornenburg and Page (1996), p. 302.
14. Dornenburg and Page (1996), pp. 63–4.
15. Dornenburg and Page (1995), pp. 267–70.
16. Qtd. in Dornenburg and Page (1996), p. 303.
17. Baudrillard p. 113.
18. Baudrillard, pp. 4–8. Consider, for example, Pierre Macherey's contention that great art displays its own contradictions and thus reveals fissures in dominant ideology: fusion cuisine seeks to hide those very fissures in the creation of a 'harmonious' whole.
19. Qtd. Dornenburg and Page (1996), p. 64.
20. Dornenburg and Page (1995), p. 64.
21. Hutcheon, p. 11.
22. Hutcheon, p. 17.
23. Jameson, p. 49.
24. Jameson, p. 49. Jameson's almost paranoid language of a system always already co-opting individual expression is eerily echoed in a recent soft drink commercial that shows Generation X skaters being relentlessly, if haplessly, followed by a group of suited marketing types using their cell phones to call in every move for immediate exploitation in trendy advertisement campaigns – like that of the commercial itself.
25. Jameson, pp. 4–5.
26. Jameson, pp. 31, xxi.
27. Olalquiaga, p. xvii.
28. Thompson.
29. Fabricant.
30. Fabricant.

317

19th-century Food Historians: Did they Search for Authenticity or Use the Past to Embellish their Present?

Valerie Mars

It can be argued that, in the 1800s, the accumulation of change, social, technical and economic, increased exponentially with the century. Unsurprisingly this influenced not only how food was prepared and served but it also influenced attitudes to cooking and eating. Traditional service, for instance, with its accompanying bills of fare, was in decline by the last quarter of the century to be replaced by new service etiquette with its new-style menus. When breaking with past ways of life, a typical strategy is to re-discover and select what is relevant or useful to the present. This can be seen in works less ephemeral than cookery. Victorian artists, architects and craftsmen selected styles to borrow and recreate. Interior décor and tableware brought an eclectic selection of styles to Victorian dining-rooms. Tradition was not thrown away but was selectively remodelled.

How did 19th-century, and particularly late Victorian, culinary historians rise to these challenges? In interpreting the past did they find out how the dishes they discussed were actually cooked? Did they see the history they wrote as the continuation of a long on-going tradition or did they adopt the prevailing evolutionary view of Victorian man as having arrived at the pinnacle of human progress?

Sharp divides between past and present have been described as disjunctions. Nineteenth-century disjunction is a feature of the growing individualism evident as the 19th century proceeded as opposed to the longer term orientations appropriate to more traditional hierarchies.[1] As Chris Brooks argues, this particular disjunction has origins reaching as far back as the 17th century when it first began to be evident.[2]

Many 19th-century authors who wrote about past foodways could not be described as historians and most appear to have known little about cookery. Not all wrote books that were exclusively devoted to culinary history, but their contributions reveal contemporary attitudes to the subject.

John Conrade Cooke, for example, in the preface to his 1824 book *Cookery and Confectionery*, is of the opinion that '…the whole of Roman Cookery seems to have been borrowed from "the kitchen of Macbeth's witches".'[3] Similarly Kirwan's chapter on 'History Ancient and Mediaeval Cooking Compared to Cookery of the last half Century', quotes Jean le Clerc on Apicius's 'extraordinary dishes and strange ragouts' that would 'burn up the blood'. Garum is described as a 'nauseous condiment'.[4] He declares that Roman cookery disappears in the fifth century, when culinary art is extinguished.'[5] Then he gives the monks credit for its revival.

It is not that the conclusions of such writers seem so odd to today's historians, it is the style of unquestioning assumption that separates this writing from 18th-, 20th- and 21st-century approaches. Their views, for the most part, offered as authenticity made manifest, were most productive and wide-ranging during the last quarter of the 19th century. They will be more fully considered but for comparison some earlier books are also discussed.

Continuing traditional foodways

Before discussing published histories it should be asked how far 19th-century men and women considered their own foodways as a continuation of a long tradition. Isabella Beeton's *Beeton's Book of Household Management* notes 'ROAST BEEF has long been a national dish in England.'[6] Similar provenance was given to other iconic dishes such as grilled mutton chops, the 18th and 19th centuries' bachelors' fast food[7] and the beef steaks which sustained members of the Beefsteak Club (a patriotic men's club which thrived from 1735 to 1867).[8] Among the English middle- to upper-class the long tradition of roast beef and mutton continued to be a mark of good living. Puddings are also noted as a particularly English dish and, like roast beef, was celebrated in prose and popular verse, such as the well-known *Roast Beef of Old England.*

319

Recipes for 'made dishes' although not included in popular, usually male, traditional rhetoric, were also integral to such long-lived culinary repertoires. An historian's 'long 18th-century' would include 18th-century dishes, found in three recipe books, that continued 18th-century cookery well into the 19th-century.

Among these, Hannah Glasse's *Art of Cookery* is recorded by Virginia Maclean as being continuously in press until 1843 or possibly 1852,[9] whilst Elizabeth Raffald's *The Experienced English Housekeeper*, which was first published in 1769, had a final edition in 1834. However, the most constantly in-print work to carry an 18th-century traditional style into the 19th was *A New System of Domestic Cookery. Formed upon Principles of Economy And Adapted To The Use Of Private Families*. It was written by Maria Eliza Ketelby Rundell, who was born in 1745. She wrote up her lifetime's culinary repertoire in 1806, when she was 60. It continued in various editions to about 1886. These books, if used as the basis of a personal repertoire adopted by a young cook, could have been in use for a lifetime. Similarly the manuscript recipe books that were handed down in families often recorded even longer culinary time spans than did printed works. How many of the earlier recipes in these collections were still being cooked is not easily answered.

In the same way cooking techniques have frequently a much longer life than that of the particular book in which they are written. To repeat a truism, cookery is essentially a craft. Texts follow practice, so that day-to-day cookery is by no means necessarily text based: true roasting in front of a fire, for example, uses skills that were practised long before cookery books were written.[10]

There is a length of time when cuisine changes from the known and practised to the strange and incomprehensible so that beyond a few generations some English recipes do not seem to have survived within 'transmittable memory'.[11] As the 19th century was a time of fast social change it can be argued that this time span decreased. Older recipes become strange dishes that belong to that 'other country'.[12]

Charles Herman Senn, a practising cook and author of the quaintly titled *Ye Art of Cookery in Ye Olden Time*, lists dishes from *A Queen's Closet Opened* of 1662 that have been long forgotten and these dishes that were still current, such as chicken pie, pigeon pie, boiled rump of beef, potted venison, stewed eels, dressed crab, strawberry cake and pancakes.[13] He reproduces Joseph Cooper's 1655 recipe for a codling tart, which, he notes, 'has retained its popularity to the present date'.[14] Some of the writers discussed below certainly understood something of both past and contemporary cuisine but for many the past was a strange country with a disagreeable cuisine.

Antiquaries

19th-century writers of culinary history inherited some interesting work on the subject. These works dated from the second half of the 18th century, when studying the past became the occupation of the newly named 'Antiquaries'. Rosemary Sweet describes antiquaries as important actors in the eager pursuit of knowledge and understanding during this period of the 'English Enlightenment'.[15]

Typical of this scholarly approach is the 1765 *Historical Account of Coffee* by John Ellis. His main purpose, as agent for the island of Dominica, was to promote coffee growing on the island yet the promotional does not intrude into the carefully researched historical section of his text. He begins with the earliest account he can find, from the French King's library, of coffee sent from Persia to Aden in the 9th century. He has notes on how it is drunk in Turkey without sugar but with spices such as star aniseed, lesser cardamoms or bruised cloves. There follow many more detailed descriptions of coffee making and of its arrival in London and Paris.

This meticulous approach is also found in two books with manuscripts reprinted by members of the Society of Antiquaries. In 1780 Samuel Pegge reproduces *The Forme of Cury, a roll of ancient English Cookery. About A.D. 1390, by the Master Cooks of King Richard II, presented afterwards to Queen Elizabeth by Edward Lord Stafford... Illustrated with notes, and a copious index, or glossary. A manuscript of the Editor, of the same age and subject, is subjoined.* These additional texts are of feasts given by Archbishop Neville and Archbishop Warham.

Samuel Pegge's notes[16] are not as interesting as the glossary with his rediscovery of the *Forme of Cury*. There are also recipes, from the Arundel collection, but recorded without comment in another collection of manuscripts from the Royal Society library by John Nicholls.

One book however was to offer a particularly fruitful source of plunder for 19th-century historians. This was Rev. Richard Warner's *Antiquitates culinariæ: or, curious tracts relating to the culinary affairs of the old English with a preliminary discourse, notes, and illustrations. MS. Notes.* Warner's work ranges from the Old Testament to 16th-century England. It is a study with meticulous footnotes, by an author whose stated intention is 'to point out the several gradations of refinement which have occurred in the *science of eating, in our own country,* from the humble table of our *Celtic* ancestors; to the studied Epicureanism of the present times.'[17]

Warner's book is in the same Enlightenment style as that of previous authors. He compares Abraham's calf dressed with butter and milk[18] to a Caliph's dish mentioned in Ockley's *History of the Saracens.*[19] And he concludes: 'Though it does not boast any of the *tricks* of *Modern cookery,* nor rise perhaps to the *modern* idea of good cheer [sp.] yet presents a very pleasing picture of good living.'[20]

Sometimes however, this thoughtful approach is almost abandoned as when describing some of the recipes in the *Forme of Cury* as 'unintelligible to a modern as the hieroglyphics of an Egyptian pillar'. He does finally relate these recipes to another cuisine concluding that almost all the recipes 'would now only be relished by those accustomed to the high-seasoned dishes of the East and West Indies'.[21] There is no suggestion, in any of these works, that the authors tasted any of the recipes they recorded. And things were not about to change in this respect.

Following the antiquaries

321

A book that stands alone in time and style, attributed to William Beckford, is *The School for Good Living: beginning with Cadmus the cook and king, and concluding with the union of cookery and chymistry.* It is filled with firm views and much anecdote. Unlike Warner, it is a work intended to promote gastronomy as a study: 'It is a part of history no less curious than interesting, to observe the rise of alimentary science, tracing it from the age of pounded acorns to the refinement of modern luxury.'[22]

He regrets that historians have been more interested in generals who have been destroyers of mankind instead of cooks and 'gastrologers'[23] who have sustained them.[24]

Beckford was the first of a variety of new culinary historians and writers offering works as diverse as were their reasons for writing culinary history. These writers reflected much of the change and reaction found in 19th-century ways of thinking, living and working. Their varied works contrast markedly with their 18th-century predecessors, whose history, can be seen as being closer to modern evidence based scholarship.

The antiquaries' approach seems almost to disappear in the 19th century, to be replaced by a more chronocentric approach to culinary history, a trend that continued unabated until the founding of the Early English Text Society in 1864. This society was 'for the purpose of bringing the mass of old English literature within the reach of the ordinary student'.[25] In 1870 they reproduced Andrew Boorde's *A compendyous regment; or, A dyetary of helth*. In 1888 they added *Two Fifteenth Century Cookery-Books*. Like the antiquaries, members were largely professional men. Food history, at least as reproduced manuscripts, joined other subjects as worthy contributions to the general body of symbolic capital evidenced in the libraries of these men.[26]

Culinary history is the subject of a series of essays in *A Book about the Table* by John Corday Jeaffreson, a work that is a mixture of thoughtful interest and curious views.

Typically, this field was dominated by male writers, but in 1882 Robina Napier edited *A Noble Boke of Cookry* from a manuscript in the Holkham collection. Her introduction suggests she understood practical cookery, unlike others with a tendency to pontificate at a safe distance from the kitchen. Napier intends her readers to understand that this manuscript is not dealing with the quaint and ridiculous, but is concerned with rational instruction. She notes that there is nothing new: '... for here are the same birds, beasts and fishes' the same courses, and even the same names for various dishes, that we find in a modern cookery book. 'We see too, with pleasure, that the same principles and the same care were recognised as necessary for good cookery in the 13th and 14th centuries as in the 19th. "Clene vesselles", "fayre watur", "luk welle to it" and "boille yt softlie" were then as now the first and most important of culinary principles. But on closer examination much will be found to surprise and amuse the curious reader.'

322

Yet she is not entirely detached from a contemporary evolutionary view of attainment: 'Who would have guessed that the most highly civilised of modern game pies is only an improved and ornamented "coffyn"?'

In the same tradition is W. Carew Hazlitt's *Old Cookery Books and Ancient Cuisine*, a bibliographic work that offered more material than any of its predecessors. His approach to researching early works is summed up in his 'Introductory':

> It naturally ensues from the absence or scantiness of explicit or systematic information connected with the opening stages of such enquires as the present, that the student is compelled to draw his own inferences from indirect or unwitting allusion; but so long as conjecture and hypothesis are not too freely indulged, this class of evidence is, as a rule tolerably trustworthy and is moreover, open to verification.[27]

A gastronomic pinnacle? Using the past to glorify the present

It was the most entrepreneurial of cooks, Alexis Soyer, who took disjunction to an extreme. Soyer, chef and master of self-promotion, saw the value of culinary history as a means of glorifying his achievements. He not only appropriated Adolphe Duhart-Fauve's work,[28] *The Pantropheon, a history of cuisine from the earliest times*, but he also added the last few pages on 'Modern Banquets' to demonstrate the superiority of his own banquets and to give an account of his famous *Hundred-Guinea Dish*.[29] Soyer offers an extreme example when comparing past with present cookery. But instead of considered comparison he prefers ridicule to glorify the present by giving emphasis to an evolutionary idea of progress. Though this is one of the recurring themes in 19th-century works, not all subscribed to this developmental approach. An unusual theory on gastronomy, as a measure of progress, can be found in J. L. W. Thudichum's *The Spirit of Cookery*. He offers his readers a short review of the historical literature for them to select works for further study. He then notes that

> The History of human culture, or that kind of development which passes as under the unsuitable name of civilisation, includes the history of the science of food-preparation; and this branch affords sometimes interesting solutions of doubts. Which no other history can solve.

Then he offers his theory:

> that the state of culture of every nation could be estimated comparatively by *its confectionery*, even when we knew little of its cookery, for confectionery is the most advanced and refined part of cookery, and thus enables the expert to draw a conclusion backwards regarding the kind of cookery out of which it originated.

323

He then compares Indian confectionery to macaroons and meringues.[30] Predictably, the macaroons and meringues triumph.

Victorian England was jingoistically promoted as the pinnacle of civilisation. Anti-French propaganda comparing plain English food with the perceived deceptive intricacies of French *haute cuisine* was at its height during wars with France and was not, and still has not, been forgotten. John Russell Smith nailed his colours to the mast in 1847 with his pseudonym 'Beef Eater'. He offers this general principle: 'in proportion as civilisation advances, so does man become more fastidious in his diet.'[31]

Male chauvinism

If the past was to be discredited so were women as writers on cuisine, whether in the past or the present. A. V. Kirwan, the author of *Host and Guest*, was of the opinion that Mrs Glasse's work was written by Dr Hill. He tells the reader he does not possess a copy, despite suggesting he may have a substantial collection of cookery books.[32] Thudichum enlarges on this theme, by agreeing with Dr Johnson that women could not 'make a good book on cookery'.[33] His introduction to Lizzie Heritage's *Cassell's Universal Cookery Book*, whose readers would have been women, is condescendingly didactic.[34]

Food histories as symbolic capital

Food history was to have a useful role in gastronomic writing in an age when higher thoughts were considered appropriate to claims of higher social status[35] and when an interest in gastronomy could be seen as unworthy. As an unworthy topic, it was not considered suitable for polite conversation. Instead free-floating opinion larded with assorted anecdote was a favourite style of conversation, an encouragement to didacts and bores. Many of the writers who added anecdotes to what they passed as culinary history, were simply offering material for such conversations. Abraham Hayward's 1852 *The Art of Dining, or Gastronomy and Gastronomers* included a chapter 'The History of Cookery from the earliest period to 1789, with illustrative Anecdotes'.[36] A. V. Kirwan twelve years later also includes such anecdotal culinary history in *Host and Guest: A Book about Dinners*. John Doran's *Table Traits, With Something on Them*, serves a similar purpose. Likewise Leonard Francis Simpson's *The Handbook of Dining or How to Dine based chiefly upon the Physiologie du Goût of Brillat-Savarin*, makes use of a source that was repeatedly used by many of the 19th-century writers of food history and anecdote.[37]

Similarly, women like Isabella Beeton found snippets from history that served to add genteel embellishment to a practical text. Women, who typically only instructed their cooks rather than cook themselves, could assert their superior status with these snippets. Beeton's 'Pate Brisee, or French Crust for Raised Pies' is followed by a paragraph on the water supply in Rome and the building of aqueducts.[38]

One writer, Anne de Salis, author of the *à la mode* series of cookery books, had it suggested to her that she might write 'a short treatise on the origin of cooking, with gastronomical anecdotes'. She does not want to tax her readers, telling them she has seen a copy of Robert May's *Accomplished Cook* in the British Museum and that it is 'well worth a glance'.[39] After giving an account of Coryot's bringing forks back to England, she is not the first to include this topic, but she also adds her own chronocentric opinion that Queen Elizabeth had no excuse for not using a fork, as they were available. De Salis lived up to the image of 'a la mode.' Her books offer fashionable recipes for upper-middle-class households and her culinary history, like Beeton's random collection of informing paragraphs, was not for serious study but served as a diversion, offering improving light interest, a useful resource for drawing-room conversation.

Culinary histories such as Hayward's (1852) chapter on 'The History of Cookery from the earliest period to 1789' is followed by anecdotes of Napoleon, Wellington, and other important personalities. These anecdotes reinforced the stereotypical views incorporated into histories. An example is the story of the Duke of Wellington's cook Felix, who left the Duke as he could not tolerate a lack of appreciation. He was an employer who was content to eat mutton roasted by the kitchen maid – a neat fable confirming the hero of Waterloo as a plain man enjoying plain English food. These anecdotes offered reassurance of the familiar. There are many of them, scattered throughout the literature, their themes are often anti-French or about the great and their connection with the origin of a particular recipe.[40] Hayward even includes a long story about the Duke d'Escars, who had the misfortune to die without a dish named after him.

Hayward also offers opinions on Beauvilliers and Carême.[41] He does not say on what evidence he draws his conclusions, unless the reader is to understand that these were given by the titled names he acknowledges in the 'Prefatory Notice' as supplying 'hints, recipes, and illustrative anecdotes.'[42] These 'distinguished and accomplished persons' all had titles. His book could not simply be of use to gourmets, a slightly suspect constituency. It had to earn a significant increment of symbolic capital. The ambiguous place of gastronomy in England meant the topic required elevation and history was an ideal subject for authors such as Abraham Hayward to introduce to their writing on contemporary foodways.

This essentially English and Victorian approach to food contrasts with Urbain Dubois' ideal French employer, an unashamed gourmet who is given the elevation of a classical identity, an Amphytrion , who exercises his comprehensive gastronomic knowledge to select a menu.[43] It was an approach inappropriate for reactionary Englishmen, and indeed Eustace Ude had been appalled by the gastronomic ignorance he found among young Englishmen in 1813.[44] This state of affairs did not appear to alter during the rest of the 19th century.

Cooking old recipes

The only example I have found of antique recipes being prepared and served, is from Ian Anstruther's account of the banquet and ball given two days after the disastrously failed 1843 Eglington Tournament. It was planned as an elaborate recreation of a medieval tournament; unfortunately it was washed away by a tremendous storm. An unnamed chef from London transported a feast that included boars' heads, swan, lamprey pies, primrose tarts, peacock pie and, anachronistically, a large quantity of turtle. It appears that the chef knew how to make a peacock pie but one guest certainly did not realise the crust was not to be eaten. Lady Londonderry is reported to have said it was made of the same armour as that supplied for the tournament.[45]

A theme common to most of the writers during the 19th century is the distance they put between themselves, and cooking and eating the food they describe. For male English élites, cookery was seen as something that was done by some women and servants in kitchens, well away from their employers. To find any examples of recipes that were reproduced has been almost impossible. A readiness to offer views without evidence is the norm. Even an experienced chef, Charles Senn, in his brief history *Ye Art of Cookery in Ye Olden Time*, states 'The art of cookery was scarcely known in England until the 16th century.'[46] Later in this booklet he mentions the *Forme of Cury* as reproduced by Warner and also mentions *Ye Noble Book of Cookery* in the edition published in 1882, as the best of several of the period.[47] No mention is made of Robina Napier's useful comments and the reader is given the impression that Senn has reached his conclusion simply by consulting the original text.

A suggestion that early recipes were good for Victorians to cook can be found in the introduction by George Weddell to *Arcana Fairfaxiana*, a 15th-century household book rescued from a building being cleared in Newcastle. It was reproduced in facsimile in 1890. He advises:

> the baking of meats still continues to engage the attention of the housewife. It may be interesting to some fair readers to try the methods of those ancient dames, for the food upon which such noble men were reared in the days of Queen Bess and of the Commonwealth may still be capable of making healthy bone and brain and blood. A crammed capon followed by pancakes made with cream – only think of it.[48]

Fin Bec, whose knowledge and views on cookery do not conform to the usual Victorian prejudices, was an admirer of French bourgeois cookery. He did not look back to past cookery as all of strange recipes but notes:

> It is in salads that we show our most lamentable contrast with the winter kitchen resources of the continent. The reader has only to glance at Evelyn's *Acetaria: a discourse of Sallets* to be surprised not that we have made no advance since that time, but that we have so far relapsed its richness in Salad plants.[49]

Cooking old recipes appears to be rare. Towards the end of the century in 1895 John Thudichum expresses outright disdain at the idea that he might cook. He advises writers on cookery to have 'a practical acquaintance with the culinary process, without being a professional cook in any sense'. He cites the example of French technical education for employers of technical labour. The employers' role is to be educated in culinary history, physics and chemistry, but not to be 'operative artists'.[50] From many of the authors discussed, their opinions suggest that few of them were 'operative artists.'

Conclusion

At the end of the 19th century gastronomy was still a marginalised topic, and mainstream historians effectively ignored culinary history: the author of *The School for Good Living*, would have found historians still preferred studying generals to cooks.

Finding work that is seriously involved with authentic dishes of the past has not proved fruitful: practical cookery was not the concern of these authors. Nor was the pursuit of authenticity their main concern. Rather, to use culinary history to serve their particular interests.

As a result new readers increasingly distant from the cookery of the long 18th century were offered not authentic accounts of past foodways but free-floating opinion and anecdote. Edward Spencer's publisher, in 1897, asked him for essays on food 'with plenty of plums'. Spencer asked what he should do if he ran out of plums? The editor replied,

Get some more; the museum, my dear sir, the great storehouse of national literature, is free to all whose character is above the normal standard.[51]

These authors did discover authentic works, but in the uses they made of the material they offered us more of their views and too little of the original.

Bibliography

Arcana Fairfaxiana. A manuscript volume of Apothecaries Lore and Houswifery... used, and partly written by the Fairfax Family. Reproduced in fac-simile, An introduction by G. Weddel (Mawson & Swan: Newcastle-on-Tyne, 1890).

Anstruther, Ian, *The Knight and the Umbrella, an account of the Eglinton Tournament* (Geoffrey Bles, London, 1963).

Arnold, Walter, *Life and Death of The Sublime Society of Beefsteaks* (Bradbury Evans & Co., London, 1871).

Beckford, W. (attrib.), *Gastronomy or the School for Good Living: a Literary and Historical Essay on the European Kitchen* (London, 1822).

Beeton, Isabella, *Mrs Beeton's Book of Household Management*, S. O. Beeton, London, 1861. This fac-simile of the 1861 edition (Southover Press, Lewes, 1998).

Boorde, Andrew, *The fyrst boke of the introduction of knowledge made by Andrew Borde, of physycke doctor: A compendyous regyment; or, A dyetary of helth made in Mountpyllier / compyled by Andrewe Boorde, of physycke doctour. Barnes in the defence of the berde: a treatyse made, answerynge the treatyse of Doctor Borde upon berdes* / edited, with a life of Andrew Boorde, and large extracts from his Brevyary, by F. J. Furnivall (Published for the Early English Text Society by N. T. Trübner & Co., 1870).

Bourdieu, Pierre, *Distinction, A Social Critique of the Judgement of Taste*, translated by Richard Nice (Routledge & Kegan Paul, London, 1986).

Brooks, Chris, *Introduction to The Study of the Past in the Victorian Age*, edited by Vanessa Brand (Oxbow Monograph 73, Oxbow Books, Oxford, for The British Archaeological Association and The Royal Archaeological Institute, 1998).

Carew Hazlitt, W., *Old Cookery Books and Ancient Cuisine* (Elliot Stock, London, 1893).

Cooke, John Conrade, *Cookery and Confectionery* (W. Simpkin and R. Marshall, London, 1824).

de Salis, Harriet Anne, 'Mrs de Salis', *Cookery à la Mode. The first of a series, Savouries à la Mode*, (Longmans, Green & Co., London, 1886), with further books in the series brought together in *À la Mode Cookery*, 1902.

de Salis, Harriet Anne, 'Mrs de Salis', *The Art of Cookery Past and Present* (Hutchinson & Co., London, 1898).

Doran, Dr John, *Table Traits, With Something on Them* (Richard Bentley, London, 1854).

Douglas, Mary, *In the Active Voice* (Routledge, London, 1982).

Dubois, Urbain, *Cosmopolitan Cookery* (Longmans & Co., London, 1870).

Ellis, John, *Historical Account of Coffee with an Engraving, and Botanical Description* (London, 1765).

Evelyn, John, FRS, *Acetaria. A discourse of sallets* (printed for B. Tooke, London 1699).

Glasse, Hannah, 1708–1770, *The Art of Cookery Made Plain and Easy*, fifth edition, published by the author (London, 1747).

Hartley, L. P., *The Go-Between*, first published 1953 (Penguin Books, Harmondsworth, 1958).

Hayward, Abraham, QC, *The Art of Dining, or Gastronomy and Gastronomer* (John Murray, first published 1852, this edition 1883).

Heritage, Lizzie, *Cassell's Universal Cookery Book* (London, 1901).

Jeaffreson, John Corday, *A Book About the Table* (Hurst and Blackett, London, 1875).

Jerrold, William Blanchard, pseud. 'Fin-Bec', *The Epicure's Year Book and Table Companion* (Bradbury Evans & Co., London, 1869).

Kirwan, A. V. of the Middle Temple, *Host and Guest: A Book About Dinners, Wines and Desserts* (Bell and Daldy, London, 1864).

Maclean, Virginia, *A Short-title Catalogue of Household and Cookery Books published in the English Tongue 1701–1800* (Prospect Books, London, 1981, series editor, Lynette Hunter).

Mars, Valerie, 'Beyond Beeton: Some 19th-Century Cookery and Household Books in the Brotherton Special Collections' in *The English Cookery Book, Historical Essays* edited by Eileen White, pp. 175–197 (Prospect Books, Blackawton, Totnes, Devon, 2004).

McKirdy, Michael, 'Who wrote Soyer's Pantropheon?' in *Petits Propos Culinaires* (Prospect Books Ltd, London, July 1988).

Nicholls, J. *Ancient Cookery. From a MS in the Library of the Royal Society* in 'A Collection of Ordinances and Regulations for the Government of the Royal Household,' (printed for the Society of Antiquaries by John Nicholls, London, 1790).

Ockley's *History of the Saracens*, vol. II.

Pegge S. ('An Antiquary'), *The Forme of Cury, a roll of ancient English Cookery, About A.D. 1390, by the Master Cooks of King Richard II, presented afterwards to Queen Elizabeth by Edward Lord Stafford… Illustrated with notes, and a copious index, or glossary. A manuscript of the Editor, of the same age and subject, is subjoined* (Published by J. Nicholls: London, 1780).

Raffald, Elizabeth, *The Experienced English Housekeeper* (published by the author, Manchester, 1869.

Rundell, Maria Eliza Ketelby, pseud. 'A Lady', *A New System of Domestic Cookery. Formed upon Principles of Economy And Adapted To The Use Of Private Families* (John Murray, London, from 1807).

Senn, Charles Herman, *Ye Art of Cookery in Ye Olden Time*, first published 1896 by the Universal Cookery and Food Association (this facsimile, David C. Marriott, 1985, London).

Simpson, Leonard Francis, *The Handbook of Dining or How to Dine based chiefly upon The Physiologie du Goût of Brillat-Savarin* (Longman, Brown, Longmans, & Roberts, London, 1859).

Smith, John Russell, pseud. 'Beef Eater', *Illustrations of Eating* (London 1847).

Soyer, Alexis, (and Adolphe Duhart-Fauvet?), *The Pantropheon, or, History of Food, and its preparation from the earliest ages of the world* (Simpkin Marshall, London, 1853).

Spencer, Edward, (Nathaniel Gubbins), *Cakes and Ale, a dissertation on banquets interspersed with various recipes* (Stanley Paul & Co., London, 1897).

Sweet, Rosemary, *The Antiquaries; the discovery of the past in 18th Century Britain* (Hambledon and London, 2003).

Thudichum, J. L. W. MD FRCP, *The Spirit of Cookery, a popular treatise on the history, science, practice and ethical import of the culinary art, with a dictionary of culinary terms* (F. Warne & Co., London, 1895).

Two Fifteenth Century Cookery-Books, Edited by Thomas Austin for the Early English Text Society, by N. T. Trübner & Co (London, 1888).

Ude, Louis Eustache, *The French Cook, or the Art of Cookery Developed in all its Branches*, Cox and Baylis, London, 1813. Later as *The French Cook; a System of Fashionable, Practical, and Economical Cookery, adapted to the use of English Families* (Ebers & Co., London, 14th edition, 1841).

Verral, William, *The Cooke's Paradise, being William Verral's Complete System of Cookery* (published 1759. This edition Sylvan Press, London, 1948).

Warner, Reverend Richard, *Antiquitates Culinaries: curious tracts relating to the culinary affairs of the old English with a preliminary discourse, notes and illustration* (Printed for R. Blamire, London, 1791).

Notes

1. Douglas, pp. 183–254.
2. Brooks, pp. 1–19.
3. Cooke, pp. III–IV.
4. Kirwan, p. 1.
5. Kirwan, p. 4.
6. Beeton, pp. 306–7. "ROAST RIBS OF BEEF, Boned and Rolled (a very Convenient Joint for a Small Family)". None of the writers who included their own century in their accounts ever mentioned Beeton. She was associated with the mass market and therefore not a subject for consideration.
7. Verral, p. 21. Verral when attempting to improve a country bachelor's kitchen is told: 'I seldom eat anything more than a mutton chop or so.'
8. Arnold,.
9. Maclean, pp. 58–61. Virginia Maclean records it continued with further editions until 1843 or possibly 1852.
10. Mars, pp. 175–97.
11. Brooks, pp. 1–19.
12. 'The past is another country.' Hartley, p. 1.
13. Senn, p. 21.
14. Senn, p. 21.
15. Sweet, pp. XIII–XXI.
16. In his notes on the texts Samuel Pegge investigates the reasons for English roast tradition as opposed to the absurdity of the British adopting the French mode of disguising meat in a climate that is temperate enough to allow meat to be hung except in the warmest weather. This thought may seem an odd one, but it was a rational explanation for praising of British roast beef.
17. Warner, p. 1.
18. Genesis, ch. XVIII.
19. Ockley, p. 277.
20. Warner, p. II.
21. Warner, p. XXXII.
22. Beckford, p. 9.
23. Beckford, p. 18. The author includes a Glossary of 'helenised English' for scientific precision: 'Gastrology: science of Eating'.
24. Beckford, p. 9.
25. Boorde, endnote.
26. Pierre Bourdieu, in his *Distinction, Social Critique on the Judgement of Taste*, examines choices in France in the late 1970s and describes cultural choices in relation to social status. He maps out associations of taste and ideals in relation to class, work, age and gender. The individuals questioned reveal their places on a social map by the measurement of their cultural (symbolic) and economic capital. New esoteric rules on 'taste' made overt the exercise of the new 'symbolic capital'. Bourdieu describes his term as the acquisition of professional knowledge and its subsequent conversion into reputation and status, giving the holder access to office and a position where their opinions carry weight.
27. Carew Hazlitt, p. 2.
28. McKirdy, pp. 18–21
29. Soyer, pp. 406–7.
30. Thudichum, p. 5.
31. Smith, p. 65.
32. Kirwan, p. 37.
33. Thudichum, pp. 8–9.

34. Heritage, pp. XVII–LXXI.
35. The use of the word 'status' does not here denote prestige, but is used in the sociological sense of the roles occupied by individuals.
36. Hayward, pp. 1–19.
37. Simpson, Leonard Francis, *The Handbook of Dining or How to Dine based chiefly upon the Physiologie du Goût of Brillat-Savarin*, [1825] (Longman, Brown, Longmans, & Roberts, London, 1859).
38. Beeton, pp. 617–8.
39. de Salis, p. 14.
40. Hayward, p. 18.
41. Hayward, pp. 27–31.
42. Hayward, p. III.
43. Dubois, p. XXII.
44. Ude, p. XLV. There were ten editions by 1828.
45. Anstruther, p. 222. Unfortunately I have been unable to find any of the source material for this event.
46. Senn, p. 7.
47. Senn, p. 20.
48. *Arcana Fairfaxiana*, p. XLIII.
49. Jerrold, p. 16.
50. Thudichum, p. 6
51. Spencer, p. XII.

330

'How does it taste Cisti? Is it good?' Authentic Representations of Italian Renaissance Society and the Culture of Wine Consumption in Giovanni Boccaccio's *Decameron*

Salvatore Musumeci

The pages of Giovanni Boccaccio's *Decameron* are filled with images that colorfully depict Italian Renaissance table-culture and alimentary habits – images that are conveyed to us using the literary conceit of story-telling.[1] A group of noble men and women who took refuge in the Florentine countryside to escape the dangers of the Black Death told ten stories per day over a ten-day period, each day being guided by a predetermined theme.[2] But while Boccaccio's novelle are often short humorous pieces that poke fun at the hypocrisy of the religious or at husbands who are easily hoodwinked by their wives and vice-versa, they also contain important insights into the complex social world of Renaissance Florence. Above all, we see into the ways in which this reality was communicated through food and wine, or indeed through all things that might be considered edible and consumable. Using one of these tales, that of Cisti the Baker and Messer Geri Spina, this paper highlights the metaphorical concepts attached to the culture of wine consumption and demonstrates the beverage's centrality as a mode for constructing social communities and defining social status, as well as touches upon the anxieties and concerns its consumption raised for both Messer Geri and Cisti.[3] In doing this I aim to show how wine not only ennobled Cisti and Messer Geri, but also served as a bridge that united two individuals who lived and operated within two separate and distinct social classes in a time where status and affluence colored and influenced every aspect of life in early Renaissance Florence.

Set in the city and surrounding countryside of Florence in the period around 1348, Boccaccio ensured that the memory of war and factional fighting as well as the plague and its devastation would remain fresh in the minds of his audience. The historicity and the use of contemporary details is an essential aspect of Boccaccio's *Decameron*. The city witnessed a dramatic demographic change from the later thirteenth century to the early decades of the fourteenth, with its population increasing to close to 90,000 people,[4] thus making it the fifth most populous city in Europe.[5] The Florentine chronicler Giovanni Villani, writing in 1338, notes that the city had '146 bakeries'[6] and that the city 'consumed 140 *moggia* of wheat every day'.[7] In addition to the vast amount of wheat consumed it was also estimated that wine consumption, per week, reached a gallon a head.[8] But while it appears as if the larders of citizens were amply stocked with bread and wine, the idea of a varied and balanced diet was far from reality.[9] The city was at war with Milan, the papacy and King Ladislaus of Naples; it was similarly locked in a struggle to gain and maintain its surrounding countryside, neighboring towns and cities such as Lucca and Pescia, and the port city of Pisa. Within the city partisan tensions and neighborhood politics were also liable to flare at any given moment. In a time when the Medici had not yet risen to be known as the princes or de facto rulers of the city, the patrician class was characterized by political unrest and conspiracies, family feuds, forced exiles and even an impending revolution.[10]

Florence was essentially undergoing a transition from a minor town to a major city. Daily life in and around the Palace of the Priors and the *Mercato Vecchio* was buzzing with a variety of vendors, merchants and products.[11] But at the same time, the reality of plague was quickly approaching. Those who survived the epidemics of 1340 and 1348 literally saw the city's population cut in half.[12] The psychological and demoralizing effect of witnessing parents burying children who succumbed to plague, and family members leaving weakened or sick loved ones to fend for themselves in an attempt to escape the ever increasing prospect of death by the pestilence was, as many have remarked, not without effect on the social conscience and moral fabric of the city. This reckless abandonment and breakdown of the civil and reasoning process fascinated Boccaccio in particular.[13] In an age where the citizens of Florence still recalled the wretchedness and horror brought about by the plague, where factional and familial fighting was part of the everyday and where war and rumors of war were a constant topic of discussion and source of grief from the heavy taxation that ensued, the daily life in early Renaissance Florence was hard, haunting and suffocating.

A series of concepts, which can roughly be divided between the practical and the metaphorical, were attached to the culture of wine consumption in this period. Informed and sustained mostly by religious literature, medical/dietetic treatises, folkloric practices and a thriving oral tradition, these concepts can be said to have created and to represent the nature of consumption in the later medieval and early Renaissance periods. In analyzing the story of Cisti and Messer Geri, I will attempt to illustrate the extent to which these concepts were encapsulated in one narrative of wine consumption by first exploring those ideas attached to practice and then those that were used to make wider, more metaphorical messages.

The basic plot of Boccaccio's tale of Cisti and Messer Geri can be summed up as follows: Messer Geri is hosting the Pope's emissaries during their visit to Florence. In the course of their day they find themselves walking past Cisti's bakery in order to reach their destination. Cisti, realizing that the day is hot, thinks to himself it would be nice to offer Messer Geri and his visitors a glass of his white wine as refreshment. However, a baker would never issue a direct invitation to a gentleman, so Cisti instead goes through a series of charades in order to indirectly entice Messer Geri and his guests to his bakery for a drink. This technique is effective and Messer Geri and the Pope's emissaries decide to taste Cisti's wine. When they taste for themselves that the wine is indeed excellent they return to Cisti's bakery nearly every morning for a sample of his wine. When the Pope's emissaries are due to leave, Messer Geri arranges a banquet for them and invites Cisti as well as some of the most distinguished citizens of Florence. Cisti, knowing his place in society, refuses the invitation. Messer Geri asks for a small amount of Cisti's wine to serve at the banquet, and sends his servant to collect the wine. The servant, thinking to steal some of the wine for himself, goes to Cisti with a large flask. Cisti rejects him twice, but once Messer Geri learns of his servant's actions, he sends a small flask, which Cisti gladly fills. Later that same day Cisti presents as a gift the remaining amount of his excellent white wine to Messer Geri, who is taken aback by such a gift, and the two then become friends for life.

As Boccaccio begins to set the backdrop and give life to Cisti and Messer Geri in the opening paragraphs of the story, it becomes immediately clear that there was a strong correlation between wine and status as well as wine and an individual's quality of life. The writer suggests that though Cisti was allotted, by Fortune, 'a humble calling', she had treated him very well and that 'he had become exceedingly rich', to which Boccaccio also adds 'he [Cisti] lived without want' and that among his prized possessions 'he kept the finest wines, both white and red' in 'Florence or its surrounding countryside'.[14] Boccaccio goes on to illustrate this connection twice more within the body of the story. The first is in response to the servants of either Messer Geri or the Pope's emissaries wanting to wash the wine glasses and serve the wine;[15] while the second is an explanation as to why Cisti refused to provide Messer Geri's servant with a bit of his wine that was to be served at a banquet held in the honor of the departing emissaries.[16] In both instances it is clear that the consumption of Cisti's wine was not for everyone. While we are unaware of what sort of white wine Cisti was serving himself, Messer Geri, the Pope's emissaries and eventually Messer Geri's dinner guests, we are made aware that it came from one of the finest collections in Florence or its surrounding countryside and that it was not a wine to be tasted, or worse, to be enjoyed, by servants.[17]

There is more than status at stake. Cisti makes important allusions to dietetic theory as he comes to the conclusion that it would do Messer Geri and the Pope's emissaries some good to be refreshed by a glass of his most excellent white wine.[18] They should therefore be allowed to sample his wine for its health giving and restorative properties rather than for social reasons. To the contemporary reader and wine enthusiast the pairing of hot weather and a chilled white wine is an issue of common sense. This being the case, this section of the narrative has yet to be given its proper attention by both culinary and literary scholars alike. It is important for the reader to note that both the time and season in which a wine, and foodstuff for that matter, was consumed was closely linked to an individual's physical constitution and geographic location.[19] This idea was largely based upon the work of the Greek physician Galen. Humoral theory developed the hypothesis of the four fundamental fluids thought to be present in the human body and which therefore made up and had the ability to change the body's 'complexion'.[20] The balance of the four fluids was not only believed to be altered by the intake of foods and liquids, but also by their preparation, texture and even the age of the individual who was consuming them.[21]

But while the tale of Cisti and Messer Geri is rich in the documented concepts attached to the culture of wine consumption in the later medieval and early Renaissance periods, there is also a strong presence of those of a metaphorical nature as well. These may not be as varied in number as the real concepts in Boccaccio's story but they are equally important. Within the story of Cisti and Messer Geri there is an over-arching Christological theme, which is represented in several separate but distinct parts. This is not surprising as drinking wine on a daily basis was inevitably overlaid with the symbolic role the drink played in the Mass and the sacraments as well as its function in the Old and New Testaments.[22] This link was further established by extant visual images (found in both devotional and civic art) with which fourteenth and fifteenth century Florentines would have had a lasting and continual dialogue.[23]

For Boccaccio and his readers, the most obvious of all the references would have been that of wine and bread, these being the two main components of Holy Communion or the sacrament of the Eucharist and the miracle of Transubstantiation. Boccaccio tells us that Cisti is a baker of bread and a keeper and consumer of wine. Cisti works the wheat and water together, eventually yielding the actual loaf of bread; grapes are cultivated, harvested, pressed and fermented to form the completely new and valuable substance of wine. In the same way are these common items themselves transformed, through the holy office of Transubstantiation, into a brand new and most holy substance – the body and blood of Jesus Christ.[24] Though the point of Boccaccio's story is not to say that Cisti's bread and wine are really the body and blood of Christ, his readers would necessarily have been aware of the religious symbolism of these two common substances.

334

Another metaphor is that of wine and the Resurrection of Jesus Christ. We are told that every morning while watching Messer Geri and his guests pass by, Cisti would wear 'a gleaming white apron' and, standing at the entrance of his bakery, would drink his excellent wine with 'so much gusto' that he would have inspired 'the dead to thirst'.[25] The imagery in this section is twofold in its similarities with the Resurrection. First, the way in which Boccaccio describes Cisti's dress as 'gleaming white' mirrors that of the description of Jesus' transfiguration in three of the four gospels.[26] During his transfiguration Jesus' clothes are said to have turned 'as white as the light',[27] or even a 'dazzling white, whiter than anyone in the world could bleach them'.[28] As Jesus and the apostles Peter, James and John descend the mountain on which the transfiguration occurred, Jesus hints at his crucifixion and instructs those with him not to tell anyone what they saw 'until the Son of Man has been raised from the dead'[29] or 'until the Son of Man had risen from the dead'.[30] The second image is found in Cisti's drinking of wine, or the metaphorical life-giving blood of Christ,[31] that is able to revive and even quench the thirst of a corpse.[32] This idea suggests Jesus' references, in the New Testament, to a new life that was to be had through the eating of his 'flesh' and the drinking of his 'blood', along with an eternal quenching of thirst to those who come and believe in him as Lord and Savior.[33]

The final major metaphor found within the story of Cisti and Messer Geri is an uncanny similarity to Christ's miracle at Cana.[34] The metaphor is not in the fact that water is changed to wine but in Messer Geri demanding of his servant to serve 'half a glass' of Cisti's excellent wine during the first course of the banquet in honor of the departing emissaries.[35] In the gospel account Jesus, as a guest at a wedding banquet, created a superior quality wine from a common amphora of water, to be served to drunken guests as if it were with the first course of the meal – another example, along with that of the bread and wine of the Mass, of the creation of a new and better substance.[36] In the tale of Cisti and Messer Geri the best wine is to be served at the beginning of the banquet (just as Jesus' wine was of the best quality, normally served at the beginning of a wedding feast), thus inaugurating the beginning of Messer Geri's banquet through its consumption as well as foreshadowing the new beginning in his and Cisti's relationship.

While at first glance both the contemporary practices and religious beliefs attached to the consumption of wine in the later medieval and early Renaissance periods may seem to be totally different and, in some ways, irreconcilable, in fact each example above communicates a very distinct aspect to the rich and complex culture of wine consumption in Boccaccio's period. It is important to note that each example, in one form or another, represents and communicates the prospect of change or, essentially, the idea of a new beginning. Bread and wine miraculously become the body and blood of Jesus Christ through the celebration of the Mass, and water miraculously becomes the most superior quality wine through Jesus' intervention at a wedding banquet. Boccaccio's everyday story of a wine-loving baker, who became the friend of a nobleman, uses these concepts to show that it was possible for both status and quality of life to be changed for the better, or for the worse, in the society and culture of later medieval and early Renaissance Florence, just as it was possible for the consumption of wine or food to change the 'complexion' of the individual who consumed it.

This might seem to be the place to conclude but there is more. Alongside the important religious metaphors that informed Boccaccio's story we need to pay attention to the fact that drinking wine was a daily activity, one that men and women of whatever status rarely reflected upon. Nonetheless there is good documentary evidence to suggest that wine formed a social divide as well as brought people together in the name of Jesus Christ.

The space in and around which wine was presented, served and consumed in the tale of Cisti and Messer Geri serves as a good indicator as to how the beverage played an essential role in the constructing of a social community within later fourteenth- and early fifteenth-century Florence. In fact Boccaccio spends close to a third of the tale detailing the place of this exact exchange. The emphasis is on the 'doorway' of Cisti's bakery where we are told he first enjoys his wine all to himself and then, with the addition of a 'beautiful bench', Messer Geri and his guests are invited to do the same in their turn.[37] The doorway thus serves as a link between the interior of Cisti's bakery and the busy streets of Florence, a link that was a very real part of everyday commerce within the city.[38] It also served as a place where Messer Geri and the Pope's emissaries could take a break and escape from the hot June sun,[39] to chat or collect their thoughts as they sipped Cisti's wine, perhaps to contemplate and organize their schedule of events for the day and days to come.[40] It is also important to note that Boccaccio ensured that his readers would have realized that the entire exchange was occurring in a very public space. He stressed that from the third day on, Messer Geri and his guests made it a point to call at Cisti's bakery 'almost every morning' to resample his wine.[41] Thus, what was essentially created by a series of charades, a couple of flagons of wine, a bench and a doorway became a micro-community operating within the larger city or world surrounding it.

Conversely, wine not only served as a vessel for the building and edifying of community relationships but it also served as an indicator of status. There was a clear distinction between those who drank good quality wine and those who drank acrid wine. For example, the latter would be the case for the laboring classes while the former was the 'prerogative' of the privileged.[42] Cisti called for a 'Bolognese flagon' containing a quantity of 'his good white wine' to be brought to him both when he wanted to gain the attention of Messer Geri and his guests as well as when he finally succeeded in entertaining the group for a drink on several occasions.[43] In looking to the excellent quality of the wine served by Cisti it also becomes clear that in order to better honor Messer Geri and the Pope's emissaries, he may have changed the type of wine he consumed on a daily basis. For instance, during his attempts to capture the attention of Messer Geri and therefore invite him to sample his wine we are told that Cisti called for 'a shiny metal pail of fresh water' along with 'a quantity of good white wine' (the wine glasses were already clean, as we are told they 'gleamed as brightly as if made of silver'), but when Messer Geri and his guests approach Cisti to taste his wine we see him only calling for 'a small flagon of his best wine'.[44] Therefore Cisti may have changed his daily consumption regime to accommodate the status of his visitors by mixing a smaller portion of water to wine than he was normally accustomed to do.[45]

A further distinction is made, via wine, in regards to those being served as opposed to those serving. For example, not only does Cisti tell the servants of Messer Geri or the Pope's emissaries to 'get behind him' and to 'leave this service' to him so that he can personally wash the glasses from which his guests will taste his excellent wine, but he also informs them that he is 'no less skilled at pouring wine than at baking bread'.[46] Cisti refers to the servants of his guests as 'my friends', noting them as equals in both social station and in the servicing of Messer Geri and the Pope's emissaries.[47] However, it is not clear if Cisti joins Messer Geri and his guests in tasting the wine and as such his earlier mention of the wine not being made for the lips and palates of servants rings true for him as well in this scenario.[48] It is an ironic twist of fate that Cisti goes from the collector and consumer of such an excellent wine to the server of the same wine with no recourse to enjoying its taste.

Through Boccaccio's setting of this story within the social milieu of early Renaissance Florence, wine becomes not only an item to be consumed with meals or used for antiseptic purposes but a loud and vivid example and testimony to defining both community and status.[49] However, much like the metaphorical concepts attached to the beverage, wine in these social circumstances yet again serves as an agent of change. For example, it was in Cisti's doorway, a place where individuals would enter his bakery in order to purchase a loaf of bread, that Messer Geri and his guests were served a glass of his most excellent wine. Therefore what was once a strictly defined place of monetary and product exchange now becomes the space for a different type of consumption. The doorway, in tandem with Cisti's wine, also served to alter the motion of Messer Geri and his guests. We know that before they sampled Cisti's wine they would merely 'pass by' the bakery; once Cisti attracts their attention, however, the doorway is no longer simply a place which is passed but a space where Messer Geri and his guests come, take some time off, with wine in hand, to sip, talk and relax.[50] But not only does the function of the doorway or the wine served to his guests change, but also the role which Cisti plays in the exchange is altered. It is important to note that Cisti's role at his bakery before his interaction with Messer Geri and the Pope's emissaries is one of an artisan proud of his art and his product. Once he lures them in with his charades and fine wine, however, Cisti abandons these roles to favor a more humble position towards Messer Geri and his guests, that of the function of servant. Indeed, instead of raising his status, the serving of wine has made him more akin to an innkeeper or tavern owner than a baker or friend.

337

In looking to the ways in which the language of consumption directly influenced, and in some cases dictated, the establishment and sustenance of communities and the defining of social spheres within the context of the later medieval and early Renaissance periods, it becomes apparent that there also existed underlying anxieties or concerns that also dictated or defined the culture of wine. I believe that if we were to survey these anxieties and concerns as they relate to both food and wine the results would be astonishing. Within the story of Cisti and Messer Geri there is the recurring anxiety of not over-stepping one's social boundaries and the concern of the judgment that would ensue should one deviate from his station.

The basis of this argument within the text is foreshadowed by the fact that Cisti refused to direct a personal invitation to Messer Geri and the Pope's emissaries but chose to go through a series of charades in order to indirectly invite them for a drink of white wine. Boccaccio lets us know that 'Cisti practised his art in person' and he 'considered it presumptuous to issue a direct invitation' to Messer Geri and the Pope's emissaries, being conscious of the difference in status and rank that existed between the parties.[51] These statements are in contrast to those describing Messer Geri's 'development of thirst' because of the hot June sun or as a result of his 'breathlessness' due to walking more than he was accustomed to doing.[52] So, unlike Cisti, Messer Geri is of the landed class or gentry and as such does no manual labor because he pays others to do it for him. This being said, Cisti's anxiety is defined not by a fear of rejection but by the way his intention may be viewed as trying to appropriate social privilege or status by circumventing his station and making himself an equal of Messer Geri simply by inviting him to his bakery for a drink.[53] This is further communicated within Boccaccio's tale by the fact that Cisti 'could not accept' an invitation from Messer Geri to attend a banquet, in honor of the departing emissaries, to which a number of the most important and 'distinguished citizens of Florence' had been invited.[54] Cisti was well aware of the difference in rank that existed between himself, Messer Geri, the Pope's emissaries and the distinguished citizens and power brokers who would most likely have been in attendance at the banquet. Thus, Cisti could not be persuaded to attend, as it would not be right of him to do so, 'socially' speaking of course.

In Boccaccio's construction, Messer Geri's attention, on the other hand, is not so much focused on Cisti but upon the emissaries and people of influence around him. He dealt with influential people on a daily basis and relied on their continued support for the means to stay within his accustomed socio-political circles of Florentine society. The way Messer Geri forewarned or prepared his guests as to the possible bad quality of Cisti's wine best illustrates his concern[55] – he assumed that those who practice a manual labor consume wine of very low quality. While wine was considered to be the drink of the masses, there existed obvious criteria of quality exercised by those who had the means to do so.[56] At this point it becomes apparent in the social contextualization of food and table culture in fourteenth and fifteenth century Italy that the items consumed communicated not only the social status of the consumer but were in fact an indication of identity.[57] For Messer Geri to partake of Cisti's wine, not to mention to sit and drink it publicly within the doorway of his bakery, indirectly communicated to his guests and to all those who witnessed the event that he was compromising his social standing and therefore lowering himself to the ranks of Cisti the Baker, a manual laborer.

While Cisti and Messer Geri appear to be a bit constrained by the rules of decorum and etiquette, their actions and intentions are indicative of a change in attitude and therefore deny any preconceived notions or social institutions, because the two men eventually become equals, even friends, through wine and its consumption. For Cisti the idea of inviting, sharing a drink with, and accepting the invitation of Messer Geri caused an anxiety based on a rigid division of status in the city where he lived and worked. Messer Geri appears to be more apprehensive because of the socio-political ramifications that may have occurred should he be seen drinking alone with Cisti at his bakery. Obviously, his being seen drinking wine at the bakery with the Pope's emissaries is no cause of worry or threat to his social and political standing within the city, as we are told he did this on several occasions. The inevitable consequence that would ensue should each individual freely engage one another through the public consumption of wine caused both Cisti and Messer Geri to look to indirect ways to come to a common ground, safe from judgment and social alienation.

As Boccaccio's story of Cisti and Messer Geri draws to a close we are able to witness wine's role in tying the story, and therefore its characters, together in friendship. Cisti makes a 'gift' of the last of his excellent white wine to Messer Geri, resulting in Messer Geri's elevating of the baker from manual laborer to a 'dear friend'.[58] After providing Messer Geri's servant with a good quantity for the evening's banquet, Cisti himself brought what was left of the wine to Messer Geri's house.[59] Cisti not only apologizes for having rejected the servant's first two attempts to acquire his wine, but in fact stresses that Messer Geri is now in possession of every single drop of it and that he may 'dispose of it' as he sees fit.[60] Boccaccio tells us that Messer Geri set great store by Cisti's gift and that from that day forward Messer Geri held Cisti the Baker in high esteem and regarded him as a dear and true friend of his for life.[61] There is no suggestion within the story that Cisti had an ulterior motive for unloading his remaining wine onto Messer Geri. He was not expecting to receive anything in return. Nor is there any sense of pomp or boasting as Cisti first brings forth only small amounts and then delivers all that remains to Messer Geri. Messer Geri, on the other hand, was not expecting such a gift and the way in which Boccaccio chooses to end his tale speaks of the sincerity of his extending his hand in friendship to Cisti. It is yet another exceptional way in which wine and its consumption was utilized as an agent of change for the good of both Cisti and Messer Geri. On a grander scale, the tale of Cisti and Messer Geri not only ends with its two main characters acting for the good of each other and those around them, but indicates that their generosity of spirit and magnanimity was, through wine, enhanced and their concerns and anxieties dissolved as they were able to move from inside their respective social spheres to create a level field of consumption where both baker and nobleman are equal and fully alike.

Bibliography

Arti fiorentine: La grande storia dell'Artigianato, vol II, Il Quattrocento, a cura di Franco Franceshi e Gloria Fossi (Firenze: Giunti, 1999).

Dalla vite al vino: Fonti e problemi della vitivinicoltura italiana medievale, a cura di Jean-Louis Gaulin e Allen J. Grieco (Bologna: CLUEB, 1994).

Food: A Culinary History, eds. Jean-Louis Flandrin and Massino Montanari, English ed. Albert Sonefeild, trans. Clarissa Botsford…[et al.] (New York: Columbia University Press, 1999).

Statuti delle arti dei fornai e dei vinattieri di firenze (1337–1339), a cura di Francesca Morandini (Firenze: L. S. Olschki, 1956).

Storia del vino in toscana: Dagli etruschi ai nostri giorni, a cura di Zeffiro Ciuffoletti (Firenze: Edizioni Polistampa, 2000).

The Holy Bible, New International Version (Nashville: Holman Bible Publishers, 1999).

The Oxford Companion to Wine, ed. Jancis Robinson (Oxford and New York: 1999).

Adamson, Melitta Weiss, *Medieval Dietetics: Food and Drink in Regimen Sanitatis Literature from 800 to 1400* (Frankfurt am Main: Peter Lang, 1995).

Albala, Ken, *Eating Right in the Renaissance* (Los Angeles: University of California Press, 2002).

Balestracci, Duccio, *La zappa e la retorica: Memorie familiari di un contadino toscano del Quattrocento* (Firenze: Libreria Salimbeni, 1984).

Bianchi, Maria Luisa and Maria Letizia Grossi, 'Botteghe, economia e spazio urbano' in *Arti fiorentine: La grande storia dell'Artigianato*, vol. II, Il Quattrocento, a cura di Franco Franceshi e Gloria Fossi, pp. 27–63.

Boccaccio, Giovanni, *Decameron*, a cura di Vittore Branca, II vols (Torino: Einaudi Editore, 1980).

Brucker, Gene A., *Renaissance Florence* (New York: John Wiley & Sons, 1969).

Cherubini, Giovanni, *Il lavoro, la taverna, la strada* (Napoli: Liguori Editore, 1997).

Cipriani, Giovanni, 'Il vino a cote' in *Storia del vino in Toscana: Dagli etruschi ai nostri giorni*, a cura di Zeffiro Ciuffoletti, pp. 63–92.

Cohn, Samuel K., *The Laboring Classes in Renaissance Florence* (New York: Academic Press, 1980).

Cortonesi, Alfio, 'Self-Sufficiency and the Market: Rural and Urban Diet in the Middle Ages' in *Food: A Culinary History*, eds. Jean-Louis Flandrin and Massino Montanari, pp. 268–74.

Desportes, Françoise, 'Food Trades' in *Food: A Culinary History*, eds. Jean-Louis Flandrin and Massino Montanari, pp. 275–86.

Fiumi, Enrico, 'Econmia e vita privata dei fiorentini nelle rilevazione statistiche di Giovanni Villani' in *Archivio Storico Italiano*, 111 (1953), pp. 207–41.

Franceshi, Franco, 'La bottega come spazio di sociabilità' in *Arti fiorentine: La grande storia dell'Artigianato*, vol. II, Il Quattrocento, a cura di Franco Franceshi e Gloria Fossi, pp. 65–83.

Frugoni, Aresnio and Chiara Frugoni, *Storia di un giorno in una città medievale* (Roma and Bari: Editori Laterza, 1997).

Grieco, Allen J., 'Il sapori del vino: Gusti e criteri di scelta fra Trecento e Cinquecento' in *Dalla vite al vino: Fonti e problemi della vitivinicoltura italiana medievale*, a cura di Jean-Louis Gaulin e Allen J. Grieco, pp. 165–86.

Grieco, Allen J., 'Food and Social Classes in Late Medieval and Renaissance Italy' in *Food: A Culinary History*, eds. Jean-Louis Flandrin and Massimo Montanari, pp. 302–12.

Herlihy, David, *Medieval and Renaissance Pistoia: The Social History of an Italian Town, 1200–1430* (New Haven: Yale University Press, 1967).

Hollingsworth, Mary, *The Cardinal's Hat: Money, Ambition and Housekeeping in a Renaissance Court* (London: Profile Books Ltd, 2004).

Marshall, Richard K, *The Local Merchants of Prato: Small Entrepreneurs in the Late Medieval Economy* (Baltimore and London: The Johns Hopkins University Press, 1999).

Martin, A. Lynn, 'Old People, Alcohol and Identity in Europe, 1300–1700' in *Food, Drink and Identity: Cooking, Eating and Drinking in Europe Since the Middle Ages*, ed. Peter Scholliers (New York and Oxford: Berg, 2001), pp. 119–37.

Martin, A. Lynn, *Alcohol, Sex and Gender in Late Medieval and Early Modern Europe* (New York: Palgrave, 2001).

Martin, A. Lynn, 'Fetal Alcohol Syndrome in Europe, 1300–1700: A Review of Data on Alcohol Consumption and Hypothesis' in *Food and Foodways*, Volume 11, Number 1, January–March (2003), pp. 1–26.

Melis, Federigo, *I vini italiani nel medioevo*, introd. Ch. Higounet, a cura di A. Affortunati Parrini (Firenze: Le Monnier, 1984).

Montanari, Massimo, *La fame e l'abbondanza: Storia dell'alimentazione in Europa* (Roma and Bari: Editori Laterza, 2003).

Nanni, Paolo, *Vinattieri fiorentini: Dalle taverne medievali alle moderne enoteche* (Firenze: Edizioni Polistampa, 2003).

Peyer, Hans Conrad, 'The Origins of Public Hostelries in Europe' in *Food: A Culinary History*, eds. Jean-Louis Flandrin and Massino Montanari, pp. 287–94.

Peyer, Hans Conrad, *Viaggiare nel medioevo: Dall'ospitalità alla locanda*, trans. Nicola Antonacci (Roma and Bari: Editori Laterza, 2000).

Phillips, Rod, *A Short History of Wine* (London: Penguin Books, 2000).

Pini, Antonio Ivan, *Vite e vino nel medioevo* (Bologna: CLUEB, 1989).

Pini, Antonio Ivan, 'Il medioevo nel bicchiere: La vite e il vino nella medievistica italiana degli ultimi decenni' in *Quaderini Medievali*, 29, June (1990), pp. 6–38.

Pinto, Giuliano, 'La vitivinicoltura nella toscana medievale' in *Storia del vino in toscana: Dagli etruschi ai nostri giorni*, a cura di Zeffiro Ciuffoletti, pp. 27–61.

Shinners, John, *Medieval Popular Religion, 1000–1500: A Reader* (Ontario: Broadview Press, 1997).

Siraisi, Nancy, *Medieval and Early Renaissance Medicine* (Chicago: University of Chicago Press, 1990).

Siraisi, Nancy, *The Clock and the Mirror: Girolamo Cardano and Renaissance Medicine* (Princeton: Princeton University Press, 1997).

Unwin, Timothy, *Wine and the Vine: An Historical Geography of Viticulture and the Wine Trade* (London and New York: Routledge, 1996).

Villani, Giovanni, *Cronica, con le continuazioni di Matteo e Fillippo*, a cura di Giovanni Aquilecchia (Torino: Giulio Einaudi Editore, 1979).

Welch, Evelyn, *Shopping in the Renaissance: Consumer Cultures in Italy, 1400–1600* (New Haven and London: Yale University Press, 2005).

Wilson, Hanneke, 'Italy: Medieval history' in *The Oxford Companion to Wine*, ed. Jancis Robinson, pp. 371–73.

Wilson, Hanneke, 'Tuscany: Ancient and Medieval history' in *The Oxford Companion to Wine*, ed. Jancis Robinson, pp. 720–22.

Wilson, Hanneke, *Wine and Words in Classical Antiquity and the Middle Ages* (London: Duckworth, 2003).

341

Notes

1. I would like to thank Robin Musumeci for her encouragement and for graciously reading and commenting on various portions of the draft. I would also like to thank Evelyn Welch, Dario Del Puppo and Allen Grieco for their time and assistance during the writing of this paper. Translations, unless otherwise noted, are my own.

2. The dates of the Black Death are 1347–49.

3. Those interested in a complete reading of the story see Boccaccio (1980), pp. 720–25.

4. 'Stimavasi d'avere in Firenze da novantamila bocche…'. Villani (1979), p. 206.

5. The four larger cities were Paris, Venice, Milan and Naples. Brucker (1969), p. 25, 51.

6. 'Aveva allora in Firenze centoquarantasei forni'. Villani (1979), p. 210.

7. '…e troviamo per la gabella della macinatura e per li fornai, che ogni di bisognava all città dentro centoquaranta moggia di grano…'. Villani (1979), p. 210.

8. 'Troviamo per la gabella delle porte che c'entrava l'anno in Firenze da cinquantacinque migliaia di cogna di vino, e quando n'era abbondanza circa diecimila congna piú'. Villani (1979), p. 211. For estimates see both Fiumi (1953), pp. 207–41 and Willson (1999), p. 721.

9. Grieco (1999), p. 302.

10. The reference is to the Ciompi revolt of 1378.

11. For an excellent study of consumer cultures in Italy in the years spanning 1400–1600 see Welch (2005).

12. For a list of years that either witnessed plague or famine see Herlihy, p. 105. See also Brucker (1969), pp. 26–7.

13. 'E in tanta afflizione e miseria della nostra città era la reverenda auttorità delle leggi, cosí divine come umane, quasi caduta e dissolute tutta per li ministri e essecutori di quelle, li quail, sí come gli altri

uomini, erano tutti o morti o infermi o sí di famigli rimasi stremi, che uficio alcuno non potean fare; per la qual cosa era a ciascun licito quanto a grado gli era d'adoperare'./'In the midst of so much affliction and misery, all respect for the laws of God and man had almost completely broken down and dissolved in our city. Those ministers and executors of the laws, who were not either dead or dying, had so few assistants that they were unable to perform any of their responsibilities. Therefore everyone was free to conduct themselves as they pleased'. Boccaccio (1980), p. 20.

14. 'Al quale quantunque la fortuna arte assai umile data avesse, tanto in quella gli era state benigna, che egli n'era ricchissimo divenuto, e senza volerla mai per alcuna altra abbandonare splendidissimamente vivea, avendo tra l'altre sue buone cose sempre I migliori vini bianchi e vermigli che in Firenze si trovassero o nel contado'. Boccaccio (1980), p. 722. On the economic significance of wine in the later medieval period see specifically Melis (1984), pp. 3–29 and 31–96, Pini (1989) and Pini (1990), pp. 6–38.

15. 'Compagni, tiratevi indietro e lasciate questo servigio fare a me, ché io so non meno ben mescere che io sappia infornare…'/ 'My friends, stand aside and leave this service to me, for I am no less skilled at pouring wine than at baking bread…'. Boccaccio (1980), p. 723. The picture of the ritual involved in the preservation, presentation and consumption of wine also hints at a thriving culture of connoisseurship that also existed in the later fourteenth and fifteenth centuries in Italy. The first reference to this connoisseurship is the fact that Cisti kept wines. Boccaccio (1980), p. 722. The second is the affirmation by Messer Geri and the Pope's emissaries that the wine was excellent. Boccaccio (1980), p. 724. The final testimony is the fact that Messer Geri ordered his servants to pour 'un mezzo bicchier'/'half a glass' of Cisti's wine to each of his guests during the 'prime mense'/'first course' of the banquet that was to honor the departure of the Pope's emissaries. Boccaccio (1980), p. 724. See also Phillips (2000), p. 105.

16. 'Messere, io non vorrei che voi credeste che il gran fiasco stamane m'avesse spaventato; ma, parendomi che vi fosse uscito di mente ciò che io a questi dí co' miei piccoli orcioletti v'ho dimostrato, cioè che questo non sia vin da famiglia, vel volli staman raccordare'./'Sir, I don't want you to think that I was surprised on seeing such a large flask this morning. But since you may have forgotten what I have shown you, during these past few days, with the help my little flagons, namely, that this is not a wine fit for servants, please allow me to refresh your memory'. Boccaccio (1980), p. 725.

17. We do know that the two most popular white wines during this period were Vernaccia and Trebbiano, of which Vernaccia was the more favored. Wilson (1999), p. 721

18. '…e essendo il caldo grande, s'avisò che gran cortesia sarebbe il dar lor bere del suo buon vin bianco…'./'seeing that it was very hot, he thought it kind to offer them some of his delicious white wine…'. Boccaccio (1980), p. 722.

19. 'Le altre due variabili che si dovevano prendere in considerazione erano in un certo qual modo collegate tra di loro poiché la stagione nella quale si consumava un alimento o una bevanda e il luogo geografico nel quale si effettuava il consumo erano entrambi collegati con il caldo o il freddo che regnava nel posto e al momento nel quale si mangiava e si beveva. Secondo questa dottrina si dovevano mangiare e bere cose fredde d'estate per controbilanciare il caldo e, inversamente, mangiare e bere cose clado d'inverno'./ 'The other two variables that need to be take into consideration were the season in which a food or beverage was consumed as well as the geographic location in which this consumption took place. Second, this doctrine stated that one had to eat or drink cold items in the summer in order to counterbalance the heat and conversely to eat and drink items considered hot in the winter'. Grieco (1994), p. 181.

20. These are blood (hot and moist), choler (hot and dry), phlegm (cold and moist) and bile (cold and dry). Albala (2002), p. 5. See also Adamson (1995), pp. 10–18 and Siraisi (1990).

21. 'For example, hot and moist wine would violently distemper children, making them sick. But for the cold and dry aged body, wine was nourishing'. Albala (2002), p. 156. See also Grieco (1999), pp. 305–06. An interesting study on alcohol consumption and the aged in Early Modern Europe is Martin (2001).

342

22. Pini (1989), pp. 22–4. See also Wilson (2003), pp. 33–43, 156–58, 168–69 and Unwin (1996), pp.81–85, 134–65.
23. Two classic examples are the images of a drunken Noah on Giotto's bell tower and the blood of a crucified Christ being collected into bowls or chalices by angels in Jacopo di Cione's *Cristo crocifisso fra la Vergine e San Giovanni con quattro angeli*.
24. According to Canon 1 of the Fourth Lateran Council of 1215 'There is one Universal Church of the faithful outside of which there is absolutely no salvation. In which there is the same priest and sacrifice, Jesus Christ, whose body and blood are truly contained in the sacrament of the altar under the forms of bread and wine; the bread being changed [transsubstantiatis] by divine power into the body, and the wine into the blood, so that to realize the mystery of unity we may receive of him what he has received of us'. Shinners (1997), 6–7. See also Matthew 26:17–30, Mark 14:12–26 and Luke 22:7–38.
25. 'E avendo un farsetto bianchissimo indosso e ungrembiule di bucato innanzi sempre...ongni mattina...cominciava a ber sí saporitamente questo suo vino, che egli n'avrebbe fatta venir voglia a' morti'. Boccaccio (1980), p. 722–23.
26. Matthew 17:1–9. Mark 9:2–10. Luke 9:28–36.
27. Matthew 17:2.
28. Mark 9:3.
29. Matthew 17:9.
30. Mark 9:9.
31. John 6:53–6.
32. John 6:35. John 7: 37.
33. See notes 32.
34. The miracle at Cana is found solely in John 2:1–11.
35. Boccaccio (1980), p. 724.
36. John 2:10.
37. 'all'uscio'/'doorway' and 'una bella panca'/'a beautiful bench'. Boccaccio (1980), pp. 722–23.
38. This scenario is echoed in Franco Franceshi's work on Renaissance workshops as a place of both commerce and sociability as is further attested to in both Françoise Desportes' work on the food trades and in Hans Conrad Peyer's work on public hostelries. Franceshi (1999), pp. 65–83, Desportes (1999), pp. 275–286 and Peyer (1999), pp. 289–94. To a lesser extent in Bianchi and Grossi (1999), pp. 27–63.
39. 'era giugno'/ 'it was June'. Boccaccio (1980), p. 722, note 6.
40. 'Drinking wine helped to bond individuals and groups by facilitating conversation and easing social interaction. Phillips (2003), p. xx. Cherubini (1997), pp. 191–224.
41. 'quasi ogni mattina con loro insieme n'andò a ber messer Geri'. Boccaccio (1980), p. 724.
42. Cortonesi (1999), p. 272.
43. 'un picciolo orcioletto bolognese nuovo del suo buon vin bianco'. Boccaccio (1980), p. 723.
44. 'ongni matina in su lora che egli avvisava che messer Geri con gli ambasciadori dover passare si faceva davanti all'uscio suo recare una secchia nuova e stagnata d'acqua fresca e un picolo orcioletto bolognese nuovo del suo buon vino bianco e due bicchieri che parevano d'ariento,sí eran chiari... E cosi detto, esso stesso, lavati quatro bicchieri belli e nuovi e fatto venire un piccolo orcioletto del suo buon vino, diligentemente diede bere a Messer Geri e a' compagni...'. Boccaccio (1980), p. 722–24.
45. 'Undiluted wine was practically never drunk in the middle ages. Drinking pure wine does not come about until the nineteenth century'. Personal communication via email from Allen Grieco (Thursday, 18 August 2005).
46. 'Compagni, tiratevi indietro e lasciate questo servigio fare a me, ché io so non meno ben mescere che io sappia infornare...'./' My friends, stand aside and leave this service to me, for I am no less skilled at pouring wine than at baking bread...'. Boccaccio (1980), p. 723.

343

47. Compagni'. Boccaccio (1980), p. 723.
48. See notes 15 and 16.
49. Hollingsworth (2004), p. 52.
50. 'passar...passare'./'pass..to pass'. Boccaccio (1980), pp. 722–23.
51. '...dove Cisti fornaio il suo forno aveva e personalmente la sua arte esserceva...ma avendo riguardo alla sua condizione e a quella di messer Geri, non gli pareva onesta cosa il presummere d'invitarlo ma pensossi di tener modo il quale inducesse messer Geri medesimo a invitarsi. Boccaccio (1980), p. 722.
52. 'Messer Geri, al quale o la qualità o affanno piú che l'usato avusto o forse il saporito bere, che a Cisti vedeva fare, sete avea generate...'. Boccaccio (1980), p. 723.
53. Using the case of Zuco Padella, a peasant who is verbally berated for stealing and consuming his master's produce, Montanari provides his readers a scenario that vividly illustrates how real the link between society and consumption was in early modern Europe. Montanari (2003), pp. 108–10.
54. 'A' quail, essendo espediti e partir dovendosi, messer Geri fece un magnifico convito, al quale invitò una parte de' piú orrevoli cittadini, il quale per niuna condizione andar vi volle'. Boccaccio (1980), p. 724.
55. 'Signori, egli è buono che noi assaggiamo del vino di questo valente umom: forse che è egli tale, che noi non ce ne penteremo...'./'My lords, it would do us well to taste the quality of this gentleman's wine; perhaps it will be of such a quality and give us no cause for regret...'. Boccaccio (1980), p. 723.
56. See also the reference to a culture of connoisseurship in note 15.
57. '...la corrispondenza fra 'qualità del cibo' e 'qualità della persona' non viene percepita come un semplice dato di fatto, legato a situazioni occasionali di benessere o di bisogno, ma postulata come verità assoluta e per così dire ontological: mangiar bene o mangiar male è un attributo intrinseco all'uomo, così come intrinseco (e auspicabilmente immutabile) è il suo stato sociale'./'...the relation between 'quality of food' and 'quality of person' was not a simple fact tied to the chances of well-being or need, but rather an ontological postulate: to eat well or poorly was an intrinsic character of man (and hopefully an unalterable one) and social status'. Montanari (2003), p. 110.
58. 'Mersser Geri ebbe il dono di Cisti carissimo e quelle grazie gli rendé che a ciò credette si convenissero, e sempre poi per da molto l'ebbe e per amico.' Boccaccio (1980), p. 725.
59. Boccaccio (1980), p. 725.
60. '...io non intendo d'esservene piú guardiano, tutto ve l'ho fatto venire: fatene per innanzi come vi piace.'/'...I no longer intend on keeping it for you and so I have had all of it delivered to you: dispose of it as you like.' Boccaccio (1980), p. 725.
61. Boccaccio (1980), p. 725.

Protecting Authentic French Food Heritage
(*Patrimoine Culinaire*)

Lizabeth Nicol

> The French... have surrounded food with so much commentary, learning and connoisseurship as to clothe it in the vestments of civilization itself... Rating restaurants is a national preoccupation. Cooking is viewed as a major art form: innovations are celebrated and talked about as though they were phrases in the development of a style of painting or poetry... A meal at a truly great restaurant is a sort of theatre you can eat.
>
> Richard Bernstein, *The Fragile Glory: A Portrait of France and the French*

One of France's greatest treasures is its cuisine. For centuries a national consciousness of a deep appreciation of food – its history, production, preparation and enjoyment – have helped to define an essential aspect of French identity. An important part of their heritage is devoted to and founded upon food. Eating in France is not simply seen as necessary for survival and health but also as a statement of culture as expressed by Richard Bernstein in *The Fragile Glory*,

> The French... have surrounded food with so much commentary, learning and connoisseurship as to clothe it in the vestments of civilization itself... Rating restaurants is a national preoccupation. Cooking is viewed as a major art form: innovations are celebrated and talked about as though they were phrases in the development of a style of painting or poetry... A meal at a truly great restaurant is a sort of theatre you can eat.[1]

The French take their cuisine seriously. They spend a great deal of time on choosing just the right product whether it be fish, meat, bread, cheese, chocolate or wine. Eating a meal is seen as a pleasurable social activity. Hours are spent around the table eating, drinking and discussing the food but also in animated general conversation. 'In France one must not just eat and drink, but talk also. Talk stimulates new ideas about food.'[2] They want to know all the details concerning their food: where it comes from, how it was produced, how long it took, who produced it, how it should be cooked and served. They are justly proud of French cuisine.

But as Sanche de Gramont so aptly points out in his portrait of France, it is the link to the land that makes the difference:

The first condition for a great cuisine is in the land, and France can fortunately provide a high quality of almost everything edible, like pré sale lamb, Charolais beef, Normandy butter, …..the ingredients are plentiful and varied. Good food has been available ever since the Gauls became sedentary and pastoral, sat on bales of hay and ate pike with vinegar and cumin, raised their Cambrésis geese, and discovered that wild asparagus tasted good.[3]

The French have always worked their land, maintaining a time-honored agricultural tradition unlike other developed nations of the world. With more surface area devoted to agriculture than any other nation in western Europe, blessed by nature with a variety soils and micro-climates (temperate to Mediterranean), France is the EU's largest agricultural producer and second only to the United States as the world's largest food exporter. Agriculture remains an integral aspect of French society. As revealed in a recent poll in the French consumers publication, *60 Millions de Consommateurs*, although the main function of farming is to nourish the nation, second in importance was preserving and defending the gastronomic and cultural heritage.

Diversity of the land is also at the heart of the notion of 'terroir' – a food's link with the soil or earth in which it grows. Braudel describes French landscape as a patchwork or mosaic of soils, sub-soils and micro-climates. He sees the French farmer as 'the architect and labourer of these gardens and fields, orchards and villages, no two which are ever exactly alike,'[4] as we can also say of the foods being produced. There are a vast number of regional specialties available as Jonathan Fenby points out,

346

> Each product has its specific local link. The best butter comes from the meadows of the Charente, the sweetest melon from Cavaillon in the south, and your favorite wines from any one of a hundred individual vineyards, each with its own taste. Those green lentils from Le Puy have an Appellation d'Origine Contrôlée to honour and protect their excellence, as do poultry from the wetlands of the Bresse east of Lyon, nuts from Grenoble, potatoes from the Ile de Ré in the Atlantic, and the olive oil from Les Baux-de-Provence and from Nyons in the foothills of the Alps. These are national treasures, as much a part of France's glory as Notre Dame or the nuclear strike force.[5]

France's culinary glory, however, has been fading in recent decades due to the pressures of progress and globalization. The industrialization of food production, mass marketing techniques and the emergence of fast-food chains have started to erode the gastronomic traditions of France. The number of farms has been in constant decline (3–5% per year from 1.6 million in 1970 to 680,000 in 1997) although production has increased due to modernization of farming methods. Shopping and buying habits have changed. In the past, the French shopped mainly at outdoor markets and local specialty shops (bakers, butchers, grocers), but a recent INPES survey shows that

79.7% of today's food is purchased in supermarkets and hypermarkets, followed by local shops at 40.1% and local outdoor markets 32%. Confidence has been shaken by recent food scares – mad cow disease, dioxin, hormones, salmonella, and genetically modified frankenfoods.

But all is not lost in this gloom and doom scenario. A recent *Crédoc* survey on what today's French population considers to be important for eating well reveals that food quality, freshness, and taste are the most important priorities along with a balanced diet and respect for the environment. The same survey reveals that a majority of French feel that industrialized agribusiness is responsible for the 'malbouffe' or loss of good quality food. But Jean-Robert Pitte, professor of geography at the Sorbonne, puts forward the idea that stopping the homogenization of products and developing a respect for regional diversity is compatible with modernized agriculture, the agribusiness and mass marketing. He cites Edouard Leclerc, head of one of France's biggest supermarket chains as being a convert to this idea by distributing many local products from small companies through his *Nos Regions ont du Talent* brand.

Studies also show that there has been a revival of interest in authentic regional products and a survey by the French Institute for Nutrition shows that the French attach several criteria to products which claim to be 'authentic.' The product will have a history, roots from the past that link it to a certain area or region. It will be produced with traditional know-how and time-honored techniques that have been handed down through generations. It will be of superior quality. It will be of the 'terroir' – the climate, rainfall and nature of the soil – all contributing to the unique flavor of the product. For the French all of these have a decisive influence on the authenticity of a product.

Few people defend their own culture and lifestyle more forcefully than the French. When it comes to their food heritage they have decided that it is worth preserving and protecting. In 2004 the Food Museum awarded

> the people of France with the first National Food Heritage award for their successful dedication to preserving their culinary traditions and history at all levels through national initiatives.
>
> The French people's continuing love of their land, farm and food traditions is manifest in their support of countless societies dedicated to promotion of local specialties, their patronage of local fresh food markets, and their willingness to financially sustain rural areas and quality food ingredients.

Following is a discussion of just a few of the varied forms of protection and preservation this food heritage has taken including AOC (*Appellations d'Origine Contrôlée*), the European Union PDO, PGI and TSG, *Label Rouge, Syndicat Interprofessionnel* and *Confréries* (Professional Associations & Societies), *Sites Remarquable du Goût* and Museums, Food Guides, and the *Inventaire du Patrimoine Culinaire*.

The AOC (*Appellation d'Origine Contrôlée*)

The AOC was one of the first legal actions taken by the French to guarantee the origin of a product and its authenticity. In fact, the first step was taken in 1905 with the passage of a law to stamp out fraudulent use of information on certain products. The government was required to define geographical zones and production methods but this was only partially successful due to lack of specifications concerning quality.

In July 1935 in response to a crisis in the wine industry, a law creating the AOC was passed and a national body (which became the Institut National des Appellations d'Origine or INAO) was designated to carry out all procedures related to certification and guarantee of product authenticity. As stated by the INAO, 'all AOC are considered to be the property of the Nation and part of the national heritage and will be treated as such by the State with the same rights and duties as national monuments, which are protected by their own specific legislation.' Initially the AOC concerned only wine and *eaux-de-vie* but in 1990 this was extended to cover dairy and other food products.

The purpose of the AOC is to protect a product that has a duly established reputation. AOC status identifies and guarantees a close link between the product and the terroir, taking into account both natural factors (geographical limits, geological elements, climatic conditions) as well as local expertise, techniques, methods of production and local customs.

As an example, let's look at *jambon de Bayonne* and *piment d'Espelette*. *Jambon de Bayonne* has been known in France since the 16th century. Rabelais included it in the Grandgousier menu and Henri IV ordered it to be delivered to him in Paris. Rules that concern the production of *jambon de Bayonne* were established in 1587, amended in 1840 and again in 1876 and are still in effect today. This high quality ham comes from the traditional breed of 'black' pigs fed on a diet which includes corn, acorns, and chestnuts. The leg is massaged after slaughter to remove all traces of blood. It must be cured in the Adour Basin with salt from the local salt flats (Salies-de-Béarn or Mouguerre). Stored at 3–4° C for 8–12 days before being cleaned and desalted, it is then cured for 2 months in a cold chamber. It is then cleaned again and air dried for 7–12 months at 14°C. Its flavor is very much dependent on the local climate and effects of the southerly wind or *foehn*. During this last process the producers may grease the muscular part of the ham and rub it with *piment d'Espelette*, which will give it a reddish/ochre color and special flavor. It carries the mark of the *lauburu* or Basque cross.

In 1999, the *piment d'Espelette – Espeletako Bippera* became the first spice to be granted AOC status. A native of Mexico, it was brought back to Spain by Columbus and has been cultivated in and around the town of Espelette since the 16th century. The mild ocean climate and slightly acidic soil of the Basque country provide ideal growing conditions. The peppers are planted out in April or May and hand harvested from mid-August through October. They are then strung on cord and made into garlands that hang under the eaves and from the doorways in the village. They dry naturally in the sun for about 2–3 months, are then broiled in an oven and ground into powder or made into a paste. Espelette pepper has a perfumed flavor mildly hot and slightly smoky. It is rated 4 on the Scoville scale, stronger than paprika and not as hot as cayenne. *Piment d'Espelette* is the only spice to have been granted an AOC.

There are 468 AOC for wines, eaux-de-vie and ciders. In the dairy products area 4 butters, 1 cream and 47 cheeses are covered (28 cow's milk, 3 sheep's milk, 11 goat's milk). Meat and poultry products include 6 lamb, 4 pork, 5 beef and 31 poultry and fowl. There are 29 covering fruits and vegetables, 12 for olives, 1 honey, 1 spice and 1 essential oil. As noted by Jonathan Fenby, 'The AOC accolade has even been extended to a foodstuff not consumed by humans, the 100,000 tonnes of hay harvested each year on the plain of Crau at the mouth of the Rhône which is exported as far away as Hong Kong for the delectation of thoroughbred racehorses.'[6]

The Protected Designation of Origin (PDO), Protected Geographical Indication (PGI) and Traditional Specialty Guaranteed (TSG)

In 1992, the EU created a system to protect and promote authentic traditional and regional food products, inspired by the French AOC and the Italian DOC (*Denominazione d'Origine Controllata*), which covers the 25 member countries of the EU. An informational campaign called EAT for European Authentic Tastes has been organized to explain the system.

PDO products, as with the AOC, are closely linked to the idea of *terroir*. Therefore, the essential qualities of the product will be directly related to its place of origin. The raw material must be from the specifically defined area, where it must also be produced, processed and prepared using traditional methods. Examples are Champagne or Roquefort cheese. It should be noted that at present there is no protection for these names on products both made and sold outside the EU. The United States usually opposes protection of geographical designations of origin as many of the products that are protected elsewhere are commonly-used generic terms in the United States. In the United States, for example, one can buy American champagne and Roquefort cheese.

PGI products require the product be produced in the geographical area or region of the name it bears. However, it is more flexible than the PDO as it requires the link to occur in at least one stage of production, processing or preparation in the defined area. This means, for example, that the raw material may come from another region. Examples are Italian Terre di Siena olive oil, or German Black Forest ham (*Schwarzwalder Schinken*).

TSG products are linked to traditional characteristics or production methods rather than to a specific region and thus are the most lenient of the three. They must be produced either from traditional materials or using traditional techniques. Examples are *jamon de Serrano* from Spain and Italian Mozzarella.

349

The *Label Rouge*

The *Label Rouge* was founded in 1960 and celebrates its 45th anniversary this year. This coveted red label, recognized by 4 out of 5 shoppers, guarantees by law that the product has been produced under very specific conditions that will give it superior quality and recognizably better taste than similar products available for purchase. The name *Label Rouge* is the property of the Ministry of Agriculture and Fisheries. Products are only granted the *Label Rouge* after rigorous and exhaustive evaluation and are both tested and tasted on a regular basis by third party certification agencies to ensure compliance. Bernard Sauveur of the National Institute for Agricultural Research points out, *Label Rouge* 'meets the requirements of the French present-day consumer, namely a superior and objectively accepted quality, a traditional way of production, traceability of the product, the insurance of independent controls and a fair price.'

It covers a vast number of products such as meats, poultry, prepared meats, seafood, fruits and vegetables, dairy products as well as such items as smoked salmon, Guérande sea salt and rose garlic (*ail rose*) from Lautrec.

Chicken is probably the best-known *Label Rouge* product and must meet strict conditions and requirements. The breed must be suited to living outdoors with no over-crowding. They must be slow growing as they must live for a minimum of 81 days (nearly twice as long as an industrially raised variety). The feed must be at least 60% grains and no animal-derived products are permitted (fishmeal, growth stimulants). The processing plant can be no more than 100 kilometers or 2 hours away and the chicken must be sold fresh with an expiration date of 9 days.

350

Confréries and Inter-Professional Associations (*Syndicats Interprofessionnels*)

Confréries, a type of guild or brotherhood, and Inter-Professional Associations are another form of defence and protection of authentic products and often go hand-in-hand with the AOC as they carry out the application procedures and requirements.

There are well over 100 *confréries* in France and many were founded in the 1950s and 1960s. Some are very small with a very limited number of members and others have memberships numbering in the thousands. Almost all demand that their members take an oath of allegiance to uphold the authenticity and standards of the product concerned, which represent almost every imaginable product from apples to walnuts as well as techniques and methods of production. There are two guides available: *101 Confréries de France* by J-P Branlard and *Les Confréries de France* by Bernard Tardif.

Likewise, there is an Inter-Professional Association for every region of France and every aspect of French working life. In the agricultural area they represent not only every type of food stuff and aspects of processing and production. Examples are the Syndicat Interprofessionnel des Laits de Conserves (concentrated and powdered milk products) founded in 1945 with 13 members, the French Inter-Professional

Association for Multi-Destination Fruit and Vegetable Processing (AFIDEM) with hundreds of members throughout France or The Inter-Professional Association for the Development of Seed Breeding-Southwest (ASEDI-SO) with 12 international seed breeding groups and 3 associations of seed farmers.

Sites Remarquable du Goût and Musées du Goût (Museums of Taste)

The *Sites Remarquables du Goût* was created by the Conseil National des Arts Culinaires (CNAC) under the auspices of the Ministries of Culture, Agriculture, Tourism and Environment. Each of the *sites* must concern reputed products with historical links, be presently available and in active production. There must be an aesthetic aspect (beauty of the architecture, village or countryside). They must be easily accessible to visitors and open year round. There are over 100 *sites* listed as being *remarquable du goût*. France has more food-related museums than any other country in the world. They are far too numerous to list but they cover everything from strawberries in Brittany, truffles in Périgord, mustard in Burgundy to olives in Provence. There is a guide available: *Les 100 meilleurs Musées gastronomiques de France* by Jean-Paul Branlard.

Guides gourmands

Guides concerning authentic regional products are indispensable for consumers who want to find the 'real' thing. *Le Guide Ferniot Hachette des Bons Produits* lists over 1500 addresses of local artisans and producers as well as tasting notes and tips on local sites of gastronomic interest. Michelin has published a series of guides for the regions of France, which covers restaurants but also boutiques, markets and where to find the best local products. The *Bible des Gourmets* by Dominique Lacour contains over 3000 addresses of the best specialties of the local terroir. The *Guide Champérard: Guide Gastronomique de France* by Marc de Champérard lists over 4250 artisans, producers and boutiques as well as restaurants and hotels. *Le Guide des Gourmands 2004* by Elisabeth de Meurville lists over 1500 that have been verified and tasted. This guide also gives the Coqs d'Or awards and has been in publication for the past 16 years. *Les Trésors Gourmands de France* by Gilles Pudlowski and Maurice Rougement lists what he considers to be the 50 treasures of France with in-depth information about their history and the artisans who make them, with beautiful photographs.

The Inventory of French Culinary Heritage (*L' Inventaire du Patrimoine Culinaire*)

Of course, it would be impossible to speak about preserving France's authentic food heritage without including the massive 22-volume survey of regional products, an initiative of the CNAC and sponsored by the French gouvernment. The inventory covers all aspects of history, traditions, local expertise and recipes. Written and edited by American food historians in Paris, Philip and Mary Hyman, Bruno Laurioux,

Laurence Bérard and Philippe Marchenay, it is a veritable tribute to the culinary heritage of France.

These are only some of the means of protection that have been taken but they demonstrates the true Gallic spirit. The French simply refuse to lose this most essential part of their past and have taken effective measures to ensure that the profound changes that are taking place and affecting their countryside and lifestyle will not mean the disappearance of some of France's most enduring treasures.

The French truly agree with Slow Food founder Carlo Petrini when he says 'Food history is as important as a Baroque church. Governments should recognize this cultural heritage and protect traditional foods. A cheese is as worthy of preserving as a 16th-century building.'

Bibliography

Bernstein, Richard, *The Fragile Glory: A Portrait of France and the French* (New York: Knopf, 1990).

Braudel, Fernand, *The Identity of France*, Vol 1, History and Environment (London: Collins, 1988).

De Gramont, Sanche, *The French: Portrait of a People* (New York, G. P. Putnam,1969).

Pitte, Jean-Robert, *French Gastronomy: The History and Geography of a Passion*.

Vial, Bernard, *French Agriculture in the Context of Europe* (Washington, D.C. French Embassy Publication).

Zeldin, Thedore, *The French* (London: Flamingo, 1984).

References

60 Millions de Consommateurs N° 381, Survey on the Relationship between Consumers and Farmers, March, 2004, pp 16–17.

60 Millions de Consommateurs N° 387, Crédoc Survey on Eating Well, October, 2004, pp 14–15.

Institut National de la Recherche Agronomique (INRA), Bernard Sauveur, *Les Critères et Facteurs de la Qualité des Poulets Label Rouge*, 1997.

National Institute for Prevention and Health Education (INPES), *Survey on French Consumer Buying and Eating Habits*, 2002

European Authentic Tastes (EAT) <http://www.eu-authentic-tastes.com>

Institute National des Appellations d'Origine (INAO) <http://www.inao.gouv.fr>

Label Rouge <http://www.label-rouge.org>

Notes

1. Bernstein, p. 168.
2. Zeldin, p. 303.
3. de Gramont, pp. 367–368.
4. Braudel, p. 65.
5. Fenby, p. 98.
6. Fenby, p. 101.

Imaginary Restaurants with Real Food in them: Reflections on the Quest for Authenticity in South-East Asian Food

Roger Owen

This paper assumes food habits to be an aspect of our instinctive urge to develop cultural images of the world that make sense to us. It then suggests routes along which this assumption could be explored – in particular, one leading to the conclusion that a desire for 'authentic' food reflects a failure of cultural nerve among those who demand it. This is no bad thing, since cultural health implies constant questioning of our own assumptions about what 'makes sense', especially in times of rapid change. Foodways, however, are only partly cultural; their roots are quite literally in the real world. For the sake of good taste as much as good health, we therefore demand that anyone who supplies or cooks our food has acquired a technical knowledge of what they are doing plus an informed sympathy for the context in which they are doing it. That is authenticity worth having.

I

Authenticity: the word suggests approval. Statements that employ it seem to be statements of fact, but really they are value judgments. Authenticity is a kind of truth, and interesting truths are usually complex. Human beings by their nature prefer complexity. Simplicity may be reassuring, comforting, even satisfying, for a while, but not for long.

The everyday food of most people in South-East Asia is perhaps superior, in terms of freshness, nutrition and actual cooking, to the junk food of many people in the West today, but it is simple to the point of monotony, monotony that can be relieved in two ways: daily by snacks and street-food, and communally by periodic feasting. Almost all the South-East Asian food we are now accustomed to in the West originates from these sources – that is, if it has any claim at all to authenticity. Even among the snacks and the festival dishes, Westerners have shown themselves to be picky. If you look at what a Javanese or Balinese villager eats on a feast day, I suspect you may not be in a great hurry to join him, or at least that your selection from what's on offer will be different from his. Yet he, like us, is choosy about what he eats. A traditional English Sunday lunch, centred on roast beef and Yorkshire pudding, with apple pie and fresh cream to follow, probably contains no basic ingredients that are not already familiar to at least a majority of South-East Asians; but they, of course, combine and cook them in very different ways from the traditional English cook, and would probably find the lists of ingredients in the English recipes rather too brief.

Clearly, the urge to eat when we are hungry is one of our deepest and strongest instincts. The urge to give a dinner party is more complicated. We share some of our food habits with the animals – the 'lower' animals even – but every one of these habits has become encrusted with cultural additions and refinements. Our food behaviour is a tangle of contradictions because, like almost everything else we do, it draws on so many other aspects of behaviour, each of which has to strike its own balance between culture and instinct. All species, apparently, exercise their sense of taste: as long as food supplies are more or less adequate, no creature eats the whole range of foods that are available to it and potentially nourishing. Many, even under the stress of hunger, are very reluctant to eat unfamiliar or 'spoiled' food. The Viking colonies in Greenland are said to have died out because they refused to eat fish. The early British in Australia nearly met the same fate because they refused to listen to what the aborigines were trying to tell them. There are stories of Moslems who find that by mistake or trickery they have eaten pork and evidently enjoyed it; but on being told that it was pork, they have been violently sick. On the other side, Western guests at Arabian feasts who have been offered an eye of the sheep always claim that their fear of insulting their hosts was greater than the repulsion they felt for such culturally strange food, and that when they ate it they rather liked it. I saw something similar happen at our own dinner-table recently, when the first course was a small whole seabass, steamed. Our Japanese guest, using chopsticks, delicately picked out the eye of the fish and passed it to the young Italian sitting opposite, saying this was the most delicious part. The Italian hesitated a little, then ate it and agreed that it was indeed excellent.

The desire not to be put down in front of fellow-guests is surely an example of cultural behaviour based on instinct; so is the fear of offending a host. All species learn, by one means or another, which foods they should or must eat to remain healthy, and many apparently learn from their parents or peers. A popular example used to be sparrows' ability to peck the tops off milk bottles. (Sparrows seem to be almost extinct today in southern Britain, though the disappearance of old-fashioned milk bottles preceded their decline by so many years that it would be risky to trace a connection.) Many species share food they have found or killed, but many others hide it away; humans have developed both habits to great heights of elaboration. I don't recall any examples of animals trading food with each other, and this is hardly surprising, for trade demands a skill that only we have fully acquired: the trick of assessing the relative attractiveness of two things against some objective standard of value.[1] We often do this very crudely, assuming that bigger or newer means better; but still, we do it, and we have this strange knack from (I believe) the same peculiarity of our brains and nervous systems that gives us language.

Our problem, as humans, is basically the same as that of a mayfly: to stay alive, for a century or a day, we have to construct inside our heads a model of the world around us that makes sense to us – i.e. it enables us to continue our lives more or

354

less successfully. A key factor in this success is our awareness and recognition of other members of our own species. As humans, we have exceptionally large and energy-hungry brains and nervous systems, and we put these to good use in satisfying their exorbitant demands; in return, they give us various pleasures and satisfactions, which, though trivial when set against the pains and fears of human existence, keep many of us happy most of the time. But we have learned to use our brains to do much more. We invent worlds which are as significant for us as the real world, in which our perceptions and acts, because they are driven ultimately by real instinct, become absolutely compelling: these invented systems compose what we call culture. Animals – even sparrows – seem to possess some rudiments of cultural behaviour, and bird-brains are indeed now known to be more highly-organised than we used to think they were, but cultural elaboration has been carried by *Homo sapiens* to far higher, and often far madder, heights. By and large, though, food culture has until recently shown off our species at somewhere near its best.

II

By 'somewhere near its best' I mean that food habits have acted, and very largely still act, as identifiers of human groups, mostly quite small ones, with the result that they have tended to promote fellowship and conviviality. Of course, food prescriptions and taboos identify non-members of 'our' family or nation as foreigners and strangers, but this is usually harmless. Vegetarian guests notoriously expect vegetarian food to be prepared for them but are usually not expected to cook meat when they invite carnivores to dinner; still, this doesn't really put anyone out – put them outside the group, I mean. But this may point us towards a possible explanation of the value we put on authenticity in food. Suppose we make rendang with pork instead of beef? What could be wrong with that, if it tastes just as good? Nothing, really; rendang is often made with chicken, duck or jackfruit instead of beef, and pork rendang is perfectly easy to cook and tastes excellent. But many of us would say, 'This is delicious, but it's not proper rendang. Rendang is Sumatran-Malaysian, specifically Islamic, therefore never with pork.' Or why not substitute yoghurt for coconut milk in a Thai green curry, as Sri Owen does in her *Healthy Thai Food*?[2] The publishers wanted to keep coconut milk out of the book altogether, but compromised because some dishes just won't work without it. Green curry of chicken, on the other hand, needs a sour sauce, and the original recipe achieves this with tamarind. Yoghurt is sufficiently sour already for the tamarind to be dispensed with. In a blind tasting, most people accustomed to Thai food could probably tell which ingredient had been used, but the difference in flavour is slight and the fact that South-East Asian cuisines use scarcely any dairy products matters less than the fact that people using the cookbook want to avoid saturated fats.

What can we say about the decision to include this inauthentic ingredient? Any form of human behaviour can be located somewhere on a continuous line between

355

culture and instinct, so we are dealing here with relatives, not absolutes; we may disagree at what point on that line an 'authentic' act becomes 'inauthentic'; but I suggest that what we are arguing about is the culture/instinct opposition. There is a cultural element here, of course, but the desire to avoid harming ourselves is fundamentally instinctive (though, as we all know only too well, it is easily overridden by temptation or addiction). Green curry made with yoghurt is a variant on the original recipe, but it preserves the intention of the original, the sourness that balances the sweetness, heat and saltiness of other ingredients. Rendang made with pork wilfully disregards the purposes of the original (which are, to make tough buffalo meat tender, and to enable it to be kept for a week or longer without refrigeration), and breaks a major dietary law in the area of its origin. There are instinctive elements here (the religious instinct: the need for security and guidance in life; the need to belong to a group), but culture is surely much stronger.

This opens up the whole question of why people want to eat foreign food. Many people of course abhor it; I remember the deep misgivings with which, as a student at Oxford, I first entered a Chinese restaurant at the age of *twenty-one*. I was with four or five other first-year undergraduates, and we had a very convivial evening; it's a little sobering, perhaps, to realise that today a restaurant of that type and class would give me much worse misgivings, but for totally different reasons. Many years later, my wife Sri and I lunched with the late Barbara Tropp, who owned the China Moon in San Francisco; she told us the restaurant had been successful because, in a city famed for its Chinese food, it was considered to serve real, regional, Chinese dishes. But she said the best meals she had there were in the kitchen, with the Chinese cooks, who saved all the tripe and offal that no good American would dream of eating, or, by the public health authority, be allowed to eat; these, they assured her, were the best bits, and they proved it by cooking them superbly well. Was she, I wonder, not quite boasting, but claiming a secret knowledge that we couldn't share? I've eaten similar food myself in parts of Indonesia, in the course of research, and it did taste a lot better than I expected, but I felt that once was enough – enough to entitle me to tell the tale. We should bear in mind, too, that the producers of fine food and drink often can't afford to consume the product themselves, and therefore talk up the cheap stuff that is their daily bread. (Gerald Mars has a good story about this kind of thing in Emilia Romagna, though I am not sure if he has published it. The plot turns on outsiders who came to the farmhouse door wanting to buy 'the real stuff – the stuff you keep for yourselves' – which of course was rotgut, as they found out after paying dearly for it. Serve them right: you shouldn't try to buy authenticity. It should come as a gift – one that is sometimes quite undeserved.)

Eating foreign food, with knowledge and understanding, does not absolutely require first-hand acquaintance with the culture that produced it, but the experience will be richer – more complex – if you have made that acquaintance. Testing in my mind the truth, or at least the persuasiveness, of that statement, I recall the re-discovery of seventeenth- and eighteenth-century music performed on 'period instruments'. Musical textures and layers of sound and harmony that had vanished in the hubbub of giant symphony orchestras were suddenly revealed. It was pointed out that we were still not hearing what the original audiences and congregations heard, because to recreate their experience we needed eighteenth-century ears and brains unsullied by Brahms and Britten. Yes; but the aesthetic experience is just as valid for us as for them, and is perhaps all the richer for us because we know how Western music has developed in the subsequent two centuries. From the eater's point of view, unfamiliar food should not only give pleasure in itself but should stimulate intellectual curiosity as to exactly how the human nervous system responds aesthetically to tastes, flavours and textures. This doesn't require elaborate cuisine; our responses to boiled rice and boiled potatoes will do quite well to start the enquiry going.

III

Cooking foreign food, however, is something else. I think we might call it 'cross-cooking', by analogy with cross-dressing. In that world, we find men and women wearing the other sex's clothes, a phenomenon that implies much about our cultural habits and expectations. Cross-cooking is in its way equally titillating and scandalous. It causes us to forsake, occasionally or even permanently, the most deeply-ingrained markers of our cultural identity: the foods that we usually eat. Similarly, both activities require improvisation and substitution if they are to achieve convincing results. Thai food produced in a modern kitchen in London or New York will never be or taste exactly like Thai food cooked in a Thai household. But, as with men in women's clothing, it's the obvious inauthenticity that is alluring: so faithful in every detail, so assertively different in effect. I don't mean the finished dish – that may be good or bad – but the cook, the kitchen, the cookbook, everything that produced the dish. Even if you go and live in Thailand, I think it will be a long time before you cook with a Thai accent. And long before that, you will have written a cookbook – in your own language.

357

Indeed, we can hardly be surprised if we find that cultural habits, including food-ways, vary as much and as meaningfully around the world as languages do, and change as swiftly and unpredictably. But whereas acquiring a foreign language requires hard work (if one is past the age of seven or eight years) and one's achievement is always subject to the acid test of effective communication with a native speaker (telling jokes and making love were, according to my teachers of the skills of TEFL, the ultimate peaks – though neither featured in our final assessments) – whereas, I say, language learning is tough, other forms of interculturalism are fun. Instead of endless comprehension exercises, you eat strange food and learn to find it delicious; if you wish to proceed to higher studies, you learn to cook it – the equivalent of speaking – and you may even aspire to the high ground whereon foreign language and foreign food meet: the written word, in the form of the exotic cookbook.

You are now in the position of Eliza Doolittle at the embassy ball. You have to persuade people that you are the Real Thing; and if you succeed, some expert will say that your knowledge of Thai food is *too good*, and he can tell that you were born – Australian. In my career as a teacher of English, I was quite often corrected by my students, particularly the Dutch, whose knowledge of English grammar and English spelling was well in advance of mine. On such occasions, I would remind them that they had an unfair advantage over me: they had been taught English, whereas I had had to pick it up as best I could, during the taxing processes of early childhood. Nevertheless, I maintained that I was the authentic English speaker. How does this pan out – so to speak – in food habits?

Obviously the people who spend real money on acquiring foreign tastes, and devote real effort to learning how to reproduce them in their own kitchens, do this because they like the food; they may enjoy showing off to their friends as well, but they wouldn't go to all that trouble and expense if they found the results horrible-tasting. Though the delight we all take in boasting about gastronomic exploits in faraway places is not to be ignored, there is plainly a real appreciation in some countries of the world for the food and cooking of other countries. Borrowing takes place at all levels from snack bars and fast food chains to posh hotels and famous restaurants, but in all these places, I suggest, we shall find, however 'naturalised' the food may have become, however dumbed-down, denatured or cheapened, it brings with it a significant amount of cultural baggage that is not strictly necessary to either the cooks or their customers; and this baggage, some of it smuggled in, some of it brazenly flaunted, is all in the name of authenticity. The clearest examples are the décor, and the language of the menu, and we need not enlarge on these here; they have always given eating-places of all types huge scope for pretentiousness. But we do not see (for example) a Turkish menu decorated with a picture of a guitar-player wearing a sombrero. That would be costume-fusion, and we have all known since we were children playing at dressing-up, that borrowed fashions in clothes remain forever outlandish: an Englishman in a kilt is a cartoon Scot.

Fortunately, food is more forgiving than clothes. Yet 'fusion food' still rouses controversy. I take this as sign of our reluctance to confront the new global culture that is emerging, or rather rushing out at us, from the meltdown of cultural differences all over the world, the disappearance of minority languages, the rise of the universal supermarket, the crossfading of politics, entertainment, education, work and (if there's any time left over) leisure. But look at the people who are digging in to defend cultural purity – fundamentalists of all persuasions, puritans as malicious as Malvolio – do we want to be like *them*? Shakespeare knew that after his death Malvolio would triumph and would close the London theatres. Whether Shakespeare guessed that, only a little later, he himself would be an ikon of an emerging global culture, I neither know nor care. The point is that globalisation started a long time ago, and still has a long way to run, though the pace is quickening. We have to live in our own interesting times, and to distinguish between what is worth preserving and what is not. The criterion is not: 'is this a perfect copy of *Ponye Gyi Wettha Hin?*' (a Burmese pork dish cooked in a black bean sauce[3]), but 'was this dish cooked with a knowledge of its country and culture of origin?' (the black beans fermented with salt; the pork cut up before cooking begins, since it will be eaten with the fingers; the proportions of garlic, ginger, and chillies appropriate to the people who are to eat the dish – piquant, but not so as to offend a guest unaccustomed to chillies; a real Burmese, or at least a real Thai, fish sauce, not soy sauce; equally, a mindfulness that this is a festival dish and must be generous in quantity and quality).

Whether we shall like our globalised paradise when we've got it is quite another thing, but I suspect we shall have no choice. One of the functions of culture is to give us the illusion of choice – something restaurant menus are good at. Maybe we should just cease worrying, and rejoice that we were born on a planet that can sustain us, for the time being anyway, on such a huge variety of nice-tasting foods. And on authenticity in South-East Asian food, Alfred Russel Wallace must have the last word. Writing in the 1860s about his seven and a half years of travel, botanising, bug-collecting, shooting and stuffing animals and birds, and eating, all through the islands from Singapore to Papua and back, he wrote of the village of Teluti in the Moluccas: 'The orang-kaya [the richest man in the village] has fine clothes, handsome lamps, and other expensive European goods, yet lives every day on sago and fish as miserably as the rest.'[4]

359

Notes

1. A possible exception to this rule, suggesting a breakthrough by capuchin monkeys, was recently observed in a US laboratory. See *The New York Times Magazine*, 5 June 2005, or: <http://www.nytimes.com/2005/06/05/magazine/05FREAK.html?ex=1119844800&en=4739c47c9c70abc3&ei=5070&pagewanted=all>.
2. Owen, Sri, *Healthy Thai Food* (Frances Lincoln, London, 1997), p. 124.
3. Example taken more or less at random from Marks, Copeland, and Aung Thien, *The Burmese Kitchen* (Evans & Company Inc., New York, 1987), p. 105.
4. Wallace, Alfred Russel, *The Malay Archipelago* (Oxford University Press reprint, Singapore, 1989), p. 365.

Attempted Authenticity in Medieval Arab Cookbooks

Charles Perry

Authenticity is elusive even today, when we can, say, get a bead on the tabbouleh at our corner restaurant simply by hopping a plane to Beirut and sampling the dish on its home ground. Centuries ago, when travel was far more difficult, cookbooks often included recipes named for regions or population groups. Were those names deluded or – to be more charitable – mere suggestions of exoticism?

And if the recipes did represent authentic dishes, to what degree had they been assimilated to the author's cooking tradition? It has been supposed that *pullus parthicus* in the 2nd-century Roman cookbook of Apicius was a Parthian dish because it contains asafetida, Persia being one source of this spice. But even ignoring the fact that other dishes in the book also call for asafetida, we are entitled to cock an eyebrow simply because the recipe uses the ultra-Roman seasonings lovage and *liquamen* (fish sauce).

Five important cookbooks have come down to us from the medieval Arab world, and in them I count 98 recipes with regional or ethnic names. Since there are no contemporary recipe collections from the regions or social groups in question, the idea of assessing how authentic the recipes are has a quixotic ring. I will proceed anyway.

One is a little skeptical about the *sulāqa fārisiyya* in a 10th-century book, since *sulāqa* is an Arabic and not a Persian name. Theoretically it could translate a Persian word, but it is not reassuring to be told 'the first to make it was Abu Samin 'Abdullah ibn Samin,'[1] with his thoroughly Arab name.

Still, the only dish in these books that seems utterly improbable is *al-turkiyya*,[2] which appears in a 13th-century North African book. It's a stewed chicken stuffed with two pickled lemons and ten olives, ingredients typical of North Africa but quite unknown in Central Asia. North Africa being the only part of the Arab world where olives are added to dishes as they cook, rather than eaten on their own, no Turks could have picked up this idea on their way to the Maghrib. Add the fact that only a paltry number of Turks lived in North Africa, and it's an open question how the dish got such a name.

A glimmer of authenticity exists in a 10th-century recipe for a stew named *nabati-yya*.[3] With its flower-like lattice of egg, it seems to be a *narjisiyya*, and in fact it is preceded and followed by *narjisiyya* recipes. The distinctive feature seems to be that it contains *itriya*. This was a small soup-type noodle, something like the Italian *orzo*. Its name is Greek, and the Nabataeans – who lived in north-west Arabia and Syria-Palestine – were under substantial Hellenistic influence and would certainly have used *itriya*. What makes things more interesting is the fact that the recipe calls for '*itriya* made of white dough,' which is the only passage in the Arab cookery literature that implies making *itriya* oneself; elsewhere it seems to be a dry pasta bought in shops.

Still, there's no way of telling how far this recipe may have been adapted to the tastes of Baghdad's court.

The North African dish *badī'ī* (from *badī'*, 'marvelous') certainly was adapted to the tastes of the eastern Arab world. On its home ground, it was meat cooked with eggs and cheese.[4] A 13th-century Syrian book, which identifies *badī'iyya*[5] as 'a dish of the North Africans,' shows the same general idea, though the cheese was not a fairly soft one, as in the west, but a firm cheese which was first poached and then fried. At the end, however, Syrian taste decisively wins out and 'much tail fat' is poured on the dish. The fat-tailed sheep which were the source of this favorite eastern Arab ingredient were not raised in North Africa or Spain. For that matter, the one other North African dish that shows up in eastern cookbooks, couscous, sometimes got a final, inauthentic topping of lamb fat.[6]

From the Crusaders, the Syrians learned what they called *al-shiwā' al-faranjī* (the Frankish roast[7]): 'Rub a scalded lamb with salt, sesame oil and rose water, and skewer it in one piece on a big lance. Take coals and put them in a place the length of the lamb, to right and left, with no fire under the lamb, and roast the lamb patiently. It comes out beautiful, well done, marvelous. Moisten it with a little sesame oil and rose water, and take it up.' The exoticism was that to the Syrians roast lamb meant a leg, shoulder or rack, not a whole animal, done in a tandoor oven, rather than over a fire in the baronial European manner (the fact that the fire should not go directly beneath the lamb seems well observed). But the writer could not refrain from basting the meat Syrian fashion with sesame oil and rose water.

One recipe shows such a distinctive technique that it has an unquestionable ring of truth: 'a dish with which the Arabs (viz. Bedouins) take pains.'[8] It instructs to dig a hole the size of your lamb meat 'and deeper,' line it with potsherds and flagstones and kindle a fire in it until the stones are quite hot. Then the coals are removed and a lattice of sticks is laid over the hot stones, the lamb being arranged on this. The whole thing is covered with 'the copper tray of the Arabs – and if there is none, an ordinary tray' and its edges are sealed with clay. Fire is laid around and on top of this lid until the meat is done. This is a variation on the ancient earth oven or pit barbecue.

Certain other dishes appear in more than one book, in recipes that give no reason to believe one was copied from another but which show a basic similarity. For instance, two recipes for *jurjāniyya* are stew flavored with raisins and pomegranate seeds.[9] Another *jurjāniyya*[10] is chicken in yogurt flavored with mustard – but it is also flavored with pomegranate seeds, suggesting that pomegranate was the characteristic seasoning in the region of Gorgan, Iran.

The name *kurdiyya*[11] refers to meat which is first boiled and then fried. One recipe refers to kid and the other to chicken, so evidently this cooking technique, rather than a particular recipe, was associated with the Kurds. In a book written in 13th-century Spain (or possibly North Africa), there are two recipes for 'Jewish chicken'[12] and also two for 'Jewish partridge'.[13] Three of the four are topped, as most stews are in this book, with the *takhmīr*, a layer of beaten eggs, but with the distinctive, and suggestive, addition of chopped livers (in one case giblets as well). A dish called *sanhājī* appears in two unrelated recipes,[14] which have in common that you throw in, apparently, every kind of meat and fowl you can get your hands on and stew them with vinegar and soy sauce. This suggests that the Sanhaja Berbers at some point outgrew the puritanism of the Almoravid empire they founded.

Some foreign recipes were accepted to the point that they were no longer thought of as regional. This is clearly true of the ancient Persian dishes that formed the basis of Arab haute cuisine, and of the Turkish dish *qāwūt* (wheat fried in butter)[15] and *gata*,[16] an Armenian bread with a short dough filling.

Finally, three recipes are associated with the Saqāliba, the slaves of northern European origin (not all of them Slavs, despite their name) who were an established feature of Moorish Spain. They are a lamb stew (*tafāyā*), a boiled lamb dish and one simply called *saqlabiyya*, the dish of the Saqāliba. They have in common that they are made with cheap cuts, such as breast, trotters, sausage and tripe, and that they call for heroic quantities of garlic: one to four heads per dish. The use of offal enlivened with a loud, coarse flavoring does suggest the cuisine of a slave class.

Notes

1. Ibn Sayyar al-Warraq, *Kitâb al-Tabīkh* كتاب الطبيخ, ed. Kaj Öhrnberg and Sahban Mroueh (Helsinki; Seuran Toimituksi, 1987) p. 113.

2. Ibn Razin al-Tujibi, *Fadālat al-Khiwān* فضالة الخوان, We 1207, Staatsbibliothek Preussischer, Landesbesitz, Berlin, p. 51b.

3. Al-Warraq, p. 181.

4. *Manuscrito Anónimo*, ed. Ambrosio Huici Miranda, in *Revista del Instituto (Egipcio) de Estudios Islamicos*, no. 9, 1957; pp. 6 and 14.

5. *Kitāb al-Wusla ilā al-Habaīb*, #1278, كتاب الوصلة الى الحبيب, al-Maktaba al-Waqfiyya, Aleppo; p. 9b. The different form of the name in these two 13th-century books reflects the different naming convention in west and east.

6. Ibid.

7. Op. cit. p. 59a.

8. Op. cit., p. 59b. Another MS of *K. Wusla*, Sinā'a 74 (Dar al-Kutub, Cairo), adds 'it is better and more elegant than (tandoor-) roasted meat.'

9. *Kitāb Wasf al-At'ima al-Mu'tāda* كتاب وصف الأطعمة المعتادة, translated in *Medieval Arab Cookery* (Totnes: Prospect Books, 2001); p. 306; Ibn Jazla, *Minhāj al-Bayân* منهاج البيان (not a cookbook but a medical encyclopedia which contains some recipes), British Library, no. Add 5934; p. 58a.

10. *K. Wusla*, p. 55b. A corrupt recipe titled *jurjāniyya* also appears in *K. Wasf*, *Medieval Arab Cookery*, p. 359; the mysterious ingredient *labī rās* لبير اس is likely to be *habb rummān* حبرمان, pomegranate seeds.

11. *K. Wasf*, *Medieval Arab Cookery*, p. 355; *K. Wusla*, p. 50a.

12. *Manuscrito Anónimo*, pp. 26 and 28.

13. Op. cit., pp. 26 and 27.

14. *Manuscrito Anónimo*, p. 10; *Fadlālat al-Khiwān*, p. 62a.

15. *K. Wasf* gives a simple, archaic recipe following one tarted up with sesame, honey, barley sugar, almonds and hazelnuts, *Medieval Arab Cookery*, p. 423.

16. This occurs in *K. Wasf* and several MSS of *K. Wusla*; see *Medieval Arab Cookery*, p. 463.

Meat Foods of Mountain Jews of Daghestan

Zoya Ramazanova and Magomedkhan Magomedkhanov
edited by Robert Chenciner

Magomedkhan has previously given three papers at Oxford Food Symposia. ('Traditional Table Manners in Dagestan', with Sergei Luguev, 1989; 'Feasting after Fasting in Archib Village, Dagestan', 1990; 'Aromat Argentina – Oowaakhh! Flavourings of some Dagestan Mountain Dishes', 1992) He is a senior researcher at the Institute of History, Archeology & Ethnography of Daghestan Scientific Center of Russian Academy of Sciences. He is leader of the Archi, one of the smallest of Daghestan's 31 ethnic groups 1,000 strong, with their own language, famed for their shepherds. Zoya is also an ethnographer and a senior colleague of Magomedkhan. She is a Lak, one of the main ethnic groups of Daghestan who are some 120,000 strong. Laks are celebrated for their intellectual achievements, and of course have their own language. Daghestan's languages are as, or more, different than, say, English and French. This paper comes from Zoya's fieldwork collected from Mountain Jews on Magomedkhan's ethnographic expedition in 2003. They visited the villages where only a small number remain. Most have moved from the country to Derbent city or to Israel.

Mountain Jews (self-nomination *'Juhurum'*) are one of the ethnic groups of Jewish national formation, which, on the territory of Daghestan and Azerbaijan, started in VI-VIII centuries AD, [by the way, during the same period when the Khazars were in the region. This is not intended to imply that the Mountain Jews are related to the Khazars]. They speak in so-called 'Tat' language, which belongs to the Iranian group of Indo-European family of languages [unlike the Khazars who spoke a Turkic language]. According to Soviet census in Daghestan in 1926 there lived 11,600 Mountain Jews and 200 'Tats' (Muslims who spoke the same language as Mountain Jews). In contrast, the 1979 census found that in Daghestan there were only 4,700 Mountain Jews and 7,400 'Tats' (!?). The 'Disappearing' of Mountain Jews and increased numbers of 'Tats' was the result of anti-Semitic policy of the Soviet regime, which welcomed the formal self-recognition of Mountain Jews as 'Tats'. Since 1980 the population of Mountain Jews of Daghestan decreased as a result of emigration to Israel and other Western states.

Mountain Jews settled in Derbent city and 23 nearby villages where, similar to other ethnic groups, they formed special quarters (districts) among Tabasarans, Lezgins, Kaitags, Kumyks and other Daghestani peoples.

Having lived for about 1500 years among other Daghestani peoples they assimilated Caucasian manners, behavioural norms, traditional methods of agriculture and trade, and a lot of traditions and particularities of material culture in house-building, clothing, and of course, food.

The economy of Mountain Jews was based on trade, crafts and agriculture. As farmers, they mainly cultivated vegetables, fruits and vines. Cattle breeding as a business was not a tradition of Mountain Jews. At the same time in the villages of Derbent and Kaitag regions every family had one or two cows or buffalos, a few sheep and as many chickens as possible.

Mountain Jews of Daghestan eat more lamb than beef or chicken or fish.

With regard to fish, those who live in the Derbent area use *kutum*, a deep burgundy-coloured fibrous estuary fish from where the Sulak and Samur deltas meet the Caspian, as a ritual food for weddings, but only in dried form and as a snack with alcohol. One of the reasons why Mountain Jews do not have fish as a staple food, even though they live near the Caspian coastline, seems to be that, as is also the case with other Daghestanis, they do not like the mess that surrounds cleaning a fish. But the exception is sturgeon which is eaten as delicacy and which requires relatively easier cleaning. ('Dying For Caviar', Robert Chenciner, *OFS*, 1997; 'Little Known Aspects of North East Caucasian Mountain Ram and Other Dishes', Robert Chenciner & Dr Emile Salmanov, *OFS*, 1987.)

Bugleme is a cooked fish dish, using *kutum*, or *sazan*, a freshwater Caucasian carp or bream. The fish is cleaned and cut into pieces and put into a glazed earthenware bowl with previously prepared onions. For 1 kilo of fish you need 1.5 kilos of onion in small pieces, which are rubbed with salt and glazed over a slow fire for 1 hour. The onions lose both weight and size (as my yarn and carpets). In addition to fish and onion you put into the ceramic bowl several whole potatoes, sour berries (barberries, or if not available, *alicha* plums or *kuraga* apricots), dry mint, salt, pepper and enough boiling water to cover the fish. Then the bowl is placed in a copper cauldron with water in it, and the copper cauldron is covered with a cover, so that the dish is cooked for 40 minutes as in a bain-marie.

For meat foods, Mountain Jews use both fresh and dried meat. For one family the approximate average amount of meat to last for the winter-spring period is calculated as four to five sheep, and one cow divided between two families. Mountain Jews do not buy fresh meat until their dried meat is finished, except for extraordinary situations, for example, special religious feasts, *shashlik* for important guests, or for funeral ritual food (about which we hope to have more information).

Tara, Inhvara Pol, Plov, and *Chudu* were used as ritual dishes, for example in *Peysakh* (Passover), or for weddings.

Tara is made of roasted onion, forcemeat, spices, sorrel and a little water. 'Forcemeat' means 'meat stuffing' or in Russian '*myasnoi farsh*'. All this is cooked over a slow fire. When the forcemeat is almost ready, add rice and fennel and *kindza* (a bitter minty leaf herb). The consistency of *tara* is something in between soup and porridge. The dish is eaten with fingers, dipping in pieces of bread.

Inhvara Pol is a sort of *khinkal* dumpling, but the dough or paste consists of more than 50 per cent wild garlic and is bound with eggs, not water. The dough is cut into two-inch-long pieces, boiled and served on a separate large plate. The lamb meat is boiled separately and served on a separate plate. There are 4 more cups with: 1) crushed walnuts; 2) boiled eggs; 3) stewed dried apricots – *kuraga*; and 4) garlic mixed with bouillon.

Chudu is made with fat meat cut into small pieces with a special knife. With roasted onion, a lot of pepper and *zelen'* (mountain greens), the meat is put into the centre of a thick pancake, the ends of which are sealed, so in the middle of *chudu* there is a hole for the steam to escape.

The preservation of meat in autumn for winter and spring was accompanied by a special ritual called *Sugum*. The householder sent an invitation to *ravvin* (the rabbi), neighbors, relatives and other respected local people, to participate in 'drawing out sinews from meat' and making sausages. Unmarried young people were invited as well. They cut up the meat, made sausages, cleaned onion and garlic, cooked *shashlik*, and sung and danced.

In the *sugum* ceremony, the housewife was the most respected and important person. She made a portion of liver and pieces of meat, and sent her daughters with plates on their heads to distribute them to neighbors, relatives or poor widows. In return those who received the gift gave back to the girls something symbolic – an egg, a piece of garlic or onion, etc. It is worth adding that the characteristic tradition of Mountain Jews was to share any non-staple food with their relatives and community members. For example after a cow or buffalo was born it was good manners to send their neighbors a plate of boiled milk and eggs. Those who received that gift returned the plate with water in it, as a symbolic wish that 'the cow would not be dry, and give a lot of milk'.

The technology of making and drying preserved meats in a shaded and slightly windy place, is the same as elsewhere in Daghestan. Carefully washed and salted *kishki* intestines are filled with cut meat spiced by *tmin* (mountain caraway), *chabrets* (mountain thyme), some flour, garlic and pepper. Men friends would visit the household to congratulate them for making an ample reserve for winter, and for having *shashlik* and wine. Meantime the women worked at drawing out the sinews, and making sausages and *kaurma* (fried pieces of meat overflowed by fat and preserved in a ceramic container in a cool, fresh, and dark place). Preserved *kaurma*, as well as dried sausages were used as a filling for *kurze*, a kind of ravioli, for *chudu* a kind of pizza, for pies, and for different varieties of soup.

Sausages were boiled for *khinkal* (dumplings) and soup, or roasted with potato and spices. A special type of sausage made immediately after an animal was slaughtered consisted of liver, very small pieces of potato, inside fat, salt, red and black pepper and a little wheat or corn grits.

In every Mountain Jew's house one could see several new and several years-old dried sheep fat-tails hung along the balcony. As was the opinion of all other Daghestanis, it was one of the best reserve foods in case of hunger, and it was believed that the older the dried sheep fat-tail, the better its medicinal value.

Internal fat was roasted and poor fat preserved in ceramic jars. Roasted fat was used for deep-frying or as a sauce for soups, *khinkal* and other mealy dishes such as porridge.

As examples, here are three more variants of stew-soups:

Khoye-gush is made from one-inch cubes of fat meat, potato, roasted onion, spices, over which water is poured to just cover the ingredients. It is then cooked on a slow fire. When the dish is ready, chopped fennel and/or *kindza* are added as garnish. *Khoye-gush* is eaten with a spoon.

Boz-bash is made from fat meat cut into very small pieces, with a lot of onion added, plus red and black pepper and pieces of sour 'bread' made of dried *alicha*, a type of plum. The mixture is boiled.

Yagni is a stew-soup made of meat, potato, *zelen'* (mountain greens), black and red pepper, a bit of *kuraga* (sour apricots), boiled in water. The soup is eaten by dipping in bread with fingers.

It was considered that the best time for meat preservation was in late autumn, when the first cold days began. Good quality fresh lamb was available at a cheap price only in summer and autumn, when animals were pastured in the high mountains.

In winter and springtime mutton as a rule decreased in quality, so, as was the case with other Daghestanis, Mountain Jews preferred to eat dried meat.

Autumn days spent preserving meat were happy days filled with social visiting, as there was more than enough delicious food such as *shashlik*, *dolma* and of course *khinkal*. Poor members of the community also were grateful to get a piece of liver or internal organs.

Chicken was considered to be very delicious, though not essential for family well-being. As Professor Mikhail Mamatovich Ikhilov used to say 'one chicken is not enough for a family, two is expensive'. He was a Mountain Jew and Daghestani ethnographer who wrote his dissertation on the 'History and Ethnography of Mountain Jews' in 1949; the section on Mountain Jews in *Peoples of the Caucasus*, Vol. I in 1960; and the book *Narodnosti Lezginskoi Gruppi* – 'Peoples of the Lezghin ethnic family' in 1967. He worked with the present authors in the Daghestan Scientific Center until his death in 1995. (Ikhilov M.M. Gorskiye evrei. Avtoref. diss. kand. ist. nauk. M., 1949; Ikhilov M.M. Gorskiye evrei // Narodi Kavkaza.T.1, M., 1960, S. 554-561; Ikhilov M.M. Narodnosti Lezginskoi gruppi: Etnographicheskoye issledovaniye proshlogo i nastoyashego Lezgin, Tabasarantsev, Rutulov, Tsakhurov, Agulov. Makhachkala, 1967)

For rice-*plov*, the chicken is stewed separately. When small pieces of chicken meat are almost ready they are sprinkled with flour, vinegar, green herbs and egg-yolk . The dish is called *chetirma* and eaten with rice-*plov*. Chicken meat was also used as the meat ingredient in different types of soups. The characteristic feature of chicken dishes of Mountain Jews is that they add egg-yolk or whole eggs. Rice also appears in a soup called *dyush-pere* made of beans with very small (less than 1 inch) ravioli, stuffed with minced lamb or beef as available.

Slaughtering is a very important act in Jewish food culture. For kosher food the animal must be slaughtered by a special butcher at the Synagogue or by the r*avvin* (rabbi) who has to know which animal is permitted for kosher food and how it must be slaughtered according to Jewish customs. For example it is forbidden to make pieces of carcasses by breaking bones. Violation of kosher customs means that the meat is *trephine* (*harum*, or forbidden).

It was forbidden to eat pork and horse meat. There were certain days when meat food was not permitted, for example meat food was forbidden in the fast-period before *Peysakh* (in Russian *Paskha*). Meat and milk foods could not be eaten at the same time.

Meat food can be divided into four groups depending on the type of cooking:

a. Boiled: *khinkal, kurze, boz-bash, yagni*

b. Roasted: *shashlik* or *shish-kebab, lyulya-kebab*

c. Stewed: *yapragi* or *dolma, tara, bugleme, khoye-gusht*

d. Baked: *chudu*

Finally, we can say that Mountain Jews' food culture has many similarities with Daghestani traditional foods, but at the same time they preserved a number of specific tastes and dishes, such as their own way of using spices, and dusting with flour.

367

Saucing the Dish of Authenticity: Mrs Charles Dickens's Menus and her Husband's Writings

Susan M. Rossi-Wilcox

As I realize now, I began this project in search of authenticity. Four years ago when I visited the Charles Dickens Museum at 48 Doughty Street on a dreary December day, I had expected to purchase a recipe card for plum pudding, that stodgy dessert which inhabits the pantry of popular culture. Through the seasonal retelling of *The Christmas Carol*, the distinctive aromas that Dickens described of the Cratchit family's festive meal still represents much of what is secular about the holiday. Dickens's plum pudding recipe would be the most genuine I reasoned, but to my utter surprise, the little shop contained no information about food, even though their guidebook mentioned Catherine Dickens's published menus. As the ghosts of Christmas past haunted me, I wrote to the director and obtained a photocopy of the only known edition published in 1852. The seemingly unremarkable menus and odd selection of recipes became more and more unsettling to me, and I wanted to put the book into a context that helped me understand their life together and why a woman who was so unfit to be married to this famous author had remained by his side for 22 years. Would Catherine's slender books of menus offer delicious clues?

The symposium's theme, authenticity, has provided an opportunity to look back at my work, *Dinner for Dickens: The Culinary History of Mrs. Charles Dickens's Menu Books*, as a case study. Ostensibly the book is about a high-profile couple's dinner parties, but in piecing together the wealth of archival information, it reads as a biography of Catherine Dickens as reflected from their well-polished dining-room table – or perhaps more accurately, as she withstood the heat outside of the kitchen. In the 1850s when Catherine wrote her menu books, Charles was hailed nearly world-wide as a literary genius, yet the strong-willed writer and his passion for a young actress would ultimately create a scandal that ended in the Dickenses' well-publicized separation in 1858. After Charles's death in 1870, his biographers would reduce Catherine to an incompetent homemaker, mother, and companion in an attempt to legitimize Dickens's brutish behavior in tearing apart his own family. Often the menus and recipes in her books were used as evidence.[1]

Background to Catherine Dickens's publications

It is not surprising that Catherine Dickens's publication concerns the culinary arts, as critics have long acknowledged, her husband's fiction abounds in references to food and drink as metaphor.[2] Yet, when one looks at the complexity of their lives in the 1850s, it is remarkable that she managed to compile the menus, let alone produce so many editions. She began the project when Charles was working feverishly as editor and co-owner of the magazine *Household Words*, finishing *David Copperfield*, and preliminarily shaping *Bleak House*. In addition, social reform issues, the founding of the Guild of Literature and Art, and a theatrical production for Queen Victoria occupied his time and added social obligations for Catherine. Bradbury and Evans published her first edition in the early part of 1851 and the second edition in October while she was in her first trimester of pregnancy. She managed to completely revise the work for a new edition in 1852, published just a month before she gave birth to their tenth and last child.[3] By 1854 Catherine had updated the menus, doubled the recipe appendix, and shortened her pseudonym. They retained the price of one shilling. Judging by the extant copies, the volume was reissued again after minor editorial changes in 1856 and 1860.[4]

Catherine probably wrote her menu books for the same readership as her husband's magazine. The majority of the 164 menus in the 1851 edition (and those in the subsequent editions) suggest small family dinners that would have been served routinely. The few elaborate multi-course bills of fare may reflect the dinner parties they hosted at Devonshire Terrace in Regent's Park before moving in October 1851 to Tavistock House in Russell Square. Her publication conforms to her husband's desire to improve standards for British cooking and his advocacy of famine-relief foods such as American corn meal, nutritious soups, and an increased use of fish. Catherine's Scottish heritage is visible in the recipe section, particularly in the 1854 edition onwards, as are her adaptations of a few foreign dishes after they lived abroad.

Her publications are entitled *What Shall We Have For Dinner? Satisfactorily Answered by Numerous Bills of Fare for from Two to Eighteen Persons by Lady Maria Clutterbuck*. This does beg the question of why she did not (or could not) use her own name. Although I discuss their financial stress during this time in the book, it remains an open question. Catherine took her pseudonym from a theatrical role she performed with her husband's amateur acting troupe in the farce *Used Up: A Petit Comedy in Two Acts*. The plot works well as a backdrop for the book's facetious introduction. By adopting the name of the character Lady Clutterbuck, the Dickenses played humorously with social expectations. The device mimicked a trend to claim aristocratic respectability. Etiquette manuals were particularly ripe for alleged authorship and the few writers with actual titles unwittingly lent credibility to the pseudonyms.[5] By adding 'Maria' for the 1851 and 1852 editions, Catherine and Charles created a more personal fiction. The two page introduction, believed by scholars to have been written by Dickens, maintains the play's farcical tone. Through the voice of Sir Jonas Clutterbuck's widow, their life and his 'virtues' of 'a very good appetite and an excellent digestion' are disclosed, and she was indebted for the 'many hours of connubial happiness'. While Sir Jonas was not considered a gourmand, he had 'great

369

gastronomical experience' and attended his share of banquets and corporation dinners having been an alderman for thirteen years.[6]

According to Lady Clutterbuck, the ideal arrangement for happy 'domestic relations' was to make home-dining more attractive than the popular men's clubs. Apparently the road to a rocky marriage, or worse still – more frequent business in the city was 'a surplusage of cold mutton or a redundancy of chops'. She confessed 'a delicacy forgotten or misapplied' can embitter a husband's daily life. The unfortunate wife begins dreading the 'matutinal meal,' which is 'only exceeded in its terrors by the more awful hour of dinner' itself. With the spirit of public service, she 'consented to give the world' the bills of fare approved by her late husband. Consoled as she was, her 'attention to the requirements of his appetite secured [her] the possession of his esteem until the last'.[7] Perhaps the relationship indicates a respectful, if loveless marriage for Lady Clutterbuck, but it certainly implies a childless one. In addition the prose inculcates what became a growing moralistic attitude that husbands should expect their home to be their tranquil castle and their wife the silent keeper of its orderliness.[8]

Catherine's menus and recipes

Putting the fictitious introduction aside, what can a collection of mid-Victorian menus reveal about its author? After all, there is a vast difference between reading a menu and eating the meal, and a far greater gap between reading Catherine's menus and understanding the social dynamics surrounding their dining-room table. While bills of fare reflect the chef's, cook's, or homemaker's creativity, they also make a statement about the writer's worldliness and financial status. To this end, some of the questions that interested me were: What are the Dickenses' food preferences? How did they change over time? And how can this be verified?

Catherine's menus would indeed pull back the dining room curtains to allow a glimpse of her family enjoying dinner, in part, because there is a wealth of documentation in diaries, household inventories, and letters. There are well over 14,000 extant letters penned solely by Dickens and published in twelve volumes in addition to those written by many prominent guests to their home. Rarely does this much archival material exist for a Victorian middle-class family.

The majority of the bills of fare Catherine compiled are for small family groups like her own. That is, out of the 164 to 174 menus in the various editions, over seventy menus were created for two or three persons, nearly forty menus for four to five diners, and about thirty menus for six or seven persons. Given the Dickenses' household with three adults (Catherine, her husband, and her sister Georgina Hogarth), the older children, in-laws, and visitors, these expanding menus could readily accommodate the variable configurations at the nightly dinner table. They probably gave more dinner parties than most middle-class couples since they enjoyed entertaining. When her bills of fare switch from an uneven number of diners to those for ten persons or more, Catherine implies a more formal structure associated with small dinner parties.

The remaining menus designed for up to twenty persons may reflect larger family gatherings for birthdays or holidays and those to entertain colleagues and friends.

The underlying assumption, however, is that Catherine's menus represent the dinners she would have *liked* to serve her family and guests, rather than those she may have *actually* served them. In order to identify the patterns and frequency of dishes in her menus, I created databases for each of the publications. Traditional pairings of foods and sauces among the roughly 1,400 entries per book began to emerge and oddities like turkey legs, for example, which at first seem ubiquitous, could be quantified to a few entries. Inconsistencies in editing also became evident. Rice blancmange (as given in the recipe) sometimes appears in her menus as 'ground rice pudding' or 'cold ground rice pudding,' but should not to be confused with 'rice pudding'. Even with the title variations, the recipes appear infrequently as dishes in Catherine's bills of fare. Asparagus soup, one of the most popular, she only suggests for nine of the 174 menus, and others, like Spanish salad dressing or Scotch broth, are not listed. Likewise, the sauces Catherine recommends in the recipes, such as pungent brown sauce with leg of mutton, or caper sauce accompanying boiled mutton, she does not include in the bills of fare. Perhaps these are errors in the menus or she did not necessarily subscribe to the combinations, but it is more likely that her menus tend to omit items that were understood. Dinner suggestions, then and now, are so imbedded in their own culture and time, that a reader subconsciously supplies the excluded items. Breads, butter, condiments, beverages, fresh or dried fruits and nuts would have completed the Dickenses' meals, but Catherine never mentions them. Her contemporaries only rarely provide that information, and often only in the general introductory remarks. These exclusions make one realize that even bills of fare are a short-hand sketch of the meal since only the most important items are given.

Catherine's practicality as a menu planner is evident from her first publication. A third of the menus provide foodstuffs available all year long. These menus designed for two to ten persons offer convenience by using common pantry items and those easily attainable at market. She seasonally set up housekeeping in different homes and clearly knew how to expand menus or produce company meals on short notice. Judging by how often pantry lists continue to be given in today's culinary magazines, we still appreciate this approach. Catherine's mainstays include soups from root vegetables, or first courses of sole or salmon, and entrées prepared from beef, mutton, and fowl. Cold storage vegetables (carrots, onions, turnips etc.), those with two growing seasons such as spinach and those available nearly year-long, like watercress, fill out the courses. In these menus, Catherine relies on steamed puddings, starch-based custards, and jam tarts for desserts. She often ends the meal with a cheese dish.

However, Catherine is not indifferent to the calendar. Her bills of fare also celebrate the change of seasons. Starting with the 1852 edition, she reorganizes all the menus into seasonal groups, and under each menu adds the time of year they could be served. By framing the menus, she both accounts for seasonal availability and provides a fairly reliable calendar of the local markets and household gardens. Her spring menus feature the first tender asparagus shoots, while early summer dishes highlight delicate peas, juicy cucumbers, and crisp cabbages before later harvests of cauliflower and broccoli. Only rarely does she suggest vegetables such as artichokes and brussels sprouts beyond their apparent availability. As one might expect, her husband held strong opinions about seasonality: 'I abhor the idea of – whether it be for Winter peaches, Spring lamb, Midsummer ice, [or] unnatural cucumbers,' Dickens once commented.[9]

Undoubtedly helpful comments and reflection guided Catherine's re-evaluation of the menus from the first edition, and allowed her to heavily revise the 1852 and 1854 publications. She changes food stuffs with the growing availability of fresh fish and produce brought by the expansion of the railroads in the 1850s. The table summarizes the overall changes in the editions. One should note that, as of this writing, neither the first editions of the 1851 or 1852 publications are extant, nor are there known copies for the intervening years: 1853, 1855, 1857, 1858, and 1859. If her work was printed beyond 1860, no copies have been located to date.

French recipes have a long precedence in British cookbooks, but for the Dickens family, living in France made the most indelible impression on them. Catherine adds French titles and dishes to her 1854 edition. The new items include *Blauquet* of Veal, *Vol au vent* of Sweetbreads with Cockscombs, Pig's Feet with Truffles, Kidneys *à la brochette*, Beef *Croquits*, and Fondue (a cheese soufflé). She uses *ramiquins, timballes,* and adds more *au gratin* dishes in her menus. Catherine also adds more variety in the food stuffs. Salmon trout, red mullet, and curried skate make their appearance, as did broiled bones and marrow bones, and the larding of roast pheasant and fillet of beef. Catherine's sauce repertoire expands. This is not to suggest that she, or their cook, adopt French reductions that transform an amalgamation of ingredients into Parisian classics; her sauces are British with bright, seasonal components. With less reliance on shrimp and oyster sauces as standards that appear in her earlier editions, she adds capers, fennel, and celery for three new sauces. She embraces a wealth of soups and provides some of the recipes in the expanded appendix. Aspic and jellies become more prominent in her menus, and for the first time she suggests a garnish of plover's eggs.

Condiments, such as lemon juice and cayenne for fried oysters, were probably not new to the Dickenses, but Catherine adds them for clarity in 1854. Potatoes are as ubiquitous as in the earlier menus; however, she shifts from 'mashed and brown potatoes' to simply 'mashed potatoes.' Turkey leg entries are dropped altogether and there is less boiled fowl mentioned. She begins appreciating isinglass for molded desserts like strawberry curd jelly and stone cream, unlike the original edition where Italian Cream for example, was not stabilized with gelatin. She concludes the meal with more fashionable savories, such as radishes served with spring onions, 'hung beef' grated on buttered toast, and thin slices of German sausage garnish with a salad of young

Changes in the Known Editions of Catherine Dickens's Publications

	1851 (2nd ed.)	1852 (new ed.)	1854, 1856, & 1860
Total Menus	164	174	170
for 2–3 diners	74	73	72
for 4–5 diners	36	39	37
for 6–7 diners	29	32	32
for 8–10 diners	20	25	24
for 14–20 diners	5	4	4
Dishes Omitted from Retained Menus	—	15	20
Dishes Replaced or Preparation Changed		28	186
Recipes in Appendix	27	27	48

373

greens. Anchovies and sardines are now accompanied with chili vinegar, which may denote a change in personal preferences, dining fashions, or both. Not only does the 1854 edition profit from the family's residence in France, but Catherine is more willing to promote British dishes. Her new entries include Baked Irish Stew, Peas Pudding, Roast Duck with Peas, Small Mutton Pies, and Chicken Salad. She adds a few desserts such as Queen's Pudding, Trifle Pudding, Brown Bread Pudding, and Strawberry Jam Creams. For some, she provides the recipes. These new instructions are of interest, since the earlier (1851, 1852) recipes that Catherine chose usually give less precise measurements, fewer techniques, and often omit baking temperatures or characteristics of the finished dish. By the 1854 edition this information is often provided. (The last two editions in 1856 and 1860 are basically reprints with minor editorial changes.)

Verification of Catherine's menus

The beauty of working with menus is that the writer's concept of well-designed meals and favorite dishes are recorded. Yet, the difficulty is proving that any of the menus or dishes were served by the compiler. The attraction of this menu project is that Catherine's revised publications offer a nine-year record for the high-profile couple and fortunately in their case, many sources may be tapped for verification. Take for example Catherine's most frequent conclusion, 'toasted cheese'. As a culinary cousin to rarebit or fondue, toasted cheese is served with buttered slices of bread or toast from a type of chafing dish with a hot water reservoir to hold the temperature of the creamy mixture prepared from seasoned grated cheese browned on the surface with a hot salamander. Toasted cheese was so strongly associated with Dickens that his son Charley once commented on 'how many dinners begun with a glass of Chichester milk-punch; how many were finished with a dish of toasted cheese'.[10] Indeed, a listing in their 1844 house inventory records both a cheese toaster and salamander.[11] The frequency with which Catherine suggests toasted cheese in her first menus seems to confirm their son's statement. Nearly a third of the small family meals that she creates for the 1851 edition, end with toasted cheese. It is tempting to believe that friends point this out, since she does reduce the entries substantially the following year and continues to substitute other savories in the 1854 edition. These early menus may suggest how beloved her husband's toasted cheese was for informal dinners, and by contrast how willing Catherine was to explore other savory options. In none of the editions was toasted cheese ever suggested for the larger formal menus serving 14–20 persons that would have required a more celebratory finish.

Sometimes the Dickenses' invitations are unclear about a gathering for a home-cooked meal or one eaten out. Charles's arrangements for 'curry-eating engagements' with close friends are a good example.[12] Catherine does serve curries. About twenty of her menus list seafood or meat curries and she provides a recipe for salmon curry [à la Soyer] in all five editions.[13] Curries provide variety within the meal rather than represent an ethnic dinner with condiments. Her rabbit curry 'smothered in white sauce' is an over-the-top Victorian treatment in the first edition, but she quickly abandons it. Unlike Soyer whose recipe she borrows, Catherine shows no seasonal preference either to help cool in the summer or to warm in the winter.[14] A meat-and-potato-gal, she sometimes forgets to add rice to the bills of fare that include curry (as suggested in the recipe), but she repairs most of those omissions by 1854.

Another of Charles's invitations appears to corroborate Catherine's testing of new recipes. Mark Lemon, a family friend and an editor for *Punch* magazine, was summoned to dinner with the cheerful lines 'the baked Irish Stew-time next Monday, is 5'.[15] Was this a test-run for the baked Irish stew recipe that found its way into Catherine's publication that same year? We will never know, but Dickens's note offers an intriguing overlap with their meals and the revision of his wife's book. This recipe, which I attribute to Catherine, is interesting in its own right. It reads more like a reminder of a familiar favorite than an actual set of instructions: 'An ordinary Irish stew, with a little gravy added, and baked until nicely browned; about half an hour'.[16] Why did Catherine include it? The scant recipe seems absurdly simple, but it may highlight a change in technology by the 1854 edition when more reliable ovens could replace some of the stovetop cooking and browning methods requiring the cook's full attention. True, the oven is recommended in Catherine's first publication (1851), but she gives alternatives, such as 'put them into the oven or before the fire to brown' when making potato balls, or her recipe entitled lamb's head and mince that was made 'brown in a Dutch oven or with a salamander'.[17] These now rather old-fashioned methods are rarely provided in the recipes she chooses for the edition written only three years later.

I attribute the briefest recipes to Catherine since some of the lengthy ones have been identified where she lifted them nearly verbatim from popular cookbooks. She acknowledges borrowing from Alexis Soyer and 'Meg Dods' (Christian Isobel Johnstone) in the recipe's or dish's title. I have identified two other cookbook writers, Sarah Josepha Buell Hale and Eliza Acton from whom she also borrowed.

One recipe that runs the full gamut, from Catherine's menus and Charles's fiction to their own table, is mutton stuffed with oysters.[18] Judging from her husband's invitation, the mutton dish was a particular favorite.

> I have been writing all day, and mean to take a great, London, back-slums kind of walk tonight, seeking adventures in knight errant style. Will you come with me? And as a preparation, will you dine with us at a quarter before 5? – Leg of mutton stuffed with oysters.
> Reply 'Yes'.[19]

375

Dickens often gallivanted around the city to observe the nightlife, which he captured as memorable scenes and characters in his writing. Nearly 15 years after this invitation was issued, he used the mutton preparation to set the stage in *Little Dorrit* where young John Chivery, the son of the prison's turnkey, was invited to dinner by Mr Agent Rugg, the debt collector. 'The banquet was appointed for a Sunday, and Miss Rugg with her own hands stuffed a leg of mutton with oysters on the occasion, and sent it to the baker's.' Although their guest did not eat much, Miss Rigg 'took kindly to the mutton, and it rapidly diminished to the bone.'[20] As food for thought, the leg of mutton serves Dickens's fictitious table and informs his readers of cultural elements and personal traits about the characters.

Contemporary cookbook authors were not immune to a culinary fiction where art imitates life imitating art – all in a single recipe. Eliza Acton had probably never met Catherine and Charles judging from his rather formal letter to her.[21] Presumably she had sent them a copy of her new publication, *Modern Cookery in All its Branches* that had been issued in January of 1845. She attributed a dish to a lovable character in *Martin Chuzzlewit*, by dubbing the recipe 'Ruth Pinch's beefsteak puddings, à la Dickens' (see footnote for recipe).[22] In the novel, the 'cheerful, tidy, bustling, quiet little Ruth,' who kept house for her older brother Tom', was a popular persona.[23] Acton's recipe quantifies Dickens's version of the dish, which was made with a pastry crust of butter and eggs, rather than suet and water. Dickens uses this combination to set up the humor he unfolds six chapters later when John Westlock, who was smitten with Ruth, teases her about her choice of ingredients. Acton, who apparently appreciated the culinary joke of the young lovers, memorialized it as a 1½ imperial pint (3¾ cups) pudding.

Thus with a ruthless pinch of historic salt, I would like to close by mentioning a few inconsistencies in the Dickens's record in light of the original question posed: How do Catherine's menus reflect her own family's eating habits? For one, Catherine only has two entries for venison in all the menus in all the editions, but venison is mentioned in more of their correspondence than any other meat. Their notes thank friends for a haunch hanging in the larder or invite guests to partake in a series of meals from the home-butchered game. Doubtlessly venison was a treat to be shared, but judging by the extant record, the Dickens family enjoyed venison more often than her bills of fare would indicate. Likewise, a dinner invitation attempts to seduce a friend for turtle soup at their home by saying 'the notice is short because the turtle won't keep and its [sic] not a thing to be trifled with', but Catherine never offers the soup in her menus.[24] She only offers a mock-turtle version. Commercial preparations of this labor-intensive starter, as well as other gifts like pâté that they enjoyed, would have been available from tavern or hotel kitchens.

More problematic is her limited fruit selection. Commonplace stone-fruits as peaches, apricots and so forth, from backyard gardens or the marketplace are unrepresented in Catherine's bills of fare. These would have been typical tart fillings like strawberries, currants, raspberries and other preserves that she did suggest. The most surprising omission, however, is pears. Their absence is difficult to explain since a pear tree grew in the Devonshire Terrace garden when she first compiled the menus.[25] Pears were a popular fruit. About 150 varieties were listed in the 1850s horticultural catalogues.

Despite the discrepancies, when verification was found for menu items, it made this research as rich as the plum pudding of my original quest. Through her menus, one learns that Catherine presented the hearty pudding at times and in ways that seemed inauthentic to our notions derived from popular culture. She first recommended it as fried plum pudding in 1851 and boiled thereafter. Moreover she did not necessarily offer the lovable, but stodgy dessert during the Christmas season. For the holidays, the upscale couple would have showcased fancier sweets and architectural jellies like those she suggests in her large dinner party menus. Plum pudding, after all, was both a dish and a device used by Dickens to describe the Cratchit family's dire circumstances and the blessing of sharing the best food they could manage with those whom they loved. As we realize, this is a sentiment espoused by Dickens in both his art and his life.

376

Works cited

Acton, Eliza, *Modern Cookery in All Its Branches* (London: Longman, Brown, Green, Longmans, 1845).

Attar, Dena, *A Bibliography of Household Books in Britain 1800–1914* (London: Prospect Books, 1987).

Clutterbuck, Lady Maria, *What Shall We Have For Dinner? Satisfactorily Answered by Numerous Bills of Fare For From Two to Eighteen Persons* 2nd ed. (London: Bradbury & Evans, 1851).

———, *What Shall We Have For Dinner? Satisfactorily Answered by Numerous Bills of Fare For From Two to Eighteen Persons.* "new ed." (London: Bradbury & Evans, 1852).

Clutterbuck, Lady, *What Shall We Have For Dinner? Satisfactorily Answered by Numerous Bills of Fare For From Two to Eighteen Persons* "new ed." (London: Bradbury & Evans, 1854).

Dickens, Charles, *Martin Chuzzlewit* (Maryland: Penguin Books, 1968).

Forster, John, *The Life of Charles Dickens,* J. W. T. Ley, ed (London: Whitefriars Press, Ltd., 1928).

Greaves, John, *Dickens at Doughty Street* (London: Trinity Press, 1975).

Hood, Annie, 'Kentish Food, or Food of Kent,' *Petits Propos Culinaires* 45(1993).

House, Madeline and Graham Storey, eds., *The Letters of Charles Dickens,* vol. 2 (Oxford: Clarendon Press, 1969).

House, Madeline, Graham Storey, and Kathleen Tillotson, eds., *The Letters of Charles Dickens,* vol. 3 (Oxford: Clarendon Press, 1974).

Johnson, Edgar, *Charles Dickens His Tragedy and Triumph,* vol. 2 (New York, Simon & Schuster, 1952).

Lane, Margaret, 'Mrs. Beeton and Catherine,' in *Purely for Pleasure* (London: Hamish Hamilton, 1966).

Rossi-Wilcox, Susan M., *Dinner for Dickens: The culinary History of Mrs. Charles Dickens's Menu Books including a transcript of What Shall We Have For Dinner? By Lady Maria Clutterbuck.* (Totnes: Prospect Books, 2005).

Storey, Graham, Kathleen Tillotson, and Nina Burgis, eds., *The Letters of Charles Dickens,* vol. 6 (Oxford: Clarendon Press, 1988).

Storey, Graham and K.J. Fielding, eds., *The Letters of Charles Dickens,* vol. 5 (Oxford: Clarendon Press, 1981).

Storey, Graham, Kathleen Tillotson, and Angus Easson, eds., *The Letters of Charles Dickens,* vol. 7 (Oxford: Clarendon Press, 1993).

Soyer, Alexis, *The Modern Housewife or Ménagère* (London: Simpkin, Marshall, & Co., 1850).

Tillotson, Kathleen, ed., *The Letters of Charles Dickens,* vol. 4 (Oxford: Clarendon Press, 1977).

Notes

1. For example statements like 'It seems rather doubtful whether she had brought her catering up to that standard at Doughty Street. According to letters written by Dickens they appear to have lived mostly on chops!' by J. Greaves (1975) 55. Or M. Lane's remark that 'A fondness for some of her [Catherine's] own recipes alone would account for the monstrous alteration in her appearance by the end of the Devonshire Terrace period,' about her Italian Cream recipe. (1966)185.

2. See publications: Chris R. Vanden Bossche, 'Cookery, not Rookery: Family and Class in David Copperfield,' *Dickens Studies Annual* 15 (1986) 89–109; William Ross Clark, 'The Hungry Mr. Dickens,' *Dalhousie Review* 3 (1956) 250–257; Simon Edwards, 'Anorexia Nervosa versus the Fleshpots of London: Rose and Nancy in Oliver Twist,' *Dickens Studies Annual* 19 (1990) 49–64; Sarah Gilead, 'Barmecide Feasts: Ritual, Narrative, and the Victorian Novel', *Dickens Studies Annual* 17 (1988) 225–247; Barbara Hardy, 'Food and Ceremony in Great Expectations', *Essays in Criticism* 13 (1963) 351–363; Margaret Lane, 'Dickens on the Hearth,' in *Dickens 1970,* ed. Michael Slater (London: Chapman & Hall, 1979) 154–171; for an analysis of food in Dickens's magazines see James E. Marlow, 'Social Harmony and Dickens' Revolutionary Cookery,' *Dickens Studies Annual* 17 (1988) 145–177; for Dickens's portrayal of cooks see Leicester Romayne, 'Cooks a la Boz,' *Dickensian* 2 (1906) 173–175.

3. Storey (1988) ix.

4. The 1851 (2nd edition) is catalogued in the National Library of Ireland and on microform at the New York Public Research Library; The British Library owns a copy of the 1852 ('A New Edition') and the Charles Dickens Museum (London) archives has a photocopy of that edition. The Schlesinger Library at Harvard University houses an 1854 ('A New Edition') by 'Lady Clutterbuck.' The Beinecke Rare Book and Manuscript Library at Yale University recently purchased the 1856 edition. This may be the same one Slater cited from Jarndyce's catalogue No. 83 (Winter 1991–2). See Michael Slater, *Dickens' Journalism: The Uncommercial Traveller and Other papers 1859–70* (Columbus: Ohio State Univ. Press, 2002) 420, 421. The New York Academy of Medicine owns an 1860 edition.

5. Attar (1987) 52–54.

6. Clutterbuck (1852) v.

7. Clutterbuck (1852) v, vi.

8. Attar (1987) 12, 57.

9. Dickens's 7 Nov. 1847 letter to G. Lewis. Storey (1981) 190.

10. Johnson (1952) 23.

11. Tillotson (1977) 710.

12. Dickens's 9 Oct. 1848 letters to J. Leech and F. Stone. Storey (1981) 422.

13. Soyer (1850) 274.

14. Soyer (1850) 81.

15. Dickens's [13] Jan 1854 letter to M. Lemon. Storey (1993) 243.

16. Clutterbuck (1854) 60; Rossi-Wilcox (2004) 72.

17. Clutterbuck (1851) 41, 49; Rossi-Wilcox (2004) 62, 67.

18. 'Leg of Mutton with Oysters' Parboil some fine well-fed oysters, take off the beards and horny parts, put to them some parsley, minced onions, and sweet herbs boiled and chopped fine, and the yolks of two or three hard-boiled eggs; mix all together, and make five or six holes in the fleshy part of a leg of mutton, and put in the mixture, and dress it in either of the following ways: tie it up in a cloth and let it boil gently two and a half or three hours according to the size, or braise it, and serve it with a pungent brown sauce. Clutterbuck (1851) 44; Rossi-Wilcox (2005) 64.

19. Dickens letter to D. Maclise. House (1969) 152.

20. Dickens (1968) 143, 144.

21. Dickens's 11 July 1845 letter to Miss Acton. Tillotson (1977) 330.

22. To make 'Ruth Pinch's celebrated pudding (known also as Beef-Steak Pudding à la Dickens), substitute six ounces of butter for the suet in this receipt, and moisten the paste with the well-beaten yolks of four eggs, or with three whole ones, mixed with a little water; butter the basin very thickly before the crust is laid in, as the pudding is to be turned out of it for table.' In all else proceed exactly as Small Beef-Steak Pudding given below.
'Small Beef-Steak Pudding
Make into a very firm, smooth paste, one pound of flour, six ounces of beef-suet, finely minced, half a teaspoonful of salt, and half a pint of cold water. Line with this a basin which holds a pint and a half. Season a pound of tender steak, free from bone and skin, with half an ounce of salt and half a teaspoonful of pepper well mixed together; lay it in the crust, pour in a quart-pint of water, roll out the cover, close the pudding carefully, tie a floured cloth over, and boil it three hours and a half. We give this receipt...as an exact guide for the proportions of meat puddings in general.'
[for the pastry crust] 'Flour, 1 lb.; suet, 6oz.; salt, ½ teaspoonful; water, ½ pint;'
[for the filling] 'rumpsteak, 1 lb.; salt, ½ oz.; pepper ½ teaspoonful; water, ¼ pint;'
[Bake in a moderate oven about 350°F] '3½ hours.' (Acton 369).

23. Dickens (1968) 766.

24. Dickens's 2 March 1844 letter to T. Beard. Tillotson (1977) 59

25. Forster (1928) 156.

378

Eggs and Soldiers, English Tea, Smoked Milk, and *Pain Anniversaire*

William Rubel

A look at Culinary Authenticity inspired by arguments about language between Alice and Humpty Dumpty in Lewis Carroll's *Alice Through the Looking Glass*:

> 'And only ONE for birthday presents, you know. There's glory for you!'
>
> 'I don't know what you mean by "glory",' Alice said.
>
> Humpty Dumpty smiled contemptuously. 'Of course you don't – till I tell you. I meant 'there's a nice knock-down argument for you!'
>
> 'But 'glory' doesn't mean 'a nice knock-down argument," Alice objected.
>
> 'When *I* use a word,' Humpty Dumpty said in rather a scornful tone, 'it means just what I choose it to mean – neither more nor less.'
>
> 'The question is,' said Alice, 'whether you CAN make words mean so many different things.'
>
> 'The question is,' said Humpty Dumpty, 'which is to be master – that's all.'
>
> Lewis Carroll, *Alice Through the Looking Glass*

The possibilities for combining ingredients is unlimited. What is not unlimited is our vocabulary. The vocabulary we use to talk about food is only a tool to help us record practice, and communicate with each other. The word itself is not the dish. In his argument with Alice, Humpty Dumpty identifies the real issue – it is a matter of who is to be in control – an academy, or usage. The Anglophone world decided a long time ago on usage. Anyone has the right to make up a new word in English, or to assign a new meaning to an old one, and if others adopt the innovation, then that use is taken into the lexicon. Alice, being only a child, had a right to be outraged at Humpty Dumpty's use of language towards her – we don't make understanding difficult for children – but glory CAN mean anything that any of us want it to mean, for it is an empty shell awaiting the meaning we give it. Our job, as scholars, is not to reject Humpty Dumpty's use, but look around and see who else, if anyone, has adopted it.

The intellectual framework for decentralized control over meaning is found in the *Oxford English Dictionary*. Roughly, it says that there are many authenticities. A waiter in a restaurant may mean one thing by 'port,' and a sailor another. A 16th-century cookbook author may mean one thing by 'seethe,' and the author of a late

20th-century romance might mean another. One might question the poetry, but tall does mean small, on the other side of the Starbuck's counter. Words are understood in terms of context. This is not the approach that modern culinary culture has been taking. Instead, it has tended to define culinary terms narrowly, and thus banish to conceptual limbo foods that don't fit a generally accepted definition for a given culinary term. Alan Davidson, in *The Oxford Companion to Food*, infers an editorial role to generally accepted definitions. Specifically, he says of a particular gazpacho from Malaga, that 'It is only one of numerous gazpacho derivatives which would probably not be recognized as gazpachos in the sense in which the term has entered the culinary vocabulary.'

Authenticity, and its linked star, the authentic, always exist in relation to something, but authenticity may be evaluated from multiple perspectives, and may thus wander from the object to which it is associated. For example, an ancient Roman sculpture standing bright and white in a museum may be authentic, in the sense it is two-thousand years old, but if we ask, would it have authenticity to a person from its period, the answer is, 'no,' as it is missing its glass eyes and bright paint, and so stands, from their perspective, unfinished.

Authenticity is a concern of many fields. It is an active concern of classical musicians. What do we make of Bach solo violin works played with a modern Italian bow, rather than a Baroque German bow?[1] Collectors in all fields, from fine art to tin toys, are concerned about authenticity – with each collecting discipline having its own customs. In the realm of furniture, for example, how much restoration an article of furniture is allowed before the piece is no longer considered authentic varies between subspecialties.[2] In photography, the print an artist makes at the time the negative was created is thought of differently, and priced differently from a print the artist makes from that same negative thirty years later – it is authentic, but is penalized for its different authenticity. In the culinary world, the analogy to this situation might be the difference between a dish made for a family celebration while living in one country, and the same dish made thirty years later for a demonstration before an audience in another country.

Since authenticity in the culinary arts concerns how we think about foods that real people really cook and eat, I have chosen to explore aspects of culinary authenticity through stories of a few foods. Every dish is a world of meanings, and each of these worlds is authentic unto itself. Here, then, to having a wonderful glory!

Eggs and soldiers
Authenticity within the family
If a documentary filmmaker were to show an English family with young children at breakfast, what better dish to indicate its Englishness than *eggs and soldiers*? I have English friends in America who serve it to their young children several times a week. *Eggs and soldiers* is simple to make. It is a soft-boiled egg set in an egg cup besides

pieces of toast cut in narrow slices, so tiny fingers can march them up and down in the egg. One of the variations possible with *eggs and soldiers* is the timing of the eggs. Foods are not just looked at. We take them into our bodies. We become accustomed to specific, and subtle, combinations of taste and texture in the dishes that we eat often. This is the most fundamental level of authority that underpins authenticity – personal practice. *Eggs and soldiers* is a dish that binds families through subtle variations in the recipe, for example, whether the egg is boiled for four minutes, or for four-and-one-half minutes.

While thirty seconds may seem small to an outsider, the difference matters to families. There is only one authentic *eggs and soldiers* per family, only one preparation that means 'home'.

Pasta with mayonnaise, Pasta with ketchup
Culinary culture

Two years ago, I took the bus from Oxford to London. I had the sweetest of drivers. We talked about many things, including food. The driver was concerned about the junk food his daughter eats when living with her mother, but, he said, when his daughter is with him on weekends, she eats well. For example, she eats pasta with a little bit of ketchup.

I became friends with a Neapolitan academic, a young woman doing post-doctoral research in the California city where I live. Of the food she ate at my house, she said that it was more Neapolitan than the food in Naples – in a sense, more authentic than its source. To return hospitality, Mara invited my wife and me to her house for dinner. She served pasta with mayonnaise topped with grated American cheese, an orange cheese selected over other choices, including *Parmigiano Reggiano*, on the principle that 'cheese is cheese.'

That there was pasta at Mara's table is consistent with her family's culinary traditions. She did not serve a baked potato, kasha, or a large bowl of rice. Mara's pasta has the authority of cultural authenticity. The English bus driver's pasta with ketchup echoes a classic Italian pasta sauce. Both my Italian friend, and the English bus driver, created their dishes out of common modern industrial ingredients.

When the little girl, the daughter of the bus driver, grows up, it will have to be with fondness that she recalls spaghetti with ketchup. Should she become a London barrister she will, of course, have already leaned that this is not something to serve to one's fellow barristers, or to a boyfriend who grew up in a professional family. Her father's pasta sauce is so clearly not encompassed by all those beautiful cookbooks featuring Italian food, so clearly not the sauce taught by TV chefs, that it falls under the pale of authenticity's curse – the inauthentic. And yet, to her, if she grows up to be a woman with a big heart, it will always be the sauce of her father's love, and no pasta sauce, no matter how fine the tomatoes, how fresh the basil, how perfect the homemade noodles, will ever touch the authenticity of her father's ketchup pasta – a

381

dish of love, care, and concern offered by a father who might not have had a great education, who might not have had a sophisticated palate, but who tried his best. And this is, in fact, of course, the soul of authentic country cuisines – trying one's best with locally available resources.

When I was close to finishing this paper, I told this story to a friend, by way of explaining to him what I was writing. 'But my mother made pasta with ketchup too,' he said, laughing. Larry's mother, born in China, living in California, used ketchup as the base for a sauce that also included ground meat and garlic. Larry does have a big heart, and thinks back with fondness on his mother's pasta, but having passed over to the social class that determines the international culinary vocabulary, has never made it. Would he make it for a girlfriend on a first date? 'With the hint of a blush,' he answered with a laugh.

English tea
Authenticy, class, and presentation

> Having breakfasted one morning at about this eventful period of time, on her customary viands; to wit, one French roll rasped, one egg new laid (or warranted to be), and one little pot of tea, wherein was infused one little silver scoopful of that herb on behalf of Miss Tox, and one little silver scoopful on behalf of the teapot – a flight of fancy in which good housekeepers delight.
>
> Charles Dickens, *Dombey and Son*

English tea – black tea served with lemon or milk – highlights one of the limitations of modern recipe notation. It does not make explicit factors extrinsic to the recipe that may be essential marks of authenticity to those who are close to the recipe's source. It assumes one understands the social context in which the recipe will be used, and that you know the marks of authenticity peculiar to that context.

There is not one English tea; there are many English teas, but the differences between them have more to do with presentation than with the tea. Charles Dickens' focus on the silver spoon in his description of Miss Tox's tea in *Dombey and Son* is a focus that is essential to reconstructing Miss Tox's tea. Accoutrements are essential to an English tea's authenticity. Does one serve the tea in a mug or cup? And if a cup, is it porcelain? Is the teaspoon silver or stainless steel? Is there a toast rack? Cloth or paper napkin? The underlying recipe, 'one teaspoon per cup, and one for the pot,' fails to touch the actual recipe for making a comforting tea for a man of the old working class, nor does it explain the precise nature of the elaborations that are essential as one moves up the hierarchy of social status to prepare tea that the recipients will recognize as being correct. A culinary lexicographer would classify the many English teas, correlating details of service, including the order in which the milk is added to the cup,[3] in such a way that a filmmaker would be able to find the right recipe for the right character.

Jadvyga zucchini blini[4]
Innovation in the context of subsistence farming

Jadaviga, 'Jadza' to her friends, lives in a small village sixty kilometers from Vilnius, Lithuania. While Lithuania is now an independent country, in Tolstoy's *War and Peace*, Vilnius was the first Russian city occupied by Napoleon, and Jadze lives a short drive from the border with Belarus. She grows most of her own food, and is minimally dependent on the market economy. Blini – a thick tortilla-sized pancake – alternates with rye bread as her staple bread. When Jadza is eating blini, she makes a pile of them in the morning for use throughout the day.

During the Soviet period Jadza took buckwheat from the collective farm, and used that for her blini, but as she no longer has access to this free source of flour, and as tastes have changed since Independence, she makes them out of wheat flour purchased in the market. Her blini recipe is wheat flour, whey, eggs, grated potato, and soda. Most of Yadze's neighbors leaven their blini with yeast, but Yadze, a woman of strong opinions, does not. Whey gives her pancakes a distinctive flavor. Yadze eats blini by tearing off pieces, and using them to scoop up food, for example, scrambled eggs, in the way country families in Mexico use tortillas. The blini of her childhood were made with rye flour and a sour starer.

One year, on a visit I made during the late summer, I was surprised to see zucchinis growing in Yadza's kitchen garden. A friend had given her seeds, she had planted them, and the large squashes they produced compared favorably with her yield from potatoes. Yadza started growing huge zucchinis – massive marrows – which she fed to her pigs, and also began to incorporate into her blini in lieu of potato.

The authority for Yadza's blini in general, and her zucchini blini in particular, comes from her standing as a country woman for whom blini is often her staple starch.[5] Like the other changes to her recipe over time, the change to zucchini was dictated by external circumstances, structured by local tradition, and colored by personality.

Alan Davidson's *Oxford Companion to Food*, has this to say about blini, 'A blini is about 10 cm (4 inches) in diameter, and rather under a centimeter thick. Blini, to be authentic, should be made from a batter of BUCKWHEAT flour leavened with yeast, and further lightened with beaten egg white and whipped cream.'[6] Davidson's blini exist in the context of a meal in which the blini 'are served after the cold *zakuski*. They may be followed by consommé, then pies and then the main meat course…' This is not the blini of a country woman who stores her whey in a galvanized bucket, and uses her pancakes in lieu of cutlery to eat her one-course meals. Conceptually, the encyclopedia format is probably not the best way for the culinary arts to create a systematic presentation of world food. The dictionary that classifies by reporting common practice is better able to describe the complexity of culinary languages and avoids the problem of what to do with the many exemplars of a given dish that fall outside of a single generalization.

Polenta integrale, Zea rostrata valsuganensis[7]
Authenticity and cultivars

> The nourishment of those poor creatures consists of the refuse of the garden, very coarse bread, a kind of meal called polenta, made of Indian corn, which is very nourishing and agreeable, and a little oil; but even in these particulars, they seem to be stinted to very scanty meals.
>
> Tobias Smollett, *Travels Through France And Italy*[8]

The recipe is so simple. Polenta, salt, and water in a ratio of your choosing, such as 1:3 or 1:4 or 1:6, depending on how dense you want the porridge to be. There are two methods for making it. Either boil the polenta, stirring often, until done; or set it in a pot on low heat, on a stove, or in a terra cotta pot in front of a fire, stirring occasionally, until done.

When American cookbook authors present polenta, they often present it as a food implicitly tied to place. Typical of the literature, Marcella Hazan, in *The Classic Italian Cookbook*,[9] writes, 'In country kitchens, *polenta* was more than food, it was a rite. It was made daily in an unlined copper kettle, the *paiolo*, which was always kept hanging at the ready on a hook in the center of the fireplace....' Hazan implicitly promises that if we follow her recipe, what we make in the pot in our kitchen, though it not be touched by fire, and perhaps not elevated to the dignity of a rite, will nonetheless taste the same as the polenta of this mythic old Italian countryside.[10]

Though it is now accurate to speak of a single maize polenta of Northern Italy based on yellow dent corn and a refining process that leaves only the endosperm, until recently there were many polentas. It is unlikely that an Italian country farmer who cooked over an open fire made polenta from refined dent corn. As we have no idea where Hazan's country family lived, let us imagine they lived in the Valsugana Valley in the foothills to the Alps. Until the nineteen-seventies, farmers in the Valsugana Valley, grew a red flint corn called *Zea rostrata valsuganensis*, and locally is either *Rostrato rosso della Valsugana* or *Spin rosso della Valsugana*. Each family made their own selections when saving seeds, so there will have been many landraces, all but a few of which were lost when universal affluence overtook the Valsugana.[11]

Spin rosso della Valsugana was ground into a coarse flour, and then cooked into polenta. Whole grain polenta made with a red flint corn has a different look, taste, and texture than does polenta made from refined dent corn. When one changes the taste and texture of polenta one also changes the taste and texture relationships between the polenta and the stews and sauces it was served with. As this polenta is not bright yellow – it is a little pink – the aesthetics of dishes made with it also differs.

By looking for culinary generalities – polenta in general – rather than to an historically accurate polenta tied to the grain of a specific time period in a specific region, or household, we are allowing to take place subtle, and insidious transformations of meanings. The conceptual simplification of culinary categories simplifies our conception of taste-possibilities, as surely as does the loss of landraces. It also, inadvertently, falsifies the culinary record.

EU protected name schemes
Enshrining authenticity in law

One of the most famous schemes for defining authenticity with respect to a food product is the French system of classifying wines on the basis of where they are grown. This is the French AOC demarcation – *Appellation d'Origine Contrôlée*. This system implies that the principle factor that controls taste is place. More broadly, it associates authenticity with where something is made – and under this guise the EU permitted Newcastle Brown Ale to be registered under EEC regulation No 2081/92 , the EU's regime for Protective Geographic Indicators (PGI). Thus, when, a couple of years after being granted PGI status, Scottish Courage, the corporate entity, decided to close the brewing plant that was the basis for the registration and move it across the river to Dunston, though only two miles from Newcastle-Upon-Tyne, Tyne and Wear, they were forced to apply to the EU to revoke their PGI status.

Official registrations under the EU's PDO (Protected Designiation of Origin), PGI (Protected Geographic Indication), and TSG (Traditional Specialty Guaranteed), are all part of the current interest in identifying authenticity with place – and then in linking current practice to past practice. There is a commercial aspect to the EU program – an attempt to protect names from competition, and thus build in a premium price for producers. In some cases this may build in a premium price for a single producer, like Newcastle Brown Ale, but more often it builds in a premium for any producer in a region.

The underlying philosophy of authenticity that underpins these registrations is articulated in the PDO (Protected Designation of Origin) for *Pane di Altamura* from the Puglia region in Italy. The registration states, 'In conclusion, despite the changes and adaptations that have taken place, the bread currently baked in Altamura in the Murgia region may be regarded as descending directly from the bread of those peasants and shepherds according to a breadmaking tradition that has continued unbroken since the Middle Ages.'[12]

We have no idea what the bread of a shepherd living in and around Altimura would have been like in the Middle Ages, except that it would have had little, if anything, to do with the bread being registered. Whatever the form their bread took, and it might well have been a flatbread, it would have been a mixture of grain cultivars – not one of which is grown today – and weeds.[13] It is illegal under current EU regulations to replicate a field system from the Middle Ages and sell the flour for bread.

The breads of Altamura that were authentic to discrete producers and time periods are not being protected under the EU registration scheme. These would include virtually all the breads that form the intellectual basis for the application – the breads of peasants and shepherds from different time periods, including the recent past, working by hand with flour they grew in their own fields, and baked as they actually baked bread, given differing levels of material culture for different social groups in different time periods. A scholar/baker who revived breads from earlier periods of Altamura's history would not be able to sell them as authentic breads of Altamura.

While the EU registrations vary in specificity, taken as a whole, they are codifying current commercial practice, and thus exclude innovation. New cultural trends in baking may come to Altamura, a brilliant innovative baker may open a bakery, others may follow that baker's lead, but unless Commission Regulation (ED) No 1291/2003 is revoked or amended, it will never be an 'authentic' *Pane di Altamura*.[14]

EU regulations lead to the actual legal banning of authenticy's implicit other as they are based on the concept of a single authenticity, rather than on the concept of multiple authenticities in the context of dynamic change.

Pain anniversaire
Change of social structure – change in meaning

If you take the road through the Alps from Grenoble to Briançon, the last village you get to on the Grenoble side of the mountains is Villard d'Arène. At an altitude of 1650 meters,[15] it is one of highest continually occupied villages in the French Alps. The village was founded towards the end of the eighteenth century. Isolated for much of the year, difficult to get to even in the best of times, situated above the timberline in marginal land, it was a village of pastoralists and subsistence farmers. Rye was the only grain they could grow. As wood was scarce, families could afford to fire the bread oven only once a year. And so, around pig-killing time, the men of the village gathered, drew lots to determine the ordering of the firing, and set the day that baking would begin. During a period of about a week each family baked a year's supply of rye bread. They mixed the dough with hot water in tubs, producing a bread that most of us associate with Russia. The villagers called it *pain bouilli*.

Between the founding of the village in the late eighteenth century and 1961, every household made the bread once a year. It was easily preserved in the mountain air in the form of a desiccated loaf. *Pain bouilli* is such an extreme form of a food that was the product of a very specific geographic and cultural situation that it highlights what is true in general, that one cannot really replicate dishes that are tied to subsistence agriculture[16] because one's relationship to the ingredients, and the making of the dish, are completely different. One way to think of this: When we see the bread on the table, our sweat is not in it.

In 1961, the modern world caught up with Villard d'Arène. For some time it had cost more to produce *pain bouilli* than to buy bread in a bakery. From subsistence bread it had become a luxury. 1961 was the last year the entire village made the bread, and a few years later the tradition ended, to be revived in recent years, by villagers who no longer make a living from agriculture, as a bread baked twice a year in village festivals – largely for tourists. Rather than let the bread dry out, villagers who make it for their own consumption store it in the freezer.

The recipe for a hot-water 'Russian Rye' and the recipe for *pain bouilli* are the same. And yet, to record them as the same bread would mean losing the cultural memory of a group of people whose situation dictated they bake large loaves of rye bread once a year. Here is the recipe for *pain bouilli*. Follow a recipe for making rye bread that uses 100% rye flour mixed with hot water, and leavened in a wooden box. Make a loaf that weighs six or eight pounds (3–4 kg). Let the loaf sit in a cool dry place for six months, and then begin using it. As one begins to chip at that loaf, a constellation of authentic dishes will find new life.

Milk of the Samburu
Authenticity as it was

The Samburu are a tribe of nomadic pastoralists who live in northern Kenya. They are related to the Masai, whom one might call their more famous cousins. Milk is the preferred staple food. It is many years since the modern world began encroaching on Samburu culture, and to speak of the Samburu as living the ancient life of the pastoralist, untouched by modern life would be false. On the other hand, many features of their ancient way of life are intact, including the taste of their milk.

The Samburu keep cows, goats, sheep, and increasingly, camels. The animals are milked into wooden containers. What differentiates Samburu milk from the milk we are used to, is that as they live where water is scarce they sterilize their wooden milking containers with burning sticks, rather than with water. Milk is served fresh, lightly fermented, like *kiefer*, and fermented, like yoghurt. There is rarely surplus, so preserved milk products are not common.

To sterilize the wooden milking container, it is rinsed, leaving a small amount of water in the bottom. A couple small sticks are put in a fire. When the ends begin to burn, they are popped into the container, and its lid is then replaced. The container is shaken, the top removed, the sticks taken out, and they are fired again. This is repeated until steam builds up in the wooden container and the containter's lid pops off with a little 'puff.'

All the woods used to clean the containers have medicinal qualities. For the purpose of cleaning the container, the taste they leave behind is the quality that is sought after. Of the primary woods used, there is a hierarchy, with *sarai (Balanites orbicularis)* providing a mild sweet, lightly smoky taste, and *loisui (Zanthoxylum usambarence)* leaving the strongest and least favorite taste. Of the seven woods used by the Samburu in the region around Wamba, the area I know the best, the woods are favored in the following order:

sarai (Balanites orbicularis)
lngeriyioi (Olea africana/europaea)

ldumei (Maerua crassifolia)
lgilai orok (Teclea simplicifolia)
lgilai (Teclea nobilus)
lmasei (Tarenna graveolens)
loisui (Zanthoxylum usambarence)

Between the different types of milk, the different types of woods used to clean the container, the degree to which the milk is fresh or fermented and, if fermented, the nature of the particular strains of fermenting bacteria, every family's milk is different. All this is under immediate threat from modernization. Already, on my last visit, in 2004, for the first time women selling milk in the villages were using plastic containers – and they were using them expressly to exclude the taste of smoke so their product would appeal to ethnic groups from other parts of Kenya.[17]

Conclusion

Every dish made by every person is its own complex world of taste, texture, and association. Every dish is imbued with its own authenticity. Pasta with ketchup is not an authentic pasta of an Italian peasant's farm, but it is an authentic pasta of an urban English city. In fact, if we looked for it, we are likely to find it all over the world. We do not degrade our culinary vocabulary by cataloging the culinary world as it is, in fact, we enrich that vocabulary, just as English is enriched by every addition to its language. The more broadly with think of what really makes a dish, and the more carefully we record and classify authenticities, the more dynamic a foundation we will establish for future culinary generations.

It should not be a surprise that just as the life of the subsistence farmer came to an end in Europe, there was a revival of interest in foods that could trace their origins to the countryside. But the countryside can no longer serve as a living source for culinary inspiration, or as a living measure of culinary authority. It is already barely possible to make an accurate record of foods that were common only forty years ago. Everywhere, there is simplification of ingredients, and an imposition of mechanical regularity on culinary products. Even in the countryside.

We will soon all have to turn our intellectual energies away from what was – and begin inventing new things. The more open the intellectual framework for describing culinary experience, the more broadly we understand authenticity, the closer we embrace the eccentric, energetic, and creative Humpty Dumpty, a talking egg who was not afraid to define his own path, the stronger will be our journey into the next phase of culinary invention.

388

Notes

1. The Baroque German bow can play true chords, while the modern Italian chord cannot. Some argue that chords in most Bach violin works were intended to be played as chords, not as arpeggios, and so an 'authentic' hearing of Bach works for solo violin requires the use of the German Baroque Bow.

2. 'What Price Authenticity?', William Hamilton, *New York Times*, June 16, 2005 discusses the difference in attitude towards restoration between the disciplines of Modern American furniture, and antique American furniture. The article discusses a heavily restored modern piece of furniture that sold at auction for $3.8 million dollars, but if it had been an 18th-century piece it would not have been considered authentic because of the extensive restoration.

3. The Queen of England, according to the fact-checkers at the American magazine *Saveur*, pours the milk into her teacup first. The young wife in George Hitchock's film *Rebecca* also pours her milk into the teacup first, and so it can be assumed that Hitchock's fact-checkers ascertained that this was the proper way for a young woman living in an English country house in the 1940s to make tea. One can be certain that for Miss Tox the order in which Mr. Dombey placed the milk in his cup was the order in which she placed milk in hers, as the Queen's practice today determined this aspect of the service recommended by *Saveur* in their recent article on cream teas.

4. As the standard flour for blini in Lithuania is now wheat flour, blini made from wheat flour are simply called 'blini.' When they are made with rye or buckwheat, then this is mentioned in the name. The Lithuanian spelling for blini is blyni.

5. As it turns out, after a couple of years, Yadze stopped growing zucchini and went back to focusing on potatoes, so this was an experiment of short duration, and was thus not adopted by neighbors.

6. Of the three recipes for blini included in the Joyce Toomre's edition of Elena Molokhovet's *A Gift to Young Houewives* (Indiana University Press, 1998), pages 320–322, two use buckwheat flour, one uses wheat flour, and none call for whipped cream or egg whites.

7. I asked my friend from the Valsugana who grows *Spin rosso della Valsugana* for his family's polenta to send a kilo to an American miller/farmer. This maize is now in limited commercial production in the United States. It is not commercially available in Italy.

8. <http://www.gutenberg.org/dirs/etext00/ttfai10.txt>.

9. Hazan, Marcella, *The Classic Italian Cookkbook: The art of Italian cooking and the Italian art of eating* (Alfred Knopf, New York, 1979), p. 204–205. Marcella Hazan refers to 'polenta flour.' This is typical of recent cookbook authors. While she differentiates between a fine- and coarse-grain, she does not clarify whether this is a whole grain flour, or whether bran and other parts of the grain may have been removed. In fact, commercial polenta is almost invariably only the endosperm.

10. The transformation of meaning implicit in moving a subsistence starch from the center of a poor person's plate to a side dish of the urban elite is a separate issue of authenticity.

11. The story may be more complex than this. Other varieties of maize may also have been grown. So far, this is the only one I have identified.

12. Commision Regulation (EC) No 1291/2003 of 18 July 2003 <http://europa.eu.int/eur-lex/lex/LexUriServ/LexUriServ.do?uri=CELEX:32003R1291:EN:HTML> Commission Regulation (EC) No 1291/2003 of 18 July 2003, Official Journal L 181 , 19/07/2003 P. 0012 - 0019

13. I am extrapolating to Southern Italy from the work John Letts has done with late medieval grains in England. See his work, Letts, John B., *Smoke Blackened Thatch: A unique source of late medieval plant remains from Southern England* (The University of Reading, 1999).

14. Neapolitan pizza has also been protected by the EU. While one might have expected, over time, for the nature of Neapolitan pizza to shift, as we have, historically, seen other foods shift in character, today's culinary culture appears to be looking for a new Classical Cuisine, one in which definitions are unchangeable.

15. Maget, Marcel, *Le Pain anniversaire à Villard d'Arène en Oisans* (Edition des Archives Contemporaines, Paris, 1989). This work fully documents the breads in this village. It is based on historic research and field visits to the village between 1948 and 1968 when the last bread was baked following the

exigencies of the traditional village cycles.

16. This applies to any food that depends for its meaning on a complex social setting – a medieval banquet provides another example. In a medieval banquet the food that was set in front of your place related to your social position, and it therefore carried a message that we cannot feel.

17. I brought a piece of *sarai* back from Kenya, and have done some experimenting with it, and with fruit woods. Custard made from lightly smoked milk is delicious.

390

The North American Indian Restaurant Menu: The Triumph of Inauthenticity

Colleen Taylor Sen

Until modern times, India did not have a tradition of public dining or a restaurant culture. The restaurant as a distinct institution developed in at least two places: Paris at the end of the 18th century and China during the Sung dynasty (960–1279). Restaurants, unlike taverns or inns, offer diners a choice, or, as the French food writer Anthelme Brillat-Savarin put it, allow people to eat 'when they wanted, what they wanted, and how much they wanted, knowing in advance how much this would cost.'[1] Restaurants in post-revolutionary France and Sung China had extensive printed menus, sometimes listing hundreds of dishes; served alcohol beverages; were elegantly decorated; and had private rooms in addition to common dining areas. Haifeng and Hangchow, the great capital cities of Sung China, were home to hundreds of restaurants, many serving regional delicacies. Their patrons were wealthy merchants and officials who valued connoisseurship and experimentation: 'Mobile, experimental, and egalitarian in temper, little influenced by dietary taboos, they brought about the creation of a Chinese cuisine.'[2]

However, in India, an equally ancient civilization, the literature contains no accounts of similar sophisticated dining establishments. Eating out was tolerated largely as a necessity rather than valued as a luxury or new experience. Hindu and Muslim religious and social prohibitions related to food imposed restrictions on what one could eat, who could prepare it, and with whom one could eat. Many wealthy merchants were orthodox Hindus or Jains who were subject to extremely stringent dietary restrictions. Foods forbidden to Jains, for example, include meat, eggs, onions, garlic, root vegetables, fruits with seeds, and alcohol.

The Indian subcontinent always had establishments that served traveling pilgrims and merchants, students and other people living away from home, and no doubt housewives who wanted a break from cooking. Merchants and other travelers carried their meals with them or stopped at inns that provided a place to rest and basic meals. Hindu temples served, and still serve, vegetarian meals to pilgrims and other worshippers as an outgrowth of the offerings made to the deities. Some temples, notably those at Udupi in Karnataka, became famous for certain dishes. Texts from the Mauryan dynasty (300 BC to AD 300), when India was the wealthiest country in the world, describe public inns, taverns, and shops that served cooked meats and sweets. Later European visitors to India marveled at the abundance of markets, shops and bakeries 'where almost every variety of cooked food and uncooked victuals could be bought at a reasonable price.'³

These traditions continue to this day. In Punjab, Haryana, Rajasthan, and other states in northern and central India, highways and main roads are lined with *dhabas* – small wayside stands patronized by truck drivers that serve five or six dishes in large brass pots and sometimes offer a bed for the night. Some *dhabas* are strictly vegetarian; others serve meat dishes. Typical dishes are *palak paneer*, spinach with cheese; *malai kofta*, vegetable balls in a creamy gravy; and *mahkani dal*, a rich black bean stew, accompanied by *chapattis* or *nan* (flat wheat breads). The standard *dhaba* drink is *chai* – tea boiled with milk and spices to produce a strong coarse brew. The patrons traditionally sit on hand-woven rope cots. In the past decade, *dhaba* food has become fashionable among young urban Indians, and some have even gone upscale by adding air conditioning, tables and chairs, and printed menus. In Chicago, New York, and other North American cities, *dhaba* denotes a small eatery that provides quick and cheap food around the clock to taxi drivers from the Indian subcontinent and elsewhere. Meat dishes feature prominently in their menus, which are posted on a wall.

In south India, people living away from home could take their meals at military hotels, which serve meat and egg dishes, or Udupi hotels that offer only vegetarian fare.⁴ Udupi restaurants open early in the morning to serve breakfast, an important meal in south India. Their menus feature *idlis*, steamed lens-shaped breads made of fermented rice and lentil flour; *dosas*, large pancakes also made from rice and lentils; *sambar*, a thin spiced soup of lentils, potatoes and other vegetables; and coconut chutney. The proper accompaniment is foamy south-Indian-style coffee, which resembles French *café au lait*. Additional items are added for dinner. In the 1930s K.K. Rao opened Woodlands restaurant in Madras to serve south Indian food in a more elegant setting. The prototype of middle-class south Indian restaurants, Woodlands opened branches in India and abroad. One of its specialties was an enormous yard-wide paper-thin *dosa* that has become a south Indian restaurant staple.

India also has a long tradition of street foods that are eaten on the spot or taken home for a light meal taken in the late afternoon. Many items are fried. Typical north Indian snacks include *samosas*, pastries with a meat or vegetable filling; breads, sometimes filled with vegetables; *pakoras*, chopped vegetables deep fried in chickpea flour; vegetable patties; and *chaat*, a blend of boiled, diced potatoes and chick peas flavored with lime juice, tamarind, coriander, and spices. Some stalls serve meat kabobs, roasted on skewers and served with Indian flat breads. In western India, vendors specialize in crunchy deep fried snacks and roasted spiced nuts. The most famous stands are those on Mumbai's Chowpatti Beach, where a local specialty is *bhelpuri*, a spicy snack made from crispy noodles, puffed rice, tomato, onion, boiled potatoes, coriander and tamarind chutney.

The emergence of the restaurant in India

Western-style restaurants came to India in the late 19th century. Around 1890,

Federico Peliti, an Italian confectioner, opened his eponymous restaurant in Calcutta (the capital of British India from the early 18th century until 1912), which became a favorite lunch spot for the city's business community. After World War I the Swiss Angelo Firpo opened his famous restaurant on Chowringhee, Calcutta's main street. Such establishments remained centers of Calcutta social and culinary life until the 1950s and 1960s when many closed down. Their menus consisted mainly of Western-style dishes, plus a few quasi-Indian dishes such as mulligatawny soup and curry. A 1944 luncheon menu from Firpo's (a popular spot among American servicemen during World War II), for example, features steak and kidney pudding, sausage and mashed potatoes, a selection of cold meats, hamburger steak and onions, lasagna au gratin, cold meat pies, and fried bekty (a local fish) with tartare sauce. A third of the menu was devoted to alcoholic beverages. Calcutta, once home to more than 80,000 Chinese, also had a thriving Chinese restaurant culture. Restaurants such as Nanking and Beiping served Chinese regional cuisine as well as a chili-enhanced Indian version. After the India-China war in the early 1960s, many Chinese emigrated abroad and the number of restaurants diminished, although Indian Chinese food remains a staple on club and hotel menus. Today Thai food is replacing Chinese food as a fashionable alternative among urban foodies.

In the countryside, travelling officials took their meals at *dak* bungalows. The cooks often had to produce meals on the spot using local ingredients, so that omelettes, roast chicken, and chicken curry were standard fare. The British also left behind a legacy of clubs, such as Delhi's Gymkhana Club and Bombay's Byculla Club, which served mainly Western dishes with a few Indian touches, such as a mulligatawny soup, kabobs, or a curry.

Hotels in large Indian cities had dining rooms that served Western food to tourists, travelers, and people who wanted to entertain outside their homes. However, until Independence in 1947, India had no restaurants where middle-class Indians and tourists could order Indian cuisine from a menu and dine in an attractive setting. In 1947, India's most famous restaurant, Moti Mahal, opened near the Red Fort in New Delhi. Its founder was Kundan Lal Gujral, a refugee from Peshawar (now part of Pakistan) near the Afghan border. Kundan Lal was the inventor of tandoori chicken and butter chicken, and the creator of the tandoori style of cuisine that has become a hallmark of Indian restaurants in India and abroad.

In Kundan Lal's native region, a common method of preparing chicken and goat was to roast pieces of meat on skewers over hot coals in a tandoor or tanoor, a large clay oven buried in the ground that originated in Iran or Central Asia. In Delhi, he experimented with different designs until he came up with an aboveground version that would work in a restaurant kitchen. To make the food more palatable to Indian tastes, Kundan Lal created a distinctive blend of spices that includes ground coriander seeds, black pepper, and a mild red pepper that gives tandoori chicken its characteristic red color. Pieces of chicken were marinated in this mixture and yogurt and roasted

393

on skewers in the tandoor. To please richer palates (and, some claim, to use left-over tandoori chicken), he created butter chicken — pieces of roasted chicken cooked in a tomato, cream and butter sauce. Other menu items included tandoor-roasted breads, rice pullaos, kabobs, and various curries. The early menus of Moti Mahal did not organize the dishes into distinct courses.

Many of the refugees who came to New Delhi in 1947 following the partition of British India into India and Pakistan were enterprising Punjabis, who launched small businesses, including food stalls that did not require a lot of capital. Some of them expanded into small neighborhood restaurants and eventually into more sophisticated establishments. The restaurant chains Kwalities and Gaylords are the best known examples.

A mainstay of their menus was the food of Punjab, a rich agricultural region known as the breadbasket of India. Punjabi cuisine is simple, robust and closely linked to the land. The staple is wheat, made into bread, supplemented by dairy products and cauliflower, peas, carrots, greens, and other seasonable vegetables. Over half of all Hindu Punjabis are vegetarians. Spicing is straightforward rather than subtle; a common sauce is based on onions, tomatoes, garlic and ginger. A distinctive feature of Punjabi cuisine is the use of *panir* – milk solids pressed under a weight and cut into cubes – as a replacement for meat in dishes with peas, spinach and other vegetables. The Punjabi national dish is thick black *makhani dal*, a rich stew of black lentils, kidney beans, butter, and cream.

As Camelia Panjabi noted in her 1996 paper to the Oxford Food Symposium, this style of cuisine was taught at the catering colleges set up by the Government of India in the 1960s. As the graduates moved into the workforce, they introduced it into five star hotels, which in the 1970s and 1980s became centers of dining and social activity for newly affluent urban dwellers.

Another important landmark in the creation of the modern Indian restaurant was the founding in 1913 of Karim's in Old Delhi by Haji Karimuddin, a descendant of cooks who worked for the Moghul Emperors. Today the fourth generation operates the restaurant, which has two other branches in the capital. The founder's goal, stated on the menu, was 'to bring the Royal Food to the common man.' Recently Karim's has become a fashionable place for tourists and locals (it even has its own website: <http://www.karimhoteldelhi.com/profile.html>), but in the past it was mainly a haunt for aficionados of the north Indian Muslim style of cooking, sometimes called Moghlai. Since this term is widely used on Indian restaurant menus, it requires some explanation.

The original food served at the court of the Moghul emperors (1526–1857) was a fusion of Persian and Indian culinary styles. Elaborate Persian meat and rice dishes were transformed in Indian kitchens by the addition of aromatic spices such as cardamom, cloves, cinnamon, and nutmeg and rare and expensive ingredients, including like rosewater, saffron, and thinly pounded gold and silver leaf.[5] Cooking techniques were complex: Some dishes took hours or days to make and involved adding spices at many points in the cooking process. Each dish was made with its own distinctive spices. To make *biryani*, for example, long-grained rice was parboiled, sometimes in meat broth; pieces of lamb or chicken were cooked in a mixture of onions, ginger, crushed almonds, spiced yogurt, and clarified butter; the meat and rice were layered in a pot, sprinkled with saffron threads and baked slowly in an oven the aromas to penetrate the rice. Before serving, the dish was decorated with nuts, raisins, and gold foil. Pilaus or pulaos are a less complex but more delicate rice dish often made with vegetables instead of meat.[6]

Another typical dish was *rogan josh*, an aromatic meat curry with a creamy gravy, which can be made with as many as twenty spices. *Qorma* or *korma* was a richly spiced dish in a gravy made of ground almonds and cream. (*Korma* also refers to a method of cooking similar to braising in which meats are marinated in yogurt and spices and then cooked over very low heat until a thick sauce is formed.) The Moghul kitchens also served many varieties of *kabobs* (a Persian word meaning 'without water') – ground or whole pieces of meat flavored with spices and grilled over coals or baked. Meals were accompanied by a variety of flat breads, mostly made from wheat flour and sautéed in ghee, deep fried or baked in a tandoor, and sometimes filled with meat, vegetables and spices.

On contemporary restaurant menus the word Moghlai or Moghul has become synonymous with meat dishes in rich gravies, often with such fanciful names as *Akbari murgh masala* (Akbar's spiced chicken), *Jahangiri qorma* (Jahangir's korma), or *Shahjahani murgh* (Shah Jahan's chicken). Because it is not economic for kitchen staff to spend hours grinding spices or days cooking dishes, these dishes are usually only an insipid version of the original. Some cooks use just one or two spice mixtures for a wide range of dishes.

395

The modern Indian restaurant menu in North America
In North America, restaurants serving the food of the Indian subcontinent can be categorized in the following way:

Standard north Indian/Pakistani restaurants;
South Indian vegetarian restaurants;
Dhabas;
Sweet and snack shops;
Restaurants serving regional specialties (Gujarati, Kerala, Hyderabadi, Bengali, Goan) either exclusively or along with standard dishes;
Upscale 'fusion' restaurants.

This paper will focus exclusively on the first category, since they are the most widespread and are what most Americans and Canadians would equate with an Indian restaurant. Typical names such as Taj Mahal, Moti Mahal, Taj Palace, Jewel of India, and Maharajah imply a continuation of the imperial culinary tradition. Their menus are exclusively in English, the *lingua franca* of Indians, although some places include Hindi names to lend authenticity. There is no equivalent to the separate menus in Chinese that are available in many Chinese restaurants. The cook may adjust the 'spiciness' at the request of the customer but except in rare cases, he will not prepare special dishes for discerning gourmets, as the chef in a good Chinese restaurant might do. Many North American Indian restaurants serve a lunch buffet for a fixed charge.

Research is needed on the history of Indian restaurants in North America. The earliest restaurants were probably opened in New York City by Bangladeshi seamen who jumped ship and have a tradition of serving as cooks, first for the Portuguese, later for the British. In the 1960s and 1970s Indian businessmen began to open restaurants in large North American cities. Their models were Gaylords and Moti Mahal, which would have been familiar to their Indian clientele.

However, some significant changes in the menu were needed to attract and retain non-Indian customers. What meals are eaten and what constitutes a meal vary widely throughout the Indian subcontinent; generally, middle-class people eat four meals a day: breakfast; lunch, which is often the main meal of the day; a late afternoon snack with milk or tea; and dinner, which is similar to but smaller than lunch. Dishes are not served sequentially but are laid in the table simultaneously, though there may be two or three groupings. Food is not portioned on a plate; it is served in dishes from which diners help themselves or are served by a female member of the family or a servant.

No single dish dominates an Indian meal, as it does in the West, where a leg of lamb or roast beef may have pride of place. An Indian meal is centered on a starch, either rice or grain.[7] Grains are usually accompanied by pulses (beans, peas, and lentils) prepared as *dal* – a boiled, spiced, soup-like dish that is universally eaten throughout the subcontinent. Small amounts of meat, fish, and vegetables enhance the taste and texture of the main grain. Only 25–30% of Indians are vegetarians, though the proportion varies widely from 5% in Kerala and West Bengal to 70% in Gujarat. However, meat is expensive and thus limited, and even the affluent eat relatively little meat by Western standards. The vegetable and meat dishes are accompanied by small portions of condiments, such as yogurt, fruit and vegetable chutneys, and sweet, sour, or pungent pickles. The standard drink is water; wine or beer are rarely consumed with a meal except among very Westernized people. In some parts of India, a meal concludes with yogurt or buttermilk to aid digestion. Soup, salads, and desserts are not part of a traditional Indian meal.

Although the early Indian restaurants such as Moti Mahal and Karim's initially preserved the Indian meal pattern, North American restaurant owners had to fit Indian dishes into the standard Western restaurant format of appetizers, soups, salads, entrees/main courses, side dishes, breads, and desserts. But because Indian dishes do not naturally fit into this pattern, the restaurateurs came up with some inventive solutions. The contemporary North American Indian restaurant draws upon a heterogeneous assortment of levels and traditions – snacks and street food, home-style dishes, tandoori cuisine, quasi-Moghlai food, and various regional cuisines.

Appetizers: Since this concept is alien to an Indian meal, restaurant owners converted street foods and snacks into appetizers. Popular items include *samosas* and *pakoras*; *shami kabobs*, fried patties made from ground meat and chickpeas; and *bhel puri*, which is sometimes classified as a salad. Some restaurants offer patrons free baskets of *papads* or *pappadum* – crunchy flat disks made from spiced lentil flour originally from south India – to nibble on while they wait. Others sell them as appetizers with coriander and tamarind sauces,

Soups: The most common menu items are mulligatawny and *shorbas*. Mulligatawny soup, a British creation, was originally a thin, very spicy lentil broth called *milagu-thannir*, or pepper water, in Tamil. Indian cooks in British households transformed it into a rich meat soup flavored with onions, spices, and sometimes coconut milk or cream. Mulligatawny soup became a standard opening course at formal dinners in British India and a part of mainstream British cuisine. (Recipes can be found in many 19th-century English cookbooks, including those by Eliza Acton and Mrs. Beeton.) The version served in North American Indian restaurants is a watery lentil or vegetarian soup that bears little resemblance to either of the original versions.

397

Arabic in origin, the word *shorba* is employed throughout the Islamic world, including Persia, to denote a substantial meat-based soup. *Shorbas* are served at the end of the day to break fast during Ramadan; during Moghul times, they were part of court banquets. In Indian restaurants the word is used interchangeably with soup, as in a tomato *shorba*. Pakistani restaurant menus often feature chicken corn soup, a borrowing from Chinese restaurants.

Salads, Sides and Accompaniments: *Dal*, the *sine qua non* of an Indian meal in India, is missing from many restaurant menus or else is relegated to the status of a soup or a side dish. In a concession to North American tastes, many Indian restaurants serve a house salad made of lettuce, which is virtually never eaten in India. Occasionally they serve *raita* — whipped yogurt with chopped cucumbers or potatoes — a standard north Indian condiment. Some, but by no means all, restaurants offer chutneys and pickles.

Main Courses: The largest part of an Indian restaurant menu consists of entrees (main courses), often divided into vegetarian and nonvegetarian dishes. Vegetarian dishes typically include such Punjabi dishes as as *palak paneer, malai kofta, alu matter gobi, saag* or *matter paneer*, which are also the mainstays of lunch buffets. Most Indian restaurants do not serve pork or beef. Goat meat, called mutton in India, is only occasionally found on North American Indian menus.

Alternatively, dishes may be organized by the style of cooking: curries, tandoori, Mohglai, kabobs, and the like. Curry is a universal term for any meat, fish or vegetable dish in a gravy. But curry also has a precise meaning: In British India, curry was a stew made by frying pieces of meat, usually chicken, in onions and ready-made curry powder and then adding water or broth and sometimes tomatoes to make a thin gravy. Curry was a popular dish at British clubs and army messes, where it was served with plain boiled rice and accompanied by nuts, raisins, chutney and other condiments. Today a classic curry is rarely found in Indian restaurants in India or abroad.

Popular restaurant Moghlai dishes include *korma, rogan josh, biryanis,* and *pulaos,* although these are pale imitations of the originals. Tandoori dishes feature prominently and some restaurants display the tandoor behind glass so that patrons can watch their dishes being made. Chicken, lamb, fish, shrimp, paneer, and vegetables are all baked in the tandoor. Kabobs are sometimes classified as tandoori dishes, sometimes as Moghlai dishes. The most popular are *boti kabobs,* chunks of meat, usually lamb; *seekh kabob,* minced lamb formed into long ovals on skewers; *pasanda* or *pasinda kabob,* long thin strips of lamb threaded on skewers; and *chapli kabob* (sometimes called *bihari kabob*), flat pieces of pounded meat.

Most menus include a few dishes from other regions of India, although the selection is very limited. For some reason, chicken or lamb *jalfrezi* and *vindaloo* figure prominently. *Jalfrezi* is a dry, hot Anglo-Indian dish in which meat is marinated in dried spices and cooked with chilies, onions, and green peppers without a liquid. *Vindaloo* (from the Portuguese *vinha de alhos,* vinegar and garlic) is a famous hot and sour Goan dish that is authentically made with pork. Some restaurants serve south Indian breakfast specialties such as *idli, dosa,* and *sambar* as main courses.

Breads: Menus may feature as many as twenty breads, which are very popular among North American diners. Although there are hundreds of kinds of breads on the subcontinent made from many varieties of grain, including millets, sorghum, rice and lentils, and corn, restaurant breads are usually flat, unleavened or slightly leavened north Indian wheat breads: puffy *chapatti* and *phulka; parathas,* sautéed on a griddle; deep-fried puffy *puri; bhatura,* a round deep fried bread; and *nan* or tandoori *roti* baked in a tandoor.

Desserts: Indians have the world's largest collective sweet tooth. Every festival, wedding, birth, social visit, or other happy occasion is an excuse to eat sweets. Most are made of sugar, milk, and clarified butter. In India, however, sweets are rarely served as a dessert course following a meal at home. Only a handful of sweets regularly appear on Indian restaurant menus: *gulab juman,* a Bengali sweet made from *chhanna* (farmer's cheese) balls in a sugar syrup; *rasmalai, chhanna* disks in a milk sauce; mango or pistachio *kulfi,* cones of frozen milk flavored with mango or pistachio; carrot *halwa* made from sugar and semolina; *kheer,* a kind of rice pudding; and ice cream.

Drinks: Many restaurants serve *lassi*, a yogurt drink that can be either sweet and mango-flavored or salty. An increasing number of restaurants serve wine and beer, sometimes from India. A standard restaurant beverage is *chai*, also called *masala* tea or *masala chai* – a concoction of inferior-grade tea leaves, milk, water, and spices boiled together.

Conclusion

The standard North American Indian restaurant is a hybrid creation, drawing upon many culinary traditions and levels, which reflect their owners efforts to adapt Indian dishes into a Western meal template. However, as the menus become standardized, this style of cuisine is becoming a distinctive cuisine on its own, just as American-style Chinese or Mexican food have done.

Bibliography

Achaya, K.T., *Indian Food: A Historical Companion* (New Delhi: Oxford University Press, 1994).
——, *A Historical Dictionary of Indian Food* (New Delhi: Oxford University Press, 1998).
Burton, David, *The Raj at Table* (London: Faber and Faber, 1993).
Conlon, Frank, 'Dining out in Bombay,' *Consuming Modernity: Public Culture in a South Asian World*, ed. Carol A. Breckenridge (Minneapolis: University of Minnesota Press, 1995), pp. 90–127.
Das Gupta, Minakshie, Bunny Gupta, and Jaya Chaliha, *The Calcutta Cookbook* (New Delhi: Penguin, 1995).
Davidson, Alan, *The Oxford Companion to Food* (Oxford: Oxford University Press, 1999).
Freeman, Michael, 'Sung,' *Food in Chinese Culture: Anthropological and Historical Perspectives*, ed. K.C. Chang (New Haven: Yale University Press, 1977), 141–192.
Gujral, Monish, *Moti Mahal's Tandoori Trail* (New Delhi: Roli Books, 2004).
Panjabi, Camelia, 'The Non-Emergence of the Regional Foods of India,' unpublished outline of paper presented to the Oxford Food Symposium, 'Food on the Move', September 1996.
Prakash, Om, *Food and Drinks in Ancient India* (New Delhi: Munshiram Manoharlal, 1961).
Sen, Colleen Taylor, *Food Culture in India* (Westport: Greenwood Press, 2004).
——, 'In Delhi, it's the Moti Mahal,' *Christian Science Monitor*, October 5, 1988.
Spang, Rebecca L, *The Invention of the Restaurant* (Cambridge: Harvard University Press, 2001).
Westrip, Joyce, *Moghul Cooking: India's Courtly Cuisine* (London: Serif, 1997).

Notes

1. cited in Davidson, p. 660.
2. Freeman, p. 175.
3. Conlon, p. 93.
4. In Indian English, the word hotel denotes 'any establishment, even a roadside stall, open to all and serving meals'. Nigel B. Hankin, *Hanklyn-Janklyn, or A Stranger's Rumble-Tumble Guide to Some Words, Customs, and Quiddities Indian and Indo-British* (New Delhi: Banyan Books, 1992), p. 88.
5. Despite the lavishness of meals at the court, described by Abul Fazl Allami, *A'In-I-Akbari*, vol. 1, trans. H. Blochmann (New Delhi: Atlantic Publishers, 1989), the emperor Akbar led an austere existence. According to Abul Fazl, he ate only once in 24 hours, frequently fasted, and would have

been a vegetarian had he not been under so much pressure. One of his favorite dishes was *khichri*, a simple dish of rice and lentils, which was a favorite of his descendants.

6. However, the distinction between biryani and pilau is not clear cut and is the subject of debate on culinary message boards.

7. On average, Indians get 92% of their calories from grains and vegetable products and only 8% from animal products (meat, diary products, eggs), around one-tenth the level in China and the U.S. Food and Agriculture Organization of the United Nations, FAOSTAT: FAO Statistics Databases. Available at uttp://apps.fao.org.

400

Authentic Food: A Philosophical Approach

Nicholas Silich

What do we mean when we talk about food or cookery as being authentic? We generally think of something along the lines of local dishes prepared by local people, or the way a dish was originally prepared. If we look at cookery programs on television, the presenters often say that a foreign dish is authentic, in spite of their having made it themselves: that it is genuine. To put it more abstractly, we use authentic when it comes to food in the sense of, really proceeding from its reputed source or author.

If we look at this from a philosophical point of view, in order to practically produce authentic food according to that definition, we would have to know the reputed source or author of the way of cooking something. This leads to the obvious problem that, if we follow it through to a complete conclusion, we do not know the source of most dishes, or indeed, who the author of a recipe was. Why is steak and kidney pie more authentic just because we make it the way our grandmother did? Why is an onion soup authentic because we use a pound of butter – which I recommend strongly – rather than 1 ounce? I would surmise that it is more authentic, but I do not know that it is. But to the philosophically inclined, such guessing is just not quite enough.

This is why I want to suggest a different usage of the term authentic when it comes to food. As it seems to be a recurring pattern in philosophy, I will have a look at what the Greeks said. The Greek equivalent of authentic describes a person who does a thing himself. That is exactly the usage I propose to use. Practically, that means that, if we have the raw ingredients and prepare, chop, cook, season and do whatever else is involved in cookery ourselves, it is more authentic than sticking a pre-made meal in the oven. It is more authentic still, if you plant and harvest your own plants, or rear your own animals and slaughter them yourself. Equally if you go out yourself to hunt, fish and gather.

Unfortunately this only works in an ideal world: we do not all have the possibilities and indeed the time to do it all ourselves. So we have to find a way of adjusting the original Greek idea to our needs. What would the next best thing to preparing food yourself be? Knowing how to do it and understanding what happens. A dish you eat and know how to prepare will be more authentic to you than one you know nothing about; your Grandmother's steak and kidney pie is still more authentic to you than the one you get at a supermarket. Knowing the farm your leg of lamb comes from is more authentic than just getting one at random, also knowing how it is bred, slaughtered, disjointed, hung &c. A problem that can arise from allowing knowledge rather than just doing, is that, to a chemist, artificial food could be the most authentic. The only answer is that, with any definition of authenticity, I suggest the main criterion for what we eat remains taste – and that I am happy not to be a chemist.

The consequence of this is that food in general gets more authentic the more we occupy ourselves with it. Look at where it comes from, what has been done to it and how we treat it. Go to farms and see for ourselves what happens there; go to slaughter-houses or butchers' and see how animals are turned into nondescript pieces of meat. Go fishing, hunting and gathering to see how animals behave if left to their own devices. Authenticity is, in this sense a quality of eaters rather than one of the food eaten.

Eating in Eden: *The Jonny-Cake Papers of 'Shepherd Tom'*

Keith Stavely and Kathleen Fitzgerald

In January, 1879, the *Providence Journal* invited Thomas Robinson Hazard – or, as he liked to call himself, Shepherd Tom – to share his thoughts on 'white Indian meal', which, the paper noted, was 'very nice, as all Rhode Islanders know'. Hazard began his published acceptance of the Journal's invitation by excluding the city with which the paper identified itself, along with most of the rest of Rhode Island, from the domain of white cornmeal authenticity. 'Nowhere else on the globe' but in Newport and Washington counties (the latter being due west across Narragansett Bay from Newport) 'was the real article ever to be found'. The implication, not entirely whimsical, was that only some, not 'all Rhode Islanders', were capable of authentic participation in the state's traditions of cornmeal cookery. Hazard proceeded to compose almost four hundred pages, in twenty-six 'bakings', in amplification of this claim to culinary supremacy and purity for the small subregion – within what was already the smallest state in the federal union – in which he had himself lived his entire life.[1]

Full understanding and appreciation of *The Jonny-Cake Papers* requires some basic orientation to its author's family history and life experiences. From the late 17th century, the Hazards were major landholders in southern Rhode Island, an area known as the Narragansett Country. Thomas Robinson Hazard's great-grandfather, Robert (*d.* 1762), was, in a manner characteristic of the region, a large-scale commercial farmer. Utilizing the labor of African and Indian slaves and indentured servants, Robert Hazard produced enough cheese, wool, and horses to export large surpluses to the West Indies, itself a society based entirely on slave labor.[2] Hazard's grandfather, also Thomas (1720–1798; nicknamed College Tom), declared his opposition to slavery in the 1740s and freed his own slaves. While this gesture produced a brief period of estrangement between College Tom and his father, the quarrel was soon patched up, and anti-slavery College Tom ran his farm pretty much as slaveholding Robert had run his, with major production of wool and cheese and commercial marketing of at least the cheese. Although College Tom's farmhands were not slaves, this was more a matter of the form than of the content of labor relations, for he remained in effect the master of a number of Africans, who 'had descended with the land and were dependents upon the estate'. One of these African slaves-in-all-but-name was a cook, Phillis, whose death was recorded in 1772.[3]

Shepherd Tom's father, Rowland Hazard (1763–1835), was the fifth child of College Tom. Rowland became a merchant engaged in the West Indies trade that had long been central to the Rhode Island economy. His firm operated from both Newport and Charleston, South Carolina, which was where he met and married Mary Peace, the daughter of a merchant also engaged in the West Indies trade.[4] Beginning in 1804, he invested an increasing portion of his maritime profits in a woolen textile manufacturing enterprise in the South Kingstown district of the Narragansett Country. By the time he turned his manufacturing interests over to Shepherd Tom and two of his other sons in the 1820s, he could claim to be the first industrialist in Rhode Island who had 'achieved a fully developed factory system'.[5]

Thomas Robinson Hazard, Shepherd Tom, was Rowland Hazard's second son. He was born in 1797 in the household of his grandfather, College Tom. Although the grandfather died before Shepherd Tom was two years old, he nevertheless passed much of his childhood in this agrarian milieu, or at least so he leads us to believe in *The Jonny-Cake Papers*. At age fifteen or sixteen, after schooling in the Philadelphia area (the family had long been Quakers), he began working in his father's woolen textile manufacturing business (he also devoted himself to sheep husbandry, whence his nickname). In the 1820s, with his father's assistance, he established his own woolen mill in the neighborhood (the primary family enterprise was taken over by two of his brothers). In 1840, shortly after his marriage, he sold his mill and purchased a large 'gentleman' farm in Portsmouth, just north of Newport, where he resided until his death in 1886. Besides farming, Shepherd Tom devoted himself during these later years to numerous reform causes. He wrote many books and articles, culminating in *The Jonny-Cake Papers*.[6]

404

Culinary authenticity remains a primary concern throughout *The Jonny-Cake Papers*. It frequently takes the geographic form already noted. A gentleman in Providence to whom Shepherd Tom had sent some Narragansett cornmeal – the gentleman's wife had complained that it was 'impossible to obtain eatable Indian meal' in Providence – had written back thanking him for this 'invaluable present of real Indian meal'. This emphasis is applied to other foodstuffs besides cornmeal and Jonny cake. The 'real Rhode Island turkey' grew to be 'large in size and black and shiny in aspect' as a result of its being bred in 'the salubrious and genial Gulf Stream atmosphere' that, as nowhere else, not even in the town of East Greenwich that bordered the Narragansett Country to the north, 'prevails in the southern part of the Ancient Atlantis, now called Newport county and Narragansett'.[7]

But the most important arena of culinary authenticity was not spatial but temporal. 'With proper materials and care', Hazard concludes his 'First Baking', 'a decent jonny-cake can be baked on a coal stove', but it would be 'by no means equal to the old-time genuine article'. This is the case 'for the simple reason that wood fires in open fireplaces have become… things of the past, and good, careful, painstaking cooks extinct'.[8] In general in *The Jonny-Cake Papers*, to be authentic is to be a thing of the past and extinct. To be a thing of the present and extant is to be inauthentic. The focus of this contrast is invariably Phillis, Shepherd Tom's grandfather's 'never-to-be-forgotten unparalleled colored cook', who always used 'pure' ingredients and who did everything 'thoroughly' and 'carefully'. Present-day cooks, on the other hand, invariably employ ingredients 'of questionable purity' and proceed 'without preparation… pell-mell', with results that are 'too horrible to mention or abide'.[9]

For Shepherd Tom, the Jonny-cake of his boyhood made by Phillis provided nourishment of the finest kind, both spiritual and physical: Phillis 'probably made as good a jonny-cake in her day as any other artist known, whether white or black, or in short, as was ever made outside of heaven'.[10] (References to heaven notwithstanding, Hazard, like most educated Victorians, is more apt to allude to the Greek than the Judeo-Christian pantheon: he jests that 'the Greeks of old' gave to Narragansett corn meal 'the name of Ambrosia'.[11]) But in his description of the best way to grind the southern Rhode Island white Indian corn meal that is Jonny-cake's main ingredient, we begin to detect an inconsistency in Hazard's portrayal of this authentic New England food. The milling style he endorses is so fastidious a process ('The object of the miller…was…how well he could grind it, let the time required to do it be what it might'.[12]) that it calls to mind less Shepherd Tom's alleged boyhood world of self-sufficient farming, based on simplicity and thrift, than the contemporary world of wealth and leisure, the leaders of which have the time and money to expend on fussy epicureanism.

Hazard describes in minute detail the reasons that the meal ground at Hammond's Mill, 'situated on the site of the elder Gilbert Stuart's snuff mill, just above the head of Pettaquamscutt pond', is far superior to any other. But to deflect the impression that his tastes might be overly refined, he attributes to Phillis the preference for this product. This rhetorical ploy requires him to grant to Phillis a degree of executive power not usually associated with household servants in general nor with African American cooks in particular: Phillis could not be 'induced by any persuasion to touch meal ground at any other mill, for the reason, as she averred, that the mills in the more immediate vicinity made harsh feeling round meal, whereas that particular mill made soft feeling flat meal'.[13] Shepherd Tom uses Phillis to articulate his preferences for unusual, costly, or labor-intensive culinary practices and products.

Hazard continues with an insistence on the relative advantages of Narragansett granite for making mill stones. Those with a smooth grain, 'being of a finer grade, made the [preferred] flat meal' whereas those others 'being coarse grained, made round meal'.[14] To put it another way, the finer the grain of granite the finer the grain of, well, grain.

We might be unsurprised to find that the wealthy Hazard family went to some lengths, at their ex-slave Phillis's command, in search of the perfect mill to grind their corn. But it must come as a jolt to hear Hazard catalog any number of southern Rhode Island families as 'amateurs in jonny-cakes, who lived within a few rods only of [an inferior] mill' ('Coon's old mill, now Wakefield', just such a one as we might now find quaintly portrayed on antiquarian postcards), toting 'their grists on their shoulders, or on horseback, way off to Hammond's or Mumford's mills, some eight to twelve miles distant' in search of flat meal.[15] American culinary authenticity has become in this instance not a celebration of the foods and tastes which can only be obtained by self-sufficient farming, but instead, albeit with a sack of grain on one's or one's horse's back, a 19th-century version of the modern search for the perfectly-made latte or grilled steak.

As with the intricate maneuvers of the latter-day latte-maker, the 'old-fashioned Narragansett miller' possesses a technique which is precisely, almost choreographically, executed:

> See the white-coated old man now first rub the meal, as it falls, carefully and thoughtfully between his fingers and thumb, then graduate the feed and raise or lower the upper stone, with that nice sense of adjustment, observance, and discretion that a Raphael might be supposed to exercise in the mixing and grinding of his colors for a Madonna, or a Canova in putting the last touch of his chisel to the statue of a god, until, by repeated handling, he had found the ambrosia to have acquired exactly the desired coolness and flatness – the result of its being cut into fine slivers by the nicely-balanced revolving stones.[16]

Hammond's Mill undoubtedly would have counted many local farmers among its clientele. But in the scene Hazard describes, it functions not as an 'authentic' local mill, but as a popular specialty shop. Hazard's nostalgic rhetoric is so persuasive, so skillfully employed, however, that the reader is likely to be, as Hazard fully expects, easily recruited into the ranks of those who believe that this 'genuine' Jonny-cake, made by 'the old-fashioned Narragansett method of making and baking... should by all means be preserved, if possible.'[17]

Thus supporting his argument for Jonny-cake's authenticity with the twin cultural pillars of skilled craftsmanship and historic preservation, Hazard proceeds to describe how Phillis 'after taking from the chest her modicum of meal, proceeded to bolt it through her finest sieve',[18] and then to make it up into Jonny-cakes:

> [She] carefully knead[ed] it in a wooden tray, having first scalded it with boiling water, and added sufficient fluid, sometimes new milk, at other times pure water, to make it of a proper consistence. It was then placed on a jonny-cake board about three-quarters of an inch in thickness, and well dressed on the surface with rich sweet cream to keep it from blistering when placed before the fire. The red oak jonny-cake board was always the middle portion of a flour barrel from five to six inches wide. This was considered an indispensable requisite in the baking of a good jonny-cake.... The cake was next placed upright on the hearth before a bright, green hardwood fire. This kind of fire was indispensable also. And so too was a heart-shaped flat-iron that supported it, which was shaped exactly to meet every exigency. First the flat's front smooth surface was placed immediately against the back of the jonny-cake to hold it

in a perpendicular position before the fire until the main part of the cake was sufficiently baked. Then a slanting side of the flat-iron was turned so as to support the board in a reclining position until the bottom and top extremities of the cake were in turn baked, and lastly, the board was slewed round and rested partly against the handle of the flat-iron, so as to bring the ends of the cake in a better position to receive the heat from the fire… When the jonny-cake was sufficiently done on the first side, a knife was passed between it and the board, and it was dextrously turned and anointed, as before, with sweet, golden-tinged cream, previous to being placed again before the fire.[19]

Phillis is described as being even more fastidious than the 'white-coated' old miller. There must be no deviations whatsoever from the process as here outlined. The choice of ingredients and equipment, the exact choreographing of every stage and step, no matter how minute – all this bespeaks the pedantry of the connoisseur here and now, as he writes, rather than any actual, unselfconscious practice of an earlier day.[20]

There is another contradiction built into the author's self-presentation. At the very opening of his chronicle, when Hazard speaks of white Indian meal being found 'nowhere else on the globe', we encounter a rhetorical strategy designed to promote old-time agrarian simplicities but propped up by assertions of cosmopolitan knowledge and experience. Is old 'Shepherd Tom' a globe-trotter? A bit later, introducing his grandfather's 'old cook' Phillis, he mentions that she was 'originally from Senegambia, or Guinea'. A casual reference to a household servant and an equally off-hand mention of the lucrative transnational trade networks that brought Rhode Island slave traders to the west coast of Africa and their captives back to Rhode Island – these belie Hazard's attempts to enshrine the extremely simple Jonny-cake as the symbol of the virtues of plain living supposedly exemplified by such 18th-century Narragansett farmers as Hazard's grandfather, College Tom.[21]

By the time Hazard was writing his description of Hammond's Mill, the small, old grist mills of New England (as opposed to the mammoth, new cotton and woolen mills of the region) were being deployed as picturesque symbols of the traditional American farm way of life that had been displaced by industrialization. This particular mill, as we have seen, was singled out by Hazard for its New England-style excellence, easily conflated with authenticity, based on its components (the finest Rhode Island granite) and its operative (that unhurried Yankee craftsman). So what is added rhetorically by mention of the detail that the mill was 'situated on the site of the elder Gilbert Stuart's snuff mill'? Is Hazard's reference to the family farm of America's premier portrait painter a calculated maneuver to assert a creditable genealogy, one with considerable social cachet? The mill descended from Gilbert Stuart's snuff mill is at the same time being designated as an authentic example of unpretentious Yankee values, located, as it is comfortably described, 'just above the head of Pettaquamscutt pond'.[22] Simple and quaint, but also socially successful, are us.

'Shepherd Tom' was, in reality, as we have stated, Thomas Robinson Hazard, scion of a wealthy, land-owning, mercantile, and (by Hazard's day) industrial clan. But, like some politicians of our time, he chose to present himself as a simple farmer of plain tastes and wants. He was, in this guise, hugely popular among Yankee Rhode Island readers of the late 19th century. As discriminating in his tastes as any aristocrat, and as willing to expend time and money in search of quality goods and services, his contradictory assertion of his simplicity was accepted because the form his epicureanism took was a newly invented, peculiarly American form of refinement, now cleverly packaged as refinement's opposite, the plain-style, democratically-approved 'real article'.[23]

The creators of authentic Rhode Island Jonny-cake resemble in their artistry, Hazard avers, the best of Italian Renaissance and neoclassical painters and sculptors. (Reflecting the Romantic ideals common among the educated classes of the late 19th century, Hazard fails to acknowledge either the commercial motivation or the artisanal workshops which supported these 'solitary' geniuses.) It follows that a lack of attention to detail (a lack of craftsmanship), an absence of individuality, a large scale and a fast tempo must be among the constituent elements of inauthenticity. Such, we can see, is the case when Hazard discusses the poor milling that results from the use of a 'burr stone': 'Rushed through the stones in a stream from the hopper as big as your arm... coarse, uneven... hot as ashes and as tasteless as sawdust.'[24]

Elsewhere, Hazard speaks at greater length about what constitutes inauthenticity in food preparation, when he complains of 'these hurrying, money-getting and universal-thievery, food-spoiling and food-bolting days'. These words begin to identify the social processes that had transformed New England in the course of the 19th century. Just prior to this outburst, Shepherd Tom describes contemporary methods of lard extraction and marketing. They involve dragging 'wounded, sick, and dead hogs out of... ankle-deep filth' in railroad cars, throwing them, 'unwashed, into great steam boilers, and thus extract[ing] the lard, which was afterwards skimmed and separated from the refuse, &c., and clarified, when it was labeled as the purest and best of lard, and sent to market to regale the appetites of the snobs and epicures in our great cities.'[25]

Railroads, great cities, great steam boilers. The present from which Shepherd Tom is recoiling is the world created by industrialization and urbanization. Earlier on in *The Jonny-Cake Papers*, he glances at another of the massive and interlinked social changes of the 19th century when he laments that 'since the introduction of coal fires, cooking stoves, and French and Irish bedeviling cooks, the making and baking of a jonny-cake has become one of the lost arts'. The Irish and French bedeviling cooks serve here as shorthand for the immigrant groups that came to New England beginning in the 1840s at the behest of manufacturers in need of a labor force. They are to be invidiously compared, as ever, with Phillis.[26]

In its horrified reaction to the present, in its strident nostalgia for the lost world of early-national Rhode Island, and in its determination to 'reconstruct' the past for the few with sufficient discrimination, *The Jonny-Cake Papers* identifies itself as one of the productions of the Colonial Revival movement of the late 19th century, along with Harriet Beecher Stowe's four novels with a New England setting, Alice Morse Earle's antiquarian inventories of daily life in the colonial era, the proliferation of historical societies, museums, 'restored' houses and even entire villages, and myriad other cultural phenomena.[27]

It is an intriguing spectacle: this son and heir of one of the pioneering New England industrialists rejects the shallow, inauthentic, alien industrial society the foundations of which his father had helped to lay and which he and his brothers had continued to erect, seeking to replace it with the authentic, close-knit, sublimely nurturant (in its food and cookery) slavery-based society of his grandfather. But how 'authentic' was Shepherd Tom's portrayal of the world of his grandfather? We have already been suggesting that Hazard's representations of past methods of food processing and preparation are suffused with the self-consciousness and sophistication of the latter-day epicure. There are further problems arising from the sorts of uses of historical evidence that nostalgia always allows itself. On the simplest level, Hazard leads the reader to believe that his grandfather and Phillis were alive and directly influencing him during his childhood. 'Never while I live', he assures us, 'whether in this world or the next, shall I forget... Aunty Phillis' apple dumplings, made with a thin crust, and a cat-head apple quartered and cored, in each of them, as big as a good sized pumpkin.' But since, as mentioned above, Phillis's death took place twenty-five years prior to Shepherd Tom's birth, he is obviously relying here not on memory but rather invention, or perhaps artful reconstruction based on family lore. For all we can tell, his tales of Phillis's supreme achievements as a cook amount to embroidered, 'ye olde' history of the same sort that led to the creation of 'authentic' Colonial Revival parlors in late-19th-century homes, stuffy rooms crammed with a hodge-podge of 17th-century artifacts in a manner only a Victorian could love.[28]

409

More broadly, there is the question of the accuracy of Shepherd Tom's overall representation of the society of the Narragansett Country prior to the American Industrial Revolution. By placing Phillis at the heart of his account, he acknowledges the centrality of slavery to that society, and he supplements this with several anecdotes about other ex-slaves in his grandfather's household. But of course, Phillis is encouraged to fulfill herself as a great cook, and College Tom's other ex-slaves are also shown generally enjoying themselves. All in all, the impression that is left is that Narragansett preindustrial slavery was similar to the antebellum South as Shepherd Tom had characterized it in an 1848 newspaper piece in favor of Colonization: 'the masters are in general humane'.[29]

Beyond the question of slavery, or rather alongside it, Shepherd Tom generally adopts a hail-fellow-well-met tone throughout *The Jonny-Cake Papers*, and he tries hard to lend an air of homely rusticity to all aspects of pre-industrial life. His intimate knowledge of the lard and hogs of the good old days – Phillis fried smelts in 'pure leaf lard'; he himself kept 'an old Berkshire sow' on his gentleman farm – helps to create this impression, as do his frequent references to everyday village institutions such as bakeries, taverns, and saddlers' shops. He repeatedly treats us to such moments as the one in which 'Capt. Bill Rodman' cut 'a pompous English traveler' down to size, in the course of an evening of democratic conviviality at 'Joe Runnell's' inn in the village of 'Little Rest'.[30]

Shepherd Tom concludes the penultimate 'Baking' of *The Jonny-Cake Papers* with a portrait of a farmstead clearly designed to represent the social ideal he is counter-posing to the degenerate, industrialized present. It is the establishment of 'Sammy Holden, a plain, unpretending old farmer'. In Holden's arrangements, all is orderly and productive. Livestock and crops suffice to feed and clothe the family comfort-ably and also 'leave quite a surplus to send to Newport markets'. On their annual autumn trips to market this surplus, the Holdens always procure 'quite a number of interesting and instructive books to be read aloud by one of the family during the long winter evenings'. If the neighbors ever need assistance, Holden 'and his boys, who were always up to their farm work and never hurried, used to go without saying nary a word, and hoe out their unlucky neighbor's corn, potatoes, or what not, that they saw suffering, or mayhap mow and put up his hay and oats'. The obvious moral is that 'were all the people on earth like the Holdens, they would be ten times more comfortable than millions are now; whilst all the money now spent for jails, peniten-tiaries, criminal courts, and gallows might be saved.'[31]

410

So what is needed is a society of self-sufficient, prosperous, self-educated, neigh-borly, independent freeholders. There is indeed historical basis for this as a valid description of much of New England society in the 17th and 18th centuries, and there is also some historical basis for it as a description of Narragansett Country life during Shepherd Tom's childhood. His distant cousin, Nailer Tom, recorded in his diary in minute detail the year-by-year functioning of just such a thriving, self-suf-ficient farmstead, the family assisting and being assisted by its neighbors in a dense network of local exchange of produce and labor. This is in fact the society that the Industrial Revolution had rendered 'extinct'.[32]

But what Shepherd Tom chooses to ignore is that such agrarian self-sufficiency had harbored within itself, in its very prosperity, the seeds of its own destruction, and that his own family had played a major part in hastening this process along. The Holdens had 'quite a surplus to send to Newport markets'. As these surpluses grew, the fortunes of people like the Holdens and Nailer Tom became ever more linked to the workings of the marketplace. Some in Narragansett, such as Shepherd Tom's own planter great-grandfather Robert, were sending agricultural commodities not just to Newport but across the seas. Agrarian prosperity metamorphosed into mari-time commerce and slave-trade prosperity. Nailer Tom's mother was the daughter of the Newport slave trader Abraham Redwood.[33] Robert Hazard's grandson became an export-import merchant. Mercantile prosperity then, as we have seen, further transmuted into the Industrial Revolution, and all the attendant ills that Shepherd Tom decried. The world of Shepherd Tom's grandfather, however superior had been its food and cookery, could not be counterposed to Shepherd Tom's own world. Just as the grandfather had produced the grandson, the grandfather's world had produced the grandson's world.[34]

The quest for authenticity in *The Jonny-Cake Papers* was undertaken by someone who had benefited greatly from the 19th century's interlocking network of trade, industry, and agriculture, a world of larger, faster, and cheaper modes of production and a greatly increased supply of products for consumption. Embedded in such a world, Hazard's nostalgic recollections amounted, as did most nostalgic cultural commentary, to an attempt to escape responsibility for the authentically unsavory ramifications of industrial life, through the baking of a highly selective, inauthentic taste of the past.

Bibliography

Coleman, Peter J., *The Transformation of Rhode Island, 1790–1860* (Providence, RI: Brown University Press, 1963).

Conforti, Joseph A., *Imagining New England: Explorations of Regional Identity from the Pilgrims to the Mid-20th Century* (Chapel Hill: University of North Carolina Press, 2001).

Coughtry, Jay, *The Notorious Triangle: Rhode Island and the African Slave Trade, 1700–1807* (Philadelphia: Temple University Press, 1981).

Hazard, Caroline, ed., *Nailer Tom's Diary: Otherwise The Journal of Thomas B. Hazard of Kingstown Rhode Island, 1778 to 1840* (Boston: Merrymount Press, 1930).

——, *Thomas Hazard son of Robt call'd College Tom: A Study of Life in Narragansett in the XVIIIth Century* (Boston: Houghton Mifflin, 1894).

Hazard, Thomas Robinson, *The Jonny-Cake Papers of 'Shepherd Tom'* (Boston: Merrymount Press, 1915).

——, *Miscellaneous Essays and Letters* (Philadelphia: Collins, 1883).

——, *Recollections of Olden Times: Rowland Robinson of Narragansett and His Unfortunate Daughter. With Genealogies of the Robinson, Hazard, and Sweet Families of Rhode Island* (Newport, RI: John P. Sanborn, 1879; rpt. 1998).

Jones, Daniel P., *The Economic and Social Transformation of Rural Rhode Island, 1780–1850* (Boston: Northeastern University Press, 1992).

Kulikoff, Allan, *From British Peasants to Colonial American Farmers* (Chapel Hill, University of North Carolina Press, 2000).

Stavely, Keith and Kathleen Fitzgerald, *America's Founding Food: The Story of New England Cooking* (Chapel Hill: University of North Carolina Press, 2004).

Stewart, Peter Crawford, 'A History of the Peace Dale Manufacturing Company' (Master's Thesis, University of Rhode Island, 1962).

Van Broekhoven, Deborah Bingham, *The Devotion of These Women: Rhode Island in the Antislavery Network* (Amherst: University of Massachusetts Press, 2002).

Notes

1. Hazard, T. (1915), p. 17. Prior to this edition, the work was published serially in the *Journal*; then, in 1880 (bakings 1–12) and 1882 (bakings 13–26), as two separate booklets; then again in 1888 as a single book.

2. Coleman, pp. 13–14; Jones, pp. 6–7; Hazard, T. (1879), pp. 16, 13. In 1774, 10% of the rural population of Rhode Island were slaves, as opposed to a slavery rate of 1–3% in Massachusetts and Connecticut. In Newport and Washington counties specifically, the 'ratio of slave to free labor... was higher than in parts of Maryland, Delaware, and Virginia'. See Kulikoff, p. 249; Van Broekhoven, p. 2.

3. Hazard, C. (1894), pp. 93–103, 78–80, 118. In the closing decades of his life, College Tom moved beyond his personal disavowal of slaveholding to become involved in a larger effort to abolish slavery in Rhode Island; ibid., pp. 170–89.

4. Hazard, T. (1879), pp. 189–91; Stewart, pp. 2–3. For the centrality of maritime commerce (and the slave trade) to the economy of colonial and early national Rhode Island, see Coleman, pp. 7–70.

5. Stewart, pp. 23–26; Coleman, pp. 95–96; Hazard, T. (1879), pp. 192–93. For maritime commerce and the slave trade as the source of much of the initial capital investment in the Rhode Island textile industry, see Coleman, pp. 71, 73.

6. Hazard, C. (1930), pp. 195 (3 Jan., 1797), 196 (2 Feb., 1797), 447 (27 May, 1815), 451 (20 Aug., 1815), 538 (23 Mar., 1820), 558 (8 May, 1821); Hazard, T. (1879), p. 82; Hazard, T. (1883), pp. 123, 187, 192–93; Hazard, T. (1915), pp. xiii, 326, 331; *Dictionary of American Biography*, ed. Allen Johnson and Dumas Malone, vol. 4 (New York: Scribner's. 1931), pp. 473–4; *American National Biography*, ed. John A. Garraty and Mark C. Carnes, vol. 10 (New York: Oxford University Press, 1999), pp. 443–5.

7. Hazard, T. (1915), pp. 23, 72.

8. Ibid., p. 30.

9. Ibid., pp. 362, 24.

10. Ibid., p. 18.

11. Ibid.

12. Ibid., p. 19.

13. Ibid., p. 18.

14. Ibid., p. 19.

15. Ibid.

16. Ibid., pp. 19–20.

17. Ibid., pp. 30, 23.

18. Ibid., p. 24.

19. Ibid., pp. 28–30.

20. For similar treatments of other foods besides Jonny-cake, see ibid., pp. 24–7 (smelts and eels), 27–8 (brown bread), 72–4 (turkey and pork).

21. Ibid., pp. 17, 18. For an overview of Rhode Island's role in the slave trade, see Coughtry.

22. Hazard, T. (1915), p. 18.

23. For an analysis of this dynamic in late-19th-century New England foodways as a whole, see Stavely, pp. 146–7, 278–9.

24. Hazard, T. (1915), p. 19. A burr stone is made from a form of fresh-water quartz that is found only in northern France. It is considered by many to be the best quality stone for milling. So Hazard is claiming that, compared to Narragansett granite, the generally-accepted best is no good at all. See Howell, Charles, 'Millstones, an Introduction', <http://www.angelfire.com/journal/pondlilymill/paper.html>. 11 July 2005.

25. Hazard, T. (1915), p. 55. Note how Hazard distracts attention from his own epicureanism by accusing others of it.

26. Ibid., p. 18. Irish and other immigrants began to be employed in the Hazard woolen mills in the

1850s, after Shepherd Tom's retirement; see Stewart, pp. 45, 97, 122.

27. For a recent survey and analysis of the Colonial Revival, see Conforti, pp. 203–62.

28. Hazard, T. (1915), p. 108; above, n. 3.

29. Hazard, T. (1915), pp. 59–62, 67–8, 82–7; Hazard, T. (1883), p. 38.

30. Hazard, T. (1915), pp. 24, 28, 143, 142. Leaf lard is 'the highest grade... from the fat around the kidneys'; *Columbia Encyclopedia*, 6th ed. (New York: Columbia University Press and Bartleby.com, 2001), <http://www.bartleby.com/65>. 11 July 2005.

31. Hazard, T. (1915), pp. 367–70.

32. See any number of entries in Hazard, C. (1930); for example those for 1804, when Shepherd Tom was a boy of seven (pp. 238–52), or those for 1806, when he was nine (pp. 269–81). For an overview of the largely self-sufficient colonial New England family farm, see Stavely, pp. 120–9.

33. Hazard, C. (1930), p. vii. See Jones, p. 7: 'The Narragansett planters... tended to marry with the Newport merchant elite'.

34. For an account of how social relations in another part of Rhode Island, the northwest, were more thoroughly based on self-sufficient farming, with only limited ties to the marketplace until well into the 19th century, see Jones, pp. 7–17. As we have just seen, Hazard predicts a huge surplus were institutions of social control such as jails and criminal courts unnecessary. Where would the money 'saved' then be expended but in the very commercial ventures that had undercut Holden-like self-sufficiency?

Haroset

Susan Weingarten

Haroset is a food with symbolic significance, which is used at the Jewish Passover *Seder* meal. From biblical times Passover was celebrated in Jerusalem by eating the paschal lamb together with unleavened bread and bitter herbs. Following the destruction of the Second Temple in the year 70 CE, the Passover rituals were recreated in a new way as the *Seder*. This meal commemorates the exodus of the Children of Israel from slavery in Egypt to freedom, and has been widely celebrated by Jews in their homes up to the present day. The *Seder* ritual includes reading a text, the *Haggadah*, pointing to and eating symbolic foods, and drinking four cups of wine.

Among the symbolic foods eaten at the *Seder* are the 'bitter herbs,' to remind the participants of the bitterness of slavery. These were originally some form of endives or bitter lettuce, common in Palestine in the spring. Once the Jewish diaspora spread north, grated horseradish was often substituted for the bitter lettuce.[1] *Haroset* was made to dip the bitter herbs into, and take away some of their bitterness. It was said to resemble the mud or clay for the bricks which the Jews made as slaves in Egypt.[2]

As a child I learned the ingredients of *haroset*:

> Apples, raisins
> Chopped up fine
> Cinnamon, nuts
> And sweet red wine.[3]

This is the present-day authentic Ashkenazi *haroset*, but there are many variations which developed over the centuries, particularly in Sephardi communities.[4] Indeed, in practice today and throughout history there is no one ingredient which is common to all versions of *haroset*, although we can point to the geographical distribution of certain ingredients.

The Talmudic sources

From the very first time the Jewish legal codes were written down we find detailed discussions of the rituals of Passover, which get a whole section to themselves in the 3rd-century Mishnah, as well as in the subsequent Palestinian or Jerusalem Talmud [JT] and the Babylonian Talmud [BT]: Pesahim, the Passover laws.[5]

The earliest written evidence of *haroset* is to be found in the Mishnah. However, this only describes *haroset* in terms of its function and symbolism, not its ingredients or taste.

They bring before [the leader of the *Seder*] unleavened bread [*matzah*] and lettuce and the *haroset*, although *haroset* is not a religious obligation. R El'azer b Zadoq says: It is a religious obligation.[6]

Thus the Mishnah mentions the *matzah*, the bitter herbs and *haroset* as belonging to the *Seder* ritual 'even though *haroset* is not a religious obligation,' merely, it is implied, a custom. However it then quotes the contrary view of Rabbi El'azar b Zadoq, a rabbi who lived before the destruction of the Temple, who says that *haroset* **is** a religious obligation. Rabbi El'azar was a spice merchant in Jerusalem, and other sources quote him as saying that merchants would cry the spices for *haroset* in the streets of Jerusalem, where Jews would come on Passover to eat the paschal lamb in the days when the Temple still stood.[7] Thus the evidence for the use of *haroset* is now put back to a time before 70CE, and it is clear that it is older than the new form of the Passover *Seder* meal. Rabbi El'azar, then, saw spices as an essential ingredient.

The Mishnah adds:

On all other nights we dip our food once, on this night we dip twice.[8]

The Mishnah is alluding here to the usual practice all over the Roman empire of dipping bread into a condiment at a meal. But at the *Seder*, it says, we dip twice – referring to an initial dipping of ordinary herbs into salt water and the later dipping of the bitter herbs in *haroset*.[9] However, there is no discussion of what *haroset* is.

Both the Talmuds expand the Mishnaic discussion of *haroset*.

415

The Jerusalem Talmud: *haroset* as *dukkeh*

The 5th-century JT notes that *haroset* is called '*dukkeh*' because it is pounded [*dukhah*].[10] Yemenite Jews, who were cut off for many years from the mainstream Jewish community, relied on the JT as their religious authority unlike other Jews, for the Babylonian Talmud did not reach them for many hundreds of years. They have preserved the tradition of the JT and to this day they call *haroset* '*dukkeh*.'

The JT goes on to quote Rabbi Joshua b Levi, a 3rd-century Palestinian rabbi, as saying that *haroset* must be thick like mud or clay, while others say it should be liquid, 'in memory of the blood.' Blood from the Passover lamb was used by the Jews to mark their houses before they left Egypt. They dipped bunches of hyssop into the blood and painted it on the lintels of their houses as a sign for the Destroying Angel to pass over them and spare their children. The mention of blood may also refer to the first of the ten plagues in the book of Exodus, when all the water in Egypt was turned to blood.[11]

It is also clear from the JT that it was usual to put spices in *haroset*. However, there is no mention of other ingredients.

In the Babylonian Talmud, finalised in the 7th century, Rav Ammi claims that *haroset* is used as a dip for the bitter herbs to counteract the harmful *kappa* they contain.[12] (It is unclear what *kappa* is – unhealthy juices or some form of worm are the alternatives proposed by medieval commentators.) Other rabbis, however, saw symbolic meaning in the *haroset*. Thus Rabbi Yohanan thinks that *haroset* is a memory of the clay for the bricks which the Jews made as slaves in Egypt. We have already seen that the JT also presents *haroset* as a memory of the clay. Rabbi Levi suggests that *haroset* preserves a memory of the apple-tree in the biblical book, the Song of Songs (8.5):

> *Under the apple-tree I aroused you; there your mother conceived you, there she who bore you conceived you.*

Although Rabbi Levi does not actually say that apples should be included in the *haroset*, it is clear that for him apples are closely connected to *haroset* through the Song of Songs.

These two rabbis are both Palestinian, so the BT here may be reporting a debate which actually took place in Palestine, but was not preserved in Palestinian sources.

What is to be done with these differing opinions? The BT carries on to cite Abbaye, a 4th-century Babylonian rabbi, who succeeds in reconciling them, and writes that *haroset* must be made both acrid and thick: acrid like apples and thick like clay. But note that here too apples are not quite presented as an ingredient: they have become a taste-memory.

The BT reports that the rabbis decided the debate in favour of Rabbi Yohanan. Thus *haroset* is to be seen as a memory of the clay, rather than the apples. Rabbi Yohanan is then quoted again, saying that the spices in the *haroset* are in memory of the straw used for making bricks, while the *haroset* itself is in memory of the clay.[13]

Thus the BT associates *haroset* with apples, but rejects the view that this is the major association, and does not actually speak of apples as an ingredient. It says that the important thing is that *haroset* should be thick like clay (but may be acrid too), and that spices should be added.

We shall see that later rabbinical commentators relate back to what is written in the Mishnah and the BT, and some of them also relate to the JT as well.[14]

The Song of Songs

The Song of Songs, attributed to King Solomon, is a series of love-songs which include some of the most beautiful descriptions of the coming of spring in the Land of Israel. It is read in synagogue on Passover, the spring festival.

Songs mentions many fruits and spices, as well as wine, milk and finest oil. The fruits appear both growing on the trees, and as ready to be eaten. Thus there are vineyards and blossoming vines, green figs on the fig tree, an orchard of pomegranates in bloom, gardens of luscious fruits and nut-trees. The lover arouses his beloved 'under the apple tree,' where her mother conceived her.

Fruits ready to eat include raisin cakes and clusters of grapes, fragrant apples, pomegranates split open or giving their juice. There is date honey, and the lover compares his beloved to a date palm, with its clusters her breasts, and says he will 'climb the date palm.' Many spices and perfumes adorn the lover and his beloved: nard, myrrh, henna, frankincense, saffron, sweet calamus and cinnamon 'with all aromatic woods' – indeed 'all the choice perfumes.'

Accepting Songs into the Bible (not without much debate), the rabbis interpreted this love-poetry allegorically, as representing the love of God for the Jewish people. Thus in the midrashim, rabbinic exegesis on Songs, the Jewish people is associated allegorically with a number of fruits: with pomegranates, grapes, figs, nuts and apples. We shall take just one example, that of the apple-tree.

In the midrash on the book of Exodus, which tells the story of the first Passover and how God saved the Israelites from slavery in Egypt, the apple-tree is intimately woven into the biblical Exodus narrative by the writers of the midrash, using the verse from Songs (8.5): *Under the apple tree I aroused you*, and expanding on it. The Egyptian authorities had declared that all male Jewish babies were to be killed. Midrash Exodus Rabbah tells the legend of how they were saved:

> Israel was delivered from Egypt because of the righteous women who lived in that generation. What did they do? When they went to draw water, God arranged that little fishes should enter their pitchers, with the result that they found them half-filled with water and half with fishes. These they carried to their husbands and then set two pots on the fire, one for hot water and the other for the fish. Then they fed them, washed them, anointed them, gave them to drink and slept with them.... As soon as they had conceived they returned to their homes and when the time of childbirth arrived they went out into the fields and gave birth beneath the apple-tree, as it is said: *Under the apple-tree I aroused you; there your mother conceived you.* God then sent down an angel, who washed and beautified the babies like a midwife.... He also provided them with oil and honey to suck.[15]

417

The apple-tree, then, became intimately associated with the Passover narrative, and in particular with God's mercy, and this is why Rabbi Levi and later rabbis relate the *haroset* to the Song of Songs.

The Babylonian Ge'onim

Following these talmudic sources, later rabbis dealing with the laws of Passover mention ingredients, and sometimes taste, in their discussions of *haroset*. We shall trace these discussions throughout the ages in different Jewish communities.

The first sources belong to Babylonia, which was to become part of the Sephardi diaspora. Following the closure of the BT, leadership of Babylonian Jewry was taken over by rabbis called *ge'onim*. Among the first of these was Amram Ga'on (*d.* 875), who headed the Jewish academy at Sura.[16] He writes:

> They bring before him [sc. the leader of the *Seder*] *haroset* – *haliqa* – which they make in our part of the world from dates.

It is clear from this information about dates that R. Amram is noting a local custom – and perhaps implicitly differentiating himself from other customs, or from the talmudic minority view of Rabbi Levi that *haroset* is a memory of apples. Rav Amram also notes another name for *haroset*: '*haliqa*.' Jews from Iraq still today call their *haroset* '*haliq*' or '*haliqa*,' and it too is deliciously sweet.

Sa'adiah Gaon (882–942), who headed the Babylonian academy at Pumbedita, wrote a commentary on the Passover *haggadah*. He says:

> You must prepare a sauce of dates, nuts and sesame and knead them together with vinegar.

He too says this is called *haliq*. To this day Jews from Babylonia make their *haroset* from dates, nuts and sesame. Sa'adiah was so influential that he appears to have authorised his local custom as authentic. He was presumably relying on the opinion of Rabbi Yohanan that clay, rather than apples, is the most important *haroset* symbol, a view which we saw was accepted by the BT. In other words, what was important was the consistency, rather than the ingredients. However, he does also say the *haroset* should include vinegar, so it will have some acidity, which the BT says is in memory of the apples.

Sephardi tradition of the Middle Ages

Rabbi Moses ben Maimon (called RaMbaM after his initials, or Maimonides), perhaps the greatest of all rabbinical commentators, was born in Cordoba in Spain in 1135 but fled to North Africa – first Fez, then Cairo. Early in his life Rambam wrote an influential commentary on the Mishnah.[17] Here he gives us a recipe:

> *Haroset* is a mixture which has in it acidity and something like straw in memory of the clay. We make it like this: soak figs or dates and cook them and pound them [*dukkin*] till they get soft, knead them with vinegar, and put in spikenard or thyme or hyssop without grinding them.[18]

Rambam has added some new ingredients to *haroset* – figs, as well as the dates of the *ge'onim*, and thyme and hyssop as alternatives for spices. We saw above that hyssop was used by the Israelites in Egypt to mark their doorposts with blood, so that the Destroying Angel would pass over them. Rambam has included this memory in his *haroset*, perhaps because the JT says that *haroset* is in memory of the blood, although he does not actually say so. His *haroset* is cooked, and he specifies that the spice or herbs are not to be ground up, so that they will be like pieces of straw.

Years later, when Rambam came to write his Code of Laws, he gives a different recipe:[19]

> And how do you make *haroset*? You take dates or dried figs, or raisins or some-thing similar, tread on them and put vinegar in them, and spice them with spice like clay with straw, and bring it to the table on Passover eve.

Rambam thus clearly accepts the view of Rabbi Yohanan in the BT who says that *haroset* is in memory of the clay, but not the view of Rabbi Levi who says it is in memory of the apple. He does, however, appear to accept the compromise of Abbaye who says that *haroset* should be like clay in consistency and like apples in acidity – in the Commentary on the Mishnah he actually says *haroset* must be acidic, and while he does not mention acidity in the Code, he does specify that *haroset* should be made with vinegar.

We saw that the Babylonian Ge'onim said their local custom was to use dates. Rambam also uses dates, but he adds some new ingredients. In his Commentary to the Mishnah he added figs. In the later Code, written in Egypt, he specifies dates, dried figs and raisins 'or something similar.' If it is the consistency which is important, then the ingredients can be varied according to what is available. This is true for the spices too – he no longer specifies anything in particular. What is important is that they should be like straw in clay. The combination of sweet fruits with vinegar will have given a sweet-sour *haroset*.

419

The border between Ashkenaz and Sepharad? Italy and Provence

Italy
Rabbi Zedekiah b Avraham Anav lived in Rome. In his 13th-century commentary on the Passover *haggadah*[20] he quotes both Sephardi and Ashkenazi authorities, but unfortunately does not specify his source for *haroset*. Rabbi Zedekiah says there must be *yeraqot*, herbs or vegetables, in his *haroset*, and adds an ingredient I have found nowhere else, 'blossoms from trees' – perhaps because not very many fresh fruits would be available in the Northern Italian spring. Maybe he is thinking of the blos-soming trees in Songs, although he does not say so. He stresses the acidity of *haroset* (in memory of the apple), identifying it with a contemporary acidic food and giving it the vernacular name of *aigros* from the French *aigres* – an acidic fruit or vegetable.[21] Modern scholars have pointed out that sour tastes were popular in medieval Europe.[22] 'Sour apples' are given as an example of acidic fruits for his *haroset* – thus apples here are a suggestion, rather than a necessary ingredient. Like a number of his contempo-

raries, he suggests cinnamon and spikenard as spices.[23]

But perhaps the most interesting ingredient is a small amount of 'clay or crushed potsherd in memory of the clay.' His is the first, but by no means the last, evidence for the practice of putting ground potsherds into *haroset* in the quest for authenticity!

R Ovadiah b Abraham, from Bertinero in Italy, (*c.* 1450–*c.* 1516), eventually became leader of the religious Jewish community in Jerusalem. In what became the standard commentary on the Mishnah he writes:

> *And haroset*: you make this from figs, hazelnuts, pistachios, almonds and several sorts of fruits. Put in apples, and pound it all in a mortar and mix it with vinegar and put on it spice: cinnamon and sweet calamus, in the form of long thin threads, in memory of the straw and it must be thick in memory of the clay.[24]

Rabbi Ovadiah has expanded the ingredients here, adding hazelnuts and pistachios, without giving any rationale, like his other Italian colleague. The spice sweet calamus [*qaneh*] appears in Songs. Here too the decorative thin threads of spice, in memory of the straw, are placed on top, not mixed in with the rest of the ingredients. The combination of figs and vinegar will have given a sweet-sour taste, unlike the sour *haroset* of R. Zedekiah.

420   Provence

At the turn of the 13th and 14th centuries, Rabbi Manoah b Shimon Badrashi from Narbonne in Provence, wrote in his commentary on the Rambam:[25]

> Our custom is to make it like this: take chestnuts, peel them, cook them and pound [*dukkin*] them well in a mortar. And afterwards take almonds and remove their thin skin and pound them with a few walnuts. And take dried figs, raisins without pips, dates and tread them, each separately. Take sour apples, peel them and crush them well and afterwards mix everything in the mortar with a pestle and make them into a paste. Pound with strong wine vinegar little by little so it is well mixed and season with spices e.g. ginger, sweet calamus, and *teven misha* called *ashqanant*,[26] and nails of cloves [*qofer*] and a little spikenard called *ashpiq*, after they have been ground.

Rabbi Manoah begins saying 'it is our custom,' implying that he knows it is different from others. This is the first time we have come across chestnuts in *haroset*, and he gives no other authority for what was clearly a major new ingredient. The figs, raisins and dates are standard now, and acidity is given by sour apples and vinegar. *Teven misha* and cloves are new ingredients. He calls cloves 'nails of *qofer*' (medieval French *girofle*).[27]

The Medieval Rabbis of Ashkenaz (northern Europe)

The famous Rabbi Shlomo b Isaac (RaShI) of Troyes in France (1040–1105), wrote a seminal commentary on the BT. Since it is unclear whether he really wrote the commentary on this particular chapter of BT Pesahim, or whether it is only attributed to him, we will call it the Rashi-text.[28]

> *In memory of the apple:* because [the Jewish women] used to give birth to their children there without pain, so that the Egyptians would not know about them, as it says: *Under the apple tree I aroused you. To make it thick:* To take it and crush it a great deal so that it will be thick. *And you must make it acrid:* To put in it apples and wine ... you must make it acrid in memory of the apple and you must make it thick in memory of the clay. *Spice: yeraqot* which you put in the *haroset* in memory of the straw which you crush in it finely in memory of the clay.

Here in the 11th century, our Ashkenazi Rashi-text's *haroset* has sour apples crushed to a thick paste, with wine and *yeraqot*. *Yeraqot* may refer to herbs or to any vegetable. Since they come under the heading of 'spice' and are in memory of the straw, it is tempting to translate them here as herbs. We have seen that herbs are added to Rambam's later Sephardi version of *haroset*. The Rashi-text says that *haroset* must be made acrid with apples and wine: this wine is clearly a dry wine, so this is another sour *haroset*.

R Shemuel b Meir [RaShBaM],[29] Rashi's grandson, writes:

> *To make it thick:* Crush many *yeraqot* in it to make it thick. *And you must make it acrid:* Put in apples in order to make it acrid and you must make it thick in memory of the clay. *Spice:* spices which you put in the *haroset* in memory of the straw

Rashbam adds that you put *yeraqot* in the *haroset* to make it thick. We saw that the Rashi-text wrote *yeraqot* in the context of spices, perhaps referring to herbs, but here since the *yeraqot* appear as an explanation of making the *haroset* thick, it is more likely that Rashbam is referring to vegetables in general. Perhaps these were cheaper than other ingredients and could be used to provide bulk rather than flavour. Again, this is a sour *haroset*.

Reply to Rashi – the Tosafot: 12th–14th centuries

The Tosafists were Rashi's successors as commentators on the BT. They write as follows:[30]

> ... *Teshuvot ha-Ge'onim* explains that you should make *haroset* from fruits that

the community of Israel is compared to in Songs: *Under the apple-tree I aroused you; like a pomegranate spilt open; the fig tree puts forth her green figs; I said: I will climb up into the date palm; nut: I went down to the nut grove.*

The Tosafists then add: *and almonds: because God took care of the end.*

The Tosafists here produce an innovation which will prove very important for the development of *haroset*: they write that *haroset* should be made from fruits to which Israel is compared in Songs: apples, pomegranates, figs, dates and nuts. Thus we now have authority for widening the range of ingredients, based on an expansion of Rabbi Levi's quotation in the BT about the apple from Songs. If one ingredient from Songs is recommended, why not the rest? This is not a case of fruit which is merely mentioned in Songs – the Tosafists here specify fruits which are allegorised in the midrashim on Songs as symbolising the Jewish people. Thus more symbolic foods are added to the *Seder* table. It is perhaps ironic that it is an Ashkenazi source which does this, for Ashekenazi *haroset* has today the fewest variations in ingredients. However, the *Teshuvot ha-Ge'onim* the Tosafists quote, sadly now lost, from its name was a Ge'onic, and hence Babylonian source. The expansion of the possible fruits leads to sweetening the sour taste.

Scholars of Ashkenaz after the Tosafists

Rabbi Asher b Yehiel [the ROsh], lived in Northern France and was the leader of the German Jewish community. He fled to Spain in 1303 and became spiritual head of Spanish Jewry, but although he moved from Ashkenaz to Sepharad, he still followed the Ashkenazi tradition. His major work was a commentary on the BT, where he writes about *haroset*:

> *Spice* is in memory of straw. The explanation is: like cinnamon and spikenard [*sanbal*], which are like straw.

His son R. Jacob b Asher, [Tur], continued the Ashkenazi tradition in Spain, as a codifier of Jewish law. He writes:[31]

> And the *haroset*: This is in memory of the clay with which our fathers were enslaved. Therefore it must be made thick like clay… and it says in the Jerusalem Talmud one person says to make it thick, but one person says to make it thin in memory of the blood. And the explanation of Rabbi Yehiel is both this and this: at first you make it thick, and afterwards you thin it down with vinegar. And you put a spice in, like cinnamon and ginger [*zangbil*] which are like straw, in memory of the straw which they mixed with the clay

Rabbi Jacob adds a new aspect to *haroset*: Rabbi Yehiel's reconciliation of the conflicting opinions in the JT that *haroset* should be thick like clay or thin like blood. You simply make it thick at first and then thin it down with vinegar afterwards. This is still done at the *Seder* table in some homes today. The spices he specifies are cinnamon and ginger [*zangbil*], although his father writes cinnamon and spikenard [*sanbal*]. Given the similarity between *zangbil* and *sanbal* it is possible this was a copyist's error. However, from now ginger becomes a common ingredient of *haroset*.

Moving back north again to 15th-century Germany, our next evidence of *haroset* comes from R Joseph b Moshe, who quotes as his authority R Israel b Petahiyah Isserlin.[32]

Rabbi Joseph adds a new ingredient to his *haroset* – pears. He knows and cites the view that the ingredients should be the fruits to which Israel is compared in Songs, but, he says, 'most of the people in our country' are also accustomed to take pears 'which are common here,' and he does not object.

The Sephardi world: the controversy over potsherds as an ingredient of *haroset*

We saw that in the 13th century the Italian Rabbi Zedekiah wrote that some people use crushed potsherds as an ingredient of their *haroset*. Clearly this custom continued, though we have no further textual evidence of it before Rabbi Joseph David from Salonica, who wrote the *Beit David* (1740).[33] The *Beit David* writes that Jewish communities in Salonica and Italy put a little ground potsherd or crushed stone (called *kallirimini*) in their *haroset*, allegedly following Rashi and Rashbam. This custom was fiercely attacked some years later by Maharam di-Lonzano, who is cited by the famous and authoritative Sephardi Rabbi Hayim David Azulai (the HiDA, 1724–1806):

> I was astounded to see something as crazy as this – maybe now on [the festival of] Purim they will let blood from people in memory of the command to exterminate the Jews! Surely we should turn misery into rejoicing, and bad to good!
>
> This mistake must have been caused by a scribal error in the commentary of the Rashbam and Rashi on this chapter. There it says 'the potsherd [*heres*] which they crush finely is in memory of the clay.' I checked this in a very old manuscript and it says there 'and the *haroset* which they crush finely is in memory of the clay,' and this is what it ought to be

Present day *haroset*

Geographical distribution

When I began to collect recipes for *haroset* I found sixty-three on a single internet site, so I decided I could not collect them all. Instead I chose to take one example from each Jewish community.[34] Overall, if we plot the different sorts of modern *haroset*

423

on a map of Jewish diaspora communities, we can see that there is a geographical distribution of *haroset*. Apple-based *haroset*, as already noted, is used by Ashkenazi communities. Date-based *haroset* is used by most Sephardi communities – Iraq, Iran, North Africa and Yemen. Some of these communities, such as the Iraqis, and the Iraqi diaspora communities in India, make the same *haroset* as Sa'adiah Gaon in the 10th century. Others have their own particular addition – e.g. pomegranates are used by Persian Jews. But in the transitional area of the Balkans, in Greece and Turkey, *haroset* is raisin-based. As we have seen, the 12th-century expansion of the rationale for the ingredients to include every fruit that the Jewish people were compared to in the Song of Songs, opened the way for these variations.

Innovation and authenticity

In the present day there are many innovations in *haroset* recipes, in keeping with modern trends of seeking the new and exciting, rather than preserving old traditions. But some of the old traditions were, of course, innovations in their own day. We have seen throughout history that not all such innovations are approved by rabbis when they arrive, and some are strongly censured. We saw such objections to using ground-up potsherds as an ingredient of *haroset*. However, this custom too continues to the present day. My father's neighbour in synagogue, Menahem Pariente, whose family comes from Gibraltar and who was himself born in Lisbon, brought me his Hebrew and Spanish *Haggadah* (1813) where the ingredients for *haroset* are listed as:

424

> Almonds, figs, apples, nuts and the like, and well-pounded spices, mixed with the dust of potsherds ground very fine.[35]

Menahem tells me they boil their potsherd before grinding it up.

Because Ashkenazi *haroset* is almost always the same, and also because it is the most common in the United States, there is some danger that it will eventually become the dominant *haroset*. I met an Iraqi woman who told me 'we don't have proper *haroset* – only dates and a few nuts and sesame seeds'. For her 'proper *haroset*' was Ashkenazi *haroset*, and she was amazed and pleased to find that hers was very similar to the authentic *haroset* of Sa'adiah Ga'on.

Some families are giving up making *haroset* – a combined 'Ashkephardi' sort with both apples and dates is sold in jars in Israeli supermarkets. On the other hand, there is a threat from excessive innovations – the authenticity of 'Golden Mango *haroset*' seems dubious. But just as in the Middle Ages people would add what was locally available and the rabbis would approve it in retrospect, so people are still adding new local ingredients: bananas are popular. And although these were not part of the original *haroset*,[36] there is an attempt to authenticate them: they go black, and this makes the *haroset* look more like mud, I was told.

I also found one innovation which innovates precisely because it aims at being ultra-authentic. We saw that rabbis who discuss apples in *haroset* consistently say that these are used to make the *haroset* acrid. In pre-modern times apples were presumably more liable to be sour than at present, when most apples are bred to be sweet, particularly in the USA. Thus a 21st-century internet discussion of *haroset* by the American Rabbi Howard Jachter[37] protests that the Talmud could not possibly have meant the apples we know when it said *haroset* must be acrid in memory of *tapuah*, the apple.[38] He solves his problem by quoting a different text, not related to *haroset*, where the Tosafists say that '*tapuah*' does not mean apple, but citron (etrog, a fruit used on the Jewish festival of Sukkot.) Thus Rabbi Jachter includes citron, rather than apple, in his *haroset*, an innovation made in the name of authenticity.

Notes

1. See on this the excellent article by A. Schaffer, 'The history of horseradish as the bitter herb of Passover', *Gesher* 8 (1981), pp. 217–37.
2. The Hebrew word I have translated here as clay or mud is *tit* which is usually translated into English as 'mortar.' This however is a mistake, arising from the Authorised Version (King James) translation of Nahum 3.14, which gives two different Hebrew words for the same thing, clay or mud. The translators of the AV solved their problem by writing 'clay and mortar' giving rise to the mistaken identification (at least in Anglophone communities) of *haroset* as 'mortar' which is used to stick bricks together, rather than the mud or clay used to make them, which is clearly what most rabbis meant.
3. Sadie Rose Weilerstein, *What the Moon Brought* (no place, 1942).
4. Jews who originate from Northern and Eastern Europe are called Ashkenazim; Jews originating from Spain and Portugal, North Africa and the Near East are called Sephardim.
5. For a brief explanation of the Talmudic literature, see my paper 'Nuts for the children: the evidence of the Talmudic literature', *Nurture: Oxford Symposium on Food and Cookery proceedings* (Bristol, 2004).
6. Mishnah Pesahim x, 3
7. In a parallel Talmudic source, the Tosefta, Rabbi El'azar is quoted as saying to some merchants of Lydda 'Come and buy your spices for the religious requirement [of *haroset*].' Cf. Tosefta Betzah iii 6; BTPesahim 116a; JTPesahim 37d and parallels.
8. MPesahim x, 4. This is also quoted in the *Haggadah*.
9. On the history of dipping foods at the *Seder*, see J. Tabory, 'The history of the first dipping on Passover eve in the period of the Mishnah and the Talmud', *Bar Ilan* 14–15 (1977), pp. 70–8 (in Hebrew).
10. JTPesahim x, 37c–d.
11. Blood on lintels: Exodus 12. 21–3; plague: 7.20f.
12. BTPesahim 114a–116a.
13. Cf Exodus 5.6–18.
14. Modern Jewish religious law is based on the Babylonian Talmud: it is unusual for rabbinic commentaries to relate to the Jerusalem Talmud.
15. Midrash Exodus Rabbah 1.12.4 with parallels in Palestinian midrashim and BTSotah 11b etc.

16. D. Goldshmidt (ed.), *Seder Rav Amram Ga'on* (Jerusalem, 1971).

17. The Rambam made a number of later alterations to his commentary on the Mishnah, which are noted in the edition by Y. Kapah (Jerusalem, 1963–1968) but apparently not to this section.

18. Y. Kapah (ed.), *Perush le-Mishnaiot*, Pesahim 10, 3 *ad loc.* (Jerusalem, 1963).

19. *Mishneh Torah*, Zemanim 2, Hilkhot Hametz uMatzah, viii, 11 (ed. Mossad HaRav Kook, Jerusalem, 1957).

20. S. Buber (ed.), R Zedekiah b Avraham, *Shibbolei haLeqet* [The Gleaned Ears] (Vilna, repr. Jerusalem, 1962), p. 184, sect. 263.

21. Aigres: qv A. Darmesteter, *Les gloses françaises dans les commentaires talmudiques de Raschi* (Paris, 1929) sv.

22. B. Larioux, 'Cuisines médiévales', in J.-L. Flandrin, M. Montanari, *Histoire de l'alimentation* (Paris, 1996), p. 466.

23. Both appear as common spices in the 14th-century *Viandier* of Taillevent. See on this B. Laurioux, 'Spices in the medieval diet: a new approach', *Food and Foodways* 1 (1985), pp. 43–76; T. Scully, *The Art of Cookery in the Middle Ages* (Woodbridge, 1995, repr. 2002), p. 85.

24. Bertinoro on MPesahim x, 3 9 *ad loc.*

25. Rabbi Manoah b Shimon Badrashi, *Sefer haMenuhah* (repr. Jerusalem, 1967), sect. 7, 11.

26. This is identified by as I. Löw, *Die Flora der Juden* (Wien/Leipzig, 1923 repr. Hildesheim, 1967) II, p. 213 as *Cymbopogon schoenanthus*.

27. It may be that Rabbi Manoah associated cloves with the spice called '*qofer*' which appears in Songs 1.14, where, however, it refers to henna, and not to cloves. For *qofer* see Löw above, sv, and Y. Feliks Spice, *Forest and Garden Trees* (*Plants in Biblical and Rabbinic literature* vol ii), (Jerusalem 1997, in Hebrew), pp. 76–77. Feliks notes that this wrong identification is given in the medieval dictionary called the Aruch.

28. The Rashi-text is to be found at the side of BTPesahim 116a.

29. The commentary of Rashbam is to be found below the Rashi-text at the side of BTPesahim 116a.

30. The Tosafists' commentary is to be found on the other side of the same page, BTPesahim 116a.

31. *Tur, Orah Hayim, Hilkhot Pesah* (repr. Jerusalem, 1960), sect. 473.

32. Y. Freimannen (ed.), Joseph b Moshe, *Sefer Leqet Yosher* (Berlin, repr. Jerusalem, 1964).

33. R Joseph David, *Beit David, a commentary on the Arba'ah Turim* (Saloniki, repr Jerusalem, 1990).

34. I hope to publish these in my forthcoming book on *haroset*.

35. Jacob Meldula, *Orden de la Agada de Pesah, en Hebraico y Español, segun uzan los Judios españoles y portuguezes, traducido del Hebraico y Caldeo* (Amsterdam and London, 1813).

36. Bananas originate in South-East Asia and appear in Palestine following the 7th-century Arab conquest. See on this I. Löw, *Die Flora der Juden* (Wien/Leipzig, 1923 repr. Hildesheim, 1967), II, pp. 253–6.

37. <http://koltorah.org/ravj/*charoset*.htm>

38. In fact apples have been found in Bronze Age Mesopotamia and from the 10th century BCE in Palestine. See on this D. Zohary, M. Hopf, *Domestication of Plants in the Old World* (Oxford, 1994), pp. 162–6.

Authentic? Or just expensive?

John Whiting

The quest for 'authentic' cuisine is an exercise in nostalgia. With our culture in a state of constant flux, authenticity has become the holy grail whose sacramental promise is the recapitulation of lost absolutes. In Marshal McLuhan's famous metaphor, we accelerate into an uncertain future with our eyes fixed on the rear-view mirror, scouring the planet for once-plentiful foods that have become priceless, i.e. both scarce and expensive.

The linguistic root of 'authenticity' is 'authority'. Its Greek source, αυθεντικος [authentikos], is derived in turn from αυθεντια [authentia], which Liddell and Scott defines as 'absolute sway'. French *restaurateurs* exemplify it by forming associations to dictate the precise ingredients of an 'authentic' bouillabaisse or cassoulet – peasant dishes that originated as catch-alls. 'Lor', there ain't no recipe for soup!' a southern cook exclaimed to my father almost a century ago. 'It jes' accumulates!'

When we attempt to arrest or reverse culinary change, we become mired in logical contradiction. The search for absolute authenticity is problematic even with a dish 'invented' by a single chef using the ingredients of his own era; but when it is the simple fare born of stark necessity and constantly varied as abundance or scarcity dictated, the quest becomes an arbitrary and empty ritual.

Generations of migrants have taken their culinary traditions with them into geographical areas where familiar ingredients were unobtainable, thus making compromise imperative. Fortunately for human pleasure as well as survival, our palates are infinitely adaptable. Calvin W. Schwabe's *Unmentionable Cuisine* demonstrates that the most unlikely of comestibles may be judged not merely acceptable but even delicious – *De gustibus* in spades![1]

Haute cuisine, like *haute couture*, is a badge of status that has evolved from a *sine qua non* of human survival. Together they determine the face and figure that the affluent present to the world. Today's massive shift in culinary emphasis from the vital to the cosmetic has had three interlocking effects: [i] Never before have so many consumers aspired to be gourmets. [ii] Gastronomy is now a major industry with a large and prosperous clientele, requiring a complex network of specialist producers and suppliers.[2] [iii] This network is globally interactive, so that any country's most prestigious restaurants are likely to be as ethnically indeterminate as its airline terminals.

Reacting against 'fusion' cuisine, culinary purists have launched a crusade for authenticity, demanding the utmost fidelity to tradition. And yet culinary tradition has always been fluid: many of the foods which the campaigners attempt to preserve or recreate were in the first instance a utilization of the ingredients that were most readily available, prepared with the simple tools that were at hand. The substratum of peasant cuisine is grinding poverty. As John Berger observes at the beginning of his perceptive analysis of global peasantry, *Pig Earth*, 'Peasant life is a life committed completely to survival.'[3]

Two remarkably similar memoirs of life in southern French villages were written by expatriate Englishmen. Unlike their fellow-countryman Peter Mayle, who achieved fame and fortune by transforming a Provençal ruin into a redoubtable playpen, Peter Graham and James Bentley were fully integrated into their respective communities. Graham identifies his in the title: *Mourjou: The Life and Food of an Auvergne Village*. James Bentley, in *Life and Food in the Dordogne*, chose not to reveal his locale, and so it took a certain amount of detective work, together with GPS navigation, for us to reach the tiny village of Turnac, at the end of a cul-de-sac within a horseshoe bend of the Dordogne known locally as the Cingle de Montfort.[4]

Both Graham and Bentley devote their opening chapters to demonstrating that until recent times peasant life was a struggle to wrest a living from limited resources. In his second chapter, 'Seignurial Extravagance', Bentley writes,

> Looking at the food of the Dordogne inevitably plunges us into social history, a history of resentment and bitterness, self-indulgence and deprivation.'[5]

428

Graham is equally unequivocal:
> [T]he Auvergnats…were poor. Before that again, they just about survived at the subsistence level; and before that, in the eighteenth and early nineteenth centuries, they often starved.'[6]

Survival through the winter was precarious. Joyeuse, an ancient village in the Ardèche, has a *Musée de la Châtaigneraie* devoted to what was virtually the only plentiful year-round food. These weren't the *marrons* that are glacéed and packed in pretty boxes, but the more common *châtaigne*, a multiseeded variety that challenged a housewife's ingenuity.[7] As an edible souvenir, the museum sells cakes made from chestnut flour; even loaded with sugar (which few peasants would have had in the larder), they are a taste most easily acquired through dire necessity.

The transmutation of peasant lead into gourmet gold is a complex and fascinating story. It could be said to have begun in the 1860s when the phylloxera aphid, an accidental but ultimately profitable American export, threatened the very existence of the French wine industry.

Having inadvertently created the need, enterprising American vine-growers were quick to meet it by supplying French vintners with aphid-resistant root stock. This necessary importation called into question the unique excellence of French wine, and so a '*vin du terroir*' strategy evolved which declared the locale to be more important than the vines and took the form of a geographically based certification called *appellation contrôlée* (AC). Applied to foodstuffs, it would become the stratagem for promoting French culinary tourism, aided and abetted by the rapid growth of the auto industry; thus Michelin with its Red Guide was able to capitalize on both the object of the journey and the means of transport.

Coming up with a *cuisine du terroir* to go with the *vin* was problematical: to bourgeois taste, authentic peasant food was repugnant. Jean Pierre Poulin, in *Manger aujourd'hui*, reiterates that

> The peasants ate mainly bread....Meals mainly consisted of soups, where a fundamental feature was a piece of stale bread left to soften in the stock.... Sometimes a little meat or, even better, fat or oil, was added for taste.[8]

It was counterproductive to strive for an authenticity that prospective consumers would find distasteful, and so tourist-motivated traditions were invented which gave familiar bourgeois dishes some semblance of local colour. Hermann Bausinger, quoted by Denis Chevalier in *Vives Campagnes, Autrement*, states unequivocally that

> From the 19th century onwards, there were a great many typical villages in the Alps or around the Mediterranean which were devoted to reconstructing and even inventing examples of the past.[9]

429

The fruits of this Orwellian revision might have been titled *The 1984 Cookbook*. Rachel Laudan summarizes its ingenious machinations:

> It made no sense as history. But the French Terroir Strategy was a brilliant marketing device that satisfied modern yearnings for a romanticized past by advertising tradition and exploiting modern methods of production and distribution....The strategy did wonders for big wine growers, restaurant owners, and those producers who could upgrade their products to appeal to sophisticated urban tastes.[10]

This imaginative proliferation of bourgeois gastronomy had no effect on the still meagre diet of the peasants: 'Well into the twentieth century, they...continued to eat a diet that...had nothing to do with the food served to culinary tourists.'[11]

The peasant diet – undernourishing and unappetizing – remained unchanged until the rise of what Laudan calls 'Culinary Modernism', which applied the technology of mass production to the propagation, preparation and distribution of food. It is this, she asserts, that 'brought to an end, at least in the West, a two-tier system of eating', in which the wealthy ate the best that was available and

> the poor who made up more than 80% of the population...survived [on] grains perceived as less desirable...with only the occasional bit of meat....Not until the large scale arable and livestock farming and efficient distribution networks associated with Culinary Modernism brought down the price of white bread and meat did their diet become richer.[12]

Unfortunately the new refinement would eventually replace one set of ills with another. Hungry French peasants would discover that the long-envied white bread with its diminished fibre was a mixed blessing – and now the Third World's bowels are also having to deal with it. Meanwhile, sweet drinks have replaced white bread as the leading source of calories in the average American diet.[13] In Britain, sugar manufacturer Tate and Lyle, one of the country's most prolific engines of obesity, is rewarded with the biggest share of Common Agricultural Policy (CAP) subsidies: at £227m, it gets four times dairy producer Meadow Foods, the second on the list. (Prince Charles' Highgrove estate and Duchy Originals – models of both sustainable and organic production – get a measly £680,835.)[14]

Laudan acknowledges in passing that Culinary Modernism had its problems:

> Migrants often suffered a decline in living standards, even if in the end they or their descendents ended up better off. The increasing distance between producer and consumer, between farm and kitchen left room for the careless or unscrupulous to adulterate food. Newly ploughed land lost fertility without careful husbandry. More highly processed foods were calorie-dense and obesity began to replace deficiency diseases. And many people worried that the world simply could not produce enough wheat and meat for all those who wanted it.[15]

There has been progress, of a sort—the adulteration is now acknowledged microscopically and incomprehensibly on the label. Over 30 years ago, Dr. Benjamin Feingold presented extensive research to the American Medical Association linking food additives to children's learning and behaviour disorders.[16] There were follow-up reports, some confirming Feingold's conclusions, some rejecting them. Then in 2002 a UK government-sponsored MAFF study came to light that had been conducted by the Asthma and Allergy Research Centre, stating unequivocally that *all* children could benefit from the removal of certain specified artificial food colourings from their diet. Having come to this embarrassing conclusion, the report gathered dust for two years until the Food Commission obtained a copy, brushed off the cobwebs and reported it in their *Food Magazine*.[17]

There is financial as well as chemical adulteration. Developed countries protect their indigenous agriculture with trade barriers and tax-supported subsidies such as the Common Agricultural Policy (CAP). The Third World is justifiably resentful of such economic discrimination; but when the barriers are finally broken down, it will not be in order to widen the margin of subsistence for Asian and African farmers, but rather the profit margins of the multi-national food industry: they will invest their capital wherever the farmers can most easily be swindled.[18]

If present economic trends continue, Western agriculture will surely follow the pattern of Western manufacturing. As the agro-industrial giants shift their production to countries where cheap farmland and even cheaper farmers are ripe for exploitation, small farms the world over will become as scarce as small factories. The only ones to remain viable will be those that process their own products and are maintained by artisans who are able to climb aboard Slow Food's Ark of Taste before they are drowned in the flood of ever-cheaper mass-produced imports. Thenceforth their hand-made output will be affordable only by the rich consumers of gastronomic luxuries.

In her earlier 'A World of Inauthentic Cuisine' Laudan's enthusiasm for Culinary Modernism is boundless: '[T]he industrialization of food got underway in the 1880s....A disaster? By my lights it was a triumph.'[19] If triumph it was, it would seem to be turning into tragedy. In the gourmandizing First World, even the media are waking up to the fruits of our cornucopia consumption; but since their *raison d'être* is compulsive shopping, the solutions they offer are not those of dietary restraint but of alternative excesses. Laudan takes umbrage at a Slow Food spokesperson's remark that 'our real enemy is the obtuse [obese?] consumer', but the observation would be echoed by many analysts of human behaviour. It relates to our collective greed, an instrument upon which the food industry has become a virtuoso performer. Those who supply us with virtually everything we eat have learned to manipulate our biological instinct to over-consume today in anticipation of hunger tomorrow. Goaded on by the constant stimulus of advertising, we fatten ourselves against the famine that never materializes.

The threat is greatest in the long-deprived Third World, who are beginning to suffer the ill effects of fast-food feasting. The world-wide prevalence of obesity is already above the critical threshold set by the World Health Organisation (WHO) for epidemics needing intervention.

431

> Paul Zimmet, an Australian physician and researcher who specializes in the study of noncommunicable diseases, wrote in 1996 that 'the [non-insulin-dependent diabetes mellitus] global epidemic is just the tip of a massive social problem now facing developing countries.'... Rates of obesity and diabetes have skyrocketed around the globe, but particularly among traditional peoples in transition... [T]he rapid introduction of processed foods and other conveniences is certainly the proximate force behind this trend.[20]

So much for the transitory and illusory benefits of Culinary Modernism. The saddest cases are those native societies to whom post-colonial policy or an abundant natural resource has brought both prosperity and habitual leisure. Micronesia, a U.S. protectorate; Nauru, grown rich from the mining of phosphate deposits; and certain Native American tribes that a loophole in the law has allowed to open Vegas-style casinos – all have seen gross obesity and its attendant diseases proliferate by geometric progression.[21]

In our own time, *terroir* has been adopted by the Slow Food movement and made a strategy for identifying, preserving and promoting artisanal foods throughout the world.[22] Its aims are ambitiously multicultural and egalitarian: Terra Madre 2004 in Turin was a unique gathering of four thousand small farmers and food producers from 130 countries on six continents. Such a rallying of the world's threatened artisans had never been achieved; alas, by the next attempt much of the diversity may well have vanished.

In collaboration with the regional authorities of Piedmont and Emilia Romagna, Slow Food has established a University of Gastronomic Science with campuses in Pollenzo and Colorno. Its purpose is to turn out graduates capable of directing food production, promotion and marketing, as well as humanistically trained teachers who understand and can communicate the central importance of food in cultural history.[23]

432

The Pollenzo campus is housed in a neo-Gothic complex built in 1833 for the first Italian Agricultural Association. Such massive expenditure requires massive support, which must come in large part from massively rich gastronomes. The magnificently restored buildings also house a first-class restaurant, a wine bank consisting of thousands of rare vintages, and a hotel of considerable comfort. Once settled in, the dedicated bon vivant need never leave the premises.

For the consumer, the products of ethical authenticity come at a price. Cheap food in an industrialized urban society is possible only with mass production and distribution carried out by virtual slave labour on the farm, in the factory and at the check-out – every supermarket bargain has been dearly paid for. Since a primary motivation of Slow Food is to provide a living wage for skilled artisans using the best ingredients, the relative cost of their products inevitably goes ballistic. This is reflected in the events organized by Slow Food's local branches, or 'convivia', at which a not-for-profit tasting of comestibles certified in its Ark of Taste is likely to cost as much as an ample restaurant meal. These products may have been authentic staples of the peasant diet, but you'll find few peasants at the Slow Food table.

Rachel Laudan, in her review of Carlo Petrini's *Slow Food: The Case for Taste*, dismisses Slow Foodies as Culinary Luddites who rewrite history to suit their appetites:

Petrini's is an Italy as artificial as a Maui beach resort with its trucked in sand

and palm trees or a Disney Magic Kingdom with its oversized Mickey and its undersized castle. Instead of white sand and Mickey, we have tiny rural restaurants that offer up wonderful food, shops that offer artisanal bread, cheeses and salami.[24]

Taking the micky with a vengeance! Unfortunately for her argument, Laudan has singled out one of Slow Food's more seductive attractions. These delightful inns, some a century old or more, have been searched out, not made-to-order, and you'll find hundreds listed in its annual guidebook, *Osterie d'Italia*. After you've experienced their generosity, hospitality and general excellence – and at the cost of a nondescript *autostrada* rest stop – you'll be in no mood to inform the management that Petrini's theory of authenticity and sustainability is logically flawed and historically inaccurate.

But you may well have spotted Rachel dining at the next table. In her provocative essay for the first issue of *Gastronomica*, in which she plays devil's advocate on behalf of 'modern, fast, processed food', she confesses to being a closet gourmet whose culinary tastes were formed under the tutelage of Elizabeth David, Richard Olney, Paula Wolfert and *Saveur*.[25] Her public rejection of their counsel is tantamount to biting the hand with which she feeds herself. But it should come as no surprise; more than one post-modern architect has chosen to live in a thatched cottage.

Rachel Laudan's conclusions may be open to doubt, but the seminal questions she raises remain largely unanswered by the Gastrocrats (which is why she necessarily occupies a disproportionate amount of space in this paper). Placating our consciences while titillating our palates is one thing; feeding the world is another. Genuinely sustainable agriculture on a global scale would be fundamentally at odds with the entire socio-economic system of which the existing food industry is a seamless part.

This fundamental contradiction appears to be not just a product of nineteenth century capitalism, but a part of our socio-economic structure from the very beginning. Agriculture has always been a potentially dangerous and self-contradictory solution to the problem of human sustenance. Ronald Wright, in *A Brief History of Progress*, summarizes the conflict with dramatic clarity:

> The invention of agriculture is itself a runaway train, leading to vastly expanded populations but seldom solving the food problem…The food crisis…has merely been postponed by switching to hybrid seed and chemical farming, at great cost to soil health and plant diversity.[26]

In other words, the multinational food industry is a primary impetus towards over-population, obesity, pollution and greenhouse gasses. The burgeoning Third World is placing demands on the agricultural ecostructure that go far beyond any that our planet has yet experienced. As fertile soil and unpolluted water grow ever scarcer, sustainable agriculture, long dismissed as a starry-eyed fantasy, is becoming the only game in town.

Some isolated efforts at sustainability, both individual and collective, have had a measure of success. In the depths of the Great Depression a best-selling American wish-book was *Five Acres and Independence: A Handbook for Small Farm Management*,[27] which set out to free the family from the devastation of a mismanaged economy. Real independence was of course illusory: unless he were to return to the stone age, the solitary farmer was reliant on the tools, seeds and materials evolved by the very system from whose control he sought to escape.

Sometimes a prosperous community with a leavening of campaigning intellectuals can produce a radical alternative. Berkeley, California is such a place: for well over a quarter-century it has furnished us with shining examples of local organically grown seasonal produce, prepared to a high standard. As with others that have followed suit, its success has depended in large measure on prosperity, geography and climate. And what is 'local'? California, covering 770 miles of latitude and three miles of altitude, encompasses an infinity of ecologies. Living off local seasonal foodstuffs in Greenland would be, as it were, a different kettle of fish; and as for the Sahara...

Even in Berkeley, most food is still peddled in the same old packets. Demand for organic produce may be growing by an encouragingly large proportion of itself, but in Europe and the U.S. it has fluctuated within about 2–4 per cent of the total market. Fashion may raise it by a percentage point or two, but its significantly greater cost will continue to put it beyond the means of any but the comfortably well off. Industrial agriculture is likely to expand exponentially until the oceans rise, the oil is exhausted, the rivers run dry and the soil is depleted.

Meanwhile, the mills of the gods grind ever faster and coarser. Twenty years ago my wife heard a food industry spokesman on TV who nailed his colours to the mast with a resounding thwack:

> Two hundred years ago everybody made their own clothes. Nowadays nobody makes their own clothes unless it's their hobby. The same thing will happen with food: I estimate that within 50 years dinner will be something people will go out and buy, and nobody will cook, unless it's their hobby. We in the food industry are working towards that.

With the global food industry setting the menu, our cuisine is being ripped apart and processed to anonymity as inexorably as is our clothing in the hands of the rag trade. Now that all of life's needs and wishes are available under one roof, can we expect more than a few rebels to reject the food that comes pouring through the same flood-gates as their clothes, their cars and their computers?

Eating healthily, ethically and aesthetically is not an easy option for the impecunious – and in the apparently prosperous West they are on the increase:

Over the past 25 years the lives of working Americans have become ever less secure. Jobs come without health insurance; corporations default on their pension obligations; workers lose their jobs more often, and unemployment lasts much longer than it used to.[28]

Europe with its shrinking job market and swelling welfare rolls is not far behind.

Until recent times, the primary means of transmitting culinary traditions from generation to generation was mother-daughter apprenticeship. Once the continuity is broken, as it was by the English Enclosures and the Scottish Clearances when peasants were driven off their lands and out of their kitchens,[29] much of the legacy was reduced to legend. Those recipes that were written down become the gold standard by which authenticity is measured.

Traditional recipes are a part of history and, like other historical documents, they may be spurious. In the case of modern *cuisine du terroir*, many of them are the products of inventive genius—the art world would call them fakes.[30] In Gertrude Stein's succinct words, 'History tells us history tells us'.

Even a genuinely authentic recipe is only a freeze-frame, a snapshot taken at an arbitrarily chosen moment in a spatial/temporal continuum. It is McLuhan's rearview mirror par excellence. As John Thorne shrewdly observes, it glosses over the 'muddles and mistakes and wrong turns' that have preceded every culinary advance, whether in the castle or the hovel:

435

> [V]ery few cooks are willing or even able to evoke the ferment, the confusion, the groping before the moment that shaped the dish. What we get instead is a rationale that works backward from the finished dish, a rationale that makes everything seem as if it had all been clear and obvious from the start.[31]

A by-product of this linearity is that authors of cookery books rarely cross-reference each other's recipes.[32] Thorne, taking as an example the simple Italian dish *risi e bisi*, compares in detail a number of authoritative modern sources in which the rice and peas, together with other widely varying ingredients, may end up as anything from soup to risotto.[33] To add to the confusion, the further back one goes the more likely that the ingredients themselves would have differed in texture and flavour from their modern mass-produced equivalents – or even, indeed, from the latter's luxurious gourmet-targeted alternatives.

Step-by-step, stand-facing-the-stove recipes of the sort favoured in lifestyle pages are fundamental to the food industry, which requires that every stage in the manufacture of its culinary clones be carried out in accordance with a veritable encyclopaedia of explicit instructions. Skilled labour is superfluous. As Eric Schlosser documents in *Fast Food Nation*, supermarkets have phased out their trained butchers; many restaurants, working from freezer to microwave, no longer require even short-order cooks, let alone chefs.[34] It is a system designed by geniuses to be executed by idiots.

Before the era of celebrity chefs and food factories, how did recipes evolve? *New Yorker* business columnist James Surowiecki argues in *The Wisdom of Crowds* that 'under the right circumstances, groups are remarkably intelligent, and are often smarter than the smartest people in them.'[35] If we were to apply his principles to the evolution of cuisine, they might read as follows:

The 'collective intelligence' of a community of domestic cooks will probably result in a better dish than would be produced by most of them working on their own. But four conditions must first be met:

1. Diversity. A group of cooks with many different points of view will make better collective decisions than when everyone follows exactly the same recipe.

2. Independence. 'People's opinions [must not be] determined by those around them.'

3. Decentralization. 'Power does not fully reside in one central location, and many of the important decisions are made by individuals based on their own local and specific knowledge rather than by an omniscient or farseeing planner.' In other words, there is no 'boss cook' whose word every housewife follows.

4. Aggregation; i.e. a community of cooks tasting each other's dishes and learning how results were achieved which most of them prefer. If the end product of this interaction is preserved in manuscript, it may at some future date be pronounced 'authentic' – and woe betide the cook who, through changing taste, ingredients or lifestyle, dares to alter it![36]

What, exactly, is culinary authenticity? The very concept is caught in a pincers movement. On one flank, the food industry has hijacked traditional recipes, transforming them into artificial travesties in which only the names survive. In a counterattack to restore integrity, gourmet purists have taken simple dishes adjusted over the centuries to keep them practical and economical, and frozen them in the past, converted into luxurious prescriptions requiring exotic and costly ingredients.

Those of us who wish to eat well on limited means must redefine authenticity in accordance with new criteria. If the concept is to have any relevance to our daily diet, it must be founded, not on inflexible catalogues of rare ingredients and arcane procedures, but on an inventive, creative and adaptive attitude towards making and partaking. Beyond the recipes, we must strive for authenticity in ourselves. In other words, we must become culinary artists.

'Chefs are artisans, not artists,' Alice Waters protests.[37] Or, as a Balinese once put it to John Cage, 'We don't have any art, we just try to do everything as well as we can.' But artists, like cooks, are good at muddling through. When they can't afford canvas, paint or marble, they come up with 'found objects'. We regard Picasso's post-war use of junk as delightfully witty and inventive, a mark of his originality and nonconformity, forgetting that conventional artists' and sculptors' materials had become extremely scarce. He worked with what was to hand.

So did Julia Child. In the late 1950s when she was writing her contributions to

Mastering the Art of French Cooking, American housewives had access only to the most basic of ingredients. Making extensive use of the U.S. Army's Post Exchange in Paris, she jointly authored a book which might have been called (as she says in her Foreword) *French Cooking from the American Supermarket.*[38]

Now that the exotic is commonplace, Julia Child's pragmatism has become a rod with which to beat her (cut, of course, from a pollarded, locally-grown organic birch). But let the purist whose cupboard is empty of inauthentic produce be the first to strike a blow. Gourmets with more taste than income have always lived in two parallel worlds. If we were always to eat by the uncompromising standards of *cuisine véritable* – nothing but the very best! – and hygiene – nothing but the freshest and the cleanest! – we would spend a fortune on ingredients and then be forced to throw half of them away.

In practice, there is the *sans pareil* of which we sing the praises, and then there is what we can afford for everyday. On the one hand, Jeffrey Steingarten flies the seven skies with a bottomless purse, seeking out the rarest and the finest of everything edible; on the other, John Thorne tells us what he does with the mass-produced American chicken thighs that even the Chinese reject. He also confesses ruefully that for a while he had to give up his favorite mail-order coffee, brewing instead what came in cans from the local supermarket. For John, 2002 was not a vintage year.

'We have more than enough masterpieces,' wrote Jane Grigson; 'what we need is a better standard of ordinariness.'[39] Carve it on every kitchen wall! M. F. K. Fisher's Dijon landlady, Madame Ollangnier, was notorious in the local markets for buying their cheapest merchandise, however unpromising:

> Storekeepers automatically lowered their prices when they saw her com-
> ing…Up would come the trapdoor to the cellar, and down Madame would
> climb…[S]he would pick up a handful of bruised oranges, a coconut with a
> crack in it, perhaps even some sprouting potatoes…And yet…from that little
> hole, which would have made an American shudder in disgust, she turned out
> daily two of the finest meals I have ever eaten.[40]

What was eccentricity in Madame Ollangier has become necessity for a growing army of the economically challenged. A friend surviving on an avant-garde musician's income lives in an urban area with the usual mix of food sources. He buys his household's fresh produce from neighbourhood ethnic markets – much cheaper than 'bargain' superstores. Both he and his wife cook well and his family eats with great pleasure and integrity. Most of their staples, however, come from Asda; shopping elsewhere, he has determined, would cost him an extra forty pounds a week. Though he believes firmly in eating locally and seasonally and supports artisanal producers in the various European countries to which he often travels, when he is at home, living day-to-day, he refuses to sacrifice his family's comfort and well-being to abstract principle.

My friend exemplifies the dilemma facing those who must watch the pennies but are possessed of both a palate and a conscience. There are of course others worse off, such as those whose jobs have been exported or their pensions stolen. The trickle-down effect in our laissez-fairyland is draining more and more of the once-middle class into an economic slough. In the West our land-based peasantry has virtually disappeared, but a new proletariat is emerging for whom the manufactured environment is the unnatural world from which they must somehow wring a precarious subsistence. As the supermarket bargain bins become the last wilderness in which to forage, they must revert to the ancient pragmatism of peasant inventiveness.

My thanks to Rachel Laudan for her inspiration, encouragement and tolerance.

Bibliography

Apple, R. W., Jr., 'Keep These Kids From Eating Veggies? Try', *New York Times*, 6 July, 2005.

Bentley, James, *Life and Food in the Dordogne* (New York: New Amsterdam, 1986).

Berger, John, *Pig Earth* (London: Bloomsbury, 1979).

Caballero, Oscar, *Text and Pretext in Textures: el Bulli, Soler & Adrià in Context* (Spain: Gourmand Books, 2004) <http://www.gourmandbooks.com/caballero.htm>

Campbell, Denis, '90% of children 'set to be couch potatoes'', *The Observer*, 29 May 2005, <http://observer.guardian.co.uk/uk_news/story/0,6903,1494947,00.html>

Child, Julia, Louisette Bertholde, Simone Beck, *Mastering the Art of French Cooking* (New York: Knopf, 1961).

Curtis, Mark, 'Brown's doleful role at Gleneagles', *Guardian*, 9 July 2005, <http://www.guardian.co.uk/comment/story/0,3604,1524757,00.html>

Feingold, B. F., 'Hyperkinesis and learning disabilities linked to artificial food flavours and colours', *American Journal of Nursing*, 75, 797–803, 1975.

The Food Magazine, Issue 59, Oct/Dec 2002, pp. 1, 3.

Fisher, M. F. K., *Long Ago in France* (London: Flamingo, 1993).

Graham, Peter, *Mourjou: The Life and Food of an Auvergne Village* (London: Viking, 1998).

Kains, M. G., *Five Acres and Independence: A Handbook for Small Farm Management* (New York: Greenberg, 1935).

Keating, Matt, 'Nature loses out to nurture, say researchers', *Guardian*, 1 June 2005.

Krugman, Paul, 'America Wants Security', *New York Times*, 23 May 2005.

Laudan, Rachel, 'Desperately Seeking Authenticity: But what would an 'authentic' cookbook really look like?', *Los Angeles Times*, 19 December 2001 <http://www.whitings-writings.com/laudan_authenticity.htm> (with the author's permission)

———, 'Slow Food, the French Terroir Strategy, and Culinary Modernism. An Essay Review of Carlo Petrini, trans. William McCuaig, foreword Alice Waters, Slow Food: The Case for Taste (New York: Columbia University Press, 2001), xxiv + 155 pp.', *Food, Culture and Society*, 7 (2004), pp. 133–146. [ms. copy from author; footnotes not paged]

———, 'A Plea for Culinary Modernism: Why We Should Love Modern, Fast, Processed Food', *Gastronomica* 1 (February 2001), pp. 36–44 [ms. copy from author; footnotes not paged; available online in pdf for $12 at <http://caliber.ucpress.net/doi/abs/10.1525/gfc.2001.1.1.36>]

_____, 'A world of Inauthentic Cuisine' (Oregon State University website, seminar on Cultural and Historical Aspects of Foods, 2000) [earlier version of *Gastronomica* article above; available free online at <http://food.oregonstate.edu/ref/culture/laudan.html>]

Mathiason, Nick, 'So who's milking it?', *Observer*, 26 June 2005 <http://observer.guardian.co.uk/business/story/0,6903,1514504,00.html>

Petrini, Carlo, trans. William McCuaig, foreword Alice Waters, *Slow Food: The Case for Taste* (New York: Columbia University Press, 2001).

Prestowitz, Clyde, 'Globalization Pyramid Game', *Boston Globe*, 31 May 2005.

Richardson, Paul, *Cornucopia: A Gastronomic Tour of Britain* (London: Little, Brown, 2000).

Schlosser, Eric, *Fast Food Nation: The Dark Side of the American Meal* (Boston: Houghton Mifflin, 2001).

Schwabe, Calvin W., *Unmentionable Cuisine* (Charlottesville: University Press of Virginia, 1979).

Shell, Ellen Ruppell, 'New World Syndrome', *The Atlantic Monthly*, June 2001

'Slow Food Goes Academic', *Fine Food Digest*, vol. 5 no. 1.

Spencer, Colin, *British Food: An Extraordinary Thousand Years of History* (London: Grub Street, 2002).

Suroweiki, James, *The Wisdom of Crowds: Why the Many Are Smarter Than the Few and How Collective Wisdom Shapes Business, Economies, Societies and Nations* (New York: Random House, 2004).

'Sweet drinks are main source of calories in the US', *Food e-News* Edition 237: 25 May–01 June 2005.

Thorne, John, *Simple Cooking* (New York: North Point, 1996).

Toussaint-Samat, Maguelonne, trans. Anthea Bell, *A History of Food* (Oxford: Blackwell, 1992).

Wright, Roger, *A Short History of Progress* (Edinburgh: Canongate, 2005).

Notes

1. Schwabe, passim. His Berkeley feasts were legendary.
2. Laudan (2004).
3. Berger, p. xi.
4. Alas, we were to learn that the Reverend James Bentley had died the year before; but his wife gave us hospitality, obviously touched that we had thought so highly of him as to seek out his anonymous village.
5. Bentley, p. 26.
6. Graham, p. xiii.
7. Toussaint-Samat, p. 716.
8. Quoted in Caballero, p. 46.
9. Ibid.
10. Laudan (2004).
11. Ibid.
12. Ibid.
13. Sweet drinks: research presented at the Experimental Biology Conference in April 2005.
14. Mathiason.
15. Laudan (2004).
16. Feingold.
17. *Food*, pp. 1, 3.
18. Curtis.
19. Laudan (2000).
20. Shell.
21. Ibid.
22. Petrini.
23. *Slow*.
24. Laudan (2004).
25. Laudan (2001).

26. Wright, p. 108.
27. Kains.
28. Krugman.
29. Spencer, p. 246.
30. History aside, a 'fake' recipe may still be delicious!.
31. Thorne (1987), p. xxii.
32. The honourable exceptions that Thorne cites include Elizabeth David, Alan Davidson and Diana Kennedy.
33. Thorne, pp. xxi–xxix.
34. Schlosser, pp. 154, 6.
35. Suroweiki, p. 4.
36. My childhood experience of church potluck suppers suggests that Suroweiki is on to a good thing.
37. Apple.
38. Child, p. vii.
39. Richardson, p. 277 (he does not identify the author in the text, but he told me later that it was indeed Jane Grigson).
40. Fisher, pp. 12–14.

Catherine de' Medici's Fork

Carolin C. Young

The myth that Catherine de' Medici (1519–89), with a fleet of Italian chefs and a dinner fork, sparked a culinary revolution when she arrived in France to marry the future Henri II (r. 1547–59) in 1533 is one of the most oft-repeated in history. However, in *Savoring the Past*, Barbara Ketcham Wheaton meticulously laid out numerous arguments against its truth.[1] To summarize these with my own nuances:

(1) Catherine was but one of myriad Italian imports that her father-in-law, François I (r. 1515–47), brought to France. In addition to crate-loads of Italian artworks and antiquities, he sponsored artists including da Vinci, Cellini, Fiorentino, and Primaticcio to join his court. Italian bankers, merchants, advisors, doctors, and musicians also made their home in France, which had developed an increasing Italomania from the time that Charles VIII (r. 1483–98) first invaded the peninsula.

(2) With a few notable exceptions, Catherine exerted little court influence until after her husband's death in 1559. The fourteen-year-old bride was merely a pawn in a complex game of political jockeying played out between her 'uncle' (actually her cousin), Pope Clement VII, and François. Moreover, her husband was the king's second son, not heir to the throne.

When Clement died a year after Catherine's wedding, but before paying the balance of her hefty dowry, the French grumbled that they had allowed a lowly merchant's daughter marry into the royal family (conveniently ignoring that her mother, Madeleine de la Tour d'Auvergne, had been one of France's noblest and wealthiest heiresses).

Catherine failed to get pregnant for more than a decade so they threatened to replace her. Even after giving birth in 1544 to the first of ten babies, Catherine smoldered in the background while her husband's glamorous mistress, Diane de Poitiers, dictated everything from politics to Henri's visits to his wife's bed.

(3) Documented evidence that a tangible, Italianate shift in French cooking, either in the form of recipes or lists of provisions, does not exist. Stephen Mennell stresses this last point, adding that, in his opinion, because early cookbooks appeared primarily in the vulgar languages rather than in Latin they must have been addressed to cooks more than to high-born gourmands, and, therefore, reflect actual culinary practice.[2]

This evidence should seemingly have rung the death knell on Catherine's tale.

Nevertheless, using an American search engine, the words 'Catherine de Medici' and 'fork' yielded 855 responses in a mere three seconds. The story turns up in such influential places as a leading French culinary study guide and in the most recent French and English language biographies of Catherine.[3] It is often the only culinary history 'fact' that non-specialists proudly claim to know.

Catherine's fork warrants closer scrutiny if only because so many people believe in it. Regardless of factual veracity, a story ascends into the realm of myth if it resonates as metaphorically true. Conversely, anachronistic events that fail to grab the popular imagination quickly drop from the collective memory. What, then, lies at the symbolic core of Catherine's myth? Where did it originate?

Ostensibly unique to Europe and its former colonies, forks are so ubiquitous to Western diners that they practically embody 'civility' itself. Why has European history credited an innovation so emblematic of its civilization to one of the most vilified personalities in its annals?

Catherine de' Medici, after all, is a very loaded character upon whom to attribute the spread of fork-use – especially if she didn't do so. However innocent she was upon arrival, by the time she died in France she had governed the nation through one of its most turbulent periods, including seven civil wars of religion. She almost certainly (although no one has ever proven it) played a pivotal role in orchestrating the St. Bartholomew's Day Massacre of August 1572, a horrific bloodbath that left thousands of French Protestants dead.

442

Narrations of the queen's wickedness grew increasingly colorful over time, reaching their nadir in the 19th century when Jules Michelet dubbed her 'that maggot which came out of Italy's tomb' and Alexandre Dumas embellished rumors of her various poisonings and plottings into *La Reine Margot* and *Les Quarante-cinq*, which remain classics today.[4] Tales of her heinousness took on such lives of their own that, collectively, they are called 'The Black Legend'. They continue to overshadow the work of numerous apologists, who have attempted to realign Catherine's reputation with the documented facts.[5] Of course, the more lurid version of Catherine's biography not only makes a better story but also exculpates French national guilt for widespread religious persecution by conveniently blaming a foreign (and female) scapegoat. Still commonly accepted as 'truth', Catherine's tenacious 'Black Legend' spills into almost any discussion of the queen. No myth connected to her can be properly understood without looking for traces of this potent fable.

The fork is but one of many items whose introduction to France has been attributed to Catherine. Wheaton notes that the queen has also been credited with importing parsley, artichokes, lettuce, and glazed earthenware in addition to Florentine perfumes, fireworks, embroidery, cuisine, pastry, confectionery, and liqueurs.[6] Broccoli, green peas, tomatoes, fruit sorbets, underwear, side-saddle riding, folding-fans, handkerchiefs, and nicotine must be added to the list as well as pasta, which, in Catherine's day, purportedly 'conquered the French.'[7]

Ignoring the New World imports, Catherine's fork succinctly encapsulates the broader idea of her Italianizing influence. It does not, however, appear in the earliest version of Catherine's culinary legend cited by Wheaton: the entry on '*cuisine*' in Diderot and D'Alembert's 1754 *Encyclopédie*, which explains that refined dining arrived in France via the Italians, principal inheritors of ancient Roman excess, who came over the mountains to France during the reign of Henri II.[8] 'One of the least debts,' the author continues, 'we owe to that crowd of corrupt Italians who served at the court of Catherine de Medici,' then adding that earlier French kings had successfully curbed any latent epicureanism.

This heavy-handed editorializing succinctly conveys multiple layers of meaning. It summarizes French culinary history with the convenient *aide mémoire* of a well-known personality; by nostalgically conjuring a lost, golden age prior to the Italian cultural invasion, the author reprises a centuries-old French nationalistic theme; and this implicitly criticizes French cuisine of the author's era as overly refined and decadent, a viewpoint famously shared by fellow *Encyclopédie* contributor Jean-Jacques Rousseau, who advocated a simple, back-to-nature diet in such novels as *Émile*.[9]

This back-handed swipe at 18th-century French court cuisine depends upon the reader's acceptance of Catherine's 'Black Legend'. In this context, her general greed and depravity color the claim about her overzealous gourmandise (and that of her Italian favorites). The subtle dig at French cooking would be lost if the Italianizing influence were attributed to, for example, the perennially beloved François I.

However, like all good myths, the legend of Catherine's culinary revolution contains more than one grain of truth. In fact, an earlier reference to Catherine's culinary innovations in France, albeit an oblique one, dates back to one of her contemporaries. In 1602, Barthélemy de Laffemas, sieur de Bautort, a valet and commerce advisor to Henri IV (r. 1589–1610), published a treatise about the silk-manufacturing industry in France, which he credits to Catherine and compares to other significant novelties unknown to previous generations: turkeys; artichokes; cauliflower; new types of grapevines, honey-producing bees, fruits, and metals; silver-mining, printing presses, and cannons.[10]

The fork also made its first published appearance in France during Catherine's lifetime. C. Calviac's *La Civile honesteté pour les enfants*, explaining the differences between French, Italian and German dining etiquette, states that Germans always eat soup and anything liquid with spoons; the Italians use forks; and the French, either one or the other, according to whim.[11] Catherine's name never appears, yet a utensil not previously discussed in France, and acknowledged to be Italian, had become sufficiently common to mention as an acceptable implement. Significantly, Calviac's publication date of 1560 coincides with the queen's leap into the foreground of French politics.

When François II (r. 1559–60) inherited the throne after Henri II's untimely death on 10 July 1559 Catherine put aside royal protocol, which required widowed

443

queens to stay near their deceased husbands for forty days, in order to orchestrate events on behalf of her son. Fifteen years old and in fragile health, the king, although legally considered a major, obviously needed serious help. Catherine cleverly engineered that the Duke and Cardinal of Guise, uncles of the king's wife, Mary Queen of Scots (r. 1542–86), might run his Council instead of more probable but troublesome candidates.

In another, highly visible break with tradition, she immediately donned, and, except at her sons' weddings, for the rest of her life dressed in, the black mourning of Italy instead of the white customarily worn by widowed French queens. Known for her luxurious tastes, she always dressed in Florentine style.

That Calviac's text mentions the fork, albeit without Catherine's name, at this very moment, succinctly encapsulates the queen's influence up to that date, which was opaque but far greater than generally assumed.

To insure that his niece's trousseau would impress, Clement VII had dispatched the bride's great-aunt Caterina Cibo, Duchess of Camerino, from Rome to Florence to supervise its preparation.[12] She, in turn, sought assistance from the renowned Isabella d'Este, one of the greatest taste-makers of the 16th century.

By Catherine's 1533 wedding forks were common among well-born Italians but, with the exception of rare ginger or suckett forks listed on royal inventories, such as that of King Charles V (r. 1364–80), virtually unheard of in France.[13] At his death in 1492, the bride's great-grandfather, Lorenzo the Magnificent, had owned eighteen, considerably fewer than many of his Florentine contemporaries.[14] So, it is highly probable that Catherine got packed off to France with more than one fork in her trunks.

The bride's aunt, together another female relative, Maria Salviati, also guided their young charge in matters of protocol. Prior to her departure, the 'duchessina' played a prominent role in numerous official entertainments and, as her last act before leaving, hosted a banquet for Florence's distinguished ladies.[15] Seven years earlier, Eustachio Celebrino da Udine had in Venice published the first instructions specifying that a fork be laid at the place of every diner.[16]

Catherine arrived in Marseilles with sixty galleys filled with nobles, servants, cooks, and supplies. The Pope himself accompanied her to perform the ceremony and to host an official wedding feast that offered France a first-hand taste of Roman opulence. Although François I had grandly fêted the last major French-Italian intermarriage, that of Catherine's parents, at the Château d'Amboise in 1518, such an eminent and extensive Italian entourage had neither attended, nor proffered hospitality on a papal scale.

The wedding dazzled bystanders, who recorded shimmering brocades; the bride's ermine-trimmed gown; her staggering jewels; her theatrical cousin Cardinal Ippolito de' Medici's Turkish-clad entourage; and a raucous post-wedding party, at which court ladies, spurred on by a Marseillaise courtesan, purportedly dipped their bared breasts into goblets of wine.[17] With such wonders to behold it is hardly surprising that any forks wielded at the proceedings failed to get mentioned. Unfortunately, no record of the menu, nor of any forks, has yet come to light.

François I had already begun to hold Italian-style entertainments that Catherine later became famous for. Typically, a classical theme unified poetry, set to music; ballet; and an elaborate presentation of food into a multi-sensory spectacle. Florence's Biblioteca nazionale contains a drawing, attributed to Primaticcio, depicting a faun, Sylvan and Pan carrying platters of food, probably made as a preparatory sketch for a masquerade held for the marriage of the Duke of Nevers to Mademoiselle de Vendôme in 1539.[18]

Her father-in-law's example inspired Catherine; but she, in turn, was known to teach him Italian dances and singing rounds.[19]

When Henri and Catherine subsequently became King and Queen of France 'an infinite stream of Italians came to the new Court', the Imperial ambassador reported to Charles V (r. 1519–56).[20] Italians in the royal employ rose, as did, in opposition to Diane's insatiable greed, visitors to the queen's household, which was managed by her Florentine chief *maître d'hôtel*, Luigi Alamanni.

Catherine's strongly pro-Italian positions, particularly of Henri's territorial campaigns, earned her the nickname, 'the Italian Queen of France.'[21] The queen wielded little power in comparison to the royal mistress but attained prominent positions for her Strozzi cousins; other *fuorusciti* (Florentines exiled by Cosimo de' Medici), who had swelled France's population; and many Italians who had arrived with her in 1533. So too, Laffemas asserts that Catherine diligently fostered Italian skills in her widespread properties, an effort whose effects, he explains, only realized their potential under Henri IV because of the ensuing civil wars.

445

On 10 June 1549, the City of Paris honored Catherine with a feast that, although ostensibly medieval in character (roasted swans being the most expensive menu item), also featured New World turkeys and many 'Italian' items that she became famously associated with: artichokes, asparagus, cucumbers, peas, parsley, and special tools for crimping tablecloths and napkins into fancy shapes.[22] The first known mention of a cadenas, containing fork, knife and spoon and with a built-in salt, dates to approximately the following year.[23]

It was, however, the years after Calviac's 1560 publication that shaped the queen's immortal image as an unrivalled hostess and as a world-class villainess.

On 5 December 1560, François II died and the throne passed to nine-year-old Charles IX (r. 1560–74). Powerful nobles, pitted into factions of ultra-Catholics and Protestants, coveted the crown for themselves. Catherine dexterously played these rivals against each other and was declared Regent.

Entertaining constituted a key tool in the Queen Mother's strategy of reconciliation, which sought (not altogether successfully) to keep peace by checking both parties. Her feasts and balls not only often commemorated hard-won treaties but also forced erstwhile combatants to physically break bread and dance together.

Frances Yates, Barbara Wheaton and Roy Strong have written extensively on Catherine's 'magnificences', as her festivals combining song, dance, drama, and food were called.[24] Regarded as the queen's most original contribution to French culture, these grand parties anticipated the collations organized by Louis XIV (r. 1643–1715) at Versailles both in style and in intent. In her own era, Pierre de Bourdeille, seigneur de Brantôme noted:

> She [Catherine] has such a knack that no matter what spectacles were offered at Court, hers surpassed all the others. ... And if such shows were expensive, they also gave great pleasure, and people used to say that she wished to imitate the Roman emperors, who studied how to exhibit games to the people and give them pleasure, and so amuse them that they had no time to get into mischief.[25]

When Catherine's eldest daughter, Élisabeth, married to Philip II of Spain (r. 1556–98), visited her in Bayonne in 1565, critics noted that no expense was spared for the celebrations and that a great deal of money was borrowed. Brantôme, who rightly understood that this was no mere family reunion but a diplomatic entente with France's most threatening rival, defended Catherine:

> [T]he Queen said she had done it to show other nations that France was not so totally ruined and poverty-stricken by reason of her recent wars as was supposed; and that; since she was able to spend so much on frivolity, she would be able to do far more for affairs of consequence and importance ... And so it was for good and sufficient reason that our most Christian Queen made this splendid festival; for be assured that if she had not done so, the visitors would have derided us and returned home with a poor opinion of France.[26]

The Bayonne festivities occurred as the highlight of a nearly two-and-a-half year trek through France to crusade for a peace, uniting both religions under one crown. Abel Jouan, a sommelier in Charles IX's 'cuisine de bouche', published an account of the trip in 1566, which records that, typically, the king made his Solemn Entry in one town, then dined publicly in another. Unfortunately, except for occasional local specialties – oranges and peppers in Brignoles; in Angoulême, 'the best trout ever' – Jouan describes little of what was eaten or how.[27]

However, a first edition copy of Bartolomeo Scappi's *Opera*, now at the Bibliothèque nationale in Paris, and bearing Catherine de' Medici's royal arms, suggests that, at least by the time of its publication in 1570, the queen, or someone in her circle, followed Italian culinary fashions.[28] In addition to an encyclopedic recipe collection, the book contains the first printed illustration of a fork together with a knife and spoon.

This book's early presence in France points to another difficulty in evaluating the extent of an 'Italianizing' influence there. Fluency, particularly in the Tuscan dialect, was considered a sign of refinement at the Valois courts.[29] The prevalence of Italian as a *lingua parla* means that Scappi didn't need to be translated into French in order to have an impact.

As previously stated, Italian servants increased steadily throughout this period. Jacqueline Boucher has shown that between 1570 and 1589 the percentage of Italian chambermaids employed at the Queen Mother's residence rose from ten to eighteen percent.[30] At her death, 33 per cent of her *maîtres d'hôtel* were Italian. Moreover, French culinary instruction, now as then, emphasizes hands-on training rather than the study of books.

It is both possible and very likely that the French elite embraced Italian cuisine and manners as enthusiastically as they did architecture, art, music, dance, literature, and theatre. However, to openly adopt an 'Italian' habit was to conspicuously pledge allegiance to the Valois – an increasingly dubious prospect as events unfurled.

In 1578 Henri Estienne published a treatise decrying the corrosive effect of the Italian language upon the French, especially in the speech of courtiers.[31] Scholars conjecture that this same man probably also authored the virulent diatribe against Catherine entitled '*Discours merveilleux de la vie, actions et déportemens de Catherine de Médicis*' (Fantastic Treatise on the Life, Actions and Misdeeds of Catherine de' Medici).[32] Written in 1574, fresh on the heels of St. Bartholomew's Day, the text goes far beyond blaming the Queen Mother for this brutal atrocity, which marked an irredeemable exception to her usual policy. It condemns Catherine as a 'Machiavellian', a poisoner of the black arts, and a power-hungry Italian mother. These claims gathered a veneer of authenticity with time and lie at the root of Catherine's 'Black Legend'.

The *Discours merveilleux* exemplifies the wildly unreliable but vastly entertaining anti-royalist propaganda that circulated freely with the help of an explosive publishing industry and a crown too weakened to enforce censorship or libel laws. Because these documents, written with strong biases and political objectives, and often at a far remove from events, survive, while the personalities they damned do not, they are often misread as 'truth' rather than as records of popular hearsay.

The attenuated elegance of Catherine's marvel-inducing festivals provided ample fodder for critics. In June 1575, the Protestant chronicler, Pierre de L'Estoile, reported that at a grand wedding feast for a brother of Queen Louise (wife of Henri III, r. 1574 – 89, the third of Catherine's sons to reign) the Queen Mother ate so much – especially of her favorites: artichoke hearts, cockscombs, and kidneys – that she made herself ill.[33] Her frequent stomach ailments were commonly attributed to gluttony.[34]

At the most excessive of Catherine's celebrations – a banquet at Chenonceau in May 1577 that marked the reconciliation between her youngest son, the Duke d'Anjou, and his brother, the king. L'Estoile recounted that, in a titillating reversal of normal court etiquette, instead of gentlemen serving the ladies, on this occasion France's most

447

beautiful and high-born women waited upon the men; and, more scandalous still, did so half-naked and with their hair unpinned in long, flowing tresses.[35]

Although conservative in her own sexual morals, Catherine's political expediency overcame personal scruples when it came to the damsels who surrounded her. In imitation of François I's famous '*petite bande*', she gathered at her side charming court beauties; gorgeously attired them; and then encouraged them to seduce important leaders from both factions and to report back to her. Known as the 'flying squadron,' they mesmerized Brantôme and offended L'Estoile. Whether or not the Queen Mother literally asked them to serve the banquet topless is more debatable. Boucher hypothesizes that L'Estoile's claim is hyperbole intended to express his disapproval for the new fashion for plunging décolleté necklines, a style that he specifically criticized the following June.[36] Nevertheless, tales of bare-breasted princesses tend to get repeated, which demonstrates the difficulty of establishing what actually took place .

However, none of these salacious anecdotes place a fork in Catherine's hand. Rather, that appears to be a later attibution in a case of guilt by association. A satire called *Les Hermaphrodites; ou l'Isle des hermaphrodites nouvellement descouverte*, which mocks Henri III, describes curled, crimped, waxed, and unnaturally powdered hermaphrodites, who awkwardly eat artichokes, asparagus and peas with little pronged forks even though they spill more onto their lace collars than they get into their mouths.[37] Frequently quoted as a literal portrait of late Valois dining, its author, Thomas Artus, sieur d'Embry, did not publish it until around 1605, after Henri IV, the first of the Bourbons, had said his mass and retaken Paris.

Although raised in the same nursery as the Valois children, the new monarch sought to discredit his predecessor and promoted himself as the rugged, garlic-smelling king on horseback who (whether or not he ever actually said it) stood for 'a chicken in every pot, every Sunday.' Written by one of his courtiers *L'Isle des hermaphrodites* forwarded this agenda.

By no means an effective king, it has been noted that Henri III 'would have made a very good prince, if he had encountered a good century.'[38] Serious research separating his myth from reality has only begun.[39] Henri's unrelenting correspondence belies his reputation for laziness. Although viewed as a decadent partier, contemporaries considered him un-kingly for abstaining from wine because of his health. Nevertheless, his love of extravagant costume and jewels; his failure to produce an heir; his favoritism of a select circle; and that group's perceived 'Italianism' resulted in the still widespread belief that Henri ignored matters of state to partake in debauched orgies with his favorite, pampered pretty boys.

In truth, Henri III, who rightly distrusted the high-born princes surrounding him, elevated men whose loyalty he could count on. That he showered too many titles, honors, and riches upon them created jealousy. So did the increasing wealth of Italian bankers, who bankrolled the troubled crown.

The Queen Mother's cronies competed against Henri III's favorites in their conspicuous consumption. On 26 January 1580 René de Biragues, the Italian-born Chancellor of France elevated by Catherine, hosted a collation that featured 'between eleven and twelve hundred dishes from Faenza' (i.e. glazed earthenware), filled with dried confitures and dragées arranged into castles, pyramids and other fanciful shapes.[40] L'Estoile reported that court pages and lackeys, 'being insolent in nature,' broke these beautiful ceramics into pieces.

At the start of his reign, Henri III instituted an intensely unpopular new protocol that restricted access to the monarch, especially at meals.[41] Only noble appointees could serve the king and a balustrade attempted to keep courtiers at a distance. Resistance to the edict, which anticipated Louis XIV's rigid etiquette, proved so intractable that in 1585 the King had to reissue and expand its regulations.

L'Isle des hermaphrodites exaggerated gossip about Henri III that spread during his lifetime. The 'hermaphrodites' (a word then used metaphorically to connote any-one whose behavior strayed outside accepted gender stereotypes) referred to Henri's favorites, also called the '*mignons de couchette*.' L'Estoile explained that during Henri's reign the word '*mignon*' lost its earlier connotation of 'minion' or 'vassal' and came to mean 'beloved' or 'darling.'[42]

Numerous diatribes against the '*mignons*' accuse them of being 'Italian sodomites.' although no evidence proves their homosexuality.[43] Italy did not yet exist as a nation but references to Italians, especially in the context of nasty, biased jibes, were com-monplace throughout Europe.[44] Among the most popular of these prejudices was the belief that all Italian men were effeminate and/or gay.

As recorded by L'Estoile, poems and *pasquils* making fun of the king's 'hermaph-rodites' and blaming Catherine for the spread of 'Italian vices' peaked in 1578 after some of the more flamboyant *mignons* killed each other off in a famous duel.[45] Coincidentally or not, the earliest known surviving fork with a Paris hallmark has a slightly indecipherable date mark believed to be that of 1577–8.[46]

A post-mortem inventory taken at her *hôtel particulier* in Paris proves that Catherine also owned forks.[47] One example, with a rock-crystal handle, came *en suite* with matching nefs, covered-cups and a vase. She also owned a full service of coral-handled forks, knives and spoons. (Catherine died at Blois, not in Paris, and like other nobles of her time, carried the majority of her possessions with her when she traveled. Therefore, she likely owned further examples.)

The officers charged with inventorying Catherine's Parisian holdings reported an incident illustrative of the fork's dissemination in France and Catherine's relationship to this phenomenon. When news of the Queen Mother's death reached Paris, the Duchess of Montpensier, sister of the Duke and Cardinal of Guise (whom Henri III had recently had assassinated) and chief propagandist of the ultra-Catholics, moved into Catherine's *hôtel particulier* with her son, the Duke of Mayenne, who was run-ning the capital's open rebellion against the king, and her daughter-in-law.[48] In spite of the crown bureaucrats' tremulous protests (recorded in detail), the Duchess of

449

Mayenne boldly appropriated some of Catherine's things, including the late queen's rock-crystal fork. Detractors publicly mocked forks but even her worst enemies privately began to adopt them.

Of all the Italianate habits derided by critics, the fork most conjured Valois decadence because, even in Italy, it had never entirely shed the virulent disapproval with which the Church Fathers had greeted it. It arrived, it is said, with a Byzantine princess, who was married to the Doge of Venice in the 11th century. St. Peter Damian (1007–71) cited her two-tined, gold fork as a vain and depraved affectation.[49] Two hundred years later, St. Bonaventure (1221–74) retold the tale. The fork, it is worth noting, resembles nothing more closely than the Devil's trident.

Pasquale Marchese points out that although many 15th-century Florentines owned dozens of forks these never appear on the detailed provision lists compiled for public feasts and are rarely depicted in dinner-themed paintings commissioned by these same patrons.[50] It seems that forks only came out at smaller parties or *en famille*, perhaps because of lingering Church censure.

Even in Venice as late as 1573, the Inquisitors of the Tribunale del Sant'Uffizio questioned Paolo Veronese about, in addition to Germans, monkeys and dwarves, the inclusion of a two-tined fork in the painter's 'Last Supper', which he promptly renamed 'Feast in the House of Levi' in order to get out of trouble.[51]

'God protect me from forks,' Martin Luther purportedly said in 1515.[52] Among Protestants in Northern Europe, for whom the fork stank of papal dissipation in addition to Byzantine excess, ecclesiastical condemnation of the utensil continued through the Thirty Years' War (1618–38).

As a diabolical symbol, the utensil fits perfectly in the hand of Catherine de' Medici, wicked witch of the 'Black Legend'. This metaphoric truth more than any factual evidence best explains the persistence of Catherine's fork as an enduring theme.

Viewed in archetypal terms, the legend of the queen's fork and that of the Byzantine princess are, in fact, the same. Both tales describe a powerful, foreign bride who forces a decadent innovation upon the natives. Like Greek myths, the heroine is mutable but the essence of the story remains the same.

Damian's un-named princess, usually assumed to have been the bride of Doge Domenico Selvo; but sometimes thought to be Maria, sister to Emperor Romanus III Agyrus, who married the eldest son of Doge Pietro II Orseolo and who died of plague in 1005, cannot be identified because 11th-century interchange between Byzantium and Venice, analogous to that between France and Italy in the 16th century, resulted in numerous strategic intermarriages.[53] Moreover, a manuscript illustration in the Rabanus Maurus *Glossaria* of 1023 at Montecassino clearly depicts two men dining across from each other at a table, each with fork and knife.[54] This not only proves an awareness of forks almost half a century before Damian's account but shows that the spread of fork-use cannot be solely attributed to women.

The Surrealist poet René Crevel in 1931 perhaps best captured the fork's hidden, psychosexual symbolism in *Mr. Knife and Miss Fork*, which tells the story of a young girl, who fantasizes that the knife is her father and the fork, the red-headed English adventuress who ran away with him.55 Drawn to grown-up words that no one will explain, she imagines that Mr. Knife tells Miss Fork, 'You are like death, Cynthia, you are a whore like death'.

That Western civilization has credited two immigrant brides and a cross-dressing king with introducing the fork hints that beneath the surface of this 'civilizing' utensil lurks an obscured but never obliterated threat of female dominance, sorcery, and the Devil.

Select Bibliography:

Amme, Jochen, *Bestecke: Die Egloffstin'sche Sammlung (15.–18. Jahrhundert) auf der Wartburg* (Stuttgart: Arnoldsche, 1994).

Artus, Thomas, sieur d'Embry, *Les Hermaphrodites; ou L'Isle des Hermaphrodites nouvellement descouverte* (Paris: ca. 1605).

Benporat, Claudio, 'A Discovery at the Vatican: The First Italian Treatise on the Art of the Scalco (Head Steward)' in *Petits Propos Culinaires* 30 (Nov. 1988), pp. 41–5.

Beaujouyeux, Balthasar de, *Balet comique de la Royne, faict aux nopces de monsieur le Duc de Joyeuse & madamyselle de Vaudremont sa sœur* (Paris: Adrian le Roy, Robert Ballard, & Mamert Patiffon, 1582).

Bimbenet-Privat, Michèle, *Les Orfèvres parisiens de la renaissance. (1506–1620)* (Paris: Commission des travaux historiques de la Ville de Paris, 1991).

Bonnaffé, Edmond, *Inventaire des meubles de Catherine de Médicis en 1589. Mobilier, tableaux, objets d'art, manuscrits* (Paris: Auguste Aubry, 1874).

Boucher, Jacqueline, *La cour de Henri III* (Rennes: Ouest-France, 1986).

Boucher, Jean (attributed to), *La Vie et Faits Notables de Henry de Valois. ... Où sont contenues les trahisons, perfidies, sacrileges, exactions, cruautez & hontes de cest Hypocrite & Apostat, ennemy de la Religion Catholique*, 2nd ed. (Paris: D. Millot, 1589).

Brantôme, Pierre de Bourdeille, seigneur de, 'Memoirs of Catherine de Medici,' in *Memoirs of Marguerite de Valois, queen of France, wife of Henri IV; of Madame de Pompadour of the Court of Louis XV; and of Catherine de Medici, queen of France and wife of Henri II* (New York: P. F. Collier & Son, 1910), pp. 336–363.

Cabanès, Augustin, *Mœurs intimes du passé*, 12 vols. (Paris: Librairie Albin Michel, 1920–1936).

Calviac, C., *La Civile honesteté pour les enfants, avec la manière d'aprendre à bien lire, prononcer et escrire: qu'avons mise au commencement* (Paris: Richard Breton, 1560).

Chevallier, Pierre, *Henri III, roi shakespearien* (Paris: Fayard, 1985).

Cimber, L. and F Danjou [Louis Lafaist], ed. *Archives curieuses de l'histoire de France, depuis Louis XI jusqu'à Louis XVIII*, first series, vols III and IX (Paris: Beauvais, 1835–36).

Cloulas, Ivan, *Catherine de Médicis* (Paris: Fayard, 1979).

Cordellier, Dominique, gen. ed., *Primatice, maître de Fontainebleau*, catalogue to the exhibition held 22 Sept. 2004–3 Jan. 2005 at the Louvre (Paris: Réunion des musées nationaux, 2004).

Crevel, René, *Mr. Knife Miss Fork*, trans. Kay Boyle, illus. Max Ernst (Paris: The Black Sun Press, 1931).

Diderot, Denis and Jean le Rond d'Alembert, *Encyclopédie, ou dictionnaire raisonné des sciences, des arts et des métiers*, vol IV (Paris: Briasson, David, Le Breton and Durand, 1754).

Dumas, Alexandre, *Les Quarante-cinq* (Paris; Robert Laffont: 1992).

——, *La Reine Margot*, ed. and trans. by David Coward (Oxford: Oxford University Press, 1997).

Estienne, Henri, *Deux dialogues du nouveau français italianizé et autrment déguizé, principalement entre les courtisans de ce temps* (Geneva: 1578).

L'Estoile, Pierre de, *Mémoires-Journaux de Pierre de L'Estoile*, vols. 1–3 (Paris: Libraries des Bibliophiles, 1875).

Frieda, Leonie, *Catherine de Medici* (London: Phoenix Books, 2003).

Gourarier, Zeev, 'Modèles de Cours et usages de table: les origines,' in Sylvie Messinger ed., *Versailles et les tables royales en Europe*, cat. to the exhibiton held 3 Nov. 1993 – 27 Feb. 1994, Musée national des châteaux de Versailles et Trianon (Paris: Réunion des musées nationaux, 1993), pp. 15–32.

Hale, John, *The Civilization of Europe in the Renaissance* (New York: Athenium, 1993).

Heller, Henry, *Anti-Italianism in Sixteenth-Century France* (Toronto: University of Toronto Press, 2003).

Knecht, R. J., *Catherine de' Medici* (Harlow, Essex: Pearson Education, Ltd., 1998).

Marchese, Pasquale, *L'invenzione della forchetta. Spilloni schidioncini lingule imbroccatoi pironi forcule forcine e forchette dai Greci ai nostri forchettoni* (Soveria Mannelli (CZ): Rubbettino Editore, 1989).

Masterpieces of Cutlery and the Art of Eating, cat. to exh. held 11 July to 26 Aug. 1979 at the Victoria and Albert Museum (London: Victoria and Albert Museum, 1979).

Mennell, Stephen, *All Manners of Food: Eating and Taste in England and France from the Middle Ages to the Present*, 2nd ed. (Urbana: University of Illinois Press, 1996).

Rousseau, Jean-Jacques, *Émile: or, On Education*, trans. Allan Bloom (New York: Basic Books, 1979).

Scappi, Bartolomeo, *Opera di M. Bartolomeo Scappi, cuoco ... divisi in sei libri* (Venice: F.e M. Tramezino, 1570).

Solnon, Jean-François, *Catherine de Médicis* (Paris: Perrin, 2003).

Strong, Roy, *Art and Power: Renaissance Festivals, 1450–1650* (Berkeley: University of California Press, 1984).

Wheaton, Barbara Ketcham, *Savoring the Past: The French Kitchen and Table from 1300 to 1789* (Philadelphia: University of Pennsylvania Press, 1983).

Yates, Francis A., *The Valois Tapestries* (London: Warburg Institute, 1959).

452

Notes

1. Wheaton, pp. 43–51.
2. Mennell, pp. 65–6; 69–71.
3. <http://www.restocours.net/Bac1/Techno/Cours/histoire%20de%20la%20cuisine.htm>; Solnon, p. 324; Frieda, p. 362.
4. Michelet in Knecht, p. xii; Dumas *La Reine Margot* and *Les Quarante-cinq*.
5. For an abbreviated summary of historians for and against Catherine see Knecht, pp. xi–xii. .
6. Wheaton, p. 43.
7. Solnon, p. 324.
8. Wheaton, p. 47; Diderot & D'Alembert vol. 4, p. 538.
9. For a summary of French anti-Italian pro-Franck intellectuals see Heller, pp. 34–6; Rousseau, p. 345.
10. 'Lettres et exemples de la feue Royne-mère (Catherine de Médicis) comme elle faisoit travailler aux manufactures, et fournissoit aux ouvriers de ses propres deniers, par Barthélemy de Laffemas Sieur de Bautort, valet de Chambre du Roy, et Controlleur General du Commerce de France' in Cimber and Danjou, vol. IX, p. 123.
11. Calviac, p. xxiiii [sic].
12. Mariéjol, pp. 25–28; Cloulas, pp. 50–7.

13. Gourarier, p. 24.
14. Marchese, pp. 79–80.
15. Mariéjol, pp. 49–52; Cloulas, pp. 18–19; Frieda, pp. 47–49.
16. Benporat.
17. Mariéjol, pp. 26–7; Frieda 49–52.
18. Cordellier no. 22, p. 124.
19. Frieda, p. 56; Cloulas 67–8.
20. Frieda, p. 87.
21. Cloulas, 'La reine italienne', pp. 79–118.
22. Account ledgers from the Archives royales reproduced in Cimber and Danjou, pp. 416–22.
23. Gourarier, p. 20.
24. Yates, pp. 53–72; Wheaton, pp. 49–50; Strong 98–122.
25. Brantôme, p. 354.
26. Ibid., p. 352.
27. Jouan, pp. 23–4 & 55.
28. BnF cat. no. RES-V-1664, ex-libris Abbé Fauvel.
29. Boucher, p. 104.
30. Ibid., pp. 99–101.
31. *Deux dialogues du langage français italianizé et autrement déguizé, principalement entre les courtisans de ce temps* (Geneva: 1578).
32. *Discours merveilleux*, reprinted in Cimber & Danjou vol. IX, pp. 1–113.
33. L'Estoile vol. I, p. 64.
34. Frieda, p. 242.
35. L'Estoile vol. I, p. 188.
36. Boucher, p. 122.
37. Artus, p. 161.
38. Solnon, p. 401.
39. Chevallier's extremely scholarly biography is thus far the best; Jacqueline Boucher's reassessment of Henri III in her works regarding Italians at the court are equally important.
40. L'Estoile vol. I, p. 350.
41. Chevallier, p. 263; Gourarier, p. 16.
42. L'Estoile vol. I, p. 142.
43. Ibid. vol. I, pp. 70–77, 115–21 & 143–50.
44. Hale, pp. 52–66.
45. L'Estoile vol. I, pp. 16–17, 231, 243–54; 259–60; 266–67.
46. Bimbinet-Privat no. 21.
47. Bonnaffé, pp. 92.
48. Ibid., pp. 24, 33–4 & 164–5.
49. Marchese, p. 47.
50. Ibid., pp. 79–91.
51. Ibid., pp. 138–9.
52. Amme, p. 13.
53. Cabanès, p. 248; Marchese, p. 43.
54. *Masterpieces of Cutlery* no. 3.
55. Crevel, unnumbered.